enigma
books

ALSO PUBLISHED BY ENIGMA BOOKS

Hitler's Table Talk 1941-1944
Hugh Trevor-Roper, ed.

In Stalin's Secret Service
W.G. Krivitsky

Hitler and Mussolini: The Secret Meetings
Santi Corvaja

The Jews in Fascist Italy: A History
Renzo De Felice

The Man Behind the Rosenbergs
Alexander Feklisov and Sergei Kostin

Roosevelt and Hopkins: An Intimate History
Robert E. Sherwood

Galeazzo Ciano

Diary

1937-1943

Preface by

Renzo De Felice
Professor of History, University of Rome

Original introduction by

Sumner Welles
U.S. Undersecretary of State, 1937-1943

enigma books

First complete and unabridged English edition.
Translated from the Italian by Robert L. Miller and co-edited by
Dr. Stanislao G. Pugliese for 1937-1938
Translated from the Italian by V. Umberto Coletti-Perucca and edited
by Hugh Gibson for 1939-1943, extensively revised by Robert L. Miller and
co-edited by Dr. Stanislao G. Pugliese

©**enigma books** 2002
©Doubleday 1946
Published by arrangement with Doubleday, a division of
The Doubleday Broadway Publishing Group, a division of Random House, Inc.
©Rizzoli Editore SpA 1980

Publisher's Cataloging In Publication Data
(Prepared by Donohue Group, Inc.)

Ciano, Galeazzo, conte, 1903-1944.
[Diario.]
Diary, 1937-1943 / Galeazzo Ciano ; translated from the Italian by Robert L. Miller
and co-edited by Dr. Stanislao G. Pugliese for 1937-1938 ; translated from the Italian
by V. Umberto Coletti-Perucca and edited by Hugh Gibson for 1939-1943, extensively
revised by Robert L. Miller and co-edited by Dr. Stanislao G. Pugliese ; preface by
Renzo de Felice ; introduction by Sumner Welles.

p. ; cm.

Includes index.

ISBN: 1-929631-02-2

1. Ciano, Galeazzo, conte, 1903-1944—Diaries. 2. Italy—Foreign relations—1922-
1945—Sources. 3. Fascism—Italy—History—Sources. 4. World War, 1939-1945—
Sources. 5. Fascists—Italy—Diaries. 6. Cabinet officers—Italy—Diaries. I. Gibson,
Hugh, 1883-1954. II. Miller, Robert L. III. Pugliese, Stanislao G., 1965- IV. Title.
V. Title: Diario.

DG575.C52 A3 2002
940.53/2/0924 B

Printed in Canada

Galeazzo Ciano

Diary

1937-1943

Table of Contents

Editorial Note

This volume of my husband's Diaries, like the preceding one, is absolutely authentic and also reproduced in its entirety.

Nothing has been altered or omitted.

It is my wish to be so that the whole truth could be told at last whether it was good or bad and through the notes my husband left we could reconstruct the five most interesting years in the history of Italy and of the world.

Edda Ciano Mussolini
From the 1980 Italian edition

Publisher's Note to the American edition

This new edition of the complete *Diary* of Galeazzo Ciano encompasses the corrected spelling of Italian and foreign names, as well as all the corrections and additions made to the text in the 1980 Italian edition. Enigma Books has made an entirely new translation of the years 1937-1938 and extensively revised and edited the translation of the years 1939-1943. We have restored all the passages omitted from the original 1946 U.S. edition.

The endnotes are intended, for the most part, to help the reader identify the individuals mentioned in the *Diary* who may not be clearly identified in the text regarding the positions or functions they occupied at the time. We have also sought to avoid, with few exceptions, any additional historical notes which would be obviously insufficient, given the vast amount of material now available pertaining to Ciano and the period.

All references to the speeches and writings of Mussolini and the correspondence between Mussolini and Hitler are made from the *Opera Omnia di B. Mussolini*, edited by Edoardo and Duilio Susmel, and published by La Fenice-Volpe, in Florence, Italy. The *Diary* is usefully complemented by the collection of documents in *L'Europa verso la catastrofe*, published by Mondadori and mentioned by Renzo De Felice in his Preface to this edition.

Our aim in presenting this American edition of Galeazzo Ciano's *Diary* is to be as complete and as close as possible to the original text, as compiled and edited by Renzo De Felice for publication in Italy in 1980.

Robert L. Miller
Publisher
January 2002

Preface

Renzo De Felice

The *Diary* of Galeazzo Ciano is offered here for the first time, over thirty years after it was first published, in a single text which includes both parts that the dramatic history of the original manuscripts had kept editorially separated.

Ciano kept his diary during the entire period he was Minister of Foreign Affairs, from June 10, 1936 until February 8, 1943. The daily diaries in which he wrote were to take very different paths. Those from January 1, 1939 to February 8, 1943—thought to be the most important ones documenting the political attitude of her husband—were safely smuggled into Switzerland by Edda Ciano in January 1944. Excerpts were published the following year in the Western press. Also in 1945 a very incomplete one-volume edition was published in the United States, since the publisher judged many parts of the text to be of no interest to American readers. A few months later in April 1946, Rizzoli published the first Italian edition, much more complete but not without certain omissions and mistakes of one kind or another. Some of these mistakes were due to the haste with which the edition was prepared (based on photocopies of the originals); that edition was subsequently corrected during its various reprints. Nevertheless, until now the best edition of that part of the *Diary* has been the French translation published in Switzerland in 1946 by La Baconnière in Neuchâtel. Since that edition was prepared directly from the original pages, it is more accurate than the Italian edition and does not include its many omissions.

The first part of the *Diary*, covering the years 1936-1938, followed a different itinerary. The various daily diaries that could not be safely taken to Switzerland fell into the hands of the Germans and were destroyed later on. The copies of the German translation appear to have been destroyed as well. The photocopies secretly made by Felicitas Beetz, the famous German agent, of the period from August 23, 1937-December 31, 1938, were saved by Edda Ciano in 1947. These photocopies (where the annotations for the following days of 1938 are missing: January 15-18, 21, 22, 27, 28; March 30-31; June 25-26; July 6-9; December 12-13; are thought to have been already torn out of the original manuscript) were used to prepare the Cappelli edition, which was published in August 1948. A few years later, in 1953, Carlo Ciucci, who had written the preface to the *Diary 1937-1938*, published three sections (part of the annotations of November 28, December 1 and 3, 1938), which had been cut at the time of the publication of the first part of the *Diary*. These three sections do not appear in the American edition of that part of the *Diary* published that same year.

Without having access to the original manuscripts, this edition is made up of the first part—1937-1938—based on the Cappelli edition with the additional parts added by Ciucci, and for the second part—1939-1943—on the last Rizzoli edition (the fifth edition of 1971) integrated and corrected on the basis of the Swiss edition.[1] Even with these limitations this may be considered a new Italian edition of the *Diary*, at least for those sections that are known to us today. It is possible that sections from 1936 and the first seven months of 1937 may still be in German or American archives even in the German translation; it is also possible that the current text could be further improved upon once we have access to the original manuscripts that have survived and the photocopies of the others.

The reader should be aware that the *Diary* in its current form must be read—even though it is a single, independent body of work—in light of the collection of documents that were being compiled at the same time by Ciano himself. This collection also underwent a number of vicissitudes after July 25, 1943, which also led it to being "scattered" from an editorial point of view, like the *Diary* itself, of what may be considered as the most important part of the "Ciano papers." While the *Diary*, as we have mentioned, was in part published by Rizzoli and in part by Cappelli, the collection of documents was published in January 1948 by Mondadori under the title *L'Europa verso la catastrofe. 184 colloqui...verbalizzati da Galeazzo Ciano.*[2] The same publisher issued a new edition, updated and corrected by Rodolfo Mosca.

Without a doubt, it is universally acknowledged that Ciano's *Diary*, as a memoir and a source, is a document of prime importance to understand and reconstruct the history of Italy during the years it encompasses. The *Diary* occupies a central position, especially regarding foreign policy because of Ciano's office during this period. Just as Mario Toscano, one of the eminent scholars of diplomatic history, wrote many years ago:

> It was…in effect written on the spur of the moment, when events had just taken place or were actually taking place and it reproduces with complete accuracy not only events of great interest, but impressions, moods, the "atmosphere," a whole collection of elements that can certainly not be culled from the official documents but which very effectively reproduce an environment and place the "document" in its true frame.

It is important to point out that—as Gaetano Salvemini had noted and as Toscano mentions—a few pages of the *Diary*, certainly those regarding the Greek campaign, had been later rewritten by Ciano. This probably took place after Mussolini removed him from the Palazzo Chigi and named him Ambassador to the Holy See once the fortunes of war were clearly turning against the Axis. Salvemini, who noticed the problem first, wrote:

In New York I was able to examine the photographs of the Ciano *Diary* page after page. I discovered that the sheet that had October 27 (back) and October 28 (front) [1940] had been torn off by Ciano himself. And that he had corrected the date of October 26 to the 27th, and wrote in some unimportant lines at the date of October 27, which he had written in, and a few more unimportant sentences at the date of October 28, which he had also written in. Obviously the original pages of October 27 and 28 had information that was not convenient for him to keep on record.

Nor may we underestimate what was written, in less detail, but more drastically, by Ramón Serrano Suñer, a friend of Ciano's and his colleague as Minister of Foreign Affairs of Spain:

> I have absolutely no doubt that his diary is authentic; I mean actually written by him. But I am also convinced that he revised and corrected it, probably at the time he was ambassador to the Vatican. I don't wish to point as proof to the serious contradictions that it represents compared to what we know about his life, but even the photocopy of the original, which I have examined, and that is full of additions and where lines are crossed out...With the changes he made after the fact he hoped to save not his own life but that of his country...

The claims made by von Ribbentrop, on the other hand, are completely unreliable when he says that there were actually two Ciano diaries, one of them a forgery perpetrated by Ciano himself "in order to create a 'peace alibi' for himself, showing that he was opposed to the 'war frenzy' on my part and that of the Führer" and to attempt to blackmail Hitler and thus avoid being punished for his "wrongdoing." It is clearly stated in the Goebbels diary that, at the start of 1943, the Germans knew Ciano was thinking of writing his memoirs and they were certain that these would be hostile to them. Even when one takes into account the relentless hunt by the Germans to seize the Ciano *Diary*, what von Ribbentrop states remains, as we said, unreliable, because of the mutual hatred between the two foreign ministers and because of the circumstances in which Ribbentrop wrote his accusation (during the Nuremberg trial when it was in his interest to deny any validity to the *Diary*, which was being used by the prosecution against him), and also because the news that was supposed to be the basis of the statement itself and which, in the best of cases, can only prove that Hitler and Ribbentrop were in possession of the translation not of the *Diary* of 1939, as the latter claimed, but of the compiled documents that, as we said, Ciano had assembled with the view of integrating them into the *Diary*.

Even if the *Diary* had been edited by its author, its value as an historical document remains, and fully justifies the importance serious scholars have attributed to it by using it in their studies, which remain fundamentally sound even many years later. The best example being the excellent essay published in 1953 by Felix Gilbert, *Ciano and his Ambassadors*, which was fortunately reissued about ten years ago. It may be assumed that the corrections and changes made to the *Diary* concern more the role Ciano played in the events than the substance of those events and are therefore tied to his personal biography. The same could be said about the pages of the daily diary of 1938 that appear to have been ripped out. Rather than make assumptions (which can also be legitimate) concerning the changed pages, and most of all about the content of those that were removed, we find it instead more useful to attempt an initial explanation of a problem that is often mentioned in passing by those who have written about Ciano or have used his *Diary* to discuss isolated issues, without examining it in detail: that of the intent and the *feeling* with which the *Diary* was written and therefore the question of its inner validity in depicting Ciano's personality and its influence on the way he describes facts, situations, people, states of mind.

Ciano was, without a doubt, very proud of his *Diary* and held it to be a document of the greatest importance. In a way one could almost say that he overvalued it to the point of deluding himself that, once it was published, it would have modified the way he and his policies were thought of, leading therefore to his being "rehabilitated." He would say so himself in the "introduction" to the *Diary*, which he wrote on December 23, 1943 in a Verona jail, and that was subsequently smuggled out. But, pleased with himself, he had also told several of his friends and acquaintances the same thing, in much less dramatic circumstances, while things were going relatively well for him. As he showed Orio Vergani the *Diary* opened to the page concerning the German aggression of the Soviet Union, he asked:

> "Do you think it's interesting? Do you think it would be a real scoop for your paper?"
> He was standing next to me, following my eyes as they raced across the page. He asked as if he were joking:
> "How much do you think an American agency would pay for it?"
> "Does Mussolini know you're keeping this diary?" I asked.
> "He knows and he doesn't know, the way he does about everything. If you feel like it come in the afternoon, during the quiet hours, between four and six. You can read everything you want!"
> "I think von Mackensen would be the one most interested in reading it."
> "I'm positive that he never shall read it, or that when he reads it will be too late."

And he had also spoken in much the same terms to Dino Alfieri, who remembered the episode this way:

> Two or three times, in the middle of the conversation, he accompanied me to the sitting room next door, which is called *of the Victories*…he would sit at the large table, open the elegant and huge safe which stood at his right, and take out a few daily diaries…He would open one or the other at random, and quickly look over a few pages. "This is the best work of my life. This is the summary of the history of Italy of these last years, part of the history of Europe, and a bit of the history of the world." He would stack the volumes one on top of the other and he would feel them as if he were attempting to gauge their weight. "You used to be president of the Association of Authors and Publishers and worked with them. How much do you think they'd pay me to sell them the copyright?" We made assumptions in the millions and millions. He was greatly

amused and excited by this and would imagine what effect the publication would have produced. "No, for now nothing doing. This diary will be published after my death. The events are recent, the comments are too sincere, the people are too openly targeted. You are in here as well. I wrote down some interesting things you sent from Berlin." He would pause and the burst out laughing: "Think of what a bomb it would be if I published it now! Instead my children will see to it. I leave them this task, which is actually quite a nice inheritance. Tell me again, how much do you think they'd offer me today?" He had fun imagining that with that kind of money he would have lived like a country squire all his life, sailing off the coast of Leghorn, fishing the greatest quantity of *occhiate*, his favorite fish.

His close friends were not the only ones who knew Ciano kept a diary: he also made no mystery about it with foreign visitors, sometimes even letting them read excerpts from it, as for instance with Sumner Welles, during their first meeting in February 1940.

His intention certainly during the last period of his life, in 1943, after he was dismissed from the Ministry of Foreign Affairs, but probably even before, was to use it along with the compilation of documents (most of them were minutes of conversations) which he also personally saw to, in order to write his memoirs someday. This intention perhaps, along with a lack of time, and a sensitive temperament geared more toward impressions than analysis, explains the writing style of the *Diary*: quick and short notations, much more concerning events and things said by others than his own observations. A temperament that induced Giuseppe Bottai to write:

> No essay of this kind is less "intimate" than this one; a style of writing that is completely external to the author, notations made of facts, meetings, conversations overheard; not an autobiography, which of those facts, meetings and conversations repeats the images and echoes of the inner consciousness of a man. From page to page one searches unsuccessfully for an experience, a political judgment, a moral criterion, leading to a single historical interpretation of the chronicle of the events he experienced.

Ciano told Orio Vergani once:

> I write without the slightest literary pretense, as you can imagine. I may not have the ability to do so and in any case I don't have the time. I must make do with a few quick notations. But not a single day goes by that I don't feel that I must write something.

And in the "introduction" he wrote in jail in Verona he would state:

> …perhaps in the very sketchy manner, from which the superfluous has been completely removed, lies the quality of my diaries. Events have been photographed therein without any embellishment and the impressions are the first ones, the most authentic, before any critical judgments and retrospective memories had any time to exercise their influence. I was in the habit of jotting down the main events day after day, from one hour to the next, and perhaps one shall discover repetitions or contradictions, just as life in fact often repeats and contradicts itself.

From this point of view, other partially published or still unpublished diaries by other top fascist leaders—we are thinking in particular about those by Giuseppe Bottai, of which he published a segment in *Vent'anni e un giorno*, and the still-unpublished diary by Dino Grandi—are extremely different. They are larger, more detailed, if not in facts at least in first-person opinions. When these shall be published, not like Ciano's *Diary*, in the *heat of battle*, but decades after the events they recount, those diaries will certainly produce less *noise*. For historians they nevertheless shall be—despite the passage of time and the progress made by scholarship—an even more precious source. As far as foreign policy between the two world wars is concerned, the Grandi diary is probably the most important. Neither of the two diaries, however, by Grandi or Bottai, perhaps because of the way they are written (especially Grandi's, in a broad, expansive and well-reasoned type of writing that easily becomes repetitive), has the ambiguous fascination of the Ciano *Diary*. It is the kind of mysterious charm one gathers from a news item whose choice over another we do not understand, of a statement reported without any explanation, of a line of reasoning barely initiated, all of which allow the reader to discover, below the surface, a whole sequence of events. This also opens up many problems to the historian that are often tied to Ciano's personality and how it influenced his way of understanding events, situations, people, and moods. Even more so since, in the absence of a truly scientifically based modern biography of Ciano,[3] the only way to understand his personality, the best source (besides the *Ciano una lunga confessione* by Orio Vergani, a book written with intense humanity, balance and intelligence which doesn't hide the compassion of an old friend) still remains—despite, and probably because of, its ambiguity—his *Diary*.

In the closing lines of the "introduction," Ciano was careful to state "not a single word of what I have written in my diaries is false, or exaggerated or inspired by partisan resentments. Everything is just as I saw and heard it." If we except the revisions made during the final period and the pages torn out, which are part of another kind of logic, we can believe what he says. Ciano, in his own way, when he was writing his *Diary*, was sincere. Bottai, who had lived through much of the same events and knew the persons mentioned in it well, has written on the subject:

> Everything in it is exact… Those who knew him and had direct knowledge of the events can vouch for it. Everything in that scrapbook of daily notations is "objective," but precisely in the manner in which the adjective is used as a noun to describe the camera lens: a merciless glassy eye, which "freezes" images without emotion. It's true that what is missing is the finishing stroke; but even the personal touch of the author, who in the act of recording reality, gives it a coherent and organic interpretation of his own. Things are looked at, not seen; words are heard but not felt.

A fairly harsh assessment, which is however more or less correct, that does not take into account the problem of the conscious and unconscious limits of both his objectivity and sincerity.

The explanation is rather simple for the obvious character traits. Even though he didn't write for publication (not for a long time at least and certainly not during his lifetime) and thinking he would possibly use it to write his memoirs, as he kept his *Diary* Ciano most probably took some precautions. He must have weighed a few words, used nuances for some comments generally employing the device of attributing a number of assessments and compromising opinions to third parties. Especially during the first years when things were proceeding well and he was more than hopeful and actually convinced that he would take over his father-in-law's job at the head of the regime, such a precaution could only have one reason. Later on, as things began to turn for the worse and the relationship with his father-in-law began deteriorating, he could also have other reasons. But for now, the only reason had only one name: Mussolini. Undeniably the Duce knew his son-in-law was keeping a diary and there is no reason to think he found out through third parties. Ciano made no mystery about it and one may well imagine he had told his father-in-law as well. He admitted, as we have seen, in discussion with Vergani, that Mussolini knew about it. The ambiguous way in which he told him [Vergani] doesn't appear important. In the *Diary* there are various notations, which prove without a doubt that Mussolini knew his son-in-law was keeping a diary, to the point that he clearly asked him to take notes regarding certain subjects. During the final period when the relations between father-in-law and son-in-law had seriously deteriorated (to the point that when, in February 1943, Ciano was dismissed from the Ministry of Foreign Affairs, he had already taken the diaries out of the Palazzo Chigi one year earlier, fearful, as he told Vergani, that the *Italian* and not just the German police were interested in getting their hands on them) there is an ambiguous and revealing annotation in the *Diary*. At the date of November 6, 1942 we read:

> Mussolini asked me if I was keeping up the diary. When I answered in the affirmative, he said that it would be useful to us to document how the Germans have always acted behind his back in the military and political areas. But what does this strange question really hide?

"But what does this strange question really hide?" It is absurd to think Ciano would believe that had Mussolini actually been thinking of breaking away from the Germans he would need the *Diary* as documentation. The strangeness of the question and the fear it created in Ciano, revealed in this annotation, have only one possible explanation: the danger that someday under any pretense, Mussolini would ask to read the *Diary*. Such a fear was completely justified in 1942, but we think Ciano had harbored it even when things were going well between him and his father-in-law. Having a basically insecure personality, but at the same time wanting very much to be "a dutiful pupil" and under pressure to prove himself as completely deserving of the Duce's trust, Ciano must have always been bothered by the idea that Mussolini could request a read of his diary, thus forcing him to a certain caution when writing, a caution that was very much in tune with what—according to all those who knew him well—was his fundamental character trait, namely cunning. As Alfieri wrote about him:

Intelligent and quick by nature, he wanted to be cunning by calculation and reason. "Nobody is going to put one over me," he'd say. "I'm the one who is going to outsmart them all."

The discussion, which in our opinion is more complex, is that of the unconscious limitations to Ciano's sincerity in writing his diary. In summing up we could say that these were the consequences of his awareness of having an inordinate capacity to assimilate and understand the meaning of things, of his *impudence* as the "incorrigible street urchin from Leghorn" (Mario Luciolli), of his "loves" and "hatreds" and, in the end, of the fact that he was not a real fascist.

Little can be said about the first two limitations. It is obvious that at times they drove him to misunderstand what he was told or was reported to him (Bottai in *Vent'anni e un giorno* picked up on one of these misunderstandings which is an excellent example of this character trait), to draw hasty or even erroneous conclusions, and also making easy statements that are much too arrogant and final. It should however be clear that both could turn out to be correct and at times indicative of a keen mind possessing considerable intelligence.

The third limitation, the "loves" and "hatreds," demands closer attention. Of the "loves," those which are obviously of interest to us here, Ciano would have above all *one* and only *one* which was stronger than any other—even though many readers may find this statement strange: the one he felt for Mussolini. This was a "love" made of admiration, devotion and—despite the family ties and the long, daily contact—not without a certain inability to separate Mussolini from the Duce. A "love" which from the beginning included the added conviction of being smarter than the Duce and with time would also combine a kind of impatience and a tendency towards being argumentative. But it still was "love," in any case. A "love" that during the first years up to the war, and also some time later, stands out from every page of the *Diary*, even those that at first appear to be the most critical ones, a love that on a different level, Orio Vergani has insightfully defined as Ciano's "Mussolini imitation," his unconscious transformation into his father-in-law's model, which he never would give up, even when the political disagreements with Mussolini became irreconcilable. It reappeared almost hysterically during the night of July 25-26, 1943, when Ciano, having been told the news of the coup d'état and of Mussolini's arrest, broke down sobbing: "He was a great man, a real genius. He could have still done a lot of good for Italy... Why did he treat us all this way?" A cry that, even though in completely different circumstances, can only remind us of a similar one Ciano writes about in the entry for July 4, 1938:

> I listened on radio to the Duce's speech at Aprilia. When I heard his voice I started to cry like a child.

It has been said that at some point Ciano "felt himself overtaken by the terrible fate of becoming the Duce's antagonist." Actually, nothing could be more to the contrary. Even when the political antagonism between the two men reached its apex, Ciano never was nor felt he was Mussolini's *opponent*. Even his own participation in the "conspiracy" of July 25 (which he sought and imposed on its most important participants who were otherwise not inclined to it, because of what he, at least up to a time, had represented within Mussolini's policies, to avoid giving an exclusively political act personal or even family overtones), was not a form of opposition. Goebbels would write in his diary that "Ciano was the leader of the conspiracy against his own father-in-law" and that "he was a scoundrel and despicable traitor, as never before witnessed in history," "the Satan of the Fascist movement and the curse of Italy." However, nothing confirms the fact that by underwriting, supporting and voting for the Grandi agenda, Ciano had other motives than that of following the impulse of his judgment and conscience and to be acting "patriotically": "to do whatever was possible to save Italy and remove her from the domination and the arrogant behavior of the Germans." From documents available we cannot conclude that he had any other motivations. If we may add something, it is that just like most of those voting in the Grand Council for the Grandi agenda, he did not quite understand the consequences of the action in which he was taking part. Grandi, on the other hand, had analyzed the situation realistically, considering all its potential consequences and quite openly saw in the Grand Council's vote the first act of an operation that in a very short time meant that Italy would be in a *de facto* state of war with Germany, placing the Allies in front of a *fait accompli*. For Ciano giving back a whole series of powers to the Crown was intended only as a means to take Italy out of the war in the most painless manner possible and probably without even implying the political end of Mussolini.

It is absolutely necessary to get to the bottom of this "love," since in many cases it becomes a key to an accurate reading of the *Diary*, most importantly where a number of statements attributed to Mussolini are concerned. Those statements appear incredible, grotesque, or morally revolting, so much so that the simple fact of recording them has been seen as proof of Ciano's "rebelliousness," of his deep antagonism toward his father-in-law, when in reality it was not like that at all, certainly not during the beginning years of the *Diary* when they appear frequently and many are quite serious. In recounting them Ciano was not in any way seeking to brand Mussolini; on the contrary, since he was under his father-in-law's spell and devoted to him, he intended them to be read as sayings for "posterity." We should also not exclude the possibility that Mussolini would sometimes speak that way because he *knew* Ciano kept a diary and that he would have written them down as gifts to posterity.

It is also important to thoroughly understand Ciano's "hatreds," not so much the small everyday dislikes, but those that were rooted deep within him. If some of them, such as his hatred for von Ribbentrop following the Salzburg meeting of August 11-13, 1939, are clear, obvious, and justified in a sense, the same cannot be said for others, which, since they are not readily apparent and identified, could deceive the reader and lead to a misunderstanding of facts and personal situations, to taking literally and for granted statements it contains which must, on the contrary, be filtered through Ciano's personality and his "hatreds." As we said, these "hatreds," which are not *commonplace*, not directly personal, but quite specifically political, if they are not identified as such, may also lead to distortions. The two most significant examples concern Italo Balbo and Dino Grandi.

Between 1937 and 1940, the years containing the greatest number of entries and where negative judgments are the harshest, Balbo and Grandi were, one way or the other with different nuances depending on the circles they moved in, the two most popular and respected Fascist leaders; along with Ciano and Bottai, they were the "classics of Fascism" (to use an expression of Ciano's reported by Bottai), which while on the surface appears affectionate, even though a bit light hearted, actually indicates his desire to promote himself to the level of the "great leaders" of the original Fascist party. From different and opposing political viewpoints, they were, besides Ciano, two of Mussolini's most obvious potential successors. This was the main reason for the hatred on the part of the *heir apparent*, his swiftness to never miss an opportunity to bad mouth them, even with foreigners (he once told Serrano Suñer, who expressed the wish to meet Grandi, that he wasn't worth it: *he's of no interest and his intelligence is smaller than a mosquito's*) and to gather and write down in his diary any gossip or opinion which was derogatory about the two, especially if coming from Mussolini, who had his own reasons to express negative opinions (especially about Balbo) that were certainly different from those of his son-in-law.

To Ciano's credit we must say that once he found himself swept up in the struggle, at the end of August 1939, to prevent Italy's entry into the war as Germany's ally, he was able to overcome at least one of his "hatreds," and acknowledged that Grandi was the best diplomat Italy had, sought his experience and his counsel, and kept him at his side during those dramatic days, even though he knew Mussolini was totally opposed to his former foreign minister and former ambassador to London becoming further involved in foreign policy. Once Ciano happily reached the life raft of *non-belligerency* he readily expressed his gratitude. At the same time he significantly omitted any mention in his *Diary* regarding Grandi's role during those days and once the moment had passed, he resumed his negative notations about him.

The fourth unconscious limit to Ciano's sincerity in his *Diary*, as we have already mentioned, lies in the fact that he was anything but a real fascist. The product of a traditional catholic upbringing, he spent his youth in a nonfascist atmosphere and then in diplomatic circles, the *enfant gâté* of a certain Roman aristocracy that flattered his vanity and his taste for beautiful things (and beautiful women). Fascism had barely touched him even though it turned him into one of the regime's top leaders. He basically was and considered himself a conservative bourgeois, the typical representative of a new power elite. Just as Bottai noted in his diary, he proclaimed himself "a bit out of habit and innate inclination, a genuinely *reactionary* and *hang'em high* type." To him fascism meant a regime and the regime meant power. And he understood everything in terms of power. Thus his complete indifference and insensitivity toward those issues that were, for the real fascists, old and young, the true ideals, the problems within fascism; toward their worries *as fascists* regarding the failure of corporatism, the deeper orientations of the regime, or the "post Mussolini" period to come. If anything did break through his indifference and insensitivity at times, it was the desire to manipulate for his own power-oriented purposes those groups and debates that surfaced from time to time among the new fascist generations, but that were tainted in his eyes by a deep distrust for anything new, *revolutionary* or *left-wing*. A distrust that he did not hide even from those friends whom he knew failed to share his feelings, since they identified with those ideals and problems as being the essential expressions of fascism's future. He even went so far as scolding them and above all—as in the case of Bottai—for their leanings toward "some youthful extremist tendencies."

In reading Ciano's *Diary*, one must keep these limitations in mind because failure to do so could lead to mistakes and misunderstandings, not only regarding his personality and some of his positions, but more importantly for the value of some statements and opinions which he records. First and foremost those attributed to Mussolini, who was deeply involved in certain problems, quite dramatically at times even though also contradictorily. Therefore if we fail to bear in mind the specific act of recording reminiscences or the privately critical manner (because they were foreign to his cultural and moral world) with which Ciano wrote them, it becomes difficult to properly evaluate them as far as a true understanding of fascism goes and one can see them as clichés, almost as *jocular statements*, or ravings, emotional and irrational outbursts rather than expressions for the most part unacceptable to us but not without their own specific logic, not to be taken lightly as jokes or expressions of a deranged mind. This could lead to losing its true historical value.

Thirty-five years have passed since the fall of fascism and after all that has surfaced and has been written about it both in Italy and overseas, it is probably impossible to read the *Diary* as it was when first published because we do not believe in the existence of any *keys to reading the text*, and we rather think that—unless they appear spontaneously, sparked by the interest and sensitivity of the reader—they will inevitably lead to a mistaken reading of reality and the construction of an image having little in common with that reality and we shall therefore not propose any. We do hope that the information and the facts we offer may foster as much as possible a reading *from the inside* of this important historical document and the reality it depicts, a reality of which many of us carry the burden today, even those who have not lived through it, and that it is necessary to know and understand it as well as possible, not only in its external and apparently grotesque manifestations or in the brutal and *material* ones, but rather through the more intimate and moral ones, because it is on the moral level that it was at its most dramatic, and its negative consequences, so often undetected today, are the heaviest.

Introduction

Sumner Welles

I first met Count Ciano in Rome on February 25, 1940, and I saw him for the last time on March 19 of that year. During most of the intervening period I was away from the Italian capital. Gauged by time alone my knowledge of him both as a man and as a statesman must be regarded as exceedingly slight. Yet in the circumstances under which I knew him, and in the nature of the discussions which brought us together, I find a measure of justification for undertaking to write this introduction to Count Ciano's Diaries and to offer my own estimate of its author.

In the early winter of 1940 I was sent by President Roosevelt as his personal representative to visit the capitals of the Allied nations and of the two Axis powers in order to report to him upon the situation in Europe and upon the possibilities for the establishment of a just and lasting peace. As is now well known, no such possibilities existed. The Nazi government was already fully prepared for an immediate all-out offensive, and the German onslaught was inevitable unless the French and British governments were willing to submit to a Hitler-dominated Europe. The Soviet Union was not to be invaded until more than a year later, and Japan's aggression upon the United States was still almost two years away.

The prospects for the Western democracies already seemed very dark indeed, although not yet so hopeless as they became a few months later.

The ability of the United States to arrest the catastrophe was tenuous. European public opinion generally believed that American sentiment was largely isolationist and that it would prevent President Roosevelt from undertaking any effective measures of assistance to England or to France when Germany's full war effort was finally exercised. The Axis governments were convinced that, should the United States finally rouse itself from its lethargy, adequate military preparation, even for self-defense, would prove to be so long delayed as to be of no practical value. Only one thing could have prevented the German offensive in the west, and that was the knowledge on the part of the Nazi leaders and of the German General Staff that the United States was fully armed as well as determined to use force if necessary to prevent the outbreak of a new world war.

In such circumstances the maximum of what the United States could hope to accomplish was to prevent the entrance of Italy into the war at the side of Germany. Even though Italy's so-called non-belligerency was being notoriously utilized to render all assistance short of war to the Germans, an actual declaration of war by Italy would necessarily imply a far greater threat to France and to Yugoslavia, as well as a vital thrust at the British life line through the Mediterranean to the Suez Canal.

With the exception of a very small group of Fascist leaders, the Italian people as a whole, as well as every potent influence within Italy, were vehemently opposed to a declaration of war. While this opposition was primarily due to a general fear and hatred of Germany and of its Nazi government, it also stemmed from the popular conviction that, however great the artificially engendered friction with Great Britain and with France might be, the future of Italy would be far more secure in a world in which the Western Powers remained to the fore than in a world in which Nazism had become the sole authority. Finally, there was a great mass of Italian public opinion which was hostile to the thought of war because of its realization that Italy would commit a fatal error by taking part in a war of which the outcome was problematical, and as a result of which, whoever the victors might be, the Italian people had nothing to gain and everything to lose.

Count Ciano shared the viewpoint of all of these groups. Of all the men possessing high authority within the Axis governments, he was the only one who made it clear to me, without subterfuge and without hesitation, that he had opposed the war, that he continued to oppose the war, that he foresaw nothing but utter devastation for the whole of Europe through the extension of the war, and that every effort which he personally could undertake would be exerted to prevent the entrance of Italy into the conflict.

His efforts, of course, were futile, as were the efforts of all other Italians. One man, and one man only, the Dictator Benito Mussolini, made the decision which plunged Italy into the holocaust and brought about the tragedy from which the Italian people have already so grievously suffered, and from which they will continue to suffer for many years to come.

Italy had prostrated itself before Mussolini. He was thus enabled to achieve an almost complete control over every form of activity in Italian life. From top to bottom the Italian social system had become wholly corrupt through the corroding influence of Fascism. The structure had already become so rotten by 1940 that no effective means existed whereby the will of the Italian people could combat the fatal determination of their dictator.

The members of what was politely termed the Italian government were no more than Mussolini's lackeys. Count Ciano himself was wholly subservient to him. Count Ciano was a man who lacked neither personal dignity nor physical courage, and yet I have seen him quail at an interview with Mussolini when the Dictator showed irritation. The will of the Duce, however perverse, however ignorant, and however blindly mistaken the Fascist leaders knew him to be, was law. For no one in Italy from the King to his ministers, from the generals to the industrial magnates, dared to oppose him.

I first knew of the existence of this *Diary*, now for the first time published in full, from Count Ciano himself. He showed it to me and read me excerpts from it in my first conversation with him. There is no question of its authenticity, nor have I any reason to believe that in the last tragic days before his execution as a "traitor," at Mussolini's order, he had the opportunity or the desire to make any changes in what he had previously written. The record stands as he wrote it down day after day from the beginning of 1939 until he was removed by Mussolini from his position as Minister for Foreign Affairs in the early winter of 1943.

I believe it to be one of the most valuable historical documents of our times. To some who have read mutilated passages previously syndicated through the press, the *Diary* has proved a disappointment because of its lack of those sensational revelations which they had apparently anticipated. But those who will read the *Diary* in its complete text will obtain an opportunity to gain a clearer insight into the manner of being of Hitler's Germany and of Mussolini's Italy, and a far more accurate understanding of the degradation of the peoples subjected to Hitlerism and to Fascism during the years when almost the entire world trembled before the Axis partners.

They will find in the *Diary* a hitherto unrevealed picture of Germany's machinations during those fateful years. They will see perhaps more vividly than before how stereotyped was Hitler's course in utilizing his most solemn pledges to other governments, and by no means least to his ally, Italy, as a means of deluding them as to his real intentions.

Notwithstanding the recent assurances emanating from the Japanese war lords that the attack upon Pearl Harbor was carried out by a small group of militarists without the knowledge of Japan's responsible officials, the readers of this *Diary* will see how the government of Japan actually notified the German and Italian governments that the United States was to be attacked four days before the date of the assault upon Pearl Harbor.

They can read the unvarnished account of the devious preparations made by the Fascist government for its perfidious invasion of Albania and for its even more treacherous attempt to invade Greece.

There is scarcely an event in the dreary list of maneuvers and countermaneuvers in eastern Europe and in the Balkans, which is not graphically portrayed in this *Diary*.

But what is perhaps most valuable of all is the picture which the *Diary* presents of Italy under the climactic stage of Fascism.

The partially unconscious analysis of Mussolini, undertaken by a man who was not only his son-in-law but who also obviously admired him, and who loyally served him until only a few months before his death, could hardly be more devastating.

As Count Ciano states in one entry, "action," no matter what kind of action it might be, was the only spring to which Mussolini's nature responded. The Dictator's obsession that Germany's armed might could overcome every other force in the world, his black rancor, his ruthless cruelty, his dense ignorance of the world at large, his gross failure to comprehend the power which men's passion for freedom represents, and, above all else, his utter contempt for the Italian people themselves, stand out unforgettably in the passages of this *Diary*.

To those Italians who actually believed in Mussolini and who sincerely regarded him, at least during the years prior to World War II, as Italy's savior, these appraisals of his fellow countrymen made by Mussolini in complete confidence to his son-in-law will come as a revelation:

"The Italian race is a race of sheep. Eighteen years is not enough to change them. . . . We must keep them disciplined and in uniform from morning until night. Beat them and beat them and beat them. . . .* To make a people great it is necessary to send them into battle even if you have to kick them in the pants. This is what I shall do."

But, as is natural, it is the author of the *Diary* himself who is most clearly depicted in these pages.

Galeazzo Ciano, Count di Cortelazzo, was born at Leghorn on March 18, 1903. He was the only son of Costanzo Ciano, who served with gallantry as a captain in the Italian navy during World War I. The elder Ciano was one of those most responsible for the initial success of the Fascist movement. Promoted to the rank of admiral and ennobled immediately after Mussolini rose to power, he subsequently served for many years as Minister of Communications and as president of the so-called Fascist Chamber of Deputies. Today he is best remembered for the immense fortune which he accumulated through the opportunities offered him by his controlling influence within the Fascist party and, in particular, during the years when he held office as Minister of Communications. Galeazzo Ciano graduated in law at the University of Rome in 1925, and during his university years, which coincided with the first period of Fascism, also worked as a dramatic and art critic on a Roman daily newspaper. Strangely enough, during these years he adopted a critical attitude toward the Fascist party, of which his father, whom he greatly revered, was already an outstanding leader.

Immediately after his graduation he entered the Italian Diplomatic Service. During his first five years in the service he was stationed at Rio de Janeiro, Buenos Aires, Peking, and the Vatican City. It was at the close of this period that he married Mussolini's daughter, Edda. Simultaneously he became an ardent Fascist.

From then on his rise was rapid. Serving briefly as Consul General at Shanghai, he was promoted in 1932 to be minister to China. By 1933 he had again returned to Italy and, receiving an appointment as a member of the Italian Delegation to the London Economic Conference in June 1933, he was immediately thereafter made chief of Mussolini's press office. In 1935 he was promoted to be Undersecretary of State for Press and Propaganda. Shortly thereafter he was named a member of the Fascist Grand Council. The following year, at the age of thirty-three, he was appointed Minister for Foreign Affairs.

In his *Diary* Count Ciano shows himself to be precisely what he was in life—the amoral product of a wholly decadent period in Italian, and, for

---

* The revised translation of this passage dated February 7, 1940 is "They only understand the stick, the stick, the stick."

that matter, in European, history. To him morality in international relations did not exist. He was wholly seized of the concept that only might makes right. The question whether the Italian people should be consulted before the nation was plunged into war, since it would be their lives which would be lost, and since it would be they who would make the sacrifices involved, simply did not occur to him.

Yet where he showed himself far superior to the man who was his father-in-law, his political chief, and finally his executioner, was in his ability to see clearly where Italy's real security lay. He appears to have had no illusions from the time of the German occupation of Austria as to the danger inherent to Italy in German ambitions and in the extension of Hitler's sway. Time and again in his *Diary* he emphasizes his belief in the accuracy of the reports which come to him of the indications given by members of the Nazi hierarchy of Germany's ultimate intention to seize Trieste from the Italians and to occupy Italy's northern plains.

The *Diary* proves that, as a statesman, Ciano saw the major issue accurately. He was under no illusions as to what a German-dominated Europe would imply for Italy. He was convinced that only through the defeat of Germany could any world order be established in which a sovereign Italy could survive.

But what is equally apparent is Ciano's total inability to change the course upon which Mussolini had embarked. He relates the warnings against Germany which he gave to Mussolini and the occasional efforts which he made to establish some better relationship between Italy and the Western Powers. There is, however, never a sign that either his advice or his efforts were fruitful. During the earlier years in which he held high office he was wholly under Mussolini's sway. During the last two years of his life at times he made attempts to rally support among the members of the Fascist Grand Council in order to block Mussolini's growing subservience to the increasingly overbearing German taskmaster. Finally, at the crucial meeting of the Fascist Grand Council, on July 25, 1943, he took a leading part in the *coup d'etat* against Mussolini, and the Dictator was at length overthrown. It was then far too late. The Armistice was consummated, but the Italian people were already prostrate.

Had Count Ciano possessed either moral courage, the true patriotism which in his *Diary* he not infrequently claims for himself, or the tough ability possessed by so many of the leaders in the Risorgimento, he would have resigned his office in August of 1939, when Mussolini ordered him to obey the German demand for the Axis alliance, and joined from outside Italy in the fight against the egregious policies of the dictatorship.

But such a course would have been wholly contrary to Count Ciano's manner of being. Family ties hemmed him in. The corrupting effect of Fascism upon his character, the decadent atmosphere in which he lived, all combined to render impossible any such hazardous exploit on his part. However much he opposed Mussolini's uninterrupted March toward disaster, however clearly he foresaw the inevitable results, he invariably acquiesced until the final tragedy was already at hand.

As an individual, Count Ciano, like most human beings, possessed his qualities and his defects. He was sincerely attached to his parents, and to all those who had been close to him in his early youth. He was a devoted father to his three children.

Of medium stature, well set up, with aquiline features, he possessed both dignity and personal charm. In intimate conversation or at informal gatherings there was not the faintest trace of the pompous and self-conscious Fascist dignitary who appeared in public and who so sedulously aped the absurd mannerisms of the Duce himself. As a companion he was frank, often surprisingly outspoken, and possessed of a keen wit and of a mordant sense of humor. He spoke well and fluently and with no inconsiderable knowledge of modern history. He was keen in his perception of the relative significance of men and of events.

Corrupt in a financial sense he undoubtedly was. Whether he was personally responsible for the assassination of several enemies of the regime in the earlier years of his tenure of the Foreign Office, as has often recently been alleged, I have no conclusive evidence. But I am inclined to the belief that Count Ciano possessed many of the qualities of the men of the Italian Renaissance, and that such crimes would have by no means been outside the bounds of his toleration.

The final passage in this *Diary*, written by Count Ciano in his prison cell in Verona some two weeks before his execution, is the most revealing epitaph that can be written for him.

Galeazzo Ciano was a creature of his times, and the times in which he had his being are the least admirable mankind has known for many centuries.

Glossary of Terms and Abbreviations

Carabinieri — Military police unit and elite police force in peacetime.

Catholic Action — *Azione Cattolica* - Catholic lay organization

Croix de Feu — French right-wing organization

CTV — *Corpo di Truppe Volontario* - Italian volunteers in Spain

Dodecanesus — Italian islands in the Aegean

Dante Alighieri
Society — Italian cultural association

DIE — *Direttorio degli Italiani all'Estero* – Office of Italians overseas

GIL — *Gioventù Italiana del Littorio* - Fascist youth organization

GUF — *Gruppi Universitari Fascisti* – Fascist University Groups

Forest Militia — Fascist conservation police

ILVA — Major Italian industrial complex

Lateran Pact — Concordat between the Holy See and the Fascist government signed in 1929.

MVSN — *Milizia Volontaria per la Sicurezza Nazionale* - Fascist Blackshirt Militia

ONB — *Opera Nazionale Balilla* - Fascist children's organization

OVRA — *Organizzazione Volontaria Repressione Antifascismo* - Secret political police

PPF — *Parti Populaire Français* - French popular party of Jacques Doriot, pro-Fascist and collaborationist

Regime Fascista — Fascist daily in Cremona, published by Farinacci

SDP — *Sudeten Deutschen Partei* - Nazi party in Sudetenland

SIM — *Servizio Informazioni Militari* - Italian military intelligence 1934-1943

SA — *Sturm Abteilungen* - Nazi party storm troopers

SS — *Schutz Staffeln* - Nazi political police and military units

Tercio — Foreign legion in the Spanish nationalist army

23 Marzo — MVSN division

3 Gennaio — MVSN division

1937

August 22, 1937

In order to protect my writer's vanity, should these notes be published one day—please bear in mind that they were jotted down by me, in fits and starts, between meetings and phone calls. I was obliged and wanted to kick literature out and I limited myself to taking very short notes on the matters of which, I am, at once, either actor, author or spectator. The facts themselves will generate the interest rather than the hurried writing style.

August 23, 1937

Starting today I intend to keep this diary on a regular basis. The Duce told me that democracy is to Slavs what alcohol is to Negroes. Total destruction. Afterwards, there is the need for exceptional regulations following intense revolutionary upheavals.

Ingram[4] made a friendly move regarding the torpedo attacks in the Mediterranean. I replied brazenly. He left almost satisfied.

The Chinese want airplanes for Shanghai. I practically said no. I reminded them of their behavior during and after the sanctions. Now they can no longer count on our goodwill.

August 24, 1937

I took Suvich[5] to the Duce. His report on his mission to Washington was unremarkable and wordy: Prolixity is often a characteristic of Venetians.

Bocchini[6] spoke to me of various matters, and then of his next visit to Germany. I gave him instructions for the Duce's trip. Nothing new concerning the internal situation.

Received Medici[7] regarding his dispute with Italo Balbo and Prince Colonna. Advised absolute calm. He must not create, even though in the right, annoyances for the Chief!

The transfer of the *Montecuccoli* to China has been approved. Good in Spain. The offensive continues victoriously. I cabled to have the water cut

1

off at Santander to speed up the surrender, which is almost at hand. Perhaps tomorrow.

Starace[8] telephoned me, furious with Badoglio[9] for the things he said to the Federal secretary of Asti. Criticizing the Spanish enterprise. Personally against myself and Russo.[10]

August 25, 1937

Santander fell today under the fire of our Legions. I gave the Duce the news at the airport as we waited for the flyers in the Damascus-Paris race. He was pleased. He told me that today he felt I would bring him good news. Today was a great victory. I think that the prisoners will be more than 50,000. I think back to the days of Guadalajara. Many were really frightened at that time. Russo and I discussed it. We both got very worried in the process. But we kept the faith.

I persuaded the Duce to give Albania 60 million, over a period of four years, for various construction projects. My visit to Tirana convinced me of the necessity of thoroughly taking care of that area. We must create stable centers of Italian interest for them. One never knows what the future holds. We must be ready to grab opportunities when they arise. We will not withdraw like in 1920. We have absorbed several hundred thousand Albanians in the south. Why could not the same take place on the other side of the Adriatic coast?

I read an article on the peace of Amiens at the beach. Very interesting on the eve of my negotiations with Great Britain. It leads to reflection on many analogies.

August 26, 1937

The victory of Santander has taken on great proportions. It is not the beginning of the end—still distant—but it is a hard knock for Red Spain. I gave orders to bomb Valencia tonight, with the planes at Palma. We must seize the moment to terrorize the enemy. The Duce told me that he will make the Guadalajara defeatists pay. Alluding to Balbo. But he will forgive him or, as usual, turn a blind eye.

Russo sent me a beautiful letter on behalf of the Militia, grateful for my work and my support in bad times. I sent a handwritten reply.

Exchange of cables between myself and Bastico.[11] Received Federzoni,[12] retour d'Amerique. The account of the trip was banal and personal.

August 27, 1937

I cabled Bastico, tactfully, to obtain the flags and cannons taken from the Basques. I envy the French, the Galerie des Invalides and the Germans, the Military Museum. No painting is worth a flag taken from the enemy.

Ingram informed me of Drummond's[13] delayed return, hence also a delay in the talks (the outcome of which makes me very dubious). I advised him to tell the press that the delay is due to his brother's death. Otherwise there will be the customary speculation.

I promised Hotta[14] that we will not supply arms to China and shall facilitate Japanese requests. I am, personally, preparing the Duce's visit to Germany. Today he approved the first draft of the program. I recommended to Starace, Alfieri[15] and Sebastiani[16] the choice of persons in the entourage. Be careful about the uniforms. We must look more Prussian than they.

August 28, 1937

Filippo[17] has returned from Bled where he handed to Stoyadinovich[18] the photographic proof of the French-Czech conspiracy against him. He will go to the conference of the PE [Petite Entente] with his blood boiling. My tactics have succeeded.

The Duce has gone to Riccione. I saw Cupini,[19] who is back from his flying triumph in Paris. He asked me for a command in Spain and I immediately gave it to him.

Conde[20] complains against the navy's obstruction in the transfer of the two destroyers and two submarines. I stopped the legalistic opposition of our navy with a dressing down in a telephone call to Cavagnari.[21] The Duce approved. This Spanish enterprise is hampered by the constant opposition from the navy, engaging in passive resistance. The air force is doing very well. The army is steady. The militia is enthusiastic. But, after all, the Duce and I alone are responsible: or rather, are those who deserve credit. One day it will be acknowledged how great it is.

August 29, 1937

Sunday in Rome. Rain, hotel, solitude, a book. I have the feeling (reinforced by hotel life) of having gone back ten years: Sunday as a bachelor. I did not miss it.

August 30, 1937

Father's birthday. Telephoned him my good wishes. May God preserve him for a long time to come.

Decided, in principle, to dispatch 5,000 men to Spain, essential to replenish the current formations. I fear that the European reaction will be very strong. Also the negotiations with London will run a serious risk.

Rosso[22] told me this morning that the Soviets want to get out of Spain because of the situation in China and that they will reduce their help to a minimum. It would be a great advantage.

Summoned Russo and Pariani[23] for the mobilization and the preparation of the volunteers.

Received Revel[24] on the Albanian matter. He also gave me the funds for the construction of the legation. Our embassy in Tirana must also emphasize our supremacy. Something similar to what the British High Commission was in Egypt.

I saw Stein,[25] on his way to Geneva. I confirmed our views and gave him a faint smile. On the eve of a possible recognition of the Empire, we should encourage Russia's hope of the weakening of the Axis. Later on, the Duce's visit will destroy their hopes completely.

August 31, 1937

I am pleased that the Duce has come back to Rome. This is now more necessary than ever.

The Naval blockade yields very remarkable results: four Russian, or Red, steamers sunk, one Greek captured, one Spanish shelled and forced to take shelter in French port.

Lunch by the sea at Revel's with Prince Umberto, who had requested my presence. Very kind, as always for some time now, but the conversation was dull, incoherent and monotonous.

Medici told me he had spoken openly to him this morning regarding Balbo, and to have pointed out that the man from Ferrara's loyalty to the monarchy was doubtful. He instead apparently spoke well of mine instead, and the Prince apparently nodded in agreement.

Speaking of Balbo, Bastianini[26] told me of a conversation that he had with him in Tripoli. In brief, he supposedly professed fondness and loyalty toward me. He also spoke on behalf of his friends. *Timeo Danaos*. But, what do these declarations really mean? The swearing of loyalty should be made to the Leader; those made between Party members smell of conspiracy. And all that I entirely repudiate.

Visit from Ricci,[27] who is nearing the end of his days at Balilla. The Duce told me upon returning from maneuvers. Visit from Bottai,[28] to make contact.

Magistrati[29] communicated to me the final program of the Duce's visit to Germany. Grandiose event. All well, and the outline of the press release is excellent.

This evening I will go to Viareggio by train. Tomorrow is Deda's birthday.[30] Visit to the children and my parents.

September 1, 1937

Viareggio. Ponte a Moriano.
All well.

September 2, 1937

The Duce approved the program of the visit to Germany and he gave me the text, to be translated, of the speech that he will give in Berlin. Excellent.

Great activity by the navy: three ships torpedoed and one seized. But international opinion is turning hostile. Above all in England following the attempt to torpedo the destroyer *Havoc*, fortunately not hit. It was the *Iride*. We are already in deep trouble.

The Duce pretends to be angry with Egypt because of military preparations. When I pointed out that they only existed on paper, he replied that he intended to create a motive for a dispute at the right moment. "Egypt will be of use to me. We must already start saying that they are the ones muddying the waters."

Arrighi, a representative of Doriot,[31] asks me that the subsidies continue and requests weapons. Predicts a winter of conflict. Judges La Rocque[32] a traitor at the service of the French popular front.

Received von Hassel:[33] unpleasant and untrustworthy.

I asked Buti[34] and Pietromarchi[35] to prepare a plan of action for Geneva. I am not very confident but we must leave no stone unturned. If the Empire is not recognized now, the question will carry on until next fall. Serious complication.

September 3, 1937

Full orchestra: French-Russian-British. Motive: Piracy in the Mediterranean. Responsibility: Fascist. The Duce is very calm. He looks toward London and does not believe that the English want a clash with us. He told me the reason for his conviction. Napoleon, before going to Russia, had the atmospheric precipitations of the previous 25 years studied, in order to know the period of the first snows. He was unfortunate: that year it snowed a month in advance. Mussolini, before beginning the Ethiopian enterprise, studied the composition of the English population divided by age. He learned that for 22 million men there were 24 million women, and 12 million citizens over 50, the age limit of bellicosity. Therefore, predominance of the static masses over the active masses of youth. Quiet life, willingness to compromise, peace.

He told me of an amusing incident: Baldwin,[36] to continue reading a detective novel during an entire Sunday afternoon, did not open an envelope containing the instructions relevant to the Hoare[37]-Laval[38] plan. The delay was sufficient to spark polemics in France and to have the plan fall through.

Coming back to current matters, we remain calm and we have a plan ready for every event. But also this storm will pass just like the others. I secured an agreement not to send reinforcements to Spain until after the League of Nations recognized our African Empire. Either they refuse to recognize us, and we are free to act, or they recognize us, and we are free just the same—according to the Fascist doctrine that what is done is done.

We will give money to Doriot: not arms.

September 4, 1937

Full day. Many meetings throughout the morning and the evening. Poliakov.[39] I had the impression that London did not clearly see the question of the recognition of the Empire, without which there is no possible accord. Pol. took note and will speak to Chamberlain.[40]

I gave orders to Cavagnari to suspend naval action until further orders. But the storm seems to be abating.

Conde brought me a cable from Franco,[41] who says that if the blockade continues for all of September it will bring the solution. This is true. But now we have to suspend it.

An exhibition of the Fascists Abroad. Much progress. The crowd applauded the Spanish and, for the first time, also the Germans.

September 5, 1937

Parade by Starace and the Young Fascists. Very successful. The younger generation must be entirely under the Party's control. I said this to the Duce, who already felt that way.

Afternoon: Viareggio, Ponte a Mariano. My children are two adorable treasures. Father is doing better. Deda is well.

Conversation with Balbo: he offered me, not an olive branch, but an entire forest of olive trees. For a moment he was even sincere.

September 6, 1937

The Duce has hurled abuse against America, country of blacks and Jews, disintegrating element of civilization. He wants to write a book: The Europe of 2000. The races which will play an important role will be the Italians, the Germans, the Russians and the Japanese. The other nations will be destroyed by the acid of Jewish corruption. They refuse even to have children because it's painful. They do not know that pain is the only creative element in the life of nations. And also in that of men. I saw Ingram and mentioned the removal of the Ethiopian stumbling block at Geneva. I consider this to be essential for the resumption of talks.

I received the Soviet indictment. The Duce approved my plan: Russia wants to sabotage the conference. Seeing that the Mediterranean conference was about to meet they have launched another plot, and this time against the international agreement. I pleaded this cause with Blondel[42] and Ingram: the latter appeared to be of the same opinion; both seemed to be shaken.

We await the Russian counter-reaction. The atmosphere darkens once again. For the moment the Bolsheviks have made a false move. We have scored a point.

September 7, 1937

Much work, many people. I spoke with Massimo[43] to discuss our reply to the French and British governments. Basically we are in agreement. The official letter was drawn up this evening. Tomorrow I will show it to the Duce. As foreseen, London and Paris are upset by the Soviet gaffe. Must take advantage: force against Russia, indulgence towards the others.

I received the judges of the Poets of Mussolini competition. Comical scene: Sarfatti[44] did not want to award the very fine poem by Fanny Dini, whom she accused of having plagiarized her lyrics. What trouble literary women are!

Farinacci[45] wants to go to Germany with the Duce. But does the Duce, who has supposedly given his consent, really want him? And then, for what reasons?

September 8, 1937

Naturally the Duce does not want Farinacci in Germany and he told me to arrange things that way.

The official letter, drawn up by me, approved at Palazzo Venezia, has been adopted along its main lines also by Germany. No Nyon: instead we are ready for discussion at the Committee of Nonintervention in London. The wording is advantageous: it is not simply a refusal but contains also constructive wording. Albania is in step; Bulgaria and Yugoslavia move together and could perhaps join us.

I told Ingram that I based my proposal on points made in our last conversation. He is also interested in backing it because of his part in its authorship. That flaccid and false British functionary was so flattered that, feebly, he will do it. Touch someone in his personal vanity and you cannot go wrong.

At the beach, conversation with Helfand, the Russian delegate. This little Jew, intelligent and refined, understands the gaffe his government made (today, second letter that confirms the accusation), but he must defend Moscow and he does it with dignity. He spoke of incontestable evidence against us. I believe that this has arisen from the decipherment of cables. I faced him with arrogant composure. He said that I am treating Russia as I wouldn't treat Lithuania. I replied that I cannot, but the Duce can.

Saw Castellino[46] and Malaparte.[47]

Meeting with Guarneri[48] and Lessona[49] for the economy and foreign exchange of the Empire.

Decided to resume the financial backing of the Rexists (250,000 per month).[50]

September 9, 1937

Delivered the letter. Long talks with Cerruti,[51] too optimistic regarding the French inclinations towards us. According to him they are dying to throw themselves into our arms. I don't believe it at all. At least not for the moment.

Ingram left a memo on British intentions regarding the recognition of the Empire. Rather negative. Without such recognition the possibility of an agreement with London is remote. Pity!

Galli:[52] Turkey, as usual, is waiting for the English. Under these circumstances my visit to Ankara will be postponed until better times.

I spoke at length with Appelius[53] about Ethiopia. About old times, and about today. I miss that war.

We will not answer the Russians. There is a precedent: Venice let Papal bulls accumulate, leaving them unanswered...

September 10, 1937

Grandi[54] is preparing to return to London. I gave him the instructions to resume contacts. The situation is once again difficult: we must give battle once again.

Berti[55] and Gambara[56] gave a long report on the situation in Spain. Tomorrow I will take them to the Duce. We still have a long way to go and victory could once again elude us. We must hurry up and win. For many reasons.

Marinotti[57] first-rate man, but a bit talkative and self-possessed, like someone who feels he is successful. All in all a man to keep in mind and, if necessary, to make use of.

September 11, 1937

Meeting between Grandi and the Duce. The latter took stock of the situation. If possible he still wants the agreement. But if Great Britain maintains an offensive course of action he is ready for the harshest of reactions.

Afternoon, meeting between the Duce and Berti. Summary of the situation in Spain. Overall, satisfactory. The Duce means to wait several weeks to decide whether to dispatch new troops. If there is no winter lull and Franco act, the Duce will help him.

Violent rage from the Duce at the first news from Nyon. The last telephone call from Bova[58] calmed him slightly.

Received Bocchini: nothing new.

September 12, 1937

Ceremony of the Young Fascist Women. Very good.

Plane to Pisa. Horse racing in Livorno. Edda and Ciccino[59] at the race. Father well.

September 13, 1937

Ingram and Blondel handed in the conclusions of Nyon. I prepared a reply in which, without requesting to participate, the right to parity is stated. I will certainly manage to trap them. Either they cooperate with us or the scheme still fails because of them. I await Berlin's consent before sending our reply.

Ricci carried out a beautiful parade. But the Ballila organization, as it is now, cannot last.

Terruzzi,[60] returned from Spain, very critical of Bastico's command. He believes that a decisive operation is possible for mid-October. Frankly, I do not. The Duce is fed up because of the huge revolt in Goggiam.

September 14, 1937

The Duce telephoned at 7 in the morning to add to the letter the request that Germany should also participate in the Mediterranean patrol. Berlin refused. That would have put the entire matter—quite simply—into the cauldron once again. As things stand, Nyon will fall into place.

Zenone[61] will become a director to the SNIA. A fascist in certain industrial groups is useful.

Teruzzi met with the Duce. The Duce was in good shape: aggressive and anti-British. Of the English he said: "A nation which thinks with its arse."

September 15, 1937

Franco asks for four submarines to be placed at his disposal. Two will go immediately and the other two shortly.

The letter has been judged as very clever, but the environment is bitter and hostile. Bova telephoned from Geneva to say that Eden[62] and Delbos[63] are ready to accept our requests but they would like us to make the first move. Impossible. We must just wait. They will come to us.

Wedding between Farace[64] and Catherine of Russia.[65] A lot of royalty present at the wedding: some taking part at the service and in secondary positions. The priest invited the bride to follow the example of her great ancestors and mentioned her namesake, the notorious Catherine. The groom did not appreciate it...

Lunch with the Prince of Piedmont. Dim conversation. I was seated near Princess Mafalda. She is not beautiful; she has neither intelligence nor personality. But she likes men, as all women do.

September 16, 1937

Nothing new in the London-Paris-Geneva area. They are waiting in vain for us to make a move.

Lunch with Volpi,[66] Cini,[37] Pirelli.[68] Considerable concern within industrial groups. They say that "stocks" are empty and that we could sustain a war only for a short period of time.

Victory in China appears quite certain. I agree. When all is said and done the Chinese will flee. And when they start running no one can stop them. The anticommunist agreement is on the fast track.

The Duce is worried that the French police could be on the trail of the perpetrators of the assassinations in Paris. Em.[69] tells me that this is impossible. Anyway, we are not involved. They are Frenchmen working for Met.

September 17, 1937

The Duce told me that Ricci would be sacked, with the words: whoever is against the Party is against me and will be broken. He added that he had slipped the news to Alfieri, who is a "chatterbox," so that the news may be passed on to the perennially restless Balbo and Bottai.

He then spoke, displaying more optimism to me about the situation in East Africa. The revolt is not growing and measures to crush it—gas included—have been ordered.

Ricci is wearing his camper's medal. He didn't mention it and neither did I.

I wrote a letter to Grandi to clarify matters and to ask for exact information.

A chance lunch with Balbo, joined by the talkative Cini. He is considered an intelligent man. I wonder if he really is or is not really a great hustler.

September 18, 1937

Ingram and Blondel brought me the additional agreement for the sea planes and surface ships, and they took advantage for a weak attempt to resume the conversations about Nyon. I prepared a conciliatory reply and managed to have the Duce agree to it, while he remains extremely uncompromising. Meantime, it is to our advantage to announce that they made the first move. The press, though, must avoid speaking of Canossa and of genuflections, otherwise it will encourage more inflexibility. I will hand over the letter tomorrow.

Libohova[70] brought me a letter from King Zog. He is happy with the recent pro-Albanian steps.

September 19, 1937

I watched from the window of the P. V., together with the Duce, the funeral of Prospero Colonna.[71] The Duce was in a good mood and made some comments. The weather was hot and rainy. Funeral weather. When it's sunny no one thinks of the dead. He told me that Tittoni[72] refused to follow funerals in the winter for fear of following the dead into the grave.

I gave the note to the two chargés d'affaires. They seemed relieved from a burden. I also added a few conciliatory words.

The Duce is calling often to find out new developments in the diplomatic battle being waged. In the meantime he is getting ready for military action. Bruno[73] will leave for Palma on the 22nd. And with him the entire Biseo[74] squadron. I envy them. But I am, at least for the moment, nailed to this desk.

September 20, 1937

No official reaction from Paris and London. The press is good. The reply will be for tomorrow.

Doucich[75] came to make a farewell call. He is a pompous and vain poet who never believed in an agreement between Rome and Belgrade. Now he pretends to be an old friend. Stoyadinovich, who is nobody's fool, fired him with good reason.

Buffarini[76] gave me the customary report on Italian affairs. Things are in good order. He led me to understand that yesterday, at Lucca, Edda was not warmly received. I am sorry. She's a great girl, but she lacks know-how and does not like crowds. So she is not liked. And it's a shame because she has great and rare qualities.

September 21, 1937

Blondel and Ingram delivered a note to me which gives us considerable satisfaction, even though the word "parity" is carefully avoided. The Duce approved my reply and the press release: we accept a technical conference to modify the conditions of Nyon according to our wishes. It is a great victory. From accused torpedoers to Mediterranean policemen, with the exclusion of the Russians, whose ships have been sunk.

I am furious with Parini.[77] He sent a proclamation to the Italians in Germany without even telling me. He has lost all sense of proportion. He is ready for rotation. I think I will substitute him with De Cicco,[78] an old and trusted Fascist party member.

Nicolas Franco[79] returns to Spain. He is happy with his work and is optimistic about the situation. He feels the conflict will be over by next spring. I might add that he has been mistaken before.

September 22, 1937

A completely quiet day.

Positive reactions to the conclusion of the Nyon negotiations. The Duce, without saying anything, let it be understood that he is very pleased.

September 23, 1937

The preparations for the visit to Germany are now complete. I personally even saw to the details. The Duce told Alfieri that my organization is close to his ideal.

Inauguration of the Augustus exhibition and of the Exhibition of the Revolution. For the latter the Duce gave instructions to reduce the part about the intervention and the war and to reach the creation of the Empire. It is his concept of permanent revolution.

I spoke to Parini. He will become minister to Cairo. Ghigi[80] goes to Vienna. Salata[81] comes back home.

Lessona reported the situation of the Empire. Numerous, but contained uprisings. He fears, though, that at Mascal something bigger may explode. If the entire country blows up it would be very serious. But I don't think so. However, what is happening prevents demobilization and that is bad for our finances.

September 24, 1937
Departure for Germany.

September 25, 1937
Munich.

September 26, 1937
Maneuvers in Mecklemburg. Interesting, but I expected more.

September 27, 1937
Essen. Visit to Krupp. Very much impressed by industrial power.
Arrival in Berlin. Triumphant.

September 28, 1937
Potsdam. The tomb of Frederick II. Sans-Souci. The New Palace. Napoleon also stayed there. He came here fighting.

Parade at the Maifeld. Beautifully choreographed: much emotion and a lot of rain.

September 29, 1937
Departure.

From a formal point of view the trip added nothing to the Berlin Protocols. But the presence of the Duce in Germany helped make friendship for Fascism more popular. I don't yet dare say that for Italy. The personal success of Mussolini is indisputable. He captured the German crowds with his magnetism, his voice, and his impetuous youthfulness.

Will the solidarity of the Regimes not be sufficient to keep two nations whose race, culture, religion, and tastes are exact opposites really together? No one can accuse me of hostility towards the pro-German policy. I was the one to start it. But, I ask myself, should Germany be considered as a goal, or rather a useful place to maneuver? Current events, and above all Mussolini's political loyalty, make me tend to believe in the first possibility. But will not events develop in such a way as to once again separate these two nations?

We shall see. Today the Rome-Berlin Axis is something very real and extremely useful. I will try to extend the line between Rome and Tokyo and the system will be complete.

It is not appropriate to make forecasts for the far distant future.

September 30, 1937

Return to Rome: triumphant. They could have done without the arches and laurels. These symbols are reserved for victors at war, not for those who return from a train journey.

The people's enthusiasm was wonderful. They were happy to welcome their Duce. Each person felt they had offered abroad the most precious possession the country has to offer. And the joy of the masses was, this time, the sum total of everyone's happiness.

October 1, 1937

Ciccino's birthday.

To Ponte a Moriano, a day spent with the family, with Deda, the children and my parents.

October 2, 1937

The Duce has gone to Rocca.[82]

In the afternoon I received Blondel and Lord Perth to hand over the note. I don't believe we can agree to take part in a conference without Germany. I will now wait for the opinion and the decisions of the Duce.

Conde, on Franco's behalf, has requested the recall of Bastico. We will concede that to him. Bastico spoke to me about the situation in Spain. Franco's position is good, but the outcome is not yet settled. He asks for reinforcements for the Volunteer Corps. In the present conditions he does not feel it capable of carrying out decisive operations. A withdrawal of the volunteers would place the nationalist position in danger. Cavagnari presented me with the decisions to control the Mediterranean: good.

October 3, 1937

Sunday at Castel Fusano. A beautiful Mediterranean autumn day: warm and a little misty.

October 4, 1937

Sent to the Duce a draft copy of our reply to the French and British initiative.

This morning I received the Duke of Aosta,[83] who gave me an account of his trip to England. According to him the agreement should be possible. But, if forced to do so, England can make war and make it well. He repeated the words used by Grandi.

In the afternoon a long-winded De Vecchi,[84] the cordial Buffarini and Guarneri hardly encouraging on the currency situation.

At the beach: a nice swim by myself.

October 5, 1937

De Vecchi resumed the next installment of his report. He is unbearably boring. Long talks with Pariani regarding the situation in Spain. His opinion is to send Alpine troops in force to break through at Valencia. But what would be the French and British reaction? Is it wise to take initiatives which could lead to a conflict? I think not. First of all, because Germany is not ready. She will be three years from now. And secondly, because we are lacking in raw materials and ammunition. And finally, because a conflict of that kind would make everyone hate us. However, the Spanish situation is serious and demands a rapid solution. I will speak to the Duce about it.

Helfand and I talked at length. These Russians cannot swallow the Rome-Berlin Axis. They hope for a improvement in relations. For the moment I don't see that it's possible. On the contrary...

October 6, 1937

I informed Berti his assignment to a command in Spain. He spoke to me at length on how he sees the situation. In brief: still a very long conflict ahead. Perhaps more than a year, unless we assign an entire expedition corps, and particularly Alpine troops which can maneuver by surprise in the mountains in winter. As things stand, and if such a dispatching is not possible, he asks for the withdrawal of the infantry and to reduce contribution to specialized services, and to the Artillery, Engineer Corps, and air force. I will speak to the Duce tomorrow: Berti gave me the impression of a man who will not give us trouble, but neither does he have any brilliant surprises in store for us.

He has asked for Teruzzi's scalp, and he will perhaps get it. Talks with Bocchini: information on Russian espionage and a diatribe against Balbo. Nothing new.

I saw the Duce upon his return from Rocca. He gave me the text of the note with a few changes. We shall hand it to the French and British on Saturday.

Galli is on his way back to Turkey. I gave him instructions to drop the project of my visit to Ankara. It is not the right time.

October 7, 1937

Meeting between Berti and the Duce. The new commander will send a report by Saturday the 16th, with an overall judgment of the situation and his proposals. Decisions will be made on the basis of this report, and in the meantime we might also examine further international developments. Teruzzi will not return to Spain. I will speak to the Duce tomorrow to see that he receives recognition for his work which will help him fend off the wave of the usual critical vultures.

Lord Perth and Blondel have asked me for the answer to their note. I told them that the delay is due to the speech by Azcárate[85] who stated at Geneva that Valencia will not do away with the Red Volunteers. Now the note is in Berlin: once we will have approval of the wording, we shall hand it in. One must always give the impression that the Axis is solid.

The Japanese begin to buy airplanes from us.

October 8, 1937

(Replaced Parini with De Cicco and made other changes.)

Nothing noteworthy today. The note will be handed over tomorrow. In the meantime tension has increased. There is no doubt that the Spanish problem is heading towards an international crisis: either a break or a clearing of the air. Many anti-fascist forces are working for the former alternative. But nations today do not want war.

October 9, 1937

I gave the letter to Lord Perth and Blondel today at midday.

No comment and only a few words to set the time of publication. Blondel appeared to be somewhat shaken by our refusal. Lord Perth was indifferent and only spoke to ask me the name of a medicine for rheumatism that I had recommended to him last year and that, it appears, worked well for him. He is very English.

Turati[86] spoke to me about the living conditions and the progress made in the Empire. Nothing to be happy about. But the minister is more at fault than the Viceroy.[87] One must have faith and let the person in charge do his job. Or otherwise replace him. But not torment him with small matters and constantly tie his hands.

October 10, 1937

Sunday at the beach. Nothing of importance.

October 11, 1937

Nothing of particular importance. We await the French and British reactions to the note. For the moment, little in the press and nothing official. Grandi told me on the telephone that it was a day of clarification. A clearing of the air.

The Duce, who follows closely and calmly with extraordinary sense of decision, called me a second time this evening. He spoke of various matters. He thinks that a committee of six powers (Italy, France, Great Britain, Germany, Portugal and Russia) could resolve the matter of the Volunteers and that of belligerency. In the meantime he wants fresh impressions from Spain. Anfuso will provide them soon. I suggested that it would be appropriate to withdraw the ambassador from Paris, for reciprocity. He agrees. He thinks of withdrawing him on the anniversary of the twelve months' absence of Chambrun.[88]

October 12, 1937

Visit from Starace, who announced the imminent sacking of Lessona. I too had understood this from a speech made by the Duce.

The Duce insists on withdrawing Cerruti. He is right. To begin with I have sent a good counselor to Paris: Prunas,[89] so that he prepares for the deputyship.

The French and British reaction to my note is weak. The Delbos "take action" is already losing its edge. I think that they will limit themselves to continue an exchange of views.

Berlin will make a nonaggression declaration to Brussels. Perhaps we should do the same, to not be cut out of the game.

I saw Russo regarding the new Black Shirt troops for Spain. For the moment I am against sending them. Too dangerous.

October 13, 1937

I accompanied Teruzzi to see the Duce, who promised him a position. I am happy that this old and loyal soldier is rewarded: he did well in Africa and in Spain.

Lowentau[90] sent me a cable, requesting a clear declaration regarding our policy towards China. I replied that we are, and will continue to be, neutral, but the Chinese attitude towards us prevents a more active demonstration of goodwill.

Conversation with Dupuy[91] of the *Petit Parisien*. Spectral analysis of Italian and French relations. On our part there is goodwill to improve them. But in Paris they don't wish to do anything positive in this direction. For quite some time official France has not had a friendly attitude towards us. How might we change the present situation? In any event it is not worth breaking all ties and closing all doors.

October 14, 1937

Edda is back.

London and Paris have accepted the fundamental concepts of the note. I am surprised. After recent threats, this French-British retreat leads one to think about the decline of these two nations. A time will come, or perhaps it has already arrived, when we may dare everything and play the ultimate game.

Volpi told me of his trip to Yugoslavia. But he didn't speak to me about Yugoslavia: he spoke about *himself* in Yugoslavia. Therefore, it was not very interesting. He would like the Ministry of the Colonies, but he denies it, blushing like an embarrassed school boy. He would be a good minister and he would do well. With all his faults he is a talented man.

Revel confirmed to me the enactment of the tax on stocks at the next Council of Ministers. The Stock Exchange has fluctuated wildly during these last few days, in anticipation of tax measures. The Duce attributes this to the fear of war and wants to close the stock markets, which he defined as "morning rallies of antifascism." The measure seems too extreme to me. The experts advise against it.

Fagiuoli[92] asked me what to do about Visconti.[93] Fire him. Valentino[94] is happy with our situation in Poland. He proposes a visit by Beck[95] to Rome. Nothing against it, as long as the Germans are in favor. I believe they should be. I will discuss it with the Duce.

October 15, 1937

I sent instructions to Grandi for the Non-Intervention Committee. Some concessions must be made. Therefore, three points should be made: we are ready to discuss the evacuation plan for our Volunteers; ask the parties in conflict what their intentions are and, if positive, then set an evacuation plan; at the same time obtain the recognition of belligerent status.

I spoke to Lord Perth in a conciliatory manner. He was very pleased. The man has gambled on an agreement with us and wants to win. He asked me about our forces in Libya. I replied that we will discuss this during the British and Italian negotiations.

The Duce has gone to Villa Torlonia. He was very pleased and he closely follows the development of events.

Logusiano[96] brought me a Romanian decoration. There was no reason to give it to me, apart from the desire of close friendship.

October 16, 1937

I accompanied Ciccino to his first day of school. How time flies! I remember as if it were yesterday went I first went. I cried when I was taken away from old Emilia and I calmed down only when the caretaker's husband, wearing a garbage man's uniform, threatened to arrest me. And yet almost thirty years have gone by! Ciccino will study well. He has a lot of self-respect and is extremely proud.

Grandi's declarations, who has diluted my instructions too much, got a good reception. We are in a clearly advantageous diplomatic position. I saw the ambassador of Poland who, in the name of Beck, came to inform me of the clearly anti-Italian activity carried out by the French at Geneva. There is nothing to be done. Internal politics divide these two nations. And their jealousy as well.

The minister of Greece came to make an act of faith (in the Greek meaning of the word) after having opposed us during the Nyon accords. He protested a little against the intrepid De Vecchi who persecutes the Greeks and has apparently inaugurated the castor oil method in the islands! He is an old lunatic who will continue to give us trouble.

I accompanied the Duce home and I gave him an extensive account on the situation. He is pleased. He had prepared an anti-Belgian *Informazione Diplomatica*. I managed to stop him. It would have been troublesome, also towards Germany.

October 17, 1937

Nothing special. Filippo, who has returned from Spain, tells me what we already knew more or less. That our soldiers are tired and also that Franco cannot wait to get them out of the way, retaining keeping the air force and artillery. He is envious of our successes and fears those of the future.

October 18, 1937

Police parade and maneuvers in the afternoon. Very well done. It is a small perfect armed force, equipped with all of the most modern weapons. With a police force like that, if loyal, movements in the streets are no longer conceivable: within a few minutes any insurrection would be stopped. In reality the modern state always has the means to defend itself, as long as the leader is willing to use them.

Himmler,[97] was present and full of admiration.

I received Ricci, for whom I had some good words. He made some mistakes, but remains a good organizer and a loyalist.

I confirmed my talks with Dupuy to Blondel, who had asked about them.

October 19, 1937

Council of Ministers. Approval of the law adding 10% tax on corporations. Medici and Benni[98] were not enthusiastic.

Franco asks us for a division to liquidate the northern front. We agreed to it.

October 20, 1937

Von Hassel accompanies Raumer, Ribbentrop's[99] chief of his ministerial staff, to see me. He is coming to propose that Italy, join the pact between Germany and Japan as an original signatory state. This follows my own contacts with Tokyo. In principle I will declare myself favorable. However, I will ask to be told and eventually participate in, the secret accords that I understand to exist between Berlin and Tokyo.

Mais il y a quelque chose qui cloche. Neurath,[100] it seems to me is going nowhere. And von Hassel, remarkably, is in agreement with him. They don't want to do anything that would worry London and they also fear Ribbentrop's personal success.

October 21, 1937

The Ribbentrop affair, as I had anticipated, is turning into a mystery. Neurath, playing the opposite card, called for Attolico.[101] He was hoping that we would not accept. Seeing that we have accepted, he is discouraged. He spoke of eventual repercussions in London. Then he went to Berchtesgaden and returned to Berlin. Conclusion: Ribbentrop will come tomorrow, but Neurath does not support his mission. Attolico, as the former Freemason he is, immediately took sides with Neurath. The Duce is right, as always. The minds of these old men cannot be changed. The men need to be changed. And it is deplorable to see how in Germany, the Minister of Foreign Affairs does not follow the directives of the Führer. From the telephone call between Neurath and von Hassel, it emerges in an overwhelming way.

Today I was moved by the story of a girl, who was asking me for help. She told me how she was forced into prostitution and used words of a simple, unmistakable truth.

I saw the film on the life of Zola. Good technically, poisonous as far as content. It is the exaltation of anti-militarism. I will have it banned.

October 22, 1937

Meeting with Ribbentrop, in the presence of von Hassel and Raumer during the second half. Then meeting with the Duce. I recorded the account of the two meetings. In principle, our joining the pact between Germany and Japan has been approved.

But from Berlin, Attolico, driven by Neurath, made opposing pressures. Here, von Hassel was very hostile to the matter. When Ribbentrop arrived at the airport, he said to one of my secretaries "this evening I will write one of the most amusing pages in my diary." These opposing currents in German foreign politics are dangerous.

The fall of Gijon is very good in Spain. This will give the possibility to Franco to overthrow the forces on the front in Aragon and, let's hope, to accelerate the developments of this damned war.

October 23, 1937

I called Prince of Hesse[102] to Rome and I will send him to the Führer to find out his thoughts on the Tripartite Pact.

In London the situation has become complicated, following Russia's refusal and the ambiguous attitude of the French and British. The Duce, on my advice, has personally written *Informazione Diplomatica* n. 4.

I received the ambassador of Japan regarding the Tripartite Pact. I took minutes of the meeting.

Gerbore[103] told me he has found out that the German police are suspicious of Magistrati's ideas. Maybe because of activities carried out by Renzetti.[104] I sent Gerbore to Berlin to inform Massimo. The matter is troublesome because, given the bonds between Massimo and me, it creates a general feeling of mistrust. It is hard to change in German minds the reputation that we once had.

Mrs. Patrone[105] cries and asks for her son, held in prison in Russia. I will do everything possible to accelerate an exchange with Grigoriev.[106]

Dinner in Ribbentrop's honor at Villa Madama.

October 24, 1937

I drafted Grandi's instructions for the meeting of the Committee which will take place on Tuesday. We must not give in on the unanimity question: otherwise we will give Russia a clear position of advantage. On the other hand, should we give in we will find France and England becoming more intransigent. Also Ribbentrop, who, regarding England, is as amorous as a betrayed lover, feels the same way. In a meeting held yesterday evening with him, he expounded to me the need of a military alliance between Rome-Berlin-Tokyo in anticipation of the inevitable conflict with the Western Powers. He said that Hitler advises to not abandon Majorca, ever again it is an extraordinary new pawn in our Mediterranean chessboard.

Classic Sunday afternoon: I played war with Ciccino and Dindina[107] with their toy soldiers. We had the whole neighborhood running for cover with our canon sound effects!

October 25, 1937

Ribbentrop called me to say that the Führer sees no problem that the agreement be signed in Rome rather than Munich, as Ribbentrop himself had proposed given his position as ambassador in London. The Duce approved and wants the signing to take place as soon as possible. If the Japanese don't split hairs too much it could be signed on the 6th. Unexpectedly, a Grand Council meeting will follow which will decide our leaving the League of Nations by the 18th, second anniversary of the sanctions. This is how Italy remembers and avenges itself. On the other hand, those of us who are against the League are already so numerous that we could establish a League of the Nations that are not part of the League of Nations.

I protested to Drummond about the activity of British agents in Jerusalem among Ethiopian political refugees. Should this continue we will give freedom of action once again to the Arab language radio. Drummond, who is a sincere convert, will cable also to second our point of view to the London Committee.

October 26, 1937

Meeting with Hotta to draft the pact.

Nothing else of any importance.

October 27, 1937

This morning I received Henry Gris, a Lithuanian journalist who had insulted me some months ago in *Esquire*. He was very embarrassed and turned red, above all his ears and around his chin. I spoke to him courteously and at length; this worked to make him even more timid.

Arrival of Hess[108] and a delegation. Meeting with Hess. I wanted to make it clear to him that in Italy the most fascist ministry is the Ministry of Foreign Affairs. I knew that I was opening a Pandora's box. He immediately went on the war path against Neurath and against German diplomats connected to the Diplomatic International. I took advantage to ask for von Hassel's head since he had been playing both ends against the middle for too long. I have documented the reasons for our mistrust in the man. Hess nodded and will speak to the Führer about it. He asked me for suggestions about a successor. I told him that a Party man would be fine. The alliance between the two countries is based, above all, on the identity of political systems that determines a common destiny.

Simul stabunt, simul cadent.

October 28, 1937

The rally at the Foro Mussolini was grandiose and picturesque: the most beautiful of all that I have ever seen. Starace is a great direction. The Germans were moved by the Duce's speech and by the rally, and were blinded by our colors and by our sun.

Meeting with Stein in the afternoon, for the liberation of Markov.[109] Not much politics and, as usual, apocalyptic prophecies if we continue our friendship with Germany. The Great Flood if the pact with Japan also comes into being.

Something new: Perth tells me, in a letter, that Eden would be happy to meet with me in Brussels. It is interesting that the move should come from him. I believe that it would be wise to go. The Duce, whom I telephoned, also shares this opinion. It is a good way to put aside the matters of the Far East: all of the floodlights of world publicity will be shining on the talks between Ciano and Eden.

October 29, 1937

This morning medals were awarded to the widows of those who died in Spain. A successful ceremony. But, to see so many people in mourning, and to look into so many red eyes, I had to examine my conscience, and I ask myself if this blood had been spilled for a just cause. Yes: that is the answer. At Malaga, at Guadalajara, at Santander, we defended our civilization and our Revolution. And sacrifice is necessary when bold and strong spirits must be forged within nations. The wounded were very proud. One of them who had lost both hands and one eye, said: "I ask only for another hand so that I may return to Spain." It sounds like a reply from an anthology, and I heard it from a boy of twenty, struck down by enemy weapons, who was happy because the Duce paused with him for a moment. The Germans that were with us learned something.

The Duce does not believe that I should go to Brussels. All things considered, he is right. The unprepared meeting with Eden, would be useless and perhaps damaging for the disappointment that it would create. If it is to be, the occasion can always we found later on. I spoke to Perth about it. He was not very convinced by my arguments. Personally he wanted the meeting, which, according to him, would have clarified the situation a lot.

October 30, 1937

In the morning, I had a meeting with Philip of Hesse. He is back from Berlin after having spoken with Hitler, who is actually very annoyed with Ribbentrop, not because he claimed responsibility for the Berlin-Tokyo-Rome Pact, which the Führer approved of, but because contrary to his instructions he had hidden everything from Neurath. Now the matter is sorted out: Ribbentrop will win after all.

Hess wished to see me outside the Ministry. I met him at the Grand Hotel. He was excited and nervous. He told me that Mrs. von Hassel[110] had spoken to him in terms very hostile to Italy. Hess, a loyal man, was indignant. He intended to leave immediately for Berlin to demand Hassel's head. The removal would have been facilitated also by the fact that the ambassador was also leaving for Berlin to complain about Ribbentrop. The Führer would then fire von Hassel, his complaint as an excuse. I advised him not to go. Write. An unexpected visit would be the cause of to other interpretations. The dispute would appear to be between him and us: not between him and his embassy. He wrote. Hassel is truly an enemy of the Rome-Berlin Axis and is hostile towards fascism. He goes around saying that Streicher,[111] visiting here, went to the German School and showered a little girl with compliments who he judged to be the most beautiful and the most intelligent. She was the only Jew in the school...

October 31, 1937

Inauguration of Guidonia.

Strong reaction in Paris at Cerruti's departure. It was a situation that needed to be cleaned up. We did, and we did well. If, recognition is to be obtained from France, it will certainly not be obtained because of smiles and weaknesses. As Cerruti had wanted. The Germans much appreciated the move.

November 1, 1937

Tokyo agreed to the formula of the Three-Power Pact. The signing will take place next Saturday at 11. The Germans and the Japanese, with whom ironing out the particulars is extremely meticulous and long, wanted to decide upon even the smallest procedural details. The matter is very important. The alliance of three military empires such as Italy, Germany, and Japan tips the scale, with an unprecedented armed force. London will have to review all of its positions.

Meeting with the King of Greece.[112] Courteous, modest, fairly open. He also wanted to speak to me about politics, which he dislikes. I described the situation in Europe, and I told him very calmly and very resolutely, that while we desire peace, we are ready for any eventuality should our rights and national positions not be recognized. The Rome-Berlin Axis is a source of power to be taken into account. Nations must take a position: either as our friends, or as our enemies. Nothing separates Italy from Greece: therefore I count on Greek friendship. He was disturbed. And even more so when I told him that we can already fully count on some friendly states in the Balkans. My allusion to Yugoslavia was obvious. Fate is sealed: the Serbs will have Salonica, we shall take Tirana and Corfu. The Greeks sense, and fear all of this. I sense that my good words did not cancel this idea, which, however, I have been working for some time to bring about.

November 2, 1937

Eden's speech was very hostile. But this was to be expected. The man cannot accept the Ethiopian failure and tries to fight back. I drafted *Informazione Diplomatica* n. 5. It is a good reply. An even better reply still will be the one on Saturday, when we sign the anticommunist Tripartite Pact, so to speak, which is in reality clearly anti-British.

Talks with Balbo. As always he is sour and untrustworthy. He counts upon the Party and tries to save his accomplice: Lessona.

November 3, 1937

The Duce was making fun of Grandi, who is actually counting too much on the Committee of Non-Intervention and sends bulletins to the Stefani agency, which the Chief has qualified as "bulletins of Austerlitz."

In Brussels, Aldrovandi[113] read the speech for the Nine-Country Conference. Apparently he was received in deathly silence, but they all realized that his proposals were the only realistic ones.

The ambassador of Japan again asked me for assurance regarding our attitude towards the Soviets. Facts speak for themselves. As do torpedoes.

Admiral Bernotti,[114] back from the maneuvers at Biserte for the application of the Nyon accords, told me that the English Admiral was courteous while the French Admiral was extremely unpleasant. The French high command is more sympathetic to the Nationalists in Spain.

November 4, 1937
Mass at S. Maria degli Angeli and the usual War Memorial ceremony. Victory Day.

November 5, 1937
I received von Ribbentrop at the station. Hassel looked very bitter.

Meeting with Minister Irimescu.[115] I mentioned of the pact that we will sign tomorrow and I said that Romania will be closely affected by it. Because of the same worrisome Bolshevik proximity, Bucharest must orient its sympathies towards the new powerful anticommunist system.

Meeting with Ribbentrop, Hotta, and von Hassel. Some details relating to the signing ceremony were agreed to. The English, it seems, are very uneasy about Tokyo signing this pact. They feel the system closing in on them.

I told the Turk that I will not go to Ankara until the conditions for such a visit are realized, namely the recognition of the Empire. I was quite cold toward him.

November 6, 1937
This morning we signed the Pact. One could sense an atmosphere very different from the usual diplomatic ceremonies. Three nations engaged down the same path, which could lead to war. A necessary fight if we want to break this mold that suffocates the energy and aspirations of young nations. After the signing we went to see the Duce. Few times have I seen him so pleased. It is no longer the situation of 1935. Italy has broken its isolation and is at the center of the most formidable political and military alliance that has ever existed.

In the afternoon a three-man meeting between the Duce, Ciano, and Ribbentrop. It was a meeting of great interest: I took minutes in a notebook.

In the evening gala dinner at the Palazzo Venezia. The two very pro-fascist Japanese military attachés were beaming. They wish the military pact well. They were happy when I told them, in the presence of the Duce, that they will have to occupy Vladivostok, which is a pistol pointed against Japan.

November 7, 1937
The Duce complained that Aldrovandi had approved a second invitation addressed to Japan for them to participate in Brussels. He is right: it was a little waltz with the League that we could have avoided. The Duce hates the reputation that Italy had, and wants to cancel it with a policy which is as sharp as the blade of a sword. To cut a long story short: I cabled Tokyo to

say that, right after the Japanese refusal, we will pull out of Brussels. The conference will be cancelled.

Ribbentrop has left. Hotta, Hassel and I were at the station. The Duce asked Ribbentrop for Hassel's head.

I am sad for father. He is weakening by the hour. I had much hoped for a recovery but it seems to me that the medicine is useless. This strong, heroic and generous man is now a tired old man. I suffer a lot: he loved me more than anyone and sacrificed a lot for me. May God perform a miracle.

November 8, 1937

The following scene took place in my office this morning. Stein walked in and said: "My government has instructed me to tell you that it considers your participation in the Tripartite Pact as contrary to our pact of 1933 and as an unfriendly gesture towards the Soviets. I have nothing else to say." I replied: "I take note of your communication. I will inform the Duce. I have nothing else to say." I got up and I showed him the door, where both of us made a cold and low bow.

The Brazilian ambassador will recommend joining the Tripartite Pact to his government.

The minister of Hungary asks in the name of Kanya[116] a meeting of the States belonging to the Protocols of Rome. We have nothing against this in principal. It would be good to have it in Budapest in January. I also think that it is wise to give the impression that the Roman block is very strong. In the afternoon the Duce returned. I briefly conferred with him.

November 9, 1937

The Tripartite stir continues. I have thought a lot of future developments. It is not worth requesting that small countries join because it must remain a pact of giants. But three countries interest me: Spain, which must represent the extension of the Axis to the Atlantic, Brazil, to shake up the whole South American democratic system, Poland, as an anti-Russian bulwark. It is worthwhile to wait a bit for Spain. Brazil needs to be worked on right away and I cabled Lojacono.[117] For approximately a year I have financed the Integralists with 40 contos per month. If at these times of struggle there is the need for greater intervention, I will give the ambassador more money.

In the evening dinner at Wisochy's[118] where I met Beck's wife, and I spoke at length with Logusiano, who resigned in the hope (perhaps useless) of being appointed Minister of Foreign Affairs in the next Cabinet. I demonstrated to him that Romania can do nothing else but join our formidable anti-Russian system. The Russians are a danger to them, as allies more than as enemies. They may as well secure our friendship and our protection straight away.

November 10, 1937

The Duce personally drafted *Informazione Diplomatica* n. 6 as a reply to Chamberlain.

Pertinax[119] harshly attacked the men leading the government in Poland. I told Ansaldo[120] to take their defense. They will be grateful. An insult to the country is unpleasant, but personal attacks are upsetting. And so it is the right moment to work. In the meantime Russia makes it easy. Because its warning to Poland to not join the Tripartite Pact demonstrates all the more to that country that it belongs with the Fascist States.

I called for the Commission preparing for the welcoming receptions for Hitler to meet on Monday. The visit will take place in May, but it must be planned well in advance if something worthwhile is to be prepared. The street decorations worry me above all. In our country, they have always been banal, provincial similar to the period of King Umberto I.

Conferred with Solmi[121] who would like to organize a Law Congress. It seems harmless enough.

November 11, 1937

A new request for a meeting in Brussels has arrived from Eden. I sent for Drummond and told him that I thought I could not accept, both because of the venue, the environment, which has indirect pro-League overtones, and because of the practically comatose condition of the conference itself. But one must not think that I do not wish to meet with Eden. On the contrary: I would be delighted. But somewhere else, after careful preparation to avoid any undue expectations or disappointments that could result from such a meeting.

Anfuso has cleared up a faux pas made by Salata in Vienna. Salata was instructed to present two British documents compromising Schmidt[122] to Schuschnigg[123] and he began asking for confrontations, retractions, etc. A scandal which would have compromised our Intelligence Service. Anfuso covered everything up. Schuschnigg told him that if and when we want, he will show Schmidt the door. Very good, because he is untrustworthy.

November 12, 1937

The press made a lot of noise about my meeting with Perth. God only knows what would have happened had I agreed to meet with Eden. But it should be said that something is happening and a certain thaw has at last begun.

Hotta thanked me for our attitude at Brussels. He asks, though, that we not withdraw the delegation which is still needed to prevent decisions hostile towards Japan.

I received the Brazilian ambassador. I told him that we are favorable to Vargas'[124] policies and I promised him the support of the Italians. Those, especially those residing in San Paulo, who for local reasons are not too favorable towards Integralism.

Meeting with Phillips.[125] A long explanation of the situation that has been created by the Tripartite Pact. He was impressed by Delbos' book, *Experience Rouge*, in which the author describes the Soviet preparations of the Spanish Revolution.

November 13, 1937

Interesting conversation with the Duce. He took his cue from one of my comments for a head-on attack on the bourgeoisie, which is still antifascist. In fact, for a number of evenings the Argentina theater is the center of an antifascist rally in the form of a production of "Napleone Unico" by Pagnol, a play in which the situations, characters and lines lead to easy analogies. He accuses the intellectual classes and the bourgeoisie of cowardice, laziness, and love of the quiet life and he declared that as long as he is alive he will keep them on their fcct by "kicking them in the shins." "When Spain is over with, I will invent something else, but the character of the Italians must be forged in combat." He banned the play. Plato censured Odysseus, and even music if it seemed sluggish and depressing.

Barella[126] spoke to me about the newspaper *Il Popolo d'Italia.* He cannot manage to get it distributed: something that is connected to the antifascism of the bourgeoisie. Even the Duce's own articles, unless thousands of lire are spent on creating sales and the Party organization is not enlisted into action, do not manage to increase sales. To think that the Duce is convinced that Italian readers await his articles impatiently. The bourgeoisie is often disgusting.

It is that same bourgeoisie that is already all excited about the nonexistent negotiations with London. I would like to reestablish the truth of the matter with an *Informazione Diplomatica.*

November 14, 1937

A tough anti-Japanese motion has been prepared in Brussels. The ball of thread begins to unravel against Tokyo. Nothing can be more dangerous than to be caught in this system of collective security. When a finger remains caught in the gears the entire arm is lost. I drafted the declaration of a contrary vote which Aldrovandi will make tomorrow. I transmitted it to Hotta, who then told me that Tokyo is about to recognize Franco and he asked me information on the condition of White Spain. At the same time he asked me if we were ready to formally recognize Manchukuo. I have nothing against this, in the present state of affairs, but it would be wise to coordinate it with Berlin.

Conde talked to me about the assignment of the two ships *Pepe* and *Poerio* to the Spanish navy. Cavagnari is making it difficult because the September installment for the two submarines sold has still not been paid. Our naval officers have always opposed our initiative in Spain. They hate anything that could put a single boat of their fleet at risk ... They are great experts on that international law which they should despise in order to fight a war properly.

Don Juan,[127] heir to the throne, has asked to see me. Much caution is required even though I believe in the restoration in Spain.

November 15, 1937

Long meeting with Chiang Kung-Pao.[128] I thought he had aged, and away from his environment, he is less brilliant than I remembered him. I developed this theory with him: Japan will militarily overthrow you, the democracies give you no practical help. The only salvation for you can be found the direct negotiations through Italian-German mediation. The sooner the better. I understand that the Chinese are counting on the vastness of the land, but they forget that the vital points of China are on the coast or the rivers where the Japanese navy is operating freely. He cabled my point of view to Chiang Kai-shek.[129]

In the afternoon, meeting of the committee for the reception of the Führer. I demand that everything be perfect, therefore I have started the organization six months ahead of time. Yesterday, everyone responded eagerly. The most delicate problem is that of the relations with the King: the Führer had Hess tell me that he does not want to stay at the Quirinal Palace. He will have to go there at least once. I think I will divide the visit into two halves: visit to the King and visit to the Duce. Much tact will be needed. The matter is difficult and criticism is easily unleashed.

November 16, 1937

Mussolini was very pleased with Aldrovandi's declaration at Brussels: a clear no. "I have at last the diplomatic service that I like," he told me. And he spoke to me at length of the need to change Italy's image as a disloyal country. Bismarck used to say that one could not engage in politics with Italy because it is disloyal both as a friend and as an enemy. Demonstrations like yesterday's prove that Fascist Italy is no longer the Italy of inside arrangements, the whore of the Democracies.

Chiang Kung-Pao asked me to sound out in Tokyo, in my name, possible conditions for peace. He led me to understand that the recognition of Manchukuo could be granted.

Von Hassel spoke to me against Schuschnigg. He is said to have expressed himself with one of his ministers, to be favorable to an agreement with Prague and therefore with the Western Democracies. I said that I didn't believe that information: Schuschnigg knows it would mean we would abandon him and therefore the end of Austria.

I took Don Juan, future King of Spain, to see the Duce. The Duce told him that it is easier to make a social policy with Monarchies than Republics, because they require less compromise. He advised basing the regime on the rural masses that are more loyal and less nervous than those in the cities. He said to give an Imperial spirit to Spain. Today's civil war is a consequence of the psychological breakdown of 1898, which determined the break up of the Spanish spirit and desperation about a future no longer worthy of the past.

November 17, 1937

I accompanied Cerruti to see the Duce, on a farewell visit. At least this was the atmosphere even though the situation is officially different. The Duce attacked French policy toward us. Cerruti defended it with remarkable courage. He gave Laval credit for the fact that oil sanctions were not applied during the Ethiopian war. The Duce said that those sanctions would have meant war.

Which was the only reason France did not want them. We shall not forget how much London did two or so years ago with the help of Paris. When Cerruti said that Italy is enemy number 1 for France, Mussolini replied. "Great honor. I want to be feared and hated, rather than tolerated or protected." In discussing the French army, the Duce cited the book by Paul Allard and advised Cerruti to read it. At the end of the meeting everyone's opinions were unchanged and France's stock did not even rise by one point!

November 18, 1937

Nothing remarkable, except for the inauguration of the Textile exhibition. A prodigy of Fascism's will.

November 19, 1937

Lessona told me of his being torpedoed. He was very sad. He asked for it. He has never been sincere, nor a friend to those who had helped him. He has always tried to harm people. He falls among enemies, who will continue to attack him now that he is unsaddled. Teruzzi is thought of as a loyal, mediocre executor: and then more loyal than mediocre.

Three-way meeting with the Duce and Chiang Kung-Pao. The Duce repeated more or less what I had already told old Kung-Pao. The only way out is through the Italian-German mediation. Nothing can be expected from the Chinese arm: less still from foreign armies. Kung-Pao will cable his government.

Perhaps this is the path towards mediation. They are depressed in Shanghai. Cora[130] cabled to say that he saw T. V. Soong[131] looking depressed for the first time. The matter strikes me because T.V. Soong is a strong personality. I cabled Cora to speak to him according to the instructions that I had sent on October 28, and along the lines of my talks with Chiang Kung-Pao.

November 20, 1937

The Duce has taken measures because of a clearly pro-French article in the newspaper *La Tribuna*. He said the author, Scardaoni,[132] was "the son of slaves."

I received the Japanese envoy, Baron Okura,[133] and I accompanied him to see the Duce. He didn't tell us anything of great importance and limited himself to expressions of gratitude for our solidarity with his country.

Volpi was, so to speak, pleased that he didn't end up with the "misfortune of going to the Colonies." Though, he was disappointed when I told him that the present situation would have to continue for some time. He still had some hope...

The Brazilian ambassador had nothing new to say about his country. Vargas is searching for a Brazilian formula. He had better find it. Otherwise his movement will shatter rapidly. The secret of rightwing dictatorships is their advantage compared to other regimes, they consist precisely in having a national formula. Italy and Germany have found it. The Germans in racism. We in Roman Imperialism.

November 21, 1937

I saw with joy at Palazzo Venezia two wonderful fascist faces: Teruzzi and Ricci.

Halifax's[134] visit to Germany provides more proof of the confusion in the foreign policy of the Reich. Too many roosters inside the chicken coop. There are at least four foreign policies. By Hitler, by Göring,[135] by Neurath, and by Ribbentrop. Without counting the minor ones. It is difficult to synchronize them properly. Neurath is a heavy load and slows things down.

I am thinking about recognizing Manchukuo. Neurath slams on the brakes. If the Führer knew, he would approve. But the Wilhelmstrasse is the most resilient remnant of the old regime. In Italy as well, besides, it took fifteen years to conquer the Palazzo Chigi. And only I know how hard I must work to make these goats march in step with Fascist timing...

Meeting between the Duce and General Visconti Prasca.[136] This man is a real Francophile: he studied in France and believes in the French military high command and in French military efficiency. During the meeting, many well-known things were restated, the Duce laid out two interesting thoughts: 1) That an army must be political. Not make politics. But every soldier must be the bearer of a fragment of a political ideal. Otherwise, what you have are employees subsidized by the state. On the basis of these ideas Badoglio finds the present army of the Reich more powerful than the army of the Kaiser, even though its equipment, discipline and preparation are not as good. 2) That the falling birth rate in France has its true origins in the 2,500,000 dead in the Napoleonic Wars and in the laws that abolished the rights of primogeniture, thus encouraging having only one child.

November 22, 1937

The Duce has raised doubts in my mind regarding the political loyalty of A. Pavolini.[137] I replied that I would reject any suspicions unless documented in an absolutely trustworthy manner.

Brief talk with the Duce. The construction of a new Ministry of Foreign Affairs was decided in principle. I am sorry to leave the Palazzo Chigi, of Mussolini's tradition. But the new building will be part of the creation of the Duce's Rome.

In the afternoon, a meeting with Guarneri and Revel. Both are very pessimistic about the monetary situation, which, according to them, makes war out of the question. They ask for two years of tranquility and ten years of peace. That seems too much to me.

On the Duce's orders I sent a cable to Attolico announcing to the Führer our intention to bid farewell to Geneva on the 25th of this month. Besides, a move of this kind, made by us after the obvious failure of Halifax's visit to Berlin, will be useful to reinforcing the Axis, or better, the triangle. We will not assemble the Grand Council. A cable from me to the secretary of the moth-eaten League will suffice.

November 23, 1937

Received a letter from Neurath, giving an account of Halifax's trip. It seems to me that the results are completely nil. We were right in not going to Brussels.

From Paris, Prunas reports that the tombs of those who died at Bligny have been desecrated. If there are still hearts that beat for France, in Italy, I think that this kind of news will be enough to cure them forever. Alfieri, whom I informed of the matter, and who has a brother buried in Reims, reacted with a violence I didn't expect from someone with his mild nature. In the meantime I sent a copy to Del Croix[138] and to Rossi.[139] If the violations continue, we will ask for the repatriation of the remains. And we will send the French theirs.

November 24, 1937

The Führer approves our exit from Geneva in principle. But he does not wish that the move be connected to the anticommunist pact. He prefers that the failure to recognize the Empire be given as an excuse. Berlin still hesitates about Manchukuo. The Führer is still too influenced by the democratic restraint of the Wilhelmstrasse.

I gave Ghigi instructions for his mission to Vienna. He was not very up to date on the situation and seemed to be a bit frightened. I defined the duty of Italy's minister to the Ballplatz like this: a doctor who has to pump oxygen to a dying patient without the heir noticing it. With the outcome in doubt, the heir interests us more than the dying patient.

November 25, 1937

We have decided to attack France following Campinchi's[140] speech. I am not entirely sure of the authenticity of the text, but the Duce decides to fire away. And he keeps the cartridge of the outrage of the tombs in Bligny in his back pocket.

The Duce is thinking of leaving Geneva on December 18, with a Grand Council meeting ad hoc. Not before, so as to avoid any embarrassment to Stoyadinovich on the eve of his visit to Italy.

For one thing Berlin told us that for the moment they will not recognize Manchukuo, while giving us freedom to act as we please. We will recognize it. In a few days time, not now, so as to not spoil the party between Germany and Japan. Besides, we must do it in return for the recognition of the Empire.

Anfuso in Vienna. He will bring Schuschnigg a Czech document which contains serious statements made by Hornbostel[141] (Schmidt?) which are hostile to the Axis and favorable to the Western Democracies. I advised the Chancellor that this is a dangerous game. I also sent a copy of the document to Göring as well.

November 26, 1937

The Duce read in a British intercept that Pirelli is making poisonous statements against autarchy. I had warned him about Pirelli's political grayness. This is now confirmed.

Franco, upon the Duce's request, is giving us 100,000 tons of iron. This is good because for one thing the ILVA could produce more. And also because it proves the sincerity of Franco's feelings towards us. Many are beginning to have doubts. I, honestly, do not. I much doubt, instead, the honesty of Sangroniz[142] and of other elements of the Ministry of Foreign Affairs. Also they are a part of the diplomatic international.

Dinner at Ambassador Hotta's, in honor of Okura. Hotta told me that our conduct at Brussels has definitely convinced Tokyo that we are sincere and therefore it would be wise to resume talks about a military consultation pact. I let him understand that we will recognize Manchukuo. The Japanese military are crazy about us. The military attaché yesterday evening spoke of a war waged against England. Since he lives in Addis Ababa street, he said that he hoped to soon go to Tunisi street, to Cairo street, and in Tokyo to Singapore street. The naval attaché begs us not to deliver to the USSR the very fast cruiser in construction at the Orlando works. The Japanese apparently are willing to buy it. They fear its speed, if it is sent to Vladivostok.

November 27, 1937

The sudden removal of Schacht[143] is good: the full Nazification of the government begins. Let's hope that he will be followed very soon by someone else. Saw Cini, Marziali,[144] Felicioni,[145] Baroni.[146]

Today, again in a British intercept, we found evidence of Guarneri's doubts regarding the financial situation. The Duce told me that he is watching him, given the Italian Manufacturer's Association environment that he comes from. I informed the Duce of my conversation with Guarneri several days ago. I confess that I am very calm regarding the situation: but even if I wasn't I would become so through contact with the calm coolness of Mussolini. He has always been right. And this time, furthermore, he is associated with winners in every area: Spain, China, Africa… In a few days, perhaps Monday, we shall recognize Manchukuo. Realistic policy. And also regarding the Chinese this is the best time to make the move. They have so many problems that there will be no reaction. Besides, if the war continues, shortly there will be no China left at all. It was difficult to wage war from Nanking: it will be impossible to do so from Chungking, with the country invaded, without communications and without revenue. It seems to me that, from many indications, China is going towards a partition. To avoid it, they should make peace: at any price.

November 28, 1937

Tomorrow Manchukuo will be recognized. I communicated this to Hotta this morning; he was very pleased. We are gaining ground. The loyal and benevolent politics that we conduct tie us closer to our friends that would become distant if we hesitated. Our conduct at Brussels has won the match with Tokyo. Tomorrow's move will be just as good.

Sunday at the beach with Edda. And for the first time the children ate at the table with us. It creates the feeling of a family. And therefore I like it.

The Duce authorized me to give the Japanese copies of the plans of Singapore sent by Perego.[147] We must make the gift appear as a special favor, as proof of our already active collaboration.

November 29, 1937

I summoned Blondel to show him a shameful vignette in the paper *Aux Écoutes*. I said that I was speaking strictly from a personal viewpoint: but I did point out that by insulting the sacred person of the Duce good relations will certainly no be reestablished between our countries.

Opening of Chamber. Grand ovation for father, who appeared in good enough shape, even if a little pale and much older. Coolness of the Chamber towards the recent ministerial nominations.

I reported to the Duce on the meeting between Schuschnigg and Anfuso. The Chancellor admitted that Hornbostel had in fact said those things, but he defended him regarding Italy: he speaks against the Axis because he is anti-Nazi. The Chancellor was very impressed by the effectiveness of our intelligence service. He asked if we spent billions. Instead we spend very little, but we have in Emanuele, a man who is fantastic.

November 30, 1937

Talks with the ambassador of China. He wanted explanations regarding the recognition Manchukuo. He feared that a similar move could hinder our possible mediation in the conflict. I told him that instead it should facilitate things. China should, though, recognize Manchukuo to make peace. Italy, by its gesture, has improved the situation.

We spoke to the Pole of the situation in general. He asked me his usual unintelligent questions.

Nothing else.

December 1, 1937

The Duce blew a fuse with Popular Culture, because it sent the film "Squadrone Bianco" to Egypt. It was a stupid thing to do. With our pro-Arab policy, how can one give the Egyptians the spectacle of Arabs being scientifically massacred by our troops?

I gave the plans of Singapore to the Japanese military attaché. He was very impressed by this gesture. We must actively work on the leaders of the Japanese general staff to reach a military agreement which should close the match with England. England, obviously, is not disarming. This is why Percy Loraine[148] told a diplomat at Istanbul that when England is ready it will destroy us and crush the Duce. He exaggerates. And we don't have to wait necessarily for this perfect preparation, of which I am a bit skeptical. Perhaps the weapons will be ready, but the men?

December 2, 1937

Nothing important.

At lunch the Duce warmly told stories about his youth. He said that his father would become attached to his debts and would keep them, at least in part, out of principle, even when he was able to pay them off. A couple of days ago, the Duce had paid his father's last debt.

When the Duce engages in conversation he is delightful. No one uses richer or fresher metaphors than he does.

Gave instructions to Grandi to protest against certain anti-Italian statements made by Sir Percy Loraine. He will have discuss it personally with Chamberlain.

December 3, 1937

Meeting with Bocchini. Nothing new. He is working on the preparations for Stoyadinovich's visit: there was the threat of a Croatian attack, but the man has already been identified and will be arrested. I will tell the minister of Yugoslavia at the end of the visit. Meeting with the Duke of Aosta. He feels the great burden of responsibility. And this is a good sign. But he still seems to be a little disoriented. He is a nice man, to whom I sincerely wish success.

The Jews are burdening me with anonymous abuse, accusing me of having promised Hitler that they would be persecuted. This is not true. The Germans have never spoken to us on this issue. Nor do I believe that it would be in our interest to unleash an anti-Semitic campaign in Italy. The problem does not exist here. They are few and, apart from some exceptions, good. And besides, the Jews must never be persecuted as "such." This only creates solidarity of all of the Jews in the world. They can be attacked on many other pretexts. But I repeat, the problem does not exist here. And maybe, in small doses, Jews are as necessary to society as yeast is necessary to make bread.

December 4, 1937

The Duce informed me of his decisions regarding the new naval construction projects. I am very pleased. I sent a handwritten letter to Göring, who, since last January, had insisted on the construction of two new 35,000-ton ships. The meeting between Grandi and Eden is very interesting. In fact I think that, especially after the Tripartite Pact, London is seeking a mutual understanding with Berlin and is also ready to make enormous sacrifices. But France? Anyway, in a few days time we will drop the bomb of our exit from Geneva. Since the Führer is committed to declaring that Germany will not reenter in the League, the London negotiations will be delayed. As far as we are concerned us I sent instructions to Grandi similar to those of the summer: either a complete agreement, with recognition of the Empire, or we are better off waiting.

The Pope gave me the Piana Grand Cross. Pizzardo[149] wrote me a very affectionate letter; I replied with equal warmth.

December 5, 1937

The meeting between Neurath and Delbos at the station in Berlin looks more like a purely formal gesture.

The preparations for Stoyadinovich's visit are complete. He will arrive this evening at 9:50 p.m. I will go to the station with the Duce. I have taken care of even the smallest details of the visit. I want this man, who has proven himself to be our sincere friend, to have an exceptional welcome. Firstly, because I consider the Belgrade Pact to be fundamental for our politics. The alliance with the Slavs allows us to look at the possibility of an Anschluss with serenity. The King, after the signing, told me that he considered this act to be the most important made by the Regime. And out of personal sympathy for Stoyadinovich. He is a strong, full-blooded man, with a resonant laugh and a strong handshake, he is a man who inspires confidence. He has much confidence in himself and rightly so. Of the political men that I have encountered so far in my European wanderings, he is the one I find the most interesting. This visit is a bitter pill to swallow for the French and the English. From an intercepted telephone call between the British press agent and a journalist, it emerges that the British embassy is spreading the rumors that we are about to take advantage of Stoyadinovich's weakness for pretty ladies to bring him further on our side. This is partly true.

The Duce laughed when I told him that, besides the official visits, I had prepared some dances with the most beautiful women of Rome society.

I informed Hotta of our new naval program and I vaguely mentioned our exit from Geneva, which will take place on Saturday the 11th.

December 6, 1937
Very busy with S[toyadinovich]'s visit. Meeting with me. Then, with the Duce. Initially S[toyadinvich] was very awkward. Then he loosened up and spoke with his natural frankness. The conversation between the two men went well. There was a good connection.

Yesterday in Turin, Anfuso's first contact with the French Nationalists. The Duce approves the establishment of arms deposits on the border.

December 7, 1937
More on the visit. Second meeting with the Duce. Recorded. Everything fine.

December 8, 1937
Visit to the Pontine cities. Stoyadinovich is more and more taken with the game. He begins to enjoy the idea of dictatorship. He adopted the Roman salute and wears his coat inside out showing the suede lining because it is "more military."

December 9, 1937
Visit to Milan. The working classes, with intelligence, have understood the importance of the event and welcomed the guest with great warmth. They also gave me an affectionate welcome. I find it effective to end the visit of a foreigner in Milan. For one thing he sees the strong creative rhythm of this city. Secondly, in contact with the workers he realizes that the regime has truly permeated the masses and destroyed the Marxist stronghold. The impression was particularly strong among the Yugoslav journalists. Those most impressed were those of the opposition.

Parenti[150] does good work and is a comrade in the mold of Starace. Therefore, ideal for this phase of the Party. The Podestà is an incompetent, it would be wise to sack him as soon as possible.

December 10, 1937

Stoyadinovich's departure. Clearly this has been a productive trip that ended this morning with the visit to the Fascist Federation and the laying of a wreath "to the martyrs of the Fascist Revolution." For a Yugoslav head of government, not bad! St[oyadinovich] returns home to form the base of his dictatorship Party. He has four years ahead of him before the King comes of age. But also afterwards he will continue, together with Paul,[151] to exercise control. He liked the Mussolini formula: Strength and consensus. King Alexander had only strength.[152] St. wants to popularize his dictatorship. Nothing new has been signed off on. But between the two countries there is much more than what comes out of the Belgrade Pact. The conversations during these few days are also fundamental for an alliance, which could be used in many different directions. One day, maybe, also towards the north. In the afternoon, hunting at the Crespi's, with... .[153] In the evening, return to Rome.

December 11, 1937

Report to the Duce on the trip to Milan. The Duce is happy and is already excited in anticipation of the Grand Council of this evening. I communicated our decision to the German chargé d'affaires and to the Tokyo embassy. The news though was already known in political and press circles. There was a leak. From what the Chief told me, the police are on his tail, in fact they already have proof against the offender, although he is not part of the administration. Bocchini will give me his name. Grand Council. It lasted for two minutes. The Duce said that everyone knows the reasons that compel us to leave Geneva. No moment could be more favorable than this one considering the sweeping Japanese victory. He opened the discussion. Starace proposed approval by acclamation. I was the first to stand, then Farinacci, Grandi, and Buffarini. Then all the others. The Duce spoke from the Palazzo Venezia. I expected a more intense speech. Instead he remained very moderate and cautious. As always, the Duce is right.

December 12, 1937

There is a kind of joy in the world about our decision of yesterday. There were more rumors going around so desperate and alarming that many people took our exit from Geneva as a routine matter.

I spoke to Grandi. I lifted his spirits because he was a bit worried. He doesn't think an agreement with London is possible. I told him that instead I view it with the same optimism as before, but that, in any case, our situation is such to allow us to consider even the possibility of a clash with perfect serenity. Naturally, I also prefer an agreement with London. Even though I fully agree with the Duce that on a historical level the Italian-British conflict is inevitable.

December 13, 1937

I was cheered by the Senate when I entered the hall!

Meeting with the Polish ambassador, recorded, about Delbos' visit to Warsaw. It was unsuccessful. Bocchini informed me of Engley's[154] conspiracy to prevent us from leaving Geneva. A vile and stupid farce which will land someone in front of the special Tribunal for the defense of the State. I hope that no one from the administration is even indirectly compromised.

Received Röder.[155] He is the best of the Hungarians. I informed him of the meetings with Stoyadinovich. He is very pleased about the separation between Yugoslavia and the other two states of the Little Entente. If Hungary wants a victory it must concentrate its efforts on Czechoslovakia, come to a full understanding with Belgrade and find a *modus vivendi* with Bucharest. I spoke to him with this in mind and he said he agreed.

December 14, 1937

I told the Duce that Balbo, at Colonna's, hurled abuse at the Rome-Berlin Axis. Accurate information: reported by d'Aieta,[156] who was present. The Chief was very indignant. Then, speaking of Balbo, he said "That's a man whose future I do not guarantee."

Nothing new on other fronts.

December 15, 1937

Council of Ministers, to approve the budget. Received Balbo, to whom I asked if it was true that he was hostile towards the policy of the Axis. He was reluctant but essentially confirmed it. He says that he doesn't trust the Germans. That one day they will abandon us. That perhaps they will be against us. He basically told me a lot of clichés. He does it to create opposition. And he was offended when I said that he was the Prince of Condé. He didn't know who he was. Not much intelligence, big ambition, absolute disloyalty, capable of anything: that's Balbo. We should keep an eye on him.

I learned from Delia di Bagno[157] that Balbo told some people not to travel to Ethiopia due to "the serious conditions of insecurity in the country." Nothing new on other fronts.

December 16, 1937

The Japanese ambassador expressed his condolences for the death of Sandri.[158] I acknowledged it but I did not lodge any protest. On the contrary, I said that I considered such an occurrence as normal in a war situation. If the Americans don't want bombs then they should leave. He was surprised and moved by our attitude.

Engely will be arrested today. From a SIM document it appears that an attempt was also made by Pilotti[159] at the British embassy. Bastianini also will be dragged in. I don't believe it. He is stupid, but loyal. Although he could have talked out of foolishness. At the bottom of many matters there is more often foolishness rather than bad faith.

I intend to ask for Guido Schmidt's head. He told the English about the intercepted information that I informed Chancellor Schuschnigg of. This, naturally, emerges from another intercept.

I told the minister of Egypt not to insist in the matter of the Coptic Church. Their press campaign will not change our decisions and will only work to worsen relations between the two countries, which, for them especially, should be kept good.

December 17, 1937

I accompanied Viola[160] to see the Duce. No new fact emerged, except for the confirmation of the withdrawal of the Volunteers on January 15, whether the battle is won or not. Viola is optimistic about the situation: he believes that Franco will be loyal to us and that our loans will be repaid. To lend credibility to his loyalty, Franco will have to, join the Tripartite Pact at the end of the war, say farewell to Geneva, and enter into a very solid agreement with us to confirm the secret one of last November. Viola believes that he will stick to these requests.

Van Zeeland came to see me.[161] He is in Rome to prepare his economic report. I wouldn't have found him unpleasant if I had not remembered that he supported the sanctions in Geneva to the maximum. He explained his ideas for the recovery of international trade. I replied that our economic policy had followed that of other countries. Starting with the so-called democracies. Today, other considerations and recent experiences push us well along the road to autarky. The sanctions are worth something in the life of our nation. Ancient history may not teach lessons in life, but personal experience must inevitably be useful.

December 18, 1937

Marzio was born.[162]

I told the Czechoslovak minister that our relations with his country depend upon those between Prague and Berlin, Prague and Budapest. We have nothing for or against the Czechs. They interest us only indirectly. But I want to give them some advice: don't believe in collective security and do not rely on friendships which are geographically distant. The minister recalled my forecasts for China and drew a parallel.

Meeting of minor importance with Berger[163] and Villani,[164] to prepare for the meeting at Budapest. A meeting of little importance: the Rome Protocols have lost their significance. I said that I would prefer the presence of Schuschnigg. Meaning, that I don't want Schmidt. Economic agreements with Germany were signed. Difficult negotiations: German bureaucracy still puts up hurdles. Hassel swallowed the bait. Maybe he already knows that the torpedo is coming at him. Hesse tells me that the ambassador who is now in Tokyo will come here. I don't know him.

December 19, 1937

Some people have interpreted the choice of name for Marzio as a political and prophetic choice, meaning war. But do they really believe that the

parties will wait the many years so that the armed youth of Marzio's generation would take to find the solution? Sometimes I ask myself if we should not
force the march and set fire to the fuse. Hitler, Göring, Hess, Stoyadino-vich,
Goebbels,[165] Daranyi,[166] Kotta[167] (Albania) and other minor people telephoned
with their congratulations. From the Royal Family, the Prince of Piedmont
(with great warmth), the Queen, the Princesses and the Duke of Aosta.

Filippo, after Vienna, will go to Spain to carry out an enquiry into our
officers who supposedly speculate with the currency and collect valuable
objects. But how long will it take to give Italians a sense of national pride,
now that the military spirit has been instilled?

Mussolini was furious at the failure of the Italian Exhibition in Berlin. He
told me that he hadn't wanted it. They went ahead anyway and it turned out to
be a fiasco. The Duce said, "I want this epitaph on my tomb: *Here lies one of the
most intelligent animals that appeared on the face of the earth.*" The Duce is proud of
his instinct, that he considers, and it has been proven to be, infallible.

December 20, 1937

The Spanish news is not good. The offensive on Guadalajara has been
postponed indefinitely because of changes of heart within Franco's commanders and the preventive offensive taken by the reds at Teruel. Our generals are worried and they have reason to be. Franco lacks the synthetic view
of war. He can lead the operations of a magnificent battalion commander.
His objective is always land. Never the enemy. And he doesn't realize that
war is won by destroying the enemy. Afterwards, territorial occupation becomes a very simple matter. Berti wants to come for consultations. He will
propose the withdrawal of most of the volunteers. After 16 months, many
are tired. One must keep in mind that only an elite can grasp and feel the
aims of an ideological war, hard-fought far from home, without immediate
and direct benefits.

I saw von Hassel in the evening. Recapitulatory conversation after his trip
to Berlin. He told me in the end that his government is preparing to withdraw
him because "the Italians are tired of him." He gave the same news to the
Duce yesterday, who replied he knew nothing about it. And I did the same.

Anyway, the situation was difficult and the scene unattractive.

Marconi's[168] daughter came to ask me for help for herself and her brother.
The hostility of the stepmother has driven them to poverty. Without money
and without circumstance. He may have been a great genius, but I only knew
him when he was already very much over the hill.

December 21, 1937

The Duce asked Berti to come and confer. I spoke to him of an article
in the *Action Française*, in which it is said that perhaps the authoritarian States
will not wait until 1941 to attack. Mussolini replied, "Precisely, I will prepare
the biggest surprise for the Italians. As soon as Spain is over with, I will
issue a statement that will remain a classic." I recalled that when in August
1935 he wanted to attack the home fleet in Alexandria and Malta by surprise.
He said to me then, "In one night the course of history can be changed." He

didn't do it because information was not precise regarding the efficiency of the English fleet and because our navy held back.

But, since then, he is meditating and maturing such a plan.

Double meeting, at the Palazzo Venezia and the Palazzo Chigi, with Nakano, leader of the Black Dragon of Japan. He was the bearer of a message from Prince Konoe[169] to the Duce. In the talks with the Duce various points were covered, but one matter focused our attention: relations with England. Nakano is an extremist. He says that between the Japanese nation and Great Britain there can never be friendship. While fighting in China, Japan is mainly faced with the Judaic and British plutocracy that wants to stop the advance of young nations. Mussolini mentioned the possibility of tighter agreements. I spoke of this two days ago with the military attaché. I think that a consultation pact can be reached. I believe it to be very useful to both parties.

Received the Foreign Press Directorate. They wish to improve the information service.

December 22, 1937

Accompanied Mizzi[170] to see the Duce. Very pessimistic picture of the situation in Malta. The denationalization action by the English is even more intense: time is moving against us. Vast English military preparations. Mizzi is convinced that Great Britain is preparing to play the revenge in a return match as soon as possible.

At lunch, Lady Chamberlain drew a totally different picture. Understanding, agreement, friendship. I replied to her that as far as we are concerned we were ready: a more complete agreement, without gray areas, and long lasting. If not, it would be better to wait until favorable conditions arise. For one thing the speeches made by Eden yesterday and the day before did not encourage a resumption of negotiations. I didn't say so, but, in my opinion it would be better to get ready to fight. Lady Chamberlain was wearing the Fascist emblem. I am too much of a patriot to appreciate an Englishwoman who makes a similar gesture in a moment like this.

December 23, 1937

I treated the minister of Greece harshly. We have received a copy of the meeting between Eden and the King of Greece. After the visit to Rome he went to London to incite the English to attack us. He spoke badly of me: he called me, ironically, the super-Metternich. Meantime, the Greeks in Dodecanesus *will pay dearly*.

At the signing with H.M. the King, who remembered in particular the various sovereigns that visited with him during his long reign. He described in lively terms certain Oriental kings who stood out for their gauche behavior. The King is a pleasant conversationalist and very interesting. Sometimes he is in the habit of going too far into detail; he then lowers and dampens the tone of the conversation.

The Duce is worried about Spain. He doesn't overestimate the Red action against Teruel, but believes, and rightly so, that it will serve to recharge the morale for the Reds. He said that the Spanish, who are descendants of the Arabs, do not know how to fight a war in its entirety: they lack the essentials and fight individually, as a patrol, or at best as a tribe.

Long talks with three leaders of the Falange. They do not attribute much importance to the situation at Teruel. They believe that in a few months the revolution could end up in total victory. They are monarchists. Anglophobes. They speak about retaking Gibraltar; they say that since the days of Philip II, all Spanish troubles are of an English nature. I did not miss the opportunity to encourage them along this wise path and revealed the dangers of Anglophilia of certain old elements nesting in the diplomatic service. They knew of them and they keep an eye on them. First, Sangroniz.

December 24, 1937

The anti-Italian offensive picks up once again in full force in London. Also the meeting between Crolla[171] and Eden was without content or results. The Duce is calm. This morning he explained to me the new air force armaments program: in June we will build 300 airplanes per month and we will have three thousand in the fleet. We must tighten our belts and arm ourselves. Everything leads us to believe that the conflict is inevitable. In which case we must not lose our greatest advantage: that of the initiative.

I asked Pignatti[172] to raise the issue with Pacelli[173] of the pro-Communist behavior of Cardinal Verdier.[174] The church is too ambiguous in some of its contacts on the Left. I realize the difficulties created by the clash with Germany, but the Vatican has gone too far and is placing its relations with us in danger. Mussolini says that he is ready to tan the hides of the priests. He adds that here it is easy because the Italian nation is not religious. It is only superstitious. Anfuso is back from Vienna. He reported on his talks with Schuschnigg, who tried to protect Schmidt. He said that he was aware of Schmidt's letter to Vansittart,[175] without exposing our secret service. He confirms that Schmidt is our friend and is trying to save his head. He will speak to me in Budapest. Apparently, Schmidt has become hysterical, since our denunciation was made. He cannot understand why we have so many English documents.

December 25, 1937

Not a peaceful Christmas. On the Duce's orders I called the Japanese ambassador and I told him this: "Moderate your behavior in Washington; sharpen it towards London. For two reasons: firstly, to separate London from America. Secondly, because we, in the case of conflict with the United States, could not do anything tangible for you, while in the case of war with Great Britain we can undertake to give you the most help." The ambassador, who is a career diplomat, therefore cautious, reserved, and God-fearing, was disturbed by my statements. He was already at lunch when I called him and he came smelling of mandarin. I fear I have disturbed his digestion. I prepared a cable to inform Auriti,[176] but I have not yet dared send it. One never knows with the cipher. We read everything coming from the English: do we really believe that the others are less capable than we are?

Then, even if they are, we must always beware. Suetonius warned us to think of the enemy as an elephant even when one is certain that he is only a flea.

December 26, 1937

I did well not to send the cable. Tokyo, or rather the Gaimu-sho, messed up. And Berlin as well. Contrary to our understanding, Hirota[177] asked the Germans to be bearers of a message to Chiang Kai-shek, containing the conditions for peace. We were informed with a delay of two days, which can be explained by our bad relations with China, making us unsuitable to perform favors. But relations are bad precisely because of our loyalty to the Japanese! I called Hassel and Hotta and I told them that we intend to participate in the next phase of the negotiations. Hassel told me that it is also the intention of his government. But at bottom he was happy about the hitch: every time there is an obstacle between Berlin and us, he is happy. Hotta, who was witness to our upright, intransigent pro-Japanese policy, was humiliated by what happened. He even spoke of resigning. He will cable his government in strong terms. But also in Tokyo the Ministry of Foreign Affairs is not up to the times. Japan makes heroic history, and its diplomats are involved in the small intrigues like clerks. I imagine the Japanese equivalents of Buti, Vitetti,[178] Cerruti, etc., shaking as ours did at the time of the Ethiopian initiative and how they behave now every time that the heroic impetus of Mussolini sweeps aside some traditional position of professional diplomacy.

I had the cargo of arms shipped by Guarneri to China impounded. I am against the shipment: One cannot run with the hare and hunt with the hounds and certain things if widely broadcast cause greater damage than the advantage of a few million earned.

December 27, 1937

I ordered the freighters containing the war material sold to China, against my advice, by Guarneri, stopped. One cannot run with the hare and hunt with the hounds. The Japanese have found out.

Berti arrived. He gave me a very unclear report on the situation, from which, though, one thing emerges: that he is in a hurry to end the Corps of Volunteer Troops. I will set the other reasons aside, but pause on one very dramatic fact: we cannot risk the prestige of Italy on 20 infantry battalions. He makes the usual remarks against the Spanish: lack of unity of command, scarce coordination, no drive, and no hurry to end the campaign.

Tomorrow we will go together to the Duce. He will listen to me and decide. I ask myself though if with all the efforts and sacrifices made we should withdraw right now while, because of the little pocket of Teruel, Franco's star is not as bright as it was some two months ago. Will we not take the responsibility of a failure of the Whites? Do we not give new courage to the Reds and to those who supply and support them? Do we not perhaps give the Spanish the possibility of getting cheaply out of a debt of recognition that they owe us? The Duce will answer these questions tomorrow. The problem deserves more careful thought. Every decision has unfavorable sides to it. This Spanish affair is long and burdensome.

December 28, 1937

I have reflected at length on yesterday's meeting with Berti. I get the impression that the man is bewildered. He doesn't believe in the Spanish undertaking, and lack of faith is the first step towards failure. I spoke with Pariani, who shares my point of view. He also thinks that today we cannot withdraw. He believes it necessary to replace Berti with Frusci.[179] I told the Duce of the conversation and I expressed my point of view in favor of remaining in Spain. To the points noted yesterday I added that a unilateral withdrawal by us would give strength and credence to those who say that Italy is exhausted and can no longer bear military efforts. This would be extremely serious: toward our friends, and our enemies.

During the four-way meeting (Duce-Ciano-Pariani-Berti) we once again listened to Berti's reasons for the troop withdrawal. The Duce opposed him. He agreed with me on all points. So we will remain in Spain. Only that the Duce will write a letter to Franco to make him understand that time for us is a factor of major importance and that we cannot stay in a war that drags on forever. We must hurry up and conclude: a military conclusion, without counting too much on the internal collapse of Red Spain. Tomorrow morning at the Palazzo Venezia another meeting of the four of us will take place.

I received von Hassel and I gave him the information of the seizure of an anti-German publication, at the same time I asked him for measures for a book recently published, disrespectful towards our army.

They have sent as chief of the military mission in Bolivia a Colonel, one and a half meters tall and as round as ball! I am outraged. But why can't the Military understand certain things?

December 29, 1937

Yesterday afternoon the Duce once again summoned to the Palazzo Venezia, myself, Pariani and Berti and handed Berti written instructions for Spain. In brief: our forces will remain until victory, they shall not be engaged to wear down the enemy but in conclusive action, need for unity of command. I have informed the Germans of all this, and asked for a common step towards Franco. After the Duce's orders, I summoned Berti to the Palazzo Chigi and in the presence of Pariani I asked the clear question: do you feel up to commanding the CTV and take it into battle? After much chatter he concluded with a "yes." Although, afterwards he asked to see me again, saying that in 15 days' time he will send a report on the basis of which we will decide. He is a man without faith: for my part, I believe that we should replace him.

The crisis of the Romanian government is a good thing. Another country which is moving nearer to us. The system of French alliances is dead. It was, right from the day that we signed the Belgrade Pact. I prepared a pro-Romanian *Informazione Diplomatica* and I cabled the instructions for a progressive *rapprochement* to Sola.[180] All of this is also positive towards Hungary, who, from time to time, has Anglophile yearnings.

Discussions with Preziosi:[181] he wanted my support to coordinate the anti-Semitic campaign. I did not agree. I am not fond of the Jews but I don't think there is need for an action of this kind in Italy. At least not for now.

December 30, 1937

Berti hurried to give orders to place the troops in reserve. The Spanish command is against it: and they are right. I cabled Frusci to do nothing until Berti arrives, which will be tomorrow evening. The Nationalist offensive on Teruel has begun and could become a great battle. Is it really necessary to withdraw right now?

Micesco, new Romanian Minister of Foreign Affairs, sent me a very friendly cable. An obvious sign of his intentions.

Meeting with Count Bethlen,[182] in Rome for a few days. A vigorous, sharp man, accustomed to being in command. We discussed Europe, concentrating on the Danube-Balkan area. He was anxious to know the true state of our relations with London. He believes that British-Italian peace would also solve the problems of Central Europe. I spoke to him of our intentions with cool calm: peace, if possible; war, if necessary. The Hungarians accept every benefit from us, it with the somewhat condescending air of the impoverished nobleman but they are not yet fully aware of our power and they have a sentimental inclination towards London, determined by two powerful factors: Judaism and snobbery. I told Bethlen that the democracies will give the Hungarians nothing more than pretty words.

December 31, 1937

The Spanish offensive is proceeding well. I telephoned Pariani asking if he thinks it useful to encourage Berti to bring our divisions in line to try to take advantage of the success. The air force in the Balearic Islands has been reinforced and has orders to shower tons of explosives behind Teruel and on cities on the coast to break Red morale.

The Duce is in a good mood. He asked Valle, in my presence, what the strength of the air force is. Before the end of year, 3,000 airplanes are scheduled, plus 750 more. He said to me that under these conditions, if the English don't come to an agreement, the day of that famous statement is drawing closer!

I complained to the minister of Norway about the cable sent by his King to the Negus and I told him that such a gesture can only seriously endanger relations between the two states. He knew nothing. He had no reaction. In answering he spat when he spoke. All of this induced me to shorten the meeting. He is an old man of seventy who retains traces of considerable idiocy.

Long talks with Bigliardi.[183] He described the navy's mood: very calm and confident in the policy of the government. No worries of having to go to war with the English. On the contrary... The new naval program was greeted with joy in the gun rooms of our ships. It has become known that I was a supporter of the new construction. This has increased my popularity, which, according to Bigliardi, is very widespread in the navy.

1938

January 1, 1938

A talk with Lady Chamberlain in the morning. She showed me a letter from her brother-in-law. Nothing new other than the usual complaints about the anti-British propaganda on Radio Bari and in the Italian press and the fact that he reiterates a general good will to negotiate with us. We shall see...

In the afternoon, a conversation with von Hassel, who informed me of some new points of the note Trautmann[184] will give to the Chinese government on behalf of Japan. These are clarifications for the most part. I took the opportunity to tell von Hassel that Trautmann is not behaving well with our functionaries in China. He keeps very much apart from them. Obviously he has not accepted the spirit of the Axis. This doesn't surprise me. He is a career diplomat, of medium stature with a gloomy personality. I remember, in 1932, how anti-Nazi he was and how disappointed he was, in 1933, when Hitler came to power.

Last night, just after midnight, a telephone call at home informed me that Teruel had been seized. I couldn't have started the year in a better way. Frusci's cables speak of a disorderly flight by the Reds. I have the feeling that if we continue to attack aggressively we could achieve great success and reach the sea. Which could mean the end of the war. But will there be this kind of drive?

Yesterday, Valle,[185] taking off from Monte Celio, bombed Barcelona. Flying time: six hours. Why didn't he tell me? He promised me next time.

January 2, 1938

I had a discussion with Host Venturi[186] yesterday to decide the fate of the freighter *Ischia*. It carries a shipment of tanks for the Chinese. It is on its way to Hong Kong. Since for technical reasons the freighter cannot change course, we had initially informed the Japanese of its position and speed so that they could seize it. They do not want to, fearing international incidents. They are letting us deliver the merchandise. But the Duce, who "intends to make allies of the Japanese military against Great Britain," had me study the best way to avoid unloading the shipment. We have decided to beach the ship on the coast of Hainan Island. Venturi says that it is a simple matter. The Duce approved. The orders have been issued.

Berti, with his first cables, dampens any enthusiasm for the victory at Teruel and still forecasts a strong resistance capability in the area by the Reds. Could he be a jinx?

With the Duce we examined the agenda of the next Budapest Convention. We must remind the Austrians and the Hungarians that they owe us closer political allegiance. These two nations are just as eager to ask for favors and at the same time they are ready shy away every time whenever they must take any kind of position that is favorable to us. Mussolini is fed up. This morning he said that when the Spanish matter is concluded he will invite Göring to Nazify Austria. I am not fond of the Austrians, but I think that we should go slowly.

The running aground of the *Ischia* is suspended following talks with Ingianni[187] and with the ship owner Lauro,[188] who have more know-how than Host Venturi, and pointed out to me all the complications this could cause. I will speak to the Duce about it.

January 3, 1938

Meeting with Perth,[189] which I summarized. I feel this conversation is quite important. It means that Great Britain does not want to close the door on negotiations. After the last cable from Crolla, and Eden's speeches, one could reach that conclusion. If a total and long-lasting agreement could be reached, we should go ahead. If not, we shouldn't.

Received the ambassador of Japan and the naval attaché on the matter of the *Ischia*. They will seize it: we will not protest. But to sink it or run it aground would be the cause of disputes and perhaps an international scandal which could reflect upon our Merchant Marine. I decided against giving this advice to the Duce. If the Japanese do not seize it, it will reach Hong Kong. Fifty tanks will not change the outcome of the war in the Far East!

I gave instructions to Mazzolini,[190] who is leaving for Egypt. Apart from normal political-diplomatic action, he must study all of the possibilities of the Italian Community in case of war with England. A few determined action squads operating by surprise could cause havoc in the cities, create chaos in the area, and maybe carry out sabotage of a military nature. He must neither write nor telephone. Come to Italy, ask for leave for family reasons.

Valle came to see me for the communiqué of his raid on Barcelona. The Agency *España* notes 60 killed. Berti cables that the offensive on Teruel is over.

I mentioned to Jacomoni[191] the name of one of the Durini[192] girls as a wife for King Zog. He insists on getting married and wants an Italian woman. But he is rather discredited here after the two previous unsuccessful attempts.

January 4, 1938

The Papal Nuncio[193] spoke to me about his meeting with Buffarini. He was very alarmed. And the Holy See was also affected by his alarm. Buffarini had apparently said that the situation regarding the Catholic Action[194] was becoming worse than what it was in 1931. He had no facts to confirm this. But I gave the Papal Nuncio a summary of the recent international activity by the Vatican. I am aware of the difficulties created by Germany, but they must not exaggerate in their connections with the popular fronts, and sometimes even with communists. This could make the Duce more annoyed towards Catholic organizations. And the Holy See must remember that it is the Axis who is fighting in Spain against communism: in that Spain which has recently experienced the massacre of members of religious orders at the hand of the Reds.

I sent to Vienna and to Budapest an outline of a declaration committing the two Danubian countries to closer adherence to the Axis, to anti-Comintern and anti-League politics. This is the right time. The Hungarians fear a *rapprochement* with Romania too much to refuse. The Duce, though, confirmed to me that he does not intend to reach an accord with the Romanians if the green light is not given by Budapest.

O' Kelly: Vice President of Ireland. Modest man, polite and good natured. Says that the next step for his country is to proclaim the Republic of Ireland. Very anti-British. I told him that our two countries will always be closer and closer for reasons both negative and positive.

I proposed to the Duce, who accepted, to send Paolucci de Calboli[195] to Japan as chief of the Party mission. He will be pleased. He has always been against the League of Nations and is an Anglophobe: he will get along well with the Japs.

January 5, 1938

The Duce told me of three conversations that he had last night at the theater. One with Bethlen, of which I took notes. He expressed the Magyar preoccupation with Germany in particular. The Hungarians still prefer a Little Entente gravitating around Paris to one centered around Berlin. Mussolini assured him that we will not come to an agreement with the Romanians without the prior blessing of the Hungarians. Bethlen was very much relieved.

Then he spoke with von Hassel, who cried about his lot and moved the Duce to pity. He told me to intervene once again with Berlin and this time to save Hassel. This is not a role that I will play out voluntarily. Hassel is an enemy and I much preferred it when the Duce ordered me to ask for his head. Anyway, tomorrow I will speak to Hassel, and then we shall see.

Finally Perth: brief summary of the positions of the two countries and confirmation of my discussion of January 3. Perth is optimistic; he told the Duce that before the year is out we will see the agreement: maybe—he says—we will see it during the first three months. The proof of the pudding... But the dawn doesn't color the sky in pink to allow so much confidence in the future.

I saw Blondel, after his leave. He told me that in governmental circles there is a good disposition, but within the public there is growing suspicion towards Italy.

Meeting with the Papal Nuncio: I reassured him. Nothing will be done against the Catholic Action. Although I did confirm what I said yesterday regarding the danger of leftist slidings of the Vatican.

January 6, 1938
Meeting with von Hassel. I spoke to him openly. I told him the reasons for our dissatisfaction towards him: things he said against Italy, his attitude during the negotiations and the signing of the Tripartite Pact. He denied the first, and he said that regarding the second matter that he was applying instructions received. He was said to have always been pro-Italian, when everyone in Germany, Party included, were against us. He added that he always worked to cancel the memory of 1915 from the minds of the Germans. But he did not ask for clemency or pity: if we wish to intervene in Berlin, we can do so on our own initiative.

I think that we should let him meet his destiny. He was an enemy before, he is even more so today. If we save him he would be an enemy made more bitter by gratitude. Secondly, we cannot disclaim responsibility for Hess and Hesse who acted upon our indication. Hassel passes and Hess remains. The second interests me the most.

The Duce, speaking of Garibaldi, said: "He was lucky to have been illiterate. Had he been literate he would have read Clausewitz[196] and he would have lost the battles!" He was in an excellent mood and enjoyed the paradox.

He ordered me to liquidate Parini for the squandering in the administration of the DIE[197]

January 7, 1938
Long discussion with the King. He wanted to speak with me regarding the work to be done at the Palace on the occasion of Hitler's visit. He mentioned a return visit to Germany. A sensitive question. The Duce dislikes this duplicate visit to his. Speaking to me about it, he said: "This is one of the times when the Monarchy reveals itself to be a useless superstructure." The Duce also added: "The Germans love me also for the solidarity of the Party, but they do not love the King because they remember that in 1915 he signed the declaration of war." I avoid giving the King an answer: but the visit will have to be made. Out of protocol and for the King's prestige. We can delay it, of course. The King told me not to trust the Germans: in the past, Berlin had always been the most untrustworthy chancellery. Austria was honest. He commended the personal honesty of the liberals: in the many years of his Reign only two fell short, a certain Maury[198] and Nunzio Nasi.[199] He criticized the construction of large ships, in which he has no faith. They are too exposed to dangers from the air as well as from submarines.

The Duce told me to wash my hands of von Hassel. Good. He listened to a report from Anfuso on the situation in Spain. Nothing new: great slowness of movement on behalf of the Whites. It seems that Teruel was not entirely occupied because the generals, reaching the Archbishop's Palace, took two hours to have lunch with the Bishop.

Meeting with Miroinescu, a pro-Italian Romanian Senator. He told me that Goga's[200] government is a transitional and transactional government in respect to that of Codreanu,[201] a kind of von Papen[202] government. He believes that a *modus vivendi* is possible with Hungary.

Meeting with Perth. Following the rumors going around on the cession of Giuba to Germany, he reminded me of the treaty of 1924 which would give the option to Great Britain. I put such rumors down as absurd and ridiculous. He was personally of the same opinion.

January 8, 1938

We spoke with the Duce of the Austro-Hungarian counterproposals for the Budapest Convention. As foreseen they are trying to avoid any responsibility toward the so called "democracies." In return they try to put in a few lines that disturb Germany and prevent the Romanian *rapprochement*. The Rome Protocols turn out to be less and less important: agreement which only have an economic content are always lacking in deeper vitality. Economic conditions change too rapidly: sometimes from one year to the next. In Central Europe, for example, the result of a harvest is sufficient. Anyway, we shall see in Budapest.

The Duce was anxious about the Empire: Goggiam is in revolt. There are 15,000 rebels. Our garrisons are besieged. Two months and a lot of troops will be required to crush the movement. The Duce says that Pirzio Biroli[203] is responsible, as well as the racial unpreparedness of the Italians. The behavior of many of our people caused the natives to lose respect for the white race.

Gervasi,[204] of the *Hearst* newspapers, asked for a loan. I gave him 20,000 lire. Naturally, without collateral. He has always been a friend. But I prefer to bribe our enemies with money, rather than encumber the spontaneity of friends.

Long meeting with Starace and Buffarini about replacing Governor Colonna.[205] It seems that we must take G. G. Borghese.[206] A bitter pill to swallow: his antifascism is rather recent. I nominated Costantino Patrizi.[207] A bit better...

January 9, 1938

Traveling to Budapest. Meeting with Villani, from which I conclude that I will find an atmosphere a bit troubled towards us. We will try to clear it up. The welcome at the station is very warm, despite the snow storm.

January 10, 1938

For me, the Conference began with two conversations: one with Schuschnigg and the other with Schmidt. As far as they were concerned, the main issue was to settle the matter of the British documents relating to the meeting between Schmidt and Vansittart. I started by being unyielding: even though it was immediately clear that the Chancellor was not prepared to give us the head of his Secretary of State. I had to give in: it was therefore worth negotiating for forgiveness rather carefully. That is what I did and I had Schmidt on my side during the political negotiations. He began by revealing that Kanya was prepared to recognize Franco, but he would have done this only if I were to demand it. The hard nut to crack for the Hungarians is the declaration about Geneva. On this point the Austrians were more inclined to give in. Instead they wanted a declaration for the independence of Austria, which I didn't feel I could make out of regard for Germany. The Hungarians asked for a declaration for the minorities. There was an anti-Romanian slant to their request, but had I accepted it, it would have above all not pleased Yugoslavia.

January 11, 1938
   This is what I wanted to avoid. The indiscriminate talk of minorities would have created renewed solidarity to the Little Entente, just now when the crisis is most acute. The Conference therefore began in a difficult atmosphere. There was friction on many issues. I made the usual general survey, with particular reference to our relations with England. It was an issue which particularly worried Kanya. I gave my report a slight touch of optimism: it was absolutely not appropriate to alarm those present at Budapest if I wanted to obtain an explicit adherence to our policy. Kanya spoke harshly of the Little Entente, and of the men who are in charge of the three states. He said that Goga has defected twice. He defined Stoyadinovich as a Balkan scoundrel. I protested, confirming that we have nothing other than reasons to be satisfied with Belgrade's policies. The Little Entente is a foible. Especially, Romania. When he wants to insult or badly define, he says: "Like a Romanian" or "a thief like a Romanian" or "a liar almost like a Romanian." These are his usual expressions.

January 12, 1938
   To arrive at a positive result regarding the Tripartite declaration, in the end I had to use strong-arm tactics. Then they gave in. They accepted practically all the formulas I proposed, with some changes that they suggested, which strengthened the document rather than weakened it, in my opinion. The negotiations took place in Daranyi's office at the Presidency, a room where a large oil portrait of Franz Joseph as a young Emperor, in 1848, stood out. History has made a lot of progress in ninety years!
   In Hungary I found a substantially favorable climate towards us among the people and the youth. The older generation, and there are many, perhaps Kanya is their typical representative, cannot be fond of us. They feel just like Princess Esterhazy, wife of former Prime Minister, who, during a dinner, told me outright that we Italians were mainly responsible for Hungarian mutilation, and that it is very easy to cut a country to pieces while it is very difficult afterwards to put it back together!

January 13, 1938
   But the young are different. They admire Italy for its warlike drive and for its social justice. The Hungary of the gentlemen landowners, the feudal Hungary, cannot want the coming of a regime that seriously and greatly improves the conditions of the masses.

The Turul, Young Nationalist Organization, wanted to nominate me Grand Master, in place of Gömböes.[208] The government was against it, using the pretext that it may have displeased... Schuschnigg. They will nominate me on another occasion. Anyhow, there was an interesting demonstration at the theater: when I got up to leave, the entire Military School, *regardless of the prohibition imposed of making any kind of demonstration*, stood up and gave the Roman salute. A clear sign of the times. The return voyage good. Much Yugoslav courtesy. Cordial welcome in Trieste. The Budapest Conference had a good echo in Italy. The Duce called me with his congratulations. This is the reward which counts the most.

January 14, 1938

I reported to the Duce on the trip to Budapest. He was pleased with the results and repeated his congratulations.

I thought that I would find him more irritated about the seizure of Teruel. He considers the matter a local success for the Reds, of little importance, and, besides, he feels it more relevant from a strategic point of view to have stopped the advance on Madrid. He would like to know Franco's precise plan. He speaks also of a possible landing at Valencia to take the Reds from behind. France and England would not move. But to do this one needs to read Franco's mind and to have definite guarantees, perhaps also of a territorial nature. I did not hide my concern. I believe that during the winter the Reds have reinforced their position. I would not be surprised to see an offensive shortly, with changes within the national front. What would happen then to our 30,000 men in Spain?

The present situation is, in my opinion, untenable. We must decide: either give the shove that brings the situation to a head, or cleverly break away, happy to have been able to write the names of the victories of Malaga and Santander on our flags.

January 19, 1938

Nothing important in the morning. Many interviews of secondary importance.

In the afternoon I received Munters, the Latvian Foreign Minister. A personality of little account. He declares himself the representative of a Fascist government, but after all he is a democrat and for the League of Nations. The secret of Geneva, for the small countries, is to provide a stage lit by the floodlights of worldwide publicity for their politicians. Munters was beaming when he said that he knew more or less all of the great figures in the world. He has toasted with "the King Emperor." This is a kind of recognition, a little muffled but in the end useful to rouse the small countries of the north.

January 20, 1938

Bose,[209] head of the Indian Congress, spoke to me at length of the situation of his Party. Until now there have been few projects. At the center there is Great Britain who is in complete control. In the provinces some departments of little importance have been entrusted to the Indians. Great Britain has excellent agents in the small and large local villages, who oppress the people with the support of English troops. Program of his Party: the independence of the country. Means to achieve this: obstructionism and passive resistance. No armed conflict. They ask only two things of us: to keep Great Britain concerned about our intentions and to inform them of the general political situation, so that they can better position themselves. In turn I suggested that Bose direct his Indian sympathies towards Italy and Japan: the two countries which have most profoundly injured British prestige. He told me that he will try; but it is difficult because the Indian nation is dominated by feeling, and therefore is today favorable to China as it was towards Ethiopia. In my opinion, and from my fleeting visits to India, I think that they are a lifeless people without reactions, who will not attain independence unless other forces knock England down. And perhaps even then some new power will take over in India. Meeting of the Commission for the Führer's visit.

January 23, 1938
Nothing new. Sunday at the beach.

January 24, 1938
I am less and less satisfied with the situation in Spain. The offensive which should have began today towards Teruel has once again been postponed. I proposed to the Duce the need for a meeting with Franco. We could have him come to Cagliari by ship and join him there, Mussolini and I. I think that a meeting would be useful to understand his intentions and his possibilities. We could better determine the lines of our policy. Because we must make a decision about Spain. Since there is much talk at this time of the radio war with Great Britain, I want to set the origins of the Arab transmission from Radio Bari straight. When I was Undersecretary of Propaganda I was asked to find a job for an Arab-Italian, the brother of a Bishop, Monsignor Cattan. I took him into the Ministry. He spoke Arabic well. We had him give a few lectures and a news broadcast. It was successful: many letters began to arrive from Palestine, Syria, and Egypt. We improved upon it. Then we had to fire Cattan because, on his own initiative, he insulted the English, with whom at the time we had good relations. But, given the success of the initiative, I didn't want to interrupt it and so I continued after Cattan's departure. However, I had no idea I had created an issue that would cause such friction with Great Britain.

January 25, 1938
A very calm day.
A meeting with Ruegger[210] with particular reference to the attacks by the Swiss press. Ruegger noted that these were extreme left-wing papers, who are enemies of Motta[211] and his government. He asks us to not overestimate them.

In Spain the Reds have once again attacked and therefore the offensive on Teruel is subject to further delay.

January 26, 1938

Nothing noteworthy.

I was interested in a report by Galli, about a discussion with Aras,[212] during which the possibility of a conflict in the Mediterranean, with its possible developments, was brought up. Galli emphasizes the possibility that Turkish troops go to Egypt, to defend the Canal, given that Great Britain could never raise a large army. It is an interesting and new possibility, which I will communicate to the General Staff.

Marzio was baptized by Monsignor Celso Costantini.[213] He received the water and salt in religious silence, without shedding a tear, which, according to the experts, is quite miraculous.

Hassel went away "on leave" this morning; he is indeed an unwelcome guest. I learned this from his daughter yesterday evening, who also told me that von Neurath was furious that Hassel had sought to justify himself with the Duce and me.

January 29, 1938

The Duce is prepared to write a letter to Franco to encourage him to do something conclusive. I encouraged him. We must put an end to this Spanish story.

Nothing else.

January 30, 1938

Nothing noteworthy.

I advised the Duce to not allow the Biseo flight to proceed to Argentina, where some hostile manifestation is being prepared against our flyers. It is not worth risking men and equipment to the considerable wear and tear of a flight of three thousand kilometers, to allow the riffraff of a second-rate country like Argentina to taunt us. The Duce approved: they will not go. Of all the countries in which I have lived, Argentina is certainly the one I liked the least, or rather, that I profoundly despised. A nation without soul and a land without color, they could not exert any charm as far as I was concerned. For quite a number of decades, when many human wrecks went to South America, the worst elements stopped at the point of arrival: there rose Buenos Aires, a boring and murky city like the river that flows through it. To an already rotten mix, in recent years, and in great abundance, there has been added the Jewish element. I don't think this has helped to improve it.

January 31, 1938

As was to be expected, disputes have begun regarding the goose step march. Above all, the old soldiers are opposed to it because they regard it as a Prussian invention. The Duce reacts violently, and he read me a speech which he will give tomorrow to explain and praise the innovation. Since it appears that the King has also expressed himself as being against it the Duce said: "It is not my fault if, physically, the King is a runt. Naturally he cannot perform the goose step march without looking ridiculous. He will hate it for the same reasons that he has always hated horses, since he has to use a ladder to get into the saddle. But the physical deficiency in a sovereign is no reason to disparage, as he has done, the army of a great nation." "They say that the goose step is Prussian. Not at all. The goose is a Roman animal, if it is true that it saved the Capitol. Its place is between the eagle and the wolf."

The Duce prepared a strong letter for Franco. Since Berti will come tomorrow, I advised him to have a meeting with him first to decide whether to send it or not.

Renato Ricci is worried about the marble of Carrara, now that France has placed prohibitive taxes. Germany, once a large buyer, has closed its markets. Another crisis is looming for marble.

February 1, 1938

Militia parade: the goose step parade march appeared in public, and was much applauded. The Duce gave a speech to the Militia in front of the Coliseum. He spoke in a military manner: he lashed out against the backbiters, whom he called sedentary, paunchy, fools and second raters. I knew to whom he was alluding: but Badoglio and De Bono[214] took it to be themselves and were seething with indignation. De Bono, most of all, said that after a speech like that he had no choice but to resign.

I accompanied Lady Chamberlain to see the Duce, to whom she showed an important letter from Neville Chamberlain. Two points: Great Britain is ready to formally recognize the Empire; the talks may begin at the end of the month. Mussolini approved and agreed. Lady Chamberlain will write a letter to her brother-in-law describing the Duce's reaction, which was clearly favorable. He gave his total consent to the project of an agreement and said that he intends to fulfill it completely, and in a manner as to build a basis of collaboration between the two Empires. He dictated the terms of the letter to Lady Chamberlain.

February 2, 1938

Meeting between the Duce and Berti in my presence. Berti, who can't see the big picture and always looks lugubrious, didn't say anything new. In a sea of useless words he drowned those few concepts, that everyone knows by heart, regarding the defects of the Spanish as inconclusive leaders. The Duce gave him the letter for Franco. An excellent, virile document which consolidates our commitments if Franco fights, but which prepares us for disengagement if the Generalissimo continues to insist in a war of grueling delay.

In the meantime Mussolini has intensified the bombings of the coast, which break the nerves of the population. Many news items indicate that the Red front is very weak. The attack of ten national divisions would be sufficient. But is Franco in the position, and would he know how, to do it? I told the Duce the impression made by his military oratory of yesterday. He was pleased. He loves the style of steel soldier and adopts it more and more. Moreover, he judges the Italian nation as being very hard, with a dramatic edge. Perhaps even sad, like its songs. Our reputation abroad has been ruined—in his opinion—by Neapolitan singers and dancers.

Meeting with the American ambassador. He fears war, but I reassured him.

Meeting with the Japanese ambassador. He told me that the Japanese are beginning to create a series of local governments in China of a provisional nature, which will eventually become permanent.

February 3, 1938

Meeting with General Ajmonino[215] to finalize the Führer's visit to the Prince of Piedmont. When H.R.H. returns to Rome I will meet up with him and together we will agree on the details.

Received Lady Listowel, wife of a Laborite Lord. She is Hungarian, very charming, she seems to be our friend and speaks good Italian. She tells me that English *feeling*[216] is rising up against us and that once the weapons will be ready, nationalist propaganda will have heated up and we should not be surprised if English should attack us. Something much more likely if Eden becomes the head of a future Liberal Labor government.

Meeting between Duce and Magistrati. Massimo minimized the German flirtation with France and summarized a meeting with Göring, who said that Nazism wants to strengthen Germany to the extreme and therefore for a few years must avoid conflict. To achieve this, one must cover the ball of steel with soft rubber. At present, he who comes close will see and feel the rubber: once the ball is slung steel will hit him. Mussolini took note. He would like to, on another occasion, ask Germany about its behavior in case of isolated conflict between ourselves and Great Britain. He repeated that he believes the conflict to be inevitable: therefore he does not want to lose the advantage of the initiative. He would be satisfied with a benevolently neutral Germany.

Bonmartini[217] bought the newspaper *Il Giornale d'Italia* and came to place it at my full disposition. He hates Balbo with all his might. But he is an individual of little account.

February 4, 1938

We have agreed to Eden's requests for greater surveillance of the Mediterranean in the fight against piracy. These are feeble measures.

I presented to the Duce the projects for the beautification of Rome for the Führer's visit. He found them to be good and approved the work carried out to this date.

Session of the Supreme Defense Commission. Meeting with Lord Lothian, Undersecretary of the Colonies, upon his return from India. At his request, I explained our point of view as to the possibilities of an agreement with England. He appeared to me to be a reasonable man. He approved the idea of a general agreement, including the recognition of the Empire. He said: "Between England and Italy there are no compromises: either the return to the traditional friendship, or conflict." I replied that I agreed. Except, though, that one cannot speak of a traditional friendship: the understanding must be on a new basis which takes into account the new power of Italy.

The lawyer Giacomo Costa, an antifascist who fled from Lipari two months or so ago, has offered his services as an informer and agent provocateur among the political exiles in Paris. He is in contact with the journalist Pascazio.[218] We shall use him.

February 5, 1938

The changes in the German government are good. It marches rapidly towards integral Nazification, which is useful to the Axis, and is one of its most powerful reasons for the similarity of the Regimes. The Duce was also very pleased: this event, which is very important, wipes the slate clean of the recent period of flirtation with France. Very good, Ribbentrop to the Foreign Ministry. From his meetings with the Duce, and with me in October-November, it was clear that he is hostile towards the English, who treated him badly. London was a failure for him; Rome, a success. He took the minister's oath in the Hall of the Victories, the day the Tripartite Pact was signed. I see, as a consequence of the incident, a reinforcement of the Axis and the Triangle. We will reach closer and more concrete understandings, and perhaps one can even think about a Conference of the Three Foreign Ministers, which could take place at Addis Ababa.

I nominated Pavolini president of the Institute of Foreign Exchange. He will do well and is loyal.

Baistrocchi[219] offers his candidacy as Commissioner for war production, in place of Dell'Olio,[220] who is by now exhausted. Balbo, during the session of the Supreme Commission, had spoken to me of General Gazzera[221] as a possible successor. I did not miss the opportunity to tell Baistrocchi, who, as everyone knows, hates Gazzera. I think that now he doesn't like Balbo either.

February 6, 1938

The compliance to British requests regarding piracy has provoked a certain relaxation in London. Eden spoke in more relaxed terms with Grandi, and dictated a note on Italian-English relations for the *Sunday Times*, a note that, in reality, was very hypocritical. I told the papers not to give it much importance. I think, more than our compliance, it was the new German government that impressed London.

Franco's offensive towards Teruel has begun. Berti cabled that it is proceeding favorably and is not at all critical. Which makes me think that things are really going well. We shall see! Recent and distant events advise not to indulge in too much optimism when the Spanish generals are running the show.

Long meeting with the Duce. I told him of Guarneri's pessimism, who said yesterday, after the Defense Commission, verbatim: "We are in bankruptcy." The Duce knew it: he does not at all share this exaggerated fear.

The situation in reality is very sound. We also spoke about the Jewish problem. I said I was leaning towards a solution which does not raise a problem that does not exist here. The Duce shares the same opinion. It would put water on the fire, even though not enough to snuff it out completely.

February 7, 1938

Grandi is ready to move right into meetings with Eden, and wants the authorization to begin talks. I made a handwritten draft of a cable, which I read to the Duce, advising calm and caution facing this British zeal for conciliation, which could also represent a maneuver by Eden, now that the change of the guard in Germany has demonstrated that British efforts to injure the Axis in Berlin will not succeed. Calm and caution: and, in any case, the talks should take place in Rome. Grandi is attempting to promote himself. He wants to be the man who made peace with England, a figure that, to many Italians, may even prove to be welcome. Not in the least. Peace or war is in the hands of Mussolini, and only he. No one must take a personal role.

I told the Duce of Baistrocchi's desire to replace Dell'Olio, who is now old and very ill. The Duce said that he will give him a successor only "when he is dead and buried." He showed some skepticism at the name of Baistrocchi, active man but muddleheaded.

Philip of Hesse is very happy with the changes in Berlin. He told me that a few hours before, Neurath and Ribbentrop knew nothing.

Good news from Spain. Remarkable breakthrough caused by an attack of three of Franco's columns in the area of Teruel. The advance continues.

February 8, 1938

After another jump, it seems that the advance has already stopped. Which, with the Spanish, is not surprising. We asked Berti if the objectives of today's action were tactical or strategic, since the Duce's intention in this second possibility was to resume bombing of the coastal cities to break the Red resistance. I received, and gave to the Duce, an eyewitness report of the recent bombardments of Barcelona. I have never read a document so realistically terrorizing. And these were only 9 "S. 79," and the entire raid lasted only one and a half minutes. Buildings pulverized, traffic interrupted, panic that became insanity: 500 dead, 1,500 wounded. It is a good lesson for the future. Useless to plan air-raid protection and the construction of shelters: the only means of escape from air attacks is the evacuation of the cities.

I sent a cable to Berlin to cut off any speculation about the so-called Italian-British *rapprochement*. Our policy is and will remain straightforward. It would be a good thing if the Führer keeps that in mind during his speech on February 20. I cabled all this to Attolico.

February 9, 1938

According to Berti's news, the Spanish have paused to prepare a second surge. The pause ought to be brief. It seems that the victory attained is considerable, even though limited to a tactical field and therefore not decisive.

The press tries to speculate on the Grandi-Eden talks, attempting to make it appear an Italian initiative which is not the case. I prepared *Informazione Diplomatica* n. *14*, which I gave to the Duce, and I had the newspaper *Il Piccolo* of Rome seized, because it continued to excite public opinion with bold titles of news of the talks in London, despite being told not to.

Grandi telephoned me and, after having read my cable of the day before yesterday, is beginning to mark time. Although no doubt that it was he who went too far. After all he is dying for a *rapprochement* with London and hates the Germans.

At the Supreme Commission I spoke on the American mentality, a problem of great importance but not only negative for us. I want to see how England will do, blocked by submarines, to stock up with only its navy and without being able to count upon the help of the neutral navies.

February 10, 1938

Received Berger and Christich.[222] The latter spoke to me of the next visit of Spaho,[223] Communications Minister, and he secretly asked me, on behalf of Stoyadinovich, that not too much importance be given to his visit by the press. He is quite an important figure whom they do not want to further inflate. Christich is fond of Stoyadinovich and was very pleased when I said that Stoyadinovich, six months after his death, will still be head of government. He is a strong man from whom no one will take power.

Pirelli is still an Anglophile and anxious for an agreement. He agreed on the psychological preparation of the Italians for the war, but he worries about the lack of gold. When I told him that, quoting Machiavelli, between gold and iron I choose the latter, he replied: "If only we had iron." Pirelli is a capitalist: he fears war and thinks of his interests, including those that he has in England.

Grandi called to say that a few steps forward were made in today's talks with Eden. We will see.

Meeting with Phillips and with Hotta, the latter so as to be informed on the progress of the talks in London. I don't want Tokyo to become suspicious of us.

Goga resigned: it seems following a French-English-Russian intervention to protect the Jews.

February 11, 1938

Agreed upon some arrangements with Volpi relating to the Belgrade Exhibition.

Grandi's reports on yesterday's talks have still not arrived. But the international press is already losing interest in an immediate agreement between Italy and England.

Tomorrow the meeting between the Führer and Schuschnigg will take place at Berchtesgaden. It will be very interesting. For one thing it is secret, truly secret. Nothing has leaked so far. And furthermore it is proof that the intentions of the Führer towards Austria have not worsened recently.

Mussolini instead is more radical. This morning he told me that he is favorable to the Nazifying of Austria. What is not integral, is not safe: Romania teaches this.

I promised 100,000 lire to Del Croix to improve the reception of the German disabled veterans, which he intended to keep quiet with the excuse of the meager financial resources of the Association. I don't like this Del Croix, and I ask myself if it is serious to continue to keep, as leader of many glorious and truly disabled former servicemen, an individual who may have had misfortune, but did not give proof of particular heroism. Everyone knows the origins of his mutilation. Neither is it possible to forget his attitude in 1924. All the more so since the soul has remained the same. The day the barometer says "stormy weather" he would drop us again.

February 12, 1938

The talks between Grandi and Eden don't seem to be very binding. I think that Great Britain wants to reach a conclusion for Spain: this is why they dangle the prospect of an agreement before our eyes. In front of which we have remained cooler than the English believe. Farinacci even replied with insults. He clearly told me of wanting to write such an article: I did not try to stop him.

"Choc" attacks me, saying that I represent the real danger for peace, not having any Latin feelings and wanting to profit from the tragedy. It is very exaggerated, but there is some truth. My conception of the Fascist Empire is not a static one. We must still go ahead. And it is correct that property owners should worry. As for Latin solidarity, it is an invention of the French that they use when others should agree to have themselves disemboweled in their place.

The first elements of the program for Beck's visit were agreed to with Wisochy. Another event that will not please Paris. Never mind!

The Romanian crisis is not clear. In the meantime someone reported to Police Headquarters in Milan claiming to be Butenko, the Soviet delegate who vanished in Bucharest. He has no corroborating identity documents. Maybe he is a madman or a trickster. Anyway, I have had him sent to Rome.

February 13, 1938

Mrs. Sarfatti wants to go to America on a lecture tour. I will speak to the Duce, even though I believe that she is one of the very few women capable of making a good impression for us abroad. She spoke to me of the Jewish question with considerable concern and was pleased to learn my moderate opinions on the issue. Besides, she was already aware of the project of a public declaration to be made shortly, of a reassuring nature.

The first news of the Hitler-Schuschnigg meeting tends to give credence to a silent Nazifying of Austria. The Anschluss is inevitable. We must only, as far as possible, delay it.

Butenko is in Rome. He asks to see me. I will do so only after identification. I called a functionary of the Legation at Bucharest to verify his identity.

February 14, 1938

Calm day. The Duce returned from the mountains, but I have not yet conferred with him. The news from Vienna confirms the process of Nazification of Austria following the meeting of Berchtesgaden.

I spoke with Pariani of our military relations with Germany. I would first like to say that Pariani is convinced of the inevitability of conflict with Western Powers. He considers the most favorable period for us to be the spring of 1939. We will have completed the preparation of the ammunition provisions, today scarce for the small-caliber guns, while France and England will go through the most difficult period of crisis. Pariani believes in the success of an instant and surprise war. Attack Egypt, attack the fleets, invasion of France. The war will be won in the Suez and in Paris. I put forward the utility of creating right away an Italian-German secret war committee. He agrees and, after the removal of Blomberg,[224] believes it to be possible. We will speak to the Duce. I suggested studying the plan to invade Switzerland in order to attack France. He agrees and believes it to be a good idea. I also suggested to have Italian troops embark, always at a surprise moment, to Port Said and Suez. It is easy to have it coincide with troop transports for East Africa. He will approve and pass my suggestions for technical study.

Cantilo, ambassador of Argentina, has become Minister of Foreign Affairs. He is not a friend of ours and is an unpleasant man.

February 15, 1938

Received Manacorda[225] and Pavolini.

The Duce has seen the agreement between Austria and Germany and he told me that he considers it an unavoidable, logical development of relations between two German countries. We must insist, when presenting the matter, that it is a matter of two German countries. To give further proof of independence, Austria should join the anti-Comintern Pact.

As far as the relations with London stand, I sent a cable that recaps our intentions: ready to negotiate, on the already-stated basis, once the Spanish problem is out of the way. For one thing, it is very interesting to note that Eden's report of the Eden-Grandi talks, is very different from that of Grandi, in that a part of the initiative is traced back to us. I won't send a copy of the document to Grandi, because his game is not completely clear.

The Duce personally drew up *Informazione Diplomatica* n. *14* on the Jewish question. The Duce himself defined the piece, which in its form is almost conciliatory, as a masterpiece of anti-Semitic propaganda. I limited myself to stating that the Jewish State, hoped for by him, should not be in Palestine. So as to save our relations with the Arabs.

February 16, 1938

Butenko has been recognized by the correspondent of the *Stefani* agency in Bucharest. I saw him this morning at the Ministry. He does not appear to me to be a man of great caliber. But he was so frightened and distraught that a judgment upon him now would be premature. He even asked that the guards, instead of staying in the corridor, remain permanently in his hotel room. To begin with I gave his declarations to the newspaper *Il Giornale d'Italia* and I am blowing up the sensation through foreign press and the radio, etc. It is a good piece of anti-Soviet propaganda not to be missed.

I drew up a long letter for Grandi after the interview with the Duce. I say that we must push forward the negotiations with London. Whatever the result may be it is important to know it. Events could then prevent the maneuver which today is still free. But, maybe, not for much longer.

Berger-Waldenegg, instructed by the Chancellor, spoke to me about the results of the Berchtesgaden talks. I thought I would find him beaten. Instead he was relaxed and hopeful for a real collaboration with Germany. I am more skeptical. I advised him to suggest to Vienna to join the Tripartite Pact. It would be proof of Austrian independence.

Meeting with Blondel: general survey and mention of a possible truce in the press.

February 17, 1938

Yesterday evening dinner at home with many diplomats. I spoke with Christich about the situation in Austria. Speaking frankly: Italy and Yugoslavia are in an identical position facing pan-Germanism. They, worse than us: because they are not as strong and because they do not have such a strong natural border barrier. Anyway, there is nothing to be done. But since the Austrian chicken has fallen, or almost, into the German pot before it was time, it is indispensable that ties between Rome and Belgrade be further reinforced and it would be better to always keep in mind that Hungary and Poland also find themselves in similar situations. Christich agreed. I think that at this point we must study an alliance with Yugoslavia. The horizontal Axis may allow the existence of the vertical Axis.

Brief chance meeting with Perth, with whom I expressed myself more or less along the lines of the letter sent to Grandi. I did the same this morning with Lady Chamberlain, who has not yet received a reply to her letter dated February 1.

Received Phillips, with whom we made the usual general survey. He asked me what I thought of the Eden-Chamberlain disagreement. I told him that I did not have specific facts, but that I would have preferred to base the agreement with London on a mutual *feeling*[226] rather than on a fight between those statesmen.

Drafted *Informazione Diplomatica* n. 15 regarding Austria.

The Butenko affair made a lot of noise and was useful to us. I will use this individual but I despise him. He is a vile traitor who abandoned his blood (a daughter) to Stalin's revenge.

February 18, 1938

This morning the Duce was rather irritated at Germany for the manner in which the problem of Austria was handled. For one thing the Germans should have advised us: instead, not even a word. Secondly, if instead of stopping at the positions reached, they thought of getting to the actual Anschluss, general conditions would be created, differing greatly from those in which the Axis was originally constituted and would require a reevaluation of the situation.

I took advantage of the opportunity of being with Hesse, after having had lunch, the two of us, with the Prince of Piedmont, to speak to him clearly as a friend. I made notes of the conversation.

Grandi was received by Chamberlain, but I don't have facts concerning the result of the talks. He was very reticent on the phone, a reticence that didn't seem to be determined only by the fear of intercepts.

February 19, 1938
Council of Ministers.

I invited Schuschnigg to specify the role played by Italy in this entire Austrian affair. These rumors of desperate appeals by Vienna left unanswered must be denied. In reality we learned of this when it was already done, when every possible alternative had vanished and there was nothing left to do except approve the work carried out by Schuschnigg.

I also cabled Berlin to make it known the Führer should be careful, in his speech, not to place the friendship of Italy and Poland on the same level, as it appeared according to information coming from Attolico. Our reaction would be very appropriate on the issue.

Grandi has made progress in his talks. It seems that we can actually begin soon. Except that Perth, on specific orders from Eden, brought me a very pointed protest about a colonial matter of rather secondary importance. Coming the day after the talks in London it seems strange. It all leads me to believe that Eden, in seeing that he lost to Chamberlain, is attempting once again to confuse the issue and stall the negotiations once more. Grandi, to whom I hinted at this over the phone, feels the same way adding that in London the confusion in the government is very strong.

February 20, 1938
The day is critical: the Führer's speech in Berlin. A crisis in London due to the disagreement between Eden and Chamberlain, particularly about the policy towards Italy.

The Führer's speech, according to what Attolico and Magistrati cabled, was good towards us and particularly directed against Great Britain. Regarding Austria, even though the word "independence" did not appear, the statements made sound fairly satisfactory. Austria is considered a national entity and not a German province. At least for now.

In London the crisis is under way. The Duce telephoned from Terminillo and wants to be informed every half hour. The situation is unstable. At 1 p.m. Eden resigned and appeared at the Cabinet meeting as a resigning minister. The Cabinet met until 6:30 p.m. and was adjourned until after dinner. Eden, sullen and alone, was cheered by the crowd shouting "Eden, Prime

Minister!" as he left. The Laborites, the Liberals and the left-wing Conservatives have already voted a motion in favor of Eden. This crisis is perhaps
one of the most important that has ever taken place. It could mean peace or
war. I authorized Grandi to take any step that might add an arrow to
Chamberlain's quiver. A cabinet run by Eden would have as its policy to fight
against the dictatorships: first of all that of Mussolini. I wait at the Ministry
for developments. At 10 the Duce goes to bed. Signs of the times: the English are working on a Sunday and the Italian leader is taking his weekend.

February 21, 1938
During a reception at Colonna's house yesterday evening I learned about
the fall of Eden. The public applauded the news. The Prince and Princess
of Piedmont were also present and he wanted to toast with me more than
once. Oddly, the English minister to the Holy See, Osborne, wanted to congratulate me and drink to Eden's resignation. From the Colonna house I gave
orders to the press not to crow: over this we must not turn Eden into a victim
of fascism. Indeed, today the newspapers present the incident as the normal
development of an internal crisis in the English Cabinet. Perth, who is reacting well, called this morning to suggest that I do what I had already done.
Meeting with Lagardelle,[227] who is back from Paris. The same old words
and the usual projects: everything is now made secondary by changes in
Great Britain.
Grandi phones in a brief account of his meeting with Chamberlain. He
confirmed that we are ready to commence talks on the established principles. It seems that instructions will be sent to Perth as soon as possible.
We set the program of Beck's visit with the ambassador of Poland. The
press must not give it an anti-French character: the fact itself is enough,
without having to add printed words to it.
Sereggi[228] invites me, on behalf of Zog, to be best man at his wedding
on April 26. I accepted. I strongly believe in my program for Albania and
anything that may increase our prestige and our influence must not be neglected.

February 22, 1938
Long Council of Ministers. When I returned to the Palazzo Chigi in the
evening, I found Perth waiting in the lobby. I took notes of the meeting. I
must add that he did not seem at all sorry about Eden's departure and he
blushed like a schoolboy when I praised him for the work he has done. It's
strange how the English blush so easily: much more than we Latins. Shyness
or modesty?
Meeting with Lessona, very worried that the Party will begin to move
against him following De Bono's report about the March on Rome Certifi-
cate. Lessona prepared a memo in his defense. Very weak: as the sole witness to his participation in the March there is only a dead man: Dario Lupi.[229]
He pleaded with me to intervene. He knows that the battle will become a
rout for him. But is it really worth saving him?

Ward Price[230] wanted an interview with either me or the Duce. I don't think that it's the right time. I limited myself to giving him general information regarding the coming negotiations and to deny rumors of the loan requested by us from London.

Things are proceeding well in Spain. Teruel has been recaptured and the troops are advancing. Berti believes it possible to reach the sea and asks Franco to deploy our divisions. The Duce sent a nice cable urging Franco to fight and laying out the dilemma of the Legionnaires: either let them fight or have them come home.

February 23, 1938

Schuschnigg sent, via Ghigi, a passage from his next speech which concerns Italy. Good, also because it denies rumors of a change in our attitude towards Austria. But what are we to do? Go to war with Germany? At our first fire all of the Austrians, all of them without exception, would join Germany against us. I thanked Schuschnigg and I also suggested that he point out that the independence of Austria finds its reasons in the will and determination of the nation and not in uncertain guarantees coming from foreign states. A country whose independence is guaranteed by a third party is virtually finished.

The fighting in Spain continues victoriously. Franco must fully take advantage of his success and seize the favorable situation which has been created by military and political events. If he also misses this excellent occasion it will be final proof of his inadequacy. Fortune is not a train that passes by at the same hour every day nor is it an honest woman who dedicates her whole life to you. Fortune is a prostitute who offers herself fleetingly and then moves on to others. If you don't know how to grab her by the hair, you lose her.

Cantilo paid a farewell visit; he goes to Argentina shortly, not very convinced of what he must do.

February 24, 1938

We spoke with Christich of the Slav minorities in the Venezia Giulia region and, to facilitate Stoyadinovich's parliamentary discussion, I told him that we are still prepared to do something in their favor. But we don't know what to do, they are tranquil people and they ask for nothing. If only the Germans of the Alto Adige region were so docile.

Blondel wanted to have a general conversation, concentrating on London and Vienna. I put forth some of our ideas regarding Austria. He had to admit that they were realistic.

Ward Price came to say goodbye to me before returning to London. He told me, among other things, that Schuschnigg told him that Italy's protection towards Austria could not turn into a practical realization, since if an Italian soldier were to step into Austrian territory a *union sacrée* would be created against us. He also said that Göring, in a recent meeting, had let him understand that if Mussolini were in Berlin he would have more or less agreed to a free hand in Austria (which is false). Göring added that anyway it is a question of German matters in which they will not tolerate the interference of other powers and according to Ward Price, that includes Italy.

The Duce telephoned to say that Schuschnigg made a strong speech along the lines of what we suggested.

February 25, 1938

The Duce was very satisfied with Schuschnigg's speech, which he listened to on the radio. Above all he was impressed by the enthusiasm of the Assembly and it made him more hopeful in Austria's vitality. In his opinion, Austrian patriotism, which had been languishing for twenty years, has been awakened and the show of uniforms, flags and banners contributed to awakening it. The Duce believes in the need to animate politics with imagination and theatricality. If Schuschnigg had presented himself yesterday with the monotonous lassitude of a ceremony and with the dragged performance of the friar, the success would not have been as lively.

Villani asked me about news of our talks with London and if we planned to discuss Central Europe. I answered no. And I confirmed to him that a possible agreement with London is not intended to substitute the Axis, but rather to be parallel to it.

I said goodbye to von Hassel. Cold, hostile, rapid meeting. I feel no remorse whatsoever for having caused the departure of this individual who badly served his country and the cause of Italian-German friendship. Maybe he even tried to overcome hostile feelings and did not succeed: he fatally and inexorably belongs to that world of Junkers, who cannot forget 1914 and who, being deep down hostile towards Nazism, do not feel solidarity towards the regime. And then he was far too familiar with Dante. I don't trust foreigners who know Dante. They want to screw us with poetry.

February 26, 1938

The Czechoslovak minister came to protest about the publication in the newspaper *Il Giornale d'Italia*, according to which Beneš[251] apparently told a foreign diplomat that since 1923 he had been advising that Mussolini be gotten rid of. The information originated with us and came from a cable by the French minister in Prague. I think that at this point we should give the document to the press, even more so following the opinions voiced by Beneš against the other states of the Little Entente; a sharp dispute can be started and perhaps even a crisis.

I received Spaho, Yugoslavian Communications Minister.

The Duce is very irritated by the fact that Franco continues to hold our volunteer forces out of action, and because Franco has not replied to his letter. Mussolini gave orders to the air force in the Balearic Islands to abstain from all operations until our Infantry is deployed. This idleness destroys troop morale; cases of indiscipline are more frequent and for the first time, desertions have started. Also the country is tired of the affairs in Spain.

To the station to welcome Graziani. The Duce was there. There were all the major hierarchies, military and civil. Only Badoglio was missing. The welcoming of the crowds was, as a whole, organized and therefore of an unconvincing warmth. In the car the Duce said to me: "Graziani will be happy with my embrace. He fought well but he governed badly."

February 27, 1938
During the flight to Florence I examined the itinerary of the Führer and I saw the preparations. Everything very well.
Then to Livorno. Finally, departure for Turin.

February 28, 1938
Wedding of the Duke of Genoa.[232] Much tension in the court circles and the Turin aristocracy about the bride who is not considered to measure up. She is not beautiful and is fairly well on in her years. And if that were not enough, the priest, when reading the marriage service, mistakenly added ten years to her age! Now there is a Freudian slip that the bride will never forget.
Afternoon with the fascists: very friendly and polite.
On the train, conversation with the Princess of Piedmont.

March 1, 1938
Nothing of particular importance during my absence.
In spite of our pressure, Franco refuses to press the advance on Teruel to the fullest and is proposing another plan, in the Belchite area, to start in ten days time. Berti would rather operate in Teruel, but he is not against Franco's project.
I tell the Duce of my trip to Turin. He agrees when I tell him that my impression of loyalty to the monarchy there is weak: when, in my speech, I spoke of the house of Savoy, the reaction was minimal. When I mentioned the Duce, the cheers never stopped.
I gave Christich a copy of the cables from Prague. From these it emerges that Beneš says Yugoslavia and Romania are "cowardly." I think that the reaction in Belgrade will be lively.
Salata informs me of new and extremely serious details of the meeting between Hitler and Schuschnigg. It seems that the Chancellor's violence was unprecedented. He threatened, at any trace of resistance, to occupy Salzburg. Now Schuschnigg has made up his mind to have a plebiscite, and place the future of Austria on the outcome of the election. In his opinion the forecasts should be favorable to the Patriotic Front. But, if it were not so, would there not be an immediate crisis? Is it worth the risk?

March 2, 1938
I learned of D'Annunzio's death at the home of Colonna yesterday evening and I received the message to accompany the Duce to Gardone. Departure at 8 in the morning. I cannot say that the Duce was very affected. He felt that D'Annunzio's lot was enviable: after a glorious and heroic life, a sudden death at an age that can be considered advanced. He told me he had learned of the incident from a telephone call from the Prefect, Rizzo,[233] who

literally said: "It is with sorrow that I give you the good news!" It was a Freudian slip which revealed the frame of mind of a policeman happy to have finally completed a mission!

The Duce extolled the military and political action of D'Annunzio, the heroic poetry and a few theatrical things, but he criticized the novels, which he considered to be burdensome documents of the nineteenth century. He said that he had more or less behaved well towards the regime, even if during the first seven or eight years he never gave his full support. I believe, though, that had he sided against it in 1924 he would have been a dangerous adversary because he had a big following among the youth.

In the evening in Brescia I received a telephone call informing me that Lord Halifax is about to receive the Negus and asks me not to place emphasis on the matter and avoid a dispute in the press. Fine; but the meeting will make a sinister impression. I communicated this to the British embassy.

March 3, 1938

The funeral took place during the morning. I accompanied the Duce by car and during the entire journey he did nothing but observe the great quantity of unnecessary iron that is found laying about the countryside. He reckons that it amounts to 5-6 million tons in Italy. He is thinking of requisitioning this "open air mine" in case of emergency. It could provide enough iron for one year of war.

Return trip. Long talk with De Bono, who spoke to me at length about the Matteotti[234] case and he told me the real truth. He, De Bono, knew nothing about it. I will remember the other details of the story without having to write them down. Why did the old man speak to me? Perhaps because he trusts my discretion completely. But I, in his place, would have remained silent, out of principle.

The visit of the former Negus seems meaningless. Meanwhile the English let us know that they will make initial contacts also with Berlin in search of a general pacification.

March 4, 1938

Franco replied to the Duce with a very extensive letter, in which he explains in grand style the reasons for the delayed all-out offensive. Actually the Red forces of the Asturias had not been liquidated so rapidly and there were still strong pockets of resistance which required the presence of national troops. Now the machinery is ready to roll and Franco makes fairly optimistic predictions for the future. He believes that the Reds no longer have the stamina to resist and that at the first serious blow they will break up. He attributes a great moral and material importance to the presence of our Volunteers. The Duce appreciated the letter for its content and its tone. He will reply tomorrow giving assurances that he will spare no efforts to extend the engagement of the volunteers. The Duce was very amused when I indicated a gross mistake in the announcement of D'Annunzio's death, drawn up by the Academy: "His lips and hands were never tired of dictating..." He attributed it to Formichi,[235] whom he defined as "the chronic enthusiast."

Grandi repeated what I more or less already knew on the London happenings. He agrees with me in reckoning that if within two months an agreement is not reached, within two Eden will be head of government, and within four we will all be in uniform.

I received the Prince of Yemen,[236] De Vecchi, the Portuguese minister, and the Dutch minister, with credentials in order. He looks like the classic diplomat, with monocle and many career memories.

Berlin sends us the report on the meeting between Hitler and Henderson.[237] The Führer was very harsh and the result totally negative.

March 5, 1938

The Duce replied to Franco with an excellent cable: good wishes for victory, a commitment to give any further assistance within the limits of our economic capability and the framework of international relations.

The news from Austria is increasingly worse: in Stiria, Nazism controls everything, both in the streets and in the barracks. It is advancing rapidly in the other provinces. There is talk surfacing of Seyss-Inquart[238] as Chancellor with the specific task of digging the grave of Austria's independence. The Duce is, now, strongly critical of Schuschnigg's speech: he feels that he lacked tact with Germany and with the Führer. He spoke threateningly without having either the possibilities or the capabilities of taking action.

Lunch at Court: once again the King spoke to me negatively of Berlin and told me not to trust the Germans, who, in his opinion, are never loyal and are perennial liars.

In the afternoon I saw Volpi about the Belgrade Exhibition and other minor issues. He is very pleased about the improved relations with London. He believes—according to what Schacht, whom he says he thinks highly of but doesn't like, told him—that Germany will be obliged to go to war for the lack of abundance. The way to avoid war is to give Germany its old colonies back quickly.

March 6, 1938

This morning the Duce had a moment of deep sorrow. He told me he feels the void left by D'Annunzio. By now he represented very little, but he was there, that old man and every now and then he had a message to add. He acknowledged that he had represented a lot in his life. Undoubtedly he contributed widely to shaping fascism into much of its current style.

Federzoni told me this morning he was going to be president of the Academy. He was not too happy about leaving the Senate. But he was putting on a brave face.

I welcomed Beck at the station. The Chief has a strong dislike for him, without knowing him, with that odd capacity that men have for hating or loving someone without ever having seen them. I must admit that this time as well his instinct is correct: at first sight Beck is not a congenial person and he creates a chilly atmosphere around him. The reception was solemn, perhaps even more than I would have liked. But there is Bastianini, the impresario for Poland who swelled the welcome. The wife, who apparently has constant reasons for sentimental tenderness towards Italy and the Italians, especially if young and of dark complexion, was exuberantly happy. He was very formal. But I don't want to judge him before having listened to him and gotten to know him better. The few words that he did say up to now did not seem to me to be very pro-German.

March 7, 1938

I received Beck. He is a moderate and cautious man, who is considerably shy. He doesn't seem to be particularly strong nor remarkably intelligent. Above all he is not clear in his presentation: his reasoning does not clearly express his ideas nor is it geometric, he is rather unsystematic, and strays and digresses further into least essential and imprecise facts. Nothing new will emerge from the visit other than a show of cordiality between the two countries and a demonstration of a possible greater understanding. We touched on all subjects with an almost impersonal interest. Above all he wanted to explain to me that Poland intends to maintain a balanced position, without any sort of compromise. He repeatedly said that the alliance with France will not work in the case of conflict provoked by the Czech problem. With regard to the Anschluss he feigned a disinterest which appears out of proportion to the importance the problem could take for Poland.

In the afternoon, he was received by the Duce. The meeting was weak. Mussolini wasn't met with intelligent feedback, so he didn't apply himself. They more or less dealt with the subjects already discussed with me.

The Duce had two interviews with the Austrian military attaché, asking him to advise Schuschnigg against the Austrian plebiscite.

March 8, 1938

Lunch with Beck at the Royal Palace. The Princess of Piedmont, who was seated next to me, did not like the Polish minister: she thought he had an ambiguous face and that his picture could easily appear in French newspapers as a pedophile. Maybe she exaggerates. But a woman's instinct should not be ignored.

The King spoke to me about the politicians before the March on Rome; he praises San Giuliano[239] above all. Of Giolitti[240] he says that he was a extraordinarily knowledgeable of business and private lives of all Italians and especially in the parliamentary world. Somewhat like a small-town mayor. But his strength was to govern through intrigue and corruption, even though he was personally honest. The King doesn't think he had any real greatness.

In the afternoon meeting with Perth, of which I took minutes. First impressions were not bad, but the starting point for the discussions is rather distant. Anyway Chamberlain is more interested than we are in reaching an agreement: it is on this card that he has staked his political future, as well as that of the entire Conservative party.

March 9, 1938

Meeting between the Duce, Ciano, and Grandi. The Duce agreed with the objections recorded in my minutes of yesterday evening's meeting. Not because he believes in eternal peace. But because he believes that the 5 years that elapse from now until the end of the Universal Exhibition are necessary to rebuild our economy.

Meeting with Beck. I told him about Schuschnigg's decision to call the vote of a plebiscite for next Sunday. He thinks this policy is very dangerous; anyway it is the last straw for Austria. This brought us to examine the problem of the Anschluss more profoundly than in previous meetings. We ended up with this formula: it being understood that the policy of our two countries consider an agreement with Germany to be a fundamental element, we must equally tighten relations that exist between us and which tie us to those countries that have a similar political position and interests. Meaning: Yugoslavia, Hungary, and Romania. To this end we will use our joint efforts to facilitate an agreement between the latter two states.

He invited me to Poland. I accepted the invitation making some reservations regarding the time of year.

March 10, 1938

I related to the Duce the conversation with Beck. The Duce was very interested. Then I accompanied the Polish guest and his wife to the station. They were both moved and Cittadini[241] reports that, when the train began to leave, they wept.

Lunch at Volpi's home with the Duchess of Guise,[242] a repainted and insignificant old woman. She bombarded me with banal questions to which I could only offer banal answers.

Prepared the speech to the Grand Council, where I spoke for two and a half hours. It went well. The Duce complimented me over and over and this confused me to the point where I can not even manage to thank him. After all, one works only to please him: if one manages it is the greatest satisfaction.

Things are going well in Spain: the offensive in Aragon proceeds safely and quickly. This time it could be the decisive battle. The Volunteer Troops are fighting marvelously.

The news is bad from Austria. The Nazis, as anticipated, are protesting against the plebiscite. Blood could be shed in the streets at any moment. This would justify a German attack. Schuschnigg's error was fatal. From the beginning it appeared clear to us that the plebiscite bomb was destined to blow up in his hands.

March 11, 1938

Full speed ahead in Spain. The communiqué and the military bulletins confirm the devastating advance of our troops. Few losses up to now and only one division employed.

Critical day for Austria. Information by phone has confirmed by the hour the mobilization on the Bavarian border and the German decision to attack. At about midday Schuschnigg agreed to delay the vote, but the Germans did not consider it to be enough and demanded his resignation. He has asked us, through Ghigi, what should be done. I have more than once conferred with the Duce. We cannot assume the responsibility of advising him one way or another. So he should act according to his conscience. The French chargé d'affaires asks to come and see me, under orders from Paris, to consult about the situation in Austria. I replied that we do not intend to consult with anyone. If he has nothing else to say there is no reason for him to come to see me. Of course, he is not coming. After the sanctions, the non-recognition of the Empire and all the other evil done to us since 1935, they want to rebuild Stresa in one hour, with Hannibal at the gates? They have lost Austria, with their politics, France and England. For us as well it is not an advantage. But in the meantime we have taken Abyssinia.

6 p.m. Schuschnigg resigns. Seyss-Inquart replaces him. Austria is no longer independent.

March 12, 1938

At 9 p.m. yesterday evening, Hesse asked me for an audience. I was having dinner at my desk. He was the bearer of a letter from Hitler for Mussolini. We went to the Palazzo Venezia. The letter is important: it contains explanations about the incident and a specific declaration on the recognition of Brenner as the Italian border. The Duce is pleased and tells Hesse to inform the Führer that Italy is following the events with absolute calm.

Grand Council. Balbo expresses fear for Trieste and criticizes German methods. Naturally he does so behind closed doors. Mussolini does it openly. He says: "If we had eight million Italians on the border, we would also do the same. At least I would. And I have also done it." He recalls the annexation of Fiume. I read the news proving Austrian enthusiasm for Nazism. Much good news arrives from Spain, which the Grand Council applauds. After the session, the Duce and I prepare the items for a public declaration that the Grand Council will vote.

This morning I drew it up and the Duce approved. We ask Berlin, through Hesse, for permission to publish the letter. The Führer arrived only after a few hours. He agreed, but asks that two paragraphs against Czechoslovakia be removed. Fine. Meeting with Perth. Put on record. I come to the conclusion that Great Britain will accept the incident with indignant resignation. Meeting with the Duce and Hesse. In Germany they are elated by our line of conduct.

Lunch with the Pirates: The Duce united around himself, at the table, all the General Staff of the ships that engage in piracy against the Reds. They spoke briefly, extolling the navy's action in the Spanish war.

March 13, 1938

Yesterday evening at the Grand Council I spoke briefly on the day's events and I presented the agenda for Austria for approval.

Today things were quiet once again. The fateful event has taken place. It was not pleasant for us: certainly not. But one day the world will understand that it was all inevitable. The Duce said that an ambiguity has been removed from the European map. And he listed the three which still remain and that, in his opinion, will have to follow, in this order: Czechoslovakia, Switzerland, and Belgium.

Christich wanted to know our opinion. And I told him quite candidly. I added that on March 25 of last year, when we signed the treaty with Yugoslavia, I was thinking about what has actually just taken place. We discussed it at length with Stoyadinovich. Now I think of the second treaty that we must enter into with Yugoslavia: unite the future of two countries in the common defense of our worlds. This without changing the friendship with Germany, which for Rome and Belgrade is, since there will be 80 million Germans in the heart of Europe, something inevitable, somewhat heavy, but very real. Shortly, not immediately for obvious reasons, Stoyadinovich and I should go for a swim at the beach or hunting for deer...

In Spain we continue to advance rapidly and victoriously.

March 14, 1938

Things go well in Spain, where the troops proceed with unexpected celerity.

Beck, returning from Naples, came to see me. We discussed the situation created after the Anschluss and we confirmed what we said during the meeting of March 9.

I saw Berger who told me to have received orders to hand over the Legation to Plessen.[243] Pleading bronchitis, he tells me that he will remain in Italy for a few more weeks. In fact, he fears for himself and his family. He was a minister under Dollfuss[244] and Schuschnigg, and, as Justice Minister, he had to sign the death sentence of Dollfuss's killers. Naturally he is still shocked by the events but recognizes the errors of the Federal government and above all says that Schmidt intended to betray everyone, ourselves included. He says that he will give me proof. Berger also affirms that Italy could not have acted differently: if so much as one Italian soldier had entered into Austria, the Austrian population, except for the Jews, would have fired at us.

I calmed the fears of that conceited cretin Ruegger who saw great dangers for us and the universe. I told him that our borders, the Brenner included, are defended not by the treaties but by the chests of 45 million Italians. In these conditions there is nothing to fear.

March 15, 1938

The Duce prepares his speech to the Chamber on the Austrian problem. It is necessary because the country has been shocked and wants to hear the Chief's word. Meeting with Villani. I confirmed the need of a much closer policy with Hungary. Meeting with Perth. Recorded. On the whole things proceed well, but I wouldn't want our devastating advance in Spain to cause anti-Chamberlain reactions in England. Who is unrelenting. He had a first jolt from the realization of the Anschluss.

The Duce read me his speech: splendid: among Mussolini's best.

March 16, 1938

The day has been filled by the eagerness to listen to the Duce's word. Magnificent speech. Deep and lasting impression. Incalculable echo. The Duce spoke with the impetus of his, sometimes contained and at other times bursting, passionate. Rarely have I "lived" one of his speeches as I did today. The country got its lashing and the gloomy are already isolated and out of the picture.

In Spain everything proceeds very well and the collapse could at this point come very shortly. There are uncontrolled rumors of dispatches that France would make in *articulo mortis*: in men and airplanes. I don't believe it. Anyway, I cabled Berlin to say that if this were to happen we would resume our freedom of action and intervene in force.

I made arrangements with Del Croix for the arrival of the German veterans. Despite the recent friction they will be very well received.

March 17, 1938

In the past few days many anonymous letters have been sent to the Duce and myself, in various tones but all of them are opposed to the Anschluss. Now they are starting to die down. The Duce noticed that they all came from Milan and remarked that not even one came from Southern Italy when the Sicilian coasts were threatened by English cannons. He attributed this cowardliness to the wealth of the North. "A nation must be poor to be proud," he concluded.

Excellent reaction in Germany to the speech. Tomorrow evening the Führer will speak and solemnly confirm the friendship with us and the promises for the borders.

I took orders from the Chief for the negotiations with England. He has basically accepted two binding formulas with deferments for Spain and for the recognition issue, which would allow us to conclude shortly. I believe it is best to act quickly because the situation is unstable and I do not have too much faith in Chamberlain's position.

I told the Papal Nuncio that Göring, in a meeting with Magistrati, was well disposed towards the Church and even spoke of a general amnesty. If possible, for obvious reasons, I want to facilitate such a reconciliation.

I wrote the letter to Attolico in relation to the meetings between British and Italians.

In Spain the offensive proceeds well.

March 18, 1938

Thirty-five years old: "Midway upon the journey…"[245]

The Duce received the German veterans. Their leader, the Duke of Coburg,[246] is an insignificant man. Of an almost handicapped physique. This goes to prove that not all Germans are those giants that Tacitus described. They also have—and I noticed it during my journey through Germany—a high percentage of half-pints.

At the Chamber, with the Duce and Starace, we discussed Balbo and certain attitudes of his. The Duce hates him. He said that he will have him meet the same end as Arpinati.[247] But to get there chatter is not enough: an incident is required, a scandal to take hold of. I asked Starace if he took the hint. He said yes and thinks to avail himself of Consul General Giannantoni.[248] I was thinking more of Muti,[249] intelligent and loyal, excellent to make Balbo slip.

I took leave of Berger. He will not return to Austria, at least for the moment.

Meeting with Perth. Everything proceeds with regularity.

March 19, 1938

Nicolas Franco asks, in his brother's name, the transfer of the *Taranto* and two destroyers, since he admits that the destruction of the *Balmes* has placed the nationals in an inferior condition as far as the fleet is concerned. There was discussion with the Duce. I said I was against the idea: it would not be possible to hide the transfer, a scandal would arise, and perhaps a change of the situation with England. Chamberlain is far weaker than ten days or so ago: we must not create new difficulties for him. The Duce has practically agreed, even though wanting a more detailed study of the situation. I believe that we could increase the air power of the Balearic Islands and, if necessary, transfer some submarines which more easily escape control.

Franco is optimistic about the situation. Though he does not believe in a freefall of the Red Republic. He foresees resistance in Catalonia and the need for action on the Rio Segre to cut off electric power to Barcelona.

The offensive resumed this evening. Still no official news, but a service note allows me to hope for better prospects of success. One year ago I experienced my worst day: Guadalajara.

I returned to see the Duce to agree upon the wording about Palestine and Arabia, included in the agreement with Great Britain. We must absolutely safeguard our prestige and our position towards the Arabs.

March 20, 1938

Speaking with Grandi, a few days ago, I said that the European situation could have perhaps interfered in the Italian-British relations. Actually, this morning Perth gave me a memorandum calling attention to the bombing of Barcelona adding that this may create a hostile frame of mind towards the continuation of the Italian-British negotiations. I replied that the initiative of the operations belongs to Franco and not to us: therefore we could have used moderating influence but not assume responsibility. Since Perth mentioned the possibility of French intervention, I made it clear that we will immediately take the toughest measures. The truth about the bombing of Barcelona is that Mussolini gave the orders to Valle, at the Chamber, a few moments before giving the speech on Austria. Franco knew nothing and yesterday asked us to suspend them for fear of foreign complications. Mussolini thinks that these bombings are perfect to break the spirit of the Reds while the troops are advancing in Aragon. And he is right. When I told him of Perth's initiative, he was not very worried; on the contrary he claimed to be pleased by the fact that Italians manage to horrify by their aggression instead of giving pleasure as mandolin players. This, in his opinion, makes us rise in the consideration of the Germans who love total and ruthless war.

In Spain the offensive proceeds well: heroic and victorious.

March 21, 1938

The plans for the New York exhibition are approved.

The troops in Spain pause on the positions reached to allow the Nationalists to pull up beside them and proceed together with the offensive.

Nothing new in the other sector. I cabled Germany asking for a degree of clemency for Neumann, the great Jewish scientist of Vienna, thrown in jail at almost eighty years of age by the Germans. To liberate him would be an act of humanity which, would produce more favorable reactions at little cost. I hope that the Nazis are not too heavy-handed in Vienna and in Austria in general. This would make the process of amalgamation, which has always been extremely awkward, more difficult. It was the same here as well, between the Piedmontese and the Neapolitans. The Piedmontese followed strong-arm tactics. They said that they would have even imposed their grammatical errors. And in fact they succeeded very quickly in their intentions. The most difficult objective was the repression of banditry, a case more political than social. The methods used were expedient: in some towns they shot the entire male population, beginning with the mayor.

Grandi telephones from London to say that the maneuver to muddy the waters is very strong, but Chamberlain holds fast.

March 22, 1938

From too many sides now we are asked to intervene in favor of people arrested in Vienna by the Nazis. We must limit these interventions. Firstly, so as not to project an image as saviors, which always creates trouble. Secondly, so as to not undervalue our recommendations which, diluted, would completely lose any effect.

Berlin asks for the agreement for Mackensen,[250] which was of course granted. I met him in Budapest and he made a good impression. Those who know him judge him to be our friend.

I received the Party Mission which is going to Spain. They do not have a precise idea of what they must do. I advised one thing above all: not to interfere with the internal matters of the Spanish.

March 23, 1938

Nothing remarkable.

Talks with Perth, who intends to give to me a more precise formula next Saturday on the various points in discussion.

March 24, 1938

I told Christich, who was leaving for Yugoslavia, that a thousand reasons pushed me to make the Belgrade Treaty: today there are a thousand

and one to consolidate it. I should like to see Stoyadinovich. We could meet up in July at the Venice Lido.

The American ambassador came to ask us to join in the constitution of an International Committee to help the emigration of political refugees from Germany and Austria. I replied that a similar request offended more our political ethics than our directives in international affairs. Phillips was surprised by my response. He saw a humanitarian aspect in the proposal. I, only a political one. The abyss of misunderstanding between us and the Americans grows deeper and deeper.

Wisochy thanked me on behalf of Beck for our behavior during the Polish-Lithuanian crisis. I replied that we were disinterested in the fate of Lithuania because the problem does not regard us. If we refuse to pressure the Warsaw government it is because we know from experience how unbearable the so-called tutor-governments are, that is, those who always feel the need to tell you that your actions will cause this or that impression. That finally, we are friends of Poland and it is our custom to agree with our friends, for the sole reason that they are our friends, even if they are wrong. But this, I added, was not the case...

March 25, 1938

Long meeting with the Hungarian minister. He wanted to know with which diplomatic instrument we intended to replace the Protocols of Rome, between Italy and his country. I have not yet reflected, but the matter does not seem difficult. Anyway, we must not go too quickly so as not to uselessly alarm the Germans. I advised Budapest to reinforce ties with Belgrade. Kanya must overcome its preconceived hostility towards the Serbs. The mentality of Ballplatz 1914 cannot be brought into the Budapest of 1938.

The Chinese would like to entrust the mediation of the conflict with Japan to me personally. We must move with much caution. The undertaking is difficult, maybe impossible. It is certain that if it were successful our prestige in the Far East would all of a sudden rise to inaccessible heights.

Cantilo has departed. He was not our friend as ambassador. I don't know if he will be as Minister of Foreign Affairs. He is a democrat, for the League, and vain, or rather, for the League *because* he is vain. He is not worth much but he is very conceited. In short, he is a perfect Argentine.

March 26, 1938

Jacomoni reports on the situation in Albania. Our penetration becomes more and more intense and organized. The program that I drew up after my visit is being carried out with regularity. I ask myself if the general situation, and particularly the Anschluss, might not allow us to take a step towards the ever more complete control of this country which *will be* ours. It seems that Belgrade is anxious for a military alliance: I think that Albania can represent the price.

I discussed the 1938 consignment with Nicolas Franco. They ask for a billion's worth of goods, with payment in kind, or almost, and very chancy. We must proceed very cautiously: we give blood for Spain. Is that not enough?

The new Belgian ambassador[251] handed me a copy of the credentials directed to the King Emperor. I was cordial with him, also because of the value of the political gesture that he made. He is a huge man, a bit halting and rather verbose. He is not unpleasant at first sight. If I had to place him in one of the two categories in which Baudelaire divided the Belgians: the braggarts and the loathsome, I would place him in the first. Which is an advantage with respect to the chargé d'affaires,[252] a perfect example of the loathsome.

Meeting with Perth. It proceeds laboriously, very laboriously. But it proceeds. The meeting was put on record.

I have taken steps with the Holy See so that they do not create difficulties in the marriage of King Zog to a Catholic.

March 27, 1938

Libohova, Albanian Minister of Foreign Affairs, brought me the official invitation to act as best man at King Zog's wedding.

With the Duce we thoroughly examined the various points of the Italian-British agreement, on the basis of the results reached at yesterday's meeting. On the whole the situation looks very satisfying and we can continue. Indeed, today I gave Perth numerous replies which he wanted and particularly about the evacuation of troops from Libya by 1,000 men per week until the two Army Corps are reduced to peacetime size, guarantees that all the volunteers in Spain leave at the end of the war, an *Informazione Diplomatica* note in favor of Chamberlain. There still remain numerous formulas to be defined; first of all regarding the recognition of the Empire. If there are no unforeseen obstacles the agreement should be signed between April 10-20.

A camouflaged airplane, of French make but without number, crashed into a mountain at Iglesias last night. Given that it presumably came from Spain and was directed to Rome, one may assume that it was a demonstrative action by the Reds of Spain. I informed Perth, and I added that an act like that would trigger a conflict.

In Spain, the advance which resumed yesterday is proceeding slowly due to strong enemy resistance.

March 28, 1938

In the morning the celebration of the air force and the giving out of the Valor medals.

Then a general survey of the Italian-British relations made by the Duce during the meeting at the Palazzo Venezia. He is satisfied with the progress of the negotiations and he gives me the green light to continue. In a short while we will be able to seal.

Ansaldo tells me that in Leghorn the anti-Anschluss agitation was caused and kept alive by the Jews.

In Spain, the Spanish are doing well, and we are going more slowly, because we have attracted upon our forces some major enemy concentration.

March 29, 1938

The Duce asks that the last meeting before the signing of the agreement with London take place at the Palazzo Venezia. This will help announce that the conclusion is near.

Perth thanks us for the decision to partially withdraw forces from Libya. He asks to not make it public yet because his government wants to hold it for the conclusion of the agreement so that the "blow" will be greater. We agree as far as Palestine and Arabia are concerned, the local troops and other minor matters. Only three or four points are not yet resolved. Maybe we will sign before April 10. This is good because it is better to distance this event from the Führer's visit.

Meeting with the Japanese and a general survey. Personally the ambassador seems very pleased with the progress achieved in the talks with Perth.

April 1, 1938

Nothing remarkable in Rome.

In Spain the victory of the legionnaires takes on a more and more strategic character and perhaps permanently cripples the resistance of the Reds.

April 2, 1938

The issue of the rank of Marshal of the Empire has repercussions. It appears that the Royal Family has said that it was illegal. Mussolini asked for the opinion of the Council of State: everything is perfectly legal. He sent it along with a very curt letter to the King. He said to me: "Enough. I am fed up to my neck. I work and he signs. I'm sorry that what you have done Wednesday was perfect from a legal point of view." I replied that we can go deeper at the first opportunity. This will certainly happen once the respectable signature of the King could be replaced by the less respectable signature of the Prince. The Duce nodded in agreement and whispered, "When Spain is over with, we shall talk about it..." And Spain will end one day. Today the Red front was smashed again. Gandesa is occupied by the legionnaires. Tortosa is the next target. Once we get there the Reds will be cut in two and they will have been thoroughly beaten.

I told Sparano, commercial attaché of Brazil and a friend of Vargas, to tell his president, whom he will see shortly in Rio de Janeiro, that we would have liked more fascist courage coming from the new government. A revolution is not consolidated if one starts to pull back.

Meeting with Perth. Remarkable progress has been achieved at this point. Generally speaking we have agreed to sign on Thursday the 14th or Monday the 18th. I would like to sign on the 14th, which is Maundy Thursday. In Belgrade as well I signed on Maundy Thursday and the treaty was successful.

April 3, 1938

I spoke at length with the Duce of our relations with Germany. In the Alto Adige region, there is propaganda which we cannot tolerate: the 212,000 Germans have acted far too arrogantly and there is even talk of a border at Ala or Salorno. I advised the Duce to speak to the Führer about it. In Italy anti-German feeling, fomented by the Catholics, the Masons, and the Jews, is becoming progressively stronger. The Axis could be destroyed at any moment should the Germans take foolish initiatives in Alto Adige. The Germans must be made to understand the need to repatriate their people. Since Alto Adige is geographically an Italian territory and since the position of mountains and the course of rivers cannot be changed, the people need to be moved.

The Duce has all but given the go ahead for the pact with London on the basis agreed upon with Perth. Public opinion will welcome it with great enthusiasm because it will also read in it a possible break away from Berlin.

In Spain, the offensive of the legionnaires continues to sweep everything in its path.

April 4, 1938

I informed Teruzzi[253] about the agreement with London, regarding the Colonies.

Made arrangements with Jacomoni for my next trip to Tirana. I asked, if it is possible, that the King come to greet me upon my arrival. We must gradually underline the nature of protectorate in our relations with Albania. I have approved the outline of a project to build the new Ministry at the Piazza Barberini. It must be worthy of the Mussolini era and of the role which it will have: the Imperial Ministry.

The ambassador of Turkey[254] and the minister of Greece[255] communicated to me their formal recognition of the Empire. I acknowledged this calmly and did not jump at giving thanks. They have delayed far too long.

The Führer, in a speech in Gratz, mentioned the possibility of not considering the new borders as military. The Duce was pleased to note the matter. If this were true the Führer would take a highly political initiative and would earn much sympathy in Italy, Yugoslavia and in Hungary, which was lost during the brusque undertaking of the Anschluss.

April 5, 1938

During the morning I stayed at home with a bad case of tonsillitis. Buffarini came to see me. He told me that yesterday the Queen, after having copiously criticized Professor Bastianelli[256] for his medical work, said: "Get rid of him. Perhaps make a Marshal of him as well, but get rid of him." This proves that the position of Marshal of the Empire to the Duce has still not been digested by the Royal Family. I was not mistaken in saying that it is a matter that is still brewing. And it will come. Buffarini also told me that many shopkeepers refuse to display the portrait of the Führer. It is indicative of a deeply rooted frame of mind.

Meeting with Perth. We await London's reply on four secondary matters, then the agreement will be completed. We might sign either on Maundy Thursday or on Easter Monday.

Bülow-Schnante[257] was favorably impressed by the preparations for Hitler's visit.

In Spain, we met unforeseen resistance in front of Tortosa. But we will get through.

April 6, 1938

An article in the *Journal des Nations* has made the Duce even more skeptical that the Council of the League of Nations will accept Chamberlain's proposal regarding the freedom of each country in granting recognition to the Empire. He instead believes that the Council will take the opportunity to give a show of strength of the League, will call Tafari to Geneva, and delay every decision. Chamberlain's position would be shaken if not altogether crushed. I immediately conferred with Perth. He remained very calm. He said that every possibility has been thought of. The British government will not ask for a decision, for which there is the necessity of unanimity, but only a recommendation, which is taken by majority. Tafari cannot address the problem of verification of his credentials. In the end Perth said that even if Geneva should end in a refusal, Chamberlain will not stop half way. I related this to the Duce who told me to go ahead with the negotiations.

Starace spoke to me at length on the question of the rank of Marshal. He also thinks that the crisis between the Regime and the Monarchy is open at this point. We reached some general agreements. He advised caution with Buffarini who talks a little too much, perhaps without malice but certainly imprudently.

Tough Spanish resistance on the outskirts of Tortosa. The Duce cabled to the air force on the Balearic Islands to attack the rear areas of the Spanish troops heavily. Franco doesn't want bombing of cities, but in this case the game is worth the candle.

April 7, 1938

I gave Gentizon[258] some information relevant to the Pact with London. Gentizon behaved well during the war and always shows understanding towards us.

The Duce told me that the King wants to send a Royal Mission, presided by the Duke of Spoleto, to the wedding of King Zog. They obviously want to hold their own. The matter is annoying because it was unforeseen and because Tirana is not London, and to straighten out that drunken beanpole of Spoleto is not easy. But I understood that the Duce wants to avoid polemics so I immediately gave orders to Jacomoni who was reluctant. In any case the King's envoy will have a second-class reception compared to the Duce's envoy.

Long meeting with Antonescu, who was the Romanian Foreign Minister. He looks like Zacconi,[259] a little younger and a little thinner. He didn't tell me anything particularly striking. He is a Francophile, with many reservations regarding the Jewish government of Blum.[260] He is anti-Russian, anti-Czech, and deep down also anti-Polish. He speaks a lot about Latinity, a theme which is often round on the lips of those who are not undisputed Latins. He would like to reach an understanding with us, especially now that the Anchsluss is a reality. This is also our intention as well, but they must first get through Budapest with an agreement on the minorities in Transylvania.

April 8, 1938

We have almost reached the conclusion with Perth today. Except for two or three details, the whole set of agreements is ready. Perth proposes that we sign on Easter Saturday. It seems that that is Halifax's desire, since it is his birthday. All very romantic...

From Spain, Gambara signals a disagreement between our command and that of the Spanish. The umpteenth clash... The Spanish may be responsible, but our men are not completely innocent either. They so often display a provincial and obstinate intolerance which is explained only by the little understanding of the world that our officials show in general. Anyway, I told the Duce that there is no cause for alarm, because we have already, on other occasions, witnessed the telegraphic intemperance of Colonel Gambara. However much the march of the legionnaires has slowed, Spanish affairs, on the whole, are proceeding well.

April 9, 1938

In fact, Gambara's cable has no repercussions. Berti cables to say that the situation is unchanged. The Reds have moved to the extreme line of resistance, before splitting into two. From Berlin, Magistrati cables that Franco had asked the Germans to withdraw their volunteers. Nothing similar has been requested of us. On the contrary, Berti asks for three hundred new officers to replace his losses, and, despite all the agreements, they will depart on Thursday.

With Perth we have cleared the last remaining points. Tomorrow we will have the final meeting.

The new German ambassador, von Mackensen, paid me a visit. I have known him for a long time. Having found out the experiences of his predecessor, he said that the success of his mission will depend upon the trust that I will have in him. At the moment there is a lot. It also may increase if he behaves well. And, naturally, the reverse is also true. I welcomed him with much cordiality and, to enable him to immediately send the "good cable"— something dear to every career diplomat—I gave him the unpublished details of the Italian-British agreement.

Villani leaves for Budapest. I told him that it is still our intention, shortly, to define, tighten and harmonize with the others, our relations with Hungary.

April 10, 1938

Still another meeting with Perth: perhaps the final one. Maybe we will see one another again to hone the agreement, but without publicizing the meeting. The Treaty is good: complete, solid, harmonious. I believe that it can really serve as a basis for the new friendship between Italy and Great Britain. Important, above all, is the document which concerns Arabia. It has been very difficult to achieve this kind of parity of position between ourselves and the British.

For the rest, nothing noteworthy.

April 11, 1938

I arranged with the Duce that Perth and I will go to the Palazzo Venezia, for the final meeting, next Thursday at 5 p.m. The Duce is pleased. I can see it and above all I found out from the King, who this morning at the signing congratulated me for the terms of the agreement, going on the information given to him by the Duce.

Berti cables that today the troops prepare the new bases of attack. Let's hope that they can reach the sea.

I saw Cobolli[261] about the blueprints of the new headquarters of the Ministry. People are cause of obstruction, but Cobolli and I hope to be able to build in the Piazza Barberini—via Veneto—via Sistina.

Long conversation with Bocchini who feels that the signing of the Pact with England will have tremendous repercussions.

April 12, 1938

Nothing remarkable.
Meeting with Medici del Vascello and Buffarini.

April 13, 1938

Concluded the agreement with Perth. There were still two or three points to be resolved. I gave assurances in principle and, finally, in the evening I went to the Palazzo Venezia. I met the Duce, who was leaving. I accompanied him in the car to Villa Torlonia. He approved my points of view. Then, by phone, I confirmed with Perth. Tomorrow visit to the Palazzo Venezia. Saturday at 6:30 p.m. signing at the Palazzo Chigi.

The agreement is of vast importance: a new era is beginning in our relations with Great Britain. Friendship on a footing of parity: the only kind of friendship that we can accept. With London, or with anyone else.

April 14, 1938

The Duce received Perth appearing a bit irritated. He had met him at the theater lately, but he had not received him at the Palazzo Venezia since the days of the sanctions. Then he brightened; he read the text of the agreements and gave his approval. Lord Perth said, wanting to be scrupulous, that Halifax in Geneva, when the recognition issue is discussed, will not repudiate the sanctionist policy of Great Britain, but will ask for an adaptation to the new situation. The Duce replied that this did not bother him at all: only practical results interest him. It would be to expect that England show repentance. On the contrary, he advised adulation to the memory of Eden. But only to the memory, though…

The Duce was pleased. Today, the Ethiopian venture is truly closed and it ends with an Imperial treaty, due above all to the iron-clad determination of one man, who alone believed and wanted it, alone, against the entire world and often against his own countrymen.

Amery,[262] small lively English politician, speaks to me about the situation. He is pleased with the agreements. He says that if they had been entered into six months ago they would have saved Austria. He now judges the

Czech situation as desperate. He says that French intervention would have feeble results, like throwing a stone at a lion that is eating a man: it disturbs the lion and doesn't save the man.

Signed an important commercial agreement with France. I removed any trace of too much political optimism from the communication.

April 15, 1938

I gave Mackensen the text of the agreements with London. At the same time I emphasized that nothing will change regarding the Axis. I also told him that no special importance must be attributed to the visit by Hore Belisha.[263] He had to go to Malta and, like a good Jew, he took advantage of the opportunity to offer himself a big slice of publicity at a low price. Judaic Vanitas.

I have ordered Gayda[264] to write an article to make it clear in a conciliatory way that the negotiations with London began before the realization of the Anschluss.

Christich, back from Belgrade, had a long meeting with me, on the situation created by recent events. The meeting was put on record. It is above all remarkable that Stoyadinovich intends to arrange and conform his policy with ours regarding a possible German attack against Czechoslovakia, reinforced by Hungary and Poland. He doesn't want to be involved: and he is right.

The Egyptians ask for equal assurances regarding the waters of [Lake] Tana. The departments raise many objections. I think that we should agree. First, because it is practically meaningless, and second, because we should do something which distances Cairo from London. At 9 p.m. I am given the news that the Nationalists have reached the shores of the Mediterranean and I inform the Duce.

April 16, 1938

The Duce also agrees about Lake Tana and we will give our approval. The Treaty is complete and ready to be signed.

The chargé d'affaires of France, today's great loser, asks to be received urgently. He is very ill at ease. He reads me a long message from his government asking to negotiate with us before Geneva. This does include a small point of blackmail: a threat, without actually saying it, to oppose the British initiative for recognition. I thank Blondel for the communication and reserve my reply after conferring with the Duce. France has also been knocked to the floor.

I give the text of the agreement to the Japanese ambassador and I assured him of the solidity of our sentiments for his country. Japan was our friend in the difficult hours: we shall not forget this.

At 6:30 p.m., we sign with England. Lord Perth is moved. He tells me: "You know how much I desired to reach this moment." It's true: Perth has been a friend. We have dozens of his reports which we obtained proving this. There is an electric atmosphere of satisfaction in the room. Many photographers and journalists. Then the minister of Egypt[265] arrives. The English treat him with a lot of respect because in this last phase of the negotiations Egypt protested against British tutelage and wanted to have its say. The crowd gathers outside the Palazzo Chigi and applauds. Perth was cheered when he left. When I go to the Palazzo Venezia my car is surrounded and I am given a hearty demonstration. The Duce is happy. He commends me and says that he will do so in public. Meanwhile the crowd has arrived at the Palazzo Venezia and he appears on the balcony.

Then we begin to work. We examine the French request and decide to give it a favorable reply.

April 17, 1938

At 10 a.m. I receive von Mackensen. I inform him of the French move and of our decision. I give him the copy of the memorandum left by Blondel and stress how we have constantly rejected every direct attempt to switch the conversations with France into three-party talks. With the Germans we must always erase the shadow of Stresa. They fear it too much, and they are prone to see it rise everywhere.

But, precisely with the Germans, things are not going so well in Alto Adige. The alien population, after the Anschluss, has acted far too inconsiderately and irredentist manifestations that we can no longer tolerate have increased. Caution counsels to act immediately, because a certain kind of agitation needs to be nipped in the bud to avoid that, once developed, it requires more drastic intervention. While yesterday in Lasa a more serious incident took place, even firearms were used. All of this is serious, coming just before the Führer's visit.

I told the Duce that I would like to attract Göring's attention to this fact at a private level. I prepared a letter for Magistrati and tomorrow I will show it to the Chief. If he agrees, I will send it.

It is not enough for the German government to take no interest in the matter and for it to repeat that common borders are intangible: it must act. It must disavow the professional agitators. It should follow our example in Dalmatia. The propaganda ceased and the Belgrade treaty prospered beyond expectations.

April 18, 1938

Aymard[266] shows me the plans for a magazine called *Audace*, which he intends to launch as soon as possible and asks me for our financial contribution, at the rate of 200,000 lire for the first year.

The Duce approved the letter for Magistrati. In the meantime new incidents have taken place and many facts in our possession led us to believe that the authorities, even though a secondary rank, are informed of the matter. This danger to the Axis must be sterilized the moment it appears, otherwise we will have serious complications. Mackensen, during the presentation visit made to the Duce, said that the Führer is determined to take radical measures against the agitators. He should. The names of the leaders of the Alto Adige irredentist activities are certainly known to him just as those of the Dalmatian agitators were known to us. A signal from him could stop all agitation. These Germans exaggerate and not just in Europe. Today I had a meeting with the ambassador of Brazil[267] to ask him to look after the opportunities of our colonial institutions. In effect, in Rio they are preparing a law against foreigners and this following the intemperance of the German community of Santa Caterina. I received ample assurance as far as we are concerned. But do these Teutons really have a physical need to exasperate all of humanity to the point of joining forces against them? They should be careful; that could still happen and this time the sanctions will be far more serious than in 1919.

April 19, 1938

I told Blondel that we can begin talks: no special topic to discuss on our part, apart from the recognition of the Empire. We therefore wait to see the French agenda to make comments and proposals. Unofficially, I told Blondel that the French press should stop saying that whatever has happened and is happening now, is aimed at weakening the Axis: this is false and just stiffens our position even more.

The Duce is also worried about reactions in Germany and doesn't want the *pourparlers* with France to end before the Führer's visit. It will be easy to create some obstacles, and dragging out the coming trip to Albania will serve the purpose well.

Czechoslovakia has recognized the Empire. Also Brazil, but with a formula which is neither fish nor fowl and to which I have already asked a modification.

Triumph in Spain: Gambara, with shock troop maneuvers, took Tortosa from behind and smashed the Red resistance. Collapse should now be close at hand and the start of talks with France should discourage the Barcelona government, now abandoned by all to its inevitable destiny. The Duce cabled Berti and Franco.

April 20, 1938

I told the Prince of Hesse to speak to Göring in my name about the situation in Alto Adige, which is becoming more and more disagreeable. Hesse was shocked by my description of facts and said that he will intervene immediately.

The Duce became violently angry, and justifiably so, against some farmers from Bari who, as guests at Party headquarters in Munich, behaved badly and even defecated on the stairs. Something indecent and enough to discredit us in an unbelievable way with German opinion. The Chief said that we must instill in our people a higher racial concept, which is also indispensable to proceed with the colonization of the Empire. He got angry with the "children of slaves" and added that if they had a distinctive physical sign he would exterminate them all being convinced of doing a favor to Italy and all of humanity.

In the afternoon I accompanied Amery to see the Chief: the meeting was not particularly important. Amery spoke about Italy, England, Czechoslovakia and of economic matters. He would like to abolish the most-favored nation clause, and replace it with preferential treatment between European nations.

Meeting with Piccio.[268] Flandin[269] lets us know that, if we wish, he is ready to stand as a candidate to the embassy in Rome.

Phillips was enchanted by the agreement with London. I gave him some news regarding the talks with France.

April 21, 1938

Monelli[270] told me of the rapid change within public opinion in Paris. It seems that the entire country is anxious for the agreement with Italy, except for the offices of the Quai d'Orsay which are still against it.

With the Duce we discuss the situation of the borders. He prepared a memorandum of which he will send me a copy. He intends—and he is right— to make the borders towards Germany hermetic. Those with Yugoslavia, semi-hermetic, because he believes a Slav-German alliance possible based upon the two irredentisms. I don't believe it. In Yugoslavia the Germans are hated, or at least feared. But I agree with precautions also in that direction. Because Yugoslavia could be invaded by the Germans. We should, though, speak clearly with Belgrade and establish an understanding of a political nature right away. In the afternoon, meeting with Mackensen. I speak to him about the repressive measures taken by the Reich in Austria and especially of the abolition of the special tariff for Trieste and the declaration of foreign shares owned by foreign residents. All of this, on the eve of the Führer's visit, can only exasperate people: the Germans must not forget that the Anschluss shocked many Italians. Mackensen agrees and will act. He asks me also about the situation in Alto Adige. I give him few explanations because I do not want to deal with this matter, of an internal nature, through diplomatic channels.

April 22, 1938

Buffarini-Farinacci-Bottai.

Meeting with Blondel who again hands me the French proposals for talks. I take my time and reserve my reply until after having conferred with the Duce. I remark though that one point will be troublesome: French res-ervations about the Italian-English agreement relating to the Red Sea.

It's clear that the Quai d'Orsay, is alarmed by the position of co-owner-ship of the Red Sea, and would like to be part of the arrangement.

Mussolini, who had just seen Nicolas Franco, seems unhappy with the proposal and says that the answer will have to wait until my return from Tirana. Which will be conveniently delayed.

Nothing must be done until after the Führer's trip.

Receive the first special envoy from Manchukuo.[271] He goes around with an interpreter because he doesn't know a word of any foreign language.

April 23, 1938

Council of Ministers.

The Duce gave me a very recent publication from Leipzig, where the issue of Alto Adige is discussed and our mountain populations are described in insulting terms.

He was indignant: "These Germans will force me to swallow the bitterest pill of my life. I refer to the French pill."

Lunch with Hore Belisha. Then three-way meeting at the Palazzo Venezia. The meeting was particularly technical and military like. The Duce explained his theories on the strength of the battalions, on motorization, and on war of maneuver. Hore Belisha greatly praised our preparation and, like a good Jew, he belittled himself as much as he could. He asked the Duce if he thought that war was near. The Duce said no. He, instead, said yes.

Meeting with Tatarescu.[272] A big man who speaks perfect French and who is more refined in spirit than in his appearance. Like all Romanians he dreads the consequences of the Anschluss so much that he thinks of the possibility of Hungary as a satellite of the Greater Reich. I was very reserved, as usual, with Romanians who are too loquacious.

Received the Naval Mission of Yugoslavia.

April 24, 1938

The Duce and I spoke at length about the issue of Alto Adige. Göring's reply arrived via Magistrati, it does not seem very explicit to me.

Later the Duce telephoned me: "I have clarified my ideas on the matter. If the Germans behave well and are respectful of Italian citizens, I could favor their culture and their language. If they even think of moving the border even only one meter, they should bear in mind that this will not occur without the harshest of wars, in which I will have the whole world join forces against Germanism. And we will knock Germany down for at least two centuries."

The Brazilian ambassador communicated to me the official recognition of the Empire. He thought of making the connections to the new laws against foreign activity in Brazil to prove that the laws are not directed against us. Von Mackensen assures the greatest of German goodwill in treating and resolving our problems with respect to the Anschluss. Mussolini's opinion of Hore Belisha was clearly negative. He said that he does not think that the British army can become a serious army while it has that "little chick" as its leader.

April 25, 1938

Trip to Tirana. The usual popular, double-barreled demonstrations, for me and the Duke of Bergamo.[273] Reception at Court. Meeting with the Queen,[274] who is pretty and has already learned to smile as is the duty of a sovereign, and with the Royal Princesses, who are vulgar, ridiculous and are fit to appear on the stage of an operetta.

April 26, 1938

Meeting with the King and reception. It is important that the King came in person to visit me at Libohova House. The importance of this gesture, going against protocol, can escape no one.

April 27, 1938

Wedding: the ceremony was carried out with greater seriousness than expected.

The Queen was radiant. The King was moved! The courtiers were so-
licitous. The people were indifferent and, in the contrast, appeared even
more tattered than usual.

April 28, 1938

Visit to the Italian enterprises.

In the afternoon, meeting with the King at Durazzo, I will draw up a
memorandum for the Duce on this and the other meetings, relating my
impressions and intentions.

I return from Albania more than ever rooted in my belief in an integral
solution.

April 29, 1938

Return trip on the *Bande Nere*. The population from Bari to Rome gives
me very warm receptions at the stations.

April 30, 1938

I report to the Duce on the visit to Albania. I will recapitulate it in a
report. But he immediately agrees with the need for a definitive solution and
says that he is even ready to go to war to have Albania. When I gave him a
magnificent sample of copper minerals from the mines of Alessio, I said:
"here are the figs of Carthage."

Berti reports on the situation in Spain. The Duce sums up and gives these
orders: the CTV stays in Spain to give proof of Italian solidarity, but it will no
longer be deployed in mass action. Only in exceptional cases will the engagement of some units be allowed. The Volunteers will leave Spain when the war
is over, or if and when the "non-intervention" makes a decision.

I resume negotiations with Blondel and I find him very accommodating. He agrees on the impossibility of concluding before the Führer's visit
and accepts almost all of my observations.

Brief meeting with Perth, in relation to the visit of the French ministers
to London. The results have been communicated to Grandi by Halifax.

Again a long meeting with the Duce, to whom I relate my activities of
today. We set the basis for a mutual respect pact to propose to the Germans
during the next visit to give content to the Axis now that the points set in
the agreements of October 1936 can be considered fulfilled.

May 1, 1938

Presented the outline of the prospective agreement with Germany to
the Chief. He agreed.

I will propose it to Ribbentrop, pointing out to him that it is in our
common interest to sign it. We have made a Pact with London, shortly we
will be making one with the French: if positions with Berlin are not set,
everyone will say that the Axis has been liquidated and that we are going
back to Stresa.

In the afternoon I work on drafting my report on Albania. It is part of
the volume of my writings.

May 2, 1938

Nothing in particular.

I visit the Führer's apartment at the Royal Palace. They have taken the opportunity to refurbish their house at our expense. The Princess and the Prince had disgraceful bathrooms. Now they will have, as they say, princely bathrooms.

The payment arrangements with Spain are initialed.

Blondel sent me the proposals for a few articles of the agreement.

May 3, 1938

Arrival of the Führer.

May 4, 1938

I will not describe the Führer's stay, since it is already reported by the papers. I will limit myself to noting some unpublished episodes, conversations and impressions.

The first thing is of an internal nature. The Court, which has no intentions of abdicating, has turned out to be useless and troublesome.

During the arrival, the country was very much disappointed to discover that the founder of Italian political power was not at the Führer's side in the triumph of the Imperial streets, conceived and realized by him. The Germans probably felt it as much as we did. Also a disagreeable incident occurred in Naples, on account of the incompetence of those officiating. The whole establishment is moldy: a dynasty which is a thousand years old does not like the look of a revolutionary regime. To a Hitler, who for them is nothing but a parvenu, they prefer any kind of little king, even from Denmark or Greece, with a bit of crown and an odd number of quarterings.

When Ribbentrop related the events, I had him speak to the Duce, who said: "Tell the Führer to be patient. I have been patient for sixteen years ..." Ribbentrop replied that the only good thing done by the Social-Democrats in Germany was to liquidate the monarchy for good.

The military parades were magnificent. The Germans, who were perhaps a little skeptical on this point, will leave with a very different impression.

May 5, 1938

Ribbentrop offered us a military assistance pact, public or secret, as we prefer. I told the Duce in no uncertain terms that I was opposed to the idea, just as I had delayed a consultation and political assistance pact.

The Duce intends to go ahead. And we will agree to it because he has a thousand and one reasons to not trust the western Democracies. But I thought it would be better to delay it, to avoid creating difficulties for Chamberlain, on the eve of the [League of Nations] Council meeting for the recognition of the Empire. The signing of a treaty, which could be interpreted in many way, including that of a secret alliance, would have made his task more difficult and handed a weapon to the opposition at Geneva.

May 6, 1938

The Führer, during the meetings with the Duce, was restrained. Hitler did not speak about politics. Whereas Ribbentrop is exuberant and at times fickle. The Duce says that he belongs to that category of Germans that cause disasters for Germany. He speaks of going to war left, right and center, without a clear opponent or a defined objective.

Sometimes he wants to destroy Russia, in agreement with Japan. At other times he fulminates against France and England. Sometimes he threatens the United States. This has always led me to consider his projects with great caution. In specific and real problems he calms down. He says that the Czechoslovak problem is not relevant today and that a form of autonomy could perhaps delay the solution for several years. He adds though, that if the matter were to be settled by force of arms, this would happen in a matter of days, and before anyone had time to react.

The Polish Corridor is accepted, for an unlimited period of time, by Germany, who indeed wishes to see the strength of Poland grow to reinforce the anti-Bolshevik barrier.

He confirmed to me what Hore Belisha had said on the subject of colonies. Hitler told Lord Halifax that the colonial problem will rise in due course, that is in a few years. For the moment Germany does not intend to accelerate it.

May 7, 1938

The Führer had more personal success than I expected. He came amid a general hostility having been imposed by the will of Mussolini, but managed to break the ice around him well enough. His speech yesterday evening helped a lot. And also personal contacts won him sympathy. Especially among the ladies.

The King is still hostile and wants to make it seem that Hitler is a kind of psychophysiological degenerate. He told the Duce and me that on the first night at the Royal Palace, at around one in the morning, Hitler asked for a woman.

This was to create much excitement. Explanation: it seems that he cannot manage to fall asleep unless he sees, with his own eyes, a woman remake his bed. It was difficult to find one, but then a maid from a hotel came and the problem was resolved. If the matter were true it would be interesting and mysterious. But, is it true? Or not rather some malice of the King, who also insinuated that Hitler injects himself with stimulants and narcotics?

May 8, 1938

Mussolini thinks that Hitler puts rouge on his cheeks to hide his pallor.

Hess and Himmler told Anfuso that at the Palazzo Venezia there is the atmosphere of revolution, while at the Quirinal they had the impression of living in an old film.

The spectacle at the stadium was magnificent. Even more than the military organization, which was perfect, the Germans had to appreciate the civil organization of the country, which is more complicated and difficult to achieve. When the civil organization is perfect and the heroic spirit awakens in a nation, military organization is easy to attain.

May 9, 1938

Florence welcomed the Führer with its heart and its intelligence. It is a sensitive city that understands everything. Hitler's speech on Saturday reversed the situation: the Italians loved, perhaps even more than the declarations of respect of our borders, the lyrical transport with which they were given.

At the station the farewell between Hitler and Mussolini was very warm. The two men were moved. The Duce said: "Now no force can ever separate us." The Führer's eyes filled with tears.

Goebbels, moving through the halls of the Quirinal, and passing before the throne, said: "Keep that piece of furniture in velvet and gold. But put the Duce on it. That one," and he indicated the King, "is too small..."

May 10, 1938

On the train the Duce and I discussed my report on Albania. He agrees with my decisions and believes that the right month to act would be May of next year. This way we would have a year for the local and international preparation. Since a diplomatic crisis will be produced and France and England will inevitably be against us, we should enter into the pact with Germany. This will also encourage Yugoslavia to great moderation. Yugoslavia, separated from its eastern and western friendships, locked between Italy and Germany, will have to grin and bear it and adopt the same attitude that we took regarding the Anschluss.

I spoke with Jacomoni and I asked him to prepare me a local action plan: public works, charitable institutions, economic organizations, sports organizations and if possible, political ones.

For the rest, nothing new, except that in Geneva anti-Italian antics are to be expected with the arrival of Tafari. Halifax and Bonnet[275] will perhaps get the better of it but they appear to be weak.

May 11, 1938

Meeting with Blondel. On all points it is easy to reach an understanding, except for Spain and the Red Sea. On Spain he tells me that no French government could pass a pact between France and Italy that does not mention the Spanish problem. And Mussolini doesn't want to mention it. For the Red Sea they would like to associate themselves with the British-Italian agreement. The same old French mania of transforming the bilateral into the collective. Blondel, on his way out, told me: "I leave with a heavy heart." I greatly reassured him, not because I am optimistic, but because I didn't want to weaken Bonnet's initiative tomorrow at Geneva.

The Spanish ambassador would not be adverse that we repeat to the French the assurances given to London, provided that we ask for similar assurances from Paris and the closing of the Pyrenees.

May 12, 1938

The Duce was totally unbending regarding the French requests. He rejects joining the agreement for the Red Sea, which he intends to consider as an Italian-English condominium and he refuses to discuss Spain with Paris.

When I told him that in that case there will be no agreement, he said that he would make one with Berlin, according to Ribbentrop's proposals. And when I added that the agreement with London might flex and perhaps break, he said that he will tighten alliance with Tokyo. And once again, the French will be responsible. God knows what I did to prevent the alliance with Berlin, which is awkward for the present and worrisome for the future. But today I think that French pettiness will cancel my efforts and that a new document will be signed in the halls of the Wilhelmstrasse shortly. Mussolini is determined.

I gave the Swiss minister an earful regarding the arrest of some irredentists from Ticino and I did it in such a way that Ruegger turned pale. Switzerland must be careful and not irritate us: its future is not rosy.

Stoyadinovich let me know that he wants to see me in June in Venice. Very well. I will speak to the Duce and set the date.

The American ambassador feared the realization of a military assistance pact with Berlin. I reassured him.

At Geneva the Ethiopian question has been buried.

May 13, 1938

I informed Perth of the difficulties in negotiations with Paris. I also told him that England should not associate France with the agreement on the Red Sea and Arabia at all. Maybe it is not even possible on the basis of article 3, which binds Italy and Great Britain to fight any attempt by a third power to establish itself in Arabia. In substance we established a condominium of two: why make it become three? Then there is the issue of Spain, and on this Mussolini will not yield. Perth tried to help reach an agreement, but he had to conclude that the French are poor negotiators.

I reported the meeting with Perth to the Duce on the *Cavour*. He is more and more anti-French. He says that it is a nation ruined by alcohol, syphilis, and journalism. He will not mention France in the speech that he will give in Genoa. And not even Switzerland whose behavior he finds unsatisfactory.

Speaking of Spain, he wants our forces to take part in a new offensive. To put them back in order he is prepared to send some officers as reinforcements; they are the most tired. But if the London Committee adds to a decision regarding the evacuation, he is ready to begin as far as we are concerned.

May 14, 1938

We arrive in Genoa at eight in the morning. The city, with the lifting fog and the sun shining, is beautiful. Flags, sirens, salvoes.

The crowd. The Chief speaks. The speech is very intense, anti-French. The crowd boos France, laughs, ironically, at the agreements with London. I compare the copy of the text of the speech that Sebastiani has with the speech as it is actually given. Everything has changed: the attack on France was missing, he was more pleasant with the English and less binding with Berlin. The mass of the people transported him. Fine: let's wait for the reactions from Paris and London. Then we'll see what tone the negotiations might have, if they continue at all.

In the afternoon at the Fascist party headquarters, the Duce speaks again: "Genoa, after Rome, is one of the four imperial cities: Pisa, Ravenna, Venice, Genoa. We too are now imperial, and we carry the flag beyond the seas, not as a seignory, or City State, or a Republic, but as a united nation. When Italy is united it cannot be anything but an Empire. When it is an Empire it can only dominate others. From today's enthusiasm I am convinced that the Italian nation is not tired, on the contrary it is ready for a new assault."

I left for Rome, after having spent the evening at the Medici's home.

May 15, 1938

The reactions to the speech, at this time, are weaker than I expected. But I think they will increase. Nothing new in the office. Peru recognized the Empire.

May 16, 1938

I caught up on the meetings and received a series of more or less interesting fellows.

All of the ministers, and especially the Danube and Balkan countries, are worried about the division of Europe in zones of Italian-German influence. I denied the rumor spread by the French press.

I told the Czechoslovak minister[276] that we hope for a peaceful solution to the Czech problem, but the matter does not interest us directly and therefore we could only have a neutral position. We did not move for Austria, it is unthinkable we should move for Prague…

Villani brought me a secret consultation pact as well as a clause of military aid in case of unprovoked aggression by Yugoslavia. I am a little skeptical about the advisability of these documents which are secret in a manner of speaking and become public when they must create annoyances. I will discuss it with the Duce in these terms.

Grandi sends me a letter for the Duce, in it he requests an appointment to State Minister. Here is a man who serves the regime disinterestedly…

May 17, 1938

I welcome the Duce at the station. In the car I inform him of the démarche made by Villani. He is also rather skeptical about the usefulness of a document of that kind. Stoyadinovich has declared to us that in no case would he attack Hungary. In the meantime the Duce wants Budapest to leave Geneva: we will speak about it later.

The Chief wants to weaken Geneva more and more, in view of the action in Albania.

I speak with Jacomoni at length about Albania and give the Chief the list of a series of measures to take to prepare the ground. We also discuss the situation with Pariani. I read my memorandum of May 2: and he agrees with everything. He believes that with good preparation it can be pulled off relatively easily.

The Duce is still very irritated at France. He wants to delay all communications with Blondel until the end of the week. I inform the Duce that in the present situation, and after his speech in Genoa, I feel my report to the Senate to be useless. He agrees. I telephone Federzoni so that the discussion does not take place.

The minister of Norway[277] gave me a statement of recognition that is so uncertain and so ambiguous that I refuse to accept it. He will cable his government to clarify the situation.

May 18, 1938

Lord Perth made a démarche about the consequences of the speech in Genoa.

The meeting is recorded. I try to separate the French position from that of the English in my reply: I don't know how well I managed. Perth, anyway, makes the move tactfully and with a certain bitterness: he was sincere in wanting the agreement and is sincere in disapproving any possible cause of disturbance.

I receive the Japanese ambassador: he thanks me, as is his custom, for a number of small things. Then he comes to the important issue: relations with England. He is pleased when I tell him that the agreements with London have not weakened our feelings for Tokyo and he is even more pleased when I do not deny that Italian-British relations have, even if indirectly, been affected by the consequences of the difficulties with Paris.

The Belgian ambassador: small matters and with great pomposity.

Cini: bulky physically, in his thinking and his laughter. He tries above all to make me forget his Germanophobia of a few weeks ago. He speaks positively of all the things he spoke badly of: even of Starace.

May 19, 1938

I find Mussolini more and more exasperated with France. He approves, on the basis of my record, the language I used with Perth. Following information from Tirana, about the exaggerated activity of the minister of Germany,[278] he tells me to let Ribbentrop know that we consider the Albanian question as "family business." The formula used by them for Austria and the Sudetenland. Consequently, "hands off."[279] He affirms that he is ready to enter Albania immediately, even at the cost of starting hostilities in Europe. He is already having military vehicles prepared.

In the afternoon I see Zanfirescu, the new Romanian minister. He is, like many of his fellow countrymen, verbose, empty and pompous. At every turn he brings up the Latin origins of his people, and he does it in such a way that at every time I am less convinced of the truth of his statements. He does all the talking, which is good because I have already read many of his cables and I have noticed that the person he quotes need only say one word to be credited with the most fantastic statements. Of all the diplomats, the Romanians are the biggest liars. Zanfirescu talks to me about the progress of negotiations between Romania and Hungary. He says that they move slowly due to Magyar obstructionism. It's possible because I know how Kanya thinks. However, I do not pass any judgment.

May 20, 1938

I saw the Duce twice. In the morning I found him to be more relaxed than during the past few days. He confirms that he does not intend to begin talking with the French and is waiting for the results of economic negotiations in Berlin. He decides on some points of our policy regarding Budapest: disinterest in the case of Magyar action against Czechoslovakia, in agreement with Berlin; help in the case (absurd and unlikely) of an unprovoked aggression by Yugoslavia. In return, Budapest must pull out from Geneva. Tirana must also pull out of Geneva, as I had suggested in my written memo regarding Albania.

Afternoon: The Duce is a little worried about Chamberlain's position. The press attacks him and there is again talk of Eden. I cable Grandi to find out how things are, and if some gesture can be made to strengthen the Prime Minister's situation. Mussolini, at my mention of a possible return of Eden, shrugs his shoulders and says: "We'll see. It will be fine for us one way or the other." He has faith in Germany's continental support.

Serious incidents in the Sudetenland, with the threat of complications with Germany. The matter is ripening, slowly and inexorably.

May 21, 1938

Norway has recognized the Empire.

I return to see the Duce in the afternoon to accompany Wisochy on a farewell call. I remained alone with him. He is happy about the commercial agreements achieved by Guarneri with Germany. He had been told by Guarneri that things were going badly: I tell the Chief what Guarneri said upon Hitler's arrival: "The Axis' funeral." The Ministry for Currency and Exchange is a Masonic center: the Duce is also convinced of it.

He speaks to me about the incidents that took place for the play "Orchidea" by Sem Benelli.[280] He says that in Italy there are still three antifascist demonstrations: funerals, the theater, and jokes. He criticized the art of Sem Benelli who displays the lowest part of humanity. "In every home there is a lavatory and everyone knows it. But this is no reason to show it to a guest when he comes to visit." I report on the Czechoslovak situation which becomes more tense following yesterday's incidents. Mussolini confirms his lack of interest for the fate of that country. In any case, he does not believe that France will mobilize. I was told that Paul Boncour,[281] when asked if he would mobilize in the case of German aggression against Prague, replied "presque." In that "presque" there is all of democracy, but no longer the greatness of France.

Meeting with Perth, which is recorded. He speaks to me about how much Great Britain has done in Prague and Berlin, and says that he considers today's situation to be very dangerous: the most serious since 1918. I confirm to him Italy's neutrality regarding the Czech matter. According to Perth, France could mobilize at any moment.

May 22, 1938

The Duce feels that the Czech situation is not as worrisome as many claim. He vents his opposition to elections and says that they have always brought trouble to humanity. The French Revolution, the Spanish War, the Austrian crisis and today also the Czechoslovak tension have all followed or preceded electoral agitation. Final, important decisions cannot depend upon that amorphous mass of the people which is irresponsible by definition. "The people do not know what they want, except earning more and working less." And yet today world peace can depend upon any drunken cretin willing to trigger an incident to exercise his "right" to vote. And all of this just to elect, just imagine, mayors in the Sudetenland!

Lord Perth asks for a very urgent meeting and I received him at 7 p.m. He is very alarmed and informs me of the communication made yesterday to von Ribbentrop. I took notes of the meeting. In brief: new advice for moderation and a confirmation that, in case of conflict, London will stand by Paris. I reassure Perth. I tell him that, apart from the fact that today new and unpredictable clashes took place, Germany will not move. I was calm and collected and I told him that the Duce is also very tranquil. This appears to be a great relief to him.

May 23, 1938

In Berlin as well, according to what Magistrati telephones, it is the English who sound the alarm. They have even gone as far as to spread the rumor that the Embassy is ready to ask for its passports. This is exaggerated because the elections took place without commotion and the situation is beginning to calm down. For one thing the incident proved two things: that Germany is not ready for a clash as some (especially Ribbentrop) would like to make one believe, and that England is terrified by the idea of a war. Mussolini says that this is normal for a nation that has a comfortable life and who has made a religion of eating and playing. Also the Germans, when you come to think of it, would have this tendency towards hedonism, but they are restrained by a heroic philosophy and by the lack of space and wealth.

Meeting with Villani. I once again present our point of view regarding the pact that was offered to us and on the basis of the Duce's instructions: I tell him that we will discuss it when Kanya comes to Italy. I mentioned their withdrawal from Geneva, but I see that Villani turns red and starts to bring up the issue of minorities.

I brief von Mackensen on the status of the talks with Blondel and on the results of the meetings with Perth. Then I clearly state that the Albanian question is "family business" for us.

Viola is optimistic on the situation in Spain. He says that Franco intends to attack in Catalonia shortly and by this action he intends to end the matter.

May 24, 1938

Inauguration of the Working Men's Club very successful.

The Duce tells me to go to Milan and gives me some instructions for the short speech that I will have to make there. I am to burn incense to Chamberlain. He wants me to rub some balm on the wounds made to the English at Genoa. If not exactly wounds, at least the irritation. Perth recommends Italian goodwill at the next meeting of the Non-Intervention Committee. I tell him that I have already sent Grandi instructions.

Bonnet sent for Prunas and he repeated general assurances in the sense of the agreement and understanding with us. The Duce also found the meeting to be very inconclusive, which took place at the private residence of the minister, because the matter was not appreciated by the bureaucrats of the Quai d'Orsay. With such men at the helm of France it is not easy to understand one another.

May 25, 1938

Nothing very significant. The French press, which is becoming too cocky towards Germany, on the Czechoslovak issue is threatening to worsen the situation. After an agreement over the phone between Alfieri and Goebbels, our press will begin the debate with the Parisian papers tomorrow.

I prepared the draft of a speech for June 2, in Milan, but it would be better to wait for developments. Now, days feel like months and the situation changes with cinematic speed.

May 26, 1938

The French-British press and some less trusted German elements have raised doubts on the real Italian attitude regarding the Czechoslovak problem. This led me to call Ambassador Mackensen to repeat to him that our point of view is not different from that presented to the Führer and to Ribbentrop. Disinterest for the fate of Prague; complete solidarity with Germany. I also offered, if Berlin likes the idea, to confirm our line of conduct with a note in the *Informazione Diplomatica*. Even though there have been no new developments, the Duce was more pessimistic today and foresees war. He said that he would go to war immediately on the German side.

Graziani speaks to me about the Empire. He is not very convinced about the possibilities of the Duke of Aosta as Viceroy. He is weak and too much in the hands of his staff. This was to be foreseen because Royal Princes are used to respect but not to command. Also Senator Gasparini[282] repeated a similar judgment to me. He is, though, more optimistic than Graziani regarding the possibility of pacifying the Empire in a relatively short time.

May 27, 1938

Berlin has still not yet replied to our offer. However, they should let us know what their real intentions are: do they want the collapse of Czechoslovakia or are they satisfied with a splitting into cantons? According to what Ribbentrop said in Rome it appears that initially they were inclined to the second alternative. Now it is known that the person who sounded the alarm ahead of time was Henderson. He lost his head and made London believe that conflict was imminent and inevitable. And his bewilderment was easily picked up by the hysterical British pacifism.

At the Committee of "non-intervention" some progress was made toward the solution of the Spanish conflict. Following the episode of one of our observers, arrested by the Reds, Grandi sent one of his customary "bulletins of Austerlitz" and attempted the usual press stunt. This happens every time the Committee meets. But I ask myself: a man can save his country once? Rare examples exist of he who has saved it twice. Why does the Comrade, Count Grandi, want to convince himself that he is saving it four times a month?

The Duce informs me of a letter received from Settimelli,[283] presently in Monaco. As soon as he got his passport, he prepares to betray. It was predictable.

May 28, 1938

Council of Ministers. Without particular importance.

The Duce informs me that he will attempt to have Settimelli brought to the Italian border, using the services of a functionary of the British police. He gives me Settimelli's letter.

At the Senate the budget of Foreign Affairs is approved by acclamation after a short speech read by Senator Crespi[284] and prepared by myself and Federzoni.

Meeting with von Mackensen. The Germans would be happy if we set our line of conduct in the form of an *Informazione Diplomatica*. But, to do this, we must know what their real intentions are. In Rome they led us to believe that a cantonization of Czechoslovakia could be sufficient for the moment. But are they still of this opinion? Or do they not instead want a dislocation of the country? Anyway, we must know. They must let us know their most intimate thoughts. The ambassador thinks that the acceptance of Henlein's[285] requests could satisfy Berlin. But he is not certain and before giving a formal reply he prefers to be sure by making a telephone call to Ribbentrop.

In Berlin, signing of the commercial agreements. The experts' forecast were pessimistic. Instead everything went well. Politics carried the day.

May 29, 1938

During the morning, ceremony for Spain. The Adriano is packed. I am received with a great demonstration. The two speakers, Milan-Astray[286] and the poet Pemán,[287] speak with warmth and color, even though their oratory appears to be vaguely grandiloquent to our audience.

In the afternoon the fascist conscripts.

I finish my speech for Milan.

May 30, 1938

The Duce approves the speech that I prepared, and says that he will give orders to the Party to create a strong wave of Francophobia throughout the country. He authorizes me to tell Perth that negotiations with France are to be considered broken, all the more because the usual idiot Parisian press (the real responsible party for the crisis) wants to give an anti-German color to the Italian-French agreements. I will also ask Perth to accelerate the implementation of the Italian-British Treaty.

The Duce also adds that he will make the agreement with France on the eve of the occupation of Albania, to be able to deliver the blow in an atmosphere of widespread euphoria.

In the afternoon I accompany the Spanish air force to see the Duce. Afterwards I receive them at the Palazzo Chigi. I speak briefly to them, saying how Italian intervention was decided and assuring them that, despite all the Committees, our solidarity will not abandon them until the national flag is flying on the highest towers of Barcelona, Valencia and Madrid.

Del Croix's Francophile enthusiasms have rather cooled since in London he was treated very badly by the French delegation, which he had painstakingly soft soaped for many years. He is getting to know them: better late than never.

May 31, 1938

In Germany there is a lot of hubbub being made over the small motor car: they will build seven million of them, and almost every family will have its own little automobile. Mussolini, commenting on a report by Attolico, said that this will encourage the hedonistic spirit, which is supposed to be instinctive in the Germans, and make the population less warrior like. Anything that is more bourgeois predisposes to pacifism.

De Bono tells me of rumors of ministerial rotations. He asks me how much truth there is in them. It is surprising how a man of 72 years of age, who from the first day of the regime has more or less occupied the top positions, still is naïve enough to believe in rumors...

Bulgaria recognizes the Empire. They had made some mention before: now, full-scale recognition.

The Japanese naval attaché[288] gives me information about a purported French-English military agreement. They also spoke of it with our attaché in Tokyo. They would like to make a secret pact with us. And I am not against it. On an historical level, Italy and Japan must march side by side for a long time.

Von Mackensen confirms the peaceful intentions of Germany in Czechoslovakia and declines the offer of an *Informazione Diplomatica*. The press has already worked well. In turn I turned down Ribbentrop's proposal of sending a commission to Alto Adige to remove the last hopes of the aliens. We will take care of that.

June 1, 1938

Nothing of particular importance.

I cable Berti to have our troops removed from Saragozza and to send a few battalions to the front line. They have now rested for more than 40 days and from news received it seems that it does not make a good impression to see the Italian forces behind the lines crowding the cabarets and brothels, while the Spanish fight in a tough battle. It's true that our soldiers have worked hard for two months and have broken through the Red lines and opened the way to the sea: all the same, fascist soldiers must not appear disinterested in fighting, at any moment or for any reason.

In Japan they are more and more determined than ever to reinforce military ties with us. The Duce also agrees.

June 2, 1938

The speech went well. Although it was not easy to warm up that environment of stupid dopes. Retired ambassadors, generals, admirals and other retired minds made up most of the audience. People, consequently, who are more favorably disposed to applaud a conservative speech which could have brought Italy back to a line of pacifism, even of the collective type.

At the station, Pirelli told me, without concealing his satisfaction, that during the afternoon discussion on politics in the Balkans an anti-German atmosphere prevailed. I immediately told Starace to place all the speakers under surveillance and, if it is the case, to take disciplinary measures. Pirelli was terrified and tried to invent some excuse which in reality worsened the situation.

I don't like these conventions. A parliamentary climate is immediately created. These old men meet up with one another again, and think with nostalgia of Chambers in the good old days, of immortal principles, and of the lodge. And in the atmosphere they forget to have, at least, hidden the green pinafore with the Blackshirt...

June 3, 1938

Report to the Duce some of the impressions of the convention. He agrees with me and says that it will be the last one. As far as the speech is concerned he liked it, and the international press, except, naturally, the French, found it favorable. The Duce confirms that he had given orders to the Party to create: "a wave of Francophobia to liberate Italians from the last subjugation: the one towards Paris." The Chief also orders me to resume sending volunteers to Spain, in small groups and in plain clothes. For the moment, 2,000.

The Prince of Hesse confirms to me that the Führer does not intend to force the situation in Czechoslovakia. But he will should the Czechs continue their provocations. He tells me furthermore, as a family secret, that the King of Greece shows signs of insanity. He is in the hands of two spiritualists whom he consults before taking any decision. He says that he is in communication with the "Red Cloud" and that he is in direct contact with her!

I deny to Plessen official negotiations for the transfer of Caproni planes to the English. There were simple private and commercial discussions. I tell him also that we will oppose a proposal of mediation in Spain and that we consider talks with France to be broken.

I had a long meeting with Perth. I took advantage of the euphoria created by the Milan speech to ask him for the enactment of the April 16 Pacts.

I took notes of the meeting. Perth appeared to be very reasonable: he is also convinced that we cannot remain engaged for our entire lives: at a certain point one must get married.

June 4, 1938

I received the new Polish ambassador.[289] I had already met him when he was Chief of the Military Mission. He is a good looking man, fairly open and a little too self assured. He says he's motivated by the best intentions toward us.

Giro, the head of the Working Men's Club in Albania, gives me his report. At this point he controls sizeable numbers. Public opinion is turning against the King and his thugs more and more. An Italian intervention, in the case of rebellion, would not encounter obstacles, and, after three days of calm, we could establish ourselves in such a way as to remove any thoughts of a reaction. The working classes, who suffer, are far removed from politics and would be delighted by any material improvement. I ordered to be ready for anything but not to act without my orders. In the meantime, create propaganda among the masses, through the Working Men's Club, welfare and sports.

The Duce is angry with Farinacci, head of the anti-Semitic faction, who has a Jewish secretary: Jole Foà. In such cases foreigners see proof of the lack of seriousness of many Italians.

June 5, 1938

Nothing new. The Duce has left for Romagna. Sunday at the beach.

June 6, 1938

Ajello[290] tells me that in Leghorn Francophobia is very violent. Apart from the memory of the Leghornese Vespers of 1917, the current problem is felt there more than anywhere else. On calm winter days Corsica seems to be within reach. It belongs to us, within the group of our islands, inhabited by our people. The Leghornese can't understand why it must belong to foreigners. And at night they secretly go to drop their nets in those waters. When Corsica will be ours, Leghorn will get an extraordinary boost.

With Cavagnari we agree on sending Admiral De Courten to Japan. Since the political pact with Tokyo will be supported by a military pact it is better to have an ad hoc man there right from the start.

General Gambara believes further use of our troops in Spain to be possible while they wait to be evacuated. We still have around 20,000 Italian fighting men, plus eighteen thousand of the Freccia division, plus a Spanish division. With these forces he believes it possible to have enough of a mass to break through towards Valencia. I told him to certainly go ahead. He is a soldier of great quality, occasionally a little tense, but intelligent and bold.

June 7, 1938

Nothing new.

June 8, 1938

A brief meeting at the beach with Stein and Helfand. They are above all interested in knowing whether there is any truth to the rumors about the coming ministerial changes. I denied all gossip. Stein said that as far as he was concerned he hoped that I will remain at the Palazzo Chigi and not go to the Party or the Ministry of Internal Affairs. Helfand added: worse could happen to us...

I received Mr. McAnemy, president of the New York Exposition. He was accompanied by the ambassador. They say that he is very important but he doesn't seem to be. He is a wrinkled old man, insipid and bundled up in an old tailcoat. He says what all Americans say. I played, as best I could, the tune of pacifism and collaboration. Without much conviction but with emphasis. Phillips was very happy.

The international press is very excited about the bombings by Franco. From a French interception it seems that in Barcelona all fuel depots are burning: 65,000 tons of gasoline. The fire is expected to last four days and all the ships have had to leave the port because the fuel oil floats in flames and is taken to the ships by the currents.

June 9, 1938

The French-British hype over Franco's bombings continues. I don't think that anything precise will come of it. The Duce, meanwhile, has decided to increase the strength of the reserves that we will send to Spain this month and in July, instead of a thousand, two thousand will go. All together, four thousand. These can be increased.

June 10, 1938

Nothing new.

Colonel Piéche,[291] of the carabinieri in Spain, is pessimistic about the duration of the war and Franco's possibilities of reorganizing the country, which, in many sectors, is still unshakably Red.

June 11, 1938

During the evening Bocchini and Buffarini came to me very alarmed about the news regarding the activity that Settimelli proposed to carry out in France. For one thing he is going to publish a sensational book. This would not have occurred had I been able to act, through Emanuele, as long as Settimelli was in Montecarlo. The Duce was in agreement. Then Bocchini proposed a possible legal solution which the Duce preferred. This solution failed. And now action seems less smooth. Although we have arranged a plan: Settimelli will have to return to Montecarlo and then we will have a greater possibility of success. I hope that an abduction by motorboat is possible. If not, we will see. Emanuele is capable, without scruples, and is always ready for action. A traitor like Settimelli does not deserve consideration.

For the rest, nothing new. Also the matter of the bombings in Spain begins to die down.

June 12, 1938

Nothing new. Sunday at Capri with Ciccino in a seaplane. Lunch with the old regulars of Aragno. The many years passed have left deep marks on their faces and their spirits.

June 13, 1938

Talamo[292] reports on the Bulgarian situation. A union with Yugoslavia is feared and many elements are already working to debunk it. Overflowing German economic and consequently political influence. Little room for us. We will try to occupy the aeronautical sector which is still relatively free.

Jacomoni brings some reports from Albania and presents various proposals. He is a man with a moderate nature: he is inclined to seek a halfway solution which maintains the King, placing him more and more under our control. But the opportunity of getting rid of him is worthwhile, in case the totalitarian solution of annexation is chosen. Of the various requests by the King, the one for a yacht is important and should be satisfied. We had better give it to him manned with an Italian crew. This guarantees the impossibility of escape in any event. Berti cables that Franco intends to proceed to Valencia on Saturday. But strong with the 14 divisions he refuses the offer of taking the Volunteer Corps into action. He reserves it to seize Madrid, which should follow shortly after Valencia.

June 14, 1938

Made the last agreements with Christich for Stoyadinovich's stay in Venice.

Prepared to ship 500,000 kg of grain to Albania, which is now suffering from a harsh famine. These are the gifts the people most appreciate.

I authorize Berti to arrange the repatriation of the most tired elements which he can replace with the 4,000 reserves we sent.

June 15, 1938

I go to Romagna. Brief meeting with the Duce, during which I bring him up to date on the rotations among diplomats which he approves. He gives me orders to send Senator Prampolini to Albania for the study of land reclamation. Lunch at the home of Anfuso in Stra. Late in the evening, I reach Venice.

June 16, 1938

Nothing significant, except for the arrival of Stoyadinovich. Very cordial.

June 17, 1938

Long meeting at the Lido. Recorded. On the whole everything goes very well. The two countries are even more united following the Anschluss. We confirm the policy of close collaboration.

June 18, 1938

Stoyadinovich departs. Very friendly farewell. The crowd holds a warm demonstration for Yugoslavia.

Brief meeting with Balbo. Acid and hostile to everything. He speaks badly of the Germans, defends the Jews, attacks Starace, criticizes the use of "voi" and the issue of the Roman salute.

I see the Duce in Riccione. He is satisfied with the results of the meeting with Stoyadinovich. He orders me to send another 100,000 kg of grain to Albania. He confirms his intention to act and to occupy it before 1939. I report the meeting with Balbo to the Duce. He reacts strongly. He says: "That man will end up like Arpinati, or even worse. If he tries to move a finger I'll have him handcuffed." He orders me not to act against Settimelli for the moment: "He'll pay later on. My enemies have always ended up in jail and sometimes under surgical knives." He confirms uncompromising autarchic politics. He repeats the need for harsh discipline: "Italy will never be Prussian enough. I will not leave the Italians alone until I have two meters of soil on top of me." He speaks against the Monarchy which he defines as "the skid of the Regime." He thinks he will get rid of that issue after the end of the war in Spain. He is in great shape morally and physically. I return to Rome by car.

June 19, 1938

Nothing noteworthy.

At the beach.

June 20, 1938

The meeting with Perth (recorded) was not very productive for the purposes of the Italian-British friendship. It is not possible for us to agree to support an armistice now, while Franco is winning. Compromise is not possible in civil war. I reported to the Duce. But I believe that this putting off til doomsday of implementing the treaty is very dangerous. France plays its game of muddying the waters. Herriot[293] told Tamburini[294] that he considers war between Italy and France to be inevitable. Volpi. I cooled down his pro-French and pro-British attitude. He guessed that we point towards Albania and he is happy. He also insists on action in Anatolia after that.

The Princess of Piedmont tried to gather information on the issue of the monarchy. She said that if she were not what she is that she would be against dynasties. She will teach her son many professions because she thinks that one day the little boy will have to work and live from his work. The Savoy family believes in divine right. She doesn't. She acknowledged to the credit of the dynasties the fact of not trying to make money and in this there is a clear anti-fascist edge. She distrusts Starace, whom she feels is an enemy. I denied this and tried to placate these anxieties by saying that there is no reason at all to be worried.

June 21, 1938

I gave instructions to Prampolini to go to Albania and study the land reclamation plan. Naturally I gave him a hint about the political objective of his mission. This excited him and he accepted with great pleasure. He will do well. Jacomoni was present at the meeting, and will introduce him to the King.

Inauguration of the Italian and German Law Congress with a good speech by Frank.[295] The anti-Axis Bottai and De Francisci[296] also applauded warmly. They have understood which way the wind is blowing...

The Mission, back from Japan, confirms the warmth of the sentiments toward us and the extraordinary military power of Japan. Contrary to what Masonic and Jewish propaganda would like to have us believe, Japan has deployed a minimal part of its forces in China. The war-making potential is still intact.

We delivered the note about Swiss neutrality.

June 22, 1938

I inform von Mackensen of the meeting with Perth, of my reply and of the Duce's decisions. He is very pleased. Every now and again these Germans need an injection of trust in us. And yet they should understand that Mussolini's Italy is upright and keeps its word. But much more time is required to overcome the clichés created by an even longer tradition of servitude, deal making, and bootlicking. We will succeed.

The Duce returns. I welcome him at the airport. I tell him that the CTV will be back in action in Spain as soon as possible. He is pleased. He approves my replies to Perth and is clearly unmovable: we will not modify our attitude toward Franco by one millimeter and the pact with London will go into effect when it pleases God. If it is effected at all. He is in a good mood because the harvests, especially grain, after many bad forecasts have picked up and are very promising.

I assure Conde, who is a little worried, of our intentions: I tell him also that the best way to prove the rumors wrong is to immediately have the Italian Legionnaires engage in combat on the road to Valencia.

With Pariani we speak about Albania: we decide on the construction of the road to the sea.

June 23, 1938

The Duce discusses economic matters and says that he intends to create monopolies for sugar, alcohol, and electric power. Fascist Italy cannot have less courage than Giolitti who, in 1906, created the railway monopoly. He criticizes generals who are orators. He says that one must never speak to soldiers about death: on the contrary, one must persuade them that they will kill and they will always be unhurt.

I see the Duke of Aosta at the beach. He looks well but the wound has still not healed. Three months after the operation is a bad sign. He intends to return to East Africa and is very dedicated in his plans and projects. On the whole he is optimistic about the situation in the Empire. He believes that expenses can be reduced and obtain equally good results if we do not rush them. He speaks badly of the colonial functionaries: 50% incompetent, 25% thieves.

Balbo, in the car, says this precise phrase which is very revealing: "In Italy we have lost the habit of being sincere." He comes to the Ministry where we have a long meeting. He is depressed. He thinks he will stay in Libya, because he has understood that it is the best solution. When you come to think of it he is a man easy to overwhelm and to outmaneuver.

Discussions with the Turkish ambassador. Recorded. I decline the offer of an Eastern Mediterranean Pact and encourage the Turks to strike with force at the sanjak of Alexandretta. France will not be able to react without engaging itself in such a way as to weaken it even more on the Continent.

June 24, 1938

I take the notes regarding Swiss neutrality to the Duce. We issued them because that's how the Germans acted. We did not feel the need. The Duce says: "When I say that Switzerland is the only country that could be democratic they think it's a compliment, when it's an awful insult. It's like telling a man that only he can be a hunchback and a eunuch. Only a country which is cowardly, ugly and insignificant can be democratic. A nation which is strong and heroic tends toward aristocracy."

I cabled Grandi and Prunas to inform them that if a raid by the Reds were to take place, as is rumored, against an Italian port, we will immediately engage in acts of war. I also informed Berlin.

I assure Villani that Yugoslavia has friendly intentions towards Hungary. They also are thinking about a pact, without simultaneous consequences, on behalf of the members of the Little Entente. Hungary must however not take the initiative of an attack against Prague, but take advantage of German actions. I draw attention to the opportunity of an understanding between Budapest and Bucharest, in order to isolate Prague and France more and more. Imredy[297] and Kanya would like to come to Rome in July. Maybe it's better to delay it for a while. Nothing is decided about Geneva. I repeat that we await Hungary's exit from the League of Nations.

June 27, 1938

Attolico, in a long report, relates some of his meetings with Ribbentrop. In short, it is about another offer to enter into a military alliance pact.

The situation, from the beginning of May until now, has changed. Relations with Great Britain have not become what we had hoped. The offer takes on a new value. Mussolini is favorable. He tells me to cable accepting a visit by Ribbentrop to Como, during which "the matter will be discussed with utmost seriousness." In the meantime he wants to prepare public opinion. He adds: "We must explain to the Germans that I will make the alliance when it will be popular. I am working to make it so." At the same time we are investigating to find out the precise relationship between Berlin and Tokyo.

I receive a visit from Lütze,[298] very amazed by the organization of the Militia, which, in truth, under Russo's command is performing miracles.

A wide-ranging conversation with Christich. Meeting with the Czechoslovak, to whom I repeat the same formula: reach an agreement with Berlin. Meeting with the Brazilian about the problem of the right to asylum.

Grandi telephones saying that in London the situation is darkening. The news of new bombings of British ships has excited public opinion. Seventeen questions will be asked at the House of Commons tomorrow. Chamberlain's position is more and more shaken. I informed the Duce.

June 28, 1938
The situation in London is becoming more and more difficult for Chamberlain; Grandi, enigmatic and anxious to not compromise himself, calls the situation very troubled. Mussolini is calm. Very calm. He does not intend to force Franco to stop the bombing. He does not wish to issue any declarations whatsoever. He awaits events with his statuary imperturbability. I saw Perth. He is very alarmed. I took notes of the meeting. He fears Chamberlain may fall. The Duce, instead, does not believe that this can take place before the English King's visit to Paris, or rather, before July 19. Then he said: "If Chamberlain falls, let's see who replaces him. I will decide what to do once positive and concrete elements come out of the situation. For the moment, I wait."

Prampolini received the final instructions for his mission in Albania. He is enthusiastic and dynamic like a boy of twenty.

Admiral Riccardi[299] reports on his mission to Malta. Nothing of particular importance. A very cordial reception, it appears.

June 29, 1938
I find the Duce very irritated regarding the rumors in the international press about my meeting with Perth. He fears that they want it to mean a threatening pressure coming from London. I propose that he have Gayda write an article based my records of the meeting. He agrees. But he adds that if the press continues to exaggerate every interview with Perth he will forbid me from seeing the British ambassador, just like he did years ago with de Beaumarchais,[300] who for a long time was not permitted to enter the Palazzo Chigi. The Duce is angry at Grandi about his recent concerns. He says: "When will you decide to stick him in a corner?"

An incident is taking shape with Brazil because Lojacono has granted asylum to Captain Foumier, who, a month or so ago, led the revolt against Vargas. In actual fact he did not have the right to do so. Asylum, at the most, can be given in flagrant cases. We will see about the developments. From here it is difficult to judge, therefore I have left Lojacono to get himself out of the mess. But I do not have much faith in his capabilities and I fear that he has already compromised himself far more than necessary.

Massimo tells to me that rumors of my move to the Party and Ministry of the Interior have much alarmed the Germans.

June 30, 1938
The Duce handed me the draft of the notes that I will give to Perth on Saturday, in reply to what he communicated to me on the 20th of this month. In brief, it rejects, in no uncertain terms, the proposal of an armistice and a unilateral evacuation. He reconfirms that he will not resume talks with France

until after the effectiveness of the Italian and British agreements are implemented. This note will turn the situation sour once again while today it tends to quiet down. But these are temporary and sporadic improvements; at bottom it is still bad. I found some procedural data in the plan for the evacuation of the Volunteers which had not been pointed out previously and that appear to be totally unacceptable. To search the Volunteers, hold them in special camps under the supervision of international guards armed with tear gas pumps, subject them to other similar and ridiculous injustice, is neither possible nor honest. I telephoned Grandi; he did as cuttlefish do: after having muddied the waters he withdrew from any discussion. I will speak about it to the Duce tomorrow. I am certain that he will refuse to subject the Black Shirts of Malaga, Santander, Guadalajara, and Ebro to such humiliations.

Received Mackensen, who brought me a photograph of von Ribbentrop with a warm dedication. I returned the gesture with mine.

July 1, 1938

Some modifications have been made to the note that I will give to Perth tomorrow evening. On my proposal the Duce removed the word "absurd," already used twice to describe the English proposals of amnesty and evacuation and he substituted it with a less aggressive one. Furthermore I will tell Perth that we will resume freedom of action until the time the pact is implemented, that we ask for the publication of documents as we await a final reply. The document is intense: a crisis in our relations with London is inevitable.

Grandi told me he had the unacceptable points of disarmament and other indignities towards the Volunteers removed from the draft for evacuation. Very well: because, after having discussed it with the Duce he was ready to cancel everything in order to defend the pride and the honor of the Black Shirts.

Berti transmits the plan of attack which will start on the 6th: the CTV will advance towards Teruel-Valencia. We'll get there. Just like we always have. In the meantime the shipments of reinforcements continue. We decided to send about 600 artillerymen.

July 2, 1938

I am not well. Regardless, I stay in the office to see Perth.

I take notes of the meeting. Perth is shocked, literally shocked in reading Mussolini's note and by my statements. He is usually quick and lively in debate; instead today he is lost, vague in his replies, and short of arguments. To use a boxing term, I should say that he is groggy.

Mackensen, to whom, immediately following, I deliver the note and give news of the meeting, is very satisfied.

I return home with a raging fever.

July 3, 1938

At home; still with a fever and unwell.

July 4, 1938

I am better. But I am still very weak and exhausted by the illness. I listen to the Duce's speech at Aprilia on the radio. When I heard his voice I began to cry like a baby.

July 5, 1938

Back to work.

I find the Duce still vibrant from yesterday. Still openly and decidedly more anti-French. He says that the Parisian press only strengthens the Axis when it mentions Mussolini turning his back on Hitler. "The day this should happen I would tell him openly. This is my style. But I do not betray." He strongly attacks the Catholic Action. He says that the priests delude themselves if they think they are a positive force in Italy. It was enough for a priest in Verona, a Catholic province, to forbid dancing, for all the youth to desert the church and crowd the dance halls. The priests from Romagna, though, are shrewd, and never forbid dancing. Besides, even Mary danced around the Ark.

Pirelli, in his disingenuous candor, came to ask for money for the Foreign Policy Institute. I spoke to him of the Congress. He played dumb. He had just returned from London, where he says he found a very tense situation. Superficially he plays the hardliner, and, grudgingly, even the Germanophile.

Agostini,[301] about Göring's Steinbocks.

Buffarini, with whom we talked about the internal situation in general.

July 10, 1938

The Duce had me ask Berti if and how many reserves he wants. He is ready to accept any request, beyond the almost 5,000 men already sent during these past weeks. The situation with London is becoming more and more complex. This—in the Duce's opinion—means a return to the Axis of the sympathies by that weak and defeatist middle-class, which, after the agreements of April 16, looked for peace in a recognition from Western Democracies. Mussolini is very irritated with these parts of the middle-class that are always ready to give in. He speaks of a third wave, to take place in October, based on the working classes and the peasants in particular. He intends to create a concentration camp with harsher methods than domestic exile.* A first sign of clampdown will be with a bonfire of Jewish, Masonic, and Francophile writings. Jewish writers and journalists will be banished from all activity. However, all of this has already been announced in the Duce's introduction in the Acts of the Grand Council. The revolution must now place its mark on the way of life of the Italians, who must learn to be less "sympathetic," to become hard, implacable, hateful: i.e., masters.

---

* *Il confino di polizia* was the official term for internal exile, a system used by the Fascist government to imprison and isolate its political opponents.

July 11, 1938

Reply to Blondel about the incident at the border. A substantially empty answer, but conciliatory enough in its tone. But I did not fail to point out more than once that the tourist who crossed the border was an artillery lieutenant. No political inference on his part nor on mine.

Meeting with Hesse, sent by Ribbentrop. Subject: the military assistance pact. Ribbentrop insists that this pact be made. I replied that the Duce and I are both in agreement but we want to see the developments of relations with London, and prepare a broad base of popular support for the treaty. In any case Ribbentrop, who says that Japan also is ready to take part in the pact, appears to want to cancel the idea of the trip to Como, which would prematurely spread too many rumors. Hesse would be given the mission to secretly conduct, unbeknown to his own embassy, the initial negotiations.

Perth informs me of London's reply to our meeting of July 2. Recorded. Nothing to do. Our point of view is not accepted: actual evacuation is demanded, to settle the Spanish issue. There is no other possibility except to wait. With all of the dangers that come with waiting.

July 12, 1938

The Duce is also unhappy with the British reply. On our part there is nothing left to say. We will await the developments of events in Spain. As far as the meeting with Hesse is concerned, the Duce, even though he takes much interest in the matter, says to delay the start of preliminary talks for the moment. The Japanese ambassador has been informed of the situation, from our point of view. I inform Mackensen of the essential part of the results of the meeting with Perth.

Baldur von Schirach[302] comes to see me. I treat him very courteously and I decorate him with the Gran Cordone di San Maurizio. It seems that some time ago he was offended because he was given a rank that he thought insufficient. This explains some of his not altogether orthodox ways with us and his useless flirtations with France. When I spoke to the Duce, he replied: "He's okay. In fact, give him also my decorations!" The Duce holds decorations in such contempt that he does not even bother to refuse them.

July 13, 1938

Action in Spain has commenced. Final objective: Valencia. First target: Segorbe. Berti made a laconic announcement. Gambara sent a cable just like him, full of fire. The Duce, in reading it, commented: "Gambara is a general upon whom I have my eyes set. I like him. He is not one of those officers who—and there are many—enter the barracks mistaking the door... they should have gone to a convent. He is a soldier who loves war. I'm sure that when he fires a cannon he does not fill his ears up with cotton wool." No news during the day. At midnight, an unofficial statement announces that "it is going well."

Sereggi brings me a project from King Zog for a revolution in Turkey. Since some rumors have already begun to spread in Tirana about our eventual action in Albania, I would not want them to be looking for a diversion. Anyway, I will examine it. I tell Sereggi that in the Adriatic I only aspire to the status quo, since I am very busy in the west. I promise help and interest in Albania. Especially in the sector of land reclamation. I confer with Prampolini who, after a first visit, is very positive about the Albanians. He will return shortly to investigate further. But he speaks of the reclamation in Durazzo as something easy to realize. He assures me that by December of 1939 we can plough, and in 5 years have complete harvests. Excellent soil. The cost, in the zone of Durazzo, very low: 3,500 hectares, 20 million lire.

July 14, 1938

The offensive in Spain is proceeding well. The Duce tells me of the publication by the paper *Il Giornale d'Italia* of a statement on the question of race. A group of scholars appear as the authors, under the aegis of the Ministry of Popular Culture. But he says that in reality he practically wrote it all himself.

July 15, 1938

Pariani's report on Germany is very optimistic. He finds that the army has made astonishing progress. Also military collaboration with us has become popular among the officers, who until last September seemed to be unenthusiastic and reserved. In the barracks the motto "believe, obey, fight"[*] has been adopted in Italian. The Duce is understandably proud. The Duce intends to carefully mold the character of the officers here as well. It is useless to stuff both the lieutenant and the captain with culture. The chiefs have to be scientists and artists, but the subordinates and the commanders of small units must have courage and sense of initiative. "All great retreats have begun with the falling back of a second lieutenant."

For the race question the Duce tells me that he will have the Party Secretary call in the "scholars" to tell them what the official position of the regime is regarding this problem. A position which does not mean persecution, but discrimination.

Civilian functionaries will have to wear a uniform. I am very much in favor of this step which reinforces discipline, and the decorum of the bureaucracy.

July 16, 1938

The action in Spain is proceeding very well. In addition to the bulletins, Gambara's notes are very significant and allow for the best hopes. Pariani is apparently of the opinion to prepare a brigade of fast tanks and send it, immediately after the occupation of Valencia, to give the final blow.

Nothing else of importance.

---

[*] "credere, ubbidire, combattere."

July 17, 1938

Doing well in Spain. The action develops rapidly and safely. Gambara's notes confirm that he is preparing to begin the encirclement of Valencia: a bold action which could produce practical results.

The Duce is pleased. He takes the opportunity to speak of the question of the double salute in the army to harshly attack the Monarchy, which, it seems, opposes the adoption of the Roman salute. He says: "My patience has been worn thin by this recalcitrant Monarchy. They have never made a binding gesture towards the Regime. I will wait because the King is 70 and hope that nature will help me." He is more and more decided to be rid of the Savoy dynasty at the first opportunity. He also speaks to me of the revolution in the way of life, especially regarding to problems of race. He is studying measures where marriages of Italians are prohibited with people of other races, including the Jewish race. He says: "All of this will increase foreign hatred towards Italy. Very well: I do all I can to turn my back to France and England, from which we get only rot."

We rejected a Romanian invitation to a conference on the Danube, which excluded Germany. The Duce declares: "I will not even go to the conference of technicians." My attitude towards Germany must be so correct so that they may call me "berreter"[303] if it is the case.

The Hungarians refuse the request of pulling out of Geneva.

July 18, 1938

The day is taken up by the Hungarians. I have the first meeting with them at the Palazzo Chigi. As I expected, Kanya made his attack against the Yugoslavs, whom, with a mentality of the old Ballplatz, he persists in calling "Serbs." He would like to cause problems between ourselves and Belgrade, using a kind of military guarantee which he asks of us in case of a Yugoslav attack. No way. We haven't the least intention of altering our good relations with Stoyadinovich to have a success with the more or less democratic government of Mr. Imredy. Yugoslavia would automatically run into the arms of France and those political-military advantages that the Axis attained in the Danube basin and in the Balkans would end. We could perhaps have the protocols of Belgrade go bust in order to occupy Albania. Then the advantage would be positive, and to raise the Italian tricolor in that land that we deserve to have can justify such a crisis. But certainly not now, to help the political games of these arrogant and petulant Hungarians.

Meeting with the Duce at the Palazzo Venezia. Verbalized. They more or less play the same tune. But also with the Duce, nothing to do. During the evening Kanya, who is very disappointed, says to me: "Hungary's misfortune is that Ciano and Göring have fallen in love with Stoyadinovich."

July 19, 1938

At the beach I read to Kanya, as far as it regards him, the minutes of my talks with Stoyadinovich in Venice. He must admit that Stoyadinovich was very explicit in excluding an attack on Hungary, if Hungary does not start a war with Prague, but follows in the steps of Germany.

We speak of Austria. He tells me that Schmidt no longer has a political position but earns 200,000 marks per year. I remind him of the discussion that I had with him in Budapest, when I did not want to deal with Guido Schmidt, whom I considered a traitor. Schuschnigg: the Hungarians would also like to do something to get him out of the prison in which he is practically held. I told of my attempts with Ribbentrop and the meager results obtained. Kanya says: "The Germans have many qualities but they are always devoid of political tact."

July 20, 1938
The Duce and I speak about Hungary. His faith in the future of that country has been shaken a lot since he met Imredy. He says that he has a false kind of energy: that is to say a dangerous man, a typical example of a ruler produced by a dying regime. His judgment on Kanya is also severe: old Hapsburg. Only openly nationalist parties will be able to tackle the serious problems which exist in that country: the agricultural question, anti-Semitism, revision. The trip to Rome came to nothing. The attempt to muddy Italian-Serb relations failed. Yesterday evening, while we waited for the performance at the Baths of Caracalla, the Duce authorized me to wait, before asking Stoyadinovich the questions we agreed upon, to meet with him. This is very good. Through diplomatic channels the demarche would have assumed an inquisitorial and unpleasant character. The Duce was very proud to show the beautiful show at the Baths. He personally took care of the details. He even set the prices of the seats, which he wanted to keep very low for the lower classes. Two lire. At the end of the performance, speaking about Imredy, he told me: "A man who responds so poorly to the people's cheering is not a leader."
Portugal recognizes the Empire.
The advance has resumed in Spain.

July 21, 1938
A cable from Berti announces that at 4 p.m. today the new attack will begin on the defensive positions of the Reds, along the Rio Palancia. Once this line is passed, we should march towards Valencia. The Spanish have placed another division under our orders, other than the Arrows. Good sign.
The Duce is irritated by Captain Weidemann's[304] useless trip to London.
It is probably the usual exaggeration by the press. But it should have been avoided. We are still practically in the dark. And perhaps the AuswärtigesAmt is in the same position. The Duce said: "If I had sent Sebastiani to see Georges Bonnet I would like to hear the Germans' comments!"
The British Sovereigns' visit to Paris does not go beyond the modest expectations as to its political outcome. It has assumed a democratic character very different from that of the Führer's trip to Italy. What the French press gives most importance to is the endless descriptions of the meals offered by the popular front. *On y mange bien en France.*[305] Even the King will leave with this slogan on his mind. And perhaps he will not end up thinking that when a people eat a lot, and well, it has less and less of a desire to die.

July 22, 1938

The offensive in Spain continues with very favorable prospects. The resistance is still tough, however.

Meeting with Guarneri. He is, as usual, pessimistic. Very anti-German. He is also worried about the racial question which, according to him, will have damaging repercussions on the economic and financial sectors.

July 23, 1938

For the moment, in Spain we do not get through. The resistance is tenacious. Gambara intends to operate with a maneuver.

At the request of Alessi,[306] I am looking after the transfer of ownership of the paper *Il Piccolo*. The Mayers, who are Jews, want to dispose of it at this point.

Nothing else noteworthy.

The Duce is in Romagna.

July 24, 1938

I go to Abetone. Then to Leghorn, where the Provincial Party Secretary tells me that the anti-Semitic measures are eagerly expected. Although in Leghorn the problem does not appear to be as serious as before. The Jews were the leaders of antifascism, and were therefore suppressed along with it.

July 25, 1938

In Spain the Reds have crossed the Ebro in two points. I don't think that they have an offensive force superior to that used in other similar attempts. But it is unfortunate that the Whites allowed themselves to be surprised with the immediate consequence being to halt our offensive on Valencia.

Lord Perth came requesting clemency for the journalist Cremona,[307] who was expelled. The reason for the expulsion is that Cremona, in speaking with other journalists, said that Mussolini cannot go too far in the anti-Semitic campaign because at other times he has taken money from Jews and even from a Jewish woman, Sarfatti. Therefore, fury… Perth asked me for another meeting tomorrow, I believe, to discuss the Czechoslovak problem.

Dindina had her ear operated on for an infection. She didn't suffer at all. I felt so sorry for her, she was under anesthetic. Then she was immediately well.

July 26, 1938

Second meeting with Perth. Verbalized, even though of little importance.

In Spain the situation tends to reestablish itself in the area of the Ebro.

Excitement about the Starace communiqué (in reality written by the Duce) on the Jewish question.

July 27, 1938

Nothing noteworthy.

July 28, 1938

Since, according to the stenographic transcript of a speech by Chamberlain, it was not clear whether he considers the evacuation of the Volunteers from Spain not only as a necessary condition, but also as sufficient for the implementation of the Treaty, I gave instructions to Crolla to find out precisely what the intentions of the Prime Minister are.

Gambara sends a tense note. It is the pessimistic influence of Berti, who would like to come to Italy to discuss... politics. Politics: they are too often an unfortunate obsession of the military.

July 29, 1938

Nothing noteworthy.

July 30, 1938

Following the Pope's speech, violently antiracist, I summoned the Papal Nuncio and I warn him; if they continue down this path, a clash is inevitable because the Duce considers the racial question to be fundamental, following the conquest of the Empire. It is to the racial unpreparedness of the Italians which we owe to the insurrection of the Amhara. I spoke very clearly to Borgongini: I explained to him the promises and the aims of our racism. He appeared to me to be very convinced. And I will add that he revealed himself to be very anti-Semitic. Tomorrow he will confer with the Holy Father. I believe that it is better to act so as to avoid a crisis, but if the Church wants it, we shall not be the losers.

Dispatches from Spain rather unchanged. We await Berti's arrival.

July 31, 1938

I am ill with tonsillitis. And stay in bed until August 7.

August 8, 1938

Back to work. General Berti gives me a detailed report on the conditions of the troops. Strange thing: this time he is less pessimistic than usual. He praises the heroism of the legionnaires. He believes though that if we do not decide to send many more new reinforcements, then it would be better to evacuate the infantry, maybe by a unilateral action. He awaits our decisions.

The Duce is very irritated about the racial question and against the Catholic Action. He orders that all Jews be eliminated from ranks of diplomacy. To begin with I will recall them to Rome. He is violent against the Pope. He says: "I do not underestimate his powers, but he must not underestimate mine. The example of 1931 would teach him. A signal from me would be enough to unleash all the anticlericalism of this nation, which has had great difficulty in swallowing a Jewish God." He repeats his theory of Catholicism as paganization of Christianity to me. "For this reason I am Catholic and anti-Christian." He refuses to see Grandi, who is waiting in the anteroom, and is dejected.

I receive the Papal Nuncio. We speak about the Catholic Action. As for the matter of race, the Pope, who now knows the real terms of the problem, is beginning to yield.

The Japanese ambassador tells me that his government intends to reach a border agreement with Russia, therefore the reaction up until now has been moderate, but if the U.S.S.R. should step up its provocations then they could result in extreme consequences. I expressed our understanding and our sympathy.

August 9, 1938

I have a meeting with Father Tacchi-Venturi.[308] We agree on the need to take direct action to avoid a conflict between the Holy See and Fascism. There is no reason for a dispute. The friction with the Catholic Action is of little importance and easy to get around, if there is goodwill on both sides. Tacchi-Venturi distrusts Starace. He says: "Who has once been a Freemason, remains a Freemason all his life."

I receive Blondel, who conveys generic expressions of French goodwill to reach an agreement. For the rest, we discuss matters of everyday business.

August 10, 1938

With the Duce I discuss the draft of the reply prepared by Franco to the Committee of Non-Intervention. Even though many things do not appear perfect, we still decide not to raise objections, all the more so since the Germans are fundamentally in agreement and Franco is in a hurry to reply.

At the beach I see the ambassador of the U.S.S.R. who comes to discuss the stalled commercial negotiations with me. I give him an appointment for tomorrow evening. I tease him about an article full of personal insults which appeared in the paper *Journal de Moscou*. I ask him if he is the author and I tell him that, having to work with fantasy, he could do better. He is very embarrassed, but denies having written it. Then, to get out of a tight corner, he says: "When I am no longer ambassador I will commit myself to writing against you." To which I respond: "I will commit myself, when you are no longer ambassador, to never writing about you." The Russian Counselor, who is quite sharp, understands and flinches.

Jacomoni talks to me about the situation in Albania and the progress of our preparation. Everything is going very well. Also the alarm of imminent action by us has subsided after my meeting with General Sereggi.

August 11, 1938

I tell the military attaché in Greece[309] to closely monitor military preparations near the Albanian border. I wouldn't want them to start setting up a serious incident at the moment of occupation, which perhaps they have already guessed. I know that they are placing canon in the Gianina area.

Meeting with the Russian ambassador regarding commercial negotiations, at a standstill on the question of the minimum quantities requested by us before agreeing to the requests for aircraft supplies.

Pater[310] and Jacomoni show me the plan for the Sports Club Theater in Tirana, which I basically approve. I want to create a first class Italian center which brings fellow countrymen together and attracts foreigners and Albanians to us. Inauguration at Christmas.

August 12, 1938
Berti goes to see the Duce. He had had a meeting during my illness and had explained the situation. Today to be the conclusion. The Duce, very clear in his explanations and very cogent in his logic, reached these conclusions: speak clearly with Franco and find out what his intentions are. If he is truly ready to renounce the help of the foreign Volunteers, then he must allow our infantry to depart with all the honors, without obliging us to the humiliating formalities of the Committee of Non-Intervention. If instead he wishes to keep them further, since we cannot operate with the present forces and since we are not willing to remain in Spain as spectators, we will send 10,000 reserves. Finally, if a crisis is brought about in the Committee of Non-Intervention and France reopens the border, we can send in one or more divisions to rapidly conclude the conflict. Berti will see Franco and give us an answer before the 20th.

Piccio reports on the mood in France. Very worried. A government minister told him that, in the case of war with the Axis, a French defeat is already considered inevitable by the leadership.

Gave Franzoni[311] instructions for his mission in Prague.

August 13, 1938
Nothing noteworthy.

August 14, 1938
I leave for Venice. By air.

August 15, 1938
In Venice with the family.

August 16, 1938
Return to Rome by plane. Good flight. Nothing of any importance at the office. The Duce, as always, is calm. He speaks to me about Balbo's trip and of the war in Spain. Since Balbo seemed worried about hidden motives for his mission, he authorizes me to tell him that the Duce desired to have in him the most competent ("which is not true," he immediately added!) observer of German air power, while there is a thrashing in the air. Balbo was happy when I told him this. Moreover he is enchanted by the trip, the Germans, by the air force, everything. Now that his vanity has been flattered, he speaks like the most convinced upholder of the Axis. The essence of his report: German air forces are very powerful, far more advanced than ours from a technical point of view.

I spoke at length with Balbo: he is in a state of euphoria from his visit to Germany. He shed his critical attitude towards everything and everybody, except towards Aosta and the Empire. Balbo is a big kid, spoiled and fidgety, high spirited and ignorant, who sometimes can be irritating. Dangerous, I don't think so, because he doesn't have the means to be so.

I received the Polish ambassador. He brought me a message from Beck regarding Geneva, a message which had no other importance than to demonstrate Polish goodwill to keep contacts with us alive.

August 17, 1938

I report my meeting with Balbo to the Duce. I confirm that he is unaware of the scheme and that he is actually pleased with what he feels is his success.

Mussolini replies: "One is always happy when one does not understand." I suggest to the Duce we dedicate an important street in Rome to D'Annunzio, rather than a tree-lined avenue in the Pincio, as the Governor did. In Rome today, which honors more or less unimportant deceased persons with main streets, Gabriele D'Annunzio, who was a marvelous Italian, deserves more.

At the beach I present Balbo to the Russian Counselor. Balbo, who loves to talk, begins a more or less pointless discussion. At the end, Helfand says to me: "Balbo is nice and also intelligent. But I am convinced that all of the rumors of anti-Mussolini aspirations are stupid: Balbo doesn't measure up to the Duce."

August 18, 1938

Nothing important other than the flight the Duce took to Pantelleria which, in the present situation of extremely high tension, will cause much comment around the world. He telephoned me upon his return. Enthusiastic about the military preparation on the island which has reached a level of extreme efficiency.

At the beach, the British chargé d'affaires[312] asked me once again, and officially, to let him know if it is true or not that we have recently provided arms to Franco's troops. I, as is best, withheld my reply.

August 19, 1938

The Duce and I plan the reply we will give to the English: since we have an expeditionary force in Spain, that this is a fighting force, that the wear on the material is equal, or rather superior, to that of the men, given that we cannot have our soldiers fight using olive branches, we have sent what's necessary so that we are not massacred by the many weapons which infiltrate—and the English know it—through the Pyrenees. This is what I will tell Sir Noel Charles tomorrow: the consequences of this reply are not difficult to foresee. In particular because Franco's note to the Committee of Non-Intervention will cause some commotion.

The report of the assistant military attaché in Berlin states that German officials consider action in Czechoslovakia to be inevitable and imminent: end of September. All the details are apparently ready. The air force supposedly will play the main role. Through political channels we have not been told anything. We will, therefore, have to maintain our positions of last May, when we were assured that any use of force was to be excluded, at least for several years.

August 20, 1938

I speak to Sir Noel Charles in the manner we had planned. The meeting was recorded. Personally he puts on a brave enough face at the reply, but I think that the reception in London will not be so cordial...

I send written instructions to Attolico to see Ribbentrop and ask for precise information on what the government of the Reich intends to do in Czechoslovakia, and this in order to "allow us to take timely measures on the western border." This communication will cause much comment among the Germans as it explains how far we are prepared to go. In reality the information coming from Berlin allows us to foresee more and more the coming crisis relating to the Czech issue. Will the conflict be localized or will France start hostilities? In such a case no other alternative exists for us than to take sides immediately with Germany, using all our resources. The Duce decided on action. Therefore, the need to fully know the facts in time.

August 21, 1938

Berti sent the account of his meeting with Franco, who rejects the idea of our dispatching new divisions, and accepts at the most the transfer of 10,000 reserves to maintain the efficiency of the current forces. Under these circumstances the Duce, after a long discussion, comes round to the idea of reducing instead of increasing the forces in Spain. Concentrate the two fascist divisions, the "Littorio" and the "23 Marzo," into one, bring the others home, meaning from 10 to 15 thousand men, negotiating this repatriation with England, whom we would confront with the dilemma: either implement the Treaty of April 16, or let it lapse. If they take the latter path, we have free rein for a military alliance with Germany.

The project seems very good to me. It serves above all to put into motion a machine which has been dormant for too long, and to unblock a situation which is deeply frozen. Franco, I believe, will be happy with such a solution. And it seems to me that the Germans also can only approve.

In the afternoon I go to Venice.

August 22, 1938

The Duce has personally drawn up the cable to Berti along the lines of what was decided yesterday evening. As is appropriate on occasions of great importance, the Duce orders me to give a copy to the King.

It appears that yesterday, the Pope made a disagreeable speech on exaggerated nationalism and on racism. The Duce, who has summoned Father Tacchi-Venturi for this evening, wants to give an ultimatum: "Contrary to what is believed," he said, "I am a patient man. It is necessary though, that I not be forced to lose this patience, otherwise I will react, destroying everything in sight. If the Pope continues to talk, I will scrape off the layer of clericalism of the Italians and before you can say it, I'll make them become anticlerical. The men in the Vatican are insensitive and mummified. Religious faith is on the decline: no one believes in a God who takes care of our suffering. I would hold in contempt a God who takes care of the private life of the policeman on the corner of the via del Corso."

Anyway it would be best if this friction could end. In the difficult international situation, a conflict with the Church would not be beneficial to anyone. I have always acted in this direction with Borgongini.

Buffarini comes to speak to me of his conflict with Starace. He feels under suspicion and is uneasy. As a matter of fact, Starace distrusts him. I will try to reconcile them: this is not the moment to trouble the Duce with palace disputes.

August 23, 1938
Nothing noteworthy.

August 24, 1938
The Duce, based on some information from Barzini,[313] is worried about the situation in Spain. He has expressed himself violently against Franco, who allows victory to slip away even when he already has it in hand. The Duce thinks that an offensive, and a victorious return of the Reds is possible. He was furious with the French press, because a satirical pamphlet, *Aux Ecoutes*, published some idiotic news of his imaginary liver disease. "This Europe is destined to perish because it has a fatal corruption: it lies."

News from Bled is good: parity of armaments for Hungary is already a remarkable advantage. If Kanya is not, as usual, dominated by his Hapsburg prejudices against the Serbs and the Romanians, an agreement on the minorities can also be reached. Anyway, the meeting in Bled has marked a new phase in the disintegration of the Little Entente. Czechoslovakia is isolated. The system of French friendships is unhinged. I bid farewell to Admiral Somigli who is leaving with two cruisers on a world tour. I spoke to him about the situation in general and, as I had explained to Cavagnari, I added that his peace mission could become a war assignment, in case of a general conflict. He quietly showed me his plan should this occur: a war of piracy and sell his skin dearly. Somigli is a man who will keep his word.

August 25, 1938
Villani, back from leave, came to see me. He was pleased with the results at Bled. He confirmed to me that the pacts for the minorities with Romania and Yugoslavia are already prepared, but left hanging because of Czechoslovakia.

He had to admit that I was right in March of 1937, when, upon returning from Belgrade, I told him that I had placed a bomb under the Little Entente. We also discussed the possibility of an imminent conflict. Not even in Budapest do they know anything specific about German intentions. They think, though, as we do, that the crisis, whatever the solution may be, will quickly follow once Runciman[314] leaves Prague.

I sent a cable of congratulations to Stoyadinovich and one to Kanya, also to emphasize the part we played in the matter.

Suvich repeats things that we more or less already know about America. He adds though, in his opinion, that in case of war America will enter into combat sooner than is generally thought.

August 26, 1938

Attolico has spoken with Ribbentrop regarding my instructions of the 20th. The reply is not completely clear. There is a great desire to act and at this point everything is ready, or almost: but the final decision does not seem to have been taken.

The Duce is indignant with Franco for the "calm optimism" with which he conducts the war. "Calm optimists," he says, "get run over by a tram as soon as the leave they house in the morning."

Borgongini Duca, on the Pope's orders, comes to discuss the announcement which, at least for the moment, will end the dispute between the Party and the Catholic Action. I nudged him a bit and he opens up about the Pope. He says that he has an awful personality, is authoritarian and almost insolent. At the Vatican they are all terrified of him. Even Borgongini himself trembles when he is about to enter the Pontiff's room. He treats everyone with arrogance: even the most distinguished cardinals. Cardinal Pacelli, for example, when he is called by the Pope must, like a petty secretary, take notes by dictation of all his instructions. He is again in good health. He eats cooked fruit and little meat. He drinks red wine in limited quantities, and does sufficient exercise in the garden. He is 82 years old and still runs the government of the Church down to the smallest details. He always repeats: "I will govern until the Conclave begins."

A mad woman arrived. Her name is Hilda de Toledano. With great mystery she claimed to be "the King of Portugal" and she offered me to place her State in the Empire of Rome.

August 27, 1938

Meeting with Charles following the expulsion of Mrs. Bastienille of *The Daily Telegraph*. I was able to cancel the order, generated in any case by a venial sin.

Nothing else noteworthy.

August 28, 1938

A reply to the Duce's cable is requested of Berti.

Nothing noteworthy.

August 29, 1938

The Duce is very angry with Franco for the anemic conduct of the war. He fears that they could have very serious surprises. "Make a note of it in your book," he told me, "that today, August 29, I predict Franco's defeat. This man does not know how, or does not want, to make war. The Reds are fighters: Franco is not."

Ambassador Rosso confirms to me his conviction that in the case of a Czech-German conflict, the Soviets will limit themselves to sending in air forces, but that they will not make a complete intervention. Helfand led me to understand the same thing yesterday, in veiled terms.

On the Czech question, which is becoming more of a burning issue, the Duce predicts that the Germans will have the Sudetens act: an insurrection will explode internally. If Beneš reacts violently, Hitler will have a plausible excuse to step in that, in the eyes of the world, will have an acceptable justification. It is unlikely that France will move. It is not ready for a war in general and even less for an aggressive war. The English will do everything to avoid a conflict that they fear more than any other country in the world.

August 30, 1938

The American ambassador, who was due to leave on Thursday, has had to delay his trip. He is very worried about the situation and asked me for our point of view. I play the same pro-German and anti-Czech music: all the responsibilities belong to Prague. In turn I ask what America will do. He replies that it is the most highly strung country in the world. Therefore it is difficult to make forecasts.

Today the United States is pacifist, but any event during the course of the war could, from one minute to the next, modify the situation.

The Duce gave orders to suspend the world tour cruise of the 7th division. This is not the time to scatter our forces. He also tells me about his project of turning the Migiurtinia into a land concession for international Jews. He says that the country has remarkable natural reserves that the Jews could utilize. Among others, shark fishing "very advantageous also because initially many Jews would end up being eaten." He is anxious to know in depth the intentions and programs of the Führer regarding the Czech crisis. I send a handwritten letter to Attolico for this purpose.

The British chargé d'affaires comes back to the question of the new aircraft supplies we sent to Franco. I reply rather abruptly, as I more or less did on August 20 on the same subject.

August 31, 1938

I accompanied Muti to see the Duce. The description that he gives about the situation in Spain, on behalf of Ambassador Viola, is rather pessimistic. It would not be surprising if in a few months things turn for the worst for Franco. Mistrust and skepticism in the country, fatigue among the troops, restlessness on the part of the other generals. Jague[315] and Vigon[316] grow in national consideration, while Franco's star no longer shines with the old light. In almost all sectors the Reds have resumed the initiative and achieved considerable advantages. The action of the passage of the Ebro raised the morale of the Reds and lowered that of the nationalists, who initially reached as far as Saragozza when they fled. The Italians are also tired. Viola proposes that not one, but both divisions be withdrawn from Spain, leaving and perhaps reinforcing the air force, tanks, and artillery. Gambara will arrive tomorrow with Berti's proposals. We will wait for those and then decide.

The Romanian minister asks for Italy's agreement on the Danube accords. He tells me that Romania will not allow, in any event, Russian troops to pass through their territory, without first having fought with every means at her disposal.

September 1, 1938

Council of Ministers. Measures against forcign Jews residing in Italy. I fly to Venice.

September 2, 1938

Return flight in the morning. The Duce is anxious because the Germans let us know very little about their plans regarding Czechoslovakia. He orders me to speak with Hesse. He wants to know how far Germany intends to push things, how much, and in what way does it expect our help. Attolico, in his reports, for the moment does not provide decisive facts: he is personally against our entering into an agreement too quickly.

Hesse agrees with us on the need for greater contact. He says to have urged Göring to work in this direction. Hesse does not open up, but says he knows important things that he cannot disclose without the authorization of his superiors. Confidentially, he says that no German initiative will be taken before October: the lines of defense are not yet ready. He will leave tomorrow morning to confer with the Führer: Ribbentrop is not very well informed.

The new ambassador from Argentina[317] makes his duty call to me. It has no particular importance.

Gambara reports on the situation in Spain. Tomorrow he will confer with the Duce. The armed forces (Berti has not yet spoken with Franco in accordance with the orders of August 22) have some ideas which do not coincide with the those of the Duce, but they do not dare to express them openly. We will see tomorrow.

Prunas sends a cable regarding a meeting between Bonnet and the German ambassador in Paris. Very precise terms: France, England, and the Soviets would intervene immediately, with American support. Will such language have a useful effect upon Germany, or has Hitler already gone to far ahead to pull back now?

September 3, 1938

At the Palazzo Venezia, meeting with Gambara, who explains the point of view of the CTV command regarding the appropriateness or not, of leaving the forces in Spain. The Duce rejects the idea of leaving one division only: equally demanding and more dangerous. Either we withdraw all of the infantry, or reinforce the two present divisions with reserves, take command of the Arrows, have them give us two Spanish divisions and with this mass, attack Barcelona. The Duce rejects this proposal and accepts the complete withdrawal of the infantry. He drafts a cable for Berti with the order to transmit it to Franco. If he agrees, fine. If not, we will find another solution, but the Duce will impose his conditions regarding the conduct of the war. The Duce is convinced that Franco has wasted the best opportunities in order to rapidly bring an end to the contest. Now the situation has changed. Time, as always, works against he who squanders it.

Attolico had a meeting with Ribbentrop. No new facts. If there is a provocation, the Germans will attack. Nothing else has apparently been decided by the Führer. It would be best for us to not request other responses. It is clear that the Germans do not want us in the game. This leaves us full freedom of action, whatever happens.

According to information from Budapest the Hungarian military foresee an imminent attack as inevitable. Kanya instead thinks it is inevitable but not imminent; in the spring.

September 4, 1938

The Duce is very antagonistic towards the Jews. He mentions the measures that he intends to have adopted at the next Grand Council and which will make up the Race Charter. In reality it is already drafted in the Duce's own handwriting. The Grand Council simply approves it by a resolution.

Regarding the concentration colony for the Jews, the Duce no longer talks about Migiurtinia, but rather of the Oltre Giuba, which presents better living and working conditions. The Duce adds: "I am getting the Italians accustomed to believing that they can do without something else: the Vatican. The contribution that it gives us materially is minimal: money does not come in from it. It meant something in a Rome of 80,000 or 100,000 inhabitants. It no longer has the minimum weight in an industrious and prosperous Rome that prepares to reach a population of a million and a half. Pilgrimages become more and more rare, small, and poor. The struggle against these great forces, judged by many this way at least, serves to give backbone to the Italians. And it also serves to show that some mountains are only molehills."

To Lucca for the race.

September 5, 1938

Borelli[318] tells me that the atmosphere in Milan is heavy. The anti-Semitic measures, and the demographic measures, have affected too many people to be popular. But the Duce, when he believes it necessary, has the courage to be unpopular. And he ends up being right.

Sola,[319] judging the current situation, says that the Romanian position is tied to the British. If London goes to war, Bucharest will follow. In that case, Russian troops will find the road into Bessarabia open. If this were to be true many plans should be quickly changed. Romania, which weighs little as a military force, is perhaps a key element geographically.

Contradictory information from Berlin: Ribbentrop intimates the resumption of negotiations with Prague, while his undersecretary tells Attolico that the crisis will occur around the 20th. The fact remains that a clear and final word has still not yet been given to us. Why?

While Pariani tells me about a meeting he had with Canaris, Chief of German Information Service, the news arrives of an initiative taken by the French military attaché to inform us of the mobilization of the reserves on the border of the Rhine. He adds that nothing of the kind has happened along the Alps. I telephone the Duce, who gives me instructions to inform Berlin, saying that the matter is indifferent to us in anticipation of hearing the decisions of the Reich. The Duce says: "Well, this is a treacherous blow by the French. It will not have good consequences."

Pariani informs me of the conditions of the army: reassuring.

September 6, 1938

Starace, yesterday evening, spoke to me about the internal situation, which according to him is a bit shaken by the recent measures. He said: "It disgusts me to pronounce this word, but there is a Quartarella[320] air blowing. The Party is solid and in order. The lower classes, the same. The rebellion is instead within the middle classes."

Cavallero[321] is optimistic about the military operations in the Empire. He anticipates being able to eliminate the last rebellious groups before Christmas. In the case of a general conflict he does not fear a large uprising by the populations. Today, the military equipment not being yet ready, he would be inclined to carry out a small range offensive action in the Sudan. In two years time, he expects to have the forces to occupy Egypt, and he is also studying a surprise action on Aden, to take that base from the English.

At the beach the Prince of Piedmont approaches me. He wants information on the situation. I brief him concerning Czechoslovakia and Spain. He maintains a very correct and calm composure. The conversation turns to Sforza.[322] The Prince is indignant that he is still a senator and that he has the Annunciation Collar. He says: "We must make him lose his position as senator. Then the Collar can also be taken away."

Hesse has returned from Berlin with a message from Hitler for the Duce. We will see him tomorrow. Specific information on the German-Czech front: none.

September 7, 1938

The early morning papers appear optimistic as far as Czechoslovakia is concerned. Prague, apparently, would be ready to accept German requests. Later though, information from German sources is more skeptical and it seems that the wave of euphoria was created deliberately by London and Paris.

I accompany Hesse to see the Duce. He conferred twice with the Führer and reads a long note dictated by him. I conserve it among my documents. In conclusion, he will attack if Czechoslovakia provokes: today he is not yet able to set a specific program.

Franco accepts, reluctantly it would appear, the withdrawal of the infantry. The Duce returns to the original proposal and offers, through Berti, to leave a division. He fears that people will conclude it amounts to a complete evacuation, and that we not abandon Franco, and instead he intends to march with the comrade until the end.

I receive Countess Castelbarco Toscanini who cries about the withdrawal of her father's passport and is worried about the reaction in America where he was supposed to conduct his next two concerts. The Duce became irritated because many Italians, and first of all the Princess of Piedmont, went to Lucerne for the Wagner concert. But the withdrawal of the passport is due to the interception of a telephone call where it appears that Toscanini attacked the Duce about the anti-Semitic policy, describing it as "stuff out of the middle ages."

September 8, 1938

The incidents at Moravska Ostrawa have once again made the little Czech boat drift to the high seas.

I receive the Manchukuo mission at the Palazzo Chigi: the leader is a timid Chinese, shadowed by two Japanese, one military and one civilian, who don't even allow him to breathe without their permission. The same scene also at Palazzo Venezia in the presence of the Duce.

I receive Blondel. He wants news regarding our position. I express myself more or less in the same terms as the *Informazione Diplomatica* n. *19*, which will be released this evening, and which was drawn up by the hand of the Duce. Blondel would like to know what commitments have been made between the Führer and the Duce. I remain enigmatic. In reality there is nothing specific. But it is clear that in any event the Duce intends to march along the line of the Axis.

September 9, 1938

I authorize Casertano[323] to finance Mizzi's[324] party, with 150,000 Italian lire, in the Maltese elections.

The Duce gives Berti instructions to conclude talks with Franco: if he prefers we will leave one division out of 9 battalions, otherwise we will withdraw all of the infantry. According to the Duce the evacuation of the forces cannot take place before the second half of October.

Sparano confirms to me what I had already said to the Duce: Lojacono, in Brazil, finds himself in an almost untenable situation. He needs to be replaced. We will call him to confer: so as to proceed step by step.

I attend the rehearsal of tomorrow's performance by the youth of the GIL. They are better than I thought. One must keep in mind that it is a preparation organized in a few weeks only and that most of these boys come from villages without any sense of discipline. Some of them don't even speak Italian.

September 10, 1938

The performance of the GIL went well. The Duce was satisfied.

Meeting with Hesse. Nothing noteworthy. He speaks to me again of the military pact. He says to have mentioned it to the Duce. I postpone the reply. Then, very confused, he says that he has to speak to me about a private matter. The Queen asked him to approach the Duce or myself in favor of her Jewish doctor, Stuckjold. It seems that the Queen is very angry about the expulsion, and also the King, who trusts this doctor very much, but does not dare to speak to the Duce. And both of them count on a friendly mediation by me… I did not make a commitment, and, smiling, I pointed out to the Prince of Hesse that the Führer would not appreciate that such missions were entrusted to him, a German and a Nazi. He turned pale.

September 11, 1938

To Ponte a Moriano and to Bagni di Lucca, for the "Poetry Prize."

Franco opts to keep a division of legionnaires in Spain, in accordance with our last proposals.

September 12, 1938

Many communications from Berlin and mainly one which proposes a secret meeting between the Duce and the Führer at the Brenner Pass, on any day *but not after September 25*. The proposal was made by Göring to Magistrati and then confirmed in Hitler's name. I spoke to the Duce about it on the phone (at Rocca delle Caminate). He replied: "It is an idea which I do not reject. We shall discuss it."

Tense news arrives from the various capitals. Switzerland and Belgium place their borders in a state of defense. In Paris there is talk of a call-up of six classes. Grandi cabled to request in the name of Chamberlain for a moderating step by the Duce towards Hitler, who, according to the English, may not be informed by his staff about the recent British steps. We let the idea drop. Mussolini says: "Such an absurdity proves that the English have unbalanced hormones." And he tells me to inform the Germans that if at this time they need action in their favor that he "is ready to go one step further than the last *Informazione Diplomatica*." I give Attolico instructions, who every now and then is assailed by war fears and would like to draw back. He will follow the order, therefore, very moderately. The Führer's speech. He seems to be very strong and certainly not conducive to a clearing of the atmosphere. He speaks about war with unprecedented determination. And this contributes to create the atmosphere. The Duce, from what he says on the phone to Alfieri, also finds the Nuremberg speech serious.

Suvich leaves Washington to go to the "Adriatica di Sicurtà." He did not appreciate the change and protested very politely.

Volpi talks to me about personal matters, of an intimate nature.

September 13, 1938

The Germans accept our offer. Attolico telephones me from Nuremberg after a meeting with Ribbentrop, and asks that we draft an *Informazione Diplomatica* to say that the eight points of Carlsbad are now superseded and that only a radical solution, based on the principal of self-determination, can end the Czechoslovak crisis. I inform the Duce about it who rapidly writes *Informazione Diplomatica* n. *20*. He dictates it to Anfuso. Then, I confer with him about his meeting with Hitler. He does not reject the idea but asks that it be delayed until the beginning of October, since he is busy with visits to the provinces. I inform Attolico.

I give instructions to Alfieri regarding the importance to be given to the *Informazione Diplomatica* and the tone of the press in general, though on this occasion it was good.

I cable Berti to establish a single division and to begin the operation to assemble those being sent home. I also ask for the exact numbers of those who return because I will need them when I speak to the English.

Meeting with the American ambassador. He wants to go on leave and tries to adapt the situation in Europe to suit his personal needs so that he can leave with a clear conscience. At least that!

Meeting with Christich. Important and put on record. He confirms that Stoyadinovich intends to conform his position to that of Italy's.

8 p.m. They cable news from Prague about an ultimatum given to Beneš by Henlein, after today's incidents. I speak to the Duce. He agrees that the situation is very serious but believes that Beneš will end up accepting. "Democracies are made to swallow bitter pills."

September 14, 1938

Already yesterday evening the first news reached about the breaking off of negotiations between Prague and Henlein. The day goes by between periods of optimism and pessimism according to the changing news. There is talk of serious incidents between the Sudeten population and the police; with scores of dead. The military attaché[325] cables from Berlin that also the air force mobilization has begun with the recall of two thousand pilots, and the concentration of the formations in fields along the border. Many diplomats are rushing into the Ministry. In general they have a gloomy outlook on events. They all ask for explanations regarding the *Informazione Diplomatica* and want to know if Italian solidarity will go as far as to join Germany in case of war. I do not give a specific answer but I let it be understood that it will be so. The British chargé d'affaires asks if self-determination means a plebiscite. Yes. In that case he says that it will be difficult to have Beneš accept it. The Belgian ambassador says: "You are asking Czechoslovakia to commit suicide."

8 p.m. Dramatic turn of events. Attolico telephones to say that Chamberlain has asked for a hearing with Hitler and will be received tomorrow at Berchtesgaden. I telephone the news to the Duce, who is surprised. He exclaims: "There will be no war. But this is the liquidation of English prestige. In two years England has hit the canvas twice."

September 15, 1938

The wave of optimism created by the news of Chamberlain's trip has been dampened by the confusing pile up of information coming from Prague and Berlin regarding the civil war in the Sudetenland. It appears that Beneš has them firing at will. And the scores of deaths continue. Some papers say hundreds. Attolico, usually optimistic, telephones to say that "if Chamberlain was not on German territory the forces of the Reich would already have given serious help to the Sudeten." I receive von Mackensen who offers thanks for the Duce's article "Letter to Runciman." He defines it as an historical document. The ambassador is rather pessimistic. He says that if Chamberlain doesn't have conclusive and rapid proposals up his sleeve, the Führer will not be able to refrain from helping the Sudeten. Together, we examine the Balkan situation, in the case of conflict, now that the neutrality of Yugoslavia is assured. We believe that neither Greece nor Turkey will make a move.

The Duce, from Rocca, calls me frequently on the phone. He is calm, he awaits developments, unconcerned and determined. But he is less optimistic than yesterday. Attolico, at 8:30 p.m., telephones to say that Berlin does not consider an intervention in Czechoslovakia to be imminent, even though news of incidents are more and more serious. Nothing is yet known about the meeting between Hitler and Chamberlain, which began at 5 p.m. and takes place in the sole presence of an interpreter. Late in the evening he gives me the first news about the meeting and the communiqué.

September 16, 1938

The interpretations of the Hitler-Chamberlain meeting differ as do the tendencies towards optimism or pessimism. In general there is the feeling of a turn for the better. The plan to have another meeting is interpreted favorably. The Duce is worried about Benes' behavior. He fears that he wants to force the Führer's hand, by pursuing a violent anti-German repression. He still hopes to provoke conflict, which for him is perhaps the only way out.

I see many diplomats. The Romanian categorically denies the news coming from the French regarding free Soviet transit in Bessarabia. The French and the Russian, at the beach, search for information that I do not give. Blondel is pessimistic. He remembers the days of '14 that he passed in the embassy in London. Even then no one wanted to die for the Serbs, and yet they did go to war. And yet the world was much happier then than it is today, and there were many reasons to preserve the peace. The Polish and the Hungarian come to thank us for the action undertaken by the Duce and to formally point out that they intend to raise the question of their minorities. The Japanese wants news. The English brings me a goodwill message from Chamberlain regarding the implementation of the Italian-British Treaty.

Attolico, whom I asked specific news also regarding the speech that the Duce will make in Trieste, calls to say that he will give it to me late in the evening.

News from Prague is better: but the fact that the Benes government remains unmovable is confirmed (8:30 p.m.).

September 17, 1938

Yesterday evening Attolico gave me the items that Hitler would like to see emphasized in the Duce's speech: accelerate the solution, have a complete solution, which releases all minorities from Czech bondage.

In the morning, after a bit of daily business, I fly to Lucca, I stay a few hours and then depart to Forlì, where, with Starace and Alfieri, I board the presidential train. I bring the Duce up to date. He concludes: "I have made the decisions. If the conflict is produced in Germany, Prague, Paris and Moscow, I will remain neutral. If Great Britain intervenes, generalizing the war, giving it an ideological character, then we will throw ourselves into the furnace. Italy and Fascism could not stay neutral."

The Duce is personally inclined to believe that the dispute will end up having a military solution. This conviction was reinforced when, in Bologna, he learned the latest news regarding the constitution of Henlein's volunteer corps and the new incidents in the Sudetenland. He remains calm nevertheless. He has one of his men tell us that he does not want to be disturbed during the night even if important news arrives "unless war breaks out." From Abano, where the train stops for the night, I telephone Rome and Berlin. The news in the press is very much exaggerated.

September 18, 1938

To Trieste from Venice on the *Camicia Nera*. Beautiful day. The sea is like a mirror and the sky an unblemished blue. Trieste greets the Duce in a blaze of sun, flags, and devotion. It was said that this city was depressed because of the Anschluss and the racial policy. I have never seen a more lively reception, nor a more explosive enthusiasm than that of the people in Trieste. The Duce speaks. Great, quiet speech. Rarely do words equal the facts. This time they do. Even if nothing happens the Duce has written a page in history today, made of courage, loyalty, and honor. There was the feeling of a turn for the better on the European political horizon. Many approvals from every capital. While the news from London, of the Chamberlain-Daladier[326] meeting, even though imprecise, allows us to forecast a full-scale withdrawal. The only negative element of the day was Hodza's[327] speech. He declared that Prague does not want plebiscites and that it is ready to resist. But for how long, if London and Paris dump them?

September 19, 1938

I accompany the Duce to Yugoslav territory. Very warm welcome. A very friendly and very significant exchange of speeches at this moment. Here is a result few believed in when I went to Belgrade in March 1937.

More optimistic news, on the whole, of the Czech situation. The Duce also the begins to favor a peaceful solution.

Flight to Rome.

I receive 100 Yugoslav workers. I speak to them in a chummy and cordial manner. Then I talk with Christich. He wants news, but I don't have much to give him. Charles wants to see me and he leaves me a generic note of goodwill regarding the Czech crisis. Without being secretive, he adds that the motive for these frequent visits is to show that contacts between Rome and London are cordially maintained.

In the meantime the Hitler-Chamberlain meeting for next Wednesday is now confirmed. And tomorrow the Führer will receive the Hungarian representative (Horthy[328] or Imredy?) and the Polish representatives. Attolico attaches much importance to this meeting. I look for the two diplomatic representatives in Rome. I do not find them. I will speak to them tomorrow morning. And I will tell them to rekindle their action: Germany must not be the only one taking advantage of this situation.

September 20, 1938

Villani and Wieniawa[329] are very satisfied with what I tell them. And I believe that there was the need for our injection because the attitude of London and Paris, faced with the Magyar-Polish requests, appeared rather discouraging. Even Berlin itself does not seem to be very eager to associate the future of the Sudeten Germans with that of the minorities from other countries.

The day goes by mostly waiting for Prague's reply, which late in the day we find out is negative. Consequently, there are new waves of pessimism.

The Duce speaks in Udine. I listen to the speech at the ministry.

Berti informs us that he is preparing the division to be repatriated, in the region of Seville, over three regiments. Everything is delayed since our divisions are still needed to stop a Red offensive. A reliable source confirms to me that our troops are tired. Very tired. And that the idea of leaving a division in Spain was not favorably received. The anonymous, and signed, letters in which repatriation is requested multiply. Signs of restlessness are mounting. I would not want that this little division of disheartened veterans gives us a big disappointment some day.

September 21, 1938

Until late there is no final news from Prague. Although is appears that Beneš is giving up. The delay in giving news according to what the Ministry says is apparently because of rear of riots.

From Spain Nulli[330] confirms that those being repatriated may be around 10,000, ready to leave at the end of September. In the meantime, no one has stated in Geneva that the Red government is sending back, in a unilateral gesture, all the volunteers. Why? Do they feel so strong? Or is this just an idealistic gesture? As far as we are concerned, I feel this takes away some of the zest from our partial evacuation. But it has the advantage of not appearing solely as our initiative, which would have certainly led to unpleasant comment: Italian fatigue, betrayal of Franco, etc.

September 22, 1938

The Duce has returned to Rome. I confer with him about the Spanish problem as well as the Czech situation. The Chief is skeptical about Spain. He believes that Franco, who has at this point lost the battle, will reach a compromise with the others. We will lose the four billion in credit: for this reason we should rake everything up, while it is possible. For the Czech problem, he insists on the need for a solution for the Magyar-Polish problems as well.

I receive the German ambassador. Recorded meeting. In the name of the Führer he thanks us for what the Duce and Italy have done. He announces a coming message from the Führer, of which the usual Prince of Hesse will deliver.

In the afternoon I receive Perth and Villani. The two meetings are recorded. Perth above all wanted to point out to me that what is being said is not true: that England will not go into war under any circumstances. This is not true. England does not desire to, but it will if Germany does not know to stop where moderation advises.

Uncertain news from Prague. Hodza resigns. Military cabinet. Red flags and demonstrations in the streets. Meanwhile it seems that the Germans are occupying the cities and border crossings. Will all of this take place peacefully?

In Spain the "23 Marzo" demonstrated great bravery. Marvelous legionnaires who protest and grumble when they are at rest and who, when they attack, have once again the enthusiasm of the first battle. And they have been there for 22 months!

No specific news regarding the Hitler-Chamberlain meeting.

September 23, 1938

Yesterday evening, on the phone, Attolico led me to understand that things are not going well at Godsberg. Faced with the vagueness of the English proposals, the Führer presents 4 precise demands. Meanwhile in the Sudetenland the cannon thunders and machine-guns are firing away. During the morning things become more complicated: Chamberlain and the Führer do not meet but the former writes a letter asking to revisit the demands and reduce them. I tell the Duce. He finds the matter very serious and replies: "When one starts to adjust things in writing it means that the situation is considered desperate and responsibility is taken in front of history." Ribbentrop telephones Attolico saying that Hitler will also reply in writing, holding fast to his point. Actually there is no news of further meetings until 7 p.m., apart from one between Henderson and Ribbentrop.

I receive the Romanian minister. He takes an important step by saying that Bucharest is beginning to become aware of the situation, understands the Magyar demands, but asks that the Hungarians not act rashly and that they keep their ambitions honest. I will do my best to encourage Romania to betray the Little Entente. I will not have much to foil because they desire nothing else. Between Warsaw and Moscow the situation becomes very cloudy.

7 p.m. Pariani telephones to say that General Marras told him that "it is for tomorrow." Attolico also confirms that "the fatal course of events" is now at hand. I telephone the news to the Prefect of Florence,[331] so that he informs the Duce who is traveling to Padua.

September 24, 1938

The telephone calls continue during the night and often the news is contradictory. In the morning I know two specific points: the general mobilization in Prague and the contents of the memorandum that Hitler gave to Chamberlain: total confirmation of his requests, with October 1 as the final date for the handover of the Sudetenland and November 25 for the organization of the plebiscites in the mixed areas. Ribbentrop assures us that until such date (October 1) troops will not enter Czechoslovakia. The Duce, who wanted to return to Rome after the first news, decides to proceed with his trip and I advised him to do this. He speaks at Belluno and explains the situation precisely. From Berlin they let us know that the terms of the memorandum were to be kept secret. At this point... From France, news of mobilization. From England, also. The Yugoslav minister confirms the neutral attitude of his country in any event.

In the afternoon, Berlin telephones that Hesse will arrive in Venice, bearer of a message for the Duce, from the Führer. I take a night flight to meet with him. Beautiful flight: Venice all lit up, in a calm September evening, it seems like a crown of phosphorescent jewels.

September 25, 1938

I receive Hesse at the Grand Hotel and we leave immediately by car for Schio, where the Duce is stopping for a few hours. He does not have a written message, nor perhaps a very specific task. He must thank the Chief for what we have done and give him Hitler's promise that whatever the need, be it defense or attack, all German forces will be at our disposal. Then bring us up to date on the situation. He repeats, as facts, all of the things that we more or less know regarding the meetings with Chamberlain and the German demands. By now the point is made in a definitive manner: if by October 1st the Czechs do not accept the terms of the ultimatum, Berlin will attack. Naturally the objective will be to destroy Czechoslovakia completely. (Hesse even mentioned the possibility of incorporating, with broad autonomy, the Czechs and Slovaks into the Reich!) Hitler still thinks that France and England will not march. But if instead they should, he is ready for war. He adds, in fact, that the military and political situation is so favorable to the Axis, that maybe it is worth playing out the match, now, that one day it will inevitably have to be played. Hesse adds that Ribbentrop is still more of an extremist in this direction. The Duce receives us in the presidential train. He is stern and calm. He listens in silence to what Hesse has to say. Then, in turn, he speaks briefly. He thanks him for the communication. He explains his point of view: France will not march, because England will not take sides with her. If the conflict should, instead, become generalized, we will take our place with Germany, immediately after England goes to war. Not before, so as to not justify her going to war. The Duce also repeated his full conviction in our victory because of the strength of our forces, and the irresistible strength of the spirit.

We return to Venice. Hesse departs for Berlin and I for Rome.

In practice: no new or conclusive element resulted from the meeting. However, the Duce and I, even though not pushing Germany towards conflict, have done nothing to restrain her.

I listen to the Duce's speech in Vicenza during the flight. Then he calls me on the phone. I suggest the possibility of a meeting between myself and Ribbentrop, to get the terms of the Italian intervention straight. He also tells me of a small, initial mobilization of 25,000 men.

Very vague news from London and Paris on the cabinet meetings which have taken place. Daladier and Bonnet will be in Paris this evening. It appears that the Czech minister in London[332] has already given a negative answer to Hitler's memorandum. People are down on their knees in the streets of England praying for peace. In Italy we wait fully aware and very calm.

In the afternoon I conferred at length with Pariani who appears to be calm enough. Still more convinced of the need for lightning-fast war. He plans to use a great amount of gas, even against fortified structures.

September 26, 1938

In the morning I went with Cavagnari to the navy offices and to the Operations Office, together with the General Staff officials we examined the situation and the possibilities. Our navy has a very tough task for which, at least at the beginning, will have to withstand the blow of two strong allied nations. Japanese intervention is considered of prime importance even if this should determine American intervention.

Many diplomats: the Belgian, the Brazilian, the Polish. There is already the smell of war in the air. The last hope for everybody is tied to the message sent to the Führer from Chamberlain after the meeting that took place this morning in London. The hope is of short duration. At 7:15 p.m. Attolico telephones to say that the meeting took place. A direct contact between the Prague government and the Berlin government with a possible mediation on behalf of London was proposed. The proposal is rejected: the Führer brings forth the date of the ultimatum from October 1, to Wednesday the 28th at 2 p.m. It's war. God protect Italy and the Duce.

I receive the minister of Yugoslavia once again to dissipate the misunderstanding created by their representative in Tirana[333] who spread rumors of an immediate occupation of Albania by us. Christich disclaims responsibility for his colleague. And then I see Mackensen who informs me of an initiative taken in Berlin by the Spanish ambassador.[334] Franco, worried about his position, thinks of reopening negotiations with London and Paris to declare his neutrality. Nothing has yet been communicated to us by Conde. How sickening! Our dead in Spain must be turning in their graves. The problem of the Volunteer Corps arises. What will they do? To begin with, I give instructions to Valle so that he begins to study the evacuation of the air force. I receive the Duce at the station at 10:50 p.m. In the meantime Hitler has spoken: nothing more than what we already knew. I fill the Duce in on the latest events: he listens to me with great seriousness and compunction. He wears a serious expression both in his face and his movements: but he is also tranquil. He shows a disgusted reaction towards Spain. He concludes, stating that tomorrow he will mobilize and start sending troops in Libya. He retires to his room as soon as we arrive at Villa Torlonia. The Spaniard has taken the step towards neutrality with Buti. Although in a reduced form. He didn't dare do it with me. Anyway, after thinking it over, neutrality is the only route that Franco can follow. Our men will remain there to fight the Reds. With a cable from the Duce we suspend the repatriation.

September 27, 1938

The Duce receives Valle, Pariani and Cavagnari and gives orders to start a mobilization sufficient to assure initially an armed neutrality. Then he confers at length with me.

He is still uncertain about the position that the French and the English will adopt after the probable declaration of war, and about their military tactics. Attack the Siegfried line? Certainly not. And since Germany, once Czechoslovakia is liquidated, will not attack the west, the resolution of the conflict without the battle of the giants is still to be believed possible. Anyway, the Duce wants that the basis of the political agreement with Berlin is established right now and that the communications of the military link-up be created. He therefore proposes that I meet with Ribbentrop. The Germans accept and suggest bringing the military as well. Keitel,[335] on their side, with Pariani and Valle on ours. We will meet in Munich, Thursday, at 12:00 noon.

Nothing new on the diplomatic chessboard, except for Berlin's confirmation that "it is for tomorrow." In the afternoon I receive Villani, to whom I repeat the usual advice to remain calm, the Japanese ambassador who, in a personal capacity, says he is convinced that Tokyo will intervene on our side, and Christich, who comes to disclaim responsibility for the minister in Tirana regarding the well-known issue. He tells me that according to the Czech minister, Russian intervention will come as an air attack against Poland.

Chamberlain speaks on the radio at 8 p.m: he sounds depressed. It is the voice of a man who has given up any hope for peace by now. Indeed, short of a miracle...

September 28, 1938

10 a.m. Four hours until hostilities are to begin, when Perth telephones asking to be received. I do so immediately. He says, and he is very moved, that Chamberlain is making an appeal to the Duce for a friendly intervention in these hours which he considers to be the last useful hours to save peace and civilization. He repeats the guarantee that England and France have already offered for the return of the Sudetenland. I ask Perth if I must consider the démarche as an official invitation to the Duce to assume the role of mediator. Yes. So then there is no time to waste: the offer deserves to be taken into consideration. I tell Perth to wait for me at the Palazzo Chigi. I go to the Duce. He immediately agrees about the impossibility of flatly rejecting Chamberlain's request. He telephones Attolico: "Go to the Führer and tell him, considering that I will be by his side whatever may happen, that I advise to delay the start of the hostilities for 24 hours. In the meantime I intend to study what can be done to resolve the problem." I return to the Palazzo Chigi. I inform Perth that the hostilities will have to commence today and confirm that our place is with Germany. He was shaking and his eyes were red. When I added, though, that the Duce accommodated Chamberlain's request and proposed a 24-hour delay, he bursts into laughter full of hiccups and runs back to his embassy. Shortly after he asks for another meeting. He brings a message from Chamberlain for the Duce

and a copy of the one directed to Hitler: a concrete proposal of a conference of 4 with the task of arriving at a radical solution of the Sudeten problem within seven days. It cannot be refused: If Hitler were to do so he would attract the hatred of the entire world and would hold all the responsibility for the conflict. Palazzo Venezia: the Duce decides to support the British request, all the more so because now the Führer, agreeing with Mussolini's request, has a phonogram of instructions. I speak with Perth to inform him, I speak with Attolico to give him the directives. Naturally I cancel the meeting with Ribbentrop and Keitel, set yesterday.

From a telephone call it appears that Blondel also is preparing to make "a démarche." Not in the slightest: we do not intend to have France. The entire issue would change color and the Germans would prick up their ears with reason. I telephone Perth: "I understand that France is getting ready to interfere. I advise you that any steps taken by Blondel would be absolutely counterproductive. See to it that this does not take place. Our work would be in danger." He agrees and will act according to my request.

3 p.m. Attolico telephones to say that Hitler is in agreement in principle but has some reservations of a secondary nature.

He places one condition however: the presence of Mussolini whom he considers to be the only guarantee. The Duce accepts. We will depart at 6 p.m. this evening to be at Munich at conference by 10:30 a.m.

I return to the Duce with the American ambassador, bearer of a very-late-in-arriving message from Roosevelt. I remain alone with the Duce. He says: "As you can see, I am moderately happy because, even though paying dearly, we could have liquidated France and Great Britain once and for all. At this point, we have crushing proof."

At 6 p.m., departure. The unanimous vote of Italy is with us.

September 29-30, 1938

The Duce is in a very good mood during the trip. We dine together and talk vivaciously on all subjects. He harshly criticizes Great Britain and its politics. "When, in a country, animals are adored to the extent that cemeteries, hospitals, and homes are made for them; when legacies are left to parrots, it is a sign that decay is underway."

"However, apart from the many reasons, this also depends on the composition of the English population. 4 million more women than men. Four million sexually deprived women, who artificially create an abundance of problems to excite or placate their senses. Being unable to embrace a man, they embrace all of humanity."

Meeting with the Führer in Kufstein. We board his carriage where all of the geographical maps of the Sudetenland and western forts are spread out on the table. He describes the situation: he intends to liquidate Czechoslovakia as it is now because it pins down 40 divisions and ties his hands towards France. Once Czechoslovakia is reduced in size, as it must be, twelve divisions will be enough to keep it in check. The Duce listens to him attentively. At this point the program is clear: either the conference succeeds soon, or the solution will be sought with force. "Besides," adds the Führer, "a time will come when united we will have to fight against France and England: this might as well happen while at the head of our countries there is the Duce and I, still young and full of life."

But all of this seems overtaken by the atmosphere which has really been created: the atmosphere of an agreement. Also the people who wave along the railway line show their joy at the event which is hanging in the air.

After a brief pause at the palace where the Duce and I reside, we go to the Führerhaus,[*] where the meeting will take place. The others are already there, gathered around a table where hors d'ocuvres and drinks are prepared. The Führer comes towards us half way down the stairs and, together with all of his entourage, reserves a treatment of marked distinction for us compared to the others. Brief, cold handshake with Daladier and Chamberlain, then the Duce, alone, moves to a corner of the room where the Nazi leaders surround him. There is a dim sense of awkwardness on behalf of the French. I speak with Daladier and then with François-Poncet,[336] about insignificant, frivolous things. Then with Chamberlain who asks me to arrange for him to speak with the Duce. He thanks him for what he has done so far. But the Duce, cool, does not take advantage of the opening and the conversation dies down.

We enter into the conference room. The four leaders, Ribbentrop, Léger,[337] Wilson,[338] myself and Schmidt, the interpreter. The Führer speaks: he thanks everyone and explains the situation. He speaks calmly, but from time to time he becomes agitated and then he raises his voice and pounds his fist into the palm of his other hand. Then Chamberlain, then Daladier and finally the Duce, who states the need for a rapid and practical decision and to that end proposes to use a document as the base of the discussion, which in reality was telephoned to us the evening before from the embassy as representing the wishes of the German government.

The discussion develops normally and is not too animated. Chamberlain lingers somewhat on legal matters, Daladier defends the Czech cause without too much conviction, the Duce prefers to remain silent and recapitulate, drawing conclusions, at the end of the dissertations by the other participants.

We pause for lunch which takes place in the Führer's private home, a modest apartment in a building full of other tenants. Inside, though, there are many paintings of great value.

The meeting continues in the afternoon and virtually breaks up into many little groups that search for the right formulas. This allows us to talk more intimately, and breaks the ice.

Daladier, above all, is talkative in personal conversation. He says that what has come to pass today is due only to the obstinacy of Beneš. In recent months he had suggested many times that Beneš grant autonomy to the Sudetenland. This would have at least delayed the present crisis. He blames the warmongers of France, who apparently insisted on pushing the country

---

[*] Nazi party headquarters in Munich.

into an absurd, and above all impossible, war; since France and England could never have done anything really useful for Czechoslovakia once it had been attacked by the Reich.

The Duce, a bit bored by the vaguely parliamentary atmosphere that is always created in conferences, moves about the room a bit absentmindedly with his hands in his pockets. Every now and again he helps in the search for a formula. In his great genius, always at the forefront of events and men, the agreement is a given by now, and while the others are still fussing over more or less formal problems, he is almost no longer interested. He is already ahead and thinking of other things.

But he takes the floor once again when it is time to bring out into the open the problem of the Magyar and Hungarian minorities. The others, all the others, would have rather not discussed it. In fact they try to avoid the discussion. But, as is always the case when there is a strong will, it dominates and the others join around him. The problem is discussed and resolved using a formula which I do not hesitate to call very brilliant.

Meanwhile bilateral meetings take place. There is the mention also of the possibility of a delay in the Duce's departure to allow him to meet with Chamberlain. But the Duce rejects the idea since he thinks that it could irritate German feelings. I speak with Chamberlain and then the Duce. We more or less say the same things: no interest towards Spain, withdrawal of 10,000 Volunteers at hand, well disposed to enact our treaty of April 16. Chamberlain mentions the possibility of a four-power conference to resolve the Spanish problem.

Finally, at 1 a.m. in the morning, the document is complete. Everyone is satisfied, even the French; even the Czechs, according to what Daladier tells me. François-Poncet, collating the document, turns red for a moment and exclaims: "Voilà comme la France traite les seuls alliés qui lui étaient restés fidèles." *

Signing, handshakes, departure.

In Italy, from the Brenner Pass to Rome, from the King to the peasants, the Duce receives welcomes as I have never seen. He, himself, says that an equal warmth was felt only on the evening of the proclamation of the Empire.

Ribbentrop has sent me a project for a Tripartite Alliance between Italy, Germany, and Japan. He says that it is the "greatest thing in the world." Always given to hyperbole, Ribbentrop. I think that we will study it calmly and perhaps set it aside for a while.

October 1, 1938

This morning, still some minor excitement. Prague informs us that Beck has sent an ultimatum, expiring at noon, for the relinquishing of the requested territories. In principle the Czechs agree, but they would like some time to conveniently prepare things. They are not in the wrong. This Polish impa-

---

* "This is the way France treats the only allies who had remained true to her."

tience is not justified: they have waited twenty years, they can wait a few days so as to avoid an incident which could once again make the situation difficult. I telephone these things to our ambassador in Warsaw and I instructed him to take steps with Beck. I personally speak to the representative in Rome.

France and England also move. While Ribbentrop, who in reality is not too happy that everything went so smoothly, telephones me to say that he will not take any initiatives in Warsaw and practically incites the Polish to attack. The ultimatum is postponed by an hour: after which, Prague yields and this difficulty is also resolved. The truth is that the Poles have become intransigent because they were not invited to Munich and because they fear revival of the Four-Power Pact.

Many diplomats, in the afternoon, among whom, Perth, to whom I mention the next resumption of contacts; Christich, who reads me a cordial letter from Stoyadinovich, and Hotta, who accompanies Shigemitsu,[339] an old colleague from Shanghai who he last saw years ago in extremely dramatic circumstances. Now he is to become ambassador in London.

October 2, 1938

The Prince of Hesse has been instructed by the Führer to explain to me why the Munich conference had the codicil of an British-German committee. Chamberlain asked the Führer for an audience and he spoke of the possible conference regarding Spain, as well as an unbelievable proposal to abolish air force bombers among the four Powers (sic!). Finally, he took a piece of paper out of his pocket with the draft of the communiqué, which he said was necessary for his parliamentary position. The Führer did not think he could refuse. And the Duce, to whom I related these things, said to me: "The explanations were superfluous. One does not deny a lemonade to a man who is thirsty."

The Duce and I examined the question of our relations with London. After what was said to Chamberlain in Munich we should not delay in negotiating with Perth. I will call him tomorrow and officially communicate to him the withdrawal of the 10,000 Volunteers. After which I will clearly propose the query: Do you now wish to enact the Treaty of April 16?

If they do so, fine. Otherwise everyone will play their own game: the Duce says to also point out that the Grand Council might denounce this treaty which has been waiting to be ratified for too long.

In the evening the Duce communicates to me, by phone, the *Informazione Diplomatica* n. *21*, regarding Hungary.

October 3, 1938

Villani asks for our support to accelerate the realization of the decisions taken at Munich concerning Hungary. From what he says, and above all from what he does not say, it is clear that the Hungarians are thinking about Slovakia. Mistake, big mistake, to which I am personally opposed. There would be a Romanian, Yugoslav, German reaction. Secondly, the Slovaks don't want it. And it is not worth canceling one injustice to commit others.

I have the meeting with Perth. I speak as agreed upon with the Duce. The arguments are so convincing that he himself cannot make any serious objections, and he tries to bring up the question of the airplanes. I advise to not raise new difficulties and to stick to the terms of our previous agreements. I confirm that it is useless to speak of a Four-Power conference, or of other visits, until relations are normalized: these may follow, not precede, the coming into force of the Treaty. I add, finally, that an answer, even if provisional, ought to be given before October 6, because the Grand Council will have to consider foreign policy and crystallize situations which at the moment have never been defined in diplomatic documents.[340]

I receive the Brazilian, the Romanian and the Portuguese. I telephone Prunas to say that if a French ambassador must come, it better not be Chambrun,[341] as the papers are saying.

He has been liquidated by his talk on the nonexistent friendship with the Duce and by the bullet that Fontanges[342] fired at his backside.

October 4, 1938

After some requests of minor importance I receive Lord Perth, at his request. He wants some clarifications following yesterday's meeting and namely: does Italy intend to no longer send troops after the withdrawal of the 10,000, and is it willing to not increase the number of nationalist pilots and airplanes? The answer to the first query is obvious, and I immediately give it. As to the second, I reserve the decision to the Duce. And I did the right thing because he rejects an undertaking which would clearly weaken Franco's position too much.

Prunas calls with the Parisian decisions regarding the ambassador, which appears to be François-Poncet. The news is rather indifferent to us. It is good that the French have capitulated, but we do not want this to excite some Italians.

A certain Kworchak[343](?), already known to me and whom the Duce sends to me, backs the idea of uniting Slovakia to Hungary. I am very doubtful of this. The Duce likes the Hungarians, in fact he says that he has sympathy for them alone in all of Europe. I don't quite trust them. After Slovakia, Croatia's time will come. And the Germans, who do not dare overlook the problem of the outlet on the Adriatic, will decide to map out this route through the Magyars, who in time will return to the inevitable traditional politics of gravitating towards Berlin. In the small map shown to me yesterday evening there was, among the claims, also Fiume. This is significant. No: our true friendship is with Belgrade.

October 5, 1938

I inform Villani that in case of Czech attack (something which we absolutely exclude) Hungary can count on the immediate dispatch of 100 fighter planes and the accompanying pilots for the defense of Budapest. We discuss Slovakia. Hungarian appetites are increasing more and more. I advise moderation. And then, to the Duce, I show how much I learned yesterday after the meeting with the Slovak propagandist, whom I discovered is a former boxer, paid by the Magyars.

The Duce agrees as well and comes to the conclusion that we must consolidate ties with Belgrade.

I see Perth and tell him of the Chief's decisions.

Chvalkovsky has been nominated Foreign Minister and is preparing to go to Prague. He has always been a friend and saw the situation clearly. Now he plans to end the problems with the three neighboring states and clearly wants to enter into the Axis orbit. "Friendship with the Axis: intimacy with Rome" is my advice, which he accepts entirely. Prague, at this point, must enter into that horizontal Axis, which should extend from Rome to Warsaw and, being very strong, could enhance the existence of the vertical Axis. I take the minister to see the Duce, who repeats the same advice to him. He says he has always been convinced that French and British help was impossible. In England they know nothing about Bohemia. Once, when he was a student in London, he was given a violin to play at a party simply because they knew him to be Czech. They got Bohemians confused with Tziganes. Now he thinks of also going to Berlin to introduce himself to the Führer.

October 6, 1938

Perth brings the British reply. It accepts in principle the coming into force of the treaty after the withdrawal of the 10,000 troops. But Chamberlain asks for some breathing space for the moment. He doesn't want to go to the Cabinet and to the House, saying: "Here it is. Take it or leave it. Mussolini set me a date." Otherwise his position, which despite the vote of confidence is shaky today, and will become indefensible. He asks for time until November 1. The Duce, who initially reacted against the English reply, ended up agreeing. Naturally, he does not intend to give any assurance for the air force and its activity.

Grand Council. Problem of the Jews. Balbo, De Bono, and Federzoni speak in their favor. The others, against. Above all Bottai, who surprises me with his intransigence. He opposes any extenuation of the measures. "They will hate us because we have driven them away. They will spurn us because we readmit them." During the break, the Duce says to me: "The discriminations don't count. We must raise the problem. Anti-Semitism is now inoculated in the blood of the Italians. It will continue to circulate and develop on its own. Then, even if I am accommodating this evening, I will be very harsh in the preparation of the laws."

October 7, 1938

I give Perth our reply. No particular reaction. Barring something new, I think the Treaty is now on its way towards ratification in a few weeks time.

Grand Council. Discussion about the Chamber of Fasces and Corporations. No participation, of particular interest, to the debate. The Duce made a veiled mention to the Albanian projects: "I was born to never leave the Italians in peace. First Africa, today Spain, tomorrow something else still." The Grand Council applauded.

Our position is set regarding the Polish Magyar demands. No Slovakia; for this, full freedom of decision: thus, maybe with Prague or maybe autonomous. Common border between Hungary and Poland, through Sub-Carpathian Russia. It seems though, that Berlin is about to make this solution difficult as well. And, from a German point of view, this is logical. Instead, I don't understand the Romanian opposition. Since Czechoslovakia, at this point, will not be much more than an appendix of Germany, are they really keen, these good Romanians, on having a common border with the Germans? Do they not understand that the Polish-Magyar contact would be a real barrier in their favor? And, in our situation, it is very delicate to say this.

October 8, 1938

Villani lists Hungary's territorial requests: the Magyar land, Sub-Carpathian Russia and a Plebiscite for the Solvaks. But news from Berlin clearly shows the silent opposition of the Germans to handing over the internal territories.

I spoke at length, and successfully, at the Grand Council on the international situation. The Duce, who listened to the speech with uttermost attention, defined the report of comrade Ciano as: "Interesting, precise, and at times, dramatic."

October 9, 1938

The Duce telephones me to tell me that he found "my report to be very brilliant and that the Grand Council appreciated it very much."

I go to Florence, and then to Ponte a Moriano with Edda and Ciccino.

October 10, 1938

The Hungarian minister dramatizes the situation and even speaks of general mobilization. I don't believe it. He tells me, in great secrecy, that some internal bands will go into action today. They have informed us and the Poles: they don't entirely trust the Germans.

I accompany Grandi to see the Duce: an unimportant meeting. Then the Duce speaks to me about De Vecchi and says: "Maybe what I am about to say will appear Mephistophelean, but it is better to do it this way. De Vecchi has always created nothing but trouble wherever I have put him. He has never known how to do anything. Now, in Rhodes, he is doing very badly. But it doesn't matter. In fact, he must be encouraged so that he does even worse. Give him the feeling of approving his work, grease the pathway so that he takes a slide so big, so permanent, so that he sees himself finished in his own eyes, more so than in the eyes of the others. And then I will be rid of him forever."

October 11, 1938

During the morning I received a long procession of people, but no important meeting took place, except for an exchange of opinions with Pierre Lyautey,[344] whom I have known for a long time and to whom I can speak openly. I told him how the French press is sinister in relations between the two countries: it has not yet understood anything of fascist psychology and less still of that of Mussolini. If there is one thing in a million that can make the Duce furious: well then it is just that issue that is bandied about. Also the atmosphere of Munich has rapidly been spoiled by the French press. I take Hesse to see the Duce. He describes initiatives taken by Poncet in Berlin for an agreement between Franco and Germany, similar to the one made with London. He also speaks of a possible consultation pact between the Four powers to be actuated should war threaten Europe. We will agree to go ahead on two conditions: that first our relations with England be regulated through the coming into force of the April 10 Treaties and that Poland is also invited. We will let France and England be the ones to escort her out. They will have to bear the indignity. Yugoslavia does not aspire to take part in the European Directorate. Stoyadinovich says that he was "le coq qui chante sur son fumier."* His "fumier" is the Balkans.

October 12, 1938

The Duce telephones me in the evening to have me put pressure on Prague for the immediate cession of the territories with a clear Hungarian majority to the Magyars. He was urged by the military attaché,[345] who told him also of Budapest's intention to mobilize tomorrow, if the Czechs continue their obstructionist maneuvers. Meanwhile, he lets me know that the new Foreign Minister Chvalkovsky has gone to Berlin and then to Berchtesgaden be place himself under the capable, and not disinterested, wings of Hitler.

October 13, 1938

Sereggi comes to bring me a personal message from the King, and also leaves me a note regarding the declarations that he has been ordered to make. Namely: that Albania is now in Italy's hands; we now control every sector of national activity. The King is devoted. The people grateful. Why do you want more? This question was not asked, but it was the real reason for the meeting. I was kind and affable. This reassured him. And above all he appreciated it when I told him, in no uncertain terms, that I have much sympathy for him and in all eventualities I consider him our man. We must move quickly with this Albania. I received Prampolini, who brought me his magnificent study of the complete reclamation of the country. He is enthusiastic with what he has seen. He judges the coastal regions to be far superior to ours and thinks, without exaggerated optimism, that from just one area of reclamation we could import 200,000,000 kilograms of grain into Italy.

Perth proposes sending the military attaché to Naples to assist with the disembarking of the Volunteers returning from Spain. We give our authorization in principle: it seems that the matter is useful to Chamberlain for the parliamentary debates which are expected to be difficult.

---

* *fumier*: dung heap.

Villani returns with the unsettled Hungarian requests. The truth is that they would like to have Slovakia, Ruthenia, everything. Create a mosaic state n. 3. They don't dare say so. Because they fear Germany. He told me that Mussolini had advised Szabo[346] to mobilize. Is this true?

October 14, 1938

Hesse asks, in the name of the Führer, if Germany can make a declaration to France similar to that made to England. Authorization on our behalf, all the more so because this will give us leeway with Paris.

The situation between Budapest and Prague gets tense. Negotiations are interrupted. Hungarian mobilization is underway. Count Czaky[347] arrives. Confers with the Duce and me. He wants authorization for the mobilization and our support for the immediate call of a conference of the Four Powers. He is very excited, above all against the Germans. He accuses the Reich of having allowed the stiff attitude by Prague towards the Hungarians. Czechoslovakia is by now a German protectorate, which Berlin intends to use to increase pressure on Romania and Hungary itself. He says that since oil has been discovered in Hungary, German policy has changed and is becoming unbearable. "But," he concludes, "before allowing ourselves to be swallowed up, we will die, down to the last one of us."

Following the Hungarian request we intervene in London, Paris and Berlin to support the proposal of the conference. I also speak with the Polish ambassador and the minister of Yugoslavia to smooth over the two difficult situations. Then Ribbentrop calls me on the phone. The Germans, as expected, are opposed to the conference. They say there will be opposition on the part of France and England, and that it is better to act behind the scenes. Since I resist, Ribbentrop ends up accepting the proposal. But Czaky comes to see me again. Budapest is worried about Berlin's behavior. They are obviously embarrassed toward us, after what they have urgently requested and obtained, but now they prefer to avoid displeasing the Germans, and abandon the idea of a conference and accept direct negotiations. All the more so, since Hitler has said he has now demobilized and doesn't intend to face a new crisis. I go to see the Duce at Villa Torlonia. We grin and bear it and approve the German idea. Although today is the first time we were in tow which annoys me a lot.

October 15, 1938

The Duce, who has obviously mulled over what happened yesterday, telephones me to propose to the Germans that an identical step be made to Prague and Budapest, to invite the two governments to resume direct negotiations. This to explain, at least in part, yesterday's change of course. Ribbentrop is against it: he says that a similar step could look like pressure, which is dangerous under the present circumstances. He asks us instead to support the Hungarian request of yesterday in Prague, minus Presburg, which the Germans like. The Duce approves. Czaky comes to say goodbye, and presses me to intervene with Prague to appeal for clemency for the forty

Hungarian rebels, made prisoners in Ruthenia by the Czechs. They are all right-wing elements. If they were to be hanged, he says, it would create as many martyrs for the opposition parties and Imredy's position, who telephoned about this, would be shaken very dangerously. I telephone Prague. In the afternoon Franzoni informs me that the Czech government received our step with utmost cordiality and that the Hungarian prisoners will be spared. At this point we can ask anything of Prague with the certainty of getting a hearing.

The Duce, having read reports from Poland, tells me to let Berlin know that we do not at all support a common Polish-Magyar border. He believes that it is not at all useful and that every German attempt of encirclement is, besides being stupid, totally absurd.

I send the message, but I confess that, as far as I am concerned, I would have seen the welding between Hungary and Poland with great pleasure. Life is long and can provide many surprises...

October 16, 1938

Nothing noteworthy, apart from a brief meeting with the Duce, during which I consign to him the Prampolini report on land reclamation in Albania, and I propose beginning the reclamation in Durazzo as soon as possible. It is the most economical, the most impressive, and useful for military purposes, and it serves to placate the not unjustified worries of the King.

October 17, 1938

I transmitted the approval of François-Poncet to Blondel. He asked me when we would nominate our representative in Paris, but I didn't respond and let the subject drop.

Receive Villani who explains the Hungarian requests. Prague should make a specific offer. Such offer will be examined by Budapest without new negotiations being initiated. If it appears convenient, it will be accepted. Otherwise the Axis powers may function as arbitrators.

I telephone Chvalkovsky in Prague to support the Magyar requests.

October 18, 1938

Police magazine: very well done. New progress compared to that of the last few years.

Nothing new in politics.

In the Grand Council: a long report by Starace, a summary by the Duce, very brilliant (anti-Catholic: he described the Vatican as the Catholic ghetto. And he said that all the Piuses had brought misfortune to the Church. He described the current Pope as "the Pontiff who will leave the greatest heap of debris behind him."). A jumbled speech by De Vecchi who greatly amused the assembly. He was unaware of what was really going on and thought he was being very successful and so he over did it, speaking nonsense, expressing himself in terms unprecedented in a political assembly.

October 19, 1938

The Duce has gone to Romagna. There is nothing new. Franzoni made the démarche with Prague. But maybe he went a little too far, immediately mentioning the possible mediation of the Axis. Apparently Chvalkovsky was impressed. I didn't mention this to Villani and he thought that all went well.

Sereggi, leaving for Albania, receives the assurance of our cordial collaboration and the promise to do something regarding land reclamation. Actually I proposed to the Duce, who still has the Prampolini project with him, that we should immediately start working on the Plain of Durazzo. There are 3,000 hectares reclaimable for less than 20 million lire. This will soothe the worries of the Albanians. It will partially prepare our future work. And will serve also for military purposes, since every landing of the troops will have to take place in Durazzo, and its immediate surroundings. Also from a psychological point of view it is useful that those soldiers and civilians landing in Albania feel that they are in a healthy and fertile land and not in a desolate swamp. A better impression would have perhaps changed history in 1920 and we would have committed ourselves more seriously.

October 20, 1938

Yesterday evening Ribbentrop called me on the phone. He told me at length that he had received the Slovak and Ruthenian representatives and negotiated a final plan to propose to Budapest. The minister of Germany will get orders to go to Kanya and strongly advise acceptance by the Magyars. I guessed, rather than learned, that the plan is not good for the Hungarians. Ribbentrop was holding back, and when I spoke about the common border between Hungary and Poland he slipped away. The Duce does not intend to put pressure on Budapest. I spoke to Villani with this in mind: "If you accept the plan, that could be called German, that's fine and we are happy. Otherwise, let us know what we can do for you."

I went to Naples to receive the Spanish legionnaires. They are very proud and not at all tired by the long campaign in a foreign country. The people greeted them well, but not with that warmth that I expected. The King, with whom I shared the car, and with whom I had a conversation at the Palace, is almost indifferent and does not have one warm word for the legionnaires. He considers today's event as one of the many ceremonies that he must take part in. He mainly discusses Cora, whom he no longer wants as Palace Prefect, and he asks me to be the one to get rid of him. On politics: little. He limits himself to repeat his skepticism of the Germans whom he judges to be untrustworthy and dangerous, and of his sympathy for the English who know how to stand by their agreements just as the Vienna of the Hapsburgs used to.

October 21, 1938

Villani, first thing in the morning, tells me about the disgust and reaction of the Hungarians to the Czech proposal. Disgust towards Germany, who made it clear that it considers its mediation efforts have thus ended, an anti-Czech reaction, because they try to withdraw 5 cities from the Magyar demands. Now, while the Hungarians are ready to compromise on Presburg and Nitra, they will not do so with the cities of the eastern zone and particularly with Kassa, to which they could not renounce without provoking a revolution in the country. The Hungarian plan to ask the arbitration of the Axis for the western zone; the Axis plus Poland for the eastern zone. I telephone the Duce who agrees, but advises to feel Germany's pulse before inviting Poland.

I met Barzini Junior,[348] to whom I give details to write the Italian chapter of a book entitled *Four Days*, about the crucial days of the Czech crisis.

The Polish ambassador, informed by Budapest, wants our point of view on the arbitration. I will tell him. Wieniawa is a cavalry general, bright enough yet without expertise, but who has the great ability of being concise and efficient. I compliment him on this and he replies: "In life one can recapture all things lost, even women, but not time." He informs me also of the negative results of Beck's trip to Romania.

Von Mackensen brings me, under orders from Ribbentrop, the document of the Czech proposal. It is clear that the Germans are acting as emissaries of Prague. He is disappointed when I inform him of the exact situation and above all turns up his nose at the idea of adding Poland. He knew nothing about it.

Hotta leaves Rome. I congratulate him on the victory at Canton. Hotta is a good man but a little cold and a bit fearful, he didn't accept the new era. We were making the triangle policy and he constantly spoke about London...

October 22, 1938

Ribbentrop telephoned from Munich about the proposal of arbitration by the Axis. He is against it and his arguments are captious. The truth is that he intends to protect Czechoslovakia for as long as possible and sacrifice the ambitions, even though legitimate, of the Magyars. According to him, arbitration is dangerous because it will end up upsetting Prague and Budapest, obliging us to resort to force, to enact the decisions. I told him that this is to be excluded because arbitration provides for the prior agreement of the parties to accept the results. He had many points against the Magyars, who had switched their position. As hostile as he is, he is nowhere near as much as the Hungarians are towards him. He will telephone again after having conferred with Hitler: he aired the possibility of a Four Power conference. And yet it was he who excluded this eight days ago!

Conde gave me a painting by Zuloaga, a gift from the Caudillo. Beautiful and vibrant remembrance of the war in Spain: "el mas Viejo requeté," with a countryside full of war and flames as background landscape.

I learn once again from the Romanian minister, through the frantic quest for friendship with us, of the eagerness of that country to escape from, or at least protect itself, from the sinister threat of Germanism. The Duce has approved the reclamation of the Durazzo Plain on the left side of the Arzen.

October 23, 1938

Very early, Villani was pleading the case of his country. He would like us to insist with the Germans for arbitration because he is certain that without our pressure they will sabotage it. The tension between the Magyars and the Germans is high even though both sides make an effort to hide it. They accuse each other of falsehoods as far as the three eastern cities, Kassa, Ungvar, and Munkacs, are concerned.

The Magyars, in support of their theory, cite the testimony of the German minister to Budapest himself,[349] who cannot though, for obvious reasons, make it public. Villani has harsh words about Germany. He worries for the future of Imredy's Cabinet and fears the coming to power of Szalazy,[350] according to him, a paid agent of Berlin.

Ribbentrop telephones in the evening. He repeats, putting the words into the Führer's mouth, what he said the evening before. He doesn't want the arbitration, because he would have shown the Hungarians what he really thought. Then he asks me if he could come to Rome at the end of the week to confer personally with the Duce and myself. I reply that it is fine. What does he want? I do not trust Ribbentrop's initiatives. He is vain, fickle, and talkative. The Duce says that all you have to do is look at his head to see that he has a small brain. And he also has little tact. These recent telephone calls have had the effect of making me not like him at all: always trying to impose his point of view. For the moment it is best to grin and bear it. But at the right time we will need to put a stop to this tendency of making policy by telephone.

October 24, 1938

Brief meeting with the Pole, who has nothing to tell me and nothing to ask me.

General Berti receives confirmation from me that he is being replaced in Spain and he seems very put out. More than his removal, he is annoyed by the nomination of Gambara with whom he has had continuous clashes. And to think that it is precisely because of these disagreements that I was induced to propose his nomination.

I see the Duce after four days of absence. He is fed up with the Czech-Magyar shilly-shallying and gives me instructions to take a clear position against the Ruthenian demands, since the French press has given an anti-German flavor to the attempt of creating a common Polish-Hungarian border. He wants a legal opinion to find out if the projected annexation of Libya could give reason to the English to quibble over the ratification of the agreement to which "I attach no importance," he says, "but it is desired by that half a million cowardly bourgeois who still exist and against whom I will launch a third attack." He speaks to me of some of his ideas regarding a Five-Power treaty about the reduction of armaments: bringing the war back on a more heroic plane, eliminating all that is too complex in the mechanism of war. In practice, to limit those weapons which are too expensive for us.

The Belgian ambassador brings me a decoration, and the Hungarian ambassador, the usual expression of gratitude.

But the negotiations do not move ahead.

Long meeting with Buffarini, who sounds the alarm over what he judges to be the dangerous ubiquity of the Party in all sectors of national life. As much as he exaggerates, there is truth to it.

October 25, 1938

Pirelli is true to himself: he comes to strike a blow for the immediate dispatch of an ambassador to Paris, since the French have made "a nice gesture." When I told the Duce, he said, "It's against this disgusting, cowardly bourgeoisie that I shall let loose the third wave during my speech today at the National Council of Fascism. He receives the Spanish ambassador who brings him a Grand Collar. The Duce reaffirms his uncompromising attitude on the subject of Spain: to end the war with a victory means preparing a heroic and Imperial Spain; to end the war through a mediation means precipitating the country into the conditions it was in when Calvo Sotelo[351] was killed and the crisis began. He also committed himself to giving more aid to Franco with arms and reinforcements: no longer with men because, firstly, they are not needed and secondly, because we are closely watched and any projected sending of Volunteers would put us in a difficult position with the English. Anyway—the Duce concluded—the end is approaching: the Reds will surrender, not straight away perhaps, but soon, because the defeat of Prague has also sealed the defeat of Barcelona. And if Franco wins militarily he will have the necessary prestige required to govern just as Kemal Pasha[352] lived for twenty years on the undisputed merit of having liberated the country with arms.

Buffarini comes to complete his complaint about Starace: according to him he places the country under the oppression of his personal-sectarian tyranny and the principle cause of the restlessness and gloominess of many areas of national life should perhaps be found in this. I have no facts by which to judge, but it is positive that everyone, as soon as they can, express themselves in this manner. It is a fact that Starace has many enemics. The Party is not healthy and, using the pretext of depersonalization, it has never been as personalized as it is now. But he also has many qualities as organizer, he gets things done, and perhaps he is loyal. Anyway, for the moment nothing can be done. The Duce supports him with a drawn sword. When the time comes, we'll see.

October 26, 1938

Yesterday evening, at the Grand Council, lively discussion regarding Balbo's proposal to grant citizenship to the Arabs. It was easy to detect a clear contradiction with the racial policy. The hardliners, like Farinacci, Starace, Alfieri, did not hesitate to take a position against him. I did the same. The project has been deferred and will be presented in a completely different form. It is interesting to notice how the Grand Council is anti-Balbo. All it took was that the measure looked like it was inspired by Balbo for a massive alignment against it to appear.

I confirm to Senator Prampolini instructions to begin reclamation works in the plain of Durazzo, on the left and then the right of the River Arzen.

Other than the advantages that I previously listed the other time, there is that very important one of allowing the concentration of the two legions of workers, which can be the bridgehead of the landing force.

I receive Berger-Waldenegg. I haven't seen him since the time of the Anschluss. He is serene, dignified and a gentleman. He has neither recriminations nor regrets. He sees the situation clearly: there are still rough edges in Austria, but everything will be straightened out in the end. The new generation will be Nazi. The most serious obstacle is created by the fight against religion. He will remain in Italy. He wants to work because he needs to. I promised to help him and I will do so as soon as possible.

October 27, 1938

Meeting with Jacomoni.[353] The preparation in Albania proceeds rapidly, so much so that maybe it would be best to quicken the pace because in the King's circles there is some alarm. The action seems to be clear: the assassination of the King (it seems that Koçi will handle it for the compensation of ten million lire), demonstrations in the streets, the bands loyal to us descend from the hills (practically all of the leaders, except for that of Kmia), an appeal to Italy for political intervention and, if the case be, military, offer of the crown to the King Emperor and later on, annexation. Jacomoni guarantees that all this can take place regularly with one month's prior notice.

The Duce hopes to talk to Ribbentrop about the fight against Catholicism: "It is idiotic and useless, and makes the Axis unpopular among the Italian Catholic masses." At the Palazzo Venezia, De Vecchi gave a long report of the military situation of the Dodecanesus, which can be summarized like this: the navy is splendid, the army is good, the air force is rotten. And I think that goes for the rest of the country.

The military and naval[354] attachés of Japan bring me the treaty of the tripartite Alliance, identical to the one provided by Ribbentrop in Munich. I still think it should be kept on ice, all the more so because Perth secretly told me of the British decision to implement the Treaty of April, starting around mid-November. We must keep both doors open. The alliance today would close one door, maybe forever, and not the least important one. The Duce, to whom I mentioned it quickly, seems to think along the same lines.

October 28, 1938

Actually, Ribbentrop came because of the three-power military alliance. We discussed it yesterday evening at the Grand Hotel. He repeated what he said last May: he has a fixation about war on his mind, he wants war, his war. He doesn't have or doesn't say what his general marching plan is. He doesn't single out his enemies, nor does he indicate the objectives. But he wants war within three or four years. I was reserved to the utmost, but I let him understand that we still have other problems to solve and perhaps other ideas about the future organization of international life. Recent events have proved the great solidarity existing between the totalitarian states. The alliance exists in point of fact. Why create rumors with a pact that would have no other consequences than to draw upon us the hatred for the aggressor?

Czech-Magyar issue. He had not understood the political importance of the arbitration of the Axis. I told him it seals the failure of every French-British influence in Danubian and Balkan Europe forever. It is a gigantic event: of an importance as great as that of Munich. Maybe he is convinced. But he is hostile to the Hungarians and defends the Czech cause with a commitment that I would call shameless.

Another meeting this morning. He repeated the concepts discussed yesterday evening and in addition agreed to the opportunity of helping Franco through final victory.

I tell the Duce. He agrees on the need to postpone the stipulation of the alliance to a later date, an alliance which would not at all be popular in Italy, above all because of the anti-German bitterness dominant in the great Catholic masses. The Duce speaks to me about France and explains how French military heroism is determined by the instinct to defend personal property: *la ferme, la cave, l'argent.** For Italians war means the defense of the borders; for the French, who are rich and in the habit of saving money, it is the conservation of their own belongings. This explains why the French are such good soldiers on the defensive.

The Hungarian minister waits anxiously for the results of the meetings with Ribbentrop. I receive him for a brief moment at the Palazzo Chigi. I don't tell him everything, because this would worry him more than necessary, but I let him understand that the German opposition to the solution they wish is strong and that I will have to work hard to remove it. Ribbentrop speaks with hostility, not only of the Magyar leaders, but at this point of the entire population. This is bad. Very bad. And, maybe, instructive. After having cultivated friendship and Hungarian illusions for twenty years, they abandon them, or rather they oppose them when helping them represents a small sacrifice. I fought with much energy. If the arbitration is to take place, I think they will manage to grab the three eastern cities from the Germans. But it will be a very hard battle.

In the afternoon the three-way meeting takes place at the Palazzo Venezia. Notes taken. Ribbentrop, who perhaps expected a pure and simple acceptance of the alliance offer, was taken aback, so much so that the Duce asks me to speak to him once again after lunch to stress the idea that postponement does not mean refusal of solidarity between the Axis powers, which is total even without a written document.

I also speak with Hesse. Ribbentrop was shocked when I mentioned the consultation pact between the great powers that was proposed by Hesse in Hitler's name on October 11. Hesse confirms the fact and gives the details: he says he received instructions from Göring, in the Führer's carriage and in his presence, while they were making the first trip to the Sudeten region. It is

---

* "The farm, the wine cellar, the money."

very strange that the Foreign Minister knows nothing, but it is not the first time that something like this happens in Germany. This further proves the existence of two rivals: Göring, who wants to organize peace, and Ribbentrop, who intends to prepare for war.

After lunch I summon Villani to my home to make some suggestions that I believe useful for the Hungarian cause. Villani, in a personal capacity, mentions the possibility of putting Aosta on the throne of Hungary. It would be interesting to establish just how much seriousness there is in this overture.

October 29, 1938

At the Villa Torlonia the Duce writes up a brief note of reply to Germany regarding the alliance: a provisional acceptance, the date being deferred and fixing the principle of the alliance as offensive rather than defensive. He reads it to Ribbentrop during the afternoon meeting and gives him a copy. Nothing new at today's meeting, after which Ribbentrop comes to the Palazzo Chigi where we set some points in relation to the arbitration of Vienna. Ribbentrop doggedly defended the Czech cause and denied the territory to the Hungarians with the same forcefulness with which, in Munich, he exacted it from Prague. Although I have the impression that, by insisting, we will manage to succeed regarding the three eastern cities.

October 30, 1938

The Hungarians come to give me useful information for the discussion with Ribbentrop about the arbitration. Leading them is Count Esterhazy whom I have already met several times in Budapest and even in Tirana where he distinguished himself as a dancer of czardas. I didn't know that the leader of the Magyar minorities in Czechoslovakia was the same Esterhazy that I had admired for his dancing virtues, and it seemed strange to me to discuss borders and such important problems with him. I had retained an admiration for the dancer! And this aristocrat at the head of the movement explained to me the many oscillations, uncertainties and fears that the Hungarians have felt in these past few weeks.

To cut a long story short: they would be happy if they could have Kassa, Ungvar and Munkacs. I will also try to improve the position of Nitra, of which the center can be considered as lost but not the surrounding countryside, which can be saved.

In the evening Mackensen comes to tell me, on Ribbentrop's behalf, that he agrees with the need to give the Magyars the three disputed cities.

October 31, 1938

The Duce approves my negotiation plans for Munich. He is pleased with what is happening. It must be confirmed that he was the first to speak of arbitration and, as always, he saw clearly. He predicts a period of relaxation in Europe. He does not want, though, to ease up on the French, with whom an insurmountable abyss must be created. This will be made easy for us if, as it seems, they are starting to behave like Celt nationalists.

Lord Perth tells me some details regarding the parliamentary discussions for the implementation of the April treaty.

I leave for Bolzano. At the station, many comrades and, notably, Starace with the entire National Directorate of the Party.

November 1, 1938

A visit to the industrial area of Bolzano, which is already very large and in full development. The appearance of the city is transformed from Nordic to Mediterranean. Mastromattei's[355] hand is perhaps a little crude, but very effective. In ten years time, or even less, it will be difficult to recognize the Bozen of old in Bolzano.

Marriage ceremony at the villa of the Dukes of Pistoia.[356] Nothing interesting except for the contrast between the old fashioned ceremonial and dress of the Royal Family in the purely twentieth century setting of the residence. Certain livery and some bows clash with the new furniture.

Cheering crowd at the station. I find Ansaldo on the train, with whom I discuss matters at length. He is the most educated and intelligent journalist that the Regime has.

Innsbruck. I make a quick tour of the city. It's cold. Few people in the streets.

Romano, the consul, says that Innsbruck suffered from the Anschluss very much: it survives mostly on foreign tourism, which has completely stopped. Anyway, the Regime is taking root in the working classes: there are no longer any unemployed. The friction that exists is of a personal nature and, at the most, could be the case of one generation.

November 2, 1938

Vienna. Ribbentrop is at the station. New atmosphere. The crowd greets me with warmth and friendliness. I remember the cold welcome of two years or so ago that the Vienna of Schuschnigg reserved for me. Something has changed: life has returned to this city and the resentment that existed towards us has given way to gratitude for having consented to this result.

At the hotel, meeting with Göring. Dressed in civilian clothes, with an expensive and loud gray suit. His tie, knotted in an old fashioned style, has a ruby ring pinned on it. Other large rubies on his fingers. On his lapel, a large Nazi eagle with diamonds. He vaguely resembles "Al Capone."

He sounds off against the Hungarians. He says that they are in cahoots with Western Democracies. That's harsh: I protest and he doesn't insist. He also mentions the possibility of a union between Yugoslavia and Bulgaria, strongly attacking King Boris.[357] The matter does not interest us. Göring believed it did because of Queen Giovanna.[358]

First meeting with Ribbentrop. He tries to pull strings as much as he can in favor of Czechoslovakia. He doesn't want to give up all three cities. Above all Munkacs, since he claims that if Hungary is to have the three cities, Romania will not be able to survive. I insist, with some vigor, as soon as I am sure that he intends to make himself the defender of Prague's cause.

He is unprepared, very unprepared, for the discussion. He is not at all well documented and his staff officer is also not up to date on the issues. This makes it easy for me.

November 3, 1938

Belvedere. First official meeting. The Slovaks defend their case rather well. The Hungarians less, that is: Kanya really badly, unnecessarily acid and argumentative, not very convincing and cold in his reasoning; Count Teleki[359] better, more documented and calm. Ribbentrop changed his attitude from the first morning conversation; he is moving closer to our point of view and in guiding the conversation he keeps to a procedure substantially favorable to the Hungarians.

Lunch and meetings with the various delegates. Afterwards, Ribbentrop and I, followed by a few staff members, go into a private meeting in the gold Cabinet. I take the lead in the discussion and, except for a few disagreements, trace the line of the new border with a red pencil. Ribbentrop's unpreparedness allows me to slice areas of territory in favor of Hungary, which, in truth, could have been the subject of much controversy.

The documents are prepared. The delegates of both sides enter. Chvalkovsky, upon seeing the map, turns pale and whispers to me: "I will have to resign tomorrow. No government could stand for a similar blow." Kanya is unperturbed, but whispers his satisfaction to Magistrati. Many Hungarians present are moved; Villani cries.

The evening with the Italians of Vienna, who are among the liveliest of our fellow citizens abroad.

Thursday, hunt on the estate of the Bürgermeister,[360] an old Nazi who spent fifteen months in prison under the old regime and who saw his 14-year-old daughter arrested and locked up for several days together with prostitutes because she had lit a nationalist fire. This explains why the government of the Reich must be harsh with Schuschnigg and his men.

November 4, 1938

Return to Rome. Welcome at the airport by many Fascist leaders and the Hungarian legation.

In the afternoon the Duce calls and, thinking he is speaking with Anfuso, gives orders to prepare a demonstration for me, believing that I was to arrive by train in the evening. When he learns instead that I have already arrived by plane he wants to see me at the Palazzo Venezia. He is very satisfied and he tells me several times.

The Duce speaks of the increasing difficulties created by the "diarchy" of Fascism and the monarchy. It seems that yesterday, during the ceremonies at the tomb of the Unknown Soldier, things grew bitter between himself and the King, because the crowd cried out for the Duce and because the band did not play the Royal March during the Elevation. The King pointed it out to him. The Duce replied that it was simply an incidental oversight. The King rebutted, bluntly, that in eight centuries the honors had always been paid to the sovereigns of the Savoy family.

The Duce sourly recounted the situation and hints that should it become possible to eliminate this state of affairs, he will not let it slip away.

November 5, 1938

I received a mission of Brazilian journalists. Blondel came to say farewell; he is preparing to leave after the arrival of the new French ambassador. Blondel is the classical average functionary, without brilliance, initiative nor courage, however scrupulous and correct. His merit is of a negative nature: in these past two years he did nothing to aggravate the situation. And that would have been very easy. Besides, he didn't have the power to do so. Instead now we will see François-Poncet. He does not come auspiciously. Yesterday the Duce said: "I will do my best to drive him crazy. I don't like him."

The Party has received orders from the Duce to take the anti-Semitic campaign to Tunisia and Nice.

November 6, 1938

Completely calm in the international sector: storm brewing with the Church.

Tomorrow the Council of Ministers will approve the law on race. In it, there is the article prohibiting mixed marriages, except *in extremis* or to legitimize children. The Pope would like the derogation be extended also for those converted to Catholicism. The Duce rejected such a request which would transform the legislation into a confessional, rather than racial law.

Then the Pope sent him a handwritten letter, which remained unanswered. Indignant, the Pontiff turned to the King and sent him a letter in which he accuses the Duce of wanting to break the Concordat. I gave a copy, that I received from Pignatti,[361] to Mussolini. The King, even though he had it since yesterday evening, has still not transmitted it. I cannot say that the Duce is very shaken. He confirmed that the pontifical thesis was acceptable, and had bitter words for the "denunciation" that the Pope to make to the King. Naturally the law, which is very harsh against the Jews, will pass tomorrow as planned.

I cable to Berlin so that a possible French-German pact does not take place before the results of Chamberlain's coming visit to Paris are made public.

November 7, 1938

Council of Ministers. Nothing particular. The Duce was annoyed at Balbo's trumpeting about the sending of colonists to Libya.

In the future these colonists will leave in small groups. All the more so since we run the risk of convincing them that they are official representatives sent by the Regime to make an impression. This happened in Littoria, where the peasants, at a certain point, refused to work because they believed they were playing a purely representative role.

Perth told me about the British decision to implement the Treaty on November 16. He will present the credentials to me and not to the Sovereign, since this is part of the ceremony and customary.

In agreement with Ribbentrop we will not accept the invitation to send our two ministers to Kassa to assist in the Magyar occupation. It would only irritate the Czechs and remove impartiality from the arbitration.

François-Poncet arrives. Only those functionaries from the ministry of whom such duty is strictly required went to greet him. Anfuso tells me, though, that there were many people at the station and also in the square and there was some applause, perhaps by the Italians. I referred this by phone to the Duce, who was obviously annoyed.

November 8, 1938

It seems to me that there is not much hope for *rapprochement* with France. The Duce, in a debriefing, gave me the outlines of what our future policy should be: "Objectives: Djibouti, perhaps through a condominium and a neutralization. Tunisia, in a more or less similar regime; Corsica, Italian, never Frenchified and therefore under our direct control, the border at the river Var. I am not interested in Savoy, which is neither historically nor geographically Italian. This is the general outline of our demands. I do not set one, nor two, nor ten years. Time will be established by events. However, always keep these goals in mind." Under these auspices François-Poncet begins his mission.

I see Count de Chambrun again. He seems to me to have declined a lot physically and mentally. At 10 in the morning he spoke as he used to at 10 in the evening, after eating and, above all, drinking.

Guariglia,[362] on his way to Paris, receives instructions to "wait and see."[363] He is a shrewd functionary, who will tie the ass where his master will tell him, but he will do it reluctantly because he is a democrat and therefore, deep down, Francophile.

An old man whom I have seen once in two years or so, announces to me that his country has recognized the Empire. With difficulty I identify him as the minister of South Africa.[364]

November 9, 1938

Council of Ministers.

First meeting with François-Poncet. He tries to be nonchalant and, going back to our fleeting contacts in Munich, to begin the conversation as if he were an old friend, dignified and sure of himself. But he is not at all. At first he just makes disjointed conversation. He speaks at length about himself and his political precedents. Then he comes to the central point of the discussion and says that his presence in Rome means that France has learned its lesson in Munich and that it intends to behave with a spirit of realism. No allusion of rivaling the Rome-Berlin Axis: he hopes to be able to move it closer to the French-British system to establish a regular Four-Power consultation. I reply, listing the evidence of our goodwill.

But between France and ourselves there is an obstacle: Spain. The position is still the one set by the Duce in his speech in Genoa. François-Poncet agrees. He explains the difficulties his government has in solving this problem. He claims that he will do his best so that an agreement can be reached.

When he left he looked very tired and seemed pensive. Navigation in Rome is difficult.

The Lithuanian minister[365] would like Italian intervention for a reconciliation between Germany and Poland.

November 10, 1938

Council of Ministers. The law for the defense of the race is voted. Starace would like to add the unconditional expulsion of all Jews from the Party. The Duce is against it. Otherwise, the law is approved, save for minimal changes, just as it was proposed by the Minister of the Interior.

In the afternoon I gather at the Palazzo Chigi all the Consuls in southern France, as well as Corsica, Algeria, etc. The Duce intends to make a policy to recover Italians residing in France. There are, today, around one million. The September crisis showed all the dramatic seriousness of this problem. The General Staff was prepared to organize eight battalions of fellow citizens to be launched against us, with moral effects that can be easily predicted. On the other hand we would have had to worry about the future awaiting the best of our fellow citizens: in part killed, in part persecuted, interned in concentration camps or sent into forced labor. Since Italian policies can still force us to face a crisis with France, we do not want a similar situation to repeat itself. All of those who wish to return will be helped to the maximum, by means of superannuation, subsidies, pensions, if necessary. The Consuls are unanimously in favor of this policy: they spent many tragic hours in September when the future of the Italians in France was extremely precarious. We must, though, guarantee work for those who repatriate. I have set a new and more extensive meeting for Saturday.

November 11, 1938

The Hungarian minister brings me a statue of Hercules, a gift for me from Kanya. He also invites me to go to Budapest in January-February. Then, almost incidentally, he mentions the possibility of disorder in Ruthenia, such as to determine the need for the union with Hungary. I advise against it in the clearest way. It would result in Germany's taking a contrary position and we ourselves, perhaps, would be obliged to recall the Magyars to the strict observance of the arbitration. Hitler told someone that at this point he considers the Ruthenian business as "his business." *E questo fia suggel.*[366] But the Hungarians are so disappointing: first, in military matters, and now as to honesty they reveal themselves to be a lot different than expected.

I have a meeting with a Jew who was my classmate in school. He was a vain boy, arrogant and insolent because of his wealth: now he is a broken and sad man. Personal cases are sad, but it is wrong to consider a great historical and social phenomenon on an individual basis. Anyway I telephoned Buffarini to draw attention to the case of the Jew married to an Aryan woman. I feel that for this gesture of detachment from the Jewish nation and religion he should be given preferential treatment. If they wish to save the family nucleus then the father cannot be placed in a position of inferiority with respect to his children.

November 12, 1938

I find the Duce to be more worked up than before about the Jews: he unconditionally approves the tough measures adopted by the Nazis. He says that in the same situation he would do even more. He is angry with the Belgian ambassador who has written a report, of which the SIM has procured a copy, saying that the Italians do not want to go to war. He personally sent 4 copies of a pamphlet regarding our war and two anonymous lines interpreted in this manner: "We are told that you say that the Italian nation does not like war, while it has victoriously fought four wars in a quarter of a century."

A measure is proposed whereby Jews born in Italy will be stateless persons.

He also received Berti, on leave. He greatly praised him and promoted him in the field to general of the army designate. He telephoned me in the afternoon to say that he was canceling the promotion because he had learned that he was a bachelor: "A general must first realize that without men divisions cannot be made."

Egypt recognizes the Empire: a recognition of vast importance.

November 13, 1938

Nothing of particular importance. The Duce criticizes the German decision to apply a fine of a billion marks. He agrees with reprisals of a personal nature but judges the valuation of seven billion lire for the life of von Rath to be excessive. In fact, absurd. He is worried about new threats against the Catholics. He says that every violence against the clergy and the churches makes the Axis unpopular, and if an open crisis was to surface and Catholicism was to be subjected to the same lot as the Jews, the Axis would have difficulty holding up. And he is right.

November 14, 1938

The Duce, who for a long time has had reservations about Albania, this morning, taking his cue from a cruise by Zog, asked me to act once again, keeping to our springtime schedule.

He was very anti-bourgeois and says that on January 3, he will make a strong speech against the Italian middle classes, entitled: "The Face and Soul of the Middle Classes." He will announce the third wave in the *Popolo d'Italia*. Because the middle classes are against the Axis without realizing that if he had chosen another policy last March he would have been beaten by Germany. Franco would have been beaten in Spain and maybe France and England would have grabbed the Empire.

The Duce tells me to write a letter to Grandi announcing our claims on Tunisia, Djibouti and the tariff revision of the Suez Canal. I write it and inform Starace. Other than being truly loyal it is good that he knows about preparatory action of the masses. Meeting for the constitution of the permanent Commission for the repatriation of Italians abroad. Other than Starace, many ministers and the presidents of the Confederation participated. There was a general responsiveness toward the problem and the struggle got off to a good start. We shall win it. I found the way to start off, appropriately, Tunisian irredentism.

November 15, 1938

Arranged the reply with Buffarini to the note of protest sent by the Holy See, very mild to be honest, after the adoption of the recent racial measures which caused a breach in the pact as far as marriage is concerned.

Through Buti I reached final agreements with the embassy of Great Britain for the implementation of the Treaty of April.

Nothing else noteworthy.

November 16, 1938

A day dedicated to peace with England. This morning, at 11 a.m., Lord Perth came to hand to me the credentials directed to the King Emperor. He was emotional and so as to not get confused he had written down the few words he had to say. Poor old man! After all, he has had some stressful moments at the Palazzo Chigi! During his mission to Rome we came close to war at least twice. Instead, today, an end was put to a crisis which was very acute and which had gone on for more than three years. I must admit that Perth worked well: intelligently and honestly. Also the action of September 28 was certainly the result of the good relations that Perth had established with me. And yet the first time that he saw me he wrote to his government (we have the document) that he had to overcome his disgust at shaking my hand, since I had directed the anti-British press campaign during the war in Ethiopia.

In the afternoon, rapid ceremony of the signing for the implementation of the Treaty. Then, at the Palazzo Venezia to inform the Duce. He was very satisfied by the fact and praised me for my work. "All of this is very important," he told me, "but will not alter our policy. In Europe, the Axis remains fundamental. In the Mediterranean, collaboration with the English as long as it is possible. France remains out. Our claims are now specific towards her."

Perth also takes a step for an official visit to Rome by Chamberlain and Halifax in the second week of January. The Duce is reluctant at first. But I insist on the moral value of this visit and he ends up by giving the go ahead.

November 17, 1938

The campaign for the repatriation of the Italians abroad is launched with all the trimmings. The Duce approved the measures that I had already adopted and my working plan. I believe the matter calls for a good fascist battle which could give us much satisfaction.

I receive the trade union leaders who accompanied the workers to Germany. In the preface of the book, published by the Confederation, I had already expressed a clearly favorable judgment on the usefulness of these mass trips, which have the value of opening the mentality of our workers and also of the Germans. Until now both nations have been in a strange spiritual position. The Germans have liked us, without respecting us. We have respected them, without liking them. Through a more precise acquaintance we may, by the fusion of both feelings, succeed at creating the true atmosphere of the Axis. And it will be easier to do this through the working classes than through the middle classes, which are more egotistical, more pacifist, more fundamentally attached in those countries that, like France and Great Britain, represent the crystallization and the defense of systems that fascism and Nazism reject and overthrow.

Vittorio Mussolini[367] was supposed to go to London but the trip has been delayed because his host had nothing better to do than to send a violent anti-German letter to *The Daily Telegraph*. I informed Berlin of the incident and the reasons why the trip was cancelled.

November 18, 1938
Villani is back at it about Ruthenia. He says that the movement is occurring inside the country, that the Ruthenians cannot live detached from Hungary, that Germany seems indifferent to this new development in the matter. It is not true. I know that the Führer has already expressed himself negatively. I told Villani clearly that I disapprove of this behavior and that if Germany asks us to join them in an invitation directed at Hungary so that it respects the terms of the arbitration, we will work in agreement with Berlin. I am very keen to avoid having the Germans think we play a double game and that it is through our encouragement that the Magyars pour oil on the fire. I also invited Villani to consider that the Hungarian position towards Geneva is intolerable at this point. They must leave the League, from which they have never had, and will never have, anything. A similar event will strengthen Imredy's position, also internally, given that the right-wing parties appear more and more active and restless.

The Princess of Piedmont told me about her trip to France and England. Nothing very important. But above all she wanted to justify herself for having attended a concert conducted by Toscanini in Lucerne last summer. She had not calculated the political significance of the gesture, to which she was induced by some Milanese friends.

November 19, 1938
Villani updates me on the situation in Ruthenia and, something important, tells me that Budapest has informed Berlin of the situation that has occurred. We await the reaction.

I begin work drafting a speech that I will make at the Chamber on November 30.

November 20, 1938
While I am hunting in Mandria (Turin), Anfuso telephones regarding the departure of 100 aircraft for Hungary. The Duce, in a meeting with the Hungarian military attaché, supposedly promised these weapons and also authorized the beginning of action in Ruthenia. This because Szabo assured that the Germans are not opposed to it. Lies. In the afternoon Berlin communicates that, interrogated by the Magyars, they had strongly advised against it and had called on them to respect the arbitration of Vienna. I agree with

the Germans. These Hungarians are behaving badly: like a Balkanized country, which they are, actually.

The fact remains that the Duce finds himself in a serious fix. He has been surprised in good faith. The promises and commitments made by him were based on the premises of German approval. This is totally absent. Every commitment is reversed. Luckily, bad weather prevented the aircraft from taking off for Hungary. If I arrive in time I will have the decision to ship the aircraft cancelled. It would be difficult to persuade the Germans of our good faith if at the same time we send the Magyars the means to carry out their aggression.

The Duce cables Berlin to contact the government of the Reich, to inform it of the truth and to agree upon an identical action.

I return to Rome in the evening.

November 21, 1938

The Germans are of the opinion that they should send a note to Budapest to appeal to them to respect the arbitration of Vienna and they send us the draft. We agree. I communicate the contents to Villani and Szabo who are saddened by the event. They acted in total good faith and truly believed that the Magyar government had German approval.

The Hungarian action will not take place. All the more so because our aircraft did not take off and will not do so for some time. Vinci[368] cables that Kanya, when he was handed the note, was crushed and, while polite, icy. He is responsible for the incident, as he is responsible for the personal hostility that has been created by the anti-Magyar attitude adopted by many German officials.

Ribbentrop, with whom I spoke on the telephone, is fully aware of the incident and has no doubts about our behavior.

November 22, 1938

Nothing of particular importance. Apart from the meeting of the Commission for the repatriation of the Italians.

November 23, 1938

The cultural pact with Germany is signed. It is an agreement that goes beyond the usual cultural pacts, the value of which is usually nil. This one really opens German doors to Italian culture in a way that has no precedents. For this reason we have given the event great exposure in the press.

The speech for the Chamber is ready. The date of November 30 remains set. Imredy resigns, as was envisaged, following the unfavorable vote of Parliament. Forecasts for the succession cannot yet be made, but there is talk of a reincarnation of Imredy himself, more to the right. It is interesting to note that Colonel Szabo has revealed himself as hostile to the present government. In Monday's meetings, while Villani disapproved of the fall of Imredy's government, Szabo did not seem at all opposed to the possibility of a Hungarist government. According to him it would be the only way to have a policy completely aligned with the Axis and, within the Axis, with Rome. He excludes that rightist extremists are, as is usually said, subservient to Germany.

November 24, 1938

The chargé d'affaires of Czechoslovakia[369] brings me a note in which it is stated that the pending questions with Germany and Poland are now permanently settled. There have not yet been the formal steps, but this is a prelude to the request for guarantee of the borders on the basis of the Munich agreement. I don't think we can refuse if we receive such a request, all the more so because Germany would easily agree.

I tell Christich of the recent incidents between us, Germany, and Hungary. He is very grateful for the communication and for the position taken. If the incursion in Ruthenia had taken place, Stoyadinovich's position would have been weakened in a moment in which it is instead necessary to support him in view of the coming elections. Christich confirmed to me that Stoyadinovich, strengthened with the majority that he will obtain, will tend more and more to place the accent on the authoritarian form of his government. During the conversation we spoke of the relations between Belgrade and Athens, and of the question of Salonica. I encouraged him to act as soon as possible towards the Aegean, which is the natural outlet of the Yugoslavs to the sea. This above all helps our action in Albania, which is progressing according to plan.

November 25, 1938

Conferred with Mosconi[370] and the lawyer Gambino[371] regarding Albania. They confirm that the old conviction that Italy will eventually take control of the country gains more and more ground. There are some sectors of public opinion that go as far as to demand this intervention. The King's situation is more and more shaky. In the circles of the Court the anti-Italian attitude has increased.

Gambara went to see the Duce. He announced an offensive on Barcelona. The approximate starting date: December 9. Gambara made an excellent report on the morale of our troops. He feels that the entire CTV, which amounts, together with the Spanish, to around 60,000 men, could have a decisive role in the coming operations. He asked for, and obtained, three artillery groups of 149 and of 100, as well as a number of men to make up for departures and losses.

In the afternoon I see Villani, who confirms that Hungary has stopped all action in Ruthenia. He speaks again of Magyar participation in the anti-Comintern pact. Very well, but it should be preceded by the withdrawal from Geneva. Villani feels that this will be easier if Kanya is replaced by Czaky. Villani reports that François-Poncet said that Hungary will one day find a gauleiter in the place of Horthy and to not trust Italy, who has already abandoned another country. Villani—as far as he says—reacted sharply.

November 26, 1938

The Duce has approved, without almost any changes, the speech that I will give to the Chamber on Wednesday.

Von Mackensen speaks to me about the Hungarian proposal to join the anti-Comitern pact. Berlin also feels such a move should be preceded by the withdrawal from Geneva.

The ambassador also talks to me about the bad relations existing between Germany and Brazil and would like to establish a parallel between the retirement of Lojacono and that of their ambassador, which is forced. They would actually like us not to send Sola. Even though I declared myself willing to examine Ribbentrop's proposals and arguments, I let it be known that no measure has been taken against us which justifies such retaliation. I also stressed the enormous amount of our economic and political interests in Brazil, as well as the friendly position taken by that country towards us during the sanctions.

November 27, 1938
Nothing noteworthy.

November 28, 1938
I find the Duce outraged at the King. Three times, during a meeting this morning, he told the Duce that he feels an "infinite compassion for the Jews." He cited cases of people persecuted, and, among others, General Pugliese,[372] who is eighty years old and laden with medals and wounds, and must remain without a servant. The Duce said that in Italy there are 20,000 people with weak backs who are moved by the fate of the Jews. The King said that he is among them. Then the King also spoke against Germany about the creation of the Fourth Alpine division. The Duce was very violent in his expressions against the Monarchy. He is considering the change of system more and more. Perhaps it is not the right moment. There would be reactions. Yesterday in Pesaro the garrison commander protested against the Provincial Party Secretary who had saluted the Duce and not the King.
Meeting about citizenship of the Arabs. A strong argument between Balbo and Starace because the former said things which were offensive about the Party's actions.
Perth comes to see me at home to arrange an announcement of Chamberlain's visit to Rome. The news should have been secret but in London they have spoken about it and the newspapers were already full of it this morning. I informed von Mackensen of the visit and its origins.
Jacomoni brings me a map with the distribution of the bands in Albania as well as the plan of action.

November 29, 1938
The Duce received François-Poncet. The frame of mind, already hostile, was aggravated by a severe cold which has been tormenting the Chief for two days. The reception was glacial. François-Poncet tried to come straight to the point and said that his government sent him here to continue the spirit of Munich. The Duce, who even pretended not to remember if at the time of Munich he had already been nominated ambassador in Rome or not, replied that relations between France and Italy are veés [*sic*] by the Spanish affair and that on the matter he is more intransigent than ever. He shifted the conversation to the internal situation in France; while Poncet, who spoke slowly trying to make an impression on his interlocutor, struggled to return

to the subject of foreign policy clinging to the Four-Power Pact. Another failure. The Duce said that the plan failed because of the French Left and that he would certainly not propose a new one. Then, with a distracted air, he said: "Il faut d'abord mettre de l'ordre dans la maison"* and he got up. François-Poncet didn't say another word. And on his way out he looked far less assured than when he came in.

I speak with Mackensen about the publication on behalf of *The News Chronicle* of the project of the Three-Power Pact. It seems that the leak came from the Japanese. Acquarone, the new Minister of the Royal House, comes to see me and says that he wants to bring a breath of fresh air to the environment. "But," he adds, "I must go slowly in matters of form, because if I remove those then there will be nothing left."

November 30, 1938

I give my speech at the Chamber. It went very well. When I spoke, toward the end, of the "natural aspirations of the Italian nation," a real tempest of acclamations and shouts broke out in the hall, "Tunisia, Corsica, Nice, Savoy."

None of it had been scripted. The Deputies spontaneously expressed their aspirations, which are those of the nation.

The Duce was pleased. I accompanied him in the car to the Palazzo Venezia. He said: "A great speech and a great day for the Regime. It is this way a problem is imposed and a nation is launched."

In fact he took the floor at the beginning of the sitting of the Grand Council and more or less said the following: "I communicate to you the next goals of fascist dynamism. As Adua has been avenged, we will avenge Valona. Albania will become Italian. I cannot and do not want to tell you when and how. But it will be. Then, for our security needs in the Mediterranean which still constrains us, we need Tunisia and Corsica. The border must be moved to the Var. I do not aim at Savoy because it is outside the Alpine circle. I instead keep Ticino in mind, because Switzerland has lost its cohesion and is destined one day to dismembered, as many small countries will be. All of this is a program. I cannot fix time frames. I only indicate the general plan. I will call those who reveal all or part of what I have said to task as traitors."

December 1, 1938

Sparano reads me a letter from the Brazilian foreign minister,[373] which narrates the abuses of power by the German ambassador.[374] He asks for our support. I don't know what we could do other than operate as mediators to clear up the incident. But I fear that the crisis is deep. The German propaganda action on their emigrated masses is of such a nature so as to seriously and justifiably make the Governor of Rio anxious.

Villani, with tears in his eyes, as has become his habit in the last few weeks, thanks me for what I said yesterday for his country.

---

* "First of all, the house must be put in good order."

I discuss the Albanian situation at length with Jacomini and the work project which now begins to look concrete. The preparation is progressing well.

The Zog regime proves to be more and more shaky and therefore tending toward collapse. We must act decidedly and unscrupulously. Besides, it is humanitarian to take one life if by doing so hundreds and maybe thousands can be saved.

December 2, 1938

The reactions to my speech are more and more intense, everywhere, and they have become hysterical in France.

Here, instead, the success is huge.

I receive hundreds of letters and cables of congratulations. The Italians now understand that the Axis has objectives which are not only German: there are also our claims, which we cannot, and will not, renounce.

The Duce, who is very satisfied as always when a battle starts, has fixed me the lines of action: have the Mussolini-Laval agreement of 1935 collapse, and synchronize our requests with German colonial claims.

Our requests are Djibouti, Tunisia, and a stake in the Suez Canal.

In the evening, conversation with François-Poncet. He affected a lot of indifference but was worried and keen to give his initiative a more friendly character than one of protest. He was captious in the conversation, of which I took notes. Singling out an isolated phrase of mine he even tried to establish that the government did not make claims. I was very reserved. After the official step, he wanted to make some comments and above all emphasize that France was not a country which had fallen so low as to be able to permanently ask for "hand-outs." On his way out he asked me if he should continue unpacking his things. Then he said: "It would be nice to be able to live in peace in Rome." I coldly replied: "This depends on you." And after a pause, smiling: "And also us." He left my office as white as a sheet.

December 3, 1938

The great European orchestra continues. This leaves us totally indifferent; in fact, we keep the dispute alive on purpose. The Duce is very pleased with what has happened. He believes that all of this is very useful for our Albanian purposes: distract local attention, allowing us a convenient preparation without stirring up any fear, and in the end induce the French to accept our going into Tirana so as to lighten the matter on them.

I see Perth twice. The first time he tells me the date of Chamberlain's visit to Rome. Set for January 11. The second time he makes a démarche for the question of Tunisia. I reply, saying what I more or less said to François-Poncet. He reminded me to observe our pact with England for the Mediterranean. I say that I will reject such a reminder until something that can be judged as contrary to such obligations can be found in my speech.

As far as the Mussolini-Laval pact is concerned, Perth also agrees in feeling that it cannot be considered to be in force.

I receive Jacomoni. Koçi is with him: the man who is about to carry out the coup against the King in Albania. Naturally, he is an old friend of the King but is unhappy about having been neglected by him. He gave me the "besa," which is the word of honor. I did not want to go into details with him: he is a vigorous and fanatical old man. He has already sent his family to Italy.

December 4, 1938

Nothing of any importance in Rome. Instead fairly serious news arrives of anti-Italian incidents fomented on purpose in Corsica and Tunisia. These conflicts benefit our game because Italian public opinion, even in those less sensitive sectors, reacts violently.

December 5, 1938

Considering Ribbentrop's coming trip to Paris the Duce and I decide not to dramatize the incidents and to put a temporary stop to the press's anti-French polemics. I make sure Ribbentrop himself is informed of this; he appears to be very satisfied. Before leaving, he had called Attolico, wanting to minimize the importance and purposes of his visit to Paris.

With Jacomoni and Giro we set some important points of the action in Albania.

The organization is proceeding well and I think that everything will be carried out according to plan. The death of the King will remove all centers of resistance and the movement will inflame the country within a few hours. I ask myself if it would not be better to act faster, because the machine is ready to go and a delay may cause problems we cannot foresee today.

A long meeting with Starace. I unreservedly gave him my opinion about some of his gestures and initiatives. First of all the projected anti-bourgeois exhibition. It is absurd to annoy people, as he does, for no reason. One cannot torment people with tea at five or the evening dress. I think that especially when politics are more rigid a larger margin of personal freedom must be allowed. Some of his measures create large areas of discontent and rebellion.

December 6, 1938

The Duce examines and approves the plan of action in Albania. But his only reservation concerns Yugoslavia. He is not at all worried about France, England and Greece. While he follows Yugoslav behavior attentively, he is worried, not just about a real reaction, which appears difficult, but about a weakening friendship towards us to Germany's advantage. It is perhaps worth speaking with Stoyadinovich and maybe study the possibility of compensation, perhaps at Greece's expense: Salonica.

Horthy invites me to a hunting party. I accept and will leave on December 19. It is worth following the Hungarian internal situation closely, which is not at all brilliant. The feudal regime continues in the present government, and only a sharp turn to the right can put Hungary back on the correct path. Yesterday Szabo extolled Szalazy and Hungarianism.

Muti returned from Spain. Things are going well enough and the next attack in Catalonia could bring resolution. I am a little skeptical: this phrase has been pronounced too many times to believe it again. Anyway the CTV, under Gambara's command, is as right as it has ever been and also relations with the air force have been conveniently cleared up.

December 7, 1938

I accompanied Muti to see the Duce. The news is good: also the clash between Bernasconi[375] and Gambara has been put right and our forces go into action in very good conditions.

Nothing else noteworthy.

December 8, 1938

The anti-French demonstrations in Italy and anti-Italian in France are multiplying. This is good because it helps make the Axis popular among Italian youth. For the moment they are student demonstrations, but irredentism has always started in the high schools.

December 9, 1938

The Duce wants the anti-French controversy to be muted somewhat because "continuing at this rate cannon will have to be put to use and the time has not yet arrived." But he said to be pleased with the results of the sample of public opinion regarding France.

We are preparing the program for Chamberlain's visit with Perth. Perth, speaking for himself, told me that he disapproves of France's behavior. He advised Poncet not to dramatize.

Barella bared his feelings against Starace to me. Also he has joined the team of those who harshly attack the Party Secretary. It is now a real popular uprising against him. I wonder, even though I have imposed on myself to take no interest in internal politics, if I should speak to the Duce. Starace, who has many positive points, has made the two biggest mistakes toward the Italian nation. He has created an atmosphere of persecution and has bored everyone with thousands of small things of a personal nature. Now Italians want to be governed from the heart. And while they are prepared to forgive even those who have hurt them, they will not forgive those who have irritated them.

December 10, 1938

Nothing noteworthy.

Lunch to honor Perth at Villa Madama.

December 11, 1938

Nothing noteworthy.

December 14, 1938

I report to the Duce on the meeting with Pignatti. He has an outburst against the Pope, whom he hopes will die very soon. He threatens to "stimulate the anti-clerical sensibilities of the people" and have Ghibelline Italy, which has never really died, come back to life. He says that in Romagna the churches were bolted shut at the beginning of Fascism and that if people go now it is only because they know that it is desired by the Duce. But he concludes by declaring the need to not provoke a crisis with the Vatican at the present time and authorizes me to deny the news about divorce and sterilization.

At the Chamber, closing ceremony. Orano[376] spoke at length and to little effect. Father, instead, had great success with a few simple phrases, full of life, as is his nature.

Christich tells me about his meeting with Poncet, which confirms to me what the minister of Uruguay[377] told me yesterday. Poncet is bitter because he thought that in coming here he would have had greater success. He had counted on his personality to remove obstacles and rekindle Francophile tendencies. Instead he has found himself isolated and has understood that he has no possibility of maneuvering behind the scenes because here the foreign policy is handled only by whoever is responsible. Since the minister of Uruguay gave me the written text of his meeting with Poncet, who had harsh words about the Germans, I will give a copy to the German embassy. That will weaken the sympathies that Poncet enjoys in some German circles.

December 15, 1938

I accompanied General Oshima, the Japanese ambassador to Berlin, to see the Duce. His visit was recommended by Ribbentrop because Oshima is, like Ribbentrop, an advocate for the transformation of the anti-Comintern Pact into a Tripartite Alliance Pact. Oshima, physically, is the image of the Samurai as they appear in old paintings or on Japanese porcelain. Interesting and hard face. Small and thickset. Extremely proud bearing. When he began to speak I realized why Ribbentrop likes him so much: they are of the same kind, enthusiastic and a simplifier. I don't mean to say careless. He attacked Russia and said that Japan intends to dismember it into many states so as to render any thought of revenge vain and absurd; he said that Japan wants to eliminate all British interest in China and the Pacific in general. He presented the English position in India in a tragic light. The Duce repeated the usual arguments on the necessity of delaying the transformation of the Pact for some time and indicated that the time to make his decisions would be mid-January to mid-February.

Giuriati, Consul General in Calcutta, tells me that on September 27, the Viceroy of the Indies[378] told him that in the case of conflict he would not know how to maintain British dominion over India.

Gave the notes of the minister of Uruguay and Poncet to Mackensen.

December 16, 1938

Lord Perth, with tears in his eyes, asked for the approval of Percy Loraine.[379] Deep in his heart he hopes that during Chamberlain's next trip the British government will not reverse its decision, but he doesn't want to show it. I am sorry that he is going. He is a man who, through a long process, has come to understand fascism and even like it. He is sincerely fond of me and I of him.

His presence would still be useful. British-Italian friendship is too weak to be subjected to shake-ups. And I don't know if this Percy Loraine is the most suitable. Some time ago he said some nasty things about Italy, and the Duce had anonymous letters sent to him containing some vile insults and newspaper cutouts with photographs of our armed forces. The auspices are not good. And to think that Perth had become such a friend to us as to cable his government (and I have the deciphered text), the day of my speech in the Chamber, that the shouts of the deputies for Tunisia and Corsica did not reach the diplomatic gallery!...

Perth recommends that pending Chamberlain's visit, the disputes with France be toned down somewhat to avoid creating major internal difficulties for the Prime Minister. I gave him assurances.

I received von Mackensen and Strautz,[380] to whom I gave a briefing regarding the interview which took place between the Duce and General Oshima at the Palazzo Venezia.

December 17, 1938

Nothing of particular importance, apart from the Duce's approval and the dispatch to the French ambassador of a note stating and documenting that the Mussolini-Laval pact of January 1935 is juridically, politically, and historically superseded. I gave a character of complete serenity to the note and I concluded with a hint at the possibility of resuming negotiations. For the moment it is better not to go too far. Above all we must not give the French the opportunity of blowing up Chamberlain's visit.

Mussolini has left for Carbonia, the new Sardinian coal area. He was very pleased with the results of the struggle for autarchy. He said that foreigners had convinced us that our country was so desperately poor that any attempt at mining the land was useless. Those same foreigners who had persuaded us that we were not a race, but rather a cowardly motley crowd of people born to serve and please nations on the other side of the mountains. A classic example of this idea is found in the report sent to the Directorate by General Berthier,[381] after his sojourn in Italy.

December 18, 1938

Departure for Hungary. In Trieste and Postumia the crowds give us a warm welcome, shouting "Tunisia, Corsica, Djibouti." They are spontaneous demonstrations of masses that have felt deep rancor rising within, according to the tradition and the instinct of the Italian people.

December 19-20, 1938

The Hungarian welcome, from the border to Budapest, is the kind which is given to a son returning home, not to a foreigner one wishes to honor. I am a little moved. It is cold, very cold, but all the same the people are in the streets, numb, red in the face, whipped by the icy wind, and they continue to shout and cheer.

I find a new atmosphere in the government as well. I speak frankly about what should be the new Magyar policy: open, certain, not equivocal, joining with the Axis. They are all in agreement, even though the atmosphere is openly hostile towards Germany. Germany is feared. Czaky doesn't hide his worry, and Imredy the same. This explains the intransigency displayed towards the Hungarian Party of Szalazy, although it is making progress among the youth. I assure the Hungarians that we will never allow Germany to act towards Hungary as they acted towards Austria. There were many other reasons, which made such politics logical, therefore acceptable. This statement of mine quiets down my counterparts, who are finally able to base their policies as follows: join the anti-Comitern Pact after Czaky's visit to Berlin; withdrawal from Geneva in May, after having provoked a crisis with the League of Nations by presenting a report on the minorities which is absolutely unacceptable; reconciliation with Yugoslavia. To this end they ask me if I would, on the occasion of my next meeting with Stoyadinovich, set the basis for an agreement. This is very good. Nothing must be done which can acquire an anti-German flavor, but it is good, for all intents and purposes, that the block between Italy, Yugoslavia, and Hungary be tightened.

The Hungarian frame of mind towards Romania is very hostile. Czaky mentioned it to me. Imredy, who had foreseen my objections, immediately interrupted. But the Regent spoke to me more openly of a possible attack against Romania, saying that the Duce in Rome had expressed his approval for such action. I watered things down. And I dropped the hint that a decision of that kind requires a reexamination in the light of the situations that have taken place.

December 21, 1938
Internal situation: not entirely clear. The anti-Semitic laws and agricultural reform will be enacted soon and the government expects great results. We shall see. But it is certain that among the youth there is a new excitement and that the entire feudal structure of Hungary begins to weigh unbearably on the new generations. The Hungarianist Party is spreading. An atmosphere of martyrdom is being created toward Szalazy, which is beneficial to him. And I do not believe the accusation that the government wants to make him sell Hungary to the Germans. Hubai, who is leading the Party during Szalazy's detention, sent me a very warm cable. I didn't reply directly to not having a document which could displease the government, but I let them know, through Vinci, that I received the greetings from the Magyar Nationalist youth with pleasure. Who knows what the future has in store!

December 22, 1938
Return trip.

December 23, 1938
I report to the Duce, who is very pleased with the results of the trip. We have a general survey and a program and set some points of discussion for Chamberlain's visit. Furthermore, the Duce confirms that at this point it is

his intention to join the triangular assistance pact, according to Ribbentrop's proposal.

We attack in Catalonia with remarkable success. The cables from Gambara are enthusiastic and also the few notes from Muti confirm success.

December 24, 1938

I send a copy of the note from me to François-Poncet, to the German chargé d'affaires, and the British ambassador. Perth reads it in part and thinks it is very moderate: the end seems to be particularly good to him. We speak of the obligation that France had with us to support our action for the conquest of Abyssinia. He says that Laval went to see him and said that such an obligation only concerned economic questions. This is not true. I told Perth that the French were fully aware of our plans for territorial conquest. I also told him of a meeting that I had with Flandin in Paris in May of 1935, when he also gave me some advice regarding the manner in which it would have been convenient to start the conflict. He suggested provoking a revolt of the Ras against the Negus, which would have given us the pretext to intervene. These declarations made quite an impression upon Perth.

Good news from Spain. The advance continues notwithstanding the counter attacks by the Reds.

December 25, 1938

Nothing new. From Yugoslavia the bad news on Stoyadinovich's situation intensifies. Even though the election results are worrisome, I am confident about the current government. I have much faith in Stoyadinovich. He is a firm man who has overcome storms far worse than this one.

December 26, 1938

France sends us a note of reply. It is a bland rebuttal of our statements, not without certain inaccuracies, naturally. I don't believe that it requires a rejoinder.

Doing well in Spain, the Italian divisions proceed rapidly towards their objectives. The Spanish are doing less well and once again show themselves to be slow and indecisive on the offensive.

The Papal Nuncio speaks to me of the situation of the Catholic Action and sounds off with a strong attack against Starace, whom he defines as "a dangerous pagan," and a vile example of immortality also in his private life. The Papal Nuncio mentions the possibility of a visit by the Duce to the Pope on the occasion of the tenth anniversary of the Concordat, but I reply that it didn't seem possible. At the most, I could go and bring a message from the Duce. But it is better to give this some thought as well.

December 27, 1938

Nothing new.

December 28, 1938

I intervened with Franco in Spain and I also had the Germans take action, to get him to move his troops. There is the possibility of a decisive victory, but the Spanish threaten to let it slip by again.

December 29, 1938

Nothing very important. Meeting with the naval attaché in Japan, Commander Ghè, who tells me about the Japanese fervor for Italy and of the anti-German resentment. Even though he is a good friend of Japan, Ghè says not to trust it too much. After the conquest of China they will need capital and tranquility and would not want to sacrifice their own interests for any foreign country.

December 30, 1938

Communicated to Lord Perth the approval of his successor.

Monelli, back from Corsica, confirms what I knew: that a Corsican irredentism doesn't exist and that the entire Party of Petru Rocca consists of no more than ten people. The others also are hardly enthusiastic: the editors of the Corsican newspapers who are the most violent against us have said that if we gave them some tourist advertising they would stop the anti-Italian campaign.

Long meeting with Alberto Giannini,[382] who returned from a long stay abroad. I haven't seen him since he emigrated, almost fourteen years ago. He has become fat and he no longer has that rebellious mind that characterized him once before. He spoke to me of the world of political exiles: wretchedly small world, without hope and without will, divided by personal feuds, compelled to act according to the wishes of their host, that is the French government. Small world of moral and material poverty destined to disappear shortly without leaving a trace.

December 31, 1938

The new Japanese ambassador[383] makes his introductory visit to me. For a career diplomat and, moreover, a Japanese, he is quite explicit and energetic. He speaks of the Tripartite Pact and immediately reveals himself to be an advocate of the reinforcement of the system. He does not hide, though, that in Japan there still exists a strong party in favor of *rapprochement* with Great Britain and America.

From Spain, Gambara and Viola report of a meeting with Franco, during which the Generalissimo was apparently persuaded to unite his efforts with ours to give the offensive in Catalonia a more concrete result. We shall see what happens in the next few days; for the moment, precious time has been lost.

Bastianini paints the internal situation in very gloomy colors and he also launches his lightning against the usual suspect, Starace. There is some truth: we do not live on a bed of roses. But Starace is not entirely responsible and it must be kept in mind that Bastianini, at the age of forty, is already a discontented, sour old man capable of speaking only of how things used to be "in his day."

1939

The Duce returned to Rome last night, and we had a long conversation. He is very unhappy about the situation in East Africa, and expresses a harsh opinion on the work of the Duke of Aosta. In fact, Asmara remains in a state of complete revolt, and the 65 battalions that are stationed there are forced to live in armed camps. Mazzetti has acted badly. He blames Teruzzi as bearing responsibility for that appointment, because Teruzzi made the decision based on personal considerations, while, when making a political appointment, one must be ready to "sell one's own mother."

The Duce spoke of the situation with the Holy See. He sees in the policy of the Catholic Action an attempt to build up a real political party, which, foreseeing difficult times for Fascism, aims at being ready to become its successor. He defended Starace; whatever he does, he does on the explicit orders of the Duce. He has rejected the suggestion of the Papal Nuncio to do something about the celebration of the tenth anniversary of the Conciliation [Lateran Treaty].

Finally, he told me of his decision to accept von Ribbentrop's proposal to transform the anti-Comintern pact into an alliance. He wants the pact signed during the last ten days of January. He considers more and more inevitable a clash with the Western democracies, and therefore he wishes to set up a military alignment in advance. In the course of the month he plans to prepare public opinion, "about which he doesn't give a damn."

I am going to write a letter to von Ribbentrop announcing our acceptance of his proposal (letter filed in the volume of official documents).

January 2, 1939

The letter to von Ribbentrop has been approved. Tomorrow I shall deliver it to Attolico together with some instructions as to what he should tell the Germans, especially about commercial relations between the two countries and concerning Alto Adige. It would be best to implement Hitler's idea to evacuate those Germans who wish to leave. I telephoned von Ribbentrop to inform him of the decision briefly. We had some difficulty speaking because of poor connections and we were not able to say very much to each other, but he was satisfied, and he agreed that by the end of the month everything can be ready, even on the Japanese side.

A conversation with the Duce and Pignatti. The Duce told the ambassador to tell the Vatican that he is dissatisfied with the policy of the Holy See, especially with reference to the Catholic Action movement. He also spoke of the clergy's opposition to the policy of the Axis, as well as to racial legislation. Let the Church not be under any illusions as to the possibility of keeping Italy under its tutelage. The power of the clergy is awesome, but more awesome yet is the power of the state, especially a Fascist state. We do not want a conflict, but we will not shy away from one, and in that case we shall arouse all the dormant anti-clerical rancor; let the Pope remember that Italy is Ghibelline. Pignatti acted in a satisfactory manner. He said that the Vatican has made many mistakes, but that the Pope is a man of good faith, and that he is the one who, more than any other prelate, is the most pro-Italian in his thinking. I have given him instructions to act very tactfully. Notwithstanding Starace, I should like to avoid a clash with the Vatican, which I would consider very harmful.

January 3, 1939

I have given instructions to Attolico on his mission to von Ribbentrop. He will leave this evening. Whereas in the past I have found him rather hostile to the idea of an alliance with Germany, today he showed himself openly favorable to it. He said that during this stay in Italy, he became convinced that nothing would be more popular among us than a war against France. During the afternoon I also informed von Mackensen, who, having just returned from Berlin, came to pay me a visit. The Polish ambassador mentioned the coming visit of Beck to Berlin to me, and a later visit which von Ribbentrop is to make to Poland. This will make my visit to Warsaw, which will probably take place during the last week of February, much easier.

At the Duce's office with the American ambassador, bearer of a message from Roosevelt, and some suggestions regarding the settlement of Jewish immigrants, for whom President Roosevelt has thought of a part of Ethiopia and the surrounding colonies. The Duce rejected this proposal, and said that only Russia, the United States, and Brazil have the material possibilities to solve the Jewish question, allotting to the Jews a part of their territories. He declared himself favorable to the creation of an independent Jewish state, and in general he promised to support it. In Spain the CTV has resumed its offensive and, it seems, with some success.

January 4, 1939

Conversation with Grandi. He is just back from a rather long vacation in Sicily, and therefore does not have much to tell me. I gave him a rather vague idea about our future alliance with Germany and observed his reaction. He declared himself to be favorable and does not believe that there can be very serious repercussions in the British world. Great Britain sees it as bound to take place. The memory of the Triple Alliance is still alive, which for a period of thirty years did not prevent maintaining cordial relations between Italy and Great Britain.

At Baghdad there have been demonstrations against our mass immigration to Libya; they think that this nucleus of Italians will break the Arabic preponderance in the Mediterranean. They are right; this is our objective; but the Duce wanted me to reassure the minister of Iraq. Since he was annoyed at the publicity that Balbo acquired through this initiative, he ordered that future immigration should take place quietly. He used this pretext to his advantage.

I have informed von Mackensen about the American proposals of yesterday. He poked fun at them, and made some sharp comments on American lack of political sense.

In Spain we are forging ahead at full speed. Gambara has executed a very brilliant maneuver. He has freed himself from the threat to his flanks and in turn has attacked the Reds on their flanks, producing a very serious crisis.

January 5, 1939

Excellent news from Spain. The only danger in sight is a possible mass intervention by the French, coming through the Pyrenees. There are already rumors on this subject. In order to avert such a threat, I have informed London and Berlin that, if the French move, this will mean the end of the policy of non-intervention. We, too, will send our regular divisions. This means that we shall make war against France on Spanish territory. I have asked the Germans to publish a note on the *Corrispondenza Diplomatica* in support of our thesis.

The Duce tells me that he has informed the King about the forthcoming military alliance with Germany. He was happy about it. He does not like the Germans, but he detests the French and holds them in low esteem. However, he considers them capable of a sudden attack against us, and therefore looks with satisfaction upon an obligation on the part of Germany to provide military aid to Italy.

Besides, times change. The anti-Italian demonstrations in France and Tunis, the gesture of Daladier, who wanted to cut our throats with a Corsican dagger, the press which insults us, create an atmosphere of hate toward France, especially among the common people. I have told Cianetti[384] to give a social flavoring to anti-French propaganda towards the workingmen. France is a bourgeois state, the defender of bourgeois privilege; this is extremely effective. Today, even Alberto Pirelli, the sad, gray-faced skeptical, distrustful Pirelli, told me of his commitment to the policy of the Axis and his aversion to the Western democracies.

Attolico, after a first conversation with von Ribbentrop, said that he prefers the 28th as the date for the signing of the alliance.

January 6, 1939

Pause in Spain. Gambara is counting upon mustering his forces in order to relaunch the attack tomorrow. I spoke this evening with the head of the Spanish economic mission Señor Annos, who has come to Rome for the commercial treaty. He is a very talkative individual, a little frivolous, very vain, but he is a Catalan and therefore at least knows the geography of his own country. He considers the victory of the past few days very important, perhaps decisive, for the purpose of getting rid of Catalonia, and therefore of the war itself.

The Duce is concerned with the Czech-Hungarian border incidents. This time it seems they are much more serious than usual. Up to now there is no direct news from the Italian Legation. The Duce wanted to have information from Grandi about the coming visit of Chamberlain, his state of mind and his intentions. But Grandi has been absent from London for twenty days. He has been having a good time in Sicily and in the mountains. When the Duce heard of this he was very resentful. He said, "That guy is all petered out; after the visit you shall fire him." But I am certain that, as has happened frequently, he will save him at the last moment. After all, he may be right, because Grandi, in spite of his shortcomings, is a good ambassador; it would not be easy to find a better successor, since our diplomatic representatives at this moment are not brilliant.

January 7, 1939

Attolico reports on his conversation with Ribbentrop, who is very enthusiastic about our decision; however, Attolico has gone too far in bringing up the economic question and that of Alto Adige as conditions to the alliance. While, as a matter of fact, the first interests us a great deal more on account of the political repercussions on public opinion, the second must be solved quietly, without useless and excessive publicity. It is sufficient that the Germans, who at this moment need men badly, take those aliens that do not desire to remain in Italian territory south of the Alpine range. I have telephoned Magistrati about this.

Prepared a very moderate toast for Chamberlain; I do not believe the situation calls for or will allow the use of too many idle words. I have seen the Japanese ambassador, who spoke to me about the alliance; he fears that Arita, the new Foreign Minister, is rather indifferent, while the Prime Minister is openly favorable. This will not have any bearing upon the conclusion of the pact, but might delay the date of signing. Meanwhile, the ambassador wishes to be received by the Duce in order to feel out the situation so that he may expedite a reply from his government. The ambassador is very favorable to the alliance, which he considers an aggressive instrument to obtain from Great Britain "the many things which it owes to us all."

Von Ribbentrop has sent me the text of the pact, as well as that of the secret conventions on the subject of the military commissions.

Gambara has been wounded, but not seriously. This is fortunate, because his role has been magnificent.

January 8, 1939

Except for certain changes in the preamble, the Duce approves the texts sent by Ribbentrop. The change was useful. One paragraph mentioned "the threat of Bolshevik dissolution" as the aim of the pact. In reality, where is this threat? And even if such a threat existed, though not to our countries, why should we be concerned about it? We should not. Every possibility of dissolution and breakdown of other peoples should be encouraged and favored by us at the proper moment.

Señor Annos has brought the Duce a message from Franco that provides a summing up of the situation and also confirming an imminent victory. The Duce was very appreciative of the message, and also praised it for the manner in which it was written, defining it as "the report of a subordinate."

Then with the Duce we examined at length actions to be taken: closer relations with Yugoslavia, Hungary, Romania, and possibly Poland, for the purpose of securing raw materials. Alliance with Spain as soon as the war is won. Claims against France. No Nice, no Savoy, because they are outside the Alpine range. Corsica: autonomy, independence, annexation. Tunisia: minority settlement for the Italians, autonomy of the Bey, Italian protectorate. Djibouti: free port and railroad, administration in common with France, annexation. Suez Canal: strong participation in the administration. Liquidation of Albania in agreement with Belgrade, eventually favoring Serbian settlement in Salonika.

January 9, 1939

I have secretly informed Starace about the treaty of alliance. He was enthusiastic about it, and said that for some time he had hoped for such a solution. It is true: even in the moments of crisis for the Axis, as, for instance, after the Anschluss, Starace was among the few who openly favored our understanding with Germany. I gave him these instructions: to stay calm until Chamberlain, to whom we must give a not too enthusiastic welcome, leaves Rome; then, afterward, steadily increase propaganda against France, so that the alliance will happen when anti-French feeling is at its height; at the news of the signing of the pact there must be enthusiastic demonstrations with a sharp flavor of Francophobia. Starace says that not too much work is needed for all this, since the change has already occurred, and thus it is easy to spark unanimous national feeling against France.

The Duce has answered quite cordially with a letter to Franco, urging him to proceed with caution up to the conclusion of the war, without accepting compromises or mediations of any kind. Also as regards the restoration of the monarchy, the Duce suggested that Franco go slow. He prefers a united and pacified Spain under the guidance of the Caudillo, head of the country and of the party. It will be easy for Franco to govern if he first achieves full military success. The prestige of a leader victorious in war is never questioned.

January 10, 1939

From the information we now have, it is clear that not all responsibility for the border clashes between the Hungarians and the Czechs is on the side of Prague. On the contrary. The Hungarian attitude is not so good. From the beginning they tried to sabotage the Vienna arbitration. This is stupid politics, since it irritates both us and Germany and certainly cannot modify the situation. I spoke clearly to Villani. I told him to urge his government to stay in line and to refrain from provoking incidents where they will not be able to count on our support and even less that of the Germans. The Duce is also very resentful, especially since the French press is using the situation to discredit the influence and action of the Axis in Central Europe. He said, "These Hungarians begin to fall in my esteem. They didn't have the courage to act when they could have acted, and now they carry on like Jesuits. . . ."

Things are going well in Spain; the offensive is proceeding at a rapid and regular pace.

January 11, 1939

Arrival of Chamberlain. In substance, the visit was kept on a minor tone, since both the Duce and myself are not convinced it is of any use. The welcome of the crowd was good, particularly in the middle-class section of the city, where the old man with the umbrella is quite popular. The welcome was colder in the outskirts, where the workers are less emotional. Chamberlain, however, is very happy with the welcome. Undoubtedly he still remembers the boos with which he was received some months ago in friendly France. . . .

6 p.m.: Conference at the Palazzo Venezia. The recorded conversations were held in a tired manner. The matters which were discussed were not the most important ones, and both parties betrayed their mental reservations. Today's conversation has been rather one of exploration. Effective contact has not been made. How far apart we are from these people! It is another world. We were talking about it after dinner with the Duce, together in a corner of the room. "These men are not made of the same stuff," he was saying, "as the Francis Drakes and the other magnificent adventurers who created the empire. These, after all, are the tired sons of a long line of rich men and they will lose their empire." Then, speaking of France, the Duce was quite offended by an article in *Europe Nouvelle*, which made unpleasant remarks about his private life. He said, "They will be the first to fall. These insults are punished with cannon fire and bombs."

January 12, 1939

Conference at the Palazzo Chigi with Lord Halifax. He is better in a tête-à-tête than in public discussion. He talks of politics with a kind of impersonal interest. The conversation turned especially to Spain. I repeated our point of view to him and he gave his. But he does not seem to be very convinced, and at heart I think he would be happy if Franco's victory were to settle the matter.

I let von Mackensen read yesterday's record. The recorded conversation of the afternoon was characterized by the deep worry which dominates the British with respect to Germany. German rearmament weighs down upon them like lead. They would be ready for any sacrifice if they could see the future clearly. This dark preoccupation of theirs has me more and more convinced of the need for the Triple Alliance. With such an instrument in our hands we could get whatever we want. The British do not want to fight. They try to draw back as slowly as possible, but they do not want to fight.

Mussolini defended Germany with strong loyalty, and he was also a bit secretive regarding his future projects and those of the Führer. Our conversations with the British have ended. Nothing was accomplished. I have telephoned von Ribbentrop that the visit was a "huge farce," totally harmless,
and I thanked him for the attitude of the German press.

January 13, 1939

No contact with the British during the morning and the afternoon; they
have gone to the Vatican. The atmosphere is now one of vague skepticism.
English newspapers defined the meeting as a game ending in no score. It's a
good characterization. I prepared a perfectly innocuous press release, which
I showed to the Duce at the Palazzo Venezia late this evening when he
returned from the Terminillo Mountains where he had gone skiing. He approved it. Dinner at Lord Perth's. Afterward, a short conversation between
the Duce, Chamberlain, and me. We spoke of the Jewish question, and it
was interesting to note that Chamberlain did not know the number of Jews
in Great Britain. He thought there were probably 60,000. The Duce said
that they were in excess of 200,000. Chamberlain is very much concerned
with the problem and he said that any further Jewish immigration to England might increase the anti-Semitism which already exists in many parts
of the country. During the meeting François-Poncet tried to get close to the
Duce, who proudly turned his back on him. The French ambassador cannot
get anything done; the Duce hates him. It has been learned from the minister of Uruguay that Poncet has said that the Duce is in the period of intellectual decay. An intercepted letter from him had this to say: "In Germany I
had to deal with real gentlemen; here, instead, I have to deal with servants
who have become masters." These are the rocks on which the Poncet mission is shipwrecked. He has been disoriented by the coolness of our reception, and so he now piles mistake upon mistake.

January 14, 1939

I accompanied the Duce to the station for Chamberlain's departure. He
is furious at the British press in general, but especially with the *Daily Express*
for an editorial by Lord Forbes, full of idiotic clichés, concerning the hostility of the Italian people toward Axis politics.

The leave-taking was brief but cordial. Chamberlain kept repeating his
thanks to me for the treatment that was accorded him during his stay in
Italy.

Chamberlain's eyes filled with tears when the train started moving and
his countrymen began singing "For He's a Jolly Good Fellow." "What is this
little song?" the Duce asked Grandi. Old Chamberlain is a pleasant fellow,
and quite aside from any other consideration I can understand the cordial
atmosphere which has grown around him.

Mussolini indirectly inspired a violent editorial in *Il Tevere* entitled "Spit-
ting on France." Tomorrow I shall propose to him that wide publicity be

given to a lengthy talk by Campinchi in a hotel in Bastia, reported to me by two of our Corsican secret agents, Grimaldi and Pietri. The speech threatens war against Italy in June and reveals exact plans of aggression by France. The report is absolutely authentic. I think that if properly used by the press, this report will go a long way toward creating a tremendous sensation, and, at any rate, will increase the wave of hatred against the French, which in Italy is already impressive.

I have sent Hitler exact copies of the two reports of the meetings at the Palazzo Venezia.

January 15, 1939

News of the troops advancing in Catalonia is more and more encouraging. General Gambara has taken on the role of leader of all Spanish forces. Rumors are beginning to circulate about French intervention in large numbers. I do not believe them. For the French to intervene now, in the present state of the war, would mean sending a great many forces or else risk being smashed along with the Catalans. They are in no position to do this; they would have to mobilize on a large scale. Moreover, a country which in the second half of the year just past has had forty thousand more deaths than births cannot allow itself the luxury of wasting the blood of its limited population. If the French intervene, so shall we. Mussolini said this morning, "If Paris sends forces we shall land 30 battalions at Valencia, even if this starts a world war."

I discussed with the Duce what I must say and do in Yugoslavia. The Albanian question was the principal point of the discussion. We agreed that it would not pay to gamble with our precious friendship with Belgrade to win Albania. Therefore, as things stand, we shall take action only if we can reach an agreement on the following basis: increase at the Yugoslav borders, demilitarization of the Albanian borders, military alliance, and absolute support of the Serbs in their conquest of Salonika.

January 16, 1939

The troops are advancing in Catalonia at an accelerated pace. Reus and Tarragona fell yesterday; today, it appears, Cervera as well. At this pace the situation in Barcelona will also become untenable. The Duce is convinced of this: he says that an exhausted army becomes paralyzed when it has its back to the sea. Victory now seems certain. For this reason we don't intend to let the French intervene. This morning I called Lord Perth and spoke to him as follows: "I warn you that if the French intervene in strength in favor of the Reds in Barcelona, we shall attack Valencia. Thirty battalions, fully equipped, are ready to board ship at the first hint. We shall move ahead even if it should start a European war. Therefore I ask you to urge the French to be moderate and to realize the sense of responsibility the situation demands."

I do not believe that France will act, even though with the taking of Barcelona a crisis will arise, the full import of which cannot be clearly understood today.

Conference with Sereggi, bearer of a letter from King Zog, who asks for a kind of mediation with the Yugoslavs regarding the treatment of the Albanian minorities living in Kosovo; if everything goes well, and if Stoyadinovich is able to march ahead with determination, I shall certainly give Zog the mediation!

January 17, 1939

The advance continues well. Many rumors of French intervention and a great deal of agitation among the French extreme political parties, but nothing serious; at least not for the time being.

The German ambassador, acting on behalf of von Ribbentrop, asked me to sound out Belgrade to ascertain whether Stoyadinovich intends to give his approval to the anti-Comintern pact. I shall try; but in my mind this is premature. There is no doubt about the intentions of Stoyadinovich with respect to the Axis and full solidarity. Personally, he would like to go even further. But I wonder if the present internal situation will allow him to make decisions of that kind, and I am inclined to think not.

Dentice di Frasso has given us information about an astonishing American invention of a very powerful smokeless, colorless, and flashless gunpowder. They appear ready to give us the secret. Dentice vouches for this claim but I am skeptical about such inventions. In any case, I am inclined to have one of our officers of the SIM take a trip to the United States in order to meet the inventor and look into the matter. It is always worth trying. Who knows?

A long conversation with Lord Lloyd,[385] to whom I repeated briefly and with some reserve what I had said to Halifax with respect to France.

January 18, 1939

Departure for Belje. Normal trip; cordial demonstrations at Trieste and Postumia.

January 19, 1939

Arrival at Belje. Hare hunt. On the way back by train, Stoyadinovich and I had a conversation. I brought up the Albanian question. At first Stoyadinovich seemed perturbed. Then he broke the ice, and spoke of the partition of Albania as the best solution.

January 20, 1939

Hunt in the forest. Good news from Spain. Stoyadinovich received it, shouting, "Corsica, Tunis, Nice!"

January 21, 1939

Final hunt at Belje. Departure for Belgrade during the evening. Stoyadinovich requested that I speak at length with the Regent and to inform him thoroughly of the international political situation. He is careful about his relations with the monarchy, which do not seem good.

January 22, 1939

Belgrade. A hunt and a long conversation with the Regent. I am particularly moved by the spontaneity of the welcome accorded me, which was very different from my last visit here. I made a report on my trip, to be filed in Rome in my volume of notes.

January 23, 1939

Return trip to Rome. Many cheering crowds at the various stations.

January 24, 1939

This morning I went to Villa Torlonia, to report to the Duce about my trip and its results. He was very satisfied. He was particularly interested in hearing that I found such widespread anti-German feeling in Yugoslavia. He was also delighted about Albania. He informed me about what had happened during my absence. Nothing very important, except for the news that the first woman was executed. There was a great deal of opposition to this punishment, fearing popular reaction. The Duce, instead, approved of it because he was convinced the masses would approve. And in reality, while the execution of a man was accepted in silence, this one was greeted with applause. The woman had murdered her own child. The crime took place in Terni.

I met Lord Perth, concerning my possible previous communication, before my departure, about French intervention in Spain. It caused alarm in London. They request that we do nothing before consulting with the British government. In principle I reassured Lord Perth.

Good, excellent news from Spain. The troops are taking up positions in the suburbs of Barcelona, so that they may occupy the city at any moment.

We ask that our Legionaries be among the first units to enter. They deserve it.

Conversation with Villani. I informed him about what I had done at Belgrade, particularly regarding Hungary. I recommended moderation regarding Romania. I do not understand how a country like Hungary, preoccupied with the German danger, does not seem to be able to see the danger of aggravating the crisis with Romania, toward which the most dangerous ambitions of Berlin seem to point. What would be the Magyar position the day when the Germans reach the borders of Transylvania?

January 25, 1939

The Duce is very anxious to get word about the occupation of Barcelona. He calls often, because he fears a repetition of what took place in Madrid; I doubt it.

I informed von Mackensen of the outcome of my trip to Belgrade, and received Lord Perth, who came to ask us to warn Franco, to refrain from taking vengeance against all his enemies after victory. I reassured him and told him that we have always tried to act as moderators. I recall that after the taking of Bilbao the Duce sent a letter which, when it is published, will do much honor to its author.

Our volunteers are overcoming the final resistance of the Lister division. Barcelona is also within reach for them, who have had the hardest task, and they are anxious to reach it.

January 26, 1939
Long conversation with the King of Bulgaria. I had not met him before. My first impression was not good, given his physical appearance. My later impression was better. We spoke at length about the international situation, with particular reference to the Danubian basin and the Balkans. He asked for news about my trip to Yugoslavia, and spoke about his agreement with that country with such feeling that I had the impression he was sincere. He was very bitter against Romania, but his intensity was the kind befitting a lymphatic person. He wants the province of Dobruja, and he wants it particularly because of great irredentist agitation. He spoke also of an outlet on the Aegean Sea, but added that this must be considered as the second step in the settlement of Bulgarian claims.

While I was at the golf club the news arrived that Barcelona had fallen. I notified the Duce at Terminillo and came to an agreement with Starace about the celebration of the event all over Italy. All that was necessary was to set the time, without any pressure, because the Italian population was spontaneously enthusiastic about the news.

The Duce, too, was deeply moved, despite the fact that he would like to show himself to be imperturbably calm.

But he has good reason to be truly satisfied, because victory in Spain bears only one name, that of Mussolini, who conducted the campaign bravely, firmly, even at a time when many people who cheer him now were against him.

January 27, 1939
The Duce has asked to see the minister of Greece in my presence. According to a report coming from Bucharest it seems that the Greek military attaché had made insulting remarks about our army in a conversation with a Hungarian colleague. The poor minister of Greece trembled like a leaf when Mussolini, with a hard, metallic face, told him that if, within three days, we were not given full satisfaction, there would be serious complications. It is his intention to hand his passport to the Greek minister, who, during this stormy scene, had nothing to say except to congratulate us on the capture of Barcelona.

Lord Perth has submitted for our approval the outline of the speech which Chamberlain will make before the House of Commons, so that we might suggest changes, if necessary. The Duce approved it and commented, "I believe this is the first time that the head of the British government submits to a foreign government the outline of one of his speeches. It's a bad sign for them."

At my suggestion Gambara has been promoted in the field to the post of divisional commander. He has deserved it, both because of his talent and because of the blood he has shed.

The Spaniards are preparing to make a political pact with Germany, of which the Germans have communicated the text to us. If it happens to be secret, like ours, there will be no objection. But if it is to be made public I consider it imperative that we be the first to release the news. Otherwise people will say that Italy makes war in Spain and Germany benefits from it.

January 28, 1939

Fagiuoli[386] reported to me a conversation he had in France with Monsieur Baudouin,[387] administrator of the salt mines in Somalia, who stated that he had been secretly put in charge by Daladier to start conversations with us about this matter. François-Poncet must not be informed about it, because in Paris he is no longer considered an authority on the Italian situation. It seems that Daladier is ready to make many concessions in these three areas: Djibouti, the Suez Canal, and the statutes regarding the Italians in Tunisia. I informed the Duce, although he also is very skeptical about these clandestine ambassadors. He suggested, however, that Monsieur Baudouin come to Rome for a possible conversation.

Long meeting with Silimbani, consul general in Tunis. French authorities are exerting a great deal of pressure, with every means in their power, to denationalize the Italians. They are preparing a *coup d'théâtre*, with the simultaneous publication of a large number of applications for naturalization, which will be the proof that the Italians want no part of their national aspirations. In order to ward off the blow and oppose the maneuver, we will organize a collective return to Italy of one thousand Italians who wish to escape the French pressure aimed at forcing them to give up their citizenship. We will create Tunisian refugees, just as there have been Austrian and Sudeten émigrés and refugees.

January 29, 1939

Nothing interesting except good news from Gambara about a further advance by the CTV toward the Pyrenees.

We captured 24 batteries and an airplane which was about to take off. Gambara is requesting food shipments, because the population is literally starving. They are sharing the rations of the Legionaries, and shout, "Long live Franco! Long live Italy!"

January 30, 1939

The minister of Greece brought his government's answer; it is an act of abject submission made in terms which leave no doubts as to the Greeks' fear of us. A guilty conscience weighs upon them, and recent experiences have proved that small countries can count only on the friendship and the enmity of their geographical neighbors.

We shipped food supplies to Barcelona. The Duce had a terrible cold, but at the same time he is very much concerned about the preparation of the militia for the parade of February 1. He is personally involved in the most minute details. He spends many a half-hour at the window of his office, hidden behind the blue curtains, looking at the movements of the various units. He ordered that drums and trumpets be used at the same time. He chose the bandleader's baton, and he teaches the movements to be made in person, and he changes the proportions and design of the baton. He is a strong believer that in the armed forces it is the form that determines the substance as well. He says that 1.4 billion men were required to defeat 60 million Germans, because the rigid Prussian military training has made them invincible soldiers. Very often he accuses the King of having diminished the physical prestige of our army in order to harmonize it with his own "unhappy physique."

January 31, 1939
The Führer's speech has produced the best impression everywhere. Even the Duce was very much satisfied with it, and he had me telephone von Ribbentrop so that he might tell Hitler that the words uttered last night have given a great deal of joy and satisfaction to all the Italian people. In fact today the Duce and I observed that the crowd applauded some officers of the SA with much warmth in the Piazza Venezia. The Axis is becoming popular. The Germans are working to this end as well as the French with their politics, based upon coarse insults and ill-concealed spite.

Conference with King Boris. Ostensibly it was to confer a decoration upon me, but in reality it was to protest politely against the exuberant activity of some members of the Italian Legation, Talamo included, who have created a difficult and uncomfortable situation. I shall intervene.

The Turkish ambassador renewed the invitation of his government that I should visit Ankara. I replied that I had not gone previously because I had become aware that the Turks themselves preferred that the visit be postponed. I had read it in a decoded cable. He became as red as a beet and said that perhaps the delay was because of the health of Ataturk. However, I was noncommittal about the invitation.

Grandi telephoned today saying that Chamberlain's speech in the House of Commons with reference to his trip to Italy has been very well received.

February 1, 1939
Review of the militia. Altogether it was very beautiful. The units are now truly ready. Masses both of men and steel. The parade, however, was boring. Nobody more than myself is in favor of the Roman step. It imposes a form which gives life to the substance itself. But eliminating the bands during the march past creates a sense of heavy monotony, even if this hammering of steps on the pavement acts by itself to create a sense of strength. The Germans blend together step, band, and drums with excellent results. We ought to do the same; it is not bad to use their own experience in view of the undeniable fact that this particular step is a genuine imitation of the Prussians. Casini[388] proposes creating an important political daily in Rome, which nowadays does not exist. I agree but it must not be owned by industrialists. Why would they need it? If a daily must be created, logically the

Fascist party should be the owner. Afterward I was visited by Pignatti, and by the Papal Nuncio. The atmosphere for the celebration of the tenth anniversary is becoming murky;[389] the Duce has no intention of answering the Pope's letter, nor of granting the changes in the law concerning mixed marriages. I asked Pignatti to find out at the Vatican because we must be sure the Pope avoids some of those sharp statements he is known to make when he speaks to the bishops if we are to accept invitations to St. Peter's.

Muti is back. Things are going extremely well in Spain. He asked for reinforcements and weapons for the final blow at Valencia and Madrid. We decided to send both.

February 2, 1939

A short meeting with von Mackensen. He says that the German government has in no way dissuaded Budapest from reaching an agreement with Bucharest. They agree with us that no opportunity should be missed to do everything in our power to have Romania become part of our system. I thanked von Mackensen for the Führer's speech and told him that we are preparing for a solemn demonstration confirming our feelings. Actually, on the Duce's orders I prepared the agenda for the meeting of the Grand Council in honor of Hitler.

I received M. Baudouin. He strikes me as being a quiet and well-mannered person. He tells me that he had a conversation with Daladier and Bonnet on Sunday and that he speaks for them. Naturally, he does not commit either Paris or Rome; his visit can be denied at any moment if we so choose. In conclusion, Daladier does not intend to make any open territorial concession; if we demanded territories there would be war. However, he is ready to make the following concessions: a large free zone in Djibouti; a share in the administration of the port; cession to Italy of the railroad in Ethiopian territory; support for our demands concerning Suez; review of the 1935 agreements concerning Tunis, provided Tunisia is not turned into an "Italian Sudetenland." I made clear that with regard to Tunis we ask but one thing: the right of the Italians to remain Italians. I reserved the right to give him an answer only after speaking with the Duce.

February 3, 1939

I report to the Duce on the conversation with M. Baudouin. He agreed that the proposals are interesting. As things stand, there are only two alternatives: either to deal on this basis, postponing the solution of the whole problem to a more favorable date, or face it now; the latter alternative would mean war. The Duce has prepared a report to the Grand Council, which he read to me. He is in favor of diplomatic negotiations; therefore, he authorized me to answer M. Baudouin that we consider the proposals worthy of consideration. He prefers that the negotiations be carried on through the ambassador. "If we reach an agreement through the mediation of a banker, suspicions of a moral character will be leveled against us." He ordered me, moreover, to keep von Mackensen secretly informed of everything.

Conversation with Baudouin. He was moved when I told him that it was through his action that the contact was made, and he understands that it is not his task to handle the negotiations to follow. We agreed that he will report to Paris and that the French government will have François-Poncet officially repeat to me everything that Baudouin told me yesterday, unless something new comes up. If there are unforeseen details to be discussed, he will write to me through Fagiuoli. I again recommended the greatest amount of discretion: should the press find out about this attempt to reach an understanding everything will fail on short notice.

February 4, 1939

While I am at the golf club I receive Gambara's cable announcing the occupation of Gerona by the Littorio division. Catalonia is now completely occupied, and there remains only the final blow at the center.

To that end we shall immediately begin to reorganize the CTV, which must again take on the task of carrying the Spanish along.

I informed von Mackensen of my conversation with Baudouin; as far I could judge he received with pleasure the news of our possible diplomatic settlement of our dispute with France.

Lord Perth is concerned about our sending fresh troops to Libya. I avoided a definite answer, but I made it a point to reassure him on two items: that nothing is done in the direction of the eastern border, and the trips of Lütze and of General Udet to Libya have no military purpose. Stoyadinovich has offered his resignation. Is this a maneuver or a genuine fall? We shall see. In any case it disturbs me.

Meeting of the Grand Council. The Duce read his report (a copy of which will go in the volume of his writings), and said that it represents a password to future generations. For the first time he prepared a document for the Grand Council and he wishes that it be included in the record under the title, "The March to the Sea." I, too, made my report, and it was greeted with hearty applause.

February 5, 1939

The Duce explained in detail what has been done for Libya: there are 30,000 men now, and 30,000 more will be sent there. In order to understand why this must be done, one need only compare the extent of our forces with those of the French in Tunisia, Algeria, and Morocco.

For the celebration of the tenth anniversary of the Lateran Treaty at St. Peter's I have been delegated to represent the government. Prince Umberto will represent the Royal House. The Duce was thinking of sending lesser officials, but Pignatti asked him not to do this, in order to avoid giving offense to the Pope, as he was already exasperated.

No definite news about the Yugoslav crisis. The Duce said that this is more proof that we can do business with only one country, meaning Germany, which, like ourselves, is not changeable in its directives and in the obligations it assumes. Stoyadinovich's position seemed to be secure; a fortnight ago he was saying that nothing and no one could get him out of power. Now, things are different. Now, the crisis interests me, not so much with regard to our relations with Belgrade, which will not change very much for a certain length of time, but rather with regard to Albania, about which we had practically reached an agreement. Anyway, we agreed with the Duce on the following formula: to forge ahead just the same. With Stoyadinovich, partition of Albania between us and Yugoslavia; *without* Stoyadinovich, occupation of Albania by us without Yugoslavia, and, if necessary, even against Yugoslavia.

February 6, 1939

Ribbentrop telephoned to tell me that a Frenchman, de Brinon,[390] has been to see him and mentioned the possibility of diplomatic agreements between Rome and Paris. He also seems to know about Baudouin's trip. I got the impression that Ribbentrop wanted us to proceed with the negotiations. I told him that we are taking no initiative, but in any case this shows that Baudouin's top-secret mission is now known. It is becoming more and more difficult to work with these democracies. Ribbentrop also spoke with optimism of the Tripartite Alliance with Japan and of the Yugoslav crisis; he believes that the new Foreign Minister is oriented towards the line of the Axis.

I saw Poncet at the Papal Nuncio's residence. He made some mention of the futility of his stay in Rome up to now, but I let the subject flag, and spoke instead of sports and art. The Japanese ambassador is skeptical about the possibility of quickly realizing the Triple Alliance; he believes that the Japanese counterproposal is an expedient which he himself advises us not to accept.

I saw the Duce at the Palazzo Venezia. He believes that the liquidation of Stoyadinovich is a real *coup d'etat* on the part of the Regent, who sought to thwart the strengthening of the Fascist dictatorship in Yugoslavia. I gave the Duce my point of view about the Albanian matter: we must work faster. He agreed with me. We shall begin immediately to recall ground troops and to concentrate the air force. We shall intensify local revolutionary preparations. The date of the action: Easter week.

February 7, 1939

The Duce is right. Stoyadinovich informed Indelli[391] that the Regent was aware of what was going on, and was, perhaps, himself at the center of the plot against him. However, Stoyadinovich has no intention of giving up. He has not yet decided how to proceed, but is determined to take revenge, and popular sentiment is more and more openly behind him. However, I wonder what he can do politically? His position was becoming stronger, but not yet strong enough to face a coalition which, with the encouragement of the Regent, was growing against him.

During the evening I saw the Duce, and we spoke at length about the situation. I repeated my views on the necessity of acting faster in the Albanian question for the following reasons: (1) the Yugoslavs now know that we are thinking of the matter, and the rumor may spread; (2) with the removal of Stoyadinovich the Yugoslav card has lost 90 percent of its value to us; (3) since the enterprise will no longer be undertaken in conjunction with Yugoslavia, but without her, and perhaps even against her, we must not give her time to strengthen her contacts with France and with England on political, diplomatic, and military grounds. Barring unforeseen circumstances, we set with the Duce the date for the attack between April 1st and 9th. In the meantime, I will meet with Ribbentrop, and perhaps mention the matter to him.

February 8, 1939

The Duce is unhappy about Japanese delays concerning the Tripartite Alliance, and he deplores the thoughtless manner in which Ribbentrop assured us that the Tokyo government had agreed. He feels that an alliance between Germany and Italy should be concluded without Japan. He observes that such an alliance would alone be sufficient to meet the array of British-French forces, and at the same time would not appear to be anti-English or anti-American.

We cabled Berlin, urging them to quickly reach an agreement with Spain, in order to counteract the *rapprochement* between Burgos and Paris. We shall then announce that we have had an agreement with Spain since November 1936.

I received De Man,[392] whose mission it is to organize a four-power conference on behalf of the King of the Belgians. I told him that it seems to me that the necessary and sufficient conditions for such an initiative do not exist. De Man expressed his point of view in a trivial way; what interested me most about him was a slight tan, which he got some place in the mountains! Jacomoni arrived, and confirmed the fact that it's time to act quickly. The air is tense in Albania; unquestionably all the chiefs are with us. But how long can the secret be kept? We studied at length the details of the operation.

February 9, 1939

The Royal Signature. Among other things the King told me that yesterday two persons had reported to him that at the last meeting of the Grand Council the Duce had deplored the meeting of November 30. I reported this to the Duce: more evidence that the Grand Council is not a completely reliable branch of government. We must change its composition and reduce the number of its members to a minimum.

I proposed to the Duce, who approved, that we put to vote tomorrow evening in the Grand Council the agenda for the celebration of the tenth anniversary of the Lateran Pact. Our relations with the Church have greatly cleared up during the last few days. I did my best to bring this about. In the evening news arrived that the Pope's condition had worsened. His death would be rather upsetting at this time. We would approach the conclave in an atmosphere of prejudice quite hostile to our purposes. We might have to expect unpleasant surprises. During the meeting of the Supreme Defense Commission I showed the Duce the transcript of the telephone call by

Pignatti concerning the last heart attack suffered by the Pope, and he only shrugged his shoulders, completely indifferent. Strange. For some time now Mussolini exhibits an increasingly strong detachment from anything related to the Church. He didn't used to be like that.

February 10, 1939

The Pope is dead. The news leaves the Duce completely indifferent. During my personal report to him he mentioned the death only in order to inform me that this evening he will postpone the meeting of the Grand Council out of respect for the memory of the Pope, and also because the public is much too concerned with the mourning to be interested in school reform.

Great resentment about Germany's wish to grab hold of Albanian oil. The evidence comes from an official communication sent to Attolico. I called Mackensen and informed him that we considered Albania just like another Italian province, and that any German intervention would create strong resentment within Italian public opinion. This fact also proves that the Albanian boil will come to a head very shortly. The Serbs have leaked the news. King Zog is alarmed and very much agitated. Some move could be made in order to thwart our action.

I went to the Holy See to offer the respects of the government at the bier of the Pope, and was received by the dean of the cardinals and by Pacelli, who is now Camerlengo of the Holy Roman Church. I conveyed the sympathy of the Italian government and of the Fascist people, and I said that the deceased Pope had forever tied his name to history through the Lateran Treaty. They liked my expressions very much. Pacelli directed me to the Sistine Chapel where the Pontiff rested on a high catafalque, and he spoke to me about the relationship between State and Church with very agreeable and hopeful expressions. Of the Pope himself we could see nothing—only his enormous white sandals and the hem of his robe; but the atmosphere created was one of infinity.

February 11, 1939

The Grand Council approved the agenda, and postponed the meeting in a display of mourning. Starace and Farinacci were opposed to such a statement, but I insisted, and Federzoni and Balbo agreed with me. The Duce, however, is always bitter about the Church. I called him in order to report what Pignatti had said; the Holy See was expecting a gesture of respect from him at the bier of the Pope, and he answered that it was too late: "That he is not interested at all in the conclave. If the Pope is an Italian, all right; if he is a foreigner, it's fine just the same."

I received Ambassador von Mackensen, who gave me the following explanations about the question of Albanian oil. They had received a proposal, but nothing had been done, and nothing would be done. The haste with which the answer was given was proof of the German eagerness to dispel anything that could upset the Axis.

The Duce praised the public assistance activity, organized by the Princess of Piedmont in Alto Adige. He said that the Princess was very fearful of him and that very often she would ask him questions and seek his instructions. Once, he said, she took out a small notebook and, following a line with her finger, asked the Duce what was the meaning of the statement that the Grand Council must now regulate the succession to the throne. The Duce answered that this would be the case only if there were a lack of continuity in the direct line, or in exceptional circumstances. She seemed to be satisfied, but the question proved how much the members of the royal family are worried about the future.

February 12, 1939

The Duce agreed to take part in the funeral of the Pope, which has been set by the nunciature for the 17th. That decision pleases me, because it will make a good impression on the conclave participants. In some American circles it is rumored that the Camerlengo has a document written by the Pope. The Duce wants Pignatti to find out, and, if it is true, to try to get a copy of the document "in order to avoid a repetition of the Filippelli incident."[393]

Calm, for the time being, in other areas.

Gorgeous Sunday of a Roman winter, warm and sunny. I spent most of it at the golf club.

February 13, 1939

General Piccio: pro-French. He reported some conversations of minor importance with Flandin and Laval, both of whom complain that they had been put in a difficult position through our requests, just when they had been able to obtain approval for the appointment of a new French ambassador to the Farnese Palace. Paul-Boncour was more inclined to be conciliatory. He said: "You have been too demanding; but we are too intransigent." Piccio says that French armaments are going to be very imposing in a very short time.

Lord Perth spoke to me again about our forces to be sent to Libya. Nothing to be done. The proportion between the Arabic population of Libya and that of the French empire is 18 to 1; that of the armed forces is actually 1 to 8. We must be in a position to defend ourselves, and such a right cannot be denied us by any clause in any Italian-British agreement.

The Duce comments on the incident between Goebbels and Froelich and says: "Goebbels is wrong, not because he took Froelich's wife, but rather because he allowed himself to be slapped in the face. You can steal a man's wife but not agree to be slapped." The commercial agreement between Italy and Germany has been signed. It embraces many points and, as the technicians say, is very satisfactory.

February 14, 1939

The Swiss minister came to express his regrets about the misdeed of his country's press, and the Spanish ambassador told me that General Jordana[394] has rejected the French suggestion to send an unofficial agent, and also France's request for a declaration of Spanish neutrality. The Duce said that with regard to Albania we must await two events: the settling of the Spanish affair, and the alliance with Germany. In the meantime, we must incite a revolt against Zog and spread the wildest rumors; like the octopus we must darken the waters. With regard to France, he repeated that it is desirable for the moment to await the development of the Baudouin initiative. Should such an undertaking not develop, we shall put the question: Will you or will you not do business? If not, we shall prepare for war without delay. He also told me that we are in possession of a secret weapon which, "though not miraculous, could, nonetheless, affect the course of the war."

The Dutch minister attempted an energetic representation with regard to the problem of the Dutch Jews, but he slowed up when I told him that we might have considered something like a gracious gesture, but never under pressure. Imagine the Dutch trying to play tough!

February 15, 1939
A little personal episode: Starace caught the honorable Martire, a former member of the Popular party, and a Fascist since 1932, in the corridors of the Chamber of Deputies in the act of trying to bad-mouth me, saying that I had the "evil eye." As his petty maliciousness was flickering out, he would have done well to tumble into bed in the dark; but he had other ideas, and preferred to try to "stab me in the back," as the Duce said later. In the final analysis, Martire was properly handcuffed and sent to jail; Ferretti, who was present at the incident, and who failed to report it, was expelled from the party. In itself the incident was insignificant, but from it the following good and bad conclusions can be drawn. Bad: the moral inadequacy of certain people whom we have admitted to our ranks, and who, in the shadows of the Littorio,[395] continue their shameful mudslinging. Good: it confirmed the Duce's psychological position towards me, since he reacted and acted with an intensity, a determination such as, according to Starace, had never been seen before. Starace also acted admirably: loyal, strong, a friend.

In the evening the Grand Council met. School reform was approved. The Duce spoke to me of the Martire affair, and expressed his regrets for not having been able to sock him in the ribs himself. And he added that seventeen years of governing have denied him "the pleasure of fighting several dozen duels."

February 16, 1939
Albania is restless. We received a cable from our military attaché to Tirana, which has somewhat disturbed the Duce, saying that the King [of Albania] wanted to order partial mobilization, and that Jacomoni had left by air for Rome. The situation is not so dramatic. I had a conference with Jacomoni, who, to tell the truth, appears quite calm. Yesterday he saw the King, who, after listening to our complaints, said that he, too, had something to say. It appears that in Belgrade they discussed the partition of Albania, but he

mentioned certain details, showing that he was only partially and incorrectly informed. He also mentioned the preparation for an internal revolt, supported especially by refugees—information that is completely false. He cited the names of many people involved; except for Koçi, these names were incorrect. He concluded reiterating his desire to reach an understanding with us, and he sent Jacomoni as his representative with full powers to seek an agreement. When I reported to the Duce by telephone he answered: "If we had already signed our pact with Berlin we could attack immediately. As things stand, we must procrastinate." Then he confirmed the instructions which I had already sent to Jacomoni two days ago, which can be summed up as follows: to keep popular agitation alive, but not fail to placate King Zog's doubts, giving him every reassurance he desires. To keep the waters muddy in order to prevent our true plans from surfacing.

February 19, 1939

The recall of Grandi from London is due to some information about him which has reached the Duce, but of which I know neither the substance nor the source. The Duce said, "It is time that this gloomy, ambiguous, and unfaithful Grandi returns to bathe in the atmosphere of the regime, and that he eventually become de-Anglicized. I will tell him personally that I have come to know things about him which have displeased me." The Duce carefully read a letter written by Nitti to Aldrovandi after the publication of his memoirs. The letter pitilessly attacks Sonnino, who is called "a bad Christian and bad Jew, and, above all, a bad minister." Mussolini himself admits that the letter is written with a good sense of humor.

The Duce is becoming more and more bitter against France, and he said that in these last months the French have reached the maximum of their perfidy and of their hate. He defined them as a "mean people." The Italians already hate France, but the Duce has every intention of increasing this hatred to an extreme in the course of the next few months. When he has waged war and beaten France he will show the Italians "how a peace in Europe should be made." He will not ask for indemnities, but will destroy all, and level many cities to the ground. He is, however, dissatisfied with the preparation of the two military departments: war and air force. While naval preparation is perfect, he does not know what is going on in the other two departments. I warn him again about Valle, who, on too many occasions, has made statements and promises, which are either not true or not possible.

February 20, 1939

On his return from Belgrade, Christich repeated to me what we already more or less knew of the Yugoslav crisis. He conferred with the Regent, who is very much intent on justifying himself with us for having double-crossed Stoyadinovich. In any case, his assurances of continued good relations with the Axis are many, and such that we cannot ignore. Christich informed me also of a meeting he had had with one of the heads of the opposition, Gavrilovic, who asked him to tell me that if he comes to power he will strengthen his ties with us. The present situation of the Cabinet is weak; either Stoyadinovich will return to power by April, or the new government will be led by the opposition.

The Duce has referred Nitti's letter to the King, and had a copy sent to me. The King generally shares Nitti's opinions on Sonnino, and, talking about Nitti, said that he was a man of clear vision and of great ability, but that these fundamental qualities were spoiled by "an unreasonable fear" which overtook him at any rustling of the leaves.

Exchange of telephone calls with Ribbentrop, in order to settle a joint action of our ambassadors with Franco to talk him into joining our anti-Comintern pact. The step will be taken when the Japanese ambassador has also received his instructions. If Franco joins, we shall put an end to the rumors which are spreading, even in Italy, about his too many intimate contacts with the Western democracies.

February 21, 1939

The joint action is no longer necessary, since Franco has decided to join the anti-Comintern pact, communicating this decision to our ambassadors, even though it remain secret until complete victory. Together with the Germans, we have accepted this solution, which is a good one because, in substance, it gives us the egg today and the chicken tomorrow.

Jacomoni referred to the Albanian situation: the King and his men have declared formally that they wish to re-establish the most cordial relations with us, but Jacomoni fears that this may be a ploy to gain time to allow the success of the King's many attempts to draw up pacts and understandings with third powers. Jacomoni feels that the situation should be changed abruptly. The Duce and I do not agree with him. I instruct him by cable to steer cautiously for some time yet, while we are waiting for certain events in the international field, which will make it easier for us to deliver our blow. Grandi returned to Rome and received with much distress the news of his recall from London. He still hopes, however, to be able to change Mussolini's decision in a coming meeting with the Duce. However, he realizes that something has happened to his relations with Mussolini, who, for some years now, has treated him coldly and with detachment.

The Fascist legions have marched into Barcelona in great form and amid enthusiastic applause. Gambara will be in Rome tomorrow for a conference.

February 22, 1939

The Duce is very happy about Franco's decision to join the anti-Comintern pact. The event is of great importance and its influence shall be felt in all future European happenings. After three centuries of inactivity Spain thus again becomes a living and dynamic factor, and, what is more important, an anti-French factor. Those silly people who tried so hard to criticize our intervention in Spain will one day perhaps understand that on the Ebro, at Barcelona, and at Malaga the foundations were laid for the Roman Mediterranean Empire.

Villani mentioned a trip by Teleki[396] to Italy for next April. I accepted with great pleasure, because I like Teleki, and I respect him as the best head of government Hungary ever had.

Christich gives me hopes about Stoyadinovich. He said that the personal jealousy of the Regent played a great role in the crisis, but he believes and hopes that in a few months Stoyadinovich will return to power again.

Arrival of Gambara. He made a very good report about matters in Spain. Either Madrid will surrender dramatically in a short time, or else at the end of March five columns will give the deathblow to Red Spain. The situation in Catalonia is good. Franco improved it with a very painstaking and drastic housecleaning. Many Italians also were taken prisoner: anarchists and communists. I informed the Duce about it, and he ordered that they all be shot, adding, "Dead men don't write history."

February 23, 1939

Attolico has sent a very interesting account of his conversation with Egyptian minister to Berlin, Mourad Pasha. He speaks in the name of his king, who declares himself to be one who hates the British, and asks whether in the event that Egypt should proclaim its neutrality and Great Britain should attempt to intervene directly or indirectly, the Axis will be ready to support the position of King Farouk. This matter is so serious that it makes me want to make a number of reservations, even though the source of information is very reliable. In agreement with the Duce I authorize Attolico to continue his conversations and to make it clear that any effort to weaken the ties between Egypt and London finds approval here.

The Duce eulogizes Gambara in lofty terms. Gambara presents his coming plan of action, which is not generally approved by the Duce, who would like to see the forces more concentrated. The Duce realizes, however, that in the present state of disintegration of Red Spain, Franco's plan to spread out the national armies all over the country might produce excellent results. He offers Gambara still another division, but Gambara refuses, and asks instead for two battalions of Alpini and a group of Alpine artillery, and these are immediately granted.

Discussion between the Duce and Grandi in the afternoon. The Duce was more clever than tough on him. In any case, he told Grandi that his mission was over, since it would lose its purpose after the signing of the Tripartite Alliance, and since he, Grandi, is becoming too Anglicized. He promised to give him another job when he leaves London.

February 24, 1939

On my way to Warsaw. Stopped at Vienna, where we had dinner at the Three Hussars. This city has a sleepy and tired appearance. Rochira[397] made the statement that high life in the center of the city has considerably deteriorated, but that the great mass of the people are working, live better, and are more and more favorable to the regime.

February 25-27, 1939

I arrive at Warsaw. The welcome of the population was characterized by curiosity and perhaps by a certain amount of sympathy, but there was no great enthusiasm. The city is gray, flat, and very gloomy, even though a tired and unusual-looking sun lighted without warming the streets of this characterless capital. I was very much aggravated with the news I have received about little anti-German demonstrations that have broken out here and there in all the Polish cities. They had been provoked by some incidents which have been taking place regularly at Danzig. Poland, in spite of all the efforts and the politics of Beck, is fundamentally and constitutionally anti-German. Its tradition, its instincts, and its interests oppose it to Germany. It is a Catholic country with large nuclei of Jews as well as strong German minorities. It inevitably contains all the elements of opposition toward Germanic imperialism. On the other hand, for us Italians it has the positive element of a general sympathy toward us, which has no practical results. The Poles are more interested in our art than in our way of living. They know our monuments better than our history. Basically, they do not consider us as we like to be considered. Too many painters, sculptors, and architects have represented Italy in Poland in the past, and continue to represent us with the inevitable servility of the artist who, in distant lands, finds a foreign Maecenas.

They love in us our artistic nature rather than the strength of our arms, in which they still do not believe entirely. We must work hard to correct the bad name the past three centuries have given us.

I have talks with just about everybody, but especially with Beck. There were no sensational elements in our discussion. Poland will continue in her policy of equilibrium, dictated by her geographical situation. With Russia, nothing more than strictly necessary contacts. With France a defensive alliance on which the Poles do not rely more than is necessary. With Germany, a good-neighbor policy, maintained with difficulty due to many spiritual and concrete differences. It will be necessary to find a solution regarding Danzig, but Beck wants this solution to emerge from free diplomatic negotiations, avoiding any useless and damaging pressure by public opinion. There is still a great deal of worry about the Ruthenian problem. The Poles are unwilling to consider Czechoslovakia's borders as final, and they still hope to reach a common border with Hungary. Concern for the Ukrainian problem presses heavily on the Polish mind, though the Poles are not talking about it; however, Beck frequently emphasizes with satisfaction, though without conviction, the assurances he has received from Hitler.

In speaking about the present situation of Czechoslovakia he defined it as "a temporary arrangement that may last for some time without, however, ceasing to be a temporary arrangement." I limited myself to a general discussion, in the course of which I stressed as much as possible the strength of the ties that link us to Germany.

I had conversations with the ambassadors from Germany and Japan, with the Papal Nuncio, and with the ministers from Hungary and Yugoslavia. I visited military organizations, particularly those relating to the air force, which made a good impression on me. I am not able to say much about the internal structure of the country, because I have not been able to observe it to any extent. But it is far from being a totalitarian regime, in spite of the fact that the only voice which counts in Poland is that of a dead man, Pilsudski,[398] and there are far too many who vie for the title of being the true heirs of his wisdom. Besides, the fact that he has remained as a posthumous dictator proves that no new force has as yet surfaced and asserted itself. Otherwise, even Marshal Pilsudski, like all dead people, would have quickly faded away.

Summarizing my impressions in terms of our own interests, it would be foolish to conclude that Poland has been won over to the Axis or to the triangle [Germany, Italy, Japan], but it would be too pessimistic to describe it as altogether hostile. When the great crisis comes Poland will remain on the sidelines for a long time, and only when the result of the struggle becomes clear will it join the winning side. And this is correct, because it is a country that has friends and enemies on both sides.

February 28, 1939

Hunting at Bialowicza, a magnificent forest, wild and primitive, and very well stocked with rare game.

March 1, 1939

Krakow: monuments and palaces, which to the Poles seem so many and so beautiful, but which in our eyes amount to very little.

March 2, 1939

Return trip. At Tarvisio I received the report of the election to the papacy of Cardinal Pacelli. It did not surprise me. I recall the conference I had had with him on February 10. He was very conciliatory, and it seems also that in the meantime he has improved relations with Germany. In fact, Pignatti said only yesterday that he is the Cardinal preferred by the Germans. At the dinner table I had already said to Edda and to my staff, "The Pope will be elected today. It is going to be Pacelli, who will take the name of Pius XII." The fact that my prediction came to pass interested everybody.

March 3, 1939

I returned to Rome. I found nothing particularly new in internal politics nor at the Ministry. I saw my staff and Alfieri, who gave me a digest of the events of the last few days. The Duce has gone to Terminillo. He telephoned me, saying that he would like to see me, and in the afternoon I went to him.

He was interested in my none-too-optimistic report on Poland. I must admit that from Rome he has always viewed the Polish situation with greater insight than those who had spent many long years on the spot. He called Poland "an empty nut." He is satisfied with Pacelli's election. He promised to send the Pope some advice on how he can usefully govern the Church. He does not, however, intend to use Tacchi-Venturi, who, in his opinion, has outlived his usefulness. We discussed the Tripartite Alliance at length.

New delays have been injected by Japanese procedure and formalism. The Duce is more and more favorable to a bilateral alliance with Berlin, excluding Tokyo. As our ally Japan will definitely push the United States into the arms of the Western democracies. He wanted to accelerate the completion of the Italian-German alliance. He said that the delay has been the cause of certain unpleasant events recently, such as the fall of Stoyadinovich. He thinks that Stoyadinovich will return to power once we sign the pact with Berlin. With reference to Albania, he approves of letting matters slide but has it in the back of his mind to act as soon as the Spanish matter is settled and the alliance is concluded—be it two or three partners.

The Duce is extremely unhappy with Guariglia, and wants him to retire very shortly with Rosso and Valentino.

March 4, 1939

I informed the minister of Switzerland that the measures taken in my absence against the Swiss journalists have been suspended. These might have been cancelled had the press taken a more moderate attitude. I saw Lord Perth—a meeting of little importance since he kept referring to the article in *Relazioni Internazionali*, which threatened war against France. I answered that the article reflected the personal opinion of its author and that, strange as it may seem, Pirelli, the magazine's editor, is a man notoriously tied by bonds of sympathy to London and Paris. On the other hand, I called his attention to the reinforcement of British troops in Egypt.

During the afternoon I saw Lyautey; it was a useless conversation. He spoke a great deal but said little. However, he said enough to make it clear that his government was very much concerned about our attitude. I was personally cordial with him, but as far as politics was concerned completely uncommunicative.

I spoke briefly to von Mackensen of my trip to Poland and gave him my impressions, which coincide with those expressed to me by ambassador Moltke.

The Duce had me refuse a dinner invitation sent by François-Poncet to meet the special mission for the coronation of the Pope. Many of its members have written against Italy, and this prompted the Duce's action.

Telephone conversation with von Ribbentrop; he is still certain of the participation of Japan in the Tripartite Pact but feels that some weeks are necessary in order to reach a conclusion.

March 5, 1939

Gambara came to say good-bye. We agreed on some details related to the despatch of the last troops to Spain. I took him with me to see the Duce, who confirmed the instructions given in previous conversations. He added that he means to keep the troops in Spain so long as there is fighting but does not intend to leave them there for police purposes. He instructed Gambara to tell Franco of his aversion to the restoration of the monarchy. "The return of the monarchy would be equivalent to plunging Spain into a new civil war within three years. The King is an ultra-discredited man, and the best that can be said of his sons is that they are morons, completely subservient to England and France." I reported my conversation with Ribbentrop to the Duce. The Duce is extremely annoyed by the delay in signing the alliance, which leaves the small countries at a loss. They see in the current fluid situation only one stable element: the rearmament of France and Britain.

Jacomoni assured us that order has returned to Albania, and that the King, after having had the greatest fear of his life, goes to extremes in showing signs of friendship for us. He has sent me his "fraternal" greetings. The fact is that none of the plotters has talked, and that the coup has only been postponed. Pignatti said that the Vatican is beginning to outline a maneuver to make it appear that Italy is opposed to the nomination of Cardinal Maglione to the Secretariat of State—a nomination which the Pope has at heart. I spoke to the Duce in order to get his authorization to issue a denial. He answered, "Tell Pignatti that I don't give a damn about the Pope, the Cardinal Secretary of State, or whoever occupies such positions." I carried out the denial just the same, though in different language.

March 6, 1939
Last night at the Colonna residence[399] I was informed through a telephone call from Pietromarchi of the insurrection at Cartagena and of the escape of the Red Spanish fleet as well as Franco's request for our air and sea co-operation to trace the eleven vessels wandering in the Mediterranean and to prevent them from crossing the Sicilian passage, should they try to go to Odessa as has already been stated. I notified the navy and the air force, and this morning at 9:00 I informed the Duce, who approved what I had done. The fleet was pursued during the day; it attempted to enter Algiers but was denied permission to do so. It now seems to be going in the direction of Bizerte.

Considerable rivalry among those seeking to be appointed to the National Council of Corporations. Names may change but not the spirit, nor is it easy to eradicate from the hearts of Italians, even though they may be Fascists, their attachment to parliament. News from Berlin indicates that the Japanese government is raising objections to signing the Tripartite Pact.

Oshima plans to resign. He stated that the cabinet should fall. What will happen after this? I don't understand. But is it really possible to take a country like Japan—which is so far away—into European political life, which has become more and more convulsed and nervous and susceptible to modification from one hour to the next by a simple telephone call?

March 7, 1939
Nothing noteworthy.

March 8, 1939
Meeting of the Central Corporative Committee at the Palazzo Venezia for the adjustment of employee wages on the occasion of the twentieth anniversary of the Fascist [party]. The Duce was very much satisfied with the measures taken, and he told me, "With this we really shorten the dis-

tance between social classes. Socialism used to say everyone equal and everyone rich. Experience has proved this to be impossible. We say, everyone equal and everyone sufficiently poor."

I saw the Japanese ambassador. He confirmed what Attolico has written concerning the Japanese answer on the Tripartite Alliance. Many reservations are made, and there is the intention to give the pact only an anti-Russian character. The answer was so unsatisfactory as to make one doubt the possibility of actually achieving this alliance. Oshima and Shiratori[400] refused to carry out the communication in an official way. They asked Tokyo to accept the pact of alliance without reservations; otherwise they will resign and will trigger the fall of the cabinet. We shall have a decision in the next few days. Shiratori feels that if the decision is favorable the pact can be signed in Berlin during the month of March; otherwise everything will be postponed indefinitely. The delay and the behavior of the Japanese make me very skeptical about the possibility of an effective collaboration between the phlegmatic and slow Japanese and the dynamic Fascists and Nazis.

March 9, 1939

At Belgrade during a royal hunt organized by the Regent Paul, I met a Croat, the Marquess of Bombelles, who was described to me as a country gentleman, friend of the Prince, and a great hunter. Today I received him in Rome, thinking that he was making a courtesy call. Instead, he went directly into the political situation and told me that he was a secret agent of Macek.[409] He spoke of the relations between Croatia and Serbia and pointed out that the chasm which separates these two countries is so wide as to make any idea of reconciliation impossible from now on. The Croats are kept in a state of moral, political, and economic servitude. If, someday, it should happen that through mobilization weapons were provided to the Croats, their rifles would fire by themselves at the Serbs. His idea of Croatia is an autonomous kingdom with an Italian prince, better still with a personal connection to the King of Italy. Bombelles was not asking for anything. He merely wanted to inform us and warn us against the politics of Belgrade, which have always been treacherous, particularly since the fall of Stoyadinovich, and are clearly favorable to the democracies and therefore against the Axis.

For obvious reasons I was quite cautious. I confirmed our adherence to the Belgrade pacts so long as the Serbs behave well toward us. However, I told Bombelles that I am always ready to keep in contact with him and that whenever the situation changes we might listen to the Croat point of view in deciding our political attitude.

March 10, 1939

The Duce was impressed by a report from Attolico which substantially confirmed two things: (1) that the Führer is fully committed to solidarity with Italy and is ready to march with us; (2) that the German people, while firmly supporting their chief, would prefer to avoid any danger of war. The Duce commented, "The German people are a military people, not a warrior people. Give the Germans a great deal of sausage, butter, beer, and a cheap car, and they will never again want to have their stomachs pierced."

Von Ribbentrop has accepted our proposal to immediately begin contacts between the two General Staffs and has proposed, in turn, a conference between Keitel and Pariani. We have accepted, and have suggested Innsbruck as the place of meeting, which should be held as soon as possible and with considerable publicity. We must let the world know that the Axis is also preparing and it does not intend to leave the initiative to the French and British, as seems to have been the case for some time.

The American ambassador has asked me whether it is true that a tripartite meeting is being planned in Berlin for the purpose of signing the alliance. I said that for the time being there is nothing in all this, but that it is possible it might take place in case developments should make it necessary for the three anti-Comintern countries to seek closer ties between them.

March 11, 1939

Gambara reported on his meeting with Franco. During the period between the 16th and 18th of this month the final action will begin. We will operate on Toledo. The meeting was militarily and even politically set in the right direction. Franco expressed himself in clearly anti-monarchist terms, and insisted that even if it should be necessary to reach a restoration it would be a matter of waiting for many years.

Slovak agitation has aroused new hopes in the heart of the Hungarians concerning the Ruthenian problem. If the Germans go into Slovakia the Hungarians intend to achieve a common border with Poland—a dream which they will not give up. Villani came to tell me this. I asked him to be calm and to wait. In the meantime the news that arrived by telephone in the evening made the crisis appear less serious, and we are told in Berlin that the Slovaks will find the solution on their own. Christich and I confirmed the celebration of the second anniversary of the Belgrade pact. He reaffirmed his belief in the return of Stoyadinovich after the present government will have failed in its negotiations with Macek. He said, "The Croat problem goes back for generations. King Alexander, who put all his authority behind it, did not succeed in reaching a solution. Certainly a government with so little authority and so short-lived cannot find it either."

March 12, 1939

Coronation of the Holy Father. I attended the ceremony as head of the Italian delegation. It is quite cold and there was considerable disorder in the organization of the pontifical protocol. The Pope was as solemn as a statue; a month ago he was a cardinal and a mere man among men. Today he seemed truly touched by divine spirit, which spiritualized and elevated him.

March 13, 1939

Nothing of any importance to us, inasmuch as the Duce does not intend to give any special significance to the Slovak crisis, which is developing and assuming disquieting proportions. Göring left San Remo in order to take part in a cabinet meeting. What can Germany's intentions be? For the present nothing has been said except that there have been vague expressions of dissatisfaction against the Prague government.

Naturally Warsaw and Budapest are also beginning to get excited.

Let us wait, because our role in this case can only be to wait for events to develop.

March 14, 1939

A long conversation with Wellington Koo[401] about the Sino-Japanese situation. Like all the Chinese, he puts his trust in the time factor in order to exhaust Japan. I advised him to come to an agreement directly with Tokyo without relying on the not disinterested promises of help that have come from the so-called democracies.

The Duke of Aosta spoke with considerable optimism about the condition of the Ethiopian Empire. I must, however, add that among the many people who have come from there he is the only optimist. He urges us to avoid a conflict with France, which would greatly set back the task of pacifying our empire and would jeopardize the conquest itself. I do not quite understand whether he was speaking as the Viceroy of Ethiopia or as the son of a French princess.

News from Central Europe is becoming increasingly serious. For the first time von Ribbentrop has spoken with Attolico and has led him to understand that the German program has been completed; namely, to incorporate Bohemia, to make Slovakia a vassal state, and to yield Ruthenia to the Hungarians. It is not known as yet when all this will take place, but such an event is destined to produce the most sinister impression on the Italian people. The Axis functions only in favor of one of its parts, which tends to acquire overwhelming proportions, acting entirely on its own initiative, with little regard for us. I expressed my point of view to the Duce. He was cautious in his reaction and did not seem to give the event too much importance. He seeks a gain in the advantages which Hungary will have upon achieving a common border with the Poles and he had me tell Budapest to move boldly. But to me this seems very little.

March 15, 1939

Events have accelerated during the night. After a meeting between Hitler, Hacha, and Chvalkovsky,[402] German troops began their occupation of Bohemia. The thing is serious, especially since Hitler had assured everyone that he did not want to annex one single Czech. This German action does not destroy, at any rate, the Czechoslovakia of Versailles, but the one that was set up at Munich and at Vienna. What credence can be given in the future to those declarations and promises, which concern us more directly? It is useless to deny that all this concerns and humiliates the Italian people. It is necessary to give them satisfaction and compensation: Albania. I spoke about it to the Duce, to whom I also expressed my conviction that at this time we shall find neither local obstacles nor serious international complications in the way of our advance. He authorized me to cable Jacomoni, asking him to prepare local revolts, and he personally ordered the navy to get the second squadron at Taranto ready.

I immediately conferred with Cavagnari, and after having cabled instructions to Tirana, I was able to speak by telephone with Jacomoni, who was on his way to headquarters. He said that tomorrow he will cable us what he thinks we can possibly do, and also foresees the possibility of handing this ultimatum to the King: either he accepts the arrival of the Italian troops and asks for a protectorate, or the troops will arrive anyway. I conferred again with the Duce, and he seemed to me to be less decided about the operation.

In the meantime Hesse arrived with the usual message. This time it is a verbal message, and not very satisfactory. The Führer sends word that he acted because the Czechs would not demobilize their military forces; because they were continuing to keep their contacts with Russia, and because they mistreated Germans. Such pretexts may be good for Goebbels' propaganda, but they should not use them when talking with us, who are guilty only of dealing too loyally with the Germans. In adding the Führer's thanks for unshakable Italian support, Hesse said that this operation frees 20 divisions for use in some other area to support Axis policy. But Hitler advises Mussolini that if he intends to undertake a large action, it is better to wait a couple of years, when the available Prussian divisions will be 100. They could have spared themselves this addition. The Duce reacted, asserting that in case of war with France we shall fight alone, without asking Germany for a single man, happy only to receive weapons and other equipment from them.

I returned to the Duce once Hesse left. I found him unhappy and depressed by the message. He did not wish to give Hesse's news to the press ("the Italians would laugh at me; every time Hitler grabs a country he sends me a message"). He continued to talk about Albania, but he has not as yet made a decision. Some doubt, which he has not yet revealed to me, disturbs his mind. He was calm, as always when the situation is serious, but he has not yet reacted in the way I expected. He wants me to return during the evening.

I received the Polish ambassador and the minister of Romania, who accept the *fait accompli* with dignity.

I saw the Duce again in the late afternoon. He is fully aware of the hostile reaction of the Italian people, but he affirms that we must, after all, take the German trick with good grace and avoid being "hateful to God and to His enemies."[403] He mentions again the possibility of a coup in Albania, but is still doubtful. Even the occupation of Albania could not, in his opinion, counterbalance in world public opinion the incorporation into the Reich of one of the richest territories of the world, such as Bohemia. I am convinced it will not come to pass. Furthermore, to Admiral Cavagnari, whom the Duce received before me, he asked only general questions regarding the possibility of making a landing, but did not give instructions of any kind. Too bad! I am convinced that our going into Albania would have raised the morale of the country, would have been an effective accomplishment of the

Axis, after which we could have re-examined our policy with regard to Germany, whose hegemony begins to take on a very disturbing shape.

March 16, 1939

Mussolini called me to the Villa Torlonia at nine o'clock in the morning. He looked sullen. He said that he had thought a great deal during the night, and that he had come to the conclusion that the Albanian operation must be postponed because he fears that, shaking the unity of Yugoslavia might favor an independent Croatia under German rule, which would mean that the Prussians would be in Sussak. It is not worthwhile to run this risk in order to take Albania, because we can have her any time we want. I can see that Mussolini has made up his mind; no use insisting. I ordered Jacomoni to let everything rest. I kept a note written by the Duce, in which he lists the reasons for the postponement of the Albanian action.

I had another meeting with the Duce. He now believes that Prussian hegemony in Europe is established. In his opinion a coalition of all the other powers, including us, could check German expansion, but could no longer roll it back. He did not count too much on the military help which the small powers could provide. I asked whether, as things stand, it would not be more desirable for us to maintain our full freedom of action to redirect ourselves in the future according to our best interests rather than bind ourselves to an alliance. The Duce declared himself decidedly in favor of the alliance. I expressed my misgivings, because the alliance will not be so popular in Italy, and also because I fear that Germany might take advantage of it to push ahead its policy of political expansion in Central Europe.

Finally, I saw the Duce for a third time during the evening. He met with de Valera, with whom he had a short and insignificant conversation. Later he received Muti, who submitted the plan for operations in Spain to begin on the 25th of this month. He approved it without discussion. Muti, who had not seen the Duce for two months, said that he found him tired and "aged many years." This is a temporary condition; but it is true that the latest events have deeply shaken him. The Duce showed me the King's speech to the Chamber of Corporations to which I contributed some minor modifications.

A large crowd of diplomats comes to the Palazzo Chigi. The most worried was the minister of Yugoslavia, who saw in Hitler's policy the marks of his Austrian origin. He said that the Germans will now aim at Budapest, and from there will launch their offensive toward the Balkans. They should not delude themselves, however, into thinking that they can subdue the Serbs without fighting, and fighting very hard. He is concerned about repercussions in Croatia, where the separatist movement will draw new life from what has happened. Stoyadinovich has emerged strengthened from the present situation, but the time for his return to power has not yet arrived. I received von Mackensen. In a matter-of-fact way I expressed our congratulations at the German success. He did not succeed very well in hiding a gesture of surprise. This time the Germans really sense that they are double-dealers.

I also met the Japanese ambassador, who was optimistic about his government's decisions regarding the Tripartite Alliance.

March 17, 1939

World opinion is very depressed. Disturbing cables come in from every capital. Even in Hungary there is no celebration on account of the occupation of Ruthenia. Worse things are feared; I saw a few diplomats: the ambassadors of Belgium and the United States. They expressed their concern to me about the future and their outrage against Berlin. I must confess that it is not easy for me to find any justification for the German action. I allowed them to infer that we were in agreement or had at least been informed, but it is such a nuisance to lie!

The Duce was anxious and gloomy. It is the first time that I see him like this. Even at the time of the Anschluss he had shown greater indifference. He is preoccupied by the Croatian problem. He is afraid that Macek may declare independence and place himself under German protection. He says, "In such a case the only alternatives are: either to fire the first shot against Germany or to be swept away by a revolution which the Fascists themselves will bring about. No one would tolerate the sight of a swastika in the Adriatic." He is thinking also of the possibility of delaying the transfer of troops to Libya, and coming to an agreement with France through London, but later he abandons the idea. Upon my advice he decided to discuss the Croatian problem with the Germans. He said, very candidly, that we could not accept a change of the Yugoslav *status quo* in Croatia without a total and fundamental re-examination of our policy.

I called von Mackensen and spoke to him calmly but with considerable firmness. I recalled that the Führer had said both to me and to the Duce that the Mediterranean does not interest the Germans; and it is upon this premise that we have formulated the policy of the Axis. If such a premise should not be adhered to the Axis would break and German intervention in questions relating to Croatia would automatically bring about its failure. My statement appeared to startle von Mackensen. He insisted that the rumors which have reached us are baseless and he assured me "that nothing has changed from the Führer's point of view." He hopes that the Duce has not taken drastically the information which has reached him. I assured him that the contrary was the case and that I was talking with him about this for purposes of clarification and so that we might always act in full harmony.

Christich asked to see me, and he denied rumors of Yugoslav military movements on the Hungarian border. On my part I denied rumors of an Italian military expedition in Albania and assured him that nothing would ever be done by Italy to weaken the territorial unity of Yugoslavia.

March 18, 1939

Audience with the Pope; I found him exactly the same as he was as Cardinal Pacelli, and, as before, he was benevolent, courteous, and human. We discussed the situation. He did not conceal his concern over the aggressive German policy and added that he was uneasy as an Italian. He was very pleased when I told him that the Duce had already taken appropriate measures to hold back the German flood into zones of the most vital interest to us. On the religious problem he declared himself optimistic as to the Italian situation. He informed me that we can reach an agreement and that he will remove Cardinal Pizzardo and will entrust the direction of the Catholic Action to a committee of diocesan archbishops. He was most concerned about Germany and intends to follow a more conciliatory policy than Pius XI, but in order to do this co-operation from the other side is necessary; otherwise what he would do would be reduced to "a useless soliloquy." The audience lasted for a half-hour. I believe that we can get along well with this Pope. I spoke at length with Cardinal Maglione. He is from southern Italy, full of talent and spirit, and in spite of his ecclesiastical education he can scarcely hide the impulses of his exuberant temperament. Maglione, too, is concerned about the German advance, but he gave a discreet hint of the French desire to reach an agreement with us, stressing at the same time the fact that he has not received any such commission nor does he intend to solicit any.

A long conference with the Duce during which we re-examined the King's speech and decided to bring it up to date. I clearly expressed to the Duce my concern about Berlin. It has increased greatly since I have had proof of German disloyalty, but he still seems to be quite favorable to the Axis. I did not succeed in convincing him even when I referred to a possible German absorption of Hungary. He said that even in such a case he would not react. He personally wrote the editorial for the *Giornale d'Italia* in which he maintains that what Germany has done is logical and that we would have acted similarly under like circumstances.

Fagiuoli brought me the transcript of a conversation with Baudouin. In it there are two interesting points: one, the French are ready to make further concessions; two, the person who revealed Baudouin's mission to the press was Ribbentrop himself on the basis of the information we had given him. Is it worthwhile being loyal with such people?

March 19, 1939

Long conversation with the Duce; during the last few days he has meditated a great deal about our discussion and agrees that it is now impossible to present the idea of an alliance with Germany to the Italian people. Even the stones would lash out against it. Our anxiety about events in Croatia is growing since all our information confirms the fact that agitation is becoming more bitter. We decided to send a cable to Belgrade in order to inform the Regent, Paul, that we have called a halt to German action and also to advise him to hasten negotiations with Zagreb, because any waste of time might be fatal.

Meanwhile, the Duce has ordered a concentration of forces on the Venetian border: should revolution break out in Croatia we shall step in. And should the Germans think they can stop us, we shall fire on them. I am more than ever convinced that this may take place. The events of the last few days have reversed my opinion of the Führer and of Germany; he, too, is unfaithful and treacherous and we cannot carry on any policy with him. Starting today I have also worked with the Duce towards an understanding with the Western Powers. But will they have at least a minimum of common sense in

Paris, or will the possibility of an understanding be compromised once more due to the unwillingness to make any concession? The Duce thinks that British irritation runs very deep at this time. "We must not forget that the English are readers of the Bible and that they combine a mercantile fanaticism with a mystical one. Now the latter prevails, and they are capable of taking action."

I sent Fagiuoli to Paris to reopen negotiations with Baudouin. The Duce plans to be specific about our demands in his speech of March 26: Djibouti, Suez, Tunis.

March 20, 1939

I received the engineer Carnelutti, a special envoy of Macek. He is of Italian origin. His brother was in the Italian consular service. He was very much excited at the beginning of the conversation and appealed to me to keep it secret because his life would be in danger. I have summarized what he said in a note. In brief, the Croats are anti-German but ready to fall into the arms of Berlin if we reject them, if only to escape from Serbian tyranny. He repeated what Bombelles has said about negotiations: to obtain concessions toward autonomy from Belgrade. If these should fail, an insurrection and an appeal for Italian military aid. The creation of a Croatian republic linked to us by an alliance pact similar to the one that we have with Albania but also including a customs and monetary union. Second phase: a personal union with Italy. The Duce ordered me to accept the Croatian program. Tomorrow I shall confer with Carnelutti.

Von Mackensen delivered an answer to my remarks of last Friday: Germany is not interested in the fate of Croatia and recognizes the pre-eminence of Italian interests. He repeated that the Mediterranean is not, cannot, nor should it become a German sea. I reported this to the Duce, who found the communication quite interesting "provided we can believe in it." Nevertheless, in spite of the fact that this morning he was very anti-German this evening he said, "We cannot change policies, because after all we are not prostitutes." He had me reject a proposal which had been made for Laval to journey to Rome which "would be of no use except as a great piece of advertising for him."

The King as usual is more anti-German than ever. He alluded to Germanic insolence and duplicity and at the same time praised the straightforwardness of the English, but in speaking with the Duce he went so far as to call the Germans rascals and beggars.

March 21, 1939

The Western Powers have lost much ground today, which was a gain for Germany. News about the attempts to constitute a "democratic bloc" has hardened the Duce in favor of the Germans. The title itself identifies our destinies with those of Germany and makes skeptics of those countries such as Romania, Yugoslavia, Poland, Turkey, and Greece, who, while remaining concerned about German progress, must preserve their internal regime built on authoritarian lines. And Germany has gained another point with us since Ribbentrop, in a letter addressed to me, renewed the solemn promise to recognize exclusive Italian rights in the Mediterranean, in the Adriatic, and in adjacent areas.

I had a conference with Carnelutti and told him: first, seek an agreement with Belgrade if for no other purpose than to gain time; second, if this should fail, and you revolt, we shall intervene at the call of the Croat government; third, abstain from every contact with Berlin, and warn us of your actions ahead of time.

The Grand Council met during the evening. The Duce talked about the necessity of adopting a policy of uncompromising loyalty to the Axis. He made a marvelous speech that was argumentative, logical, cold, and heroic. Balbo and De Bono were derisive. As a matter of fact, Balbo allowed himself to make an unfortunate remark, "You are shining Germany's boots." I reacted to this violently, and I proved to them that Mussolini's policies had always been those of a proud man. The Duce approved of what I had done, and told me that Balbo will always remain "the democratic swine who was once the speaker at the Girolamo Savonarola Lodge of Ferrara."[404]

Fagiuoli, returning from Paris, has brought communications from Daladier through Baudouin. They are rather unsatisfactory. Now it will be necessary to wait for the Duce's speech on March 26 for which both of us have added the portion dealing with foreign policy.

March 22, 1939

Christich assured me that Yugoslavia would not join the bloc proposed by London, adding that it might do so only if Italy changed its policy, joining it herself. I went with Attolico to the Duce, who was again irritated against Germany, driven on under the lash of the French press, which never misses the opportunity to exasperate his personal touchiness. Attolico talked at length about the situation and about his conferences with von Ribbentrop and Hitler. He did so wisely and courageously. He greatly stressed the fact that Germany had not desired to be dragged into a war for the reasons that Hitler has outlined as follows: armaments are not ready and will not be ready for two more years; a navy is lacking; Japan is too engaged to be able to provide any effective aid. He did say, however, that should a crisis materialize, Germany will support us. Finally, he emphasized the necessity of dotting our *i*s in our mutual relations, since the Germans are slipping, perhaps without even being aware of it, from the fact of being powerful to that of being arrogant, and might strike at our interests. The Duce analyzed the current situation with respect to Italian public spirit, and came to the conclusion that in order to continue the policy of the Axis it is necessary to set the objectives of our respective policies, to establish zones of influence and of action for Italy and Germany, and to have Germany reabsorb the German-speaking residents of Alto Adige. He also intends to write a personal letter to Hitler stating that certain events represent significant blows to his personal prestige.

March 23, 1939

Inauguration of the Chamber of Fasces and Corporations. The wording of the oath has been changed; we no longer swear allegiance to the "Royal Successors." There is a great deal of talk about this matter, and those who are most outspoken are, as usual, Balbo and De Bono, who benefit from it in order to further their petty anti-Fascist speculations. However, I do not know whether the innovation is appropriate at this time. I knew nothing about it. If I had been forewarned I should have been strongly against it. From explanations I received later on, I found out that this had always been the formula used. Nevertheless there was alarm. And how!

The Duce has decided to move more rapidly on the Albanian question, and he himself has drawn up the project of agreement which is very brief, consisting of three dry clauses which give it more the appearance of a reprieve than of an international pact. I am also preparing one with Vitetti. It is an accord that, though couched in courteous terms, will permit us to effect the annexation of Albania. The Duce has approved it. Either Zog accepts the conditions which we lay before him or we shall undertake the military seizure of the country. To this end we are already mobilizing and concentrating in Puglia four regiments of Bersaglieri, an infantry division, air force squadrons, and all of the first naval squadron.

Chamberlain has sent a letter to the Duce. He expresses his concern over the international situation and asks the Duce to help reestablish mutual trust and assure continued peace. Mussolini will answer after striking at Albania. This letter strengthens his decision to act because in it he finds more proof of the inertia of the democracies.

March 24, 1939

We discussed with the Duce and Pariani our plan for action in Albania. We agreed that it is not advisable to send an ultimatum immediately, but rather to begin our negotiations with King Zog. If he tries to resist, or to outsmart us, we will use force. The Duce was concerned about reactions in Belgrade, which must, for many reasons, be kept at a minimum.

Acquarone[405] came on behalf of the King asking me for advice on a certain matter. It seems that His Majesty would like to show some appreciation of the Duce the day after tomorrow; but what? A title of nobility would not be welcome. A nomination as Chancellor of the Empire? Very well, but what difference would this make? In any case I cannot assume responsibility for giving an answer without having conferred with the Duce, a matter which I will attend to tomorrow morning. I believe that he will turn it down. But the King's gesture is significant just at this moment, when certain people are speculating and attempting to create the impression that there is dissension between the regime and the dynasty.

March 25, 1939

As I had foreseen, the Duce refused every title and every honor. "I do not know what they could ever give me," he said. "Make me a prince? I would be the first to laugh at the idea; imagine people calling me Prince Mussolini! As for Chancellor of the Empire, all right, but what does it mean? I suppose it would mean that I would continue to be the head of the government as I am now. No, nothing doing. Tell Acquarone to thank the King for me and tell him that the only thing that I want from him is his continued co-operation."

De Ferraris[406] left for Tirana taking the planned agreement for the protectorate with him. It is not yet possible to foresee what the developments will be, but it seems probable that King Zog will give in. There is, above all, a fact on which I am counting: the coming birth of Zog's child. Zog loves his wife very much as well as his whole family. I believe that he will prefer to insure a quiet future for his dear ones. And frankly I cannot imagine Geraldine running around fighting through the mountains of Unthi or of Mirdizu in her ninth month of pregnancy.

I had a meeting with Prince Beauvau, brother-in-law of Pietro Colonna. I talked to him briefly about our situation with respect to France, and although he is a good friend of Italy he did not know nor did he understand very much about it. The speech which the Duce will make tomorrow and which is awaited by everyone will be most useful and will present the picture clearly to all of Europe.

March 26, 1939

Meeting of the Fascist militia. The past twenty years have certainly left their mark on the body, but the spirit always remains vibrant and willing.

The Duce's speech made a great impression. Only the Quadrumviri were obviously ill at ease, particularly De Bono. The Duce, who knew of this, said that De Bono "is an old idiot, with all respect for his age and for his mind if he ever had one; he was always an idiot, but now he is old on top of it."

After the news of the fall of Madrid, Franco began the attack. Tomorrow the CTV will also go into action. The expectations are excellent, even though the Reds appear from their positions to want to resist.

March 27, 1939

Reactions to the Duce's speech are rather favorable. Even in France, where the fear of war is on everyone's mind, they prefer to highlight the pacifist elements in the speech, rather than its hostile notes. The Duce was quite angry with the King this morning. The King found ways of telling him three distasteful things: (1) he disagrees with the policy on Albania since he did not see the point of taking such a risk in order to "grab a few rocks"; (2) that the offer made by Acquarone to give the Duce some honorary title on the twentieth anniversary of Fascism was decided upon in order to "forestall any repetition by the Fascists of the 'humiliation' inflicted upon the King when, without his knowledge, the Duce was given the title of Marshal of the Empire— a humiliation which the King still resents"; (3) that Conrad of Bavaria had told him that in certain quarters in Munich Mussolini is referred to as "The Gauleiter of Italy." The Duce commented bitterly on the King's words. He said, "If Hitler had had to deal with a shithead of a King he would never have been able to take Austria and Czechoslovakia," and he went on de-claiming that the monarchy does not like Fascism because Fascism is a uni-fied party, "and the monarchy desires that the country be divided into two or three factions, which could be played one against the other in such a way as to permit the monarchy to control everybody without taking sides."

Our troops have attacked in Spain and are going ahead very well.

March 28, 1939

I informed the German ambassador of Chamberlain's letter to the Duce as well as our plans for an answer which will reiterate our general desire to preserve peace and at the same time stress the need for effective and sub-stantial recognition of Italian rights.

De Ferraris has returned from Albania with a memorandum from Jacomoni. It seems that the King is up to some sort of trickery. His answer is yes and then he has his ministers say no. Nevertheless, the machine is in motion and can no longer be stopped. Either it will be carried out with Zog or else it will be carried out against him. For many reasons, primarily be-cause we Italians do not want to be the ones to start a war in Europe, I should prefer the first alternative, but if Zog does not yield it will be neces-sary to use force resolutely.

Madrid has fallen and with the capital all the other cities of Red Spain. The war is over. It is a new formidable victory for Fascism, perhaps the greatest one so far.

Conversations of minor interest with Hesse, and with the minister of Romania, who tried to affirm and to defend the necessity of the very tough pact between Berlin and Bucharest.

Demonstrations in the Piazza Venezia because of the fall of Madrid. The Duce is overjoyed. Pointing to the atlas open at the page containing the map of Spain he said, "It has been open in this way for almost three years, and that is enough. But I know already that I must open it at another page." He has Albania in mind.

March 29, 1939

I had two meetings with the Duce to make decisions regarding Albania. Since he is leaving for Calabria, and will return on Saturday, he insisted on bringing the matter up to date. (1) The army, navy, and air force continue their preparations. They will be ready on Saturday. (2) Jacomoni must, in the meantime, exert diplomatic pressure on the King, and report back. (3) At a certain point, unless he gives up before this, we shall send our ships into the territorial waters of Albania and present an ultimatum. (4) If he persists in his refusal we shall raise the tribes in revolt, publish our declarations, and land. (5) Having occupied Tirana, we shall gather the Albanian chiefs into a constituent assembly, over which I should preside, and offer the crown of Albania to the King of Italy.

No one will react. Not even Yugoslavia, which is too preoccupied with recent Croat events. This evening I talked at length with Christich; I gave him the broadest assurances regarding Croatia, but held back on Albania. He offered no objections; he proposes, as a condition, that Albania shall not be used against Yugoslavia.

Badoglio went to the Duce to say that he was in agreement with him on the Albanian undertaking; his only suggestion was that a larger contingent of forces be mobilized. We shall mobilize an additional division, and also a tank battalion.

March 30, 1939

Jacomoni unexpectedly announced that he would arrive this afternoon. But because of engine trouble he has stopped at Brindisi and will arrive tomorrow.

Laval's speech is considered by everybody to be a stiffening of the French position. I told the Duce so by telephone. He answered, "So much the better; it was just what I desired."

I received Bombelles. He brought serious news from Croatia. The secession movement is spreading extremely fast. I do not as yet quite understand the real motives for his visit with the exception of two to which he has clearly alluded: to make personal contacts with Pavelić, who was one of the most aggressive men in the country and has the means of carrying on a strong campaign in favor of Italy among the Croatian masses. I made a new appointment for Sunday, after having conferred with the Duce.

The tension between Germany and Poland, which had become so alarming during the last few days, seems now to be lessening. I am glad of it because a German move would have disastrous repercussions here. Poland enjoys a good deal of favor, and besides the Germans must not overdo things. It is now difficult to find anyone who has faith in their word. They would be completely discredited should they fail to carry out their pact of collaboration with Poland which they have reaffirmed over and over again.

Conference with Shiratori and Oshima to announce that they will present the proposals for the alliance on April 2.

March 31, 1939

After a long series of more or less useless discussions with, among others, Spoleto and Suardo,[407] I had a meeting with Pariani, Jacomoni, and Guzzoni, who has been appointed to command the expeditionary corps in Albania. Jacomoni had no particular reasons for coming to Rome, except perhaps that by his absence he would introduce a little calm into the atmosphere in Tirana, which by this time was pretty much disturbed. It would appear that the King [Zog] has decided to refuse to sign a treaty that formally and substantially violates the integrity and sovereignty of Albania. Pariani said that he preferred such a determined attitude which permits the final disposal of the Albanian question. We studied the military action and its close connection with diplomatic moves. It appears that this connection is possible. But Jacomoni returned in the afternoon after his meeting with the military heads to give me his disquieting impressions regarding the organization of the expeditionary corps. It appears that they cannot, with all their efforts, put together a battalion of trained motorcycle troops, which could make a surprise entrance in Tirana. Unforeseen difficulties arise also with regard to landing operations. In the meantime, news from Tirana confirms the fact that the King is preparing to resist—a matter which annoys me greatly, because I consider it rather dangerous to fire the first shot in this disturbed and inflammable Europe. Since the Duce will arrive tomorrow afternoon, his decisions cannot be altered, but while waiting I instructed Jacomoni to prepare a draft treaty which in his opinion might be accepted by King Zog.

Charles[408] brought me the text of Chamberlain's declaration to the House of Commons on assistance to Poland. He also asks, as a personal matter, if he might take a step in London, to say that Italy is ready to talk with France, if France will take the initiative. I reserve the right to answer after I talk it over with the Duce. Had there not been Daladier's speech I should have said yes without hesitation.

Wieniawa talked about German-Polish relations. They hope for a peaceful solution, but if the Germans follow their usual unyielding procedure the Poles will fight. Wieniawa declared that he is rather optimistic as to the resistance of the Polish armies.

April 1, 1939

The Duce returned and I had a preliminary conference with him, with Jacomoni present. He approved the outline of the treaty with some slight modifications, which are more matters of detail than of substance, but which will allow the King to save face. For an Oriental, this means a lot. We planned this line of action: tomorrow Jacomoni will appear before the King with a new outline of the treaty and will make it clear that the situation is now serious. Either he accepts, and in that case I will go to Tirana to attend the solemn ceremony to sign the treaty, naturally accompanied by a strong squadron of planes, which will be a symbol of the fact that Albania is Italian. Should he refuse, disorders will break out all over Albania on Thursday, making armed intervention on our part an immediate necessity. In this case, we shall land on Friday morning.

During the afternoon Sereggi, the new minister of Albania, came to see me. He begins his mission at a stormy time. Passing through Bari, he saw the concentration of troops and realized that the music was about to begin. I spoke frankly to him; in a friendly tone but quite firmly. He said that he agreed with us. He urged me to save appearances in such a way as to make the solution acceptable to the King and to the people. I accompanied him to the Palazzo Venezia where the Duce repeated the warning to him in more precise terms. He added that if the King should refuse to sign the pact, a crisis will be unavoidable. Sereggi decided to leave for Tirana, together with Jacomoni, in order to persuade the King. Then, on the pretext that he was not able to exchange his Albanian money, he asked Jacomoni to lend him 15,000 lire, a first installment on a bribe!

April 2, 1939

Muti arrived in Rome, and I am ready to send him to Tirana with a small team of men as enterprising and hotheaded as himself, in order to create the incidents which are to take place next Thursday evening if the King, in the meantime, has not had the kindness to capitulate. I gave him freedom of action, but he is under definite orders: to respect the Queen and the child, if it is already born; to wreak terror during the night; to hide in the woods at daybreak and await the arrival of our troops, trying, in the meantime, to prevent Zog's retreat toward the Mati, where he might attempt some resistance.

I authorized Bombelles to secretly make contact with Pavelić. As for propaganda, I am thinking things over and shall soon reach a decision, although the Duce has already approved a subsidy to be given to the Croats.

I received von Mackensen, and informed him of the Duce's letter in answer to Chamberlain. I also received Shiratori, bearer of the Japanese answer for the Tripartite Alliance. In general this answer is good. However, it makes two reservations: (1) to make known to London, Paris, and Washington that for the Japanese the alliance is directed against Moscow; (2) and to add the declaration that, in case of a European war, Japanese aid would be limited. O.K. for the second. But with reference to the first, it seems to me that such a reservation might alter the true value of the pact, and I want to set this down clearly.

April 3, 1939

I fine-tuned some details of the Albanian operation with Pariani. The situation is much more serious than we initially thought following information we received this evening. It's impossible to send in the Muti team because the airports are under very close scrutiny and the city is riddled with armed groups who are threatening Italians. In agreement with the Duce I send a cable to Jacomoni with orders to concentrate tomorrow in Durazzo the Italian women and children so that they may be protected by a warship of the Royal Italian Navy and a second cable with orders to go and see King Zog and tell him that we shall hold him personally responsible for any harm done to the lives and property of all Italians.

Later I had conversations with Mackensen and with Villani. The former has lived in Tirana and hates the Albanians; he wholeheartedly approves of our action and what we are about to undertake. Villani worries about the fate of Geraldine, but is reassured when I tell him that I gave Jacomoni orders to place her family and relatives under our protection. I send a cable to all our diplomats overseas, not to tell them to do anything but rather to inform them of the situation as we see it. Ribbentrop calls me regarding the alliance. He will give me his observations (which coincide with our own) through Attolico and adds that he hopes to welcome me to Berlin for the signing of the Pact in two to three weeks.

I give orders to Giro to assemble all Albanian emigrants at Bari to send them back to their country along with our troops.

April 4, 1939

The Duce doesn't hide his disappointment after reading a cable from Jacomoni who thinks a peaceful solution may be possible. When he is ready to take action he would prefer a solution by force of arms. But he is also not satisfied with the army that he considers "aging" and says it is "under the influence of the monarchy." At Bologna a Bersaglieri battalion about to leave for Albania was singing "we want peace not war." And the officers present did nothing… so Mussolini gets angry.

At the Council of Ministers, the Duce and I report on the Albanian situation and at the same time we explain our objectives. I receive Perth. He is worried because of the Albanian situation. I reassure him but insist on the fact that we will not permit anyone to interfere in this matter. As he takes his leave I tell him, as a parting conciliatory gesture, that we will not reject an eventual French initiative to resume the talks. He left in good spirits and better disposed about the Albanian problem, which is what I wanted.

I see Christich. After discussing the general situation and the visit to Rome of the Regent Paul, I explain the Albanian situation and underscore the fact that King Zog is a disruptive factor in our relations with Yugoslavia. I assure him that nothing final will be done without informing Belgrade. When he takes his leave Christich is quite calm even though the matter is very serious for his country. The news regarding the fate of Italians in Tirana is getting more and more alarming. We decide to evacuate them. At the Palazzo Venezia, at a meeting between the Duce, Sereggi and myself, we decide to give the King a final time limit not beyond 12 p.m. on Thursday.

April 5, 1939

Two ships will sail to Valona and Durazzo to evacuate the Italians who are now seriously threatened by the roving armed bands that Zog has commissioned to spread terror. International public opinion is calm for now: so calm in fact that I suspect they must not have paid attention to the friction between ourselves and Zog and that they actually expect a call from Zog. Germany is marching correctly: Ribbentrop told Attolico that Berlin is sympathetic to our actions at Tirana since any Italian victory reinforces the power of the Axis. Budapest has also reacted well; Villani informs me that 6 Hungarian divisions which are already mobilized are ready to go to the Yugoslav border should pressure be necessary on the Serbs. Time required: 48 hours.

I also meet with Bombelles who had a satisfactory talk with Pavelić. Now he returns to Zagreb to speak with Macek, then he comes back to Rome to define our financial contribution to the propaganda campaign. I see the Duce several times. He is calm, frighteningly so and more convinced than ever that no one will want to interfere in our dispute with Albania. Nevertheless he has decided to march and he shall do so even if the entire world were to line up against him. I repeat this to Muti who took a quick trip to Tirana and confirms our impression that Zog wants to resist with the meager forces at his disposal. Since the King is asking for another 24 hours to decide, the Duce with a cable written in his own hand sets the expiration of the ultimatum for 12 p.m. on Thursday, April 6th. At dawn Zog's son was born. How long will he remain heir to the throne of Albania?

April 6, 1939

The reactions in the various capitals, including Belgrade, are rather moderate. Christich, on the other hand, is more alarmed, but in answer to a question he declared himself convinced that the Albanian problem cannot change the relations which happily exist between Rome and Belgrade. He recommended that no action be taken without first informing Belgrade, and that somehow the existence of the Albanian state be preserved as a matter of form.

Many contradictory news despatches during the morning. Jacomoni cabled an Albanian counterproposal presented before the Duce's ultimatum, but we did not take it into consideration. Sereggi cabled to offer his resignation. From Durazzo and Valona news arrived that the Italian refugees are boarding ship normally. Fortusi and the aviator Tesci, who arrived at noon from Tirana, said that the exodus of the Italians has filled the population with terror. They crowd the streets, weeping, and accusing King Zog of having brought this calamity upon them. The Duce telephoned the order for the embarkation, saying that the order for departure would come during the evening. At my suggestion he decided to carry out this afternoon a demonstration flight by a hundred planes over Durazzo, Tirana, and Valona.

4 p.m. A cable arrived from Jacomoni. It appears that the King does not wish to take upon himself the responsibility for a complete capitulation, and intends to call the Council of Ministers to take the extreme decision of either resisting or giving up. Quite justly, Jacomoni observes that, in this way, the King puts himself outside the terms of the ultimatum, but he agreed to transmit the information, nonetheless.

The Duce, whom I have kept informed, gave the order to launch the expedition, reserving the right to announce news of its progress, if any.

From the cable offices we learn that long coded messages are sent from Tirana to the Foreign Office. We cannot stop them. I gave orders, however, that they be delayed, and that many errors in the code groups be repeated. It is well that we gain time, even though Chamberlain gave the House of Commons an account of what has happened which was very favorable to us, and has also declared that Great Britain has no specific interests in Albania.

7 p.m. Jacomoni cabled saying that he was burning the secret codes, that he had told the officials of the naval mission to leave, and that the entire legation might have to get on the destroyer, which is at Durazzo. The Duce repeats the order to attack, while specifying that the air force must spare the cities and the population.

Badoglio has written a letter to the Duce, criticizing the plan of operations. The Duce paid no attention to it. In a letter the King takes note of the communication made by the Duce yesterday, but expresses his doubts regarding the possibility of our installing ourselves solidly in Albania, basing his opinion on historical memories of Venetians and Aragonese. Evidently he does not remember that the Romans installed themselves there very well.

9 p.m. I communicated to Villani and to von Mackensen our decision to proceed with the military occupation. I received assurances from them both as to their solidarity and their absolute understanding of the motives for our action. Afterwards, I saw Christich. I informed him of the attempts to create a crisis between us and Belgrade. I gave him the fullest assurance regarding the extent of our action and of our understandings. It seemed to me that he took it all with a remarkable dose of resignation. As he went out he said, "So Zog is coming to the same end Beneš came to."

A final Albanian proposal reaches us. They would like to deal with Pariani. This is not possible, especially since Pariani is in Germany. We answered that they could send a plenipotentiary to Guzzoni.

I returned home at about 10:30 p.m. I am tired and don't feel well. I should like to rest, especially since tomorrow I must fly out in order to observe the landing of our forces. But I can't: Christich asked for another appointment. He seemed to want to say something urgent and serious to me. I was afraid that there would be a change in the policy of Yugoslavia. Instead, it was a question of new requests for clarification and for details about our action and our future plans. I tendered the olive branch. Christich himself, on telephoning to Belgrade, displayed his satisfaction over what I had told him.

April 7, 1939

I got up at 4 a.m. Farace was waiting for me in the anteroom with many communications, among which was a cable from Zog to the Duce. It confirmed his decision to reach a military understanding and asked for negotiations. We answered that he should send his negotiators to Guzzoni. The Duce, who got up during the night, which is extremely unusual, would like to have news and explanations that I am not in a position to give him because I have none.

Gabrielli,[410] the military attaché, who in the last few days has behaved very strangely, cables that Zog has forty-five thousand men at his disposal. It seems that he is exaggerating.

At 6 a.m. I left by plane. The weather is calm and warm. Buti, Vitetti, and Pavolini came with me. We were at Durazzo at seven forty-five. It was a beautiful spectacle. In the bay, motionless and solemn, were the warships, while motorboats, lighters, and tugs moved around the port, transporting the landing forces. The sea was like a mirror. The countryside is green and the mountains, which are high and massive, are crowned with snow. We saw only a few people in Durazzo. But there must have been some resistance because I saw detachments of Bersaglieri, crouched behind piles of coal, defending the port, and I saw others going up the hill in single file in order to surround the city.

From some of the windows there was occasional firing. I continued to Tirana. The streets were deserted and undefended. In the capital the crowd moved through the streets quite calmly. The legation was barricaded. On the roof was a large tricolored flag and in the courtyard many vehicles. I was convinced that in case of danger it would be easy to defend it from above and I gave orders to this effect.

I reported to the Duce, who was quite satisfied, particularly because international reaction was almost non-existent. The memorandum, which Lord Perth left with me in the course of a cordial visit, might have been written by our offices.

During the afternoon everything changed. Guzzoni received Zog's negotiators, and instead of proceeding as the Duce had ordered, suspended everything for six hours. The Duce was furious, because this delay might have very serious consequences. It is necessary for us to arrive in the capital in order to carry on our political maneuvering. Through Valle, the Duce ordered that the march resume, but meanwhile a day has been lost and this allows the usual mudslinging French press to say that the Italians have been beaten by the Albanians. We have no news about the advance of the columns. The only one who cables is Jacomoni, who is hiding with other Italians in the legation. The information he sends gives rise to more and more concern about his fate; the bandits are ransacking the Royal Palace and threaten the legation. The Duce, in a very nervous state of mind, telephones repeatedly during the night, demanding information that I am unable to give. Only in the early hours of the morning does Jacomoni indicate that the city has quieted down, but we do not know anything about Guzzoni's advance.

April 8, 1939

D'Aieta[411] telephoned at eight o'clock in the morning, saying that Jacomoni gives every assurance that one may land at the Tirana air field. I decided to leave immediately, and I informed the Duce, who approved. I arrived in Tirana at 10:30, after having flown over the armored column, which is marching on the Albanian capital. The forward elements are already at the gates of the city. I found Valle, Guzzoni, and Jacomoni on the air field, together with many units of mechanized engineers. I must admit that strong emotions have overtaken me and everybody else. I saw Guzzoni, who explained the reasons for the delay: landing difficulties, wrong fuel types, and, finally, lack of communications, because the radio operators who were recalled are not up to the mark. The situation is now excellent. I received many Albanian delegates who paid me homage. In reply I said that Italy will respect Albanian independence, insuring her political development, as well as the social and civil growth of the people.

With the news of Zog's flight to Greece all our fears vanish about resistance in the mountains. In fact, the soldiers are already returning to their barracks, after having deposited their weapons in the garden of the legation. I gave orders that the soldiers be treated well, and especially the officers. I took some steps in the direction of re-establishing order and the normal rhythm of civilian life. I gave orders that all of Zog's political prisoners be freed. These prisoners had each been sentenced to one hundred years in jail.

I distributed money to the poor. I conferred with the most important men of Tirana, in order to get a definite idea of the wishes of the Albanians and also to make decisions regarding the new form of government to be given to the country. Mixing with the troops and their officers, I found them all very proud of the undertaking.

April 9, 1939

I return to Rome to confer with and report to the Duce. Many Albanians greet me on the air field with considerable warmth. They give me Albanian flags and ask for Italian flags in return. This morning Tirana is decorated with tricolored Italian flags.

The Duce is happy. He listens attentively to my report and decides to send a congratulatory cable to General Guzzoni. He really deserves it.

Regarding the new constitutional setup of Albania, the Duce has prepared a regency project, which does not seem good to me. I tell him so, and explain my plan as follows: to create at once a government council, to announce a body of electors as of April 12, have it vote a decision which will sanction the personal union between the two countries, conferring the crown of Albania on King Victor Emmanuel III. He approves in principle. During the afternoon I draw up the document and discuss it with some jurists and other experts at legalistic hairsplitting, such as Buti, Perassi,[412] and Vitetti. All agree that while such a decision will give us possession of Albania it will make things look legitimate. This is all the more useful, because tension with Great Britain appears to be decreasing after a conference I had this morning with Lord Perth, and the Yugoslavs behave in such a friendly way as can be explained only by their boundless fear. The same may be said of the Greeks.

April 10, 1939

With the Duce we examine the project drawn up yesterday which is approved, except for a few formal variations. Program: Constitutional Assembly at Tirana on the twelfth, the Grand Council at Rome on the thirteenth, my speech to the Chamber on the fifteenth, and Sunday, the sixteenth, a great national celebration of the event.

Reaction abroad begins to wane. It is clear above all that the British protests are more for domestic consumption than anything else.

News from Albania is good; military occupation is carried out according to plan and without obstacles.

April 11, 1939

I got to work on the preparation of the speech for the Chamber. The reaction of foreign countries has toned down; with tomorrow's ceremonies we shall give the democracies a good pretext, since they ask for nothing better than to wash their hands of the whole affair.

I communicated to Pignatti the Duce's decision to erect a mosque in Rome in view of the fact that six million Italian subjects are now Moslems. After having spoken with Maglione,[413] Pignatti reported to me that at the

Vatican they are horrified at the idea, which they feel is contrary to Article I of the Concordat. But the Duce has made up his mind, and he is supported in this by the King, who is always at the vanguard of any anti-Church policy. Personally, I do not see any need for such a thing, and, at any rate, I would be more inclined to have this mosque built in Naples, since that city is the real bridgehead to our African domains. In so far as this proposal concerns the Albanians, we realize that they are an atheistic people who would prefer a raise in salary to a mosque.

April 12, 1939

I arrive at Tirana by plane at 10:30 and the members of the new Albanian government greet me at the airport. I did not know Verlaçi[414] and, had I known him, I would have opposed his nomination. He is a very surly-looking man and will cause us a great deal of problems. The crowd receives me triumphantly; there is a certain amount of coolness, especially among high school students. I see that they dislike raising their arms for the Roman salute, and there are some who openly refuse to do it even when their companions urge them.

However, things are not going as smoothly as it might appear. There is a great deal of opposition to a personal union. Everyone agrees to have a prince of the House of Savoy or, better still, they would like to have me. But they understand that giving the crown to Victor Emmanuel III means the end of Albanian independence. I have long discussions with many chiefs; the most stubborn are those from Scutari (who have been incited by the Catholic clergy) whom it will be easy to convince, however, as soon as I distribute bundles of Albanian francs, which I have brought with me. Nevertheless, things go well during the meeting of the electoral body; there is a unanimous vote that is also very enthusiastic. They come as a delegation to bring me their decision. I speak from the balcony of the legation and am particularly successful when I give assurances that the decision will prejudice neither the form nor substance of Albanian independence. Let it be understood that this success refers to the masses, because I see the eyes of some patriots flaming with anger and tears running down their faces. Independent Albania is no more.

April 13, 1939

I return to Rome and go at once to the Palazzo Venezia. I find the Duce on the roof observing anti-aircraft experiments. I inform him as to what has happened. He would like to immediately take a further step and abolish the Ministry of Foreign Affairs. I do not share his views. We must proceed gradually unless we want to antagonize the rest of the world. So far matters have run as smoothly as oil because we have not had to use force, but if tomorrow we should begin firing on the crowd, public opinion would become excited again. On the other hand, the Ministry of Foreign Affairs is useful to us in order to make the new situation legally acceptable without having to go through an endless dispute on recognitions. Later on it can be quickly eliminated. I propose to the Chief [Mussolini] the creation of an undersecretary for Albanian affairs by naming Benini to the post. I want a technical expert because it will be necessary to quickly carry out a program of public works. Only thus will we definitely link the people to us and undermine the authority of their leaders.

During the evening a short session of the Grand Council to approve the decree.

April 14, 1939

Council of Ministers. Then I work on my speech which I send to the Duce in the late afternoon. He makes a few changes to it, then he defines it: "One of the best speeches that has ever been made in Parliament."

I receive the Yugoslav. We agree to a meeting I shall have in Venice with Markovic[415] on Saturday, the 22nd.

Göring arrives. I welcome him at the station and accompany him to Villa Madama. On our way he stresses the situation of the Axis, which he defines as formidable. He harshly attacks Poland.

April 15, 1939

The Albanians have arrived. Some of them look depressed. The Duce received them at the Palazzo Venezia and addressed them. I noted that they listened anxiously for the word "independence," but that word did not come, and they were saddened. Jacomoni confirmed this later.

I made my speech to the Chamber. It went over in a big way. Later there was a meeting of the Senate which was hurried and not too imposing.

Finally, a meeting with Göring and the Duce at the Palazzo Venezia. The record was kept separately. Roosevelt has sent a message proposing a ten years' truce. At first the Duce refused to read it, then he defined it: "A result of progressive paralysis."

April 16, 1939

The ceremony of offering the Albanian crown to the King of Italy takes place at the Royal Palace. The Albanians, who seem to be lost in the great halls of the Quirinal, look depressed. Verlaçi especially appears depressed as he says, looking weary and without conviction, the words he has to say to offer the crown. The King answers in an uncertain and shaky voice; he is certainly not an orator who makes any impression on an audience, and these Albanians who are a warrior mountain people look with amazement and timidity on the little man who is seated on a great gilt chair beside which stands a gigantic Mussolini looking like a bronze statue. They cannot understand how all this can be.

I talked to the Duce about the state of mind of the Albanians. He, too, was aware of it, and he assures me that he will talk to them today about their national independence and sovereignty in a way that will send them home reassured.

I had two long conversations with Göring, one at the Ministry of the Armed Forces and the other at the Palazzo Venezia. The second of these was recorded. Although he speaks a great deal about war which he is preparing for with great attention, yet it seems to me that he does not completely rule out the possibility of peace, at least for a few years. What disturbs me the most in his conversations is the tone in which he described relations with Poland; it reminds me peculiarly of the same terms used before for Austria and for Czechoslovakia. But the Germans are mistaken if they think they can act in the same way; Poland will undoubtedly be overrun, but the Poles will not lay down their arms without a hard fight.

April 17, 1939

I accompany Göring to the station. He is rather pleased with his stay in Rome, for it has given him contacts with me and with the Duce. Generally speaking, the impression is that even Germany intends to keep the peace. Only one danger: Poland. I was impressed not so much by what he said, but by the contemptuous tone he used in talking about Warsaw. The Germans should not think that in Poland they will make a triumphant entrance as they have done elsewhere; if attacked, the Poles will fight. The Duce also sees it this way.

April 18, 1939

We received the Hungarians at the station. Teleki makes a good impression on the Duce as well; Czaky is what he appears to be: a small, presumptuous man and, more disturbingly, he apparently is a physical and spiritual weakling always trying to strike heroic poses.

The first meeting takes place in the afternoon. Nothing very extraordinary. Czaky presents the situation in detail and tries to give his words an anti-German flavor. Above all, he keeps harping on Slovakia; he hopes—or, better, he deludes himself into thinking—that Germany might make a kind gift of it to Budapest.

It is useless to summarize the conversation since it is not important. In the Duce's words: "Only a bottle of wine was missing from the table."

We begin to draw our plans of action in Albania with Benini.[416] I think he will succeed because he is a man of action and is clear in his ideas and in his judgment. The Duce, too, had a good impression of him.

April 19, 1939

The more or less useless conversations with the Hungarians are continuing. Czaky becomes more and more prolix and futile in his arguments. He specializes in saying the obvious, and in saying it as if it were a matter of great importance. Mussolini says of him that "he takes a long running start to jump over a straw."

Conversation with Perth. The British raise some difficulties connected with the title: King of Albania. Some lively arguments with Perth, in which I maintained that the change in dynasty is a matter of internal affairs in which no one has a right to interfere.

April 20, 1939

After the Duce made his controversial speech with respect to Roosevelt's message, I accompanied him to the Palazzo Venezia and showed him a very serious report by Attolico, which announces imminent German action against Poland. This would mean war; hence, we have the right to be informed in time. We must be able to prepare ourselves and we must prepare public opinion so that it will not be taken by surprise. I therefore gave instructions to Attolico to hasten my meeting with von Ribbentrop.

During the afternoon the third, and fortunately the last, conference with the Hungarians. That is to say with Czaky, because Teleki has scarcely opened his mouth. My impression of Czaky is more and more negative. Today, in a very offhand way, he declared that he was convinced that Hitler is crazy. He bases this observation on the look of the Führer's eyes, and he said such absurdities with incomparable assurance. We hope that this presumptuous individual will not be the Guido Schmidt of Hungary. The Duce has summarized the situation: (1) Italy and Germany desire some years of peace and are doing all they can to preserve it. (2) Hungary is carrying on and will carry on the policy of the Axis. (3) No one wants the dismemberment of Yugoslavia, and everyone is working toward maintaining the *status quo*. If, however, any dismemberment should come about, Italian interests in Croatia are paramount. (4) As for the Slovak problem, Hungary will adopt a watchful attitude and will do nothing contrary to German wishes.

April 21, 1939

A day particularly devoted to Albania. I have a conference with Sthyka, Albanian ex-minister to Belgrade. He gives information above all on the problem of the Kossovars, that is, eight hundred and fifty thousand physically strong Albanians, morally firm, and enthusiastic at the idea of a union with their mother country. It seems that the Serbs are in a panic over it. For the moment we must not even allow it to be imagined that the problem is attracting our attention; rather it is necessary to give the Yugoslavs a dose of chloroform. Later on it will be necessary to adopt a policy of real interest in the question of Kosovo; this will cause an "irredentist" problem in the Balkans that will absorb the attention of the Albanians themselves and will be a dagger thrust into the back of Yugoslavia.

In the afternoon a meeting of the ministers to pass the budget of the undersecretariat for Albania. It is set at 430,000,000 lire. Although I protested very much against it, I am convinced that it is a sum that will allow us to carry on a large-scale action.

A conference with Viola to discuss my trip to Spain, which is to precede the trip that Göring will make there. It would make a bad impression on the Italians if that fellow should get there before us.

At the Palazzo Venezia I greet Lord Perth. The Duce has treated him very courteously and seems to like him now. It has been decided that we will accept the credentials of his successor without the title of King of Albania.

April 22-23, 1939

In Venice for the arrival of Marković. The population gives me a cordial welcome. Evidently the Albanian question has had a particular echo in this great Adriatic city. Markovic makes a good impression on me. He is a kind, temperate, and modest man. He has all the characteristics of the career diplomat. The arrival in Venice was a great event for him. This was the first time he was traveling abroad as a minister. The applause, the flags, the bands, and an enchanted Venice full of sun and springtime had touched his spirit deeply.

Our first meeting went very well. I immediately discovered him to be reasonable and understanding, while, on the other hand, Indelli, who is an unreasonable alarmist, had led us to believe in some excitement among the Yugoslavs which does not really exist; even if such feeling existed among some elements of their public opinion it had not reached responsible quarters. Our conversation concerned the following points:

Albania: the *fait accompli* has been accepted, including our reasons for sending troops. Our decision not to have the troops go in large numbers beyond Durazzo-Tirana to the north is appreciated. I gave assurances of our disinterest in Kosovo.

Germany: there will be even closer spirit of co-operation with the Axis, without joining the anti-Comintern pact for the moment for reasons of internal policy, but without at the same time rejecting any such possibility.

Rejection of any kind of British involvement. A political formula for Yugoslavia; in case of a conflict, a disarmed neutrality with the economic support of Italy and Germany. Naturally, within the system of the Axis and gravitating principally to Rome.

Hungary: gradual improvement of relations in order not to compromise our existing obligations to Romania, the policy of which Markovic has openly and sharply criticized.

League of Nations: progressive indifference.

In general the visit has yielded excellent results. The communiqué issued at the end of the conversation has pleased our journalists and has very much displeased the French and British newsmen, which goes to prove that it is good. Markovic has made a good impression on all those who have come to know him; Stoyadinovich has been liked even more, perhaps because he is more modest and is more physically attractive. He [Markovic] is very careful to hide the great expanse of his bald pate, and to this end he mobilizes all the hair of his temples and of the nape of his neck. He said that his hairs are the only Yugoslavs mobilized in the Albanian crisis.

After my return to Rome I make a report to the Duce, who is quite satisfied. Jacomoni, following my request, has confirmed the agreement for the equality of civil and political rights of Italians and Albanians. The matter is very important, in fact as important as the annexation itself.

April 24, 1939

I received many diplomats and, particularly, the Polish ambassador, who complains about certain strong reactions by our press against articles appearing in Warsaw opposition newspapers. He finds that such stuff is not worth bothering about; perhaps he is right.

The minister of Holland, a good, very absent gentleman, whom I rarely see, comes to spin me a strange yarn. He says that he is very much alarmed over what is happening in Europe and above all over what people are whispering is yet to happen. Some officers have told him that we and the Germans have decided to divide Europe between us; Holland would belong to Germany. He asked me how much truth there was in all this. I answered him jokingly, and then I reported the conversation to the Duce, who was very much amused. They are the ideas of an official who is a little stupid and very timid, but they are nonetheless indicative of a state of mind spreading around the world.

Starace and Benini on their return from Tirana say they are enthusiastic about all they have seen, and admit that Albania is in reality far better than they had thought.

I go to the theater, where *Cesare*, by Forzano, is playing. The Duce also attends this show. He himself collaborated in the work, and some years ago, through me, he sent to Forzano the opera's scenario. Frankly, I think this is a bad opera, with neither originality nor technique. It affords neither pleasure nor interest. Besides, adulation is an art that one must practice with control. Forzano obviously goes too far, and the results are anything but those he intended to produce.

April 25, 1939

From Berlin comes the news that the Japanese still have reservations about the Tripartite Alliance; hence the signature is to be postponed *sine die*. Mussolini, whom I telephoned at Forlì, where he happens to be today, says that he is satisfied. In reality, for some time past he has considered Japanese participation more harmful than useful. I shall see von Ribbentrop on the sixth in some city in northern Italy in order to discuss common policies.

François-Poncet uses the pretext of the signing of a commercial agreement to talk to me of Italian-French relations. He says he has been informed by Lord Perth as to what the Duce said about negotiations begun with Baudouin and later interrupted. He wants us to know that the French government is always ready to continue discussions on this basis. I make sweeping reservations, but at his request I add that I do not consider anything changed in our political directives. In turn I ask him if I must consider this démarche as official. He tells me that he has made it with his government's authorization.

April 26, 1939

I report to the Duce by telephone on my conversation with François-Poncet. He doesn't seem to give it much weight. He says: "Anyway, I have no intention of starting negotiations with France until after the signing of the treaty with Germany." I received many foreign diplomats; they are all very much amazed at our foreign policy and all of them, including the more pessimistic ones, like Helfand, who is a professional Cassandra, admit that our successes have been far greater than they would have thought possible.

We decide on certain important works in Albania, among them the construction of hotels in the larger centers, and for these the Duce gives a personal contribution of a million lire.

The English chargé d'affaires sends me a brief synopsis of what Mr. Chamberlain is planning to tell the House of Commons with regard to military conscription. The project seems to me of very modest proportions.

April 27, 1939

Nothing new, except a conference with the Japanese ambassador, who says that the last word about the Japanese decisions on the Tripartite Pact has not yet been said. However, I stress the point that we must know it before May 6.

From Berlin they informed me that the Führer in his speech tomorrow will denounce the naval pact with Great Britain as well as the friendship pact with Poland. This is very serious. The situation which during the past few days had an undeniable clarity may become very dark from one hour to the next. The Duce, to whom I transmitted the information to the Rocca delle Caminate,[417] has telephoned for more details. He, too, does not hide his concern about the denunciation of the pact with Poland. However, on the other hand, the situation is less alarming regarding the pact with Great Britain.

April 28, 1939

The Führer has delivered his speech. It lasted exactly two hours and twenty minutes; it cannot be said that brevity is the foremost quality of this man. Generally speaking, the speech is less warmongering than one might have expected on the basis of information reaching us from Berlin. The first reactions to the speech in the different capitals are also rather mild. Every word allowing any hope of peaceful intentions is received by all of humanity with immeasurable joy. No nation wants war today; the most that one can say is that they are ready if it is necessary. This applies to us and to the Germans. As for the others, I do not know. I ask myself seriously whether a German move against Poland, notwithstanding the many declarations and mutual guarantees, would not, in the end, lead to a new Munich. On the other hand, the British-French war against a Germany which is on the defensive on its western border is practically an impossible one.

I received news from Japan. It appears that they have now decided to sign the alliance. I tell Shiratori that it is necessary in any case to have a yes or no quickly. In a few days I shall meet Ribbentrop and we must make our decisions, especially since the diplomatic work of the democracies has been greatly intensified in the last few days, and that the British-Soviet alliance seems now to be a concrete and accomplished fact.

The Duce returns to Rome.

April 29, 1939

Council of Ministers. Some decisions are approved to increase the power of the armed forces. The Duce is very much dissatisfied with all of them, with the exception of the navy. He has the feeling, and he is right, that beyond appearances, which are more or less carefully put on, there is little underneath. I think so too. I do not have any specific information as to the army, but the many rumors I hear are distinctly pessimistic. Also some impressions that I formed during the mobilization for the Albanian undertaking, a small mobilization after all. This has increased my doubts. The military makes a big ado with a lot of names. They multiply the number of divisions, but actually these are so small that they scarcely have more than the strength of regiments. The ammunition depots are lacking in ammunition. Artillery is outmoded. Our anti-aircraft and anti-tank weapons are altogether nonexistent. There has been a good deal of bluffing in the military area, and even the Duce himself has been deceived—a tragic bluff. Better not even talk about the air force. Valle made the statement that there were 3,006 planes in working order, while the information service of the navy says that they amount to only 982. An enormous difference! I report the matter to the Duce. I believe that it is my duty to speak with absolute honesty about such a matter, even though it will make him bitter. This will serve to avoid greater sorrow in the future.

April 30, 1939

This morning the Duce is furious once again on account of the photograph taken of the honor guard grenadiers presenting arms at the arrival of General Brauchitsch. He is right, because it is difficult to find anything more badly done. The Duce sees in this an indication of the spiritual and physical lack of discipline in the army. He explains it by saying that the army was at one time the "exclusive property of the Italian monarchy" and had, mostly, the simple function of an all-purpose police force for the preservation of public order; today, on the contrary, its main business is to wage war. This confuses many officers.

I discussed with Alfieri the advisability of accepting the title of Prince of Kruia which the Albanians would like to bestow on me. This would be the first and only thanks received so far for having given Albania to Italy. Nevertheless, my inclinations are to refuse it.

I had my first conversation with Gafencu.[418] He is a likable man, a little timid, but quite sharp. We explore the situation. I do not conceal my disappointment over Romania's acceptance of the British guarantee. What purpose would it serve if Hungary or Bulgaria attacked? He talks about relations with Budapest and stresses the intransigence of the Magyars. I agree with him on this point; the Hungarians are always absurdly insistent. I don't like their attitude toward us either. They condescend to accept favors that they first solicit. Gafencu also talks about our relations with France. He knows about my last conversation with François-Poncet. He says that Bonnet's tendency is for conciliation; that of Leger is to wait until we take the initiative. They should certainly have to wait for a long time.

May 1, 1939

The ceremony of submitting the reply to the King's speech takes place at the Royal Palace. The Duce criticizes the eighteenth-century character of the ceremony, the use of gala carriages, et cetera, and says this is the last time it is going to happen.

Gafencu is received by the Duce. The meeting starts off in a rather cool way. In general Mussolini is prejudiced against the Romanians, whom he despises as soldiers. But then he allows himself to be carried away by his love for discussion and polemics. He criticizes openly the Romanian acceptance of the British guarantee; as a result Romania assumes the role of a protected country. Gafencu explains the reasons that have led him to accept it; above all the pressure of public opinion, which has been greatly concerned over German territorial demands for *Lebensraum*. We continue to explore the general political situation; nothing particularly interesting.

In the afternoon I have a long conference with Christich. He is concerned about a possible German-Polish crisis during Prince Paul's coming visit to Rome. I reassure him, giving him some information as to my meeting with von Ribbentrop, which will take place during the week.

Von Mackensen in Rome and Attolico from Berlin inform me of Turkish anxiety about our intentions. They suggest our giving the Turks some reassurance sufficient to calm them down. Mussolini, to whom I refer the matter, approves this reassurance but says: "This is the fruit of a bad conscience. They deserve an act of aggression because of the mere fact that they fear one."

May 2, 1939

General Carboni,[419] who has the reputation of being a thorough student of military matters, today confirms reports that our armament situation is disastrous. I have received this information from too many sources not to take it seriously. But what is the Duce doing? His attention seems to be spent mostly on matters of form; there is hell to pay if the "Present Arms" is not done right or if an officer doesn't know how to lift his legs in the Roman step, but he seems to concern himself only up to a certain point about our real weaknesses which he certainly knows very well. In spite of my formal charges in connection with the results of Cavagnari's investigation of the efficiency of our air force he has done nothing, absolutely nothing; and today in his conversation with Cavagnari he didn't even mention the matter. Why? Does he fear the truth so much that he is unwilling to listen?

I received Bombelles. After what has happened with Yugoslavia we have no intention of doing anything that might weaken the unity of the state. On the other hand, it is not clear what the Croats are up to. It appears that an agreement has been reached with the Serbs. Therefore, I fully confirmed all that I had said in previous conversations regarding our active interest in the destinies of Croatia, but I said that for the moment I intended to do nothing.

My last meeting with Gafencu. We became decidedly good friends. He invites me to Bucharest in October, which is all very well, but might it not be that by October many plans will have to be revised?

May 3, 1939

To calm Turkish apprehensions toward us and above all to please the Germans, who think a countermaneuver leaning to Great Britain and France is possible, I have given the Turkish ambassador reassurances to the effect that Italy has neither economic, political, nor territorial aims with respect to his country. The ambassador was very much satisfied with my statements. This was obvious, notwithstanding his effort to hide his feelings.

Have made arrangements with Parenti so that the arrival of von Ribbentrop in Milan will be marked by particular solemnity. This is necessary in order to squelch rumors appearing in foreign papers of the strong and vocal opposition of the citizens of Milan to the policies of the Axis.

I receive Sir Percy Loraine, the new British ambassador. Our conversation is purely conventional and therefore dull. However, Loraine made a good impression upon me. In my opinion he is a naturally timid man. He is very much concerned with the environment in which he is to carry on his mission. Rome, for a foreign diplomat, is a difficult post; but this is particularly true for an Englishman who finds himself in the ambiguous situation of an unpredictable friend, *amico incerto*.[420] He must keep up the appearance of formal friendship but in reality carry on political action which is hostile toward us. Lord Perth had adapted himself so as to fit in and interpret our point of view. Will Loraine do the same? I think it is possible.

May 4, 1939

I stayed at home because I did not feel well. The Duce wrote some instructions for the conversation with Ribbentrop and sends me his notes. He emphasizes the need for a peaceful policy.

May 5, 1939

Many conversations, but none of any particular interest except one with the Japanese ambassador. The final draft of the Tripartite Pact has been communicated to Auriti in Tokyo. It is very weak. Ribbentrop is also dissatisfied with it. But the ambassador tells me it is difficult to go any further, and that we are now near the *breaking point*.[421]

A speech by Beck. It is hard to judge it on the basis of the brief synopsis we have. It does not seem aggressive or unyielding. But they are not satisfied in Berlin. The conversation with Ribbentrop will take place in Milan rather than Como. This is what the Duce wanted in order to refute the French rumor about a bloody anti-German demonstration in Milan. In the evening I leave for Milan.

May 6-7, 1939

Milan's welcome to von Ribbentrop dispels the legend which had been spread by the usual police informers that northern Italy was deeply anti-German. The Milanese population is very much flattered that the Lombard city had been chosen as the meeting place for an important event, and has shown considerable enthusiasm. I, myself, was surprised, not by the thing itself, but by the size of the demonstrations.

I have had stenographic notes taken of my conversations with von Ribbentrop.

Some comments: For the first time I have found my German colleague in a pleasantly relaxed state of mind. He did not, as usual, make many wild statements. Rather, he has made himself the standard bearer of the policy of moderation and understanding. Naturally, he has said that within a few years they must go here, and grab there, but the slowing down of the speed of German dynamism is a very significant symptom.

The alliance, or rather the immediate announcement of the alliance, was decided Saturday evening immediately after dinner at the Continental Hotel following a telephone call from the Duce. After the conversation I had reported to Mussolini the satisfactory results from our point of view.

As usual with Mussolini, when he has obtained something, he always asks for more; and he has asked me to make a public announcement of the bilateral pact, which he has always preferred to the triangular alliance. Von Ribbentrop, who from the bottom of his heart has always preferred the inclusion of Japan in the pact, at first hesitated, but then yielded, pending Hitler's approval of the proposal.

The latter, when reached by telephone, gave his immediate approval, and has personally took a hand in drafting the agreement. When I informed the Duce on Sunday morning he expressed particular satisfaction.

Von Ribbentrop managed a fair personal success, even in that useless and snobbish world of so-called society—which is required when one must give a dinner. The men in von Ribbentrop's entourage are also liked by those with whom they come in contact. They are not the usual wooden and some-what boring Germans; they are likable young men, who speak foreign languages well, and who, in a drawing room, are able to forget all their heel clicking when addressing a lady.

May 8, 1939

I returned to Rome. Starace is very happy over what I had to say to him on the state of mind of the Milanese. The Duce, too, is pleased by what has happened.

I received Christich, with whom I discussed the official meeting, and also Helfand, to whom I emphasized the fact that the pact as drafted contains no anti-Russian character. I tried to facilitate the exchange of Russian prisoners held as hostages by Franco.

May 9, 1939

Review of the troops in Via dell'Impero. The Albanians paraded in Rome for the first time; I confess that this moved me. In the afternoon the sittings of the Roman Curia are resumed; the arrangements are entrusted to the Senate. My father protested against this, recalling that the Senate was the very body which opposed Caesar, and that Caesar was killed inside those walls.

Conversation with von Brauchitsch.[422] He, too, like all the Germans, is repeating the password of peace.

Conversation with Shiratori, who was very much impressed by our treaty of alliance with Berlin. I hope that Tokyo will wake up in time to join. I doubt it.

May 10, 1939

Prince Paul of Yugoslavia arrives. The Duce, as always in such ceremonies when the subject of monarchy comes up, was critical, saying that the monarchy was the sworn enemy of the regime. He is of the opinion that a manifesto would be enough to liquidate it. Someday he thinks he will do it.

At the Palazzo Venezia there is a meeting between the Duce, myself, and Markovic. Nothing new regarding the direct relations between Rome and Belgrade. The points settled at the meeting in Venice have all been confirmed. But a new element is the clear position taken by Yugoslavia against Turkey and the proposal to form a Romanian-Yugoslav-Bulgarian bloc for the purpose of opposing Turkey. In order to achieve this, an agreement between the Magyars and Romanians is necessary. All this is quite interesting.

A conversation with Poncet at his request. He comes to tell me that the French government is happy about the fact that we are still ready to negotiate on the basis of Baudouin's proposals. But while exploring the matter he tried to save what he could in the usual French way, especially as regards Tunis. I immediately asked that he should not attempt to switch the cards on us, as this would preclude the possibility of success. And, very cleverly, he quickly drew in his oars. I cannot predict if these deals will come to any conclusion, but I do know that François-Poncet has become a very different person. His ideas on Italy and on the regime have become clearer, and perhaps he has also modified his ideas in general. He tells me that he now detests freedom of the press and that he is coming closer and closer to totalitarian ideas.

May 11, 1939

Naval review. During the sea trip I had a long conversation with the Regent, Paul. He is very much concerned about the threats of war, and I believe that he has faith in my assurances of peace only up to a certain point. He tried to give me some explanations regarding Stoyadinovich. Quite apart from the break up of his majority in Parliament, the man had discredited himself by shady business speculations, carried on partly by him and partly by his cronies. It seems that he has been able to accumulate, especially in foreign countries, vast sums of money. Paul also hinted at the possibility of a lawsuit. I advised him against it, but would not swear that my words had any effect. The Duce, to whom I told these things, commented that this thirst for wealth is a kind of disease. Otherwise it could not be explained, particularly because man's capacity to enjoy has a limit beyond which gold becomes an obstacle. Besides, as a kind of vengeance wreaked by fate, it is the richest men who can least enjoy their wealth; Rockefeller was obliged to live on milk and an orange during the last sixteen years of his life.

The King, on board ship, expressed his belief that Corsica must inevitably become Italian when the great crisis breaks out in Europe. The Duce, at the dinner at the Quirinal, spoke with some diplomats.

Nothing special except a warning to Greece because it had accepted the French-British guarantee. He used some harsh words even to Ruegger because of the attitude of the Swiss press.

May 12, 1939

This morning I found the Duce very nervous and concerned about the international situation. I believe that Daladier's speech, which was needlessly stubborn, has contributed to his state of mind. He told me that this speech makes my conversations with Poncet worthless and that therefore I should forget about them. On Yugoslavia he has also many reservations; as proof of the sincerity of their attitude he would like a definite gesture, such as their withdrawal from the League of Nations. I think this is premature, and also that we must take into account the internal difficulties which still exist in that country.

The Duce is also disturbed about Bulgaria; he instructed me to cable Talamo to sound out the real intentions of that government. The proper place for Bulgaria is in the Axis fold, but I believe that we must still make more efforts to convince that trembling king of this more than obvious truth.

There was a bit of a storm in the intellectual spheres of Albania, which explains why twenty or so persons will immediately be sent into internal exile (*confino*). There must not be the least sign of weakness; justice and force must be the characteristics of the new regime. Public works are starting well. The roads are all planned in such a way as to lead to the Greek border. This plan was ordered by the Duce, who is thinking more and more of jumping on Greece at the first opportunity.

May 13, 1939

Departure for Florence with the Yugoslavs. While on the train the German outline for the alliance pact is handed to me. In general it is acceptable. We should, however, like to add a clause regarding borders, that are to be permanently guaranteed, *Lebensraum* as concerns Italy, and the duration of the pact. I have never read such a pact; it contains some real dynamite.

The welcome in Florence was curtailed on account of a downpour that has lasted for hours and hours. I speak with Marković about the problem of Yugoslavia remaining in Geneva. He still offers some resistance, but he realizes the advisability of deserting the mausoleum at Geneva. I believe he will end up accepting our advice.

May 14, 1939

Von Ribbentrop makes one more attempt to add to the signature of the alliance a tripartite pact with Japan. I offer no objections, although I am thoroughly skeptical of the possibility and also the usefulness of the matter.

The Duce makes a very fine speech at Turin. He is calm in his delivery but emphatic in the substance of his speech. He then calls me on the telephone. We have our last discussion relative to the signing of the alliance. The Germans propose that I go to Berlin from May 21 to 24. I ask that the timing be either delayed or advanced. It does not seem to me that May 24[423] is the most appropriate date to sign such a formidable pact of military understanding with the Germans!

May 15, 1939

I return to Rome. The Yugoslav visit went well even though nothing new was decided. The Turkish threat is what particularly concerns Belgrade; we must take advantage of this psychological condition to pull the Yugoslavs more and more into the orbit of the Axis.

Useless conversation with the Belgian ambassador.

Conversation with Wieniawa. He had asked to see me several days ago so that when he did meet me his request was no longer up to date. Beck had been informed by Valentino of our complete solidarity with the Germans in case of war. Wieniawa is pessimistic; he believes war is inevitable. Besides, he has no desire to remain in Rome under these conditions; he has asked to be recalled. After our official conversation was finished we spoke as friend to friend and I advised him to be very moderate. Whatever happens Poland will pay the price of the conflict. Because there are two alternatives: either the Axis wins and Germany will absorb Poland, or the Axis loses and Poland becomes a province of the Bolshevik International. No French-British help is possible, at least at the beginning of the war; Poland would be soon reduced to a heap of rubble. Wieniawa admits that I am right on many points, but he has faith in the ultimate success that would give new power to Poland. I fear that this illusion of his, unfortunately, is shared by too many of his countrymen.

I inform Villani about the conversations with the Yugoslavs. Especially of the idea of a four-party treaty against the Turks.

May 16, 1939

Nothing new.

May 17, 1939

The American ambassador is very anxious to explain to me a conversation which the Duce had with him some days ago at the Quirinal. He is resentful, particularly because Mussolini said that America is in the hands of the Jews. He wanted to deny this, but used very weak arguments. He stressed one point, namely, that the American people, who originated in Europe, intend unanimously to concern themselves with European affairs, and it would be folly to think that they would remain aloof in the event of a conflict. I reported this to the Duce, who did not seem to be very much alarmed.

During the afternoon I received Alessandri, former President of Chile and a good friend of Italy. He has been defeated by a popular-front coalition, but he considers the Red regime to be ill-suited to his country, and foresees, he says with horror, that he will be recalled to power. Like all Americans he is anxious about the international situation, and is dreaming of a formula that may have the magic power to resolve all controversies.

Mussolini approves the final text of the alliance pact, and authorizes the bestowal of the Order of the Annunziata on von Ribbentrop. He also says that he is preparing an exchange of cables between the King and the Führer in order "to prevent the usual malicious interpretations that might be made by the French press."

May 18, 1939

Christich thanks me for the courtesies extended to the Regent, Paul, and Markovic, and asks for information regarding the Bulgarian attitude. I let him read Talamo's cable, which states that Bulgaria is ready to align itself with the Axis provided Yugoslavia does likewise and guarantees Bulgaria against Romania. In Belgrade they are increasingly concerned over the enigmatic Turkish policy, and are trying to create a Slav bloc of an anti-Turkish character. This is what we also desire.

I see Szabo and he brings me an album of photographs of Ruthenia. When I ask him he states that Hungary is already in a position to beat Romania. It only needs heavy artillery.

Guzzoni and Messe send excellent news about the situation in Albania. I take steps to effect the complete absorption of the Albanian armed forces.

Carnelutti, sent by Macek, wants information regarding our conversations with and commitments to the Regent, Paul. Nothing is changed on our part, since Belgrade has made no formal commitment to join the Axis. Then he informs me: (1) Macek no longer wishes to reach any agreement with Belgrade; (2) he will continue his separatist movement; (3) he asks for a loan of 20,000,000 dinars; (4) within six months, at our request, he will be ready to start an uprising. I make an appointment with him following my return from Germany, in order to continue our negotiations.

May 19, 1939

Nothing particularly important.

May 20, 1939

Departure for Berlin. During my trip I speak with Mastromattei, the prefect of Bolzano, to whom I show the text of the treaty. He states that the preamble with its definitive recognition of borders will strike a great blow at irredentism in Alto Adige.

May 21-23, 1939

I arrive in Berlin. There are great demonstrations, clearly spontaneous in their warmth. My first discussion with Ribbentrop. Nothing has changed with respect to what was said and decided upon in Milan. He repeats Germany's interest in and intention to insure for itself a long period of peace of at least three years. He dwells on the desirability of binding Japan to our system. He maintains that Russia is too weak to give much help to the Western democracies even if she should take their side. He speaks also of the Turkish situation. He has been influenced by the suggestions of the superficial von Papen and so he believes that the Turkish attitude has been determined by fear of Italy. I prove to him with original Turkish documents, intercepted by our secret service, that Turkish hostility is also directed against Germany. Finally, I talked to him about Yugoslavia. I tell him that our conversations in Rome have not really been satisfactory, even if they appear to be so. I declare that we shall not take the initiative in anti-Yugoslav movements, as long as Belgrade adopts a correct policy toward the Axis, but that we shall immediately revise our stand if Belgrade tilts toward the democracies.

I go on to say that an internal revolt in Croatia would not leave us indifferent. Ribbentrop approves, but I can see that he really prefers to maintain the Yugoslav *status quo*. Himmler, on the other hand, tells me clearly that we must hurry and establish our protectorate over Croatia.

We repeat more or less the same discussion with the Führer. He states that he is very much satisfied with the pact and confirms the fact that Mediterranean policy will be directed by Italy. He takes an interest in Albania and is enthusiastic about our program for making Albania a stronghold which will inexorably dominate the Balkans.

I thought Hitler was in excellent shape, quite serene, less aggressive. A little older. His eyes are more deeply wrinkled. He sleeps very little. Always less. And he spends most of the night surrounded by collaborators and friends. Frau Goebbels, who is a regular participant in these gatherings and who feels quite honored by them, was describing them to me without being able to conceal a vague feeling of boredom because of their monotony. It is always Hitler who talks! He can be Führer as much as he likes, but he always repeats himself and bores his guests. For the first time I hear hints, within the inner circles, of the Führer's tender feelings for a beautiful girl.

She is twenty years old with beautiful quiet eyes, regular features, and a magnificent body. Her name is Sigrid von Lappers. They see each other frequently and intimately.

The ceremony for the signature of the pact was very solemn and the Führer was sincerely moved

Göring, whose standing is always very high, but no longer on the rise, had tears in his eyes when he saw the Collar of the Annunziata around the neck of Ribbentrop.

Von Mackensen told me that Göring had made a scene, complaining that the Collar really belonged to him, since he was the true and only promoter of the alliance. I promised Mackensen that I would try to get Göring a Collar.

Himmler talked at length about relations with the Church. They like the new Pope and believe that a *modus vivendi* is possible. I encouraged him along these lines, saying that an agreement between the Reich and the Vatican would make the Axis more popular.

Ribbentrop is making a name for himself. In speaking to Signora Attolico, Hitler said: "Whatever has been said about him, I must now admit that this man is extremely capable."

May 24, 1939
Return to Rome.
At the station all the high Fascist officials and a considerable crowd welcome me on my arrival with warm demonstrations. However, it is clear to me that the pact is more popular in Germany than in Italy. Here we are convinced of its usefulness and hence accept it as a matter of course. The Germans, on the other hand, put into it a warmth of feeling which we lack. We must recognize that hatred for France has not yet been successful in arousing love for Germany.

At the station Anfuso hands me a cable from the King. I learn afterward from the Duce that the King had thought of conferring upon me the title of marquis, but that he had been very wisely advised against it by the Duce himself. He felt that it would not be helpful to me because of the disapproval it would arouse in the great Fascist masses. The Duce had suggested sending the cable to greet me.

I reported to Mussolini on the details and impressions of my trip to Germany. I find him quite satisfied, and, what is most unusual, he repeatedly expressed his satisfaction. Then he went on to speak of Yugoslavia. He was more than ever distrustful of it, and he authorized me to strengthen Macek's movement by timely financial aid.

May 25, 1939
I thank the King for the cable. He answers: "From 1900 to the present time I have never sent a cable to a minister. I believed that it would be worthwhile to break a tradition in order to express my own deep feelings." He then quickly made a jibe at the Germans: "As long as the Germans need us they will be courteous, and even slavish, but at the first opportunity they will reveal themselves as the great scoundrels they really are." He recalls certain bitter contacts that he had with them on the occasion of one of his trips in 1893, and he does not think that things have changed since that time.

A long conference with the Duce. He harps increasingly on the anti-Yugoslav, anti-Greek note. We decide to close the Albanian Ministry for Foreign Affairs and to remove foreign diplomats from Tirana. He is thinking also of denouncing the London pact because of the British-Turkish accord. He will bring it up for the first time next Saturday in the presence of Percy Loraine on the occasion of his presentation. The King has made a strange prophecy with unusual confidence: "The day will come," he said, "in which Italy and Germany will come to an agreement with England. Then peace and progress will really be assured." There is no doubt that the King is anti-German, but it is likewise certain that he detests and scorns the French with profound conviction.

The Duce attacks the monarchy and says: "I envy Hitler, who does not have to drag along so many empty baggage cars."

May 26, 1939

A conversation with Carnelutti, who has just returned from Zagreb. He confirms Macek's full decision to turn down any agreement with Belgrade and to prepare for the rebellion. We agreed and drew up the following points in a memorandum: (1) Italy will finance Macek's Croat revolt with 20,000,000 dinars; (2) he undertakes to prepare the revolution within four to six months; (3) he will immediately call in Italian troops to insure order and peace; (4) Croatia will proclaim itself an independent state in confederation with Rome. It will have its own government but its ministries for foreign affairs and of national defense will be in common with Italy; (5) Italy will be permitted to keep armed forces in Croatia and will also have a lieutenant general located there as in Albania; (6) after some time we shall decide on possibilities for union under a single head.

The Duce read and approved the report. He desires, however, that Macek countersign it. In the meantime, I have sent it to Zagreb by secure means. Next week we shall begin our payments via Zurich.

Mussolini is taken up with the idea of breaking up Yugoslavia into pieces and of annexing the kingdom of Croatia. He thinks the undertaking is relatively easy, and, as things stand, I agree with him. Meanwhile, I am thinking of better organizing the Albanians of Kosovo: they could be turned into a dagger in Belgrade's flank.

May 27-28, 1939

This is a crucial day in our relations with Great Britain. The Duce received Percy Loraine for his formal presentation; but soon the visit took on an entirely different character. The Duce, who ordinarily is courteous and engaging, was extremely stern; his face became absolutely impenetrable; it looked like the face of an Oriental god sculptured in stone. He began by asserting that in view of the obvious British policy of encirclement it was necessary to ask, as he now was asking, whether the April 16 agreement had any tangible value left. Percy Loraine did not expect this blow; he blushed and struggled for words, then he composed himself quite well. He asked if, while reserving the right to call for instructions from his own government, he could not at this time state his personal views. Then he began to argue with a certain professional ability. His strongest argument was the one dealing with the attitude maintained by the British during the Albanian crisis. There is no question that we have changed the status quo of the Mediterranean, yet Chamberlain had accepted the responsibility of confirming the value of the pact. The Duce countered harshly in an argumentative tone. He declared that British policies were leading all of Europe into war. Through her guarantees to the small powers, Great Britain had brought about a very dangerous aggravation of the situation.

Agreement between the Germans and the Poles could have been reached if the British had not interfered. At this point Loraine reacted more strongly; for a moment I had the impression that he was about to get up and ask permission to leave. He controlled himself with difficulty, but emphasized his regret that Mussolini's point of view was so far removed from that of the British. Mussolini answered that time will prove who is right. The Duce made a brief and cutting comment about the British-Russian alliance, and then the conversation ended abruptly. During the course of the long walk between the table and the door, Loraine sought for some human contact with the Duce. But it was impossible. He walked slowly and gravely, with his eyes on the floor and his mind elsewhere. His leave-taking was icy.

Mussolini then told me that he had meditated for a long time and that he thought the moment had arrived to clarify all positions. He handed me a memorandum, which I am to pass on to Hitler, which he had written regarding the necessity for immediate Axis occupation of Central Europe and the Balkans in case of war.

The Master of Ceremonies, who knows nothing of these conversations, and who accompanied the British ambassador home, said: "Loraine, on his way back, was red and congested and he was bothered by a nervous tic. He looked like a man who had received a slap in the face. He talked to himself all the time."

Let us see what will happen now. In my opinion the British-Italian agreement is dead and maybe Chamberlain will die with it.

May 29, 1939

A long conversation with the minister of Bulgaria. Naturally the attitude of his country was the main subject of our talks. I maintained that the geographic and political situation of Bulgaria as well as her best interests push her inevitably towards the Axis. It may be possible for Yugoslavia to remain neutral, but for Bulgaria, surrounded by enemies, such a possibility is excluded. The minister, for the most part, seemed to share my point of view. He said, however, that from the military point of view Bulgaria is as yet unprepared. I did not fail to reply that if Bulgaria adopts a well-defined policy, it will be in the interest of Italy and Germany to make up for her deficiencies. I informed Talamo of the conversation and authorized him to speak along these lines with the leaders in Sofia. I attribute the greatest importance to the Bulgarian card.

Christich informed me that Yugoslavia has asked Turkey to declare that the British-Turkish pact has no effect in the Balkans. The distrust between Belgrade and Ankara deepens.

Cavallero has been appointed vice-president of the Italian-German mixed commission, as prescribed in the treaty. I shall leave Wednesday for Berlin as bearer of the memorandum written by the Duce.

I made certain general provisions for Albania, among them the more important are the integration of the armed forces and closing of the Ministry of Foreign Affairs.

May 30, 1939

The Senate approves by acclamation the budget of the Ministry for Foreign Affairs. I received François-Poncet. He has nothing important to tell me and brings up only a few trifling routine matters, but he is trying to see the lay of the land and find out our reaction. He does not speak about continuing negotiations; nor do I. We agree in thinking that it is best to wait until the situation develops. I criticize the policy of encirclement; he answers that it is a simple, defensive action on the part of those who fear further aggressive ventures by the Axis. In his opinion, March 15, the date on which Hitler tore up the Munich protocol, is the key to the new situation. He is quite pessimistic, but does not exclude the possibility of maintaining for a long time in Europe a peace based upon the balance of power. The first experiment lasted for some time—from 1871 to 1914. He alludes to the fact that Mussolini has refused to go on with the exchange of a fragment of the Ara Pacis now in Paris and deduces from this that his mind is extremely embittered against France.

I give von Mackensen some documents provided by our secret service, which prove that the British-Turkish accord is a genuine offensive alliance against the Axis, and I informed him of the heated conference between Loraine and the Duce at the Palazzo Venezia.

May 31, 1939

Mussolini listens to my account of the meeting with Poncet with little interest. He says: "Had I accepted the fragment of the Ara Pacis the entire French press would have said that I would have to be satisfied with a few stones instead of Tunisia and Corsica." For the moment he has no intention of relaxing our relations with France. He would like, instead, to obtain from Switzerland three hundred million gold francs in order to avoid revealing the decrease of our treasury reserves, which have been reduced to three billion. In the present political situation I am of the opinion that it would be difficult to get money from Berne.

The Duce sets down some directives in principle: (1) to get Hungary and Spain into the military alliance; (2) facilitate the entrance of Japan into the Pact of Steel; (3) have Bulgaria take a position in favor of the Axis; (4) obtain a definite clarification of the Yugoslav attitude. In this connection it is necessary to note that Macek has refused to sign the Carnelutti report, saying that he has resumed negotiations with Belgrade and that he still wishes to clarify some points in the future relations between Rome and Croatia. This I have from Carnelutti. According to Bombelles, the refusal was much more categorical because Macek has made other commitments (but with whom?) and because he is a democrat and wants to avoid any deep understandings with Fascism. The Duce, to whom I show Carnelutti's letter, is of the opinion that we must wait for the results of Prince Paul's visit to Berlin. He also believes that some concessions can be made on the future state of Croatia, limiting ourselves to having a common ministry of foreign affairs and control of the army.

June 1, 1939

Our Legionnaires are displeased at the fact that the Duce will not review them. But he does not intend to change his decision: he will not come to Naples because the King is there; and he wants only a delegation to come to Rome. He will issue a proclamation. I am thinking of an assembly of the legions in September; it might be the occasion for a review.

The ambassador[424] comes to see me for one of his pointless conversations. The conversation drifts to the monarchy. I do not conceal our point of view from him, and am increasingly convinced that he is flirting with Don Juan and is also smiling to the English. I shall ask Serrano Suñer[425] for his head.

I see Loraine for the first time since the conference at the Palazzo Venezia. He says that he will go to London soon and asks if there is anything to add to what the Duce said. Nothing as far as I am concerned. But we speak again about the situation, and he does not hide the fact that the British pact with Turkey is the direct result of our occupation of Albania. Hence the trust, which was the very basis for the pact of April 16, has disappeared. We agree that for the moment there is nothing to be done; he repeats more or less what François-Poncet had said about the dangers of the present situation, which might crystallize into an equilibrium between the two blocs.

June 2, 1939
I received the Albanians at the station. They come to receive the text of their constitution-to-be, which is to unify the armed forces and abolish their ministry for foreign affairs. As rewards, we shall give them certain compensations of a personal nature, such as nominations to the Senate, ambassadorial titles, et cetera. I must say that probably for the first time since the annexation they were visibly satisfied. Which goes to show that personal benefits will frequently silence even the most noble feelings. . . .

After signing with Argentina last evening, Guarneri unburdened himself of some very pessimistic talk on the exchange situation. Our reserves are now reduced to 3,200,000,000. Five hundred more will be necessary to carry through to the end of the year. Guarneri openly speaks of bankruptcy and says that it can be avoided only by bringing imperialistic policies to an end.

The Duce said today that Guarneri's talk is just one of his usual "exhalations" which accurately express the state of mind and the wishes of certain plutocratic circles. In any case, it made no great impression on him, because he has been listening to Guarneri's false prophecies for six whole years and they all fail to materialize with perfect punctuality, as democratic prophecies always do. I personally believe, however, that the truth is somewhere in between.

June 3, 1939
Ceremony at the court for the delivery of the constitution to the Albanians. The King asks who drafted the document and observes sarcastically that there is no heraldic symbol of the dynasty on the Albanian flag. I answer that this is not quite so, because it does have the blue Savoyard sash and the crown of Scanderbeg. This convinces him, but he is still in a bad mood. I report this to the Duce, who seizes the occasion to lower his horns and attack the monarchy. Starace is also present. The Duce declares that he

is completely sick and tired of dragging behind him "empty baggage cars, which, moreover, very often have their brakes on," that the King "is a bitter, untrustworthy little man, who at this time is concerned with embroidery on the flag and does not sense the pride which comes from seeing his national territory increased by 30,000 square kilometers," and that, in conclusion, "it is the monarchy, because of its idiotic glorification, that prevents the 'Fascistization' of the army. The mediating agency for this 'glorification' is that revolting Asinari de Bernezzo."[426]

The Duce said, "I am like a cat, cautious and prudent, but when I jump I am sure of landing where I wish. I am now beginning to think whether we ought to do away with the House of Savoy. In order to liquidate it, it is enough to mobilize 250,000 men in two provinces, Forlì and Ravenna. Or perhaps the posting of a proclamation will be enough." He spoke with such directness that Starace interpreted the words of Mussolini as marching orders for party action.

In the afternoon I settled the problem of the co-ordination of Albanian diplomatic services with the Italian services. A few decorations and a few jobs were enough to accomplish this.

The operation to emasculate Albania without making the patient scream—the annexation—is now practically completed. As I have already noted, for the first time the Albanians are not so somber. Such is the advantage of cold-blooded and calculated decisions. The Duce and I have brought up the problem of the irredentism of Kosovo and of Ciamuria. The Duce defines this irredentism: "The little light in the tunnel." Meaning, the ideal spiritual motive that we must stimulate in the future to keep the Albanian national spirit high and united.

June 4, 1939
Nothing new.

June 5-7, 1939
Departure for Naples.
Serrano Suñer arrives on the *Duke of Aosta*. At the same time on the *Sardegna* comes the first contingent of the Arrow Division, which has arrived to accompany their Fascist comrades who are being sent home. Considerable excitement; the Legionaries sing war hymns; cannon and sirens fill the clear and sunny air. Serrano Suñer clasps my hands for a long time and repeats words of gratitude for what Italy has done and her way of doing it. I embrace Gambara; through him I want to hug to my breast every one of those who return and every one of those who remain in Spain, the guardians of a friendship and performers of a task that will produce glorious results.

In the evening I have a long conference with Serrano Suñer while we are driving through the panoramic streets of Naples. He is a slender, sickly man—one of those creatures suited for study and reflection; a very conscientious man, honest and full of enthusiasm. Having been caught in the whirlpool of the revolution, he has become both actor and author, and brings to his task a passionate faith. Intelligent, but still somewhat inexperienced, he wavers in his judgment between the results of the practical knowledge he has acquired and the vague and metaphysical expressions of his thinking. But it is always feeling that dominates him: he hates and loves impetuously.

France is his *bête noire*. He said that he hates her in the first place because his two brothers were killed by French bullets, and also because he is Spanish, and for this reason considers France the eternal enemy of Greater Spain.

We discuss many points: *war*. Spain fears a war in the near future because she is today at the extreme limit of her resources. In certain regions there is famine. If she can have two or preferably three years' time, she can reconstitute herself and complete her military preparations. Spain will be at the side of the Axis because she will be guided by feeling and by reason. A neutral Spain would, in any event, be destined to a future of poverty and humiliation. Furthermore, Franco's Spain intends to solve the problem of Gibraltar; as long as the British flag flies on Gibraltar, Spain will not be a completely free and sovereign nation. Spanish youth lives with the desire and hope of kicking the English into the sea, and is getting ready to do so. Spain also has accounts to square with France, that "dishonest and dishonorable France," and these accounts are called Morocco and political and economic independence.

Serrano Suñer was very happy to learn that both we and the Germans also wish to postpone the conflict for some years.

Relations with Italy. The alliance is a fact in our minds; it would be premature, for the moment, to put it in a protocol. But that is what he wishes. We discussed Germany with much restraint, especially due to the religious question. He is a believer, a convinced and fervent believer. The anti-Catholic excesses of the Germans are repugnant to him.

Portugal. He considers it to be fundamental to Spanish policy and to the Axis to remove Portugal from the British sphere of influence. Difficult as this may be, he intends to work in this direction, and also asks for our collaboration.

Monarchy. Perhaps "within twenty years Spain may have need of a king." Then if the Bourbons have behaved well, they can be put back on the throne, but not for the time being. The head of the state is Franco, and the need for a monarchy is felt in only a few quarters. Many who shout "long live the King" try to hide their opposition to the regime by this cry. Franco will act with the harshest energy against those people.

These are more or less the points Serrano Suñer repeated to the Duce during the long conference which took place in the Palazzo Venezia. The Duce reiterated his determined hostility to the restoration of the monarchy "which would become a center for opportunism and intrigue."

June 8, 1939

Percy Loraine delivers London's answer to the Duce's query. Chamberlain considers the pact of April 16 to be in full force and hopes that it might have further possibilities of development. I do not know whether such an answer will please the Duce, who is rarely satisfied with mere words and wants action, "the everlasting action," as he says. "For the time being the situation is negative; the pact between Britain and Turkey, the guarantees given to Greece and Romania, the negotiations with Moscow, are the elements of that policy of encirclement which London is directing against us."

I received a document of the highest interest from Hong Kong. It is a study made by Admiral Noble on British naval possibilities against the forces of the triangle. It is couched in pessimistic terms, especially regarding the Mediterranean, dominated in his opinion by the aerial, naval, and submarine forces of Fascist Italy.

June 9, 1939

During the evening I have long conferences with Serrano Suñer. He reacts violently against Ambassador Conde, whom he calls an imbecile, and relates that Conde had even attempted to warn him against the Duce and myself. The fact is that Conde, who is really a colossal fool, is completely attached to the monarchy and intriguing with the King and the princes for the restoration. He has served his time, and it is good for him to have a change of scenery. Suñer agrees, and will have him removed. Suñer also speaks to me disparagingly of General Jordana, as well as of the entire Spanish diplomatic corps. He does not wish to become head of the government. He says that this is a French maneuver designed to disturb his good relations with Franco, but he would like to take the place of General Jordana. Evidently he is counting on our support and for this reason he would like to hasten Franco's visit to Italy. He was somewhat prejudiced against the Axis. Mussolini's words have dispelled his misgivings and he wishes to establish contacts with the Nazis, about whom he had been somewhat doubtful before. His Catholic faith and the propaganda of some hostile elements had succeeded in rousing in him the belief that Hitler's position had been shaky.

June 10, 1939

I report to the Duce on what Suñer had told me. The Duce also would like to see him as head of the Foreign Ministry, even while holding on to the Ministry of Internal Affairs, which, in the Duce's opinion, his "fifteen years' experience constitute his best asset for leadership." I shall write a letter to Franco, which I will deliver personally on the occasion of my trip.

Naval review; very beautiful. It appears that the King of Italy has praised the Roman step, even recalling certain historical episodes that prove its high ethical value. The Duce's comment was: "I wanted to answer him: 'My dear, solemn idiot, it was precisely against you that I had to argue the hardest in order to introduce it.'"

I hand a copy of the Noble document to the Japanese ambassador. I translate a portion of it, and I can see that it makes a huge impression upon him.

The ambassador leaves tonight for Berlin, where new and it would appear better instructions have arrived for the conclusion of the Tripartite Pact.

I also gave von Mackensen the document and other cables which prove duplicitous Yugoslav wavering. Mackensen was irritated by Serrano Suñer because he did not mention the Germans in his speech. In Suñer's defense I explained this by saying that he had little diplomatic experience, and I affirmed that in Spain Suñer represents the man who has the confidence of the Axis. I suggest the idea of a trip to Germany.

June 11, 1939
Nothing new.

June 12, 1939
The Duce speaks about De Vecchi and says that for eighteen years he has had to carry on his shoulders the embarrassing weight of this individual. "On October 28, 1922 he was already willing to betray us to obtain a portfolio of some sort in the new cabinet to be formed by a coalition of different parties." After this statement he recalled, one after another, the blunders which De Vecchi had made in every one of the positions he had occupied. He aroused the wrath of God by threatening to take away the pensions of the war wounded, and then he made a speech that was a real shock to the regime. In Africa he worked hard to occupy by force territories that already belonged to us and carried out cruel and useless slaughters. In conclusion, he thinks that he is a "fearless clown," but he wishes to keep him quiet and gives him everything he asks for. He has had two of his sons-in-law given the title of baron. Mussolini laughs about it, and will end up giving him the high military rank to which he aspires.

A second conference at the Palazzo Venezia with Serrano Suñer. Nothing new. The Duce advises Franco to have a "January 3" for Spain by freeing himself as soon as possible of all those elements that are not faithful to the revolution. Serrano Suñer says that he has spoken to the King and to the Prince of Asturias. He had a good impression of the latter. Of the former he speaks ill; the King is an unreliable, domineering man, who even suggested improving relations between France and Spain in the near future, which outraged Serrano Suñer.

June 13, 1939
New tensions because of the problem of Danzig. As a matter of fact our military attaché in Paris had warned us of this in advance two days ago. This leads one to suspect that the Poles had planned some action in Danzig. The Duce receives von Mackensen, who brings a gift from Goebbels. He talks chiefly about the desirability of better relations between Germany and the Holy See for the purpose of strengthening ties with Spain. He reviews what he has done in Italy and comes to the conclusion that when the interests of the state conflict with those of the Church, the state should go ahead and take care of its own business. The Pope, he thinks, can go ahead and protest, if only "to save his own soul and maybe also mine."

We have decided on the construction of the Pater Village in Tirana with five hundred apartments to house Italians returning from abroad. In this way we shall also succeed in increasing the number of Italians living in Tirana. In Tirana the news is that everything is going well, both from the political and the military and economic points of view.

During his farewell call, Serrano Suñer asks me to have the secret police keep a close eye on the Spanish Air Force General Kindelan during his visit to Rome. He accuses him of plotting for the monarchy and wants to have proof of this in his hands in order to denounce him to Franco.

The Duce calls me in to discuss Franco's visit. He is very much annoyed by the inevitable interference of the King [of Italy], since Franco is the head of the state. Says the Duce: "This time I will not tolerate a half-and-half situation as there was during Hitler's visit. If the King doesn't have sense enough to withdraw, I will. It is necessary to put this paradoxical situation before the Italian people so that they may finally understand that there are certain incompatibilities, and that it may make its own choice."

June 14, 1939

Serrano Suñer leaves. He is visibly moved and repeats words of gratitude for me and for the Duce, as well as his love for Italy. He treats Conde coldly. Conde is scheduled to be torpedoed soon. Serrano Suñer told me that this idiotic individual had tried to influence him against the Duce and me, since he believes that we are opposed to the restoration of the monarchy. Relations between Serrano and Mackensen are now better, in fact, they are good. However, my intervention was necessary, because deep down Suñer was opposed to the Germans, and von Mackensen was offended by his none too casual forgetfulness of the German contribution to the cause of nationalist Spain.

The Duce wants us to begin defining with Spain the future program for the western Mediterranean: Morocco would go completely to Spain; Tunisia and Algeria would go to us. An agreement with Spain should insure our permanent outlet to the Atlantic Ocean through Morocco.

Dinner at the French embassy, a useless, colorless, dinner, in the traditional diplomatic manner with the usual second-rate "dear colleagues" entrusted with uncertain and presumptuous undertakings, young and hard pressed appointees and old court dames present only to gorge themselves with free food. We practically do not speak about politics. Still, the entire French press makes a big fuss over the event which, I repeat, represents nothing, absolutely nothing, and leaves our relations with France as before— even worse than before.

June 15, 1939

I go to Genoa. The fliers return from Spain.

Genoa, an unexpectedly royalist city, gives the King such an enthusiastic welcome as to lead me to reflect on many things.

I mention this to Starace.

June 16, 1939

I return to Rome. Nothing sensational.

June 17, 1939

During my absence a regrettable incident occurred in connection with an athletic parade of Nazis in Bolzano, during which the secretary of the group was arrested. Von Mackensen speaks to me about it. I immediately take steps to get the secretary of the group out of jail, and the Duce gives his authorization to do so. They acted too impetuously. Had I been present things would have gone differently. What impression will the arrest of a Nazi official in Italy make abroad? And how about the impression in Germany itself? What would we say if they arrested the secretary of the Fascist party in Berlin or in Munich?

I receive Stylla, former minister of Albania to Belgrade. I intend to use him in connection with the Kosovo problem, concerning which he is very competent. I shall create within the undersecretariat for Albania an office for irredentisms.

Bottoni and Benini just arrived from Tirana, bringing excellent news on the Albanian situation.

The Duce has gone to Riccione for a short rest.

June 18, 1939

Nothing new.

June 19, 1939

Nothing new.

June 20, 1939

Hitler asks that the head of the Nazi group in Bolzano be sent to Germany because he intends to punish him in an exemplary way. It is an elegant gesture, equivalent to publicly proving the importance that he attributes to Italian friendship.

Conference with Talamo. He says that Bulgaria continues in its uncertain attitude and that at least for the time being he does not have much hope of having it take a clear-cut position at the side of the Axis.

June 21, 1939

The officials of the commission for the repatriation of Germans residing in Alto Adige leave for Berlin. There has been some uncertainty on the Duce's part as to the advisability of sending Mastromattei; people might criticize the fact that a prefect is going to Berlin on a diplomatic mission. But this is not quite the case; he is going as an expert who is a member of a commission. On the other hand, it seems that the Germans mean business. We must not, therefore, do anything that might create problems.

June 22, 1939

At Buffarini's office I support the Slovenes' request for permission to publish some small non-political newspapers in their own language. If we really want to carry out a policy that will attract the Croats, Slovenes, and so forth, we must start by giving them the feeling that we are being intelligently liberal. We shall think of tightening the reins later on. As for the rest, there is nothing new.

June 23, 1939

I receive a letter from Serrano Suñer inviting me to go to Spain between July 10 and 18. It is worded very courteously but leads me to find in it a certain amount of reserve. This may be due to the fact, as pointed out by Gambara, that there is some rift between Serrano Suñer and Franco. We shall see. I should like to find out many things in Spain, and I hope Serrano, even though it be in the best of faith, didn't go too far in his predictions of total adherence to the Axis.

From Berlin they telephone that the first meeting on Alto Adige has produced concrete results and that the prospects are very encouraging.

June 24, 1939

Nothing new.

June 25, 1939

Nothing new.

June 26-July 2, 1939

Now that solitude has settled around me as well as within me, I wish, dear Dad, to be in your company for a while in this great room of the Palazzo Chigi, where you came so often to support me with your trusting and farseeing optimism.[427]

The cruel news of your death struck me suddenly like a treacherous blow. We had seen each other only a few days before, on Wednesday or Friday. I found you in your office in what I thought was good physical shape. You spoke with your usual liveliness and you were expounding plans and projects which you intended to carry out in the space of a few years. You did not hesitate to plan ahead, for you were now certain that your iron will had prevailed over the ailment which, two years ago, had almost overwhelmed you. And you gave of yourself sincerely, working without ever asking anything for yourself; thus the ailment struck you down stealthily.

I returned home Monday evening, after having passed some hours in the home of friends. I had no inkling of the loss that would befall me, but I was sad and a bit tired.

I went to bed at about one o'clock, or even before. I found that, contrary to his usual habit, my servant was waiting for me to say that they had telephoned from the Ministry for Foreign Affairs. This surprised me. A night telephone call, which at the time of Spain and Albania was a common thing, appeared to me, in view of the present conditions of European politics, somewhat unjustified. I learned quickly that they were calling me from Ponte a Moriano because you were not well. I had a foreboding of the truth, but I cast the thought away from me with angered rage. I called Ponte a

Moriano. A servant with a sad voice answered me and gave the receiver to my mother, who, between sobs, said at once that you, Dad, our good, great, dear father, were no more. It was a great blow. This is not a common, ordinary word which I now repeat: it was a great blow to me, physically and mentally. I felt that something was torn away from my physical being. Only at that moment, after thirty-six years of life, did I come to realize how real and deep and indestructible are the ties of blood: You, Dad, who have known from my infancy my admiring love for you, you alone can thoroughly understand my sorrow.

Do you recall, when I was a child at La Spezia, how I bade you good-by every time you left from the little terrace of our house, facing the sea? I was unable to speak and my eyes filled with tears, but I restrained myself as long as you were present, because I did not want to show my weakness to a grown-up. But my efforts were useless, and you knew very well that as soon as you had disappeared around the corner of via dei Colli and del Torretto I would have collapsed to the ground, overcome by tears and solitude. Well, Dad, the same thing has happened again. I have been overwhelmed by an unreasonable sorrow just as I was at that time, with the difference that I, no longer the child dressed in a sailor suit, proud of the ribbon which I wore with the name of your ship, but a man with quite a few gray hairs, with a heavy burden of responsibility, of thoughts and worries, with my secret sadness, which I have hidden even from you—I am a man, in short, who is not cured of his wounds in one hour, but who carries them with him forever from now on.

I rushed to Ponte a Moriano all alone in a car. Alone, not because some of my friends—who had been informed by me—had abandoned me, but because I wanted to remain with you and every other person would have been an obstacle to this, our first communion.

My trip from Rome to Ponte a Moriano was long and terrible, but when dawn came, I do not know why, a hope arose in me that perhaps I had misunderstood, and that your end had not come. I do not know, I cannot succeed in explaining the strange temptation that came to me which, however, lasted only a short time. Passing through Leghorn, in front of the *Telegrafo* building,[428] which you so carefully planned and which you loved so much, I saw the flag at half mast. For the first time, during the entire night, I wept.

Mother, overcome with a grief that only fifty years of a faithful and devoted love can explain, received me with despondent tenderness and led me to the room where you were lying calmly on the bed, wearing the gray suit in which death had overtaken you a few hours before. I would have thought that you were sleeping were it not for a small crucifix that had been piously placed upon your great heroic breast. Mother had the strength to tell me, in all its details, your tragedy and her own. The illness that overcame you when you left Leghorn, your will power in attempting to hide your ailment, the constant alternation of slight improvements and more serious attacks, the useless search for help in the deserted and impassable countryside—all this Mother told me.

And she told me that, arriving home, your home in Ponte a Moriano, which you loved so much and where you played with my children for your joy and mine, and where even on that night little Marzio slept in blessed ignorance of what was happening, you insisted on getting out of the car without help, and, realizing that even an old fighter like you could not prevail in the matter, you put your arms around the doctor, saying calmly, "Now we must die," and breathed your last. You died as a soldier, as a Fascist, as a Christian.

Dad, I do not speak to you about myself. You know and you understand that any words of mine would be an offense to our great love as well as to my own sorrow. I shall tell you about the others instead. You were and you are very much beloved. More than anybody can believe. Your friends Rodinis, Baiocchi, Caparma, and many others were affected by your passing like animals wounded to death seeking only to die in solitude. Starace arrived right after me and was terribly grieved. With his own hands he chose to place on your bed, to the right and to the left of your mortal remains, the party's insignia which you have honored so much by your work and by your faith.

Then, very shortly, the King arrived. He could not control his emotion. He spoke about you in generous terms. He greeted you with the Roman salute and his eyes filled with tears. Since he had arrived without any ceremony, in the company of only an aide in civilian dress, he laid aside all formality of his royal rank, and one could see in him only a poor old man burdened with sorrow, who wanted to weep over the coffin of a lost friend. On the stairs the King, who was going out, met the Duce, just arriving by air from Forlì. Your Chief, whom you loved so much and to whom you were always faithful, really loved you as you wanted him to love you and as on many an occasion you knew he loved you and wished that he would put it into words. But to put his love into words is not in his hard nature. He spoke to you, however, after you were dead. He stayed a long time, looking at you with steady eyes and a tense face. Then he caressed you tenderly on your head and shoulders, and twice he kissed you on the forehead. He repeated that with the death of Arnaldo,[429] your parting was the hardest blow for him. He left after two hours, only to return the following day to pay you final homage in Leghorn.

What a strange and painful thing, Dad, that I who have always obeyed you should now have the sad duty to carry out the final preparations.

Still it was necessary to go through with it, and so I gave orders that they dress you in the uniform of an admiral with the decorations of the party and of the Fascist armed forces, and that the temporary burial take place at the cemetery of the Purificazione near your loved ones, and that the final burial be prepared at Montenero. The final burial must not take place in Famedio where the other great Livornese rest. You are the glory not only of a city, you belong to Imperial Italy. Your monument will rise from the top of the hill. It will be a monument that will recall your war and your heroism. On top of it will be a beacon which will be lit every night so that we may all be reminded from a distance of your immortal spirit. I say from a distance, because it will be seen even from that Corsica which encircles our savage Sea of Leghorn and in whose freedom you have always believed.

Late in the afternoon we took you to Leghorn, and seeing you leave your home at Ponte a Moriano forever was another blow for me. I followed you in the first car and beside me was Starace who, I repeat, has been like a brother. Almost the entire journey took place very slowly, often at a walking pace, because a great crowd of grieving peasants lined both sides of the street along the way. And all the flowers of Lucca were spontaneously offered to you.

We arrive in Leghorn at about seven o'clock in the evening. The weather is beautiful: blue sky and warm air. All the church bells are ringing. The city seems to be stricken by an irreparable catastrophe, and it also seems that this is a drama that affects everyone. A silent and pensive people gathered on the sidewalks. Eyes are fixed and dry. Arms are raised in the Roman salute. Many women kneel and many are praying. This homage of love that your city pays you is such that only you could have imagined it. The love you gave the people of Leghorn during your lifetime is being repaid to you many times over if it were possible in the hour of your departure. In the hall of the Fascio, where you rest on the gun carriage fit for heroes, a great crowd passes silently and sadly. I remain near you for a long time. To look at you and to caress you lessens my sorrow, and I wish I could embrace one by one all who come to pay you homage. I recognize in their sorrow true sorrow— the sorrow which makes men brothers. The order to mount guard has been given to the best men of Italy, all those who have excelled in the last twenty years in the army, in politics, in the Faith. The war, and the revolution, the new glory of Italy, are all there beside you personified in her best men.

Innumerable touching episodes took place, but I shall recall only one, because it certainly will be dearest to your heart. An old man, so old that he appeared to be ageless, dragged himself along to pay homage to your remains and said that he wanted to honor not only your memory but also that of your father, whose cabin boy he had been on board a sailing ship.

I have returned, Dad, to see the house in which you were born. It is modest and somewhat ill-kept. This will no longer be the case in the future. I shall take an interest in it. And I shall see to it that it becomes, as it should be, a place sacred to all those people—and there are many of them—who have and will have the cult of your memory.

Yesterday, because of you, the King and the Duce met on the staircase of a modest country home. Today, again because of you, all of Italy has come to Leghorn. Never before in its history has the entire life of the nation been assembled within its walls.

The last solemn honors have been paid. The Duce came by plane from Romagna and followed on foot the caisson bearing your mortal remains. Next to him was Mother, who has courageously kept her vow to remain near you to the last, and I, myself. Meanwhile, Maria, who is not altogether well but who will get better, remained in Rome in her silent tears near the radio that broadcast the details of this occasion.

The religious ceremony took place in the cathedral. I had suggested St. Peter and Paul, the church of your childhood. But it was too small. The cathedral itself, which, when I was a child, seemed to have a boundless immensity, could not hold even a part of the high officials who were following you. As for the common people, they crowded the streets, and their attitude was so compassionate and humble that the entire city seemed to be transformed into an immense temple of sorrow. After the blessing on the Piazza there was the Fascist roll call. I am sure that among all the voices you recognized my own. "Present" is the only word, Dad, that I can say with reference to you since you left me.

If in life you might at times be or seem to be far away, now that you are no more this is not possible. You are near me and with my spirit, endlessly and inseparably. The Duce and Mother had withdrawn. I followed your remains as far as the cemetery, and as you were crossing the fatal threshold of the Purificazione the naval squadron, having arrived during the night, let the cannon thunder in your honor. For some minutes you paused near the tombs of your forefathers, as you were wont to do every time you came to Leghorn. Then you were carried to a small chapel where you now rest in a niche until such time as a worthy monument is ready to receive you. I am grateful to those who have arranged for you to be put in a niche and not buried. It was nerve-wracking to see the marble slab shut you off from the world of the living, but it would have been sadder still for me to see you buried in the earth.

The squad members and my friends led me away as I was once again overcome by my grief. Then, with Mother, I started on my way back to Rome and, my dear Dad, life must again take on its usual rhythm within and without. This is inevitable and perhaps best. But today, as I write you, I am still upset: I feel a profound loneliness in my heart and a sweet and painful sadness. Someday, if I know that it would not be contrary to your wishes and to your nature, I will speak and write about you as I wish to do and as I must, so that so many beautiful things may be made public which you have stubbornly wanted to conceal. Today I would not know how, nor could I do it. But remember, Dad, that among all those who honestly do you honor here, I do so now with my devotion, with my love, with my tenderness, which tragic fate has impressed on me profoundly, immutably, and completely.

July 3, 1939

Life goes on, and my work helps somewhat to draw me out of this great sorrow into which I have been plunged. The Duce was really paternal and uttered many expressions of great attachment and affection about my father. Then, this morning, he handed me the document that Father had in his possession since November 1926—a letter in which the Duce nominated him as his successor and gave him instructions on the measures to be taken in case of any sudden disappearance of the Chief. The Duce also spoke of his plans regarding the successor to my father in the chamber: Grandi and Farinacci. I inclined toward the candidacy of Farinacci, but this morning Starace, who has fought such a candidacy, and maybe with good reasons, came to see me. We agree on a colorless figure, such as Teruzzi or Acerbo,[430] for the nomination.

The international situation has darkened in these last few days because of the problem of Danzig. I remain calm, thinking that it is a false alarm.

The fact is that the Germans haven't said a word on the subject, which cannot be reconciled with the commitments of the pact. The Duce has outlined a plan for a solution of the problem through a plebiscite. But this seems to me rather utopian and I told him so.

Gathering at the Palazzo Chigi to discuss the question of the return of the German population from Alto Adige to Germany. Things are going well, and I believe that in a short time we shall have satisfactory results.

July 4, 1939

The question of Danzig is slowly becoming more reassuring. From Berlin no communication, which confirms the fact that nothing dramatic is in the offing.

I have seen Christich, who has taken upon himself to tell me that his country does not intend to be compromised by the pact that Turkey has made with the Western democracies. I have also seen the Japanese ambassador, who states that his government is ready to sign the pact with some reservations, more pro-forma than anything else. I have likewise seen the British ambassador, who spoke mournfully about the bitterness of our press with respect to his country. I answered that it is not the press but the facts that have created a new and very harsh state of mind between Italy and Great Britain.

The Duce received Cavallero in my presence. He said that the mixed Italian-German commission will have, in relation to the Axis, the same functions which the Supreme Commission for Defense has had for internal questions.

I have received Badoglio's report on Albania: "*Quam parva sapientia!*" and the rest.

July 5, 1939

I see many diplomats, who are preparing to go on vacation, with their minds more at rest, now that the Danzig storm seems to have blown over.

François-Poncet unsuccessfully tries to help out a journalist who has been expelled. As usual we discuss the issue of responsibility for the present situation and conclude that only time can improve it.

The Greek, Metaxas, pays a courtesy visit, but he is stunned by my reception and by all the reservations which I raise concerning Greece's acceptance of a unilateral guarantee from Great Britain, which places his country in the somewhat unenviable position of becoming a semi-protectorate.

July 6, 1939

Conferences with Villani, the Belgian, the Turkish and Yugoslav ambassadors. Nothing important. We urge Berlin to make a statement regarding the exodus of the Germans from Alto Adige. It seems that the Führer is creating difficulties, and it is easy to see his reasons. However, the statement is necessary in order to re-establish the reality of the measure, since the foreign press is attempting to falsify its nature by every possible means.

July 7, 1939

Like a good ambassador who is new to his work, Percy Loraine makes a great to-do about communicating to the Duce a personal message from Chamberlain, and succeeds in having himself conveyed to the Palazzo Venezia. The message was of no particular importance. It was a sort of low-key charge against German claims to Danzig, as well as mentioning the dangers to world peace that might come from such pretensions. The Duce debated the message immediately, point by point, and some of his arguments were truly brilliant, such as the one about Poland being the last country to speak about Czechoslovakia, since it was Poland that struck the death blow when Czechoslovakia was down on her knees, and he concluded by repeating, "Tell Chamberlain that if England is ready to fight in defense of Poland, Italy will take up arms with her ally Germany." Percy Loraine practically never opened his mouth. The second interview at the Palazzo Venezia had no more sparkling results than the first one!

During the evening I acquainted von Mackensen with what had happened, and he seemed to be particularly satisfied with the attitude taken by the Duce on the British move.

July 8, 1939

Nothing new.

July 9, 1939

I leave for Spain.

July 19, 1939

I have set down my impressions of Spain in a notebook. The Duce is quite satisfied with the report on my Spanish trip.

I summon Magistrati to Rome regarding the matter of the meeting between Hitler and Mussolini, which is set for August 4. He thinks that it is due to Attolico's endemic crisis of fear. Nevertheless, we must prepare the meeting well in order to prevent it from being totally useless. Perhaps in view of the fact that for many reasons war plans must be delayed as long as possible he could talk to the Führer about putting forth a proposal for an international peace conference. This would offer the following advantages: either the democracies will agree to sit around a table and negotiate and then they will have to wind up yielding considerably, or they will refuse, and in this case we shall have the advantage of having taken the initiative for peace, which will reveal the internal position of the others and strengthen our position in arguing for what we want. But what are Hitler's real intentions? Attolico is very much concerned and warns of the imminence of a new and perhaps fatal crisis.

July 20, 1939

The information sent by Attolico continues to be alarming. From what he says, the Germans are preparing to strike at Danzig by August 14. And for the first time Caruso from Prague announces movements of forces on a vast scale. But is it possible that all this should take place without our knowledge, indeed after so many protestations of peace made by our Axis comrades? We shall see.

By order of the Duce I have presented an ultimatum to the Papal Nuncio for the *Osservatore Romano*. Either it will cease its subtle propaganda against the Axis or we shall prohibit its circulation in Italy. It has become the official mouthpiece of the anti-Fascists.

Villani speaks of the possibility of placing the Duke of Aosta on the throne of Hungary, but I have not succeeded in finding out whether he is acting on orders or on his personal initiative, in which case the matter is not of great importance.

July 21, 1939

Massimo[431] is not so pessimistic about the situation and he confirms my suspicions: that Attolico let himself be carried away in a fit of panic without very good reasons. Naturally Massimo expresses himself with a thousand reservations and ambiguities, as he usually does. Such is his nature, which neither the years nor events will change. He is generally favorable to the proposal for a meeting. He agrees on the necessity of presenting it to the Germans very tactfully or in such a way as to avoid its being interpreted by them to mean that we would readily withdraw from our obligations towards the alliance.

July 22, 1939

I take Magistrati to see the Duce, who has drafted an announcement for the meeting at Brenner Pass. It is based on the proposal of an international conference. The Duce outlines at some length the reasons for our proposal. I am skeptical of such a conference actually taking place, but I agree on the usefulness of our move that will, above all, sow confusion and dissension into the opposite camp, where many voices against war can already be heard.

I insist on making two points: (1) that our proposal be conditional only if the Germans have not previously decided to wage war, since, in that case, it would be useless to discuss anything; (2) that Ribbentrop be queried about the matter. I am doubtful, very doubtful, about Attolico's effectiveness now. He has lost his head. I am sending a cable to Magistrati ordering him to take part personally in all the negotiations.

I receive Koliqi,[432] with whom I spoke about the problem of Kosovo and of Ciamuria. He will prepare a memorandum with a plan. I give instructions for the action that we must develop in three successive stages: (1) general broad propaganda stressing culture and religion; (2) the same for the management of public welfare; (3) covert military organization to be ready for the moment when the inevitable Yugoslav crisis comes to a head.

July 23, 1939

I tried to pay a visit to my children at Capri, but the rough sea prevented my landing. News from Spain minimizes the importance of the dismissal of Queipo de Llano,[433] which, however, was expected, and the speech was nothing but the pretext that Franco had been seeking for a long time. I remember that after having called General Queipo "crazy," Serrano Suñer said that it was his intention to kick him upstairs by sending him to the "golden exile" of the embassy at Buenos Aires. Events have permitted the realization of this idea sooner than expected.

July 24, 1939

Attolico will see von Ribbentrop on Tuesday. I am curious to find out the German reaction to our proposal. I hope that it will be favorable but I do not believe so.

Villani brings the Duce two letters from Teleki. The first to confirm the absolute adherence of Hungary to the Axis; the second raises some reservations regarding a conflict with Poland. I vaguely suspect that the first letter was written in order to deliver the second.

Villani also speaks of the dynastic question and frequently mentions the name of the Duke of Aosta. He says he speaks for himself, but he admits that such a possibility is being discussed even in government circles. He severely criticizes Czaky, whom he considers "lacking in balance, dominated by a boundless ambition, and unscrupulous."

The minister of Yugoslavia repeats for the nth time his country's act of faith in collaboration with the Axis. They evidently feel our growing suspicions, which have been increased because of Prince Paul's trip to London.

July 25, 1939

Nothing new. The Hungarian move of yesterday made a terrible impression on the Duce and on the Germans. That was to be expected. At the Palazzo Chigi I had the first meeting regarding the reception to be given Franco.

In a long visit Guarneri sounded the alarm for the umpteenth time about the monetary situation, which according to him is very bad. He is preparing an alarming report for the Duce, who listens to him with "his imperturbable pessimism," and this is what most seriously troubles Guarneri.

July 26, 1939

I talked by telephone with Magistrati about the conversation with Ribbentrop. His reaction to the proposal of an international conference was unfavorable. He will talk about it with the Führer, but it is now easy to see that nothing will come of it. In which case, it would seem to be a good idea to postpone the meeting between the two leaders. In any event, before suggesting a decision to the Duce, I prefer to await the arrival of Attolico's report that is to be sent by airplane.

I tell Villani confidentially of the impression caused in Rome and Berlin by the Hungarian note regarding non-intervention in case of war with Poland. He notes our disappointment and places the responsibility on Count Czaky, a man whom I have always judged negatively.

July 27, 1939

I go to Leghorn to attend the ceremony on the thirtieth day after Dad's death. After a month sorrow grips my soul more deeply and more desperately than the first day. I can't get used to the idea of the loss of the man whom I loved so much and who has done so much for me. May God watch over him.

I resume my work with the usual intensity. This is a relief to me. I receive Attolico's report, which I send to the Duce. The ambassador's blunder becomes more and more evident. Once again Ribbentrop has affirmed German determination to avoid war for a long time. The idea of postponing the useless meeting at the Brenner Pass is becoming more obvious to me. The Duce also shares this opinion. However, I ask the Duce to read the report before he makes any decision.

Franco submits the name of Queipo as head of the Spanish military mission in Italy, and, naturally, it is immediately accepted. This is a clever move in order to end all recent gossip, to get rid of Queipo de Llano and at the same time keep him under control.

Good news from Albania, where mining explorations are proceeding very well. The Ammi has already yielded 8,000,000 tons of iron ore and many even greater deposits are being discovered.

July 28, 1939

After reading the report, the Duce decided to postpone his meeting with Hitler and I think he did well. I telephone Attolico, who is still trying to kid us. This time Attolico missed the boat. He was frightened by his own shadow and probably, in cahoots with somebody in the German Foreign Ministry, was trying to save his country from a non-existent danger. It's too bad. This ambassador has done good work, but now he lets himself be taken in by the war panic. This may easily be explained by the fact that he is a very rich man.

It appears that Ribbentrop has requested time to report to Hitler, who had voiced his opposition to the conference. Tomorrow we shall have a reply on the postponement.

The Bulgarians are concerned about the deployment of Turkish forces. They are right. Ankara, with British help, again wants to try to play the supremacy game in the Balkans. We must take advantage of this fact to instill fear into the Greeks and Yugoslavs, both of whom still remember the stench of the Turks. Anyway, Marković has been greatly alarmed ever since news first arrived of the understanding between Turkey and Great Britain. I shall have Ansaldo write on this issue. I don't expect too much, but it is always worthwhile trying to rekindle some old hatreds which are not entirely dead.

July 29, 1939

Nothing new.

July 30, 1939

Nothing new. We have not yet been able to get a reply from Berlin regarding the Brenner Pass meeting. Flying to Capri.

July 31, 1939

Nothing new except for the postponement of the Brenner Pass meeting, which Hitler decided personally. I am happy that this meeting, which was meaningless and dangerous, has been avoided, at least for the time being.

August 1, 1939

Nothing new.

August 2, 1939

The Duce is irritated by the sending of Indian troops to Egypt. Tomorrow I shall ask Percy Loraine for an explanation and particulars as to this British decision on the basis of the accord between Italy and Great Britain.

I received the ministers of Yugoslavia and Hungary, as well as the chargé d'affaires of France, unimportant conversations.

Attolico continues to harp on his favorite theme of the meeting between Hitler and Mussolini, still insisting on the bugaboo of a sudden decision that Hitler will make on August 15. Attolico's insistence makes me wonder. Either this ambassador has lost his head or he sees and knows something which has completely escaped us. Appearances lean toward the first alternative, but it is necessary to observe events carefully.

August 3, 1939

Percy Loraine says that the information about Indian troops in Egypt was provided to our military attaché in London. This is true, but the report has not yet reached us.

Massimo writes me a private letter where he appears to disagree with the ambassador as to the danger of an approaching crisis. He advises us against asking the Germans for a clarification of their program. If Massimo, notwithstanding his considerable and very great caution, has decided to take such a step, it means that he is sure of what he is saying. I have transmitted his letter to the Duce. On the other hand Roatta, the new military attaché, informs us of the concentration of forces and movements on the Polish border. Who is right? I may be mistaken, but I continue to feel optimistic.

August 4, 1939

A brief conversation with Christich to call his attention to the danger presented by the excessive freedom of action allowed in Yugoslavia to certain emissaries of Zog. According to information in our possession, they are attempting to foment border incidents. Christich promised to intervene strongly, and I believe he will keep his word, because he is very much afraid of any possible complications.

Attolico's alarmist bombardment continues. I can no longer see through the situation clearly. I am beginning to think that I should have a meeting with von Ribbentrop. The moment has come when we must really know how things stand. The situation is too serious for us to wait passively for developments.

The Duce returns to Rome.

August 5, 1939
     Nothing new.

August 6, 1939
     I received from Christich broad assurances about the precautions that
will be taken with reference to the Albanian refugees. I confer with the Duce.
The King has expressed his intention of giving me the Collar of the
Annunziata. The Duce was evasive at first, since "the Collar may lead to
compromises that it would be better not to make," but now he is convinced
as to the desirability of my having it, and tomorrow he will write to the King
about the matter.
     We discussed the situation. We agree in feeling that we must find some
way out. By following the Germans we shall go to war and enter it under the
most unfavorable conditions for the Axis, and especially for Italy. Our gold
reserves are reduced to almost nothing, as well as our stocks of metals, and
we are far from having completed our autarchic and military preparations.
If the crisis comes we shall fight if only to save our "honor." But we must
avoid war. I propose to the Duce the idea of my meeting with von
Ribbentrop—a meeting that on the surface would be of a private nature,
but during which I would attempt to pursue the discussion of Mussolini's
project for a world peace conference. He is very favorable. Tomorrow we
shall discuss the matter further, but I am convinced that the Duce wants to
move vigorously to avoid the crisis. And he is right in so doing.

August 7, 1939
     The Duce has written a fine letter to the King to say that he approves
my receiving the Collar of the Annunziata. He writes, among other things,
"It is my duty to declare to Your Majesty that we owe to Count Ciano the
penetration of Albania from within, which has permitted us to annex it
almost without striking a blow. This in itself is worth the Collar."
     The Duce has approved my meeting with von Ribbentrop, and I have
therefore telephoned instructions to Attolico on this point. Attolico himself had thought of something of the kind and was very pleased. I have
added that the meeting between the Duce and Hitler can take place at a later
date when the negotiations between Britain, France, and Russia have been
concluded.
     We are favorably impressed by the measures taken by Franco to create a
one-party system. The proof of this is the wild fury of the French press.

August 8, 1939
     With Benini to see the Duce, to discuss the question of Albanian iron
ore. The Duce is quite satisfied with the report. He decides that in the future
I shall take a trip to Albania, during which the Collar of the Annunziata will
be conferred on me. Massimo writes in a rather soothing tone from Berlin.
He does not foresee any immediate aggressive moves on Germany's part
even though the Danzig situation is serious and dangerous.

August 9, 1939

Von Ribbentrop has approved the idea of our meeting. I decided to leave tomorrow night in order to meet him at Salzburg. The Duce is anxious that I prove to the Germans, with documentary evidence, that to go to war at this time would be folly. Our preparation will not allow us to believe that victory will be certain. The probabilities are 50 percent; at least that's what the Duce thinks. On the other hand, within three years the probabilities will be 80 percent. Mussolini always has in mind the idea of an international peace conference. I believe it would be an excellent move.

The Japanese ambassador informs me that Tokyo has decided to join the alliance. After so much uncertainty I wonder if this is true. And, if it is true, I wonder if it is for the best, since conversations in Moscow are as yet inconclusive. Besides, won't this fact make Germany more arrogant and encourage her to rush along a path of intransigence and thus bring the crisis to the boiling point regarding the Danzig problem?

The King has very cordially confirmed to the Duce the matter of granting me the Collar.

August 10, 1939

The Duce is more than ever convinced of the need to delay the conflict. He has worked out the outline of a press release himself concerning the meeting at Salzburg, which ends with the mention of international negotiations to settle the problems that so dangerously disturb European life.

Before letting me go he recommends that I should frankly tell the Germans that we must avoid a conflict with Poland, since it will now be impossible to localize it, and a general war would be disastrous for everybody. Never has the Duce spoken of the need for peace with so much warmth and without reservations. I agree with him 100 percent, and this conviction will lead me to redouble my efforts. But I am doubtful as to the results.

August 11, 1939

In my notes of meetings I have kept the transcripts of my conversations with Ribbentrop and Hitler. Here I shall jot down only some impressions of a general nature. Ribbentrop is evasive whenever I ask him for details about the next German action. His conscience bothers him. He has lied too many times about German intentions toward Poland not to feel uneasy now about what he must tell me and what they are getting ready to do.

The decision to fight is implacable. He rejects any solution which might give satisfaction to Germany and avoid the conflict. I am certain that even if the Germans were given more than they ask for they would attack just the same, because they are possessed by the demon of destruction.

At times our conversation becomes very tense. I do not hesitate to express my thoughts with brutal frankness. But this does not move him. I am becoming aware of how little we count in the opinion of the Germans.

The atmosphere is cold. And the coldness between us spreads even among our staff. During dinner we do not exchange a word. We are distrustful of each other. But I, at least, have a clear conscience. He does not.

August 12, 1939

Hitler is very cordial, but he, too, is impassive and implacable in his decision. He speaks in the large drawing room of his house, standing in front of a table on which some maps are spread out. He exhibits truly profound military knowledge. He speaks with a great deal of calm and becomes excited only when he advises us to give Yugoslavia the *coup de grâce* as soon as possible.

I realize immediately that there is no longer anything that can be done. He has decided to strike, and strike he will. All our arguments will not in the least avail to stop him. He continues to repeat that he will localize the conflict to Poland, but his statement that the Great War must be fought while he and the Duce are still young leads me to believe once more that he is acting in bad faith.

He utters words of high praise for the Duce, but he listens with a faraway and impersonal interest to what I tell him about the bad effects a war would have on the Italian people. Actually I *feel* that as far as the Germans are concerned an alliance with us is worth only the number of divisions that the enemy will be obliged to keep facing us, thus easing up the situation on the German war fronts.

They care for nothing more. The fate that might befall us does not interest them in the least. They know that the decision to go to war will be made by them and not by us. In conclusion, they promise us only a beggarly pittance.

August 13, 1939

The second meeting with Hitler is shorter, and, I would say, more concise. Even in his gestures the man reveals more than yesterday his imminent will to take action. Our parting is cordial but reserved on both sides.

I report to the Duce at the Palazzo Venezia. And, in addition to reporting to him what happened, I also offer my own judgment of the situation as well as of the men involved and of events. I return to Rome completely disgusted with Germany, with its leaders, with their way of doing things. They have betrayed us and lied to us. Now they are dragging us into an adventure which we have not wanted and which might compromise the regime and the country as a whole. The Italian people will shudder in horror when they find out about the aggression against Poland and most probably will wish to fight the Germans. I don't know whether to wish Italy a victory or Germany a defeat. In any case, given the German attitude, I think that our hands are free, and I propose that we act accordingly, declaring that we have no intention of participating in a war which we have neither wanted nor provoked.

The Duce's reactions are varied. At first he agrees with me. Then he says that honor compels him to march with Germany. Finally, he states that he wants his share of the spoils in Croatia and Dalmatia.

August 14, 1939

I find Mussolini worried. I do not hesitate to arouse in him every possible anti-German reaction any way I can. I speak to him of his diminished prestige and his playing the none-too-brilliant role of second fiddle. And, finally, I turn over to him documents which prove German bad faith on the Polish question. The alliance was based on premises which they now ignore; they are the traitors and we must not have any scruples in ditching them. But Mussolini still has many scruples. I am going to do my level best to convince him, because in so doing I am sure that I shall render a great service to him and to my country. Meanwhile, I tell Starace not to withhold the country's true state of mind, which is clearly anti-German, from the Duce. Tomorrow I shall also discuss this with the head of the police force. He must be made aware that the Italian people do not want to fight alongside Germany in order to give it that power with which one day it will threaten us. I no longer harbor any doubts about the Germans. Tomorrow it will be Hungary's turn, and then ours. We must act now while there is time.

I meet the Polish ambassador at the beach. I speak with him in vague terms and advise moderation. Our counselor at Warsaw tells us that Poland will fight to the last man. The churches are filled. The people pray and sing a hymn, "O God, help us save our country." These people will be massacred by German steel tomorrow. They are completely innocent. My heart is with them.

August 15, 1939

The Duce, who at first had refused to act independently of the Germans, today, after examining the documents that I gave him, and after our conversations, is convinced that we must not march blindly with Germany. However, he makes one reservation: he wants time to prepare the break with Germany, and he will do it in such a way as not to cut relations brutally and suddenly. He feels that it may still be possible, though perhaps difficult, for the democracies to give in, in which case it would not be beneficial to us to antagonize Germany, since we, too, must have our share of the spoils. It is, therefore, necessary to find a solution which will allow the following: (1) if the democracies attack, we should be able to break free "honorably" of the Germans; (2) if the democracies simply accept the situation, we should take advantage and settle accounts with Belgrade once and for all.

For this purpose it seems useful to set down in writing the conclusions of the Salzburg meeting. This is a document that we might either make public or leave buried in the archives, as the case may require. But the Duce is more and more convinced that the democracies will fight. "It is useless," he says, "to climb two thousand meters into the clouds. Perhaps we are closer to the Eternal Father up there, if He exists, but we are surely farther removed from mankind. This time it means war. And we cannot go to war because our condition does not allow us to do so."

The conversations I had with him today lasted for six hours. And I was brutally frank with him.

August 16, 1939

Today as well I have had two conferences at the Palazzo Venezia. I was alone in the morning and accompanied by Attolico in the afternoon. The

Duce is more convinced than ever that France and England will go to war if Germany attacks. "If they do not act," he says, "I shall send an ultimatum to the Bank of France, asking for the consignment of gold which is the thing that the French hold more dear than anything else." He is really beginning to react to German behavior toward him. Personally, I encourage him in this with every means in my power.

During the afternoon we examine at length the advisability of sending a note to the Germans, but then we conclude that it is better to make a verbal communication, since a written document might induce Germany to ask for clarification about our eventual position in case of war. This is the last thing I want to see happen.

Mussolini, impelled by his idea of honor, might be drawn to reaffirm his determination to march with the Germans. He wanted to do so two days ago, and it was difficult to prevent him. It would be a mad venture, carried out against the unanimous will of the Italian people, who as yet do not know how things stand, but who, having had a whiff of the truth, have had a sudden fit of rage against the Germans.

Starace, who is in good faith in this matter, says that when Germany attacks Poland we must keep our eyes open to prevent public demonstrations against the Germans. A policy of neutrality will, on the other hand, be more popular, and, if it were necessary later, war with Germany would be every bit as popular.

August 17, 1939

I went again with Attolico to see the Duce. For a moment the fires of the old scruples of loyalty return to the Duce, and he wanted Attolico to confirm to Ribbentrop that, in spite of everything, Italy will march with Germany should the democracies throw themselves into the furnace of war. I fought like a lion against this idea and succeeded in getting the Duce to modify these instructions so that, at least, we would say nothing until the Germans have renewed their request as to what we will do. The Duce, however, has still not settled on a precise line of action, and he is still capable of tightening our bonds with Germany even more. Yet he does realize, and everyone tells him, that our country no longer wants to have anything to do with the Germans.

A brief discussion with von Mackensen, in which I tell him what Attolico will tell Ribbentrop tomorrow.

A brief conversation with Christich, who is, as always, fearful and uncertain. Finally I receive Percy Loraine. I do not conceal from him that I consider the situation extremely serious, and I tell him that Europe needs a great deal of common sense in order to avoid the crisis. He replies that the common sense is there, but that Europe cannot tolerate recurring *diktats* from Hitler. If the crisis comes, England will fight. Personally, he would like to participate in such a fight. He is sorry about only one thing: that for the first time in history our two countries may be at war with each other. I made no reply, but I think he knows that I, too, do not wish to see this happen.

August 18, 1939

A conversation with the Duce in the morning with his usual shifting feelings. He still thinks it possible that the democracies will not march, and that Germany might do good business cheaply, from which he does not intend to be excluded. Then, too, he fears Hitler's rage. He believes that a denunciation of the pact or something similar might induce Hitler to abandon the Polish question in order to square accounts with Italy. All this makes him nervous and disturbed. My suggestions are given short shrift. He now suspects that I, too, am against the Axis, and that I have made up my mind, and he refuses to be influenced by me.

In the afternoon Count Czaky arrives suddenly. He is, as always, confused, muddled, and contradictory. He hurriedly submits the idea of making a pact of alliance with the Axis. He hopes in this way to save Hungary from a German invasion or from a "friendly occupation." I discourage him, above all because I see in this a new bond between us and Germany.

The Duce is also very reserved on the issue. Czaky has no definite ideas on the situation. He still thinks that the Germans may be bluffing. He says that 95 percent of the Hungarian people hate the Germans. The Regent himself, speaking of them, called them "buffoons and brigands," and Madame Horthy said that even she would take up arms if they had to fight the Germans. For the first time we have been approached in an official way about placing the Duke of Aosta on the throne of Hungary. The Regent would be favorable, but the obstacle is a German veto.

August 19, 1939

I arrive at Tirana, where the news of being awarded the Collar of the Annunziata reaches me. I inspect the public works of Tirana and Durazzo. In Albania much has been done along material and spiritual lines. Party organizations are excellent, especially the work done with younger people, who are now clearly oriented in favor of Italy.

There is no doubt that if we can work in peace we shall have one of the richest regions of Italy within a few years.

I am quite satisfied with what I see, but today my spirit is absent. The vicissitudes of European politics are too serious and sad to let me concentrate my attention on Albanian problems only.

August 20, 1939

On the steamer *Duca degli Abruzzi*, I reach Valona. Here, too, I am given an enthusiastic welcome. Such much poverty! Tirana and Durazzo by contrast are two thriving cities. And yet the region is very beautiful, the bay spacious, and the sea rich in fish and fishing facilities. After a few years of work all will be transformed. We were to go to Korcia, but the weather was bad and we put it off. We return to Durazzo. There was a cable from Anfuso saying that my presence in Rome during the evening was "extremely desirable." I cancel my visit to Scutari and return to Rome.

This is what had happened: in my absence, the Duce made an about-face. He wants to support Germany at any cost in the conflict which is now close at hand, and he wishes to send during the evening, through Attolico, a communication to the Germans stating this intention. In the meantime, the British have made an appeal to the Duce to settle the controversy peacefully.

Conference between Mussolini, myself, and Attolico. The Duce has made up his mind and says it is already too late to drop the Germans. If this should happen the world press would say that Italy is cowardly, that it is not ready, and that it has drawn back when faced with the specter of war. I try to debate the matter, but that is useless now. Mussolini holds very stubbornly to his idea. I use the British communication as a pretext to delay any decision until tomorrow morning. I still hope to see my point of view prevail, while Attolico leaves the Palazzo Venezia discouraged and overwhelmed with grief.

August 21, 1939

Today I have spoken clearly: I have burned all my bridges. When I entered the room Mussolini confirmed his decision to march with the Germans. "Duce, you cannot and must not do it. The loyalty with which I have served you in carrying out the policy of the Axis demands my speaking clearly to you now. I went to Salzburg in order to adopt a common line of action. I found myself faced with a *diktat*. The Germans, not ourselves, have betrayed the alliance in which we were supposed to be partners, and not servants. Tear up the pact. Throw it in Hitler's face and Europe will recognize in you the natural leader of the anti-German crusade. Do you want me to go to Salzburg? Very well, I shall go and I shall speak to the Germans as they should be spoken to. Hitler will not have me put out my cigarette as he did with Schuschnigg." I told him this and more. He was very impressed, and approved my proposal; namely, to ask von Ribbentrop to come to the Brenner Pass, speak frankly to him, and to reaffirm our rights as Axis partners. He does not want the Axis to collapse for the time being, but if it should I would not be the one to weep over it.

We telephoned von Ribbentrop, who was unavailable for some time. Finally, at 5:30 p.m., I speak to him and tell him that I want to see him at the Brenner Pass. He says that he cannot give me an answer at once because he "is waiting for an important message from Moscow (sic) and will call me during the evening." I report this to the Duce, who asks me, as he frequently does these days, what the tone of the conversation had been and what the German mood sounded like.

Another conference with the Duce. He approves the document that I have drawn up for my discussion with von Ribbentrop and we settle on four points relating to events that might present themselves. In my opinion three do not count, but one is fundamental: the one which insists that we shall not intervene if the conflict is provoked by an attack on Poland.

August 22, 1939

Yesterday evening at 10:30 there was a coup de théâtre. Ribbentrop called, saying that he would prefer to see me at Innsbruck rather than at the border, because he was to leave later on for Moscow to sign a political pact with the Soviet government. I interrupted all decisions and reported back to the Duce.

He agreed with me in feeling that my trip to Germany would no longer be timely. I spoke again with Ribbentrop to tell him that our projected meeting would be postponed until his return from Moscow.

A long telephone conversation with the Duce. There is no doubt the Germans have struck a master blow. The European situation is upset. Can France and Great Britain, who have based their entire anti-Axis policy on an alliance with the Soviets, count upon the unconditional support of the extremist masses? And will the system of encirclement using small countries continue to prevail now that the Moscow cornerstone has collapsed? Nevertheless, we must make no hasty decisions. We must wait, and, if possible, be ready to gain something in Croatia and Dalmatia for ourselves. The Duce has set up an army under Graziani's command. I have established contacts with our Croatian friends in Italy and in their own country.

In diplomatic circles there is a great deal of confusion about the Russian action. In general the representatives of democratic countries are inclined to minimize the development. During the evening I see Percy Loraine, who would like an answer to the proposal he made on Sunday. My answer is vague, but not negative. In general I reiterate our desire for peace and the Duce's readiness to influence Hitler towards negotiations.

August 23, 1939

The day is charged with electricity and full of threats. In the meantime anxiety over the German-Russian pact gives way to a more rational evaluation of this development, which to my way of thinking is not really that fundamental. France and England trumpet to the four winds that they will intervene just the same in any potential conflict. Japan protests. News from Tokyo indicates their discontent, sharpened because Japan has been kept in the dark up to now.

The Duce, following my insistent suggestions, authorized me to present to Percy Loraine a plan for a solution based on a preliminary return of Danzig to the Reich, after which there would be negotiations and a great peace conference. I do not know whether it was the emotion or the heat, but it is a fact that Percy Loraine fainted or almost fainted in my arms. He found a place to rest in the toilet.

A meeting with François-Poncet, who was rather discouraged and pessimistic. However, he, too, without underestimating the importance of Russia's defection, repeats that France will fight. Weizsäcker[434] telephones me from the Berghof to inform me of Hitler's harsh answer to the British ambassador. Another hope is gone.

A new meeting with the Duce, regarding my visit to the King. He does not wish me to show him the anti-German papers and he proposes that I limit myself to informing him of the four points which, however, have not yet been communicated to the Germans. This evening the Duce is favorable to war. He talks of armies and of attacks. He received Pariani, who gave him good news on the condition of the army. Pariani is a traitor and a liar.

In the evening, Phillips brings me a long message from Roosevelt for the King. It doesn't seem to me to be very clear.

August 24, 1939

I went to Sant'Anna di Valdieri to confer with the King. This opportunity arose because of my visit to thank him for the Collar of the Annunziata, but we hardly spoke about the Collar. He wants news about the situation. I quickly inform him of what has happened, and, with him, I do not have to attack the Germans, because in his own mind he feels openly hostile toward them. I show him the four points agreed on with the Duce regarding our attitude. He approves, especially the third: the one about neutrality. In his judgment we are in absolutely no condition to wage war. The army is in a "pitiful" state. The military review and the maneuvers have fully revealed the sad state of unpreparedness of all our great units. Even the defense of our borders is insufficient. He has made thirty-two inspections and is convinced that the French can get through it with great ease.

The officers of the Italian army are not qualified for the job, and our equipment is old and obsolete. To this must be added the state of mind of the Italians, which is clearly anti-German. The peasants go into the army cursing those "damn Germans." We must, therefore, in his opinion, await events and do nothing.

Six months of neutrality will give us greater strength. In any case, if supreme decisions should have to be taken, he should like to be in Rome, "not to be left out," and he hopes that the Duce, in case of conflict, would give to the Prince of Piedmont a command. "Those two imbeciles, Bergamo and Pistoia, have commands, and my son should have one, too, for he is as smart as the Duke of Aosta." He then added paternally that Prince Umberto likes me very much and that he always speaks of me with trust and hope.

August 25, 1939

During the night I had a telephone conversation with von Ribbentrop who, at Hitler's request, says that the situation is becoming "critical" on account of the usual "Polish provocations." His tone is less decisive and overbearing than it was before. I speak to him of the advisability of our seeing each other. The answer is evasive.

Bastianini informs me that during my absence the attitude of the Duce has become furiously warlike.

Indeed this is the state of mind I find this morning. I make use of the opinions of the King in order to dissuade him, and I succeed in having him approve a communication to Hitler announcing our nonintervention for the time being, pending a re-examination of our position, until such time as we have completed our preparations for war. I was very happy over this result, but the Duce calls me back to the Palazzo Venezia. He has changed his mind. He fears the bitter judgment of the Germans, and wants to intervene at once. It is useless to struggle. I accept and return to the Palazzo Chigi, where consternation replaces the harmony that had reigned just a few minutes before.

2 p.m. I am told of a message from Hitler to the Duce. I go to the Palazzo Venezia with von Mackensen. The ambiguous message is couched

in abstract language but leads us to understand that the action will begin very shortly and asks for "Italian understanding." I use this phrase as a pretext to persuade the Duce to write to Hitler. We are not ready to go to war. We shall do it if you will furnish us all the materiel and raw materials we need. It is not the kind of communication that I should have wanted to make, but it is something, anyway. The ice has been broken. I personally telephone it to Attolico, who will relay the information to Hitler. The German reaction is cold.

At 9:30 p.m. von Mackensen brings a brief note in which we are requested to make a precise list of what we need. During the drive von Mackensen, who is hostile to the military adventure, requests me to draw up a complete list. He hopes that this will put the brakes on his government. In fact, there has been an initial suspension: Roatta has telephoned that the mobilization and marching orders for this evening have been postponed.

August 26, 1939

Berlin is showering us with requests for the list of our needs. To prepare this we convene at the Palazzo Venezia at ten o'clock with the chiefs of staff of the three armies and with Benini. Before entering the Duce's study I remind these comrades of their responsibility. They must tell the whole truth regarding the size of our stocks and not do what is usually done and be criminally optimistic. But they are all in precisely this state of mind, the most optimistic being Pariani.

Valle, on the other hand, is very much aware of his responsibility and is honest in his statements.

We go over the list. Our needs are gigantic because stockpiles are virtually nil. It's enough to kill a bull—if a bull could read it. I remain alone with the Duce and we prepare a message to Hitler. We explain to him why it is that our needs are so enormous, and we conclude by saying that Italy absolutely cannot enter the war without such provisions. The Duce also makes some mention of his political action to follow. In transmitting our request Attolico gets into trouble. (In a subsequent discussion Attolico told me that this was not a mistake but that he had purposely done it in order to discourage the Germans from meeting our requests.) He asked for the immediate delivery of all the materiel, something impossible, since it involves 17,000,000 tons, which require 17,000 train cars to ship them. I straightened things out. Soon Hitler's reply arrives. They can give us only iron, coal, and lumber. Only a few anti-aircraft batteries. He indicates that he understands our situation and urges us to be friendly. He proposes annihilating Poland and beating France and England without help.

Once Mackensen left the Duce prepared the answer. He expressed regret at not being able to intervene. He again proposed a political solution. The Duce is really upset. His military instinct and his sense of honor were drawing him toward war. Reason has now stopped him. But this hurts him very much. In the military field he was badly served by his staff who, under the illusion of eternal peace, have lulled him to dangerous illusions. Now he has had to confront the hard truth. And this, for the Duce, is a tremendous blow.

However, Italy is spared a great tragedy, that very tragedy which is about to fall on the German people. Hitler is entering the war with an alarming scarcity of equipment and with a divided country.

The message is conveyed to the Führer at about 8 p.m. He announces that he will reply.

August 27, 1939

Halifax has informed me, very courteously, that the precautionary measures taken in the Mediterranean must not be interpreted as a prelude to hostilities against us. I answer in an equally courteous tone; I am very much interested in keeping in contact with London.

Hitler's answer: he still appears set to go to war and asks us for three things: not to make known our decision to remain neutral until it is absolutely necessary, to continue our military preparations in order to divert the French and British, to send agricultural and industrial workers to Germany. The Duce answers that he agrees to do all this and promises a reassessment of our position after the first phase of the conflict. But when will this first phase end?

This morning he seemed satisfied with his decision "to stand looking out the window," as he says. Meanwhile a singular incident takes place. The English transmit to us the text of the German proposals to London, about which there is great ado but about which we are 100 percent in the dark. Heavy stuff: Hitler proposes an alliance to the British or something similar. And this was done naturally without our knowledge. I am indignant and say so openly. The Duce is also indignant, but does not show it. He still wants to maintain an attitude of solidarity with the Germans, at least outwardly. Naturally, I do not reveal our ignorance of this document to Percy Loraine, whom I advise not to reject the German proposals and to begin to negotiate to gain time if for no other reason. We decide to make direct contact with Halifax and I telephone him.

This makes Percy Loraine and Halifax happy; the latter tells me that it is not the intention of the British to reject the offers but that at the same time they intend to safeguard existing commitments to Poland. The telephone call is characterized by extreme cordiality on both sides. The situation, therefore, is gradually improving. I have had to struggle hard to persuade the Duce to act as he has. And I must add that in this move I have been completely abandoned by the large group of men who are concerned with telling the Duce only those things that please him. Telling the truth is the least of their cares.

Starace, with his intellectual and moral shortsightedness, has the cheek to tell Mussolini that Italian women are happy about the war because they are going to receive six lire a day and will be rid of their husbands. How shameful! The Italian people do not deserve such a vulgar insult.

No matter. I am continuing my struggle alone because I am convinced that I am fighting for a good cause. War today, in view of our material situation and our morale, would be a great misfortune. I intend to avoid it at all costs.

In my conference this afternoon I found the Duce sharing my opinion. In his judgment the matter of a secret agreement with London has struck a strong blow at the Germans. He says that Hitler is acting this way because he fears that intervention on the part of the Duce might settle the crisis at the last moment, as he did last year at Munich. This would have the effect of raising his prestige, of which Hitler is jealous.

I am not sure whether this explanation is correct. For me there is a simpler explanation; namely, that the Germans are treacherous and deceitful. Any kind of alliance with them becomes a bad alliance on short notice. From London we are informed that the Cabinet meeting has adjourned but will reconvene tomorrow at twelve o'clock with a final answer to Hitler. Attolico has asked von Ribbentrop for information on the situation. He answered that there is little chance for peace and that Henderson has gone to London only to express his personal views. Could there ever be a more revolting pig than von Ribbentrop? But this is all very well, because it helps to dissipate the last scruples the Duce still harbors. Today he is much relieved. He does not speak at all about going to war during the second phase.

He says that he will do only what is necessary after having awaited the developments of the situation with a good deal of calm. It has been hard to draw him onto my side, but finally he is there, and has every good intention of staying there. The inevitable *faux pas* the Germans will make will certainly be most helpful.

Hitler, at a secret meeting, has spoken to the Deputies of the Reichstag in strong terms. However, I do not know what he said nor has Attolico been able to tell me.

August 28, 1939

The day was quiet, so to speak. There was a pause which, according to Magistrati, was caused by the German need to send troops to the western border. We had no direct contact with Berlin, where, in fact, Weizsäcker told Attolico that there was no communication in writing from the Führer to the British. Many cordial exchanges with the British, who have forewarned us of the content of the answer that Henderson is preparing to take back to Berlin in the evening. Once again they have appealed to the Duce to take pacifying action. But I do not believe that it is possible now to do more than has been done already. We might draw an unpleasant answer from the Germans. The Duce is now quite calm, as he always is after he has made a decision. He does not want to utter the word "neutrality," but this is the frame of mind that he has finally accepted. He even begins to hope that the struggle will be hard, long, and bloody for others, for he sees in this a possibility of great advantage for us.

During the night Percy Loraine sends me an outline of the British answer. It is not bad; in fact it leaves the door open to many possibilities. On the other hand, the British action has also induced Poland to become more conciliatory. This is probably the key to the whole situation.

August 29, 1939

The Duce is restless. He would like to do something. Certain articles in the English press, which speak of the necessity of Italian neutrality, have had a very negative effect on him. Meanwhile, he sets down a series of military and civilian measures of a warlike nature, which, in my opinion, need not be taken at this time. From Berlin, as well as from London, the news is better. Halifax telephones to tell me that the Führer has not rejected the English proposals and that there are still some possibilities for a peaceful solution. Attolico, who has conferred with Ribbentrop, says more or less the same thing. Under the circumstances, I persuade the Duce to send a cable to Hitler advising him to pursue negotiations. I inform Sir Percy Loraine of this and he is very happy. I receive the wife of the German ambassador to Spain, Baroness von Stohrer. She is very pessimistic about the German internal situation. She believes that the outbreak of a total war might rapidly lead to Bolshevism. She says that the German people, who "are the most ungrateful people in the world," are at this time agitated by very strong anti-Nazi opinions.

Attolico has conferred with the Führer, who thanks him for the communication from the Duce. Hitler has told the British that he is "ready to receive a Polish plenipotentiary," but that in spite of this he is still skeptical about the possibility of a negotiated solution, "since the two armies are now within rifle range and the slightest incident may cause a clash."

August 30, 1939

My first thought today is the memory of my father. He would have been sixty-three years old if an unfair death had not stopped the beating of his great heart. May God welcome him and may his generous soul be always near me.

The situation has again grown worse. The British answer does not close the door to future negotiations, but it does not give, nor could it give, the Germans all they ask for. Our only hope is in direct contacts, but time passes, and the Polish plenipotentiary does not arrive at Berlin. Instead, news reaches us of general mobilization in Warsaw, and it is not the kind of news made to calm our nerves. I continue and multiply my contacts with the English.

Percy Loraine came to my house during the night and all day he has been ringing me up, but we are not successful in changing the situation.

The Duce is convinced "that it will happen tomorrow." Naturally, the idea of a neutrality imposed on us weighs upon him more and more. Not being able to wage war, he makes all the necessary preparations so that in case of a peaceful solution he may be able to say that he would have waged it. Calls to arms, blackouts, requisitions, closing of cafés and amusement places. All this implies two serious dangers: one which is external, since it might cause London and Paris to believe that we are preparing to attack, and hence lead them to take the initiative in moving against us; the other of an internal character, because it will alarm the population, which is more and more openly anti-German and against the war. Bocchini, whom I have urged to send to our Chief *true* reports on the situation, is very pessimistic. He went so far as to tell me that in case of uprisings in favor of maintaining neutrality the carabinieri and police would join the people.

August 31, 1939

An ugly awakening. Attolico cables at nine, saying that the situation is desperate and that unless something new comes up there will be war in a few hours. I go quickly to the Palazzo Venezia. We must find a new solution. In agreement with the Duce I telephone Halifax to tell him that the Duce can intervene with Hitler only if he can bring a big prize: Danzig. Empty-handed he can do nothing. On his part, Lord Halifax asks me to bring pressure on Berlin, so that certain procedural difficulties may be overcome and direct contacts established between Germany and Poland.

I telephone this to Attolico, who is more and more pessimistic. After a while Halifax sends word that our proposal regarding Danzig cannot be adopted. The sky is becoming darker and darker.

I receive François-Poncet. The conversation is without purpose and, therefore, vague and indefinite. The wish for peace is repeated on both sides. He seeks to learn what our attitude will be, but I make no reply. He is romantic, sad, and nostalgic. I should also add that he is sincere.

I see the Duce again. As a last resort, let us propose to France and Great Britain a conference on September 5, for the purpose of reviewing those clauses of the Treaty of Versailles which disturb European life. I warmly support the proposal, if for no other reason than because it will widen the distance between us and Hitler, who wants no conferences and has said so many times. François-Poncet welcomes the proposal with satisfaction but with some skepticism. Percy Loraine welcomes it with enthusiasm. Halifax reacts to it favorably, reserving the right to submit it to Chamberlain. I insist on a quick answer, since time is pressing. But the day goes by without communications of any kind. Not until 8:20 p.m. does the telephone central office inform us that London has cut its communications with Italy.

Here, then, are the consequences of the measures taken in the last few days, or, rather, of the many statements about the meager measures taken in the last few days. I go to inform the Duce. He is affected by it. "This is war," he says, "but tomorrow we shall declare in the Grand Council that we are not marching." Tomorrow will be too late. The English and French may have then committed acts making any such declaration very difficult.

I propose calling Percy Loraine and that I commit an indiscretion. If a scandal comes of it I am willing to be sacrificed, but the situation will be saved. The Duce approves. Percy Loraine comes to see me. I acquaint him with what has happened and then, acting as if I can no longer contain my feelings, I say, "But why do you want to start the irreparable? Can't you understand that we shall never start a war against you and the French?" Percy Loraine is moved. He is on the verge of tears. He takes my two hands in his and says, "I have known this for fifteen days. And I cabled it to my government. The measures of the last few days had shaken my faith. But I am happy to have come to the Palazzo Chigi tonight." He pressed both my hands again and left happy. I inform the Duce of this by telephone. In the meantime he had given orders that the lights of the city be turned on again, to lessen the alarm.

From Berlin there arrives the German communiqué summarizing all that has happened in the last few days, including the proposals made to Poland. These are very moderate, but there is something obscure in the whole German attitude. The proposals are set forth, but at the same time it is stated that they are no longer open to discussion. In any case, all discussion is superfluous. Hitler's program as it was announced to me at the Berghof is being applied point by point. Tonight the attack will begin, since August 31 was given as the last possible date. The Duce, instead, thinks that negotiation is still possible. I do not, for I see in the communiqué a clarion call to war. At midnight Magistrati informs us that newspapers are being distributed free in Berlin with the headline, "Poland Refuses! Attack About to Begin!" In fact the attack begins at 5:25 a.m. I received news of this in the morning from Minister Alfieri and immediately afterward also from the Duce, who calls me to the Palazzo Venezia.

September 1, 1939

The Duce is calm. He has already decided not to intervene, and the struggle which has torn his spirit during these last weeks has ceased. He telephones personally to Attolico urging him to entreat Hitler to send him a cable releasing him from the obligations of the alliance. He does not want to pass as a welsher in the eyes of the German people, nor in the eyes of the Italian people, who, to tell the truth, do not show too many scruples, blinded as they are by anti-German hatred. Hitler sends the message through von Mackensen.

I receive François-Poncet and Sir Percy Loraine. It is now clear that France and England will do nothing against us. Nevertheless, I repeat to François-Poncet what I have said to Percy Loraine about our attitude. And this contact is useful to dispel any doubts. The French still insist that the Duce should take the initiative toward the conference we discussed yesterday. The English are more skeptical. But we Italians are more skeptical still, we who know how things stand and know about the rabid determination of the Germans to fight.

At 3:00 Council of Ministers. The Duce speaks briefly. Then I speak, adopting a clear-cut anti-German tone. The agenda for non-intervention by Italy, already drawn up since morning by the Duce and myself, is approved. They all reacted very well. Even ministers like Starace and Alfieri, who had been among the most vociferous warmongers, embrace me and say that I have rendered a great service to my country.

During the evening information arrives as to measures taken in London and Paris, which are a prelude to a declaration of war.

There also arrive the first bits of news on the victories achieved by the Germans. The Poles are withdrawing everywhere. I do not believe their resistance can last long.

September 2, 1939

Yielding to French pressure we suggest to Berlin the possibility of a conference. A mere hint for the information of Berlin. Contrary to what I expected, Hitler does not reject the proposal categorically. I inform the Duce. I call in the ambassadors of France and England. I telephone Lord Halifax and Bonnet personally. (I note that my telephone call to Bonnet, to judge from the tone of his voice and from the words spoken, has produced lively satisfaction in Paris.) I find much good will among the French, and maybe as much among the English, but with greater firmness on the part of the latter. One condition is put forward: the evacuation of the Polish territories occupied by the Germans. This condition is confirmed by Lord Halifax, after the meeting of the Cabinet.

It seems to me that nothing else can be done. It isn't my business to give Hitler such advice since he would reject it decisively, and maybe with contempt. I tell this to Halifax, to the two ambassadors, and to the Duce, and, finally, I telephone to Berlin that unless the Germans advise us to the contrary we shall let the conversations lapse. The last glimmer of hope has died. Daladier addresses the French Chamber in a decisive tone and his English colleagues do the same in London.

Nothing new here. The Duce is convinced of the need to remain neutral, but he is not at all happy. Whenever he can he reverts to the possibility of our action. The Italian people, however, are unequivocally happy about the decisions taken.

September 3, 1939

During the night I was awakened by the Ministry because Bonnet has asked Guariglia if we could not at least obtain a symbolic withdrawal of German forces from Poland. Nothing can be done. I throw the proposal in the wastebasket without even informing the Duce. But this shows that France is moving toward the great test without enthusiasm and full of uncertainty. A people like the French, heroic in self-defense, don't care about foreign lands it doesn't know and for nations too far away.

At 11:00 the news arrives that Great Britain has declared war on Germany. France does the same at 5 p.m. But how can they fight this war? The German advance in Poland is overwhelming. It is not impossible for us to foresee a very rapid finish. In what way can France and England bring help to Poland? And once Poland is liquidated, will they want to continue a conflict for which there is no longer any reason? The Duce doesn't think so. He tends to believe in peace in the short term, since he feels that the clash itself, being militarily impossible, will not take place at all. On the other hand, I think it will; I don't know which course the war will take, but it shall play itself out and will be long, uncertain, and implacable. The participation of Great Britain makes this certain. England has declared war on Hitler. The war can end only if Hitler is eliminated or Great Britain is defeated.

On his way to the front Hitler calls Attolico to the chancellery and entrusts him with greetings to the Duce. He was, I am told, calm and optimistic. He thinks that he will have Poland at his feet in four weeks, and in another four weeks will be able to concentrate his forces on the western front. He said nothing more. The Duce, who still prizes German friendship very much, was happy to know of Hitler's gesture.

September 4, 1939

I accompany Mackensen to see the Duce. He handed him a message from Hitler, in which the conviction is reaffirmed that the two regimes, bound together by a common destiny, must follow the same path. Hitler shows much confidence in the success of his enterprise. The Duce expresses full solidarity with Germany, and this is what he really feels. He gives in to my suggestions momentarily, but later, as is his habit, he returns to his former ideas. He is convinced that France does not want and cannot fight this war; that the French people are tired even before they begin to fight; and he is still dreaming of heroic undertakings against Yugoslavia, which would bring him to the Romanian oil, completely oblivious to the reality of our situation.

Favagrossa[435] said tonight that he would be happy if our present stockpiles allowed us to fight for three months. At times the Duce seems attracted to the idea of neutrality that would allow us to gather economic and military strength, so that we could intervene effectively at the right moment. But immediately afterward he abandons this idea. The idea of joining the Germans attracts him. The battle that I have to wage with him is hard, and at times I feel I lack the strength to pursue it, but I must fight to the end. Otherwise it will mean the ruin of the country, the ruin of Fascism, and the ruin of the Duce himself.

After a meeting with the American ambassador I succeed in getting permission for our steamships to leave port. They will be full to capacity, especially since the sinking of the *Athenia*. In addition to the economic advantages we shall also be relieved of much worry.

Von Papen has been intriguing in Ankara. I propose sending a letter of protest to Ribbentrop. This will be another cause of friction—and I hope for many more.

September 5, 1939

I tell François-Poncet that the anti-Italian measures that are being taken at Tunis, Djibouti, Oran, etc., may lead to serious incidents. He will telephone Bonnet and I promptly received assurances that all these measures have been revoked. François-Poncet suggests that a meeting take place between one of their officials and Giannini[436] in order to eliminate any possibility of friction between Italy and France. I speak to the Duce about it. After some hesitation he agreed. It is another step forward. François-Poncet believes that we can try another attempt at mediation after the occupation of Warsaw. To succeed, however, it would be necessary for Hitler to be endowed with the greatest wisdom—that sort of wisdom that does not desert one after victory. François-Poncet is doubtful because he knows the man and because, above all, he is afraid of the extremist influence of Ribbentrop, whom he qualifies as a dangerous imbecile.

Neutrality is beginning to bear fruit. Stock market quotations soar, the first orders to buy Italian goods come from France, ships resume their sailings at double the normal rates and are jam-packed. The Duce is somewhat pleased by all this, but not enough as yet. He must be told that we need a long period of prosperous neutrality in order to go to war later, as he desires, but not for another year. General Carboni paints a very dark picture of the conditions of our military preparedness, our meager resources, disorganized command, demoralization among the masses. Perhaps he exaggerates, but there is some truth in it.

September 6, 1939

The Duce is in a more tranquil mood. He still believes that the opportunity of entering the game as a mediator will appear shortly. He is therefore glad about German successes in Poland, believing that they will shorten the conflict. Today Krakow fell, and German generals paid their respects at the tomb of Pilsudski. The Duce feels that this fine gesture could never have been made by the Germany of the Kaiser. The ambassador of Poland, whom I received this afternoon, was sad but not depressed. He says that the war will go on until the last soldier is dead and that we shall yet have many surprises. What surprises, and when?

Conversation with Percy Loraine. I had asked him to let the Turks know that they keep up too much agitation against us and should be quiet if they don't want all of the Balkans to catch fire. The English will do this, especially since Loraine has sent me a very honeyed note intimating that the English will take care to avoid incidents with our submarines.

Villani comes to speak to me on behalf of Czaky about the danger of a German request for the passage of German troops through Hungary. He would oppose it, even by force of arms, although he would accept it if the Germans would agree to march against Romania. This is one of Czaky's usual fantasies to which both I and the Duce give little credence. But we must keep an eye on him, since he is an irresponsible and vain man and is also excitable—which could mean trouble.

Tacchi-Venturi conveys a report of the Pope's desire for peace and his ardent wish that Italian neutrality be maintained.

September 7, 1939

Nothing that is worth recording. Federzoni, Bottai, Bocchini and other fellow Fascists come to assure me of their unconditional support of my position on the question of the alliance with Germany. They agree in finding legal, ethical, and political reasons for our attitude.

The Duce still has intermittent belligerent flashes. Whenever he reads an article that compares his policy with that of 1914 he reacts violently in favor of Germany. He speaks of further consultations with Hitler in order to make decisions about intervention. But he will not do anything.

September 8, 1939

The Germans occupy Warsaw. The Duce is very much excited over the news. He sees in it some possibility of a rapid conclusion of the conflict through the proposals made by Hitler. But I do not believe that Hitler can have the wisdom to be moderate in victory, and I believe even less that the English, now that they have taken up the sword, are ready to sheath it to their dishonor.

Indeed, Percy Loraine repeats this to me during a conference I had with him—a conversation marked by a sincere desire for understanding with us and a calm, unbending intransigence with respect to Germany. On the other hand, Poncet, who is getting ready to leave for France, seems more conciliatory. It is clear that there is a crack between London and Paris. The French recall only too well the horrors of a war fought on their own territory to adopt without hesitation the British line of conduct.

September 9, 1939

Villani reports that the Germans have asked for the free use of the railroad at Kassa to attack Poland from the rear. The request, without threats at this time, was made today by Ribbentrop over the telephone at 4 p.m. to Czaky to say that the first German troops will be transiting tomorrow at twelve. The Hungarians do not wish to yield to the demand. They are aware that this is a prelude to an actual occupation of the country. And they are right. On my return from Salzburg I told the Duce that the Germans were using the same language with the Hungarians that they had used six months earlier with Poland: "*querelles d'Allemands*." I accompanied Villani to see the Duce. Villani is extremely anti-German. He spoke clearly. He talked of the threat that would weigh upon the world, including Italy, if Germany won the war. In Vienna they are already singing a song which says, "What we have we shall hold onto tightly, and tomorrow we shall go to Trieste." Hatred against Italy is always alive in the German mind, even though the Axis had for a time put this hatred to sleep. The Duce was shaken. He advised the Hungarians to turn down the German demand as courteously as they can.

Then, in talking with me, the Duce violently condemned German conduct. But he wishes to pursue a cautious policy, since a German victory cannot be completely discounted. I do not believe that he is wrong. I told him that I agreed with him, if the Germans would hurry. "If Germany wins before Christmas, well and good, otherwise she will lose the war."

September 10, 1939

Long conversation—the Duce, myself, and Attolico. The Duce is especially desirous to know the state of mind of the German people as regards us. Attolico reports that if the highest circles, where the truth is known, are calm and measured in their judgments, the masses, unaware of what has taken place, are already beginning to give indications of increasing hostility. The words treachery and perjury are often repeated. The Duce reacts violently and wants Hitler to publish in Germany the cable he sent the Duce which, since it is known to everyone, there is no reason to keep hidden from the Germans. Attolico also reports on the morale of Germany. It is quite depressed, even if military victories in Poland have galvanized it temporarily. During the conversation the Duce speaks with moderation and sometimes expresses himself against the Germans. Attolico, on leaving with me, shares my satisfaction in the change of Mussolini's psychology during these last weeks.

De Bono speaks of the situation of the army and defines it as materially and morally disastrous. He has recently completed an inspection on the western border, and is convinced that the present state of our defenses could not stand up against a French attack. He says that "Pariani is a traitor" and that "Starace is a sinister buffoon."

September 11, 1939

Villani reports that the Hungarians have denied the right of passage to German forces and that Ribbentrop has not reacted. He had asked for the transit of some materials but I believe that this refusal will not be forgotten by the Germans and that at some time or other the Hungarians will have to pay for it. The English continue to use all sorts of blandishments on us. Percy Loraine came to make excuses for a hostile article written by Lloyd George and assured me that the British had pulled the Turks' ears for their hostile attitude toward us. As a matter of fact, the Turks have changed their tune in the last few days, especially in the press. Loraine also says that the Polish military position is not as bad as the Germans would make it appear. The army is, for the most part, intact, and ready for the most severe tests. Can this be true? It is a fact that Warsaw has not yet been completely occupied, and recent experience has shown that fighting in cities is difficult.

Today, for the first time, the Duce alluded to the possibility of making a public declaration of Italian neutrality. Naturally, he says, this will be done in agreement with the Germans, but meanwhile we have taken one long step forward.

September 12, 1939

I received Villani early. He is very angry with the Germans. After the Germans accepted the refusal to grant transit to their troops, they had the "glorious Slovak army" make the same request. The danger is even greater. According to Villani, the Slovaks are to the Germans what the jackals are to the hyenas—accomplices and pimps, with this added, that all the Slovak minorities will raise their heads. Czaky refused in principle, and will confirm his refusal as soon as he gets his orders from the Regent. The Duce, to whom I reported the matter, also found it ridiculous, and said that "against the glorious Slovakian army it is necessary to oppose the not less glorious Hungarian army."

Clodius, the German economic agent, let Giannini understand that Berlin would like to postpone the expatriation of the Germans from Alto Adige until the end of the war. The proposal is slippery. I remember that at Berchtesgaden Hitler twice said that the withdrawal of the minorities from

Alto Adige reflected on his prestige and that for this reason he would be more intransigent with Poland. I suspect that the Germans are preparing to put one over us. The Duce is indignant. He was ready to make great economic concessions to the Germans, and remains unyielding on the question of minorities. I speak to Clodius myself but succeed in getting only this concession: that the problem be again submitted to Berlin for examination. Orders come from higher up.

I accompany Grazzi to see the Duce, who gives instructions for an understanding with Greece, a country too poor for us to covet.

September 13, 1939

Important conversation with Percy Loraine, who hands me a very friendly letter from Lord Halifax thanking me for my past cooperation and hoping that it will continue in the future. After this Loraine says, stating that he is speaking only for himself, "From various quarters I hear it said that England is getting ready to make threats against Italy because of her attitude. This is not true. We are going to leave all this to the judgment of the Duce. I should like to ask one thing only, that if a change of policy should take place we be advised in time." I answered, "No change will take place. However, we will never take you by surprise. But I, too, want to tell you one thing—be careful not to dictate to us. Our position would stiffen immediately. If anyone should dictate to us from within or without we should naturally answer from within and naturally against the one who tried to force our hand." I reported the conference to the Duce and he completely approved it. He has also given me instructions to answer Halifax's letter in a very cordial manner.

Bocchini reports on the state of mind around the country, which is improving a lot with the spreading of news of the certainty of our neutrality. Nevertheless, the country is and remains fundamentally anti-German. Germanophiles can be counted on the fingers of one hand. They are objects of scorn. The *Tevere*, an ultra-German paper, is being called in Rome "The Rhinegold." Farinacci is obstinately pro-German. Does the Rhine also flow through Cremona?

September 14, 1939

I have answered Halifax, ending my letter with a hint of a possible action by the Duce to re-establish peace.

Magistrati had a very important conference with Göring, who seems to have realized the advisability of Italy's remaining neutral. Such a position will help Germany more than our eventual entrance into the conflict. One surprising thing—Göring hinted at the impending intervention of Russia, which is to absorb a part of Poland. In fact, Russia is showing signs of worry. It is mobilizing numerous classes and Tass publishes news of Polish boundary raids and provocations. How unimaginative people are when they intend to quarrel.

September 15, 1939

I have persuaded the Duce to appoint an ambassador to London. This move will have considerable repercussion in the world and will go a long way to normalize our relations with Great Britain. I had chosen Bastianini, who, although he is not an eagle, is nevertheless a very trustworthy person and very much on the side of the policy of non-intervention. I am sure that he will render important services.

This morning the Duce returned to his idea of creating a bloc of Danubian and Balkan countries which we are to head. I have drafted a cable of instructions for Attolico. But in the course of the evening Mussolini decided to suspend the matter. He is thinking of postponing it until the end of German operations in Poland. He still believes it possible that the war can then be stopped, a European conference called, and a collective-security pact concluded among the six great European powers. I am sorry that I do not agree with him this time. In order to bring this about it would be necessary for Hitler to give evidence of a moderation of which I do not believe him capable. And then England will go ahead, carrying on the war implacably to the end, until her own defeat or that of Germany. I anticipate a bitter, hard, long, very long conflict, which will end in victory for Great Britain.

Graziani is pessimistic as to the condition of the army. Pariani, on the other hand, is so optimistic and sure of himself as to make one wonder if perchance he is not right. As for myself, however, I do not believe him.

September 16, 1939

François-Poncet has returned from Paris less optimistic than when he left here. The war will go on. It will be carried on to the end at any sacrifice. This is the spirit that predominates in France. I have had a transcript of the conversation made and have sent a copy to the King. In so far as we are concerned, unlimited smiles and polite words—a real serenade under the balcony. They are not sure of the situation and are afraid that one day they will also have to settle accounts with us. It now seems that Germany wants to attack Romania. This disturbs the sleep of the French and British. But the fact that Russia is preparing to intervene should be even more disturbing. At this time an agreement has been reached or is about to be reached with Japan. The Soviets can have a free hand in Europe. The Duce thinks that the Ukraine will have an internal uprising, will proclaim a Bolshevik republic, and be federated with Moscow. Russian intervention will thus be justified.[437]

Other happenings have today darkened the horizon of the democracies. The Turkish Minister of Foreign Affairs is going to Moscow. Lindbergh[438] makes a speech stating that whatever happens the United States must keep out of the fray. The Soviet military attaché to Berlin returns to Moscow to be received by the highest officials of the Soviet Union. The situation is developing in such a way as to make the position of the democracies precarious.

I have also seen Sir Percy Loraine. He is quite disturbed, and the information he provided confirms the coming German thrust into Romania. This means that fire will be set to the Balkans and will probably make our neutrality untenable.

September 17, 1939

This evening the Russians entered Poland. On the pretext of avoiding disorders the Bolsheviks have crossed the borders. The Poles have put up some resistance, but what can they do at this hour? The Duce comments on the news to the effect that the situation of the democracies is becoming increasingly serious. Although they are bound to action by the pact, he does not believe that France and England will declare war on Russia. Besides, the Duce does not believe that Germany wants to invade Romania; it will be satisfied to dominate it economically. I recall that during the Berghof conferences Hitler twice made the statement that King Carol will have to pay dearly for the murder of Codreanu, who, on his mother's side, was of German blood. It would not surprise me if he should want to settle accounts at this time.

From the train of the Supreme Command in Upper Silesia von Ribbentrop has talked to me over the telephone. He was calm and very cordial. He said that the Polish army has already been annihilated and that within two or three days the last pockets of resistance must give way. Russian intervention has taken place according to a prearranged plan. For the time being he was not able to say any more, but said that in a few days he would establish closer contacts with me. Although I didn't say so I have thought about eventual proposals for peace. I, too, was very cordial toward him and asked him to convey to Hitler our congratulations and greetings.

Wieniawa has informed me of the Russian invasion. For the first time he was very much discouraged, his eyes were filled with tears and showed that he had not slept for some time.

September 18, 1939

François-Poncet is gloomy. Although he does not want to admit it, he sees the situation in dark colors, but even now he refuses to rule out *a priori* the possibility of an understanding should Hitler be prepared to make reasonable offers. He says that during the first six months there have been many French-British failures, but that, just like in 1914, they would soon be corrected. He insisted that the course of the war is not quite similar to that of the other conflict and that it is not altogether certain, in view of the steady German progress, that six months more of war will be added to the first six months. The end may come quickly. Percy Loraine, whom I met at the golf club, was also unhappy. The sinking of the *Courageous*, which he had just learned about, did not help to keep him in good spirits.

A long conference with the Duce in the evening. I reported what I had learned from General Guzzoni. At the present time our first-line forces amount to only ten divisions. The thirty-five others are patched up, incompletely manned, and with poor equipment. The Duce admitted that this was so and uttered bitter words as to the real condition of the army, which at this time is so faulty. He harbors illusions about our air force. He has figures given him by Valle, which are absurdly optimistic. I advised him to start an investigation through the prefects: count the planes in the hangars and then add them up. This should not be an impossible task. And yet until now we have not been able to find out the truth.

September 19, 1939

The most important event of the day is Hitler's speech at Danzig, which may be called restrained and perhaps the precursor of a peace offensive. His references to us are friendly and cordial, which at this time have a special value. The Duce was flattered that the Führer had mentioned him twice.

From Romania comes the information that the Polish military and political leaders have, for the most part, been interned at the request of the Germans. How can we put any trust in our allies? Wieniawa, who had come to protest because Italian newspapers had spoken of the flight of Smigly-Rydz to Romania, wept when I furnished proof that the marshal, who had promised to sign a victorious peace in Berlin, had really crossed the border. I assured him that we intended to be humane and that Polish refugees would find a home and help in Italian territory.

As we had been led to expect, the conference between Grazzi[439] and Metaxas[440] has had good results. Tomorrow we shall issue a first communiqué, which will give France and Great Britain more bad news, of which they have had plenty the last few days.[441]

September 20, 1939

No information worthy of mention. Our friends the Croats are waking up and I feel that we should not neglect them. The occasion may arise for us to carry out our Croat action with the unwilling complicity of Germany and without incurring the hostility of France and England, which might welcome this new barrier to the German advance. I have spoken of it to the Duce and he has given me a hundred thousand Swiss francs to intensify our propaganda.

A long and somewhat useless conversation with Helfand, who made every effort, now that he is almost an ally of the Germans, not to speak ill of them as he has done for so many years.

September 21, 1939

Nothing new.

September 22, 1939

The Duce was somewhat shocked by the murder of Calinescu.[442] He fears there could be some mysterious foreign plot at the bottom of it. The reaction to this has been so violent as to lead one to reflect. Only weak regimes punish so severely.

I have spoken with Starace about the internal situation and told him that some of his methods do not uproot anti-Fascism; they create it. In Via Veneto during the evening I saw a person beaten up who was absolutely harmless (a patriot and a Fascist) by a small group of gangster elements protected by the fact that they belonged to the party and by the assurance that they would not be punished. They punished this Fascist, who has come from abroad, for having used "*lei*" rather than "*voi*." My presence was sufficient to end the incident quickly, but the look of the small crowd that had gathered was anything but reassuring and obviously hostile to the so-called Fascists. This unwarranted *squadrismo* action is harmful, and I am going to speak to the Duce about it. I am far from deploring beatings when they are well deserved, but it disgusted me to see idiotic and cowardly acts of violence. Unfortunately this has become a habit with so many mercenaries employed by the party hierarchy.

September 23, 1939

After a long silence the Duce spoke today to the party leadership in Bologna. I saw him immediately after his speech. And, as often happens on these occasions, he was in a state of utter excitement. He read me what he had said, and together we changed some parts that concerned our foreign policy. Regarding internal affairs, I gave him my point of view as follows: Never so much as today has the country been solidly behind the regime and the Duce. To speak of assassinations, plots, defeatism, et cetera, would be an attempt to give body to a shadow. The facts are quite otherwise. All the national resentment is directed against the person of Starace, who, in spite of having many good qualities, uses the wrong methods. "He is a vulgarian," the Duce said. "True," I answered. "Besides, we should not forget that he comes from Lecce, and that throughout all their history Milan, Turin, Rome, Florence, have never been governed by a southern man who was so typically southern. The sensibility of these cities cries out." The Duce agreed. It would not surprise me to see a change of guard, which, in view of the state of affairs, would be a very useful thing.

I received the Russian chargé d'affaires, who asked me for the approval of the new Russian ambassador, and I also received the British chargé d'affaires, who spoke to me about routine matters.

Nitti[443] has addressed a letter to the Duce, for the first time in eighteen years, I believe. I do not know its contents as yet.

September 24, 1939

The developments created by the Russian occupation of Poland have led the Duce to revise the optimistic view that he had previously held on the German situation. Indeed he now goes so far as to say that Hitler is bottled up and that by maneuvering cleverly the French and English may yet succeed in pitting Russia against Germany. The fact is that the Duce is in favor of peace only because the position as a neutral is not at all to his liking.

In the last few days he has repeated that a great nation cannot remain eternally in such a position without losing ground, and that therefore someday it should prepare to intervene. I cannot contradict him, because that would make matters worse. But he knows well by now the deplorable conditions of unpreparedness of the army, and this morning, for the first time, he admitted that Pariani has not been telling the truth. In his opinion the army has two glaring defects: being excessively attached to the dynasty and being too much concerned about personnel matters. The second is perhaps true, but there are a few other reasons for the present state of utter confusion.

Nevertheless, firing Pariani would be a good thing. I shall try to have Soddu succeed him because I hold him in high esteem. Sebastiani has said that the Chief also wants to fire Valle, but he does not know how he is going to replace him. Why not with Ricci, who is a good pilot and who has given evidence of being a fine organizer?

We have asked Attolico to consider the idea of forming a bloc of neutrals and at least outwardly trying to give the matter an economic slant. He agrees and has spoken to Weizsäcker about it.

September 25, 1939

"It's good to use a small person to kill a large one, but it is a mistake to use of a large one to get rid of a small one." Such is the diagnosis that the Duce has made of the Russian intervention requested by Germany. He is more than ever convinced that Hitler will rue the day he brought the Russians into the heart of Europe once again. They have two weapons that make them still more terrible: pan-Slavic nationalism, with which they can bring pressure on the Balkans, and Communism, which is spreading rapidly among the proletariat all over the world, beginning with Germany itself.

François-Poncet tries to find out whether the *gentle hint* for peace contained in the Duce's speech has any concrete basis in some German offer. No. Nothing new for the time being. Then he expresses himself pessimistically as to the possibilities of peace, and adds that for us Fascists it must be easy to understand how a country can struggle, and perhaps be defeated, to uphold a point of honor. It was difficult to contradict him.

Villani speaks about Hungary. In spite of the state of emergency there is a good deal of calm and the intention to fight in case the Germans should want to invade the country. Teleki calls Hitler a gangster and Czaky has sent word to me that von Ribbentrop has not concealed his hatred for me. I feel very much honored.

Meeting to take up the issue of Alto Adige. Notwithstanding many objections made by the Germans, the exodus will begin again soon. Golden bridges. . . .

September 26, 1939

We already surmised during the last few days that something was being hatched between Moscow and Berlin, and today we have had confirmation from Rosso. It seems that Ribbentrop has returned to Moscow to sign a genuine military alliance to giving Bessarabia and Estonia to the Russians and the remaining part of Romania to the Germans. Absolute silence from Berlin. As usual we are told nothing. I telephoned Attolico that he should obtain information, and after a few hours he reports that Ribbentrop's trip to Moscow seems confirmed. Hitler and his staff have returned to Berlin and, after a statement which he is to make tomorrow, he intends to go to the western front for the first time.

During the evening Moscow confirms the visit of Ribbentrop, who will arrive at 4 p.m. tomorrow. Berlin remains silent. All this is not clear. The Germans prepare to strike a blow without our knowledge—and from Vienna to Warsaw they have struck many. All this I tell the Duce, who telephones for news, and I let him understand that it is very difficult to go on like this. The alliance between Moscow and Berlin is a monstrous union against the letter and spirit of our pact. It is anti-Rome as well as anti-Catholic. It is a return to barbarism, which it is our historic function to resist with every weapon and by every means. But will it be possible for us to do so? Or has not the outcome already been tragically decided?

September 27, 1939

Berlin gives us absolutely no information. It is from the press agencies that we find out that Ribbentrop has left for Moscow. But the purpose of his trip is entirely unknown to us. Alleging that he had very little time at his disposal, Ribbentrop refused to receive Attolico. This is bad. . . .

In the morning the Duce received Commander Pecori, our naval attaché in Berlin, in order to discuss some requests made by the Germans for naval assistance. They would like submarine supply stations from us, help in locating French and British naval convoys, and, in addition, the transfer of some of our submarines for their operations in the Mediterranean. The Duce was at first favorable to the German requests, including the last point, which is the most dangerous. With Cavagnari, who agrees with me 100 percent, we sabotaged the plan. Pecori doesn't say anything very new except that the Germans will begin mass production of submarines in April. They think they can produce about twenty every month, both of small and medium tonnage. Valentino, who has just come from Warsaw, tells his personal experiences. From what he says the German air force has formidable power. It is absolutely pitiless and has constantly dropped bombs on the civilian population, but the German horrors are surpassed a thousand times by the unspeakable horrors of the Bolshevik advance.

September 28, 1939

Attolico reports that on Germany's part there is no opposition to our grouping in a political-economic system all the neutral Danubian-Balkan states as well as Spain. The Duce still has many doubts. I, on the other hand, firmly believe in the desirability of such a move, which will give us a much broader political and economic base. Nevertheless, I am of the opinion that we must wait and see what emerges from Ribbentrop's stay in Moscow before taking the initiative. We are still completely in the dark. Events in the Baltic states and in Bessarabia do not lead me to expect anything good. That man Ribbentrop is a sinister person and his influence on events is extremely dangerous.

I receive Villani. The Hungarians are restless. What can they do if the Russians enter Romania? In my opinion, they should stay put. They are too weak and too exposed to get into the game before they are obliged to do so.

September 29, 1939

We receive first through the press, and then from the ambassadors, the texts of the Moscow agreements. They deal with an outright partition of Poland, although they contain something that allows us to foresee that on the German side at least there is some intent for a face-saving formula later. The Duce, however, is rather pessimistic and believes that in view of present conditions it is almost impossible to attempt a peaceful solution. He is right. Besides, it would not be admissible that the head of the Fascist party should support a solution that will place into the hands of the Bolsheviks many millions of Polish Catholics.

I see François-Poncet, who is indignant at what has been done and how it was done. He expresses the hope that the Duce will not intervene and recommend a solution that will be inevitably rejected by France and England. François-Poncet, in addition, sees the day drawing nearer when Italy will stand beside these two powers to defend the freedom and dignity of Europe and its own national life as well. We speak of French and Italian relations. I voice severe criticism at the sordid French attitude toward us and he agrees. "What do you expect?" he adds. "The French are strange people who would like to win the lottery without buying a ticket." I am preparing the draft of a joint declaration to serve as the legal basis for creating a group of neutrals which I should like to unite around Italy.

September 30, 1939

The Duce this morning was confirming his skepticism of the possibility of negotiations, when, during the meeting of the Council of Ministers, I received a telephone call from Ribbentrop. He was more careful and more courteous than during other recent telephone conversations. He advanced three proposals: (1) a meeting between Mussolini and Hitler possibly at Munich; (2) a trip I would take to Berlin, where Hitler would like to talk to me at length about the whole situation; (3) a meeting with him at the Brenner border. But the third solution was the least acceptable. I told the Duce that it was desirable to forgo, for the time being, any idea of a trip by him. A meeting might place him in a difficult position, both internationally, should Hitler advance absurd proposals, as it is likely, and, also, with regard to Hitler himself, if the latter asked him for immediate military collaboration. Therefore, I shall go to Berlin.

I personally called Ribbentrop, who emphasizes the need that I leave immediately today, at 6 p.m. I go without any clear idea of what the Germans will propose, but I have the unshakeable and deeply rooted determination to safeguard our freedom of action. I do not believe that I can bring back from Berlin any contribution to the re-establishment of peace in Europe, but it is certain that I will fight like a lion to preserve peace for the Italian people.

October 1-2, 1939

As usual I have summarized in a memorandum in my conference book the official account of my contacts with Hitler and other high officials of the Reich.

Here I record a few impressions. I found Hitler very tranquil, relaxed, I should say. Whereas at Salzburg the inner struggle of this man, decided upon action but not yet sure of the means at his disposal and of his calculations, was obvious. Now, on the other hand, he seems completely sure of himself. The test he has passed has given him confidence for future challenges. He was wearing a field-gray jacket with his usual black trousers. His face bore traces of recent fatigue, but this was not reflected in the alertness of his mind. Hitler spoke for almost two hours and cited figure after figure without referring to a single note. With respect to Italy, his attitude was the same as before. What is past is past. From now on he looks to the future and seeks to have us at his side. But I must say that all our suggestions as to military collaboration have been discussed with the utmost discretion. What most impressed me is his confidence in final victory. Either he is hallucinating, or he really is a genius. He outlines plans of action and cites dates with an assurance that does not allow any contradiction. Will he be proved right? In my opinion the match will not be as simple as he believes: France and England still have a great deal to say. If it is to be war, it will be an implacable war. Hitler's eyes flash in sinister fashion whenever he talks about his ways and means of fighting. I return from Germany with the strong conviction that the first months of the war will lead the Germans to believe in victory, but that the longer it lasts the harder it will be.

Ribbentrop says nothing new and nothing original. He is Hitler's amplified echo. For the present he is completely pro-Russian. And he expresses himself in favor of the Communists in such a brazen and vulgar way as to make anyone who listens to him wonder.

The German people are resigned but determined. They will wage war and will wage it well, but they dream and hope for peace. The applause with which I was received clearly reveals this state of mind.

All the Italians in Germany heartily hate the Germans, *but they are firmly convinced, without exception, that Hitler will win the war.*

Göring did not show up. The tragicomedy of the unattributed Collar [of the Order of the Annunziata] continues. At this juncture, in the year 1939, we are about to have a second *affaire du collier.*

October 3, 1939

I give the Duce my report and go into all the details verbally. He does not share Hitler's confidence in victory. The French and English will hold firm. His conclusions are based on information given him by our military experts. And, besides, why hide it? He is somewhat bitter about Hitler's sudden rise to fame. He would be greatly pleased if Hitler were slowed down, and, hoping for this, he predicts that it will come about.

Nevertheless, for many months to come nothing can be changed in our attitude, which is to remain neutral and go on preparing.

October 4, 1939

For the first time in six years Mussolini speaks to me about sacking Starace. I encourage him, and Muti's name is mentioned as the one to fill Starace's place. Muti is valiant and faithful. True, he is still without sufficient political experience. But he is full of natural genius and has a strong will. If he is appointed he will do well, if for no other reason than he will be the successor to Starace, who is hated and despised.

A meeting with two ambassadors: those of France and Britain. I give them some information on the results of my interviews in Berlin. In agreement with Mussolini, I let them understand that the German conditions are hard, possibly acceptable, but in any case hard. At heart the Duce wishes for the European giants to fight bitterly against one another, and, in spite of all that is said about our will for peace, he prefers that with some measure of restraint I throw kerosene on the flames.

October 5, 1939

Hitler announces that tomorrow morning he will let us have the text of the speech he is to deliver at twelve o'clock. According to Attolico, it seems that appearances have been saved with respect to Poland. It is certain that tomorrow will be the fateful day; either peace or real war. I should not be surprised if Hitler became a little more yielding. Determined as he is to face events with force, a bit of the old socialist still remains in him, making him hesitate at the prospect of a European conflagration. Not so Ribbentrop. He is an aristocrat, or, rather worse, a *parvenu*, and the shedding of the people's blood does not worry him. The case of Hitler is different. He was a worker, and he still feels repulsed by bloodshed. He would prefer victories without spilling blood. Therefore I think that a faint though very feeble hope still exists.

October 6, 1939

I accompany von Mackensen to see the Duce to deliver the text of Hitler's speech. The Duce speaks in a very cordial tone, and tells him that Italian military preparations are proceeding at a regular and rapid pace. If the war should continue, in the spring he will be able to give help rather than receive it.

When we were alone, the Duce read Hitler's speech and commented on it very favorably. He judges it to be so clever and effective in arousing emotion as to bring about a real change in the international situation. He indulges himself in such a strain of wishful thinking that in the evening he telephones me to say that as far as he is concerned the war is now over.[444]

I do not share this optimism. There is no doubt that the speech will create some emotion in the enemy camp, which is divided by strains of pacifism. But what does Hitler offer except fair words? And how much are his fair words worth? I still have too much respect for France and England to believe that they will fall into Hitler's trap. The war did not end today; soon it will begin in earnest.

October 7, 1939

The first reactions to Hitler's speech are coming in. Though they are negative, I cannot find in them that violence which would seem to be called for by the real essence of the speech, which is fundamentally negative. The

Polish ambassador himself, while lightly reaffirming his old uncompromising attitude, this morning did not seem to reject discussion of German proposals out of hand.

Mussolini would like to do something that would get us into the game. He feels left out, and this pains him. The moment will arrive, but for the time being it is necessary to avoid taking any steps which would have little chance of success.

I gave the Duce a *curriculum vitae* of Muti. He was impressed by it. Muti is something of a warrior of the early Middle Ages.

October 8, 1939

Nothing new, except for a marked stiffening of the French and British reaction.

Only two voices were heard in England in favor of the conference proposed by Hitler: those of Lloyd George and Bernard Shaw. Which proves conclusively that the English consider Hitler's proposals absolutely unacceptable.

October 9, 1939

I have never seen the Duce as depressed as he was this morning. He now realizes that the war will inevitably go on, and he feels all the discomfort of having to stay out of it. He did what is for him an exceptional thing: unburdened his feelings to me. "The Italians," he said, "after having heard my warlike propaganda for eighteen years, cannot understand how I can become the herald of peace, now that Europe is in flames. There is no other explanation except for the military unpreparedness of the country, but even for this I am held responsible—me, mind you—who have always proclaimed the power of our armed forces." He vented his feeling on Hitler, who, he said, placed him in a situation where he had to "uproot so many men and had cast a bad light even on a man like the Duce himself." He is right. No objections to this. In the country rumors are being spread against everything and everybody, himself included. But he has always acted in good faith. He was betrayed by four or five individuals whom he unadvisedly appointed to high positions and whom he still has not punished severely enough.

I am saddened. Maria is ill in bed. She seemed thin and bloodless, as if made of ivory. May God help her. I love her very much. She is the only connection with my passing youth.[445]

October 10, 1939

I listen to Daladier's speech on the radio. It seems to me as if it were clearly uncompromising, even though it is measured and correct in its form. Mussolini doesn't share this opinion. In fact, he telephones me, rather satisfied that "the French are beginning to weaken." Frankly, I don't believe this. We shall see.

October 11, 1939

Reactions to Daladier's speech confirm my first impression of its uncompromising character. In fact, Mussolini does not talk about it any longer. François-Poncet also is of the opinion that war can no longer be stopped and that operations will soon take on a much broader scope. He does not deny the difficulties of the undertaking, but has faith in the victory of France—true confidence. I distinctly sense real conviction in his words.

The German government continues to place a thousand difficulties in the way of the evacuation of the Germans from Alto Adige. Requests and demands pile up every day. They ask quite seriously for permission to take with them even the doorknobs and the locks on the doors. In the meantime the local situation becomes more disturbed. The people who know that they must leave are beginning to consider themselves somewhat outside the law. Some incidents have already occurred. I call Mackensen and ask him to deal with the matter on a political level. We must act quickly. The Italians are following this issue with great interest and they cannot justify the delays, especially since, under Russian pressure, the Germans got eighty thousand men out of the Baltic states in a few hours.

October 12, 1939

Bombelles sends an interesting report on the situation in Croatia. Agitation is strong, and the money we provided has intensified it to the point of causing serious incidents between the mobilized Croatian troops and their Serbian officers. He feels that the situation is getting ripe rather quickly for our intervention. I discuss it with the Duce. I, too, feel that we must strike a blow in Croatia but with the consent of, or at least without the opposition of, France and England. We must make these people understand that it is in their interest if we block the path of the Germans and if we save Hungary from the double pressure of Germany and Russia. Nevertheless, we must not be in a hurry. It is an operation which will succeed, but it must be conducted like the one in Albania.

Chamberlain speaks. It does not seem to me that his speech contains any new elements when compared to those expressed by Daladier. As a matter of fact, the first impression I gathered was rather of a more determined intransigence.

October 13, 1939

Chamberlain's speech dashes the hopes of even the most convinced pacifists. One recognizes the traditional British decision in the voice of the old statesman. The Duce, after having read the original text, also concludes that every possibility for an understanding has now vanished. He was preparing to make a statement but is putting it off for the time being. Well done. This is a time to keep one's mouth shut.

In Germany the speech was received with indignation and fury. Attolico cables that it sounded like a war cry, and von Mackensen expresses himself in similar terms. The latter comes on behalf of Ribbentrop to request the support of our press on some specific points of the dispute. Mackensen is rather depressed and, all his efforts notwithstanding, he does not entirely succeed in hiding his deep antipathy toward Ribbentrop, whom he considers the person most responsible for the war.

October 14-15, 1939
Nothing new.

October 16, 1939
In the afternoon the Duce expresses himself at length on the state of the armed forces. He has to face the facts, and the situation known to everybody can no longer be ignored even by him. Finally, he said that he wishes to fire Pariani and Valle. This would be wise. He also said there will be no possibility of going to war before the end of June or July, and even then we shall have at most three months' supplies. Under such conditions it would be insane to think of war. We must know to wait, and I am sure that the Duce, who suffers to the death because of his present position, will know how to wait until the best interests of Italy can be served by such a move.

All over the world a deadly silence seems to presage bad news. When the Germans shut themselves up in their silent resentment they are preparing a blow. I believe that the cannon will be heard soon for real. The Duce was very much affected by a few documentary films about Russia which have come into our possession, and wants to begin a press campaign to explain to the Italians that Bolshevism is dead and that a kind of Slavic Fascism has replaced it. I try to dissuade him. Russian friendship is a potion that the Italians would not swallow too willingly, especially if offered in a German beaker, as it would now have to be served.

October 17, 1939
Maria's condition has become worse and the doctors have lost hope of saving her. May the Virgin Mary accomplish the miracle! There is nothing sadder than to witness the gradual extinction of a youthful life which has been filled only with purity and goodness. Fate is trying me very harshly this year.

October 18, 1939
Tonight passed tragically. The death of Maria seemed imminent and unavoidable. Later she rallied and is now somewhat better. There is a slender thread of hope, but I still cling to it. The mercy of the Virgin may have descended upon a creature who richly deserves it.

Hitler sent his ambassador to express his good wishes for the health of Maria, and Ribbentrop sent a cable.

Together with Clodius I have worked out the final clauses for the agreement on Alto Adige, which will be signed tomorrow. I have also tried to satisfy some of Hitler's requests of an economic nature for the purpose of facilitating the transfer. I believe we must do everything possible for the Germans as long as it gets us to avoid giving them our complete military support.

The Duce confirms his intention of proceeding to a change of guard within the party by substituting Starace with the excellent Muti. Better late than never.

October 19, 1939
Maria continues to improve, and this leads me to entertain high hopes.
Today France and Great Britain signed the agreement with Turkey.[446] This does not displease me, because it means Germany is losing a point. Poncet telephones to tell me, under instructions from Paris, that the agreement has no anti-Italian character, but is aimed only at the preservation of the *status quo* in the eastern Mediterranean. I don't know what this assurance is worth, but it is good that it has been given. A vast change of guard is about to take place in the government. The Duce is getting ready to make all my friends ministers: Muti, Pavolini, Riccardi, and Ricci. He dismisses Alfieri, and this displeases me, because he has been a good comrade. I shall try to keep him afloat politically, and if I do not succeed in having him appointed President of the Chamber, I should like to appoint him Ambassador to the Holy See. Starace will perhaps pass into my jurisdiction as Governor of the Aegean, but I like this less. Pariani and Valle, too, are finally leaving.

October 20, 1939
Maria is worse. I now feel that disaster is inevitable and close at hand. Anguish wrings my heart, because of my own sorrow and the deep, silent sorrow that has overwhelmed my mother's heart.

October 21, 1939
The gravity of Maria's illness continues unabated. Slight and transitory improvements render the sad fact more evident, just as the lightning shows more clearly for a moment the horror of the storm. Nothing is sadder than to have to watch this slow agony and to look on smilingly, because Maria, who is completely conscious, must not suspect the fate that awaits her. Up to this point she has not realized that death is ready to strike her, and this proves again that divine Providence is truly infinite.

October 22, 1939
At six minutes past midnight, the same hour in which my father passed into the shadows, Maria passed away. After a long and painful agony she breathed her last serenely, receiving the comforts of religion. But she had been unconscious for over half an hour.
This is a great blow, which again numbs me. Maria was a good sister. Always near me spiritually, but always discreet and thoughtful, she was for me a link with my past. Our early youth was spent in absolute intimacy, as was proper in the modest family of an officer. For a long time we slept in the same room, ate our meals together with the spontaneity of two colts who feed out of the same manger. Later on, even though life did separate us physically for a long time, it could never really separate us. Maria was proud, loyal, honest, and straight as a sword. The ailment which consumed her

perhaps at times influenced her personality, but it could not in the least change the profound characteristics of her soul. Everybody who knew her never failed to be impressed by them. Universal and deep sorrow is felt for her. Melancholy dominates my spirit, and the void which has come into my heart with her disappearance can be filled neither by time nor events. A kiss to you, Maria. May God receive you in His great arms as you deserve. Adieu.

October 23, 1939

At Leghorn for Maria's funeral. Once again, overwhelmed by sorrow, I have passed through the city of my childhood between rows of people who appeared to be suffering with me. Maria has been placed in the Purificazione Cemetery in a niche under that in which Father rests. When, a little later in the day, I returned alone to the cemetery to say an affectionate farewell to my loved ones, it seemed less hard for me to abandon my sister in that sad place, since our great, unforgettable father had received her there. And he will watch over her as he watched over us when we were children.

October 24, 1939

Life goes on its way. At the Ministry an audience with the Duce, whose attitude was paternal. Visits, conversations, the press, cables. . . . But when, after a fall, we begin to walk again, the slope seems harder to climb, and one feels that the burden weighing on the shoulders has increased.

October 25, 1939

The Duce plans to write a letter to Hitler telling him that as things stand Italy represents an economic and moral backup for Germany, but that later on it may also play a military role. I do not see the need for this document, but the Duce is a little restless and wants to do something. He also speaks of a coming meeting of the Grand Council to be held soon with the idea of informing it exactly as to what has happened. He also alludes to the timeliness of a very important speech by me to inform the country of what is taking place. If I must tell the truth it will be difficult to reach the conclusion which the Duce expects and which he imposes upon me—that is, that the Axis and the alliance with Germany still exist and are fully operative.

October 26, 1939

The speech that Ribbentrop delivered at Danzig has had damaging repercussions. It was a mediocre repetition of Hitler's speech. Loraine said that Ribbentrop is a second-rate man with secondhand ideas. I agree with him.

Mussolini speaks again of the speech that I am to make on December 16, and, in listing the arguments that I must employ to establish the reasons for our attitude, the Duce, while still wishing to maintain a pro-German line, levels the harshest charges against the Germans. It will be a difficult task, but taking advantage of his state of mind I shall try to make a speech that will go as deep as possible, save appearances as much as possible, but tell the truth and so permanently widen the breach between ourselves and the Germans.

This morning the Duce said that Hitler is creating serious risks for himself, since, forced by circumstances, he is putting all power in the hands of the military leaders. Arms in the hands of the people and power in the hands of the officers are very unfavorable circumstances for any dictatorship. The Duce discovered this in September, when anti-Fascism found in our barracks the best environment in which to grow and prosper. In time of war the influence of the party becomes very ephemeral, and the blackshirts themselves are ostracized by regular army officers. Recently we have had many instances of this.

October 27, 1939

Changes are about to take place in high positions, both in the party and the government. The Duce has decided in favor of Muti, but he is still somewhat doubtful as to Valle's successor. He is thinking of General Pinna. I advised him against this, because this man is too intimately linked with the work of his predecessor. We must choose a new man. I suggest Pricolo. For the navy, too, the Duce asked me for a nomination, and he advances the name of Admiral Riccardi. My father did not hold him in high esteem because he tried to shirk his duty during the war [World War I]. I think the best thing to do is to keep Cavagnari, who has served very well. The Duce agrees. The changes will take place on Monday.

In the international field nothing new. Increasingly strong rumors reach us about an imminent German offensive in the west. Mussolini does not believe that this will take place. On the contrary, I believe it will.

October 28, 1939

Nothing new. This year's celebration of the anniversary of the March on Rome is somewhat lifeless and lacking in enthusiasm. The Duce is the most dissatisfied and restless person among us all. He feels that events have betrayed both hopes and promises. What does the future hold in store? That depends upon us here. I am steadfast in my ideas: that if we can remain calm and if we wait and overcome our impatience, we can yet turn this unfavorable situation to our benefit. But calm and caution are required ingredients to attain these goals.

October 29, 1939

Nothing new.

October 30, 1939

The Duce tells me that yesterday, returning from an excursion to Pomezia, he informed Starace that he had been sacked. On receiving the news Starace objected to being replaced by Muti, and he proposed the nomination of certain federal secretaries of the Fascist party, friends whom he favored. But the Duce did not fall for it and insisted on the name of Muti. "After all," he said, "he was unable to make any proven accusation worthy of consideration. Only provincial gossip. I think Starace is jealous of Muti because Muti has more decorations than he."

I spoke at length with Muti, outlining directives to him. Muti will follow me like a child. In spite of my growing skepticism about men in general, Muti is one of the rare ones that I believe to be sincere.

Starace is sent to command the militia. Even there he will do damage, but certainly less.

October 31, 1939

The bombshell with the change in the ministries explodes. There is general enthusiasm because of the fall of Starace and expressions of good wishes for the new ministers. Starace and Muti meet in my office and the meeting is almost cordial.

November 1, 1939

Nothing new in foreign affairs.

November 2, 1939

At Leghorn to visit my two dear departed ones. At Florence that evening, where the Fascist militia welcomed me with considerable warmth.

November 3, 1939

The new ministry is quietly being called the "Ciano cabinet." Job hunters begin to crowd me. Foreign policy explanations are also sought. How absurd!

November 4, 1939

Nothing new.

November 5, 1939

Nothing worthwhile is happening either in Italy or abroad. In Berlin, Attolico has had a conference with Ribbentrop, who has shown himself, as usual, an out-and-out warmonger. He said that from now on there is no way to have peace but to make war. All this, beautified by many phrases about the certainty of a lightning victory, about which events make us more and more skeptical every day.

November 6, 1939

Nothing new.

November 7, 1939

Lively reaction of the Duce to the Comintern manifesto attacking the middle classes of the warring countries, including Germany and Italy as well. At my suggestion his reaction takes shape in a strong article in the *Giornale d'Italia*. Friction with Russia certainly does not help improve our relations with Berlin. But other elements also play their part in this. In the first place, the fact that Ribbentrop continues to say that England entered the war because she learned in time that Italy would remain neutral. This is a lie. If Ribbentrop is trying to find a justification for his errors, he makes a new and dangerous mistake. I wrote Attolico to clear up this point immediately. If Ribbentrop insists, we may move toward some real unpleasantness. This morning the Duce was indignant.

News from Germany, Austria, and Prague all confirm a definite worsening of their internal situation.

Conversation with Soddu. He is very well informed. He says that the present condition of our army is much worse than had been thought. He excludes any possibility of being ready in April; maybe in October at the very earliest. Soddu, too, agrees with me in believing that Germany will inevitably be beaten. He will speak about this to the Duce.

November 8, 1939

The Duce is very much impressed by what General Liotta told him about the German tendency toward alcoholism. The General went so far as to say that the "German peril can be held back only by means of the alcoholization of Germany," and "that tomorrow's world will belong to the people who drink water." However, I have wondered whether it is worthwhile taking that Sicilian peasant, Liotta, seriously who, because he offered some bottles of bad wine to the Germans, believes that he has won their confidence.

The initiatives for peace by the King and Queen of Belgium and Holland have not had any success, at least for the time being.[447]

Conference with Badoglio, who comes to place himself at my disposal. He is pessimistic as to the condition of our armed forces and states that if we work very hard for two years we may be in a position to intervene if, in the meantime, the others wear out. Badoglio is deeply neutral but on the whole he would prefer to fight against the Germans rather than with them.

November 9, 1939

The attempt on Hitler's life at Munich leaves everybody quite skeptical, and Mussolini is more skeptical than anyone else. Actually, many details of the matter do not altogether convince us of the accuracy of the account given in the papers. Either it is a master plot on the part of the police, for the purpose of creating anti-British sentiment among the German people who are quite indifferent, or, if the attempted murder is real, it is a family brawl of people belonging to the inner circle of the Nazi party; perhaps a carry-over of what took place on June 30 [1934] which cannot have been forgotten in Munich. The Duce has had a hard time composing a cable expressing his delight that the danger has been avoided. He wanted it to be warm, but not too warm, because in his judgment no Italian feels any great joy over the fact that Hitler had escaped death—least of all the Duce.

Information from several sources leads us to believe that a German attack in Belgium and Holland is close at hand. Attolico relays this information, but without vouching for it. The Belgian ambassador in Rome is very much concerned and feels that the alarm is confirmed by the intensified preparation of the Germans. On the other hand, François-Poncet is skeptical.

I have spoken clearly to Mackensen and have given instructions to Attolico on the situation which is developing in Alto Adige, where the action of German propagandists is carried out contrary to our agreements for the emigration of people of non-Italian origin. People speak guardedly of the return of Alto Adige to the Reich and hopes are aroused that may unduly embitter a situation which is growing increasingly tense. If the French and British were clever, this would be a fine moment to create a major incident between us and the Germans.

November 10, 1939

Nothing new. Speculation continues on both sides regarding the attempt on Hitler's life in Munich, many aspects of which are undeniably mysterious.

November 11, 1939

Rumors about an imminent German invasion of Belgium and Holland become more persistent. News of this sort has now been coming from too many quarters not to be given serious consideration. However, I must say two things: that nothing on this matter has been communicated to me from Berlin, and that, as a matter of fact, Hitler and Ribbentrop have always specifically excluded an attack on the neutrals for moral and technical reasons. But this, considering what has happened before, would lead one to think that anything is possible. . . .

Mussolini does not believe that such an attack will be made, but he admits that, if it did take place, Germany's actions would be totally discredited and that in Italy there would be such a wave of hatred for Germany as to make anybody think twice. The Duce in these last few days, probably because of the situation in Alto Adige, is taking positions and expresses himself more and more markedly as anti-German.

November 12-13, 1939

Nothing new.

November 14, 1939

I receive the Prince of Hesse. I find him rather depressed, in spite of his effort to show in his usual good cheer. He confirms reports that the German offensive will take place soon on the French front and not through Holland and Belgium.

Regarding the border incident with Holland, he secretly informs me that it was because of a raid by the Gestapo in Holland in order to capture, as it did, the head of the English Intelligence Service.

He tells me little or nothing about the attempt on Hitler's life at Munich. He says that those responsible must be sought in the circle of Röhm's old friends.

November 15-17, 1939

Nothing new.

November 18, 1939

The Prince of Piedmont hands me a small personal gift—the evening dress button for the Collar of the Annunziata. He takes advantage of the occasion to talk to me about a few matters: (1) he is happy over the change of guard. He does not conceal his dislike for Starace and for his followers and their ways; (2) the troops are always fraternizing with the French on the borderline, while dislike of the Germans is becoming more and more acute. The Germans also contribute to this with their behavior. Their military attaché, Rintelen, arrived unexpectedly among the Italian troops and began to ask indiscreet questions as if he were making an inspection of the front. This was resented by our soldiers, especially by the officers; (3) Hesse showed himself to be rather concerned about the situation, and also mentioned the possibility of replacing Ambassador Attolico, but the Prince, naturally, let the conversation die out.

November 19, 1939

To Turin for hunting on the Medici estate.

November 20, 1939

News from Prague leads us to believe that the situation is more difficult than what is admitted in official reports. The Duce is satisfied, especially because he thinks that a Bohemian crisis will delay or, perhaps, cancel the projected offensive on the western front. For Mussolini, the idea of Hitler's waging war, and, worse still, winning it, is altogether unbearable. He gives instructions to our consul in Prague to advise the Bohemians to side with the Communists. This will make German repression harder and will accentuate the causes for disagreement between Moscow and Berlin.

November 21, 1939

Matters are going badly in Alto Adige. The Germans, in attempting to carry out the agreement, are preparing to hold nothing short of a plebiscite. Up to this point no harm is done, provided the German population leaves immediately after having expressed their choice. Instead, nothing happens. They have the privilege of remaining as long as three years, and nothing leads us to hope that on the German side there is any intention of shortening the time. Mussolini says that he does not quite understand. Today he stated that we might get into a war with the Reich on this matter. Meanwhile, he strengthens the police and the carabinieri and also increases the border guards.

All this is very well, because the chasm separating us from Germany becomes wider every day, even in the mind of the Duce. This is a good moment for French and British propaganda to get to work. If an incident were to break out in Alto Adige our relations with Berlin would become extremely precarious.

November 22, 1939

Nothing new.

November 23, 1939
   Nothing new.

November 24, 1939
   I take steps at the French embassy and at the office of the English chargé d'affaires to protest against the new blockade measures. This protest is couched in mild terms. The Englishman takes this into account, but Poncet, who is always very brilliant, argues, saying that it is not to him but to the German ambassador that we ought to protest, since the floating mines are the cause for the tightening of the blockade. Then, since with the French, as with heaven, reconciliation is always possible, he says that he will intervene so that the transit of German coal, which in reality is what interests us, be allowed to go through without too many difficulties.

November 25, 1939
   Nothing new.

November 26, 1939
   At Dresden the Statthalter said, after a banquet attended by our Consul, that Germany must fear friends that betray her even more than her enemies. I called von Mackensen and told him that this time if there is anyone who has been betrayed it is not Germany. He sought to excuse the Statthalter, saying that by the end of the banquet he probably was not in a lucid state of mind.
   The Duce is indignant because of this phrase uttered in Dresden. The German star is beginning to pale, even in his mind, and this is what counts most.

November 27, 1939
   Attolico reports that a German government official has protested because, according to him, our navy serves the interests of the French and British, and he went so far as to say that some submarine might open fire on us also. A genuine diplomatic blunder, typical of a German mind, which I use effectively to exasperate the Duce.
   I have finished writing the speech that I am to deliver on December 16—a very insidious speech—which, if accepted in its present form by the Duce, will definitely end or at least undermine our relations with Germany, which are actually getting worse.

November 28, 1939
   The Duce completely approves of the speech which, unless something new comes up, will be delivered on December 16. He speaks to me about the new President of the Chamber. He had already chosen De Francisci. I dissuade him. It does not seem to me right that my father's place should be filled by a mediocre individual who has been rescued by Fascism. I declare myself in favor of the appointment of Grandi, and the Duce decides it this way.
   In the international field, nothing new except the increasing tension between Russia and Finland, which announces a coming attack. What is the

attitude of Germany? One thing is sure, and that is that for many years Germany has been supplying arms to Finland. I did not neglect to find ways of informing the Russians of this.

November 29, 1939
No important news.

November 30, 1939
Russia has attacked Finland.

A long conference with Sir Percy Loraine, who has returned from London. I vigorously take on the issue of the blockade and tell him that it is utterly idiotic to compromise British-Italian relations for questions of secondary importance. I have the impression that he has done his best, but that he has encountered difficulties of practical application. He speaks with tranquil confidence about the general situation. Germany, which had announced many offensive plans on sea, on land, and in the air, has not seriously carried out any of them. England is stronger every day, and more resolved to carry the war on to its logical conclusion: the end of that regime which has transformed Germany into a permanent danger to European peace.

Toward us a great deal of cordiality. He was also the bearer of a letter addressed to me by Halifax, which was very courteous but not of particular importance.

December 1, 1939
At the golf club I saw Lord Lloyd, who has just returned from a trip to the Balkans. He had nothing special to tell me except to confirm what the ambassador had told me yesterday: that England was determined to carry the war to full victory.

The German ambassador asks me again what we intend to do about the matter of the blockade. Ribbentrop showers us with cables, and wants to create a crisis between us and London at any cost. What annoys me most is that he gave orders to Mackensen to see the Duce. I have to take him there tomorrow. Such meetings always have a dangerous side to them.

General Carboni, new head of the SIM, is to meet with Canaris in Munich. My recommendation to him is that he make no serious commitment. He must say yes to the Germans on small matters so that we can say no on big ones.

December 2, 1939
This morning I called together Ricci, Riccardi, and Host Venturi to form an office of co-ordination for economic warfare. All three are 100 percent anti-German, but I thought it advisable to bring them up to date by telling them briefly what happened at Salzburg and later. They were indignant, and I am certain that they will put forth their best efforts to straighten out matters with France and England and accentuate the differences with Germany.

The Duce received von Mackensen. When the Duce speaks with Germans he can't help adopting a warlike attitude. And this morning he did it again, though not too openly. It is clear that Ribbentrop, who is beginning to flounder in the bog, is making every effort to drag us into the war. It would be idiotic not to see through his game, as it would be criminal to give in to him. In any event, the Duce has made no specific commitments and, what is more important, he clearly reaffirmed the anti-Bolshevik orientation of our policy.

In reality, all of Italy is indignant about Russian aggression against Finland, and it is only out of a sense of discipline that there are no public demonstrations. I have prepared a letter for Lord Halifax on the issue of the blockade. It is a fact that the blockade is hampering our ships, and, given the Duce's still uncertain state of mind, it is advisable to avoid any incident that might provoke a crisis between London and us.

December 3, 1939

The Duce and I have drawn up the agenda to be voted on at the next meeting of the Grand Council. The Duce is very insistent on the insertion of a clause reiterating that relations between Rome and Berlin remain unchanged—*palabras y plumas el viento las lleva!* I do not object, provided there is another clause reaffirming quite as categorically that we are going to continue our policy of watchful but armed waiting.

Mussolini is more and more restless. He feels cut out of this great struggle and in one way or another he would like to find a way to fit into it. He intends, after the Council meeting, to send a letter to Hitler saying that should he wish him to find a diplomatic solution, the Duce is ready to support it. If, on the other hand, Hitler is planning to continue the war, we will intervene in 1942, as our obligations demand. All this seems useless and dangerous to me, but it is not yet the moment to contradict him. I shall do so if he wants to carry out his project. At this moment there is nothing better than to remain inactive, completely inactive. This gives us all sorts of advantages, even along moral lines. Besides, we should not delude ourselves in any way. The Italian people are growing ever more anti-German. Even their violent anti-Bolshevik demonstrations can be interpreted as anti-German signs. The fate of the Finns would be of much less concern to the Italians if the Russians were not from all practical points of view the allies of Germany.

December 4, 1939

In all Italian cities there are sporadic demonstrations by students in favor of Finland and against Russia. But we must not forget that the people say "Death to Russia" and really mean "Death to Germany."

I showed the Duce the report of an Italian, the Grande Ufficiale Volpato, the only foreigner permitted to live in Posen.[448] With a simplicity which accentuates the horror of the facts, he describes all that the Germans are doing: unmentionable atrocities without reason. The Duce himself was indignant; he advised me to see to it that by indirect channels the American and French newspapers get the contents of the report. The world must know.

Starace brings me a report from his information service in which it is said that the German embassy is preparing news of a serious break between me and the Duce. The thing is over now. This is the tail end of an old maneuver which began after Salzburg. Starace, who wanted to give proof of his loyalty, told me that he had absolutely no intention of showing it to the Duce. I know that bird and fear his gifts. I told him that the report left me completely indifferent and that, as a matter of fact, I advised him to give the paper to the Duce. He persisted in saying he would not. But it was he who persisted, which leaves me completely out of it.

December 5, 1939

Conference with Dr. Ley.[449] His visit to Rome bears a perfect German imprint. No one had asked him to take the trip. He had insisted very much on seeing Cronetti in Venice, and as soon as he received our official permission he hurried to Rome to confer with the Duce and with me to give his trip a distinctly political flavor.

Ley is a heavyset man who in the past was a well-known drunkard living in a brothel in Cologne. He is not the best choice to undertake diplomatic missions. He repeats like a phonograph record whatever his master has instructed him to say, and shies with noticeable fright when asked an unexpected question. I have had a stenographic note made of the conference. There is nothing sensational in what he said, but he hinted at several very important things: (1) that an attack on Holland is being prepared based on the pretext that Holland is not abiding by her declaration of neutrality; (2) that Russia has been given more or less a free hand in Sweden and Bessarabia; (3) that Germany foresees conflict with the Soviets within a few years; (4) that Hitler's only thought is to continue the war.

Percy Loraine is traveling to Malta to try to influence the Admiralty to make its blockade less irksome.

December 6, 1939

François-Poncet informs me that the Allies have decided not to interfere with the coal we are importing from Germany. We have a long conversation, in which the only important point is that the French admit the possibility of the Germans breaking through the Maginot Line, though they believe they can beat them subsequently out in the open. Paris, too, holds that the German offensive is imminent. I saw Attolico, who arrived from Berlin. He can tell me very little, since the Germans now tell us very little. To him they say less than to the others. He confirms what everybody is saying, and that is that the feeling of the German people is more and more unfavorable to Italy, even though in some quarters our intervention in the spring is considered certain—a certainty presumably based on a conversation Mussolini had with Mackensen a month ago.

December 7, 1939

Nothing new. During the evening I prepared a long report to the Grand Council. I asked the Duce for permission to read all the documents and he agreed. What I revealed made a great impression; and since I believe that the

Grand Council keeps air-tight secrets. . . . I am sure that everything I said yesterday evening will slowly trickle down into the country and will have the appropriate effect.

December 8, 1939

The Duce was quite satisfied with my report. On the other hand, he was furious at Balbo, who continues to carry on a press campaign in the *Corriere Padano* [a Ferrara daily], which is so openly anti-Communist that it implies an indirect crack at Germany. "He thinks," said the Duce in my presence and in the presence of Pavolini, "that he can fish in troubled waters at home, but he should remember that I am in a position to stand everyone, without exception, up to the wall."

I receive the minister of Finland, who thanks me for the moral assistance given to his country, and who asks for arms and possibly specialists. No objection on our part to the sending of arms; some planes have already been sent. This, however, is possible only so long as Germany will allow the traffic. But how much longer will Germany consent? The minister replies that that side of the question is settled, and confides to me that Germany herself has supplied arms to Finland, turning over to her certain stocks especially from the Polish war booty. This proves that the understanding between the Germans and the Bolsheviks is not as complete as they would have us believe in Berlin and in Moscow. In reality, distrust, contempt, and hatred prevail.

December 9, 1939

Today I was somewhat troubled because the Duce wanted me to insert a statement in my speech about relations between Italy and Russia which, if not couched in cordial terms, should at least be civil. This did not seem very timely to me and was in sharp contrast with the rest of the speech. To settle the matter, a note arrived during the evening from the new Soviet ambassador notifying us that since he had been recalled to Moscow he would be unable to present his credentials on the 12th, as had been arranged. I informed the Duce, stressing the extraordinary discourtesy of such a gesture. His reaction was immediate, and if my speech is going to be changed it will be to make the pill more bitter still.

However, the Duce's attitude is always vacillating and fundamentally he is still in favor of Germany. He said today that the time will soon come when we shall demand Corsica and Tunisia from France. I answered that in that event we must be ready, because this would inevitably mean war. He was quite pleased with an English article which said that the Italian people might fight on the side of Germany for reasons of honor. This is also his point of view, and even when there are a thousand voices to the contrary, a single anonymous voice saying that he is right is sufficient, and he will cling to it and overlook, indeed deny, the others. I cannot conceal the fact that the Duce's state of mind troubles me.

December 10, 1939

Mussolini is becoming more and more exasperated by the British block-ade. He threatens countermeasures and revenge. I believe, on the contrary, that we can do very little about it. Either we have the power to oppose it, which means war, or else we keep our mouths shut and try to resolve difficulties in a friendly way. The Duce is more and more nervous, but he proudly declares that he is extremely calm. The position of playing a neutral part in a Europe that is fighting or getting ready to fight humiliates him. But I can't see a way out. Our absolute military unpreparedness, our lack of sufficient means, and our economic dependence will force us to remain in our present position for a long time, which doesn't displease me in the least. The day will come when everybody will appreciate the great advantages that non-belligerency has provided to Italy.

December 11, 1939

Nothing new.

December 12, 1939

When the Germans discovered that we were working the Lokris mine, our only source of nickel, they asked us for it. I thought I would get a strong reaction from the Duce. Instead there was nothing of the sort. If he is not ready to grant the request, he is at least inclined to yield a part of the product. It is all very well, but it is enlightening to see how these gentlemen act—that is, as bullies and robbers. How long are we going to take this?

December 13, 1939

A long conference with the King because of the Albanian decorations. We then have a general discussion. He tells me nothing new, but makes it clear that he is decidedly neutral and an out-and-out anti-German. Neither does he like the French, and he doesn't rate their military efficiency very highly. He considers it likely, although contrary to his hopes, that the German military offensive will have positive results. The Duce has me add to my speech, in addition to a confirmation of our alliance with Germany, a reference to his speech to the Fascist militia. It is necessary to make clear to the press that this reference is important because of what was said regarding international obligations, and not because of what was said against France, otherwise we are going to sink into a dispute that might become dangerous.

Von Mackensen also returns to the matter of the nickel mine. I answer with abundant proof that we can be deprived of only a part, which will involve a small amount of mineral. He is not satisfied, and I am less satisfied than he.

December 14, 1939

In the Chamber they commemorate my father's death. Grandi delivers a very noble oration,[450] and the Duce utters words which, for him, are rare. I had never seen the hall without my father. Today a great laurel wreath had been placed on his chair, but never was he so close to me as he was today.

December 15, 1939

Nothing new.

December 16, 1939

I spoke to the Chamber. My speech was very successful, even if everybody did not understand the subtle anti-German poison permeating it. The first impression seemed merely anti-Bolshevik, but in substance it was anti-German. They tell me that the German ambassador listened to it in silence, and at times was unable to conceal his disappointment. Good.

During the evening I saw Sir Percy Loraine, who is highly satisfied and pays me his compliments.

December 17, 1939

The speech continues to be discussed. It has had much success in Italy as well as abroad. Politically, it went a long way. If it was difficult to persuade the Italians to march with the Germans before, it is impossible now that they should snap into action despite their given word, since they know the whole truth and what is happening behind the scenes. Everybody knows and understands that Germany has betrayed us twice.

December 18, 1939

Nothing new. There are still many comments and all of them good, including those from Berlin, where, nevertheless, they are swallowing a bitter pill.

I have finished making arrangements for the King's visit to the Pope and for a return of the visit—an event without any precedent. It will cause a lot of talk, and it will not help draw Germany closer to us. The fight against Catholicism in Germany is being carried on stupidly and without pity.

December 19, 1939

I expected that François-Poncet would have reacted more sympathetically to my speech. Instead, during the visit that he paid me yesterday, while he did not complain about what I had said, he did emphasize that my reference to solidarity with Germany was expressed too strongly. To tell the truth, I do not know in what part of my speech nor why this occurred. The English were more intuitive and have given my speech a welcome which caution alone has restrained. As to the Italians, who were the most intelligent of all, they have completely understood my lingo. They consider my speech to be the real funeral of the Axis.

A Finnish representative asks to purchase weapons. There is no objection to this within the limits of our possibilities and on condition that they take care of the transportation themselves.

Wieniawa accuses me of being "the worst assassin in the world." According to him, in my speech I had done away with 7,000,000 Poles, who, according to him, are 25,000,000.

A long conference with Albanian senators. They present their objections and their wishes. Insignificant things of a personal and local nature, we can satisfy them about. I am convinced, especially from what they themselves have said, that matters in Albania are moving in a satisfactory manner.

December 20, 1939

The Albanians take the oath in the Senate. The Duce was beside himself because the *Osservatore Romano* announced the visit of the Italian royal family with only a brief news article. "But this is how the Vatican always acts. It's very hard to make him understand it." The Duce fumes against the Pope. "I'm becoming more and more of a Ghibelline. In the crest of Forlì there is the eagle of the Whites." Another thing that enrages the Duce is that the British have stopped our ships. I don't know what to do about this. On the other hand, as long as we advertise our solidarity with Berlin, it is difficult for the British not to apply the rules of blockade against us. Tomorrow I shall accompany Percy Loraine to the Duce. It's good that he should see Mussolini's state of mind for himself.

December 21, 1939

Visit of the King and Queen to the Holy See. The King is in a good mood and congratulates me on my speech. He is glad that I have given some annoyance to the Germans, who, in his opinion, and as he hopes, are destined to lose the war, above all if they cannot count on the full support of Russia. The visit takes place without complications, but there is some commotion when the Pope begins a speech. The King, who is very much embarrassed under ordinary circumstances, does not know what to do. He was afraid that he had to answer it, and since he does not excel at oratory he turned to me with a look of despair. I made him a sign not to move and this calmed him down. During the conversation he had with the King, the Pope criticized Germany violently for its persecution of the Church.

I met with Himmler and have quite an unimportant conversation with him. I tried to obtain information on the offensive, but the Germans now distrust me and the information was not forthcoming. The Duce was closeted with Himmler for two hours yesterday, and the latter left the Mappamondo hall very much satisfied. What can Mussolini have promised him? In discussing the conference with me, the Duce said that Himmler was anti-Russian and somewhat discouraged and that Mussolini "told him that he would never allow a German defeat to take place." This is already a lot, but I fear that the conversation has gone much beyond this.

December 22, 1939

I confer at length with Percy Loraine on the question of the blockade. We must find a solution before some incident occurs which may complicate the situation and shift the problem from the commercial field to that of prestige, where any conciliation becomes much more difficult.

December 23, 1939

A long conversation with Antonescu,[451] who was sent here by the King of Romania on a fact-finding mission about our intentions should the Russians attack the Romanian border. I answered, reaffirming our anti-Bolshevik point of view, but avoided any binding commitments at a moment when we must have the maximum freedom of action. The Romanians would like us to approach the Hungarians, because any Hungarian threat on the Romanian rear would force the Romanians to reach an agreement with the Russians. This may be possible, although Czaky's stubbornness does not give us much hope.

I gave von Mackensen an extremely disturbing document which comes to us from Prague. It is the account of a lecture given by Dr. Pfitzner, the German deputy mayor of Prague, in which German imperialistic objectives are bluntly revealed. It refers not only to the Germans' intention of taking possession of Alto Adige and Trieste, but to their ambition of conquering the Po Valley.

Mussolini was highly indignant and, since the document contained many threats against Russia, he ordered me to send the statement with an unsigned note to the Soviet embassy in Paris. I told Mackensen that if a thing like this came to the attention of the Italian people there would arise an utterly uncontrollable movement of hostility to Germany. Mackensen was greatly impressed. Every time he is invited to confer with me now he trembles, because he understands my line of action perfectly well.

December 24, 1939

François-Poncet tells me that the French government is worried about the situation in the Balkans, but this is only his personal opinion for the moment. Weygand's army, which is ready in Syria, will intervene to throw back any threat, be it German or Russian, but there is no intention in Paris of doing anything without prior agreement with Italy, whose paramount interests in the area are recognized. I cannot for the moment assume any obligations, but it is important to note that France has taken the initiative.

December 25, 1939

Nothing new.

The holiday makes me feel more sadly the absence of those who are no more.

December 26, 1939

With Mussolini we discuss Romania. He agrees to have me transmit the Romanian demand to Hungary, and he is even ready, in case of Russian aggression, to give the Romanians military support of the kind we gave to Franco in Spain. The report on the speech by the deputy mayor of Prague has made him more and more distrustful of the Germans. Now, for the first time, he openly desires German defeat, and since Marras, military attaché to Berlin, indicated that he has had news from good sources of the imminent invasion of Holland and Belgium, the Duce invites me to secretly inform the two diplomatic representatives [of Holland and Belgium]. Mussolini is thinking of the occupation of Croatia, which seems possible to me, and I told him that it should be undertaken only in agreement with the French and the British.

I inform Antonescu of our program in case of possible Russian and British complications. He is very happy about it. He tells me that he learned from the French ambassador to Bucharest that Great Britain has recently sent a note to Paris couched in the following terms: (1) Italy must again be won over to the British side; (2) Italy wants to go into the Balkans; (3) if this is the condition for the realization of the first point, England is ready to let her go ahead. The French are said to have sent a long note where they object to his, which is very possible, as it is just like the narrow and nearsighted Parisian policy. But it is a good sign that the British are in such a frame of mind.

December 27, 1939

The Germans are greatly alarmed over the Prague speech, so much so that they have called von Mackensen to Berlin for a conference. Naturally they deny the speech, but it has its logical foundation in a whole mass of German literature which has spread propaganda for a long time along the same lines expressed by Dr. Pfitzner, the deputy mayor of Prague.

The Pope has conferred upon me the Order of the Golden Spur. More than the decoration itself, I was pleased with the cable sent by Cardinal Maglione, in which he praises my work in favor of the "most noble cause of peace," and of the *rapprochement* between Church and State. On the whole, Mussolini tends to underrate the importance of the Pope's visit to the King, and never so much as in the last few days he delights in calling himself "an unbeliever." On the other hand, the event is very pleasing to the Italian people, who attribute to the visit an anti-German and anti-Bolshevik flavor.

A long discussion with Bocchini. He complained especially about the Duce's restless moods, which have already been noticed by the entire staff, and he even went so far as to say that the Duce should take an intensive anti-syphilitic cure, because Bocchini claims that the psychic condition of Mussolini is due to a recurrence of this old illness. It surprised and annoyed me very much that Bocchini should say this, although I must admit that Mussolini's present contradictory behavior is truly upsetting to anyone who works with him.

Verlaçi asks for my approval to ". . . take the initiative against Zog, who, when he shall be dead, will be less of a problem than he is today." The matter does not interest us, and I answer that only the Albanians can be the judges of the life of another Albanian.

December 28, 1939

The Pope visited the King. Everything went off according to plan. The King was pleased by the visit, and after the meeting he told me that the Pope repeated many times that he would like to improve relations with Germany but that this is rendered impossible by the increasingly uncompromising

German attitude. Immediately after the visit I went to the Duce. Today, also, he was making ironic comments on the visit of the Pope, and discounted its importance.

Czaky informs us that he will be in Venice during the first week of January. I shall try to get him to understand that it is, above all, in Hungary's interest to get along with Romania, now that the Russian danger is coming closer and becoming more obvious. If Hungary wants to live and even prosper moderately she must avoid becoming, more than she is today, a mosaic state. Past experience proves this to be very dangerous.

We have recalled Rosso from Moscow. As long as the Soviets do not send an ambassador to Rome our embassy will also be headed by a chargé d'affaires. Our decision will not improve relations with Russia or with Germany. The ridiculous and false cable from Stalin to Ribbentrop, in which Stalin speaks of Russian and German blood shed in common (but where?) proves that the collusion between Bolshevism and Nazism is becoming more and more intimate and deep. So much the worse for them, because Russia and Germany will suffer the same fate.

December 29, 1939

I see Besnard, the French representative to the 1942 Fascist Exposition. We discuss politics a bit, but he does not say anything interesting. Former ambassadors generally flatter themselves in believing that they are in a position to accomplish what the ambassadors in charge of the affairs of their country cannot do, and which they did not do themselves when they could have done so.

Sir Percy Loraine informs me that the English government intends to act more generously toward Italy about the blockade. This is all for the best and will serve to calm the Duce's nervous tension.

I am somewhat alarmed over Muti's behavior. He is a fine fellow, attached and devoted, but one who has more guts than brains. And besides, he cannot resist the temptation of basing all his actions on personal considerations. For him to favor Dick and to deceive Tom is everything. The rest does not count. He does not see the essence of a problem. Unintentionally he acts on his own and heeds less and less what I have to say. He thinks that he has won over Mussolini, but he does not understand that the latter is the coldest judge of men; he doesn't contradict his interlocutor, does not argue, never opposes, he chews people up by the most pitiless methods. Muti thinks that he is playing the cat with Mussolini, but he is really the mouse. It may be that I am creating something where there is a shadow, but I am afraid that the Duce is in a quandary as to the situation of the party, and I wouldn't like Muti to have the ephemeral and fleeting life of a political meteor.

December 30, 1939

I bring Verlaçi to see the Duce. He makes a very optimistic report on the situation in Albania and asks for a greater concentration of powers in the Italian lieutenancy. Public power must be divided as follows: the government of Tirana is answerable to the lieutenancy and the lieutenancy is answerable to Rome. In order to carry out this concentration I have thought of calling Parini to the position of inspector general of the party replacing of Giro, who has done well during the preparation but who has compromised himself with too many people.

A long conference with Maria of Piedmont. She is especially disturbed by the threat of the German invasion of Belgium. I led her to understand that in the light of our latest information it now seems very probable. She will immediately inform King Leopold. We have agreed that whenever I obtain further information I will inform her through a trusted person. She wanted to know many details of what I did at Salzburg and later addressed me in a very friendly and kindly manner. She hates the Germans with all her heart and calls them liars and swine. She has good words for the Prince of Piedmont: she says that he has undergone a sudden and complete change in his feelings and habits, and led me to understand that the child she is carrying is in fact his, without the intervention of any doctors or syringes.

Mussolini wants the Albanian plans against King Zog suspended. He gives orders to this effect, and he is right, because we would not derive any advantage from it but only blame.

December 31, 1939

Mussolini is still suffering from the usual recurrent waves of pro-Germanism. Now he would like to send Hitler some advice (his previous advice made no impression), informing him that Italy is continuing to arm. But what are we preparing for? The war at the side of Germany must not be undertaken and never will be undertaken. It would be a crime and the height of folly! As for war against Germany, for the moment I do not see any reason for it. In any case, if necessary I acquiesce in war against Germany but not in her company. This is my point of view. Mussolini's point of view is exactly the opposite. He would never have war against Germany, and, when we are ready, he would fight on the side of Germany against the democracies, who, in my opinion, are the only countries with which one can deal seriously and honestly.

For the moment we must not talk of war. The state of unpreparedness of the country is complete. We are worse off now than in September. General Favagrossa said yesterday that if he could have all the material already asked for, allowing our factories to work double shift, a sufficiently complete preparation could be reached by October of 1942. Generals Badoglio and Soddu agree that we cannot do otherwise.

Thus closes a year which, for me, has been so cruel in my personal life and so generous in my political life. In my opinion the coming year holds many surprises. Maybe we shall witness a rapid conclusion to a tragic upheaval which humanity did not want and is unable to understand. In the very fact that this absurd and inexplicable war is understood by no one, we can, perhaps, find the key to its end.

1940

Mussolini chides the democracies for talking too much about peace. This depresses public opinion and creates opinions opposed to the conflict. Hence, a keen pro-German feeling is reawakening in the Duce. This is why he sent a cable to Hitler today, a cable for which someday we are going to be held accountable.

January 2, 1940

I persuade the Duce to allow volunteers to go to Finland, where fighter pilots and artillerymen are needed. Tomorrow I will come to an understanding with the Finnish minister.

Graziani, during a conference with me, reveals himself to be an interventionist and pro-German and denounces Badoglio because of the contacts he maintains with Gamelin. I have been at odds with Badoglio many times, but this time I agree with him. Graziani, on the other hand, favors war at the side of Germany and tries to persuade the Duce to hasten it. We must watch him and neutralize his influence. I inform the Belgian ambassador of the possibility of a German attack against the neutral countries. Two months ago I told him that I did not consider this probable. Today I told him that new sources of information have led me to change my opinion. He was impressed.

The Duce regrets that von Ribbentrop has not sent his usual New Year's cable of greetings. Evidently my speech irks Ribbentrop. His anger leaves me indifferent. As a matter of fact it honors me.

January 3, 1940

The Duce has prepared a letter for Hitler. After a first reading it does not seem very compromising, but tomorrow I am going to analyze it thoroughly.

Von Mackensen brings along a bulging file containing the German government's inquiry on Pfitzner's speech, which, quite naturally, sounds very negative. The Germans would now like us to reveal the source of our information. This is not possible. We are not informers. Attolico on the other hand has written to us that he was under the impression that the investigation had produced results which, at least in part, support our contention.

I have arranged for a large transfer of diplomats. I have personally appointed the son of Badoglio. He is no ace, but his father adores him, and at this time I intend to keep his good will at all costs. He is a valuable ally to the cause of non-intervention.

January 4, 1940
Nothing new.

January 5, 1940
Von Mackensen returns to see me to find out the name of the person responsible for the Pfitzner case. I lead him to understand that it is an Italian who has already returned to Italy, and will be punished by us. He seems to accept this explanation. In reality, the document was furnished to Muti by a Czech lawyer, for whom Muti himself accepts personal responsibility. The translation was made by an employee of the consulate, named Matteucci.

After having made a few changes to it, the Duce orders that the letter he had been pondering over be sent to Hitler. It's a fine document, full of wisdom and restraint, but it leaves matters as they are. Mussolini's advice is accepted by Hitler only when it coincides exactly with his own ideas.

I am leaving for Venice this evening to meet the clever and cautious Count Czaky.

Mussolini describes the state of mind of the country as follows: "Italy has no liking for Germany, is indifferent toward France, hates Great Britain and Russia." This is a diagnosis that I can agree with only after many reservations.

January 6-7, 1940
At Venice with Czaky. I wrote a detailed report on the results of the conference, which, I consider rather satisfactory. Czaky has assured me that Hungary will not take the initiatives in the Balkans intended to spread the fire. As a matter of fact, I already knew about the Hungarian attitude. It recalls that of certain individuals who shout and gesticulate and threaten so that they may be prevented from coming to blows. The Hungarians (they proved it during the Czechoslovak crisis) are violent in their use of words but moderate in their actions. Too much, at times.

January 8, 1940
I report to the Duce, who is annoyed that Czaky should get involved about Croatia, where Mussolini's ambitions are increasingly directed.

Conversation with François-Poncet. Nothing new from him. I inform him with some caution of the results of the Venice conference. He complains about Mussolini's "kicking." "It is too bad," he affirms, "because in

France they are beginning to believe that the Duce himself is the only obstacle to an understanding between the two countries."

I receive the Prince of Hesse. For the nth time he announces that a *modus vivendi* between the Pope and the Reich is close at hand. He alludes to the possibility of a trip to Rome by Ribbentrop. I do my best to discourage it.

January 9, 1940

Colijn, the former Premier of Holland, has come to Rome to find out our opinion regarding the situation and, possibly, to establish more direct relations. He informs me about what his country has done to prevent a future German invasion. He is certain that the Dutch will fight with the energy that comes from desperation. The Prussians' breakthrough will not be easy. I tell Colijn that, for the moment, there is nothing to do but wait and see and, at the most, to be armed as much as possible. Colijn said that he doesn't believe that a German victory is possible. I let him understand that I feel the same way.

I inform Percy Loraine about the results of the Venice talks. He is satisfied with them. What we are doing for Romania has the great advantage of placing us more and more in the anti-German camp.

January 10, 1940

Badoglio, who is now politically on the right track, no longer considers it possible that we can prepare our defenses in the coming year. We lack raw the materials. It will take all of 1941, and not even in 1942 will we be able to take offensive action. In agreement with Badoglio, we will put a brake on General Graziani's ambitions. Graziani has more ambition than brains, yet he is influencing the Duce in the dangerous direction of intervention.

The Duce's letter was received by Hitler yesterday. It appears that Hitler will reply in writing. Attolico sent word to me through one of his trusted clerks that he does not believe that the Duce's suggestions will be accepted in Germany, and the feeling that we will soon enter the war on the side of Germany is gaining ground. We now see the results of Mussolini's conversations with Mackensen and Himmler. The less Germans Mussolini sees the better.

Ambassador Rosso has returned from Moscow. He does not bring much news because diplomats are forced to lead a secluded life these days. He believes that the understanding between Russia and Germany is solid, but that the Russians are not inclined to provide any appreciable support on the field of battle. He emphasizes that this is his personal opinion, because he knows nothing definite.

January 11, 1940

Attolico reports a long conference with von Ribbentrop commenting on the Duce's letter. The Germans are wondering whether Mussolini, in laying out a proposal for the reconstruction of the Polish state as a sufficient condition for the re-establishment of peace, has not discussed it with the Allies. Nothing of the sort. It is a personal conviction of the Duce, who continues to believe, and he is wrong, that the French and British do not want to make war. In the Göring circles there is again talk of a German offensive within a short time, and they expect victory. The Duce's letter has not, on the whole, been well received.

Mussolini talked to me today of "intervention alongside Germany during the second half of 1941." He, too, is becoming convinced that the lack of preparedness of the armed forces makes any kind of warlike attempt by us impossible before that time. I told Mackensen that Ribbentrop, in speaking with Attolico, denied that he had said that France and England would not enter the war. Mackensen, after remembering the Salzburg bet, beat his head and said, "I can't say anything, because Ribbentrop is my minister, but I am sorry that I should be the one with such a short memory."

January 12, 1940
Nothing new.

January 13, 1940
The Duce talks to me about Muti. He says that in the management of the Fascist party the command has gone soft and a too violent contrast exists as compared with the rigid formalism of Starace, "whom he adored." I had to agree. Muti has found bad company, is arrogant, and I don't think he will last long.

Our negotiations with the British to solve the problem of the blockade have run aground, in spite of a very courteous personal letter from Halifax, which reached me today.

We again discuss the crown of Hungary with Villani: union under one head, or else coronation of the Duke of Aosta. Doesn't matter which, so long as we proceed faster, because the question of Croatia is quickly coming to a head.

January 14, 1940
The Germans are protesting against the sale of Italian airplane engines to France. The Duce wants to forbid the exportation of war materiel to the Allies. But after a long discussion, in the presence of Riccardi, he is convinced that we will quite soon be left without foreign exchange, and hence without raw materials that are indispensable to military preparedness—those raw materials that can be obtained only with foreign money owing to the devaluation of the Italian lira. Therefore, I can speak clearly to the Germans. I draw up a note, giving our point of view. I have no illusions. The Germans will be furious, but this will make it possible to carve out greater freedom in international commerce which at this moment is quite favorable to us.

I tell Percy Loraine that it is not possible for us to agree with British proposals regarding the blockade. The Italian people will not allow their most elementary necessities to be rationed. British persistence would be equivalent to transferring the blockade problem to the political sphere, and this is very dangerous. Sir Percy Loraine, who is becoming more understanding every day, has understood the point.

January 15, 1940

Mussolini approves my memorandum, which I deliver to Mackensen during the evening. He takes it with a few words and with much disappointment, and I do nothing to modify his impression.

The Duce is sad because of the state of our armed forces, which he at last has become well acquainted with. The number of divisions that are ready are ten; by the end of January there will be eleven. The others lack everything more or less. Some are 92 percent lacking in artillery. Under these conditions it is crazy to speak of war. Mussolini, according to what he says, is discouraged to the point of feeling the symptoms of a new stomach ulcer.

I set up a special office for Finland at the Italian Ministry for Foreign Affairs. The office shall co-ordinate all our political, military, and economic efforts in favor of that Baltic nation. I entrust it to Captain Bechi.

Conference with Sir Percy. We try to settle our control problems but do not succeed. He informs me that before long the embargo will also strike at German coal, which arrives by sea. Although the Duce does not seem to give much importance to such a decision, I am really anxious because of the consequences it will have on the entire economic life of the country.

January 16, 1940

The carabinieri give the Duce an alarming report on Albania. He takes it very seriously. The command of the carabinieri is a reliable source of information but they don't see the full picture, and at times they simply pass on the observations made by non-commissioned officers. Jacomoni vehemently denies everything and is preparing, together with Benini, a counterreport. In Albania we are working methodically and without bluffing, which, in the opinion of a few persons, is perhaps a mistake. But I do not intend to change.

I prepare with Muti the agenda for the meeting of the federal secretaries of the Fascist party. We must give the impression that the machinery of the Fascist party is, as ever, in good working order. The Duce wants to add some sentences with an anti-Allied flavor, but this is a mistake, because it will harden the French and British position against us and provide us with no practical advantage.

A letter from the Princess of Piedmont thanking me in the name of her brother[452] for what I have done for him. I believe that this is a timely warning. And today Ambassador Attolico cables that the attack on Belgium is not only probable, but may even be imminent. Attolico is very conscientious in his information gathering.

January 17, 1940

Mussolini, in his present seesawing of feelings, is somewhat hostile to the Germans today. He says, "They should allow themselves to be guided by me if they do not want to make numerous unpardonable *faux pas*. In politics it is undeniable that I am more intelligent than Hitler." I must say that until now the Chancellor of the Reich doesn't appear to share this opinion.

Christich, on his return from Belgrade, renews his assurances of friendship for Italy, and insists on emphasizing that the understanding reached between Serbs and Croats this time is deep and active. However, the news that comes to us from another source is exactly the opposite.

I received de Man, the Belgian minister, who is traveling and stopped by Rome, as well as the Polish ambassador, who tells me of the daily martyrdom his country is subjected to under the terrible yoke of German bestiality.

Accompanied by Jacomoni, I discussed the Albanian situation with the Duce. Let the carabinieri think and write as they please. However, one thing is certain: for the time being Albania has not caused us the least bit of trouble.

January 18, 1940

I went with Jacomoni to see the Duce. I think the Duce, too, realizes that the alarm created by General Agostinucci, who is called the "stuffed lion" by the Albanians, is, for the most part, at least, unjustified. The meeting was useful, at any rate, to agree on certain plans for public works, especially in Tirana.

I confer with Ricci on the coal problem. The Duce told him: "I have the pleasure, and let me emphasize *the pleasure*, to inform you that English coal can no longer come into Italy." This he considers to be a good lash of the whip for the Italians, so that they will learn to depend only on their own resources. He expects to substitute our own lignite for the coal which is now imported from Great Britain. But will our own lignite be sufficient? And is the machinery to extract it complete? Ricci does not conceal his skepticism.

Percy Loraine discusses the blockade with me and commercial problems; then he becomes thoughtful and intent. He seems to want to say something but cannot decide. I encourage him to speak. He reveals to me his concern about the attitude of the Duce, whom he feels and knows is fundamentally hostile. "The Duce must be aware," he concludes, "that the Britain of today is no longer the Britain of a year ago. She is now strong and prepared for anything." It is hard for me to argue with him because I share his opinion and he knows it.

January 19, 1940

Today, François-Poncet could also not conceal his concern over the attitude the Duce is taking. The statements made by the secretary of the party, the origin of which, however, is obvious, had an unfavorable echo in France and England, because they sound like threats. Nevertheless, we must be convinced that the Allies will win the war and we must not reach the peace table looking like accomplices, albeit non-combatant accomplices, of Germany. I tried to convince François-Poncet that he was wrong, but the facts, alas, count more than words, including my own words. Even Balbo, who came to see me and who thinks along the same lines as I do, was very hostile to the declarations made by Muti on foreign as well as on domestic policy.

January 20, 1940

Meeting of the Council of Ministers characterized by a phantasmagoric display of billions which we do not have—budget plans that would take anybody's breath away—anybody but the Duce, who remains totally calm. He said that states are never shaken by financial questions; they fall either due to internal political instability or as a result of military defeats, never because of economic causes. Revel weakly objected, saying that the French Revolution failed precisely because of the assignat,* but the Duce did not encourage the discussion and cut him short, adding something about a possible advantage of inflation on a Cyclopean scale, but, fortunately, he mentioned it only academically.

January 21, 1940

Countess Potocka, with whom I went hunting wild boar last year at Bialowieza and whom I was instrumental in freeing from a Russian prison some weeks ago, came to see me. She described with dignity her life in Russia during her imprisonment, her return trip, her encounter with the Germans of the Gestapo. She wished neither to alarm me nor to seek my pity. She is too aristocratic for that. She despises the Russians. She hates the Germans. She said that Beck is not disliked in Poland, where his policies find understanding and support, but that Marshal Smigly-Rydz can never again return to Poland.

Bombelles describes the visit of the Regent, Paul, to Zagreb as "a funeral during which no one took off his hat." He says that the situation goes from bad to worse, that the Serbs are hated more and more and become less efficient, and that shortly everything will be ready for the rebellion. He proposes that I meet with Pavelic, which I neither accept nor decline. Our proposed action plan should be the following: insurrection, occupation of Zagreb, arrival of Pavelic, appeal to Italy for intervention, formation of a kingdom of Croatia, and offer of the crown to the King of Italy. Bombelles agrees and says that our military effort will be at a minimum because the popular insurrection will be complete and the Serbs will be struck everywhere and implacably disposed of by the Croats themselves.

January 22, 1940

Mussolini agrees on the need for me to have a talk with Pavelic. This will take place tomorrow at home. In principle the Croatian question seems to be moving toward a solution. It is, however, necessary to prepare the ground with London and Paris. This is a fundamental condition. Otherwise it is better to do nothing about it. We would pay dearly for it, and rather soon. Mussolini, however, turns a deaf ear to all this. Yesterday, when I asked him for assurances regarding the future which I wanted to communicate to Loraine and Poncet, he said, "One thing is certain: we shall never

---

* At a certain point in the French Revolution, because of economic pressures, the assignat was used as money.

join with them [France and England]." I was very careful not to say this to the two ambassadors as Mussolini would have wished me to.

I appealed to the minister of Romania for the release of certain Hungarians who have been accused of plotting against the security of the state. It will be a useful gesture, since a trial would exacerbate the tension between those two countries.

January 23, 1940

Council of Ministers. Military budgets. The Duce uses the occasion to speak of the international situation. All of his attacks are aimed against France and England, who "can now no longer win the war." He repeats that we cannot remain neutral indefinitely. To preserve neutrality until the end of the war "would bring us down to second rate among the European powers." He foresees that our military possibilities will enable us to make a move during the second half of 1940, or better still during the early part of 1941. Every allusion to action is directed against the Allies. He speaks of terror bombings over France, of the control of the Mediterranean. His declaration greatly impressed the ministers, some of whom heartily approved, especially Ricci and Revel. Riccardi, on the other hand, speaking later in the antechamber, said that it is absurd to plan to arm 70 divisions when the raw materials at our disposal are hardly enough to arm ten of them.

I received Pavelic. Anfuso took a stenographic record of the conference. Pavelic is an aggressive, calm man, who knows where he wants to go, and does not fear taking on responsibility in order to reach his goals. We agreed to the main points of preparation and action.

I assure Sir Percy Loraine that I am doing "something and even more than something" in favor of Finland. He was satisfied.

January 24, 1940
Nothing new.

January 25, 1940
Nothing new.

January 26, 1940
Nothing new.

January 27, 1940

The Finnish minister asks for additional supplies of weapons, especially heavy artillery; and he asks for them in a tone of desperation. If events go on in Finland as they are now, the overwhelming superiority of Russian resources will break down Finnish morale and resistance will come to an end. Perhaps the minister has painted too dark a picture, but it is certain that to hope for an unlimited resistance is a vain illusion.

Gamelin told General Visconti Prasca, who in turn has repeated to me, that he would be ready to give a billion to the Germans, provided they would do him the favor of taking the initiative in the attack. Visconti Prasca thinks the French army the best in the world. He is convinced that as of now Germany has lost the war.

January 28, 1940

The Duce has returned from Terminillo. He is not exactly nervous, but he appeared more irritable than usual. He lashes out, as usual, against France and England, because, owing to their policies, "they have lost the victory." And he takes it out on Germany for having hastened the war which, within three years, "would have been won because of the disunity among the democracies."

Even with respect to the internal situation, he is dissatisfied because of Muti. The latter has taken some disciplinary measures that have been widely discussed and have met with the approval of anti-Fascist circles, which makes Mussolini indignant. "We must act like the Church," he said, "which never strikes its members publicly. Once I denounced the Bishop of Jesi to Tacchi-Venturi for being a pederast. In spite of overwhelming proof, I was not given any satisfaction then and there, but some years later I learned that the guilty man had died in obscurity at Frascati."

I see Poncet. He is disturbed by the Italian attitude. He thinks he can recognize the earmarks of warmongering and pro-German activities. He is convinced that Mussolini is blinded by his hatred for democracy, and that one day he will end up in creating an unavoidable crisis.

January 29, 1940

After a long period I saw the King again. As usual he was very courteous with me, praising my work. He is anti-German, for such are his convictions and his nature, but he is no longer certain of a German defeat. He is doubtful about the power of internal resistance of the British Empire. He is disturbed about Italy. "With the present policy we risk becoming '*a Dio spiacente ed ai nemici suoi*.'"[453] He was sufficiently informed about Mussolini's plans for Croatia, but did not conceal his mistrust regarding the success of the undertaking if it is not preceded by a timely understanding with France and Britain.

The Duce is irritated by the internal situation. The people grumble. Food restrictions worry the population. War again casts its shadow over the country. He was annoyed about the Count of Turin, who was hoarding soap, he says, "to help wash his 35,000 whores, with whom one cannot understand what he does, given his health." He ranted about the possibility of an uprising, "When the instincts in a people are static and without ideas, only the use of force can save them. Those whom we strike will be grateful because the blow will save them from falling into the abyss toward which their own fear was pushing them. Have you ever seen a lamb become a wolf? The Italian race is a race of sheep. Eighteen years is not enough to change them. It takes a hundred and eighty, or maybe a hundred and eighty centuries."

January 30, 1940

Piero Parini points out that the professors and students of Corcia [Albania] who created disorders lately have been identified, and he believes that some harsh punishment is necessary. The Duce approves. I cable, ordering that they be arrested and deported to some island on the Tyrrhenian Sea. Albanian intellectuals are obviously those who most oppose the new situation, and it is necessary to absorb them wherever it is possible, or to deal severely with those who are unwilling to be convinced. It is not a very serious problem: a matter involving 200 or 300 persons. The Albanian people do not cause trouble. They work, earn, and enjoy a comfortable living, which they have not known until now, and most of them are satisfied.

January 31, 1940

The English ambassador informs me that while his government is increasing the shipment of supplies to Finland, it has decided not to send military units. He is pleased when I tell him that we, too, are shipping supplies and a nucleus of specialists. At the end of the conversation he hints at the worry caused by the Duce's personal attitude. England feels in the Duce's hostility something that will prevent a deep and sincere *rapprochement*. I try to deny this, but he does not listen to me, nor can I proceed on this line with an intelligent and candid man like Percy Loraine, nor go very much beyond what is generally referred to as a conventional diplomatic white lie.

Hitler has made a speech for which I see no reason, except that of celebrating the date of his coming to power.

February 1, 1940

Anniversary of the founding of the militia. Mussolini made a speech which I did not hear, but which I am told is alarmingly radical. Brief, uncompromising, ending with the statement that Italians are yearning to fight in "that fight which is bound to come." Unfortunately, nothing can be done about it. His mind is set and decided on war. The only good thing is that he has issued orders to Pavolini not to reproduce it in the press. At least there will not be a new crisis with France and England. That's something, when one lives from day to day!

Mussolini leaves for Romagna.

February 2, 1940

Nothing new.

February 3, 1940

The English ambassador delivers a memorandum regarding our commercial negotiations. The terms are not bad, but one of the clauses must be considered *sine qua non*, and that is the sale to Great Britain of ammunition and weapons. I am certain that the Duce will not like it, but Riccardi says that we must make a virtue of necessity, and reach an agreement with the English, otherwise the economic situation will become too burdensome.

February 4, 1940
  Nothing new.

February 5, 1940
  Nothing new.

February 6, 1940
  Conference with General Carboni, just back from Germany. He makes a frank and pessimistic report on the state of the country. Food is scarce, and, above all, enthusiasm is scarce as well. A great ground offensive is being prepared, but it will not be possible to start it before the end of April, after it thaws.
  I see the Prince of Hesse. He wants to confer with the Duce on behalf of Hitler, but has nothing special to say. He informs me that Göring is the most incensed against Italy, and apparently against me personally. That won't keep me awake. The real reason must be sought in the Collar of the Annunziata given to von Ribbentrop when he expected it for himself. He blames me for it. He will calm down when he gets his.
  Mussolini telephones from Forlì. He continues to object to the sale of arms to the English. He thinks that the British position is becoming more and more difficult every day. Why?

February 7, 1940
  Return of the Duce, with whom I have a long conversation. Meanwhile, he refuses to sell weapons to Great Britain. He says that he does not want to reduce the means of making war that are at our disposal, and that he intends to keep the obligations recently confirmed with Germany. "Governments, like individuals, must follow a line of morality and honor." He is not concerned about English reactions, which I forecast will be inevitable and harsh. Neither does the lack of coal weigh on his mind. He repeats that it is good for the Italian people to be put to tests that make them shake off their century-old mental laziness. He is bitter toward the people. "We must keep them disciplined and in uniform from morning till night. They only understand the stick, the stick, the stick." He does not differentiate between the social classes, and calls all those who wish to vegetate, "the people."
  I inform Riccardi of the Duce's decision on the issue of commercial exchanges with England. He is very gloomy. He had counted upon the 20 million pounds sterling that were part of the agreement, and he is afraid that we shall no longer receive any raw materials, most of which come from the British market. Von Mackensen comes to plead for the usual illegal favors that Germany demands of us as its accomplices. As usual, I am inclined to answer these secondary requests in the affirmative in order to be able to answer the larger demands negatively whenever they come, since they will, unfortunately, appear.

February 8, 1940

I inform Percy Loraine that the Duce has decided to turn down every [British] request for war materiel. The communication had a very strong effect. Loraine replied that this would destroy the basis of all negotiations and that shortly coal shipments from Germany would be intercepted. He also emphasized the political significance of our refusal. Italian-British relations are moving into a period of sharper tension. When I stated that the Duce is ready to reassess his decision in six months, he answered that by that time Europe will be reshaped for ten generations to come.

I take Prince Hesse to see the Duce. Hitler proposes a meeting of the two leaders at the border. Mussolini immediately declared that he agreed. I fear this meeting. When the Duce is with the Germans he becomes excited. Today, with Hesse, he used warlike language exclusively. He said that he intends to take his place at the side of Germany as soon as his weapons preparations allow us to be a help rather than a hindrance to the Germans. Even with Hesse he maintained an attitude of complete indifference with regard to the coal crisis about which everyone is worried. Bocchini confirms reports that the country's state of mind is becoming more and more unsettled, and he fears that regrettable incidents and disorders will take place in the near future.

February 9, 1940

Clodius, who has been in Rome for a few days on commercial matters, received the news of the Duce's refusal to England with joy. He declared that if Italian weapons were sold to the Allies a violent reaction would develop, particularly in German military circles. Clodius was unhappy over the progress of his negotiations. He asks for many things, perhaps for too many things, and gets many refusals from our officials. I only gave him assurances and good words. They cost so little.

The Duce is very proud of his "no" to the British. He repeats that states, like individuals, must have a moral standard on which no compromise can be made; the limits of decency cannot be disregarded. Selling arms to the British would have dishonored us. Naturally, I replied, it remains to be seen for how long we can continue to be unyielding on practical grounds. The sources of raw materials are in the hands of others. How will they react now?

The Duce has confirmed his statement that he is favorable to the meeting with Hitler. He also looks with favor on a trip by Ribbentrop to Rome, especially because this would allow him to visit the Pope.

February 10, 1940

Nothing new. I go to Leghorn for the anniversary of Buccari.[454]

February 11, 1940

The ceremony at my father's tomb fills me with pride and sadness. While formerly it used to be a joy for me to go to the city of my childhood, now, it reopens old wounds. My father's death has changed my life, or, rather, my conception of life. My youth was also buried in his grave.

Benini reports that Riccardi made a very courageous speech before the Supreme Commission for the Defense of the Italian State on our present monetary situation, our stockpiles, and on our real condition in going to war. In the speech he reached completely pessimistic conclusions and spoke in a tone never heard before. Badoglio objected not so much to the substance as to the form, agreeing fully with the former.

February 12, 1940

I found the Duce irritated at Riccardi's speech. According to him, what Riccardi said pleased the critics of Fascist policy so much that as soon as the Duce had left the chamber Balbo went to shake hands with Riccardi, who until then was his implacable enemy. The Duce repeats that he does not believe in the cry baby of the Ministry of Currency Exchange. Even Guarneri has been warning that we have been on the brink of bankruptcy for the past six years, but we have carried on quite well. But the Duce does not add that during that time we burned 12 billion in foreign securities and 5 billion in gold. Now our reserves have been reduced to 1,400 miserable million, and when these are gone we shall only have our eyes to weep with. Riccardi erred in the way he presented things, but he acted courageously in sounding the alarm.

February 13, 1940

Nothing new.

February 14, 1940

I communicate to Sir Percy Loraine the Duce's final decision to refuse to supply any military goods to the British, including the training planes already agreed to. Sir Percy does not conceal his disappointment and says that relations between our two countries are really moving toward a period of growing difficulties.

General Graziani, followed by the Duce, replied to Riccardi's speech at a meeting of the Supreme Defense Council. Graziani claims that the army should be thanked for not having demanded financial sacrifices of the country that might have been too heavy. The Duce assumes complete responsibility and defends the armaments program. He says that ever since 1935 Italian economists have been threatening bankruptcy and that, in spite of this, we have continued to carry on. In replying, Riccardi made up pretty well for his previous error, expressed regrets for the tone of his speech, but basically repeated what he had said on Saturday. The laws of economics cannot be changed.

Balbo accompanies me to the Palazzo Chigi. He can hardly control himself. He fully approves of my action. "Just whistle," he says, "and I'll be at your side."

February 15, 1940

Bocchini's report on the internal situation was very pessimistic. The hardship of the country is growing and all kinds of difficulties are increasing. The prestige of the regime is not what it used to be. But is Bocchini telling Mussolini all this? He swears to me that he is.

February 16, 1940

François-Poncet, whom I had not seen for a long time, complains about our press attacks, and especially those appearing in the *Popolo d'Italia*. French newspapers, for the time being, are not reacting, but relations between the two countries are suffering from this nonetheless, and the atmosphere of better understanding which we had established in the last few months has been upset once again. I used some kind words, but nothing more, since the press campaign is desired and directed personally by the Duce, my influence being very limited.

Donegani is worried about the coal problem. If our supplies are reduced or cease entirely in the next few days, industry will suffer a sudden stoppage with dire consequences in the field of production and labor.

I receive Sidorovici, leader of the Romanian Youth Movement. Some leader! He is a big hulk, a preposterous creature devoid of any interest.

February 17, 1940

News from Finland confirms the fact that the position of its defenders is becoming more difficult. The Russians are exerting more and more pressure with vast masses of men and arms. Resistance under such conditions cannot last very long. For obvious reasons we can do no more than what has already been done. Nor is it advisable for us to commit ourselves too much to a military undertaking beyond our control.

Sir Percy comes to show me certain documents of minor importance which tend to prove collusion between Nazism and Communism. I needed no such proof to be convinced of this. I conferred with the Duce on the need to stop our petty newspaper campaign against France. He promised me that he would do it—but for how long?

February 18, 1940

Last night at the Colonnas' Percy Loraine told me that March 1 is the date chosen when England would stop all coal shipments coming to Italy from Germany by sea. I talked about this with the Duce, who flaunts his indifference on the subject. He talks a great deal about national fuels and is counting on an increase of production in our lignite mines. He fools himself and others fool him. Technical experts, on the other hand (and I mean those who are really capable and honest), agree that the lack of coal will paralyze our national life to a large degree. The last few months should have taught Mussolini a great deal about the dangers of self-delusion.

Sebastiani informs me that Mussolini intends to fire Revel because of the colossal failure of the special sales tax. This was an idiotic decree because there is nothing more hateful than a tax which keeps nagging millions of taxpayers at every turn.

I talked to Casertano about Muti. He says that Muti is acting in good faith, but that power has gone to his head, and he is under the influence of a group of friends, minor leaders in the army and elsewhere, who push him into making one mistake after the other, often for their own personal gain. I don't think that Muti will last long as secretary of the Fascist party.

February 19, 1940

Nothing new in politics. The British attack on the German steamer *Altmark*, which was sailing in Norwegian territorial waters with English prisoners, has made a deep impression. I discuss it with Percy Loraine, and to his surprise I declare that the English action is justified and reminiscent of the boldest traditions of the navy at the time of Francis Drake.

I advise the Hungarian Villani to be calm, very calm. If a conflict started by Hungary should break out within a short time, we would not be in a position to give any help. Besides, even the Magyars do not approve the verbal but equally dangerous violence of Count Czaky. At the golf club on the same day Countess Bethlen suggested that I should pull the coattails of her much too intemperate Minister for Foreign Affairs [Czaky].

February 20, 1940

Göring, in conversation with Teucci,[455] spoke clearly about the Italian position, making statements that prove he is disappointed and very angry. We must keep this in mind. He is the most human of the German leaders, but he is emotional and violent and might become dangerous. In the meantime, Clodius and Mackensen have come to complain about the difficulties they are encountering in the commercial negotiations. What is it they want from us? I told them clearly that as long as we maintain a hostile policy toward France and England we shall have increasing difficulties in getting supplies of raw materials. They cannot demand, as they do, that we also renounce our Balkan markets.

Percy Loraine informs me in writing that today his government will declare in the House of Commons that German coal en route to Italy is merchandise subject to confiscation. The crisis is approaching, and all the Stefani press releases which fill the newspapers today with articles on our production and use of lignite will not be enough to remedy the situation.

Ansaldo reports on his conversation with the Duce. Nothing really new. The Duce reiterates his firm hostility toward the democracies and his idea of waging a parallel war on the side of Germany, an idea in which I believe less and less.

February 21, 1940

The Duce intends to satisfy the Germans, and at the Palazzo Venezia there is a meeting with Riccardi and Giannini. Both of them are insistent on the need to refuse goods which we ourselves lack, such as hemp, copper, and other raw materials. But the Duce decides to give 3,500 tons of copper anyway, from the amount which he is preparing to extort from the homes of the Italians. He thinks that this requisition will amount to 20,000 tons, but perhaps this estimate is too high. Nevertheless, the requisition will not be well received, and worse still if it becomes known that a part of the copper will have to be handed over to the hated Germans. I insist with the Duce that he should not requisition sacred objects in churches. He refused. "The churches do not need copper but faith, and there is very little faith left now. Catholicism is wrong in demanding too much credulity on the part of modern man."

February 22, 1940
Our commercial agreement with the Germans was easily reached after the Duce's intervention.

I see the Prince of Piedmont. I apprise him of the situation which he, moreover, knows very well and sizes up cautiously. But it was clear that he liked to hear from me what he himself did not dare say. He is very anti-German and convinced that Italy must remain neutral. He is skeptical, very skeptical, about the army's true capabilities at the present time and condition—a condition which he considers to be altogether pitiful.

February 23, 1940
Nothing new.

February 24, 1940
Nothing new.

February 25, 1940
Hitler has spoken. Contrary to English comments which pass off his speech as quite ordinary, the Duce considers that this time the Führer wants to give his peace conditions: recognition of the principle of *Lebensraum* for Germany and restoration of the colonies. I feel that these conditions appear too dishonorable for London to discuss them, but the Duce considers them acceptable. The Duce has once more confirmed that he is certain the Allies will lose the war, and his entire policy is based on this conviction. In fact, he has again spoken of claims against France, and has outlined his thesis on the need for free access to the open seas, without which Italy will never be an empire.

February 26, 1940
I received Roosevelt's representative, Sumner Welles. He is a very dignified person, a distinguished American both in appearance and in manners, who easily carries the weight of a mission that has placed him in the limelight of American and world publicity. The conversation was very cordial. I did not hesitate to inform him about events concerning which he was not informed and about my own plans. I give a normal, simple tone to the conversation and this impressed him, because he was not expecting it. He is anti-German, but is making an effort to be correctly impartial. He was glad, however, when I let him know my feelings and sympathies. Unfortunately, the conference with the Duce (recorded elsewhere) took place in a rather icy atmosphere. Mussolini stresses the aloofness that he now openly displays in his relations with the Anglo-Saxons. Sumner Welles left the Mappamondo room more depressed than when he entered it. The Duce later commented sarcastically on the interview: "Between us and the Americans any kind of

understanding is impossible because they assess problems on the surface while we go deeply into them." The Duce was not impressed with Welles's personality, but I do not agree with him. I have had too many dealings with the pack of conceited vulgarians that make up the German leadership not to appreciate the fact that Sumner Welles is a gentleman.

February 27, 1940
I travel to Naples to act as crown notary on the occasion of the birth of Princess Maria Gabriella, daughter of Prince Umberto and Princess Maria José. I also visit the work in progress for the Triennial Overseas Exposition and of the Costanzo Ciano School, an institution which I hope is worthy of the name it bears. During my absence the Duce published an editorial in italics in the *Giornale d'Italia* answering the *Daily Herald*, in which he says that in addition to being willing to join the Germans we are also ready to join the Russians if there is any intention of threatening our existence as a totalitarian regime. This made quite an impression, none of it favorable.

February 28, 1940
The Duce said yesterday to Anfuso, "There are still some criminals and imbeciles in Italy who believe that Germany will be beaten. I tell you Germany will win." I accept "imbecile" if it is for me, but I think "criminal" is unjust! In any case, it is this deep, honest conviction of his that inspires his actions. The Duce ordered that the report of the conversation with Sumner Welles be given to von Mackensen, who was very pleased. I can understand it. Mussolini defended the German line with absolute determination.

News comes from Paris that political censorship has been lifted. Here's an event that cannot fail to complicate matters.

February 29, 1940
Pavolini received orders to start a campaign against some French newspapers, mostly because of an article by Kerillis[456] on Italian neutrality. A very touchy subject. All we have to do is start and the rest will follow. I am worried.

This morning the Duce let off steam against the people of Genoa, who, like the Milanese, "reveal themselves to be incurably pro-English and at the same time somewhat vile." The reason is that in Genoa they are complaining more than elsewhere, despite the fact that Albini[457] denies it.

Again Bocchini is concerned more and more about the internal situation. Economic difficulties, political uncertainty, scarcity of food: these are the fundamental reasons of discontent.

From various sources it is confirmed that Germany is getting ready for an offensive on the western front. It cannot be immediate, however; in Göring's circle they mention the end of March, a month dear to Hitler's superstition.

March 1, 1940

The English press announces that as of today German coal will be treated as an article of contraband, and, hence, seized. We shall have moments of serious difficulty before supplies from British sources can be arranged, aside from the difficulties of making payment. The Duce has set aside for this use one billion in gold from the Bank of Italy. On the *Rex*, which is soon to leave, we shall send ingots valued at 2 million dollars. After this billion is withdrawn, our gold reserve will be about 1,300 million against the deficit in the balance of payments estimated at 4 billion for the current year. Despite these difficulties the Duce repeats that a government has never fallen on account of financial and economic difficulties. Today he praised the broad vision of Hitler's policies, who has in mind "a real plan to regulate European life," based upon an exchange of populations making political borders coincide with ethnic borders.

Revel is not at all pessimistic about the financial situation, and I am surprised. Today at the golf club he explained a fantastic theory of his to me, according to which gold will no longer be worth anything, and we shall become rich through the sale of works of art. Revel is a fool, who has begun to play the part of an extreme interventionist in order to please his master. Nevertheless, this is dangerous, because the Minister of Finance, if honest and capable, ought to act as a sort of brake.

March 2, 1940

The coal blockade is causing a great deal of comment in the international press, and also a certain amount of excitement in Italy. The Duce thinks it necessary to send a note of protest in strong terms to the British government. He dictates the concluding phrases of the harsh and threatening note himself.

I receive Sir Noel Charles, replacing the ambassador who is ill. He seeks to clarify the measures taken by his government concerning the blockade, but the explanation is of slight significance. I take advantage of the occasion to tell him—as a good friend of the English—that the measures taken on the issue of coal are the sort that will help push Italy into the arms of Germany. It would be absurd not to admit that British stock is down in our estimation.

Charles informs me, as well, of the impending despatch of new forces to the Near East, which should not be interpreted as having any connection with the Balkan situation.

March 3, 1940

The Duce approves the note I have prepared on the basis of his conclusions, a note, I believe, which is firm and to the point, and yet not such as to burn our bridges. Von Mackensen comes to see me. I give him a copy of the note. His government instructs him to say that the German press is at our disposal for an attack on Great Britain on the coal question. Berlin's game is clear. The Germans are trying to embitter relations between London and ourselves at any cost. I have not the least intention of encouraging this. I thank von Mackensen, and tell him that it is not necessary to take any further steps. We are able to take care of the matter with the means at our disposal.

Guariglia sends an interesting and clever report on Italian-French relations. He goes so far as to propose negotiations and the conclusion of an agreement. Although the report contains phrases and arguments which will certainly be unwelcome to the Duce, I decide to submit it to him anyway, because it may have a wholesome influence on his thinking.

I speak with the Duce about the eventual exportation of works of art. He is favorable, but I am not. He does not like works of art, and above all detests that period of history during which the greatest masterpieces were produced. I recall—he recalls it too—that he felt a sense of boredom and physical fatigue unusual for him on the day he had to accompany Hitler on a detailed visit of the Pitti Palace and the Uffizi.

March 4, 1940

I go with General Marras to see the Duce; the latter is very pessimistic about the German attitude toward us. He is convinced that the Germans, notwithstanding a certain formal respect for us, maintain their hatred and scorn unchanged, now aggravated by what they call the second treachery. No war move would be so popular in Germany, both for the older and younger generations, as an armed invasion pushed in the direction of our blue skies and warm seas. This and other things Marras frankly told the Duce, who is shocked by the report. The Duce repeated his theory of a parallel war and again insisted that Italy would never enter the war at the side of the Western Powers. Of this he is certain.

Bodini[458] also presents a report on his trip to Germany, but it is very superficial. Two points emerge from it: the certainty of a coming offensive, and the German conviction that they won the war last September. What bitter disillusionment this will be if they are still in the trenches during the next few winters.

March 5, 1940

The American Consul at Naples, in order to find out the state of mind of the Italian people, questioned a beggar, who answered that he does not fear war, but rather revolution. The report, which landed into the hands of the Duce, has put him in a good mood. He says: "Even the beggars are so satisfied with their lot under the Fascist regime as to fear a revolution." This was his final comment, but as Minister of Foreign Affairs I shudder at the sources of information used by consuls, and naturally this also includes our own consuls.

Long conversation with the King. I find him disappointed at the English attitude which, however, has not changed his stubborn anti-German view. "I know that I am in the German black book," he said. "Yes, Your Majesty. At the top. And if you will allow me to be bold enough to say so,

I am in it immediately after you." "I think so too. This honors both of us as far as Italy is concerned." That was the tone of our conversation. I did not hesitate to tell him that I would consider a German victory the greatest disaster for our country. He asked what we might be able to obtain from the Allies. "The preservation of Italy's freedom, which German hegemony would compromise for centuries to come," I said. He agreed.

I try in vain to moderate the worries of François-Poncet, who is very much disturbed over the resumption of the pro-German tendencies in the press, by the party, and above all by the Duce.

March 6, 1940

The Duce is more than ever irritated about the coal issue. The first ships were held up yesterday, precisely as stated in Percy Loraine's report, although some information in the press and the optimism of the Minister of Communications had caused us to hope for a postponement. Mussolini is angered at this display of force more than by the practical consequences that might derive. "Within a short time the guns will fire off by themselves. It is not possible that of all people I should become the laughingstock of Europe. I have to stand for one humiliation after another. As soon as I am ready I shall make the English regret this. My intervention in the war will bring about their defeat." The Duce, alas, is still under illusions as to our chances for quick rearmament. The situation is still very difficult and lack of coal will only make it worse. Perhaps we shall go to war, but we shall be unprepared and unarmed.

For the first time I found a person who wants to go to war on the German side against France and England. This person is no less than the intrepid Cesare Maria de Vecchi di Val Cismon! The Americans say that a sucker is born every minute; one has only to look for him. This time I have found one. Cesare Maria is, above all, a pompous and vain man, who dreams of obtaining a marshal's baton and decorations and hopes to get them through the blood of others.

March 7, 1940

The situation created by the confiscation of our coal has not changed at all, although Bastianini indicates from London a possible easing of the British attitude. Mussolini is brooding over his exasperation. Today he uttered between his teeth new and vague threats against the English. He said, "England will be defeated. Inexorably defeated. This is the pure truth, that you— yes you—should also get into your head." During our seven years of daily contacts this is the *first* time that he picks on me personally. If I considered my job more important than my conscience, I should be greatly worried tonight. Instead, I am perfectly tranquil. I know that I am honestly serving my country and Him whom I love and to whom I owe so much.

The Yugoslav minister is concerned about events in Croatia and asks us to increase our vigilance over Pavelic. I give him immediately the broadest assurances on this issue.

March 8, 1940

A coup de théâtre, dear to the low-class tastes of the Germans: von Mackensen informs me that Ribbentrop will be in Rome on Sunday, bringing with him Hitler's reply to the Duce. He adds pompously that he [Ribbentrop] will pay a visit to the Pope. I telephone Mussolini, emphasizing the inadvisability of such a move, precisely when the coal business has made our relations with London so delicate. But the Duce is very much satisfied, and all I can do is let the Germans know that we welcome the visit.

Frankly, I dislike all this. It will have a far-reaching effect worldwide, just when we ought not add fuel to the fire. Furthermore, I dread the Duce's contact with the Germans. In these last few days his hostile attitude toward the Allies has become more pronounced. The thought of war dominates him, and it will dominate him even more if the offensive on the western front begins. Inaction will then go against the grain of his aggressive temperament. Under the circumstances, Ribbentrop will need no great oratorical power to urge the Duce on a course which he, the Duce, desires with all his soul. With respect to Ribbentrop's visit to the Pope, I judge it to be a gesture as sensational as it is futile.

March 9, 1940

We were finally able to reach an agreement with the British on the issue of ships they are holding up. The ships were released with their cargoes on condition that none of our ships are to be sent to northern ports for the purpose of loading German coal for Italy. I tell Charles this evening that the agreement pleased me in a very special way, and he, being quicker than he would have me believe, replied that my remark made it unnecessary for him to ask any questions regarding Ribbentrop's visit; a visit which will be very unpopular in Italy.

I tell Pavolini to feature the news about the agreement with London in the most positive way. Ribbentrop will not like this, but it will help counteract, within and outside our borders, the unfavorable impression his visit will cause.

March 10, 1940

The meeting at the station was rather cool. The crowd, which had been gathered by the Federal secretary with some difficulty, showed a good deal of restraint. As we drove away von Ribbentrop at once stated that the fine weather we were having brought nearer the moment for action and arrogantly uttered this phrase, "Within a few months the French army will be destroyed and the English on the Continent will be prisoners of war." The same words are repeated to the Duce during the conference.

Von Ribbentrop is the bearer of Hitler's letter: a long document in which there are many unimportant things, but in which two fundamental points are emphasized—that he intends to settle the conflict militarily and that Italy's place will inevitably be at Germany's side. Von Ribbentrop dilutes these ideas into many words. Mussolini listens and promises to answer tomorrow, after having meditated over the letter as well as over the interview.

But he immediately joins Hitler, in stating that Fascism's place is alongside Nazism on the firing line. The conference was quite cordial and without excitement on either side.

After the interview, once we were alone, Mussolini says that he does not believe in the German offensive nor in complete German success. He has not yet reached a firm conclusion. He wants to think it over further. Up to now, von Ribbentrop has not scored any decisive points.

March 11, 1940

Today it was Mussolini's turn to talk. The stenographic report of today's conference [with von Ribbentrop] has been made and will be filed elsewhere. The Duce expressed himself calmly, avoiding grandiloquent statements, but could not restrain himself from alluding repeatedly to two obligations (implicit in the present state of things) which he intends to maintain, and which are above all part of his deepest convictions. He declared that, reserving his freedom to choose the date, he intends to intervene in the conflict and to fight a war parallel to that of Germany; basically aligning himself with Germany. The main reason for this is that Italy is imprisoned in the Mediterranean. Von Ribbentrop tried to dot his *i*s as much as possible, asking us to reinforce our troops on the French border in order to bring about a concentration of forces on the other side. He then proposed that within a short time a meeting between Hitler and Mussolini should take place at the Brenner Pass. The Duce quickly accepted the proposal, which I find quite dangerous because of the immediate consequences it may have, and also because of its influence on the future. I shall try to talk it over with the Duce.

Von Ribbentrop's visit had thus ended. If he wanted to reinforce the Axis, he has succeeded. If, on the other hand, he wanted to accelerate our intervention, he has not achieved his aim, although he may have secured from Mussolini some new but not very useful compromises.

March 12, 1940

This morning Mussolini insistently asked for the reports of yesterday's conversations, not yet sent in from Berlin. He says he fears that there might be some mistake, but actually he believes he has gone too far in his commitment to fight against the Allies. He would now like to dissuade Hitler from his land offensive, an idea to which he returns over and over again. Italian inaction, which already weighs heavily on the Duce, would be unbearable if German forces should engage in battle. Therefore he hopes to prevail upon Hitler, and this is the result he expects to achieve at the meeting at the Brenner Pass. I express my opposition to this.

The Germans know by now that the Duce opposes the land offensive, but they have let us know that they will go ahead just the same. It is therefore useless for us to insist. But if the German offensive is preceded by a meeting at the Brenner Pass we shall never be able to exonerate Mussolini from some measure of responsibility for the great massacre. Nor can it be denied that the Duce is fascinated by Hitler, a fascination which involves something deeply rooted in his nature: action. The Führer will get much more out of the Duce than Ribbentrop was able to get. With the necessary tact, I said as much to the Duce, who partly agreed with me, but he insisted that he cannot now decline the offer of a meeting with Hitler. He is probably right in this. I can therefore only repeat again my recommendations for caution.

March 13, 1940

Von Ribbentrop telephones and asks to set the date of the meeting at the Brenner Pass for Monday, March 18. At first Mussolini exploded: "These Germans are unbearable; they don't give one time to breathe nor to think things over." But then he concluded that in view of the state of affairs, since the meeting must take place, it had better take place at once. So I confirm to von Ribbentrop the date chosen by him. Nevertheless, the Duce was nervous. Until now he has lived under the illusion that a real war would not be waged. The prospect of an imminent clash in which he might remain an outsider disturbs him and, to use his words, humiliates him. He still hopes, but less than before, that he can influence Hitler and persuade him to refrain from his intention to attack.

Poncet would like some information. I am quite reserved with him, but I do not conceal the fact that I consider the clash now imminent. As far as we are concerned, I tell him that we shall maintain the political line that we have followed up to now.

Casertano makes a report on the condition of the party: terrible. Muti, for whom I am not going to make any effort, has demonstrated himself to be arrogant and distrustful, and, as often happens, is less devoted to me than I thought he was. All I can do is abandon him to his fate.

March 14, 1940

While playing golf, Count Acquarone, Minister of the Royal House, approached me. He talked openly about his concern regarding the situation and assured me that the King is also aware of the hardship felt by the country. In his opinion the King feels that it may become necessary for him to intervene at any moment to give things a different direction; he is prepared to do so and to do it with despatch. Acquarone repeats that the King has for me "more than benevolence—a real affection and much trust." Acquarone, I cannot say whether on his own initiative or on the King's orders, wanted to delve deeper into the subject, but I kept the conversation on general lines.

Mussolini is more and more preoccupied about the meeting at the Brenner Pass. He would like to get a document from Hitler—such as a communiqué—which would give him a certain amount of freedom of action to stay out of the war, even if hostilities should begin on the western front. This seems difficult to me, because Hitler, too, has his public opinion to consider, which would not forgive him if he lost his Italian trump. It would be better if we made the Germans understand that they are repeating the old Salzburg tune. They do and undo things without consulting us, frequently acting against our point of view. Their present behavior, as in the past, offers us a suitable pretext to insist on our freedom of action.

March 15, 1940
Nothing new.

March 16, 1940
Two conferences with Sumner Welles—at the Palazzo Chigi and the Palazzo Venezia. Stenographic reports are to be found elsewhere. The most important result is this: in London and in Paris there does not exist any of the uncompromising attitude which their speeches and the papers indicate. If they had certain guarantees of security they would be ready to give in more or less and to recognize the *fait accompli*. I think that if they really go along this path, they are moving toward defeat. If Hitler is still doubtful about when to start the attack, his doubts will be dispelled at once when he learns from Mussolini of these shilly-shallyings by the democracies. But I do not believe he has any doubts. From the haste with which Hitler wanted to set the meeting, and the fact that he did not want to remain at the Brenner Pass for more than an hour and a half, Mussolini deduces that within a short time he will set off the powder keg. Today the Duce is calmer. He intends to keep his solidarity with Germany, but he does not intend to enter the war— at least for the time being. He said, "I shall do as Bertoldo did. He accepted the death sentence on condition that he choose the tree on which he was to be hanged.[459] Needless to say, he never found that tree. I shall agree to enter the war, but will choose the right moment. I alone intend to be the judge, and a great deal will depend upon how the war progresses." These intentions encourage me, but only up to a certain point. To push Mussolini on is an easy undertaking, but to pull him back is difficult.

March 17, 1940
Welles has telephoned Roosevelt, asking for permission to undertake some vague initiative for peace, but the answer is negative. The whole tone of the telephone call gives one the impression that Roosevelt does not wish to commit himself beyond a certain point, and certainly not before he has carefully examined the results of Welles' European mission.

We leave at 1:30 p.m. Mackensen, rather embarrassed, tells me that the Führer has expressed a wish that the conversation begin between the Duce and himself alone. (Alfieri says that he learned from Frau Mackensen that Hitler wishes to keep Ribbentrop at a distance, but this seems to me to be one of Alfieri's flights of imagination.) During the trip I talked with Mussolini at length. He is calm and, at heart, happy that Hitler has called for him. He believes that hostilities will start at any moment, and he repeats to me his latest theory on our position if this should happen. Italian forces, he says, will constitute the left wing which will tie up an equal number of enemy troops without fighting, but ready, nonetheless, to go into action at a convenient moment.

During our trip the first cables begin to arrive from the capitals, where news of the trip has been announced. They express surprise and amazement. In general, they tend to connect the event to Sumner Welles's presence in Rome.

March 18, 1940

It is snowing at the Brenner Pass. Mussolini is waiting for his guest with anxious elation. Recently he has felt more and more the fascination of the Führer. His military successes—the only successes that Mussolini really values and desires—are the reason for this. While we are waiting, he tells me that he had a dream during the night "which tore away the veil from the future." But he does not say what the dream is. On the other hand, he says that this has happened at other times, when, for example, he had dreamed of fording a stream, and learned that the Fiume question was about to be solved.

The Hitler meeting is very cordial on both sides. The conference, of which a stenographic report is to be found elsewhere, is more a monologue than anything else. Hitler talks all the time, but is less agitated than usual. He makes few gestures and speaks in a quiet tone. He looks physically fit. Mussolini listens to him with interest and with deference. He speaks little and confirms his intention to move with Germany. He reserves to himself only the choice of the right moment (it reminds me of Bertoldo's tree). The conference ends with a short meal.

Later Mussolini gives me his impressions. He did not find in Hitler that uncompromising attitude which von Ribbentrop had led him to suspect. Yesterday, as well, von Ribbentrop only opened his mouth to harp on Hitler's intransigency. Mussolini believes that Hitler will think twice before he begins an offensive on land.

The meeting has not substantially changed our position.

March 19, 1940

The crisscrossing of speculation regarding the reasons for and the results of the Brenner meeting continue, and, as it always happens, the most natural and therefore truthful reasons are disregarded. In Rome yesterday the meeting was interpreted as a step toward peace, and the city celebrated, which made me think how difficult it would be to have it celebrate an announcement of war in the same way.

I saw Sumner Welles and briefly informed him about the situation: nothing but an event inside the house of the Axis which leaves things exactly as they were before. He is happy that there is no threat of an immediate military clash. This way Roosevelt will have time to study Welles's reports, and perhaps take some peace initiatives. Welles also talks about a possible meeting between Mussolini and Roosevelt in the Azores—a rather complicated project with uncertain results.

Percy Loraine is desirous of news. I put him at ease. The Brenner meeting is no prelude to surprises in our policy. This is what he wanted to hear.

In thinking over his meeting with Hitler, and while waiting to read Schmidt's reports, the Duce is convinced that Hitler is not preparing to launch the land offensive. As a matter of fact, Mussolini resented the fact that Hitler did all the talking; he had in mind to tell him many things, and instead had to keep quiet most of the time, a thing which, as dictator, or rather the dean of dictators, he's not in the habit of doing.

March 20, 1940

Chamberlain's outburst yesterday in the House of Commons, in speaking of the "two gentlemen who have met at the Brenner Pass," is very significant, but Mussolini has not attached any importance to it nor has he alluded to it. Poncet, too, has expressed himself regretfully about the meeting, and my words did little to convince him that there is nothing new. "You are mistaken," he said. "You have bet, and in fact the Duce himself has put his money on the losing horse, and now he is doubling his bet. But the French-British horse, even if he may lag behind at the beginning of the race, will win in the last lap." He spoke of the French Cabinet crisis and very skeptically about Daladier, who will not form an important cabinet because he does not care to surround himself with strong men. He feels that Reynaud is the right man.

Sumner Welles, before leaving, spoke clearly with Blasco d'Aieta, who is a relative of his. Even without undertaking any offensive, Germany will be exhausted within a year. He considers the war already won by the French and English. The United States is there with all the weight of her power, to guarantee this victory. He deplored the fact that Italy, for which he has a great deal of sympathy, should continue to get more and more deeply involved with one who is destined to suffer a harrowing defeat.

March 21, 1940

Nothing new.

March 22, 1940

Nothing new.

March 23, 1940

I receive Count Teleki at the station, and later am present at the unveiling of the signs with the new names of the streets near Montecitorio, dedicated to the memory of my father's military deeds. Mussolini, who is in a good mood these days and quite talkative, is growing more definitely pro-German every day. He now speaks openly of entering the war at the side of Germany and even defines our course of action: defensive in the Alps, defensive in Libya, offensive in Ethiopia against Djibouti and Kenya, air and naval offensive in the Mediterranean. The Duce's attitude is beginning to influence many Fascist leaders, who, either because they follow him, or out of personal conviction, are lining up within the ranks of interventionism: Muti, Ricci, and, to a greater extent, Revel and Riccardi, who is no longer telling unpleasant truths as he used to. Opposed to the adventure are Grandi and Bottai. The latter naturally are among those who hold positions that they don't want to lose; the people at all social levels want no part of the war. Starace tells me that the Duce made some very warlike speeches to him, and that this morning he said to General Galbiati, commander of the University Student Volunteers, "Hold yourself ready. Shortly we will march in the west." Starace himself adds much water to his wine. He states that the internal conditions of the country are precarious and "almost dangerous."

March 24, 1940

I play golf with Teleki. He repeats that 95 percent of Hungarians hate Germany. He desires only to keep his country out of the war and hopes that Italy may do the same. Villani again alludes to the question of the crown. He confirms the Magyar intention to offer it to some member of the House of Savoy.

Mussolini again has one of his anti-clerical outbursts. He attacks the clergy on the grounds of faith, honesty, and morals. He says that in numerous towns in southern Italy the population almost forces the parish priest to take a concubine, since only in this way will their wives be left undisturbed.

March 25, 1940

A long conference with Count Teleki. I find him objective and reasonable with respect to Magyar claims. He realizes what a danger it would be for Hungary to add a disproportionate number of foreign minorities. The very life of the country would be affected by it. Besides, he will not do anything against Romania, because he does not want to be responsible, even indirectly, for having opened the doors of Europe to Russia. No one would forgive him for this, not even Germany. Teleki has avoided taking any open position one way or the other, but has not hidden his sympathy for the Western Powers and fears a complete German victory like the plague.

In the afternoon I talked with the Duce and General Soddu.[460] The Germans offer us the immediate delivery of some anti-aircraft batteries. Mussolini plans on sending for them at once. Soddu agrees, but he does not want any German personnel. This supplying of weapons, which the Germans will hasten to reveal publicly, will make London and Paris still more acutely suspicious.

March 26, 1940

With the Duce during the morning. We do not talk about politics. He praises Friedrich Wilhelm who, by kicking the women who were walking the streets and beating the clergymen who were looking at the soldiers, created today's Prussia. During the conversation the Duce was sparkling and pungent; but he is wrong to admire the Prussians more and more as "a philosophical breed."

In the afternoon I bring Teleki in to see him, and there is more or less a repetition of yesterday's conference. The Duce makes it clear that he does not intend to remain neutral to the end, and that at a certain moment he will intervene on Germany's side. Teleki receives this declaration with very limited enthusiasm.

March 27, 1940

A visit from Poncet, who is getting ready to confer with Reynaud. He was deeply impressed by the turn that events have taken, and he wanted to know if in the present state of affairs he must consider that the die has been cast. I tried to calm him down, but did not succeed, because he is a keen man, and, besides, recent events have been far too clear and eloquent. Poncet tried again to put before us the possibility of negotiations for conditions more favorable to Italy, and he went so far as to talk about the cession of French Somaliland. I did not accept these offers, which, for that matter, were vague, and told him that Mussolini's state of mind is not much inclined to negotiation. In fact, when I told Mussolini about the conference with the French ambassador, he quickly answered that French offers are always made in bad faith and with the sole practical aim of "compromising and defaming us."

Caruso[461] presents a report about the conditions in the Bohemian protectorate. Apparently things are going better, and the ferocity of German pressure has abated. But there is a storm lurking. If one day the wind changes not one German will get out alive.

At luncheon Teleki asks me abruptly, "Do you know how to play bridge?" "Why?" "For the day when we are together in the Dachau concentration camp." This is the real state of mind of this man.

March 28, 1940

A long conversation last evening with the Prince of Piedmont. Though he is usually cautious and reserved, he revealed, without exposing himself too much, his concern about the growing pro-German direction of our policy—a concern which was made more acute, he said, by his knowledge of our present military condition. He denies that since September there has been any real improvement in our armament; supplies are scarce and morale is low. He is worried about the Fascist militia, which he thinks does not represent the volunteer spirit of the army, but is rather a group of dissatisfied and undisciplined men.

I talk about the party with the Duce. I agree with him that if we are really moving toward war, Muti is not the right man to fully develop the Fascist organizations, and to make them dynamic and responsive. Mussolini is concerned about it, but then, as is usual for him now, he concluded optimistically, "I myself will galvanize the party at the right time, and I will do it in the manner of Friedrich Wilhelm."

Another conversation with Teleki. Nothing new, but he opens his anti-German heart to me. He hopes for the defeat of Germany, not a complete defeat—which might provoke violent shocks—but a kind of defeat that would blunt her teeth and claws for a long time.

March 29, 1940

A report presented by Melchiori,[462] who has spent a month in Germany, has had a profound influence on the Duce. I do not know the value of this individual's observations. He is a shining example of amorality, greedy ambition, ineptitude, and ignorance, who does not know a single word of German and spends his time in the anterooms of the consulates and the embassy begging for secondhand information, which he then cooks up in a rather vulgar style. The trouble is that Mussolini takes him seriously. Few documents have struck him lately as much as the Melchiori report, in which even though he reaches the conventional conclusion of "an unavoidable German victory" he also points out the difficult living conditions of the German people. This report has not substantially modified the decisions of the Duce, but for the first time he admits that Germany is not resting on a bed of roses, and that the failure of the offensive or a long-drawn-out war would mean defeat, and hence the collapse of the German regime. "I do not understand," he said, "why Hitler does not realize this. I myself can feel that Fascism is wearing out—a wear and tear which is not deep, but is nevertheless noticeable, and he does not feel it in Germany, where the crisis has already assumed rather alarming proportions."

March 30, 1940

The Germans raise objections to our recognition of the government of Wang Ching-Wei. It is now too late after the cable I sent him with the intention of widening the gulf which separates our politics from the Russians. I speak to the Duce about it and point out the danger of doing something that is not welcome to Japan. He agrees, and inveighs against von Ribbentrop, "a truly sinister man, because he is an imbecile and is conceited."

Molotov's speech cannot have pleased Germany, because its tone is quite different from that used by von Ribbentrop toward Moscow.

Mussolini is irritated for the nth time at Catholicism, which is to blame for "having made Italy universal, hence preventing it from becoming national. When a country is universal it belongs to everybody but itself."

March 31, 1940

Word reaches me from many quarters that the Duce is thinking of firing me from the Ministry of Foreign Affairs. I do not believe it. In any case, if this should happen, I would be delighted to leave this job in which I have served for almost four years—and what years!—carrying my head high. Everything that I have done was done for the sole purpose of serving my country and the Duce, and whenever I took a stand which seemed to conflict with that of the Duce I did so to defend the Duce's position against offense from abroad. This has been the true—and the deepest—reason for my incurable resentment—*which I confirm*—a resentment against the Germans since the days of Salzburg. But all this doesn't count. The Duce will do whatever he wishes to do. *Dominus dedit, Dominus abstulit.*[463]

I read the entire text of Molotov's speech. On two points he is harsh with us, and this helps in avoiding the understanding which Berlin wishes us to reach with the Russians.

Mussolini is indignant with Sumner Welles because he told Chamberlain that, while not actually having suffered a stroke, the Duce looks, nevertheless, very tired and perturbed. We learned this from one of the usual cables we stole from the English embassy.

April 1, 1940

Von Mackensen, on his return from Berlin, hands me a stenographic report of the Brenner Pass meeting. It is not in the stenographic style of other reports written by Schmidt. It is a very terse summary. It appears that Hitler had raised some objections about furnishing me a copy. The ambassador, under orders from von Ribbentrop, speaks once more of Italian-Russian relations and he asks, with some hesitation, because he does not personally agree with his master, that our press publish articles "more or less praising the Soviets." I flatly refuse. We cannot take such an undignified somersault and Molotov's speech is certainly not a document that justifies such a gesture on our part. The Duce approves, and concludes that "the best we can do for Russia is to be silent, and that is a great deal."

After reading the report, Mussolini repeats that it is his intention to write to Hitler to dissuade him from attempting his land offensive, which is equivalent to putting all his money on a single card. I encourage this move by the Duce because either Hitler will attack just the same and Mussolini will be affected by it and, God willing, will find another pretext to break away, or Hitler will not attack and the war will end in the course of a few months, in a stalemate. It will end up well for us one way or the other. But von Mackensen and our embassy in Berlin agree in stating that the offensive will take place, and perhaps in a short time.

April 2, 1940

Violent turn of the wheel towards war. Today Mussolini wants to go full steam ahead toward hostilities if France and England really intend, as they announce, to tighten the blockade. As Göring, in a conference with Colonel Teucci, said that he understood the Italian position, Mussolini cabled that Göring be told that he is hastening preparations. And yet no one asked him to do so! The Duce tells me that he has drawn up a memorandum concerning our plan of political and strategic action. He will give me a copy and on Saturday he will get together with the seven men responsible who will be informed about the document.

During the Council of Ministers he also makes the statement that he favors going to war. He foresees that the war could break out at any time, and rules out "that we would prostitute ourselves to the democracies, which in any case would draw us to a conflict with the Germans" as well as our remaining neutral "which would demote Italy as a great power for a century and forever as a Fascist regime." Mussolini concludes that we shall move with the Germans with our own war aims.

He speaks of a Mediterranean empire and of access to the oceans. He believes blindly in German victory and in Hitler's word regarding our share of the booty. But even if we consider German victory as a given (and I strongly reject that idea), is it so sure that Hitler, who has never stuck to his word with anyone, will do so with us?

April 3, 1940
Nothing new.

April 4, 1940
Nothing new.

April 5, 1940
Last night I saw the German film about the conquest of Poland. I had previously refused to attend, but if I had again been absent last night, it would have looked too strange. It is a good film if the Germans wish merely to portray brute force, but it is awful for propaganda purposes. The audience, composed in part of pro-German officials and in part of self-appointed pro-German pimps, did not go beyond the limits of mere courtesy in its applause.

I gathered an impression of weakness on the part of the Allies this morning during my conversation with Dingli, the legal adviser of the embassy in London and a friend of Chamberlain. Grandi had a great deal of respect for this man, who impresses me as being of rather secondary importance. He brought a useless and very general message from the Prime Minister, one of those messages of good will destined from the start to remain unanswered. But more important than this was the man's lack of faith in victory. If this were really indicative of British morale, the fate of Europe would be tragically sealed. But I do not believe that it is.

Sumner Welles sent his ambassador to tell me that the whole story about the map is completely unfounded, and that Reynaud never spoke to him about the new territorial setup in Europe.[464]

April 6, 1940
I received from the Duce one of the eight copies of the secret report prepared by him summarizing the situation and outlining the military and political program for the future. It is a thoughtful document in which he reaches the double conclusion that Italy cannot make an about face nor remain neutral to the end of the conflict without losing its standing among the great powers. Therefore, we must fight on the side of Germany for our interests and when conditions are favorable. The military action plan is: defensive action on all fronts and offensive action toward Djibouti; air and naval offensive all around. But the Duke of Aosta, whom I saw this morning, said that it is not only extremely problematical that we can maintain present positions, because the French and English are already equipped and ready for action, but the population, among whom rebellion is still alive,

would revolt as soon as they got any inkling of our difficulties. I talked about this with the Duce and, for whatever it was worth, repeated that Italy unanimously hates the Germans.

I informed Mussolini briefly of my conversation with Dingli and he wanted me to suggest to Dingli, in his name, that he attempt to bring about a compromise peace.

April 7, 1940

A year has passed since we landed in Albania. That is a day that I remember with emotion. And, talking about Albania, General Favagrossa today refused the minimum amount needed to solve the housing problem in Albania. With all the goodwill he can't give any money because he hasn't got it. With him I made a rapid survey of the situation regarding our metal reserves. The results were very sad. Italy is losing all her foreign markets, and even the small amount of gold that we have to spend cannot be converted into the metals that we need. Internal resources are scarce, and we have already gone the limit in gathering copper pans and iron grates. Everything is gone. The truth is that we are worse off today with regard to reserves than we were in September. We have enough supplies for only a few months of war. This is what Favagrossa says. Under such conditions, how can we dare go to war?

I spoke with Dingli and told him that in the event Chamberlain is ready to offer possible conditions, we could become intermediaries for his proposals and facilitate a compromise. Otherwise, they must entertain no illusions. Italy will be on Germany's side. Dingli is satisfied with his mission and is getting ready to return to London to report. I have the vague impression that I shall not hear from him again. A man of little account.

April 8, 1940

There is alarm in Budapest. Teleki has sent one of his messengers to Rome, Mr. Baranjay, to inform us of an approach made by the German General Staff to the Hungarian General Staff. On the pretext that Russia will soon move into Bessarabia, Germany intends to occupy the Romanian oil fields and asks for free passage through Hungary. The price for this permission would be Transylvania. For the Hungarians the problem is either of letting the Germans through, or oppose them with force. In either case Hungarian freedom would come to an end. Acceptance would spare them devastation and ruin, while fighting, though more painful for the moment, would prepare for a future rebirth. Villani and Baranjay advocated resistance and hoped for Italian aid. I accompanied them to see the Duce, who reserved his answer, though in principle he advised acceptance. He repeated to them, also, that he stands firmly with Germany, that he is getting ready to fight against the French and English. We have sent a cable to Berlin to learn how much truth there is in what the Hungarians say. We have been told nothing; in fact, the Germans have so far assured us of exactly the opposite. But experience proves that this doesn't mean very much.

April 9, 1940

They did not march in the direction of Romania.

A secretary of the German embassy came to my house at two o'clock in the morning, bearing a letter from Mackensen, who asked to be received at seven o'clock in the morning. Nothing else. He arrived at 6:30, pale and tired, and communicated Hitler's decision to occupy Denmark and Norway, adding that this decision had already been acted upon. He made no comments, but agreed with me wholeheartedly when I told him that the reaction of the neutrals and especially of the Americans, would be violent. Then we went to the Duce to give him a written message from Hitler—the usual letter, in the usual style, announcing what he had already done. Mussolini said, "I approve Hitler's action wholeheartedly. It is a gesture that can have incalculable results, and this is the way to win wars. The democracies have lost the race. I shall give orders to the press and to the Italian people to applaud this German action without reservation." Mackensen left the Palazzo Venezia beaming.

Later, I returned with the Hungarians to see Mussolini. Attolico has denied the rumor of an attack on Romania. The Duce advised, therefore, that the Hungarians remain calm, and that they accede to the German requests. This was not the answer the Hungarians expected and hoped for. They went so far as to ask whether, in the case of military resistance, they could count on Italian help. Mussolini smiled. "How could this ever be," he said, "since I am Hitler's ally and intend to remain so?"

When we were alone, the Duce talked about Croatia. By now his hands are itching.

He intends to quicken the tempo, taking advantage of the disorder pervading Europe. But he was not specific, except to say that he is convinced that an attack against Yugoslavia will not lead France and England to strike at us. But what if this should not happen? Are we ready to fight? Balbo and the Duke of Aosta have talked to me about their respective sectors of operation in the last few days in such terms as to leave very little room for any illusions.

The first unconfirmed news of fighting and resistance in Norway is coming in. I hope that the news is true; in the first place, because of the reactions that such an unequal struggle will have on world opinion; second, to show that there are still people who know how to fight in defense of human dignity.

April 10, 1940

News of the German action in the north has had a favorable echo among the Italian people, who, as Mussolini says, "are like a whore who prefers the winning mate." More surprising than the speed of the German action is the French-British reaction. The Allies reply to Hitler's military success with a barrage of speeches and articles that is absolutely futile for purposes of war.

Returning from Paris, François-Poncet was very downcast today—a mood that sharply contrasts with his lively and provocative temperament. He spoke of "giving time a chance," of "lost battles and wars that were won," of "the United States that will not permit a Hitler victory." I agree.

But I should like to see more decisive action. In France, everybody, or almost everybody, is now convinced that Italy is preparing to turn against them, but nothing will be done that might provoke or accelerate such an Italian decision. They would like to leave the entire responsibility up to us. Poncet personally pointed out the dangers in precipitating matters.

Mackensen came to see me on a pretext. He wanted to know what were our further reactions to what had happened. I showered him with congratulations and good wishes, since there is now nothing else to do, even though I am absolutely of the opinion that the last word has not yet been spoken, and that we may witness a complete change in the situation—perhaps soon.

April 11, 1940

An urgent message from Hitler to the Duce. I went with von Mackensen to Villa Torlonia at 11 p.m., where Mussolini, contrary to his usual custom, was standing waiting for us. He had a bad cold, was feverish and tired, but pleased to receive Hitler's message. Today he has prepared an enthusiastic answer. In it he says that, beginning tomorrow, the Italian fleet will be ready, that our preparation in the air and on land is proceeding at an accelerated pace, and, finally, he calls Hitler's attention to the ambiguous Romanian attitude, at the same time expressing a desire to safeguard peace in that sector of Europe for the time being. Hitler received Attolico and mentioned with satisfaction the message from the Duce. He has given optimistic reports on the course of the present air and naval battle. I wonder. Only time will prove whether the Führer has acted as a strategist or has run into a dangerous trap.

This morning Mussolini was gloomy. He had returned from a conference with the King that had not satisfied him. He said, "The King would like us to enter only to pick up the broken dishes. I hope that they will not break them over our heads before that. And then it is humiliating to remain with our hands folded while others write history. It matters little who wins. To make a people great it is necessary to send them to battle even if you have to kick them in the ass. This is what I shall do. I do not forget that in 1918 there were 540,000 deserters in Italy. And if we do not take advantage of this opportunity to pit our navy against the French and British forces, what is the use of building 600,000 tons of warships? Some coast guards and some yachts would be enough to take the young ladies on a joy ride."

April 12, 1940

I go to bed with a very bad flu and remain there until the 20th.

April 20, 1940

My illness gave rise to much gossip. They talked about "diplomatic illness," and Rome is filled with rumors about my resignation. Naturally, German successes have caused many desertions in the ranks of my so-called friends. On the contrary, it was an old anti-Fascist, Alberto Giannini, who took a courageous stand by writing to the Duce, imploring him not to fire me, since this would increase the country's confusion. Mussolini reacted sympathetically and said that he wished, first of all, to do something that will cut short all these rumors; then he told Buffarini and Muti that I am the man who enjoys his full confidence.

No news from inside the country during my days of absence. A letter from Hitler to bring the situation up to date. The letter was naturally written in an optimistic tone. Hitler uses words that go straight to the Duce's heart and produce the desired effect. In the evening Prince Hesse talked to me about the coming offensive, and told me that Hitler blames bad weather for his not having been able to celebrate his birthday in Paris.

After ten days I found Mussolini more warlike and more pro-German than ever, but he says that he will do nothing before the end of August, that is, after improving preparations and after the harvest. Thus only three months remain to give us a ray of hope.

April 21, 1940

The Duce's speech from the balcony of the Palazzo Venezia was sober and controlled, while the one that he made to the representatives of the labor confederations inside the palace was radical and 100 percent Nazi. Immediately afterward, however, he asked me to try and reduce the possible consequences of his speech in the diplomatic corps, because "up to the second half of August there is no sense in talking of war."

April 22, 1940

This morning the date for Italy's entrance into this war was changed to the spring of 1941 because, according to the Duce, Norway has further removed a solution of the conflict, as well as the center of the European field of operations. Naturally this does not mean that he has in the least changed his attitude. It seems that he had a rather excited meeting with the King, during which Mussolini asserted that "Italy today is in fact a British colony, and some Italians would be ready to make this a legal fact, that is, they would make of her a Malta multiplied by a million." And he added, "I saw that old man turn pale." But alas, the King, who is so much against the war, can do no more to guard against it.

I saw François-Poncet. He was excited and depressed at the same time and talked about Italian war maneuvers so near, in fact, it seemed that they could begin any day now. I tried to set him straight a bit, and he left my room better informed on our policy, and, above all, more tranquil. I did the same thing with the American ambassador, who reveals himself more and more to be a friend and a gentleman. I did the same also with certain other foreign diplomats of lower rank.

April 23, 1940

I attempt to soothe the English chargé d'affaires who, although he is very reserved, has not been indifferent to the onslaught of alarmist rumors during the last week, which began with my illness. I repeat: Italy stands sol-idly behind Germany, but does not intend, until further notice, to make its solidarity more concrete, which does not mean that it intends to make Badoglio's few guns thunder in the place of the paper guns of Virginio Gayda. It seems to me that the French and English should be satisfied, and I believe that as long as it lasts they will certainly be satisfied.

Renzetti has spoken to me again about what might be called Göring's tragicomedy of the Collar of the Annunziata. It seems that the heart of the big marshal is still as filled with desperate sadness as when he saw the picturesque, glittering scenes of the Collar hanging from von Ribbentrop's neck. I speak to the Duce about it. We must not let the bloated quasi-dictator of the Reich suffer any longer. And Mussolini, who has sincere scorn for these honors, authorizes me to write an appeal to the King to describe the pitiful situation of the tender Hermann and to propose that a suitable pendant be given him on the May 22, the sad anniversary of the Alliance. Let's hope the King will accede to the proposal, because in the matter of the Collar of the Annunziata he is cautious and reserved.

April 24, 1940

François-Poncet has brought a sealed letter from Paul Reynaud[465] to the Duce. He was somewhat resentful that he, the ambassador of France, should be the bearer of a message and kept in complete ignorance as to its contents, and he fired a few darts at his government while at the same time speaking well of Reynaud: "He is a man who has always had the courage to tell the bitter truth, but he has all the faults of men under five feet three. He elbows his way ahead for fear that he won't be taken seriously." Mussolini read the letter with pleasure and scorn. In truth, it is a strange message, a little melancholy and a little bragging, which, I believe, very well reflects the temperament of its author. It ends with a sort of invitation to a meeting before the two nations cross swords. Mussolini intends to answer with a refusal, adding some words to take the drama out of Reynaud's vision of things. Naturally, the first thought of the Duce was to send Hitler a complete copy of the letter.

Von Mackensen, back from Berlin, comes to see me, and I go with him to see the Duce. He speaks about the Hungarian proposal for a three-nation conference, and is against it. This is a far-fetched idea of the restless Count Czaky. On his return from the Palazzo Venezia, in his car, he mentions the position of Attolico. I invite him to talk, and then he says that in Berlin they would now welcome his recall. Obviously: he is an Italian and a gentleman. As his successor, Hitler is thinking of Farinacci and Alfieri. I eliminate the first and dwell upon the second. I am sure that Mussolini will agree to the German wishes.

April 25, 1940

I speak with the Duce on the question of the ambassador to Germany. Mussolini accepts the nomination of Alfieri without any objection, and I accompany the latter to the Palazzo Venezia. The Duce at once gives him some instructions concerning his coming mission to Germany. He repeats his loyalty to the pacts, but regarding war he says that "he will enter it only when he has a quasi-mathematical certainty of winning it." Alfieri leaves the Mappamondo hall convinced that he will have to go slowly and cautiously in Germany.

Giunta[466] in the Chamber has made an inconclusive and vulgar speech of a distinctly pro-German character, and with such absurd implications that it stunned the Chamber. Mussolini, who had approved the first part of it, was struck by the cold atmosphere which the gross Germanic adoration, displayed by Giunta, created in the hall. On the other hand, Pavolini, who was making his debut as a minister, was a big success.

April 26, 1940

Barzini, Jr., was arrested. From one of the usual documents we took from the British embassy it appears that he had informed the British that we have a secret service operating effectively inside the embassy itself, and that he had said that "Mussolini is insane," and that Italian newspapermen hated every line they were compelled to write by the Fascist party. Mussolini is furious and even speaks of the Special Tribunal.

The answer to Reynaud is ready. A cold, cutting, and contemptuous letter. Tomorrow I shall hand it to François-Poncet. Tonight I shall send a copy to von Mackensen. I try to make the letter less harsh, at least in form, but my efforts had meager results, it is clear that the Duce's letter can be used by Reynaud against the remaining pro-Italian Frenchmen as proof of our provocative radicalism. The Duce also sent a brief telephone message to Hitler to advise him to hold on to Narvik at all costs.

I obtained from the Duce the nomination of Attolico to the Holy See. I do not wish to give the Germans the impression that they can so easily liquidate a man of ours who has done his duty very well. Otherwise, God only knows where it will end and who will be the next victim to be sacrificed on the Nazi altar.

April 27, 1940

After all, François-Poncet was neither surprised nor disturbed by Mussolini's answer to Reynaud. He did not know the text of the French letter, and I showed it to him. While he spoke positively of the spirit and the form of the message, he said that it was evidently written by a man who, not knowing Mussolini, thought he could win him over through an appeal to his sentimental side. This is a gravely mistaken idea which Poncet has tried for a long time and unsuccessfully to correct. His government, in turn, was prevented from correcting it by those pro-Italian Frenchmen of Laval's ilk, who are often encouraged by our own Ambassador Guariglia. Mussolini's letter, which he described as "dry," will go a long way to set things straight.

I communicate to Attolico Hitler's stab in the back. He takes it with a great deal of dignity and comes to the conclusion that it is an honor for him to end his mission in this manner. He is glad to go to the Vatican—from the Devil to Holy Water. He confirms briefly his judgment on the German situation: "A short war, a victory for the Reich; a long war, a victory for the Allies."

He tells me that Ribbentrop does not conceal his dislike for me, and that he considers me responsible for Italian non-intervention. I am proud of it.

In Berlin, Ribbentrop makes some declarations, advertised as sensational, on the Norwegian question. On the basis of a first reading it seems to me to be a case of the mountain giving birth to a mouse.

April 28, 1940

Another letter from Hitler to the Duce to bring him up to date on his military successes in Norway. These letters are, in general, of meager importance, but Hitler is a good psychologist and he knows that these messages go straight to Mussolini's heart.

The Pope addressed a letter to the Duce, in which he praises his efforts to keep the peace, and prays that for the future also Italy will stay out of the conflict. Mussolini's reaction to the letter was skeptical, cold, and sarcastic.

April 29, 1940

Mussolini says that the King was against granting the Collar of the Annunziata to Göring, but that, willy-nilly, he will do it in the end. On the other hand, he approved of the reply to Reynaud very much. From the Duce's account it is clear that the conversations between him and the King are anything but cordial. In fact, they are one continuous quarrel, in which the Duce reaffirms with all the impetuous violence of his character the need for the policy he is advocating, and the King, with the prudence that his position and character demand, strives to point out all the dangers such a policy contains. But, on the whole, Mussolini takes little account of the King's judgment, and thinks that the actual strength of the monarchy is negligible. He is convinced that the Italian people follow him [the Duce] and him alone. This morning he praised Blum, who, in an article in *Populaire*, said more or less the same thing.

A long conversation with Helfand, who now is playing the part of an official pro-German badly and weakly. I gave him information of a general character, and avoided any mention of policy which might alter the present situation between the two countries. After all, many Germans remain cool toward Moscow. Bismarck himself was saying yesterday that the Russians must not be trusted for two reasons: because they are Bolshevik, and because they are Russians, and more for the second reason than for the first.

April 30, 1940

Nothing new.

May 1, 1940

Phillips has a message from Roosevelt for the Duce. It is a warning not to enter the war, dressed in polite phrases, but nonetheless clear. If the conflict spreads, some states that intend to remain neutral will need to revise their positions at once. Naturally, Mussolini did not react well to this, considering the fact that Roosevelt is openly in favor of the French and British. At first he said little or nothing to the American ambassador, except to reaffirm the Italian right to a window on the open sea. Then he personally wrote a cutting and hostile answer to Roosevelt, in which he comes to the conclusion that if the Monroe Doctrine works for Americans, it must also be valid for Europeans.

The English have decided to have their ships avoid crossing the Mediterranean. I speak about it to Charles, and do not hide my surprise at a measure that must be a prelude to war. Fortunately, we have not gone that far yet. It is important that London avoid measures increasing the existing nervous tension. Charles agreed, but he was concerned about the speech by the Duce to the Fascist organizations on April 21. At a meeting of the ministers Mussolini reaffirmed his faith in a German victory through the formula he has adopted. "In the struggle between the forces of conservatism and those of revolution, it is always the latter that win."

Mussolini speaks to me again about a *rapprochement* with Russia.

May 2, 1940

The Duce sends a message to Hitler informing him of the situation as it has developed in the last few days. He begins with this premise: "The feeling of the Italian people is unanimously opposed to the Allies." Where does he get this information? Is he really sure of what he writes, or is it not true that, conscious of his personal influence, he is thinking of the right moment to modify the national mood at his whim? Dino Grandi is dissatisfied with the hostile reaction his speech to the Chamber has elicited from London and Paris. He recalls the pro-Axis talk which he gave in London last year, and calls it a blot on his character and on his life as well.[467] He received only three cables: one from Starace, one from Morgagni, and one from an inmate of the insane asylum in Catania, who offered to put the speech into verse for 100 lire.

The first accurate news on the German victory in Norway makes a deep impression. Chamberlain's speech makes an even deeper impression. It is so resignedly pessimistic as to admit the possibility of a German landing in England. Mussolini is exultant. He has nothing but scorn for the despatch of a fleet into the Mediterranean, convinced as he is that the Allies will never take the initiative against us.

May 3, 1940

The news from Norway literally exalts the Duce who, with ever-increasing emphasis, says he is his certain of a German victory. From Berlin come cables that are filled with positive optimism. Von Ribbentrop tells Zamboni[468] that the offensive on the Maginot Line will be as rapid as it is sure. Göring, for the first time, urges Renzetti to hasten our intervention because the war, which he admits he had reasons to be opposed to at the beginning, is now on its way toward speedy victory. I don't believe it. And even if we wanted to intervene, can we do so?

General Soddu says that now even Graziani, concerned about his responsibilities, says he is clearly opposed to any war action on our part, including that in Croatia.

Our greatest deficiency is in artillery. The Italian navy knows the dangerous task that awaits it. The Duce complains of Admiral Cavagnari's lack of
energy. Cavagnari is a gentleman and tells the truth.

Our air force is being built up laboriously. General Aimone Cat, one of
the best technicians, has expressed himself very pessimistically, recognizing
at the same time that what Pricolo has done has brought about some considerable progress. He is even more negative about our antiaircraft. Very
poor weapons, and bad functioning of our support services.

Franco sends a noncommittal message to the Duce, in which he confirms the absolute and unavoidable neutrality of Spain as it prepares to nurse
her wounds.

May 4, 1940

A new letter to the Duce from Hitler, which consists of disconnected
paragraphs. It contains details about the development of the war in Norway.
Hitler complains about the excessive speed of victory, which did not allow
him to draw in the English forces more effectively to destroy them completely. For the first time the tone of the letter is sarcastic regarding the
military capabilities of the Allies. He concludes by saying that he intends to
have victory in the west as soon as possible, and that he is impelled to do
this by hidden threats of American intervention.

May 5, 1940

I spend the day at Leghorn. I wanted to kneel down before Father and
Maria. Beautiful weather; from the windows of my home we could see Cape
Corse almost within reach. And yet at Leghorn, too, and even on the part of
those who are most enthusiastic, the Mediterranean question is not very
deeply felt. Never deeply enough anyway, to justify a war.

May 6, 1940

Audience with the King in order to obtain his signature for the laws that
have been passed. His Majesty speaks today about his opposition to Germany, not very strongly, but with a good deal of moderation, and says that
in his opinion the Italian military machine is still very weak. He advises
going slow. For this reason the King recommends our remaining as long as
possible in our present position of watchful waiting and preparation. He
has decided to give the Collar of the Annunziata to Göring, but rather unwillingly. Mussolini, who conferred with him about the matter, said: "Your
Majesty, it's perhaps a lemon that you must swallow, but everything advises
us to make such a gesture at this time."

Conference with Christich. His government receives the declarations I
made the other day with a sigh of relief. I believe that the situation will force
us to keep to them for a long period of time.

May 7, 1940

Nothing new.

May 8, 1940

Percy Loraine has returned from London. From what he says, his instructions are to do everything he possibly can to safeguard relations between Italy and Great Britain "honorably and in good faith." He mentions the fact that our press campaigns have already strengthened the conviction in large sections of English public opinion that Fascist Italy is to be numbered among its enemies. This is serious, especially when the time comes to settle accounts at the end of the war, which he is sure will end victoriously for his country. I have spoken frankly with him about our policy. The Duce intends to be true to the pacts that bind him to Berlin, but this does not mean that in the near future we are going to abandon our non-belligerency. These statements, ordered by Mussolini, disturbed Sir Percy, who, unfortunately, did not leave reassured. However, he remained very calm and altogether certain about the English future.

I give von Mackensen a record of the meeting of the British ministers in the Balkans, which was obtain in the usual way from the English embassy. I also speak of the ceremony for conferring the Collar of the Annunziata on Göring. We can have it take place on May 22 at the Brenner Pass, which will save me a speech and a solemn ceremony of reaffirmation of the Alliance—a task I find difficult and displeasing.

May 9, 1940

During the ceremony at the Tomb of the Unknown Soldier I spoke with Badoglio, who now is less anti-German than before, since the Norwegian victory has had its effect on him even while he still defends non-belligerency fanatically. In his opinion, an attack on the Maginot Line would not be successful; he knows the Maginot Line personally, and believes that a breakthrough would require six months' action and the sacrifice of a million men. In talking to me about Badoglio, Mussolini said that he has convinced the marshal of his thesis, as he had done before. I do not think this is so. In the face of the German successes, Badoglio is more cautious; but I do not believe he is convinced.

Anfuso reports that Princess Bismarck, with whom he is on very friendly terms, told him with tears in her eyes that Germany is lost, that Hitler has ruined the country and its people. She spoke so convincingly that Anfuso suspected her of being an *agent provocateur*, but then many things in what she said led him to change his mind. She used even stronger words against Ribbentrop and his policy.

May 10, 1940

This is for history: yesterday I dined poorly at the German embassy. A long and boring after-dinner conversation, as varied as one can have it with the Germans. Not a word about the situation. When we got out at half past midnight von Mackensen said that "*perhaps* he would have to disturb me during the night with a communication that he expected from Berlin," and took my private telephone number. At 4 a.m. he called me to say that within three quarters of an hour he would come to see me and together we would go to see the Duce, as he had had orders to confer with him at exactly 5 a.m. He would say nothing over the telephone about the reasons for the meeting. When he arrived at my house he had a large package of papers with him which certainly could not have arrived by telephone. He muttered with much embarrassment some excuse about a diplomatic courier who had remained at the hotel until he got the "go" sign from Berlin.

Together we went to see the Duce, who, forewarned by me, had already got up. We found the Duce calm and smiling. He read Hitler's note, which listed the reasons for the action, and concluded with a kind invitation to Mussolini to make the decisions he considers necessary for the future of his country. Then the Duce examined the accompanying papers for a long time. Finally, after almost two hours, he told Mackensen that he was convinced that France and England were preparing to attack Germany through Belgium and Holland. He approved of Hitler's action wholeheartedly.

After Mackensen left, the Duce repeated to me his certainty about the rapid success of the Nazi armies, as well as his decision to intervene. I did not fail to repeat that, for the time being, we should wait and see. This is a long-drawn-out affair, longer than we can possibly foresee now. He didn't deign to answer me. My remarks only annoyed him. During the morning I saw him many times and, alas, found that his idea of going to war was growing stronger and stronger. Edda, too, has been at the Palazzo Venezia and, ardent as she is, told her father that the country wants war, and that to continue our attitude of neutrality would be dishonorable for Italy. That is the kind of talk Mussolini wants to hear, the only kind he takes seriously.

I confer with Poncet, Loraine, and Phillips. They want news regarding the Italian attitude. They are rather skeptical and pessimistic. From certain intercepted telephone messages it appears that they are expecting our intervention at any moment. I try to calm them down and partially succeed. On the other hand, they are well aware of my thinking and how I am sincerely trying to postpone the intervention.

Poncet is rather downcast. He has a tired air, red eyes, and is unusually unkempt in his attire. Loraine is cold and determined. With an emphasis that is startling in such a phlegmatic and courteous gentleman he asserts that Germany will be destroyed. For an instant all the determination of his race surfaced in his eyes and words. Phillips said that what has happened is bound to stir America profoundly. He made no prophecies, but I should not be surprised if the United States immediately broke relations with Germany as a prelude to intervention. And the United States is a very important factor to consider, although erroneous judgments are generally made about her.

Mussolini is preparing a message to answer Hitler which is warm but not such as to commit us. I ask him to delete a phrase in which he associates himself with an accusation against the Allies to the effect that they were threatening Belgian neutrality. He listens to me and makes the change.

In leaving for Florence, Edda comes to see me and talks about immediate intervention, about the need to fight, about honor and dishonor. I listen with impersonal courtesy. It's a shame that she, who is so intelligent, also refuses to reason. I think she does well to go to the Florentine musical festival, where she can more profitably busy herself with music.

I saw the Belgian ambassador and the Dutch minister. They are sad but dignified, and both express themselves with much faith in the ability of their countries to resist. General Soddu, on the contrary, maintains that the struggle on the Belgian-Dutch line will amount to nothing, while French defense will be absolutely unbreakable. He is, in any event, of the opinion that we should not take any initiative for at least a month after the beginning of the offensive.

I saw Pavelic. The Croatian situation is getting ripe and if we delay too long the Croats will line up with Germany. Now I shall prepare a map showing the precise positions of the forces and their most urgent needs. Then we shall go to the execution phase. I have not set a definite moment; in fact, I recommended that we avoid any premature start of hostilities. We have received proof of the fact that Bombelles is a traitor on Belgrade's payroll and he will suffer the merciless law of the Ustasche.

I report the conversation to the Duce. He says that we must act quickly. He makes notes on his calendar, somewhere near the first part of June, and decides to call Gambara back from Spain to take command of the forces that will carry out the breakthrough.

No direct news from the battlefront, but from all that we hear it appears that things are going well for the Germans. What is especially surprising is the lack of Allied action in the air, while the others are bombing a hundred places.

Churchill replacing Chamberlain is seen here with complete indifference. The Duce views it with irony.

May 11, 1940

During the night some Fascists beat up an English official who had torn down an anti-British poster, and Sir Percy Loraine came to me this morning to discuss the incident. Since he had a rather haughty attitude, very much in contrast to our excellent personal relations, I answered the same way, refusing to give any explanation; on the other hand, emphasizing the fact that, while the British army is fighting hard, English officials had better go to bed, rather than wander around bars until four o'clock in the morning. We parted so frostily that I thought it necessary to inform the Duce, because of possible future developments. But this evening Loraine telephoned me, friendly as usual, closing the matter.

Nothing new here. Today Mussolini is less bellicose than he was yesterday, and more inclined to wait. It seems that the Italian General Staff has thrown very timely cold water on our present military prospects. Even Balbo has told me that we cannot gear up before two months, and before having received a specific amount of arms and supplies.

May 12, 1940

The cables sent by the Pope to the rulers of the three invaded states have incensed Mussolini, who would like to curb the Vatican, and is inclined to go to extremes.[469] In these last few days he often repeats that the papacy is a cancer which gnaws at our national life, and that he intends, if necessary, to liquidate this problem once and for all. He added: "The Pope need not think that he can seek an alliance with the monarchy because I am ready to get rid of them both at the same time. The seven cities of Romagna will be sufficient to knock out King and Pope together."

I do not share this policy of the Duce, because, if he intends to wage war, he must not provoke a crisis with the Church. The Italian people are Catholic but not bigoted. Superficially, maybe, they scorn the Church, but they are religious at heart, and especially in times of peril they draw closer to the altars. I believe that it is indispensable for us to avoid any clash, and for this reason I give Alfieri instructions to take a step that will not have any of the controversial character the Duce wanted to give it.

The King sends word that he will give the Collar of the Annunziata to Göring, but, nevertheless, he wishes to avoid sending a congratulatory cable and the notification. I shall try to find a way out. His Majesty desires that his wish be kept secret from Mussolini.

May 13, 1940

Mussolini began to talk as follows: "Some months ago I said that the Allies had lost the victory. Today I tell you that they have lost the war. We Italians are already sufficiently dishonored. Any delay is inconceivable. We have no time to lose. Within a month I shall declare war. I shall attack France and England in the air and on the sea. I am no longer thinking of taking up arms against Yugoslavia because it would be a humiliating replacement." Today, for the first time, I did not answer. Unfortunately, I can do nothing now to hold the Duce back. He has decided to act, and act he will. He believes in German success and in the swiftness of that success. Only a new turn in military events can induce him to alter his decision, but for the time being things are going so badly for the Allies that there is no hope.

Alfieri has spoken to the Pope. He will prepare a written report, meanwhile he stresses the fact that he found a clear-cut uncompromising attitude within the Church. The Pope has said that "he is even ready to be deported to a concentration camp, but will do nothing against his conscience."

I see Poncet and Loraine. No discussion of any importance. Tentative soundings more than anything else. I try not to increase their fears, but I honestly do not wish to hide the fact that the situation is growing more serious.

May 14, 1940

Letter from Hitler to the Duce. A long and calm account of military events. It is a message full of assurances: victories on land, and, above all, victories in the air, which the Germans at this time dominate completely.

Naturally, all this can only influence the Duce to intervene. He has also announced to von Mackensen his decision to join the struggle soon. "It is now no longer a question of months, it is a question of weeks and perhaps days." I, at least, hope that it is more a matter of weeks than of days, for although the fortunes of war are favoring the Germans, it is too soon to count our eggs and before making a supreme decision we must remember that Italy is not ready for war, or at least is ready for a very short war. A mistake in timing would be fatal to us.

The Duce informs me that General Soddu has spoken to the King about the question of the Italian supreme command, which Mussolini wants to assume personally. It seems that His Majesty has resisted strongly, basing his right to decide on the constitution. However, he finally consented to a compromise, meaning a delegation of powers. Mussolini showed irritation. He said clearly that after the war was won he intended to get rid of a monarchy which he does not like and whose weight he can no longer tolerate.

May 15, 1940

Roosevelt sends a message to the Duce. The tone has changed. It is no longer as it was the first time, in a covertly threatening style. It is rather a discouraged and conciliatory message. He mentions the Gospel of Christ, but these are arguments that have little effect upon the mind of Mussolini, especially today, when he is convinced that victory is within his reach. It will take more than this to move him.

Great excitement over the news of the breakthrough of the Maginot Line at Sedan. It is a piece of news that doesn't convince me completely, and I believe that it is dangerous to exaggerate information of secondary importance. Public opinion has now improved because of German victories, but the real feelings of the people have not changed.

Naturally, in political circles, one witnesses a headlong rush to show credentials of being for the war and having pro-German sympathies, and so forth. It would be laughable if the optimistic bits of news we receive were followed by others less good.

May 16, 1940

The news was, in truth, very much exaggerated. The breaching of the Maginot Line has become a breakthrough! The proof is that during the evening Sir Percy sent a British report on the operations of a rather optimistic flavor. I show it to the Duce, who is impressed, although his nature compels him to believe only news which is favorable to his own longings. Nevertheless, during the day he has shown himself to be less anxious to set fire to the powder keg.

The conference that he had with the King has also irritated him. His Majesty still maintains an obstructionist attitude with reference to intervention, saying that public opinion is overwhelmingly against it. He raised numerous objections on the issue of military command, although he yielded in the end.

Loraine brings a message from Churchill to the Duce. It is a message of good will, couched in vague terms, but nonetheless dignified and noble. Even Mussolini appreciates its tone, and he means to answer that, like England, he, too, intends to remain true to his word. An increasing uneasiness in the Vatican on account of the daily incidents caused, above all, by interference with the sale of the *Osservatore Romano*. The Papal Nuncio calls attention to these matters in a conversation with me, during which I was able to offer him only kind and vague words.

May 17, 1940

News from the French front speaks of an overwhelming German advance. Saint Quentin has been taken, and Paris is directly threatened from there. We still lack confirmation from French sources, just as we lack details on the depth of the penetration of the lines. However, all this leads one to believe that it is a very serious situation. Italian public opinion (I mean honest opinion, not the clownish politicians, who have become exaggeratedly pro-German) reacts in a strange way to this news: admiration for the Germans, a wishful belief in the rapid conclusion of the war, and, above all, a great concern about the future. Mussolini is calm and at least until now has shown no desire to hasten intervention.

Von Mackensen proposes an exchange of cables between me and von Ribbentrop on the occasion of the anniversary of the pacts, and speaks of the bestowal of the Collar of the Annunziata on Göring; it can be presented by Alfieri. But Marshal Göring insists on a cable from the King. I fear that the present situation will not allow any alternative. The King must do it.

May 18, 1940

News of the conflict is increasingly favorable to the Germans: Brussels has fallen, Antwerp is destroyed, columns of tanks running through France up to Soissons, followed, it seems, by German infantry. However, our military staff is withholding its opinion. General Soddu does not think it is a decisive battle and asks for two more weeks before passing judgment.

I give Sir Percy Loraine the Duce's answer to Churchill. It is brief and needlessly harsh in tone. Loraine receives it without comment. In turn, he gives me his usual information on the military situation, which the English continue to present in incredibly rosy colors.

François-Poncet is more concerned. He believes that during the last few hours the situation has improved, but he knows that the fate of France is at stake. He is concerned about our attitude and says that he does not "consider that it is in Italy's interest to see France crushed." He refuses likewise to believe that Mussolini will want to rob Stalin of the glory of striking at a fallen man.

Without saying anything I hand Phillips the brief and dry answer to Roosevelt's message. He receives it without comment. Tomorrow I am going to Cremona and Milan. Mussolini orders me to give a clear hint of our coming intervention, as well as to indicate unequivocally that he will also be "the only leader" of the nation at war—both as civilian and military head.

May 19, 1940

Cremona. Milan. Very warm welcome in both cities. But in Milan mention of intervention made in my brief speech, while received with enthusiasm by the Fascist militiamen, is greeted with limited enthusiasm by the great masses of the people. I have the impression that Milan, which hates the Germans tenaciously, considers entry into the war, even under present conditions, as an unwelcome necessity.

May 20, 1940

I report to the Duce on my Milan visit, and he agrees with my opinion on the situation. Today he does not speak of intervention. He fully approves the text of the speeches delivered by me yesterday along the line of his suggestions.

Mackensen mentions the possibility of a *rapprochement* between us and Russia, through Ribbentrop. I answer that there is no objection on our part, provided the Russians take the initiative by sending back their ambassador. They started the break and they will have to make the first move.

War news continues to favor the Germans. They captured General Giraud, together with his staff. François-Poncet spoke to me of him a few days ago as the great hope of France, and predicted that he would be Gamelin's successor.

All this makes a great impression on many Italians, even those whose attitude is unexpected. Even Dino Grandi came to see me, and said quite dramatically, "We should admit that we were wrong in everything and prepare ourselves for the new times ahead." I did not share his change of heart; not because I am stubborn, but because, in spite of everything, my opinions have not changed. The worth of a horse is tested in a long race, and nobody can imagine how long this race will be.

May 21, 1940

The King is nervous. This morning I went to the Royal Palace to accompany the Albanian mission, which has come to bring the Address in Reply to the Speech of the Crown. The King almost attacked me on the question of the Collar of the Annunziata for Göring. He said, "This thing has gone all wrong. To give Göring the Collar is a gesture that displeases me, and to send him a cable is distasteful for a hundred thousand reasons." On the military situation His Majesty expressed himself negatively about the Germans.

I talked to the Duce of the need to clearly present our aspirations to the Germans. If we really must leap headlong into war, we must make a specific deal. Even today the war remains for me an adventure with many frightening and unknown factors. I know these fellows too well, and I trust their written agreements very little and their word not at all. After the first of June I might see Ribbentrop and draw up a report on what our share should be at the end of the war.

May 22, 1940

I leave for Albania. I arrive at Durazzo and Tirana. A very warm welcome. The Albanians are far along on the path of intervention. They want Kosovo and Ciamuria. It is easy for us to increase our popularity by becoming champions of Albanian nationalism.

May 23, 1940

I visit Scutari and Rubico. A very promising copper mine. The public works that I visited this morning are also satisfactory. Everywhere a warm welcome.

There is no question that the mass of the people is now won over by Italy. The Albanian people are grateful to us for having taught them to eat twice a day, for this rarely happened before. Even in the physical appearance of the people one can see improved living conditions.

May 24, 1940

I mingled with the workers at Ragosina. Italian laborers mix well with the Albanians. We find the greatest difficulties in the Italian middle classes, who treat the natives badly and who have a colonial mentality. Unfortunately, this is also true of military officers, and, according to Jacomoni, especially of their wives.

May 25, 1940

Stopped at Butrinto. Very beautiful. The Canal of Corfu. Port Edda. I returned to Italy.

In Brindisi, at Bari, and later at every station, I receive a hearty welcome. The people want to know what will happen, and I hear many voices calling for war. This never happened up to a few days ago.

May 26, 1940

I report to the Duce on my trip which, on the whole, has been satisfactory. Mussolini discusses his disagreement with the King on the issue of the military command during the war. It seems that before yielding to the Duce the King put up considerable resistance.

Hitler has addressed another letter to the Duce and Alfieri sent a report on his conference with Göring. The latter raised the question of the date of our intervention and suggested our attacking when, after the liquidation of the British-French-Belgian strongholds, the Germans can throw the whole weight of their power on Paris. The Duce agrees in principle. He plans to write a letter to Hitler announcing our intervention for the latter part of June.

May 27, 1940

Long conferences with François-Poncet and Phillips. The latter was the bearer of a message from Roosevelt for the Duce, but was not received and speaks with me instead. I have made a stenographic report of our interview. In short, Roosevelt offers to become the mediator between us and the Allies, becoming personally responsible for the execution, after the war, of any eventual agreements. I answer Phillips that Roosevelt is off track. It takes more than that to dissuade Mussolini. In fact, it is not that he wants to obtain this or that; what he wants is war, and, even if he were to obtain double what he claims by peaceful means, he would refuse.

My conference with Poncet is also important, not because of its results, but as a psychological indication. He made some very precise overtures. Except for Corsica, which is "an integral part of France," he said that we can make a deal about Tunisia and perhaps even about Algeria. I answered that he, too, like Phillips, is coming too late, and reminded him of the time when France, in 1938, objected to our having even those four reefs which England had ceded to us in the Red Sea. Once more the French have been, as Machiavelli says, "more niggardly than cautious."

Poncet recognizes the faults of the French, attacks the governments of the past, and blames most of it on Léger, whom he calls a "sinister man." The conversation, naturally, was kept on an academic level.

May 28, 1940

My conference with Poncet, who is the picture of distress, and the events of the night (the Belgian capitulation) led Mussolini to speed up his planning, as he is convinced that things are now coming to a head, and he wants to create enough claims to be entitled to his share of the spoils. This is all very well regarding France. But England is still standing. And America? The Duce talks of June 10.

I see Christich; he is terrified and would like to know if we will attack his country. I can only partially reassure him. A painful conference with Sir Percy Loraine. He had come to discuss the issue of the blockade and complained about the interruption of the negotiations. I answered that all this was useless because we are on the brink of war. Although prepared for it, he did not expect such a brutal blow and grew pale. Then he recovered his bearings. "If you choose the sword, it will be the sword that will decide the future. It is good to establish this in connection with responsibilities for the war." Then he continued, changing tone, "We shall answer war with war, but, notwithstanding this, my heart is filled with sadness to think that blood must flow between our countries." I answered that this was very sad for me, too, but that I could not see any other way out.

On the situation in Flanders he expressed himself as follows: "If the Allies win, the war will end in a year. If the Germans win, it will last more than three years. But this will not change the end, which will be our victory." He spoke with firmness, but his face was very sad and his eyes at times were dim.

May 29, 1940

Today at eleven the High Command was inaugurated at the Palazzo Venezia! Rarely have I seen Mussolini so happy. He has realized his real dream: that of becoming the military leader of the country at war. Under him will be Badoglio, Graziani, Pricolo, and Cavagnari. The decision is about to be taken; after June 5 any day may be good. I reported to the Duce on my conferences of yesterday, and advised him to give solemn assurances to Yugoslavia as to our neutrality, and especially evidence that we have no interest in setting the match to the Balkan powder keg. After the war is won we can obtain what we want anyway. He authorizes me to act in this way, and therefore I talked to Christich, who, having been called suddenly, came to my room as pale as a ghost, but he left comforted.

Badoglio now appears ready to make the best of it, and is preparing for war. He still tries to gain some days in order to examine the French situation more clearly, because he thinks that there may be some surprises. He is concerned about Libya, where a French move might have a chance of success. However, the war must be short. Not more than two or three months, at least, according to Favagrossa, who is a pessimist, because our supplies are frighteningly low. We literally don't have some metals. On the eve of the war—and what a war!—we have only 100 tons of nickel.

May 30, 1940

The decision has been taken. The die is cast. Today Mussolini gave me his message to Hitler about our entry into the war. The date chosen is June 5, unless Hitler himself considers it convenient to postpone it for a few days. The message is sent in cipher to Ambassador Alfieri at Berlin with orders to deliver it to Hitler personally. At the same time I inform von Mackensen; although he was already prepared, the ambassador was overjoyed by the news. He had words of admiration for the Duce and praised my decision to take part in the war as a pilot. "In Germany," he said, "the higher-ups in the Party have not set a good example. Baldur von Schirach, at least until now, has been safely tucked away in the rear."

Mussolini plans to speak to the people on the afternoon of June 4. One hour before this I am to announce a state of war to Poncet and Loraine. The Duce wanted to omit "this formality." I insisted on it in order at least to observe the forms.

The minister of Egypt, speaking for himself, discusses an eventual proclamation of neutrality by his government. I encourage him. I do not believe that Egyptian neutrality would make a great deal of difference in the game, but, nevertheless, it might provide some advantage.

May 31, 1940

Another move by Roosevelt, this time more energetic. After reminding us of the traditional interest of his country in the Mediterranean, he states that Italy's intervention in the war would bring about an increase in armaments by the United States and a multiplying of help in resources and materiel to the Allies. I reserve my answer until I have conferred with Mussolini, but tell Phillips offhand that Roosevelt's new attempt will suffer the fate of his preceding attempts and will not move the Duce.

Alfieri telephones that he has transmitted the message to Hitler, who was "glad, in fact enthusiastic," and has reserved to himself the right of letting us know, after having conferred with his generals, whether the date chosen is satisfactory. I submit the draft of a communiqué for the declaration of war to the Duce. He approves it but advises my talking to the King about it, since the latter is sensitive and, besides, according to the constitution, it is up to him to declare war. Daladier delivers a note to Guariglia. No definite proposal, but many openings. It states clearly that every attempt will be made to avoid war, but Mussolini refuses to take it into consideration; in fact, he decides that he will not even answer it.

June 1, 1940
An audience with the King. He approves the formula that I submit to him. He has now resigned himself to the idea of war. He believes that France and England have actually been inflicted by some tremendously hard blows, but, with good reason, he attributes great importance to the eventual intervention of the United States. He feels that the country is going to war without enthusiasm. There is interventionist propaganda, but there is not in the least the kind of enthusiasm we had in 1915. "Those who talk of a short and easy war are fools. There are still many unknown factors, and the horizon is very different from that of May 1915." The King ended on those words.

Christich reports Belgrade's satisfaction at the communication of the other day, and gives the fullest assurances of complete and almost benevolent neutrality.

I gave Phillips the Duce's answer. Briefly, it is as follows: America has no further interests in the Mediterranean than Italy has in the Caribbean. Therefore, it is beside the point for Roosevelt to insist; in fact, he should remember that his pressures can only stiffen Mussolini's stand.

Mackensen brings Hitler's written reply to the Duce. The news of our intervention is received by the Chancellor with enthusiasm. He asks, however, that the date be changed by a few days, this because he intends to make a decisive attack on French airfields. He fears that the beginning of the Italian action might cause a reshuffling of the French air forces, interfering with his plan of destruction. In principle the Duce agrees, because the postponement is useful to round out our preparations in Libya. He prefers the eleventh to the eighth, since the former is "a date of good omen for him."

Poncet speaks to me about Daladier's note. From my answers he understands that there is no longer ground for nurturing hopes and illusions. Mussolini's choice will be imposed by the sword. Poncet does not insist on a reply. In fact, if the reply is to be in any way quarrelsome, better to have none at all, because, in any event, "there will always be a future, and we must not think that contacts between France and Italy will no longer be necessary after the war." He says nothing about the situation. He believes that the game is not over, and that the two great battles that Hitler must fight—the battle of Paris and above, all the battle of London—may still bring many surprises.

Bottai, who is one of the few who has not lost his head, proposed to me on the golf course today that in the face of so much official interventionism we form a new party: the "Party of the Interventionists in Bad Faith."

June 2, 1940

The Duce drafts his reply to Hitler. While the postponement is useful, especially to complete military preparations in Libya, Mussolini, who had already set June 5 as the day, is annoyed at having to change it. He selects June 11.

During the evening Mackensen urgently asks for an interview and, on Hitler's behalf, withdraws the reservations made in the previous communication; in fact, it seems that now an earlier intervention would be most welcome. This is not possible now. We have moved several divisions, and a declaration of war before June 11 would catch us during the movement. June 11 is confirmed as the final date; we only need Hitler to answer "go ahead." Having taken this decision, Mussolini becomes, as always after a decision, calm, tranquil and sure of himself.

I saw Balbo in the evening for a long talk. He is preparing to return to Libya. He has made up his mind to do the best he can, but he does not believe that the war will be quick and easy. The weapons at his disposal are sufficient only for a short conflict. What if the war should be long? At any rate, he is a soldier, and he will fight with energy and determination. Naturally, he doesn't withdraw a single one of his objections to the Axis policy. Balbo does not discuss the Germans. He hates them. And it is this incurable hatred which guides his reasoning.

June 3, 1940

Alfieri cables Hitler's "O.K." In reality the bombing of Paris and of other French airfields proves that Hitler has already started to move.

Mussolini says that the King, also, finds the date of the 11th satisfactory, perhaps because of the slight delay that will be granted to us, because it is his birthday, and because as a young recruit he was given the number 1,111. Now that the sword is about to be drawn, the King, like all members of the House of Savoy, is preparing to be a soldier, and only a soldier.

Percy Loraine comes to see me on the pretext of small daily matters. We already talk as representatives of two countries in conflict, even though our own personal relations are excellent. He is sad but calm. He realizes that the next two or three months will be extremely critical for the Allies. But if they can hold out, Germany is lost. He would like to participate personally in the war. I answer that I have no desire to discuss the matter. Now that my country is in the war, or will be soon, I do not wish to discuss his conjectures, nor can I tolerate such a discussion.

June 4, 1940

A meeting of the Council of Ministers. While all were expecting great sensational political announcements, the Duce coquettishly gave today's meeting "a strictly administrative character, such as it has never had in eighteen years." No declaration. Only at the beginning of the meeting Mussolini said, "This is the last Council of Ministers during peacetime," and took up the agenda.

I have chosen my military position in the war. I shall take command of a bomber squadron in Pisa. I have chosen this airfield because it is closest to Corsica, and because it is dear to me to fight where I was born and where my father rests in peace. The Duce approved my decision to join up as well as that of leaving Rome for Pisa, because he prefers that I become "a soldier-minister" rather than a "minister-soldier."

June 5, 1940

The Germans have attacked on the line of the Somme. As of now, information is lacking, but everybody is convinced that they will cross it quickly. French morale has not yet improved, and the defensive organization is necessarily incomplete. Have we reached the decisive battle?

As far as we are concerned, nothing has changed in our program. Only this, that the Duce, though he had previously been thinking of launching an air attack against France as a beginning, has now decided to bomb British ports in the Mediterranean and to remain as an observer toward France, unless, he concluded, "before Monday they [the French] have been subjected to a new attack by the Germans and our action against them will serve to finish the work."

June 6, 1940

I find the Duce angry at the King over the question of the supreme command. He had hoped that the King would yield it without difficulty. Instead, His Majesty has written a letter in which he repeats that he assumes the command, while at the same time entrusting to Mussolini the political and military conduct of the war. Mussolini finds this "an ambiguous formula through which he is given what he has virtually had for eighteen years." A great disappointment for the Duce, who plans to write the King that it is better to leave things as they are, and he adds, "After the war is over I shall tell Hitler to do away with all of these absurd anachronisms in the form of monarchies."

Little news about the battle of the Somme. The Germans are gaining ground, but a real breakthrough does not seem to have occurred. The French, now that they are on their own soil, fight with their traditional bravery, even if their hopes have in large part vanished. The reshuffling of the Reynaud cabinet has been interpreted as a sign of political collapse.

June 7, 1940

Nothing new in Italy. On the French front the struggle continues to be extremely harsh. Although the French have had to retreat in a number of places, there are yet no signs of an actual breakthrough. The public is following the events of this battle with unprecedented anxiety. It knows that on the Somme decisive cards are being played for the history of the world.

Almost a farewell visit from Percy Loraine. He is sad and feels intensely the gravity of the hour for his country, but he speaks with unshakable firmness about a fight to the finish, confirming his faith in victory "because the

British are not in the habit of being beaten." He is personally worried about his trip home, but I have taken every precaution to insure him and his associates perfect treatment. He is also worried about a colt he must leave behind in Italy.

June 8, 1940

The battle continues. New German successes, but still one cannot speak of a breakthrough at the front. French resistance is becoming tenacious, stubborn, heroic. Mussolini reads me the speech he will make on Monday, at 6 p.m., when the nation shall be called to listen. It is an appeal to the people in Mussolini's best classical style, in which he briefly outlines the reasons for our intervention.

The Duce is following the battle in progress with anxiety, and is happy over the resistance of the French because "the Germans are finally being weakened and will not reach the end of the war too fresh and too strong." We agree to return Ambassador Rosso to Moscow and the Soviet ambassador to Rome. Ribbentrop will be happy about this, since it was one of the great objectives of his policy. Still, there is something not entirely clear in the Kremlin's conduct toward Germany.

June 9, 1940

A rapid German advance appears to be deciding the fate of the battle irrevocably. In Badoglio's judgment, the battle will still be long and hard, because of the terrain.

The Duce was angry at the Germans this morning, because, having intercepted a telephone call, he found out that Ribbentrop had the cheek to ask for the text of Mussolini's speech. "He is the same arrogant boor," said the Duce. "I am not his servant, and I do not intend to be."

Poncet comes to say good-by. He is sad and depressed, and at this stage he admits that his country is beaten. He personally would accept a separate peace, but does not know his government's intentions. A separate peace would probably be the lesser of two evils. The continuation of the war will be a frightful destruction of civilization, of riches, of life. Poncet wept, but he stated that France wishes to save at least its military honor in a hopeless struggle, three against one, five against one. We said good-by with an emotion that neither of us was able to conceal. Poncet is a man like us: he is a Latin.

Mackensen brings the Duce a message received by air from Hitler. His best wishes for our coming into the war. He accepts the offer of the Bersaglieri, and will send, in exchange, some regiments of his Alpine troops. He describes with cool optimism the various phases of the battle of France.

June 10, 1940

Declaration of war. First I received Poncet, who tried not to show his emotion. I told him, "You probably understood the reason for your being called." He answered, with a fleeting smile, "Although I am not very intelligent, I have understood this time." After having listened to the declaration of war, he replied, "It is blow with a dagger to a man who has already fallen. I thank you nonetheless for using a velvet glove," he continued, saying that he had foreseen all this for two years, and that he no longer hoped that he could avoid it after the signing of the Pact of Steel. He was unable to consider me an enemy, nor could he consider any Italian an enemy. However, as for the future it was necessary to find some formula for European life, he hoped that an unbridgeable chasm would not be created between Italy and France. "The Germans are hard masters. You, too, will learn this." I did not answer. This did not seem to me the time for discussion. "Don't get yourself killed," he concluded, pointing to my aviator's uniform, and he clasped my hand.

Sir Percy Loraine was more laconic and inscrutable. He received my communication without batting an eye or changing color. He limited himself to writing down the exact formula I used and asked me if he was to consider it as advance information or as a general declaration of war. Learning that it was the latter, he withdrew with dignity and courtesy. At the door we exchanged a long and cordial handshake.

Mussolini speaks from the balcony of the Palazzo Venezia. The news of the war does not surprise anyone and does not arouse very much enthusiasm. I am sad, very sad. The adventure begins. May God help Italy.

June 11, 1940

A meeting of the Council of Ministers. Some war measures relating to finance and justice are rapidly adopted. The Duce wants our legislation to conform to that of the Germans.

I leave for Pisa by plane, where I take command of a group of bombers assigned to me. The first day of the war passes very peacefully on this happy yet rugged coast of Antignano.

June 15, 1940

I fly as far as Nice looking for French ships which had bombed Genoa. Very bad weather; dangerous flying. I return after two hours without having sighted the enemy.

June 16, 1940

Bombing of Calvi.

June 17, 1940

Bombing of Borgo, the airport of Bastia. Accurate targeting. The French reaction is also active and accurate. On my return to the field I am told that Reynaud has fallen and that Pétain has taken his place. This means peace. In fact, Anfuso telephones me to return to Rome at once in order to leave for Munich that evening. The French have asked for an armistice, and Hitler, before dictating his terms, wants to confer with the Duce.

I find Mussolini dissatisfied. This sudden peace disquiets him. During the trip we speak at length in order to clarify conditions under which the armistice is to be granted to the French. The Duce is an extremist. He would like to go so far as the total occupation of French territory and demands the surrender of the French fleet. But he is aware that his opinion has only a consultative value. The war has been won by Hitler without any active military participation on Italy's part, and it is Hitler who will have the last word. This, naturally, disturbs and saddens him. His reflections on the Italian people, and, above all, on our armed forces, are extremely bitter this evening.

June 18-19, 1940

During the trip by train the German welcome is very warm. At Munich a meeting with Hitler and von Ribbentrop. The Duce and the Führer are locked in conference. Von Ribbentrop is exceptionally moderate and calm, and in favor of peace. He says at once that we must offer lenient armistice terms to France, especially concerning the fleet; this is to avoid having the French fleet join the English. From the words of von Ribbentrop I feel that the mood has changed also regarding England. If London wants war it will be a total war, complete, pitiless. But Hitler makes many reservations on the desirability of dismantling the British Empire, which he considers, even today, to be an important factor in world equilibrium. I ask von Ribbentrop a clear-cut question, "Do you prefer the continuation of the war, or peace?" He does not hesitate a moment. "Peace." He also alludes to vague contacts between London and Berlin through Sweden. I speak of our requests with respect to France. In general I find him understanding, but von Ribbentrop does not want to push the conversation further because he does not know as yet Hitler's precise ideas. He says only that there is a German project to round up and send the Jews to Madagascar.

The conference then continued with Hitler, Mussolini, and the military authorities. In principle the terms of the armistice with France are set. Mussolini shows himself to be quite intransigent regarding the fleet.

Hitler, on the other hand, wants to prevent an uprising of the French navy in favor of the English. From all that he says it is clear that he wants to act quickly to end it all. Hitler is now like the gambler who, having made a big win, would like to leave the table, risking nothing more. Today he speaks with a restraint and an insight which, after such a victory, are really astonishing. I cannot be accused of excessive tenderness toward him, but today I truly admire him.

Mussolini is extremely embarrassed. He feels that he is playing a secondary role. He tells me about his conference with Hitler, not without a note of bitterness and irony, and concludes by saying that the German people have, in themselves, the germs of a collapse because a formidable internal clash will appear, smashing everything. In truth, the Duce fears that the hour of peace is growing near and sees that once again that unattainable dream of his life: glory on the field of battle is fading away.

June 20, 1940

The French have appointed the same delegates to deal with us who were sent to deal with Germany, and they ask whether negotiations can take place contemporaneously at the same time and place. This was also our idea at Munich. But Hitler was against it and specifically asked for "two commissions." The Duce thinks that he sees in this a psychological reason, mainly, that Hitler did not want the French to face Italians and Germans on the same level.

Mussolini decided yesterday to attack the French in the Alps. Badoglio was energetically opposed, but the Duce insisted. Then I spoke to him. I consider it rather inglorious to fall upon a defeated army and I find it morally dangerous also. The armistice is at hand, and if our army should not overcome resistance during the first assault, we would end our campaign with a terrible failure. Mussolini listened to me, and it seems that he will limit the attack to a small sector near the Swiss border. He was persuaded to do this also by a telephone interception of a conversation between Generals Roatta and Pintor, in which the latter declared that he is completely unprepared to carry out an attack tomorrow. This happens after nine months of waiting, and with the French reduced as they are! Had we entered the war in September what would have happened? Mussolini is very indignant with Balbo, who in Cyrenaica has met with a series of failures already, notwithstanding the large number of men and materiel at his disposal.

June 21, 1940

Alfieri transmits the German armistice terms. I examine them with the Duce and Badoglio. They are moderate terms which prove Hitler's desire to reach an understanding quickly. Under these conditions Mussolini does not feel inclined to make claims for territorial occupation. This might cause a break in the negotiations and bring about a real rift in our relations with Berlin. Hence, he will limit his demands to the militarization of a fifty-kilometer strip of the border and plans to state our claims at the moment of peace. Mussolini is quite humiliated, because our troops have not taken a step forward. Even today they have not succeeded in advancing and have halted in front of the first French fortification that put up some opposition.

In Libya an Italian general has allowed himself to be taken prisoner. Mussolini is taking it out on the Italian people, "It is the material that I lack. Even Michelangelo needed marble to make statues. If he had had only clay he would have been nothing more than a potter. A people who for sixteen centuries have been an anvil cannot become a hammer within a few years."

Hitler's ceremony for the signing of the armistice has also disturbed the Duce very much. This explains why the Germans did not want a unified commission.

June 22, 1940

We are waiting for the French delegates. There is a little delay because of some discussions, but Alfieri telephoned that the signing will surely take place. The delegates, it seems, will come tomorrow. Mussolini would like to delay as much as possible, in the hope that General Gambara, who in the meantime has attacked, will reach Nice. It would be a good thing, but will we have time? I received the Soviet ambassador. The conversation was cordial but general. I tell him that Italian-Russian relations are, above all, psychological, because there are no direct interests in conflict which separate the two countries. The ambassador addresses some questions to me about the Balkans. I say that, in principle, our policy in that area is to preserve the *status quo*.

Preparations are made for the armistice ceremony. The Duce wishes that since there has been no struggle there should not be any elaborate staging. The meeting will take place almost secretly and the press will be requested to downplay it.

June 23, 1940

The French plenipotentiaries arrived in German planes. We received them at 7:30 p.m. at Villa Incisa on the via Cassia. Badoglio does not hide his emotion. He wants to treat them with great courtesy. Among the French delegates is Parisot, who is a personal friend of his. Who knows how many times they have spoken ill of the Germans together? In the dining room, on the ground floor, there is a long table, and we sit down at one end. I have Badoglio at my right and Admiral Cavagnari at my left. We wait for the French standing up, and greet them with the Roman salute. They answer with a nod of the head. They are dignified. They do not show any pride nor, on the other hand, do they display any humiliation. Only Ambassador Noel is as white as a sheet. They sit down. I stand up and declare that Badoglio will communicate the armistice terms. Roatta reads the French translation of the terms. Huntziger answers that although he is a plenipotentiary, nevertheless, since they are dealing with issues involving the future of his country, he must report to Bordeaux, therefore he requests that the meeting be adjourned until tomorrow. I approve, and set the meeting for 10 a.m. Before leaving I shake hands with Huntziger, who was not expecting it. Then I say good-by to all the French delegates, followed by Badoglio and the others. The ceremony lasted twenty-five minutes in all.

From the Palazzo Chigi I report to the Duce by telephone; he is bitter because he had wanted to reach the armistice after a victory by our own armed forces.

June 24, 1940

Badoglio requested he be left alone to continue the negotiations. My presence would have had the appearance of a control which Keitel, at Compiègne, did not have. No opposition on my part, particularly because from telephone interceptions I saw that they were in agreement at Bordeaux. The armistice was signed at 7:15 p.m. and at 7:35 p.m. I sent word to von Mackensen. Within six hours the shooting will stop in France unless . . . I do not want to make any predictions, but I am not altogether certain that the Pétain government can succeed in imposing its will, especially on the empire and on the navy.

Today, at Constantinople, all the French merchant ships raised the English flag. The war is not yet over, rather it is beginning now. We are going to have so many surprises that we shall not wish for more.

Russia is preparing to attack Romania. This is what Molotov has told Schulenburg.[470] Germany can do no more than acquiesce, but it is clear that Russian policy is increasingly anti-German. The capital in which there is the greatest amount of conspiracy against German victory is Moscow. The situation had appeared quite different when, in August and September, the Bolsheviks signed the pacts with the Nazis. At that time they didn't believe in a German triumph. They wanted to push Germany into a conflict and Europe into a crisis because they were thinking of a long and exhausting struggle between the democracies and Hitler. Things have moved fast, and now Moscow is trying to muddy the waters.

June 25, 1940

In Italy as yet the armistice terms are not known, but already rumors are circulating which create a noticeable uneasiness. People were expecting immediate and gratuitous occupation. They thought that all the territory not conquered by force of arms would come over to us anyway, in view of the agreement. When the document is made public, the disappointment will increase even more.

Starace, returning from the front, says that the attack on the Alps has proved the total lack of preparation of our army, an absolute lack of offensive capability, and the complete incompetence of the top officers. Men were sent to a useless death two days before the armistice, using the same technique that was employed more than twenty years ago. If the war in Libya and Ethiopia is conducted in the same manner, the future is going to hold many bitter disappointments for us.

I have requested and obtained German intervention to save the life of Stoyadinovich, who, according to indications from our representative, is in the hands of his enemies and running serious risks.

June 26, 1940

After a communication from von Mackensen I took the initiative with the Soviet ambassador to discuss the issue of Bessarabia. In short, Italy has no objection to the resolution of this problem, but would prefer, in view of the present state of affairs, to see the controversy settled peacefully and without creating a new conflict in the Balkans.

June 27, 1940

It is the anniversary of Father's death. I go to Leghorn for the occasion. My sorrow is not as bitter as it was at the time of his death, but even now the wound caused by his disappearance is painfully open in my heart. My dear, great, and good father, you who have given me not only my life, but also whatever I have found beautiful in it, know that I am always close to you and that your spirit is my light and guide at all times.

June 28, 1940

Russian ultimatum to Romania. From Bucharest they ask us desperately what they should do. Yield, is our answer. We must at any cost avoid a conflict in the Balkans which would deprive us of their economic resources. For our part, we shall keep Hungary and Bulgaria from joining the conflict.

In fact, Romania yields, rather sadly, but also with a swiftness worthy of Romanian traditions as a belligerent people. I see many diplomatic representatives and give them all the Italian point of view.

The Pope intends to take an initiative for peace. I talk of it over the telephone with the Duce, who is immediately and resolutely hostile.

Admiral Cavagnari complains about the High Command. There is disorder, and no one assumes responsibility. We have lost eight submarines.

June 29, 1940

Balbo is dead. A tragic mistake has brought about his end. The antiaircraft battery at Tobruk fired on his plane, mistaking it for an English plane, and shot it down. The news saddened me very much. Balbo did not deserve to end up like this. He was exuberant, restless, he loved life in all its forms. He had more dash than talent, more vivacity than acumen. He was a decent fellow, and even in political clashes, in which his partisan temperament delighted, he never stooped to anything dishonorable and to questionable methods. He did not desire war, and opposed it to the last. But once it had been decided, he spoke with me in the language of a faithful soldier, and, if fate had not been against him, he was preparing to act with decision and daring.

Balbo's memory will linger for a long time among Italians because he was, above all, a true Italian, with the great faults and great virtues of our race.

June 30, 1940

Alfieri telephones that Hitler is going through one of his periods of isolation, which with him are a prelude to momentous decisions. Therefore, he has not yet answered the Duce's message, in which he [the Duce] offered the participation of our land and air forces in the attack on Great Britain. But does he really want our help? From information sent by Teucci, it seems that the German offensive will only be a massive air force strike, and will take place between the 10th and 15th of July.

The Duce continues his visit to the western front. This trip of his, while Hitler is visiting Paris, is generating unfavorable comments. Had I had the opportunity, I would have advised him against it.

July 1, 1940

Alfieri has gone to confer with Hitler and will also bring up my coming trip to Germany.

Nothing else is new.

July 2, 1940

Mussolini has returned from his trip to the western front, and, as I expected, he came back enthusiastic over what he has seen. He finds that Italian armaments are in good shape. He speaks with fervor of the breakthrough of the Alpine Maginot Line. As a matter of fact, there has been no breakthrough. Our storm troops carried out infiltrations inside the French fortification system and occupied towns in the valleys, while the French forts cut off the path behind them. The curtain of the armistice has fortunately fallen on all this. Otherwise, there might have been many not altogether joyful happenings. Now Mussolini considers the march on Alexandria as practically done. He says that Badoglio also feels the undertaking easy and safe.

Alfieri has reported on his conference with Hitler. I am convinced that there is something brewing in that fellow's mind, and that certainly no new decision has been taken. There is no longer that impressive tone of assurance that surfaced when Hitler spoke of breaking through the Maginot Line. Now he is considering many alternatives, and is raising doubts which account for his restlessness. Meanwhile, he doesn't answer Mussolini's offer to send men and planes to participate in an attack on England. On the other hand, he offers us air force assistance to bomb the Suez Canal. Obviously he does not trust us that much.

July 3, 1940

I ask Phillips to explain the Republican candidacy and if the United States is ready to enter the war. He replies, "In the field of foreign policy, Democrats and Republicans are almost entirely in agreement. For the moment we don't intend to enter the conflict. We are arming on a very large scale, and are helping the British in every way. However, some new fact might decide our intervention, such as the bombing of London with many victims among the civilian population." This is why Hitler is careful and thoughtful before launching the final adventure. All the more so, because, as we gather from many quarters, the Russians are preparing to take a more and more hostile attitude toward the Axis.

I spoke clearly to the Greek minister. De Vecchi cables that English ships and maybe also English planes find refuge, supplies, and protection in Greece. Mussolini is furious. If this music should continue he is decided to take action against Greece. The Greek minister tried weakly to deny it, but he left with his tail between his legs.

Limited shelling between the French and English fleets at Oran. We still have no details, but it is a very momentous event.

This Sunday I shall be in Berlin and perhaps Hitler will speak. Will it be a speech of peace or one of total war against Great Britain?

July 4, 1940

News of the British-French naval engagement is still unclear. In any case, a good part of the French fleet has been destroyed, and perhaps another part has been seized. This disturbs Admiral Cavagnari, who this morning confirmed the fact that we had lost ten submarines. It is too early to judge the consequences of the British action. For the moment it proves that the fighting spirit of His British Majesty's fleet is quite alive, and still has the aggressive ruthlessness of the captains and pirates of the seventeenth century.

Bastianini, who is back from London, also says that British morale is very high and that they have no doubts about victory, even though it may come only after a long time. Everybody—aristocracy, middle class, and the common people—is embittered, tenacious, and proud. Air force and anti-aircraft preparation is being readied on a large scale, so as to repulse and greatly reduce the enemy offensive. This explains Hitler's indecision.

Mussolini is worried about the possibility that the Germans may have got hold of certain documents among those that they captured from the French which might compromise us. So far as the Duce is concerned this isn't possible; they must be forgeries. As far as I'm concerned . . . I could not be so sure! But the Germans know very well what I think, and have no need to confirm my views with some French opinions.

Alfieri confirms my trip to Berlin for next Sunday.

July 5, 1940

The Duce gives me instructions for my trip to Germany. He definitely wants to participate in the attack on Great Britain, if it occurs, and he is concerned by the fact that France is trying to slip gradually into the anti-British camp. He fears that this may cause us to be defrauded of our booty. He orders me also to tell Hitler that he intends to land on the Ionian Islands and to tell him about the need to split up Yugoslavia, a typical Versailles creation, working against us. Through her minister, Greece gives assurances of total neutrality, of which the Duce is very skeptical, especially since De Vecchi maintains his accusations against Greece.

July 6, 1940

On my way to Berlin.

July 7, 1940

I arrive in Berlin. Warm reception. Conference with Hitler, of which there is a stenographic report elsewhere. I can add, personally, that he was very kind, extremely so. He is rather inclined to continue the struggle and to unleash a storm of wrath and steel upon the English. But the final decision has not been reached, and it is for this reason that he is delaying his speech, of which, as he himself puts it, he wants to weigh every word. As to his health—he is well. He is calm and reserved, very reserved for a German who has won.

Von Ribbentrop, too, has changed, in contrast to his attitude at Munich. Then he reflected the warlike spirit of his master. Today he is again belligerent and extreme.

July 8, 1940

A visit to the front: the Maginot Line, Metz, Verdun. The struggle has been less hard than I had thought, seen from a distance; except for a row of villages between the border and the Maginot Line, the other villages do not show any traces of war.

July 9, 1940
    Still at the front: Lille, Dunkirk, Ostend, Bruges, Flanders. Here, too, many signs of flight and very few of fighting.

July 10, 1940
    Munich. Meeting with the Hungarians at Hitler's residence. The latter clearly analyzes the situation with respect to the restless Magyars. If they are certain of succeeding alone, they can attack but they must not expect any help from Italy and Germany, who are involved elsewhere. The Magyars left dissatisfied. Salzburg. Great popular demonstration.

July 11, 1940
    Report to the Duce on my trip. He is satisfied with the results. Von Ribbentrop spoke very clearly about the Italian requests. Mussolini is in a good mood, satisfied with the results of the air and naval engagement, and optimistic about the coming action in Egypt.
    Von Ribbentrop telephones in a gruff and rude manner concerning some articles in our newspapers which have unmasked Axis intentions regarding the Balkans. He exaggerates. I know how to answer him, but for the time we must keep silent.

July 12, 1940
    Nothing worth recording.

July 13, 1940
    The real controversy in naval conflicts is not between us and the British, but between our air force and our navy. Cavagnari states that our air force was completely absent during the first phase of the encounter, but that when it finally came it was directed against our own ships, which for six hours withstood bombing from our 79s. Other information also contradicts the glowing reports of our air force. I confess that I am also incredulous. Mussolini, on the other hand, is not. Today he said that within three days the Italian navy has annihilated 50 percent of the British naval potential in the Mediterranean. Perhaps this is somewhat exaggerated.
    We are awaiting a speech from Hitler. We shall learn the decisions from him.

July 14, 1940
    Helfand, who directed the Soviet embassy in Rome for many months, must return to Moscow, but he can smell the whiff of the firing squad. That is why he has asked for help to escape to America, where he will leave his family, and, I believe, remain himself. He is a keen and intelligent man, whose long contact with bourgeois civilization has turned into a complete bourgeois. Under the stress of imminent misfortune all his Jewish blood has come to the surface. He has become extremely obliging and does nothing

but bow and scrape. But he wishes to save his family and his daughter, whom he adores. He fears their deportation more than his own death. This is very human and very beautiful.

July 15, 1940

Alfieri telephones that the date of Hitler's speech is not yet decided.

The outline of the letter that the Führer intends to send to King Carol on the Transylvanian question arrives. The Duce approves it.

July 16, 1940

Hitler has addressed a long letter to the Duce. It announces the attack against England as something that has been decided, but he definitely and politely declines the offer of an Italian expeditionary force. He explains his refusal by saying that logistic difficulties would arise in supplying two armies. Göring, as well, in a conversation with Alfieri, said that the Italian air force has too important a task in the Mediterranean to scatter its forces in other sectors. The Duce was very much annoyed by the refusal, but he finds solace in instructing the press to play up the naval battle of a week ago. However, we have received information, even from German sources, that the damage inflicted on the British navy is about nil. The Italian navy is also of this opinion, while the Italian air force tends to exaggerate. I only hope that the version given by the air force is true, otherwise it will cost us in dignity and prestige even with the Germans.

I took steps to extend full help to the Italians in France. It is really humiliating to learn that they are forced to beg the defeated French for handouts.

July 17, 1940

Nothing new.

July 18, 1940

The Germans inform us at the last moment that Hitler's speech will be made tomorrow at 7 p.m. I must leave at once.

July 19, 1940

I arrive in Berlin. Conference with von Ribbentrop. Hitler's speech will be a last appeal to Great Britain. I understand that, without their saying so, however, they are hoping and praying that this appeal will not be rejected.

Ceremony at the Reichstag. It is solemn and stagy. Hitler speaks simply, and, I should say also, in an unusually humane tone. I believe that his desire for peace is sincere. In fact, late in the evening, when the first cold English reactions to the speech arrive, unconcealed disappointment spreads among the Germans.

July 20, 1940

Conference with the Führer, a stenographic report of which is to be found elsewhere. He confirms my impressions of yesterday. He would like an understanding with Great Britain. He knows that war with the English will be hard and bloody, and knows also that people everywhere today are averse to bloodshed.

In the afternoon a visit to Göring. He looked feverish, but as he dangled the Collar of the Annunziata from his neck he was somewhat rude and haughty toward me. I was more interested in the luxurious decoration of his house than in him and his changing moods. It is an ever-increasing show of luxury, and it is truly incomprehensible how, in a country which is social-ized, or almost so, people can tolerate the extraordinary pomp displayed by this Western satrap.

July 21, 1940
    Return trip.

July 22, 1940
    I report my impressions to the Duce. He had been opposed to Hitler's speech, calling it "much too cunning a speech." He fears that the English may find in it a pretext to begin negotiations. That would be sad for Mussolini, because now more than ever he wants war. And yet today he was depressed on account of the loss of the *Colleoni*, not so much because of the sinking itself as because he feels the Italians did not fight very well.

    Halifax makes an inconsequential speech about Germany, in which Hitler's vague proposals for peace are not taken into account.

July 23, 1940
    The Romanian ministers go to confer with the Germans at Salzburg, then they will come to us.

July 24, 1940
    Nothing new.

July 25, 1940
    To Florence, to visit Marzio, who has been ill for a few days. I am glad to find him lively and gay, as he always has been.

July 26, 1940
    Our air force losses during the first month of the war amount to 250 planes; we are producing an equal amount. The question of pilots is more difficult. Their losses cannot be too easily replaced.

    I saw von Mackensen. The usual quarrel between Ribbentrop and Goebbels brings him to me. I do my best to eliminate every pretext for dragging us into this quarrel.

    The Hungarians are nervous about the Romanians' trip to Rome and to Berlin. They fear that Romania, after so many years of Little Entente and "Genevaism," might ask and be given entry to the Axis.

July 27, 1940

After a long period the Duce talks with the King. He saw him yesterday, and His Majesty's first question was "whether we shouldn't fear that Prussia might soon play a dirty trick on Italy as well." This question irritated the Duce because "it revealed that nothing has changed in the attitude of the King, who at heart still hopes for a British victory—a victory, that is, of the country where he has always kept his immense fortune."

I received the Romanians. They are simply disgusting. They open their mouths only to make honeyed compliments. They have become anti-French, anti-English, and anti-League of Nations. They talk with contempt of the *diktat* of Versailles—too honeyed. I have a first meeting with them at the Palazzo Chigi and I remind them a bit roughly of their anti-Italian past. In the afternoon another meeting at the Palazzo Venezia. Mussolini, who had received the report of the German conversations with the Romanians in time, repeated what Hitler had said at Salzburg.

July 28, 1940

Sunday, I went to Leghorn with the children.

July 29, 1940

Mussolini calls many times by telephone from Riccione to have me modify the minutes of Saturday's conversation. He wants me to delete certain anti-Russian phrases of his and substitute some rather pro-Soviet remarks. The reports are to go to Berlin!

General Favagrossa brings me up to date on the problem of our supplies. It isn't as bad as we had thought. Our greatest need is for copper and steel alloys.

July 30, 1940

From Berlin comes news of complete calm. Is it the calm before the storm? That's what Alfieri says.

I inform the Hungarians about last Saturday's talks. Villani is rather satisfied about them.

July 31, 1940

Nothing new.

August 1, 1940

Nothing new.

August 2, 1940

Nothing new.

August 3, 1940

I ask the Greek minister to withdraw his consul in Trieste, who is incurably anti-Italian. He attempts to defend him, but I have very clear proof as to his guilt and he must yield.

Soddu says that Graziani, after having emptied Italy in order to supply Libya, does not feel that he is prepared to attack Egypt, mainly because of the heat. He intends to postpone the operation until spring. I do not yet know the reactions of the Duce, but I predict that they will be violent. From Germany, too, come rumors of a postponement of the attack. Can they be true?

Four SIM agents were surprised this evening inside the Yugoslav legation. We must encourage the rumor that they were simply ordinary burglars.

August 4, 1940

Mussolini has returned to Rome. He is in quite a good mood, notwithstanding the postponement of the offensive in Libya and the reopening of an old leg wound which he suffered during the last war. He does not mention the military situation. On the other hand, Badoglio informs me that Graziani has been ordered to Rome. Meanwhile, the Duke of Aosta has begun his offensive against British Somaliland, with excellent prospects.

Mussolini speaks of our relations with Russia, and believes that the moment has come to take further steps to improve them. I agree.

From Berlin Alfieri reports that the sudden return of Hitler with the highest Nazi officials leads him to suspect that operations are imminent, about which we, as usual, have been told nothing.

August 5, 1940

The Duce is ranting against "the Italians," which happens whenever he encounters opposition to his projects. The main points he made were: decrease in the birth rate, the tendency toward alcoholism, and complacency. He says that one day he will make a sweeping speech entitled "The Secret Wounds of Italy." He will do this in order to force the nation to face its own weaknesses. He said that the main reason for the reforestation of the Apennine regions is to make the climate of Italy more rigorous. This will bring about the elimination of the weaker stock and an improvement of the Italian race.

Conclusion: the Duce is dissatisfied because Graziani, who has laid so much blame on Balbo, now refuses to face problems, and does not want to attack Egypt. Today he has called him for an accounting, but I don't yet know what the outcome is. Mussolini's uneasiness will increase if, as it appears probable, Hitler will soon launch his offensive against the British Isles.

August 6, 1940

Alfieri now says that German activity has slowed down and this time he fails to explain the reason. Could there be something to the rumors about a separate peace through the King of Sweden?

Mussolini talks a lot about an Italian attack on Yugoslavia during the second half of September. Therefore, he wishes me to put aside the Croatian problem and quickly reach an agreement with Russia, which should be of a "spectacular" character. He also raises the question of my going to Moscow. Litvinov's visit was never returned. All this seems premature. In any case, I shall talk to Mackensen about it. Regarding the attack on Yugoslavia, I do not believe that, unless something new comes up, Hitler will allow the status quo of the Balkans to be disturbed.

The Duce telephones during the evening, he is elated because our troops have entered Zeila. I do not know the real importance of this.

August 7, 1940
Nothing new.

August 8, 1940
Graziani came to see me. He talks about the attack on Egypt as a very serious undertaking, and says that our present preparation is far from perfect. He criticizes Badoglio, who does not check the Duce's aggressive spirit— a fact which "for a man who knows Africa means that he must suffer from softening of the brain, or, what is worse, from bad faith." "The water supply is entirely insufficient. We move toward a defeat which, in the desert, inevitably becomes a rapid and total disaster."

I reported this to the Duce, who was very unhappy about it because in his last conversation with Graziani he had understood that the offensive would start in a few days. Graziani did not set any date with me. He would rather not attack at all, or, at any rate, not for two or three months. Mussolini concluded that "one should not give jobs to people who aren't looking for at least one promotion. Graziani has too many to lose."[471]

Mackensen brings a plan for an dual protest to be addressed to Bern because of an obnoxious speech by a Swiss general. We agree about its general points.

According to Alfieri, the offensive across the English Channel has been delayed because of bad weather. But, according to General Marras, the delay is caused by secret conversations supposedly going on now. The Alfieri version is the most plausible.

August 9, 1940
Nothing new.

August 10, 1940
Meeting of the Council of Ministers. A long Mussolini monologue, which covered everything from the events of the war and alcoholism to his inevitable attack on the Italian middle class. "A bourgeois," he said, "is one who is neither a worker nor a farmer, and who is concerned only with his own interests." As for me, I still prefer Flaubert's definition: "Bourgeois is anything that is low." The bourgeois concept has more of a psychological than an economic value. But on this problem of the so-called struggle against the bourgeois there are many things to be said, and someday it would be well to say them.

I talked to the Duce about the difficulties that have arisen on the Greek-Albanian border. I don't wish to dramatize the situation, but the Greek attitude is very tricky. The Duce is considering "forceful action, because since 1923 he has some accounts to settle, and the Greeks deceive themselves if they think that he has forgotten."

News of further delay in the offensive comes from Berlin. Will it take place? When? And in what form? We know nothing. The fact is that the Germans keep us in the dark about everything, just as they did when we were neutral, even though we are now fighting with them.

August 11, 1940

Mussolini still speaks about the Greek issue and wants details on Ciamuria. He has prepared a Stefani despatch, which will start raising the issue. He has had Jacomoni and Visconti Prasca come to Rome and intends to confer with them. He speaks of a surprise attack against Greece toward the end of September. If he has decided this, I feel that he must work fast. It is dangerous to give the Greeks time to prepare.

The German air force has asked that our planes be sent to join in the action against Great Britain. When we offered them a month ago they were promptly refused. Now Germany asks for them. Why? I am not very favorable to this for technical and also for political reasons.

Favagrossa compares the Italian situation to a bathtub where the stopper is removed and the taps are turned off. Only from the shower, which is France, is it possible to expect a little water to run. But up to now this has not happened. We are very much concerned about tin, copper, and nickel. By the end of September we shall have absolutely nothing as far as tin is concerned.

August 12, 1940

I accompany Jacomoni and Visconti Prasca to see the Duce, who sets down the political and military lines for action against Greece. If Ciamuria and Corfu are yielded without striking a blow, we shall not ask for anything more. If, on the other hand, any resistance is attempted, we shall go the limit. Jacomoni and Visconti Prasca consider the action possible, and even easy, provided, however, that it be undertaken at once. On the other hand, the Duce is still of the opinion, for general military reasons, that the action should be postponed until toward the end of September.

From Germany news of air strikes, but nothing more. I have spoken over the telephone with Alfieri, who was more vague than usual. A new and violent outburst by Mussolini against the middle class. "After the war is over, I shall begin my attack on the middle class, which is cowardly and despicable. We must destroy it physically, and save perhaps 20 percent, if that much." And he added, "I shall strike at it, and I shall say, like St. Dominic, 'God will choose His own!'"

In Somaliland we fight and advance.

August 13, 1940

Mussolini is very resentful toward the Duke of Aosta because of the delay of operations in Somaliland. He repeats this formula: "Princes ought to be enlisted as civilians."

August 14, 1940
     In Leghorn to see the children.

August 15, 1940
     A Greek vessel has been sunk by a submarine of unidentified national-ity. The incident threatens to become serious. As for me, I consider the intemperance of De Vecchi at the bottom of it. I confer with the Duce, who wishes to settle this incident peacefully. It was not necessary. I suggest send-ing a note to Greece. This will place the dispute on a diplomatic level.

August 16, 1940
     Nothing new.

August 17, 1940
     Alfieri had an interesting conference with von Ribbentrop. It can be summarized as follows: (1) that the German government does not desire that we seek too close an understanding with Russia; (2) that it is necessary to shelve any plans to attack Yugoslavia; (3) that an eventual action against Greece is not at all welcome by Berlin. It is a complete order to halt all along the line. According to von Ribbentrop, every effort must be concentrated against Great Britain, because there, and there alone, is "the life-and-death question." This leads me to think that even German opinion feels the war is going to be hard. The Duce dictated our counterproposal himself. Natu-rally, we accept Berlin's point of view, even regarding Greece. In fact, we hold back the note we had already prepared.
     At the beach I saw Mollier, the press attaché at the German embassy, who is more talkative than the ambassador. He says that the landing is now imminent, and that thousands of landing craft are ready in the Channel ports; that the operation, which is a very bold one, will be hard and bloody, but its outcome is certain. Mollier spoke of peace by the end of September.

August 18, 1940
     Nothing very important. Only from Berlin a series of significant hints leading us to consider the decisive attack against Great Britain as imminent. Mussolini believes them to be true, and is convinced that we shall have victory and peace by the end of next month. For this reason he wants to move fast in Egypt.
     Badoglio and De Vecchi insult each other by letter, so the Duce has told me. He was satisfied, and attributed to De Vecchi statements of which he could not be proud.

August 19, 1940
     The Duce reads me a cable he has sent to Graziani. He orders him to march into Egypt as soon as a German patrol lands in England. Mussolini

takes personal responsibility for the order, knowing full well the objections that Graziani will make.

August 20, 1940

Graziani sends in a copy of a report indicating that all his generals are opposed to the offensive into Egypt. I shall show it to the Duce.

A speech by Churchill. For the first time in a year I read an English speech which is clear and forward-looking. One can feel that behind the façade of beautiful words and strong statements there is a will and a faith.

August 21, 1940

Nothing new.

August 22, 1940

Mussolini gives me a copy of some military directives he has formulated, in which the actions against Yugoslavia and Greece are postponed indefinitely. It appears that the Germans have renewed their pressure, even on our General Staff, for this very reason. The Duce at first wanted to give a copy of his directives to the German embassy, then he telephoned, countermanding his instructions. It appears that he prefers sending them to Hitler in writing.

Riccardi is now optimistic about our supplies. At the present rate of collection and acquisition there should not be any noticeable shortages until the end of 1941.

An important speech by Halifax. The British tone has changed, and the possibility of an understanding with Germany is not excluded. Could this explain the delay in the attack?

August 23, 1940

The Duce has written a letter—a summary of which goes to Hitler—and he received an interesting one from Franco. The Caudillo talks about Spain entering the war soon. He says that he has already approached the Germans to get what he needs. To us he has not specified what he had asked for.

August 24, 1940

Nothing new.

August 25, 1940

Nothing new. I am spending the day in Leghorn.

August 26, 1940

Von Ribbentrop telephoned several times. He is concerned about the turn taken by the controversy between the Hungarians and Romanians. Germany wants to avoid a crisis in the Balkans at all costs. Hence, although he does not speak of arbitration, von Ribbentrop is thinking of calling the two ministers of foreign affairs to Vienna to give them the friendly advice of the Axis toward a solution. All this is naturally to be accompanied by a threat:

whoever does not accept the advice will take full responsibility for future consequences. I agree, and the Duce approves. I have Ghigi and Talamo come to Rome in order to gather more information. We shall go to Vienna within two or three days.

Von Ribbentrop informs me that he has dealt harshly with the Greek minister, who had tried to knock on doors in Berlin. He did not receive him, and has told him it would be more useful to speak with Italy, since Germany is in perfect agreement with us about everything.

August 27, 1940

The meeting at Vienna is set for tomorrow. The Hungarians and Romanians will come on Thursday. Von Ribbentrop telephones that the Führer is of the opinion that the Romanians should surrender forty thousand square kilometers to Hungary, which has asked for sixty thousand. Mussolini has no precise ideas on the subject, and gives me full freedom of action. He is completely absorbed by the plan to attack Egypt, and says that Keitel also thinks that the taking of Cairo is more important than the taking of London. Keitel has not said this to me. The attack is to take place on September 6. What does Graziani think of it?

August 28, 1940

Hitler wishes to speak to me before I go to Vienna. Hence we go by way of Salzburg. The weather is beautiful south of the Alps and cloudy in the north. The usual reception at Berchtesgaden. Hitler is cordial and serene as always, but more tired than on other occasions. After lunch we speak first about the situation in general. I have summarized the conference in a cable to the Duce. Hitler explains the failure to attack Great Britain as due to bad weather. He says that he will need at least two weeks of good weather to overcome British naval superiority, but from everything he said it seems to me that there is now a definite postponement of the assault. Until when? Nevertheless, Hitler seems resolved to go the limit, because, he tells me, he has rejected an attempt at mediation made by the King of Sweden.

We speak little of the Magyar-Romanian question. He leaves the solution to von Ribbentrop and me. The only thing he has at heart is that peace be preserved there, and that Romanian oil continue to flow into his reservoirs.

Flight to Vienna. The city, compared to what it was a year ago, seems to be in more miserable condition: little traffic, stores that are understocked, and a heavy atmosphere. People in the streets are poorly dressed and listless.

August 29, 1940

With Ribbentrop we decide to solve the problem through arbitration. If we start a discussion we will never succeed in getting out of it. We first talk with the Hungarians. Czaky is reasonable; Teleki is hostile. Then Ribbentrop attacks the Hungarians. Courtesy is not his forte. He accuses Hungary of having engaged in anti-German policy on more than one occasion. His words are rather threatening. The conversation with the Romanian is less violent. Manoilescu[472] doesn't know what to do or what to say and seems terrified for his country and for himself. We try to make him pay a heavy price for our guarantee of his borders. He, too, is convinced that this is an excellent thing, but thinks the price is high.

The Hungarians accepted this afternoon. The Romanians will make us wait for their answer until four o'clock in the morning. In the meantime Ribbentrop and I trace the new border and dictate the terms of the arbitration. It is a difficult problem to solve; in fact, impossible to solve with any real justice. We shall try to be as fair as we can.

In Vienna they are eating less and badly. Hotels are short of supplies and disorganized to the point where they don't appear to be the same. The war weighs more heavily on this city than elsewhere. Austrian morale is not good either.

August 30, 1940

Ceremony for the signature at the Belvedere. The Hungarians can't contain their joy when they see the map. Then we heard a loud thud. It was Manoilescu, who fainted on the table. Doctors, massage, camphorated oil. Finally he comes to, but he appears very much in a state of shock.

In the evening there is a demonstration in front of the hotel. Since they went to the trouble of organizing one, it should have been bigger and warmer. Vienna is truly gray.

August 31, 1940

I went hunting with Ribbentrop.

September 1, 1940

I return to Rome. A conversation with the Duce. He is pleased with what has happened. He says that he is pleased that the war will last beyond this month and, maybe, beyond the winter, because this will give Italy time to make greater sacrifices and thus enable him to assert our rights better. Will he prove right this time? And isn't there the danger that if the war doesn't end soon it may last beyond the time that is favorable for us? This is a question that is worth asking and which many Germans, among those who have their heads screwed on, are now asking.

September 2, 1940

Nothing new.

September 3, 1940

Nothing new.

September 4, 1940

The Americans are lending 50 fighter planes to Great Britain. There is a great deal of excitement and indignation in Berlin. The Duce, on the other hand, says that he is indifferent. At the request of the Germans we stop our radio broadcasts at 10 p.m. It seems that this step was taken because it gave an advantage to British pilots through late-night programs.

September 5, 1940

Mussolini returned to Rome. He is alarmed by the situation in Romania as described by the military attaché. Yet Ghigi is much more calm. They are also calm in Berlin. Hitler has spoken, and has uttered some harsh threats against England. But he makes no mention of the blitzkrieg, and some expressions he used, such as his clownish ridiculing of Duff Cooper, for example, make me seriously wonder. He must be nervous.

September 6, 1940

The Duce is rather excited. I don't know why. He is taking it out on his generals, whom he removes, as well as on the Germans, who are preventing us from improving relations with Moscow.

King Carol of Romania has abdicated. He is paying, but only in part, for his silly buffoonery, his betrayals, and his crimes.

September 7, 1940

Council of Ministers. At the end of the meeting the Duce makes some political statements. He begins by stating that, in his opinion, the war is now bound to last part of the winter, although he considers the German landing in England as certain. As to what concerns us more directly, he has again taken up the matter of our attack on Egypt. It was to take place today, but Graziani has asked that it be postponed for one month. Badoglio was in favor of the delay. Mussolini vetoes this, taking personal responsibility for the decision. If Graziani does not attack on Monday he will be replaced. He has also given orders to the navy to make a move to seek out the British fleet and give battle. As to the more distant future, he said that he is now convinced that between 1945 and 1950 war will break out between the Axis and Russia. By that time his program to equip 100 divisions will be ready.

September 8, 1940

Graziani answered that he will obey. The attack will begin tomorrow. Many military technicians are skeptical. Among them the Prince of Piedmont, who has expressed doubts to me about the prospects and wisdom of the enterprise.

The naval encounter has not as yet taken place, because our air force reconnaissance has not yet located the route of the British squadron from Gibraltar.

September 9, 1940

The drive against Egypt has suffered a new delay. Graziani is doing his best to keep to his objective, and is preparing to begin action on the 12th. Never has a military operation been launched with such opposition from the commanders.

What is happening in London under German bombing? From here it is difficult to judge. The blow must be hard. Decisive? I don't believe it.

September 10, 1940
   Nothing new.

September 11, 1940
   The beginning of the attack on Egypt is confirmed for tomorrow. Even General Carboni, who has never been unduly optimistic, says that our advance as far as Marsa Matruk is easy, and that it is possible to reach Alexandria.
   German air action continues against London. We do not know exactly what the results are. It seems incredible, but we do not have a single informant in Great Britain. On the other hand, the Germans have many. In London itself there is a German agent who makes up to twenty-nine radio transmissions in one day. At least, according to Admiral Canaris.

September 12, 1940
   Nothing new.

September 13, 1940
   Von Ribbentrop telephones from Berlin. He wants to come to Rome next week in order to confer on two subjects: Russia and America. The trip may prove useful. I agree to it.
   Graziani must have launched his attack, but as of now we have no precise information.

September 14, 1940
   The attack on Egypt has started. At the moment the British are withdrawing without fighting. They wish to draw us away from our base, stretching our lines of communication. The Duce, who is once again in a good mood, considers the arrival at Marsa Matruk as a great victory, especially since it allows our aviation to attack Alexandria by day, with fighter escort.
   No definite news from the north. The Duce is still convinced that the landing will take place, while General Marras, who thought it certain until today, is beginning to doubt it. Maybe we shall learn the truth from Ribbentrop.
   The Russian attitude is becoming alarmingly ambiguous.

September 15, 1940
   I go to Leghorn, later to La Spezia, to preside at ceremonies in honor of my father. The statue by Messina is a work worthy of the Renaissance. When it was unveiled the image of my father seemed so powerfully alive that I was thrilled.

September 16, 1940
   Mussolini is nervous because of the slow progress in Egypt. But he is angry at Berti who, because of his slowness, may lose us our booty. The fact is that no fighting has started yet. Only some rear-guard action.
   Ribbentrop's visit has been confirmed for Tuesday.

September 17, 1940

It seems that things in Egypt are going better and better. The English are withdrawing faster than expected. According to military experts there will be resistance at Marsa Matruk. Others believe, on the other hand, that it will come at Alexandria. Mussolini is radiant with joy. He has taken complete responsibility for the offensive on his shoulders, and is proud that he was right.

September 18, 1940

Nothing new.

September 19, 1940

Von Ribbentrop arrived. He is in a good mood and pleased by the welcome given him by "the applause squad," which was very well mobilized by the police commissioner. In the car Ribbentrop speaks at once about the surprise in his bag: a military alliance with Japan, to be signed within the next few days in Berlin. The Russian dream vanished forever in the rooms of the Belvedere at Vienna, after the guarantee to Romania. He thinks that such a move will have a double advantage: against Russia and against America, which, under the threat of the Japanese fleet, will not dare move. I tell him that I disagree. The anti-Russian guarantee is very good, but the anti-American statement is less appropriate, because Washington will increasingly favor the English. As for England, von Ribbentrop says that the weather has been very bad and that the clouds even more than the RAF have prevented final success. However, the invasion will take place anyway as soon as there are a few days of fine weather. The landing is ready and possible. English territorial defense is non-existent. A single German division will suffice to bring about a complete collapse.

In the afternoon a conference at the Palazzo Venezia, the stenographic report of which is filed elsewhere. In general I find von Ribbentrop in higher spirits than at Vienna, and the main reason for his elation is the pact with Japan, which he considers fundamentally important, and which is, besides, one of his personal successes.

September 20, 1940

A second conversation with Ribbentrop. It deals for the most part with Spanish intervention, which now appears to be certain and imminent. Ribbentrop reads a message sent by Hitler to Franco. It is a partly political and partly military document, written with the convincing logic which the Führer's writings frequently display.

D'Aieta reports to me that Ribbentrop's optimistic forecasts are not shared by his associates, who think that this may be a long war. Some of them think it will be a hard war.

September 21, 1940

I went with Ribbentrop to Villa d'Este and to Villa Adriana. In the last few days Ribbentrop has wanted to meet many people both inside and outside political circles. Everybody disliked him.

September 22, 1940

Final conference with von Ribbentrop, wide-ranging in scope. Von Ribbentrop alludes to the possibility of the Axis taking the initiative in breaking diplomatic relations with the United States. Mussolini is inclined to agree. I do not, first of all because I believe we must avoid a conflict with America at all costs, and then because I believe that we would be a help to Roosevelt, who could then run for reelection as the injured party who has been attacked. Anyway, the decision is not imminent, and I hope that I shall be able to put up my oar.

Bad weather continues in the north, and along with the summer the forecasts made by von Ribbentrop fade away. The Hungarians are laying too heavy a hand on Transylvania. In agreement with von Ribbentrop, we take steps in Budapest to advise moderation which, in the hour of success, represents the greatest wisdom. However, the Hungarians are beginning to print propaganda leaflets stating: "The Trianon is dead. Vienna, too, will die."

September 23, 1940

No news.

September 24, 1940

The final text of the Tripartite Pact is agreed upon. The signature can now take place in a few days.

During the night Mackensen telephoned about de Gaulle. He appeared at Dakar with some English vessels and called on the French to give up. The governor resisted, and Pétain asked the armistice commission for authorization to send some French vessels, among them the *Strasbourg*, into the Atlantic. The Germans objected. I, too, object. We cannot clearly understand de Gaulle's attitude. In fact, I am convinced that as time works against the possibility of a British collapse, solidarity between Free France and the French colonial empire appears more obvious.

I spoke about it to the Duce, who is also thinking about occupying Corsica. He is right. If we don't get there the British will, and from Ghisonaccia the Royal Air Force will attack Italy.

Cavagnari absolutely denies that a cruiser of the *London* type has been sunk. According to him, it is one of the usual bragging claims of the air force to spite the navy, whom they make fun of.

September 25, 1940

I went to Florence on account of Marzio's operation; thank God everything goes well. At the station I received a telephone call from Ribbentrop announcing that the signature of the alliance will take place on Friday. I must leave immediately.

September 26, 1940

I am on my way to Berlin. On Hitler's order the train is stopped at Munich. Attacks by the Royal Air Force endanger the area, and the Führer does not wish to expose me to the risk of a long stop in open country. I sleep in Munich and will continue by air.

September 27-28, 1940

The pact is signed. The signature takes place more or less like that of the Pact of Steel. But the atmosphere is cooler. Even the Berlin street crowd, a comparatively small one, composed mostly of school children, cheers with regularity but without conviction. Japan is far away. Its help is doubtful. Only one thing is certain: that it will be a long war. This does not please the Germans, who had come to believe that with the end of summer the war would also end. A winter of war is hard to take. More so since food is scarce in Berlin, and it is easy to see that the window displays of the stores promise much more than what is actually inside.

Another thing contributing to the depressed spirit of Berlin life is the constant recurrence of air raids. Every night citizens spend from four to five hours in the cellar. They lack sleep, there is promiscuity between men and women, cold, and these things do not create a good mood. The number of people with colds is incredible. Bomb damage is slight; nervousness is very high. At ten o'clock in the evening everyone looks at his watch. People want to return home to their loved ones. All this does not yet justify the pessimism in certain quarters where the first war is being remembered and they are beginning to think of the worst.

But it is a fact that the attitude in Germany today is not like last June or even last August.

I had two conversations with Hitler, a formal one after the signing, the other the next day. He did not speak about the current situation. He spoke rather of Spanish intervention, which he opposes because it would cost more than it is worth. He proposed a meeting with the Duce at the Brenner Pass, and I immediately accepted. No more invasion of England. No more blitz destruction of England. From Hitler's statements there now appears worry about a long war. He wishes to conserve his armed power. He speaks with his usual decision, with less impetuousness but with as much determination as ever. Ribbentrop is more nervous. Perhaps he is in bad health, and perhaps he has other reasons to complain. He had relied too much on a lightning end to the conflict not to be disappointed. The Germans are impeccably courteous toward us Italians. Ansaldo feels that the courtesy is in proportion to the need the Germans have of us. With the Spaniards, on the other hand, the Germans are less courteous. Generally speaking, Serrano Suñer's mission was not successful, and the man himself did not and could not please the Germans.

September 29, 1940

On my way home.

September 30, 1940

I confer with the Duce. I find him in a good mood and very happy that Italy could score "a success in Egypt which gives her the glory she has sought in vain for three centuries."

He is rather irritated at Badoglio, who now seems to have taken up the role of delaying Graziani's march.

October 1, 1940

Serrano Suñer arrives in Rome. General Queipo de Llano is also at the station, but they do not greet each other and Queipo declines an invitation to lunch. In speaking of Queipo, Serrano Suñer called him "a bandit and a beast." All this has a symbolic meaning: it represents the situation of Spanish public life today.

I have a long conversation with the Duce which is recorded elsewhere. There is one point in the record of the conversation which I had to take out of the copy given to the Germans: Serrano's colorful invectives against the Germans, for their absolute lack of tact in dealing with Spain. Serrano is right. The Germans are not models of courtesy, and Ribbentrop less so than the others, even though this time there is something to be said for him. For years the Spaniards have been asking for a lot and giving nothing in return. However, Serrano could have expressed himself differently.

October 2, 1940

The Duce is very anxious about an attack to take place soon on Marsa Matruk, and is irritated by Badoglio because the latter does not think the action can be carried out in October. I speak about it with Graziani because the Duce wants to know his opinion. Graziani feels that we must still wait for some time, at least all of November, to complete our logistic preparation, which is the only real final guarantee of success.

He is afraid that the English may resist for a long time at Marsa Matruk. If our supply lines should not function well we would have to retreat. And in the desert a retreat is equivalent to a rout.

A conference with Serrano. He says nothing new but he is postponing his departure until after my return from the Brenner Pass in order to be duly informed.

October 3, 1940

Biseo, a man who really understands aviation, has painted a black picture of our air force in North Africa. Our logistic organization is bad, and we are short of pursuit planes. Although the English are numerically inferior, they cause us plenty of trouble. Biseo thinks it will be difficult to carry out our attack on Egypt to its logical conclusion.

A partial crisis in London with Chamberlain's removal from the government. Information is scarce and uncertain, nor does it allow us to make any kind of diagnosis regarding the significance of this event. A long conference with the King, who is vaguely pessimistic and fundamentally hostile to Germany. He repeats his favorite refrain on the scant feeling of security which German promises give. He is also skeptical as to the condition of our armed forces.

October 4, 1940

Rarely have I seen the Duce in such a good mood and in good shape as at the Brenner Pass today. The meeting was cordial and the conversations were certainly the most interesting of all that have taken place so far. Hitler put at least some of his cards on the table, and told us about his future plans. I have recorded the conversation elsewhere. These are my general impressions: (1) there is no longer any talk about a landing in the British Isles and preparations already made remain where they are; (2) there is hope of attracting France into the orbit of the anti-British coalition, since it is now understood that the Anglo-Saxon world is still a hard nut to crack; (3) greater importance is given to the Mediterranean sector, which is good for us. Hitler was energetic and again extremely anti-Bolshevik. "Bolshevism," he said, "is the doctrine of people who are lowest on the scale of civilization." Ribbentrop, on the other hand, was very silent and in noticeably bad health.

Anfuso, who spent much time with the Germans of the entourage and who is the most pro-German of my collaborators, is not too satisfied, and says that a spirit of adventure still seems to drive the Germans.

I had a long conversation with the Duce on the train. He said that he will soon fire Muti because he is incompetent and an opportunist; he also said that he will spur Graziani on to start the offensive sooner, and that he hates the King "because the King is the only defeatist in the country."

October 5, 1940

I inform Serrano of the results of the meeting in so far as they concern Spain, and he is only partially satisfied. Why hadn't he yet realized that the Germans have had an eye on Morocco for a long time?

The Duce approved the report on the Brenner meeting, and asks that a copy be sent to the King, as well as a summary to Badoglio. He made some negative comments about Badoglio, and declared that in the spring he will think about finding a replacement for him.

October 6, 1940

I go to Leghorn.

October 7, 1940

Nothing new.

October 8, 1940

A telephone call from the Duce, requesting that we take an initiative with Romania to elicit a request for Italian troops. He is very angry because only German forces are present in the Romanian oil regions. The step is delicate and difficult, but I imagine that Ghigi[473] will carry it through all right.

October 9, 1940
    Nothing new.

October 10, 1940
    Ribbentrop telephoned, informing me that the Hungarian government
has again asked permission to join the Tripartite Alliance. While he was
previously against it, Ribbentrop is now favorable, because we must not
turn down anyone who wants to join in the anti-British fight. Mussolini gives
his approval, though a bit unwillingly, since he does not wish to enlarge the
Tripartite Alliance. Once the Hungarians are admitted he believes we should
have to open the door to the Romanians also. I inform Ribbentrop of this,
and he receives the idea with very subdued enthusiasm.

October 11, 1940
    Nothing new.

October 12, 1940
    Return of the Duce. He is very angry at Graziani because the latter has
once more answered by delaying the Duce's order to begin the offensive.
The Duce speaks of replacing him, and mentions the names of Generals
Messe and Vercellino.
    But above all he is indignant at the German occupation of Romania.[474]
He says that this has made a very poor impression on Italian public opinion,
because, in view of the decisions taken at Vienna, nobody had expected this
to happen. "Hitler places me in front of a *fait accompli*. This time I am going
to pay him back in his own coin. He will find out from the papers that I
have occupied Greece. In this way the equilibrium will be re-established." I
ask if he has come to an agreement with Badoglio. "Not yet," he answers,
"but I shall send in my resignation as an Italian if anyone objects to our
fighting the Greeks." The Duce seems determined to act now. In fact, I
believe that the military operation will be useful and easy.

October 13, 1940
    Nothing new.

October 14, 1940
    Mussolini speaks to me again about our action in Greece, and sets the
date for October 26. Jacomoni gives very satisfactory information, especially
on the state of mind of the population of Ciamuria, which is favorable to us.

October 15, 1940
    A meeting with the Duce at the Palazzo Venezia, to discuss the Greek
enterprise. Badoglio, Roatta, Soddu, Jacomoni, Visconti Prasca, and myself
take part in it. The discussion is available in a stenographic report.
    Afterward, at the Palazzo Chigi, I speak with Ranza and Visconti Prasca,
who explain their military plans. I also speak with Jacomoni, who gives an

account of the political situation. He says that in Albania the attack on Greece is awaited keenly and enthusiastically. Albanian youth, which has always been reserved in its attitude toward us, now openly demonstrates its approval.

October 16, 1940

I receive a copy of a report from Graziani. He states that to resume his march into Egypt he will need at least two months' time. I immediately send the document to the Duce. I can imagine his indignation.

October 17, 1940

The Duce is at Terni. Marshal Badoglio comes to see me, and speaks very seriously about our action in Greece. The three heads of the General Staff have unanimously declared themselves against it. The present forces are insufficient, and the navy does not feel that it can carry out a landing at Prevesa because the water is too shallow. All of Badoglio's talk has a pessimistic tinge. He foresees the war spreading, and with it the exhaustion of our already-meager resources. I listen, and do not argue. I insist that, from a political point of view, the moment is good. Greece is isolated. Turkey will not move. Neither will Yugoslavia. If the Bulgarians enter the war it will be on our side. From the military point of view I express no opinion. Badoglio must, without any hesitation, repeat to Mussolini what he has told me.

I go to Naples. I meet Edda, who is returning with a hospital ship. I speak with the wounded. They are magnificent.

October 18, 1940

I go in early to see the Duce. I find Soddu in the anteroom. He has spoken with Badoglio, who stated that if we move against Greece he will resign. I report to the Duce, who is already in a very bad mood on account of Graziani. He has a violent outburst of rage, and says that he will personally go to Greece "to witness the incredible shame of Italians who are afraid of the Greeks." He is planning to move at any cost, and if Badoglio hands in his resignation it will be immediately accepted. But Badoglio not only does not resign, he doesn't even repeat to Mussolini what he told me yesterday. In fact, the Duce says that Badoglio only brought this up in order to obtain a postponement of a few days, at least two.

I go with Manoilescu to see the Duce. A long and gloomy lamentation over the insolence of the Hungarians, which is undoubtedly a fact but which we can hardly stop. On the other hand, after twenty years of Romanian oppression a reaction was to be expected, especially since the Magyars are at heart of a savage and harsh temperament.

From an intercepted cable it seems that Turkey is preparing to move if Greece is attacked. I do not believe it, and the Duce considers it out of the question.

October 19, 1940

Council of Ministers. The Duce discusses the situation, and leads us to understand that action is imminent, but he does not mention the date, nor does he give precise details about the direction it will take.

Anfuso returns from Sofia, where he delivered a letter from the Duce to King Boris. It was not an invitation to action, but rather information on the decision taken. It was left up to him to decide his course as dictated by his conscience as King and as a Bulgarian. He answered with a written and sealed message, but in the long conference he had with Anfuso his attitude was rather evasive, in accordance with his habits and his character. He fears the Turks above all.

October 20, 1940

I see Bismarck, who informs me of two matters, both of them very important; namely, that during the coming week Hitler will meet Franco somewhere in France, and that, during the course of his trip, he will speak with French government officials to see if he can put into practice the projects discussed at the Brenner Pass. This is not very satisfactory to me. In the long run, a *rapprochement* between Berlin and Paris could not but work against us. But is this possible?

October 21, 1940

Nothing new.

October 22, 1940

This is a sad day, more than ever because it is the anniversary of the death of my good sister, Maria.

Mussolini is back. He has prepared a letter for Hitler on the general situation. He alludes to our impending action in Greece, but does not make clear either the form or the date, because he fears that once again an order might come to stop us. Many indications lead us to believe that in Berlin they are not very enthusiastic about our going to Athens. The date is now set for October 28. General Pricolo reports that Badoglio has given orders for a limited air action. The Duce does not agree. He wants us to attack very vigorously, because he would like everything to go to pieces at the first clash. If we allow the Greeks too much time to think and breathe, the English will come, and perhaps the Turks, and the situation will become long, drawn out and difficult. The Duce can now hardly stand Badoglio, whom he considers an obstacle between himself and the troops.

I begin to draft the ultimatum which Grazzi will hand to Metaxas at two o'clock in the morning of October 28. Naturally it is a document that allows no way out for Greece. Either she accepts occupation or she will be attacked.

October 23, 1940

Nothing new.

October 24, 1940

With General Pricolo I examine the plan of the air attack on Greece. It is good, because it is energetic and bold. With a hard blow from the beginning it will be possible to obtain a complete collapse within a few hours.

During the evening von Ribbentrop telephones from a little railway station in France. He reports on a conference with Franco and with Pétain, and is, on the whole, satisfied with the results achieved. He says that the program of collaboration is heading toward concrete results. I do not conceal my doubt and suspicion. Nevertheless, it is essential that the inclusion of France in the Axis shall not be to our detriment. Von Ribbentrop also discusses an impending trip by Hitler to a city in northern Italy, to confer with the Duce.

October 25, 1940

With the Duce I settle upon our diplomatic lines of action for our move in Greece. He also approves a meeting with the Soviet ambassador immediately after the attack. It is a gesture that may calm the troubled waters, perhaps prepare the ground for the future. In the meantime, von Mackensen conveys some more particulars concerning Hitler's conferences with the French and the Spaniards, and announces the terms of a secret tripartite protocol with Spain.

The Duce sends a letter to General Visconti Prasca, spurring him into action.

Von Ribbentrop telephones. He proposes a conference and the proposal is accepted. It is to take place on Monday, the 28th, in Florence, between Hitler and Mussolini. This Führer's rush to Italy so soon after his conference with Pétain is not at all to my liking. I hope he will not offer us a cup of hemlock because of our claims against France. This will be a bitter pill for the Italian people, even more than the Versailles disappointment.

October 26, 1940

Nothing new.

October 27, 1940

Numerous incidents in Albania. Action is expected at any moment. And yet the four diplomats, German, Japanese, Spanish, and Hungarian, to whom I handed the text of the ultimatum to Greece, were rather surprised.

I have prepared the agenda for the meeting in Florence tomorrow. Hitler will be there for only a few hours, and then will leave for the Brenner Pass.

October 28, 1940

We attack in Albania and carry on a conference at Florence. In both places things have gone well. Notwithstanding the bad weather, the troops are moving fast, even without air support.

In Florence the conference, of which there is a stenographic report elsewhere, is of the greatest interest and proves that German solidarity has not failed us.

The Duce is in a very good mood. He speaks at length about the situation of the party. He rejects Ricci's candidacy, and accepts the name of Serena. He would also like to consider Marziali, the Prefect of Milan, but I dissuade him. It would be a disaster—worse than that caused by Muti.

October 29, 1940

The weather is bad, but the advance continues. Diplomatic reactions in the Balkans are quite limited for the time being. No one makes a move to defend the Greeks. It is now a question of speed, and we must act quickly.

I leave for Tirana during the evening.

October 30, 1940

At Tirana. Bad weather. I do not fly. I inspect the public works, the roads, the port. Things are going bit slowly. It's because of the rain.

October 31, 1940

Continued bad weather. I write a long letter to the Duce. Here they complain of the ill will of the General Staff, which didn't prepare for the action as it should have. Badoglio was convinced that the Greek question could have been settled at the peace table, and his attitude was affected by this prejudice. This resulted in a much weaker preparation than we were led to expect.

November 1, 1940

The sun has finally appeared. I take advantage of it to carry out a spectacular bombing of Salonika. On my return I am attacked by Greek planes. All goes well. Two of theirs went down, but I must confess that it is the first time that I had them on my tail. It is an ugly sensation.

I went from Tirana to Taranto to confer with the Duce, and then from Taranto to Rome, from where I will leave for Germany.

November 2, 1940

On my way to Sudetenland.

November 3, 1940

I wrote a report of my conversations with Ribbentrop. I have nothing to add. I saw no one except the people on the official committee, and the foresters—not enough to gather any impressions.

Only during the last night, while Ribbentrop talked to his guests, repeating his favorite motto that the war was already won, a German army major turned to me and said in his labored French: "We heard this phrase in 1914, in 1915, in 1916, and in 1917. I believed it. Yet in 1918 I wished I were dead." His calm sincerity and sadness impressed me. Let's hope that too many of them don't start thinking this way.

November 4, 1940

I leave for Italy.

November 5, 1940

On my way home.

November 6, 1940

Mussolini is dissatisfied over the way things are going in Greece. The attack on Corcia did take place, even though the results were not those that English radio bragged about. The enemy has made some progress and it is a fact that on the eighth day of operations the initiative is in their hands. Soddu has left for Albania and will take command. Visconti will remain in command of the army of the Epirus.

I don't think that we have come to the point where we must bandage our heads, although many are beginning to do so. As a matter of fact, in the evening Mussolini is calmer. The forces now gathered in the Corcia sector indicate that the Greek push may be definitely slowed up. Afterward the counterattack and success will come. Perhaps even much sooner than expected.

November 7, 1940

I confer with Benini, who has just returned from Tirana, and accompany him to see the Duce, to whom he makes a long report. On the Corcia sector our collapse began when a frightened battalion of Albanians ran away. It seems there was no treachery. Our soldiers did miracles. Entire Greek divisions were stopped by the resistance put up by platoons of custom guards, and the Greeks did not pass until the defenders died to the last man. We withdrew to a defensive line. Soddu maintains that the arrival of a few regiments of Alpine troops would definitely eliminate all dangers. In the Epirus sector Visconti is still relatively optimistic and thinks that we can position ourselves to bring about the fall of Janina. Soddu doesn't agree and thinks we ought to stop our maneuver, increase our forces, and repeat our attack.

The civilian organization is excellent. The port of Durazzo is operating at full capacity, but is not too crowded with ships. So also are the roads, which insure an intense and safe traffic between the front and the rear.

In the afternoon I went to the reception given by the Soviets. This creates a profound sensation in the diplomatic corps. It is the first time that I have crossed the portals of this embassy as Minister for Foreign Affairs.

November 8, 1940

The news given by Jacomoni does not corroborate that of headquarters, which is more pessimistic. The Duce has a long conversation with Badoglio and Roatta and makes plans for sending troops. It appears that Badoglio is gloomy and this irritates the Duce. He is especially irritated because Badoglio asks for four more months. Too long. We must act immediately and energetically. The attack by the Greeks is slowing down and they have no reserves. Grazzi, returning from Athens, confirms that internal conditions of the country are very bad, and their resistance is made of soap bubbles. According to him, Metaxas, who receives our ultimatum in his night shirt and dressing gown, was ready to yield. He became unyielding only after having talked with the King, and after the intervention of the English minister.

In the evening news is better. The Greek attack is weakening in all sectors.

November 9, 1940

The situation is unchanged on the Albanian front. The Greek attack has lost its impetus and is dying out. But we, unfortunately, also do not have the strength to resume our advance. We shall do so in a few weeks. The Duce is now very angry with Jacomoni and Visconti, who had described the operation as too easy and bound to succeed.

Hitler has made a speech. I didn't like it. Too many personal arguments to be convincing. The purpose of the speech is to raise the morale of the German people, who are disappointed by the results of the American elections. But did the Führer succeed? Mussolini plans to speak on November 18. He is aware of the fact that the internal situation has become difficult and that a word from him is needed.

November 10, 1940

An offensive thrust by our cavalry carried far in the vicinity of Prevesa has found no resistance, which proves that the Greeks have only a thin military line and having broken it we shall move on with ease. If we had two divisions in Albania today we could launch them, assured of success.

Neville Chamberlain is dead. I have pleasant memories of the two occasions I saw him, in Munich and in Rome. He was a simple man, spontaneous and human. Mussolini does not attach any weight to the event, and commented, "This time he definitely missed the bus," and he was so pleased with his own remark that he asked me to include it in my diary.

November 11, 1940

Today I received Stackic, a lawyer from Belgrade, who was introduced to me by Galeazzo di Bagno. He is on a mission from the royal house of Serbia and, more precisely, for Antic, Minister of the Royal House. It appears that Antic would like to meet me for the purpose of strengthening ties between Italy and Yugoslavia. He even talks of an alliance with far-reaching guarantees, among which is the demilitarization of the Adriatic. I referred the matter to Mussolini, who encouraged the project. I am very favorable to it. I always considered an attack on Yugoslavia a difficult undertaking and not useful for the future equilibrium of Europe. Instead of bringing home to us a mass of nervous and untrustworthy Croats, I believe it is better to create a solid basis of understanding between Italy and Yugoslavia. This would be useful if the future brings us an anti-Russian or an anti-German policy.

From Albania we receive news that the situation has stabilized. Had we had more adequate forces we could have gone far. Now we can only wait. Unfortunately, success, when it does come, will no longer be of the first magnitude.

From many sources, and especially from Moscow, comes news of a certain anti-Italian attitude, and even actual anti-Italian propaganda that the

Germans are spreading in Greece.

November 12, 1940

A black day. The British have attacked the Italian fleet at anchor in Taranto without warning and have sunk the dreadnought *Cavour* and seriously damaged the battleships *Littorio* and *Duilio*. These ships will stay out of the fight for many months. I thought I would find the Duce downhearted. Instead, he took the blow quite well and does not, at the moment, seem to have fully realized its gravity. When Badoglio last came to see me at the Palazzo Chigi, he said that when we attacked Greece we should immediately move the fleet, which would no longer be safe in the port of Taranto; why was this not done a fortnight after the beginning of operations and with a full moon?

The British bombing also did serious damage to Durazzo. The Agip tank is on fire. Fortunately the port is unscathed. It is very important to keep it from being damaged, since it is our only access to Albania. It has worked well and is still working splendidly. No slowing down or bottleneck in this harbor. I remember what happened at Massawa at the beginning of the Ethiopian campaign, and the comparison is gratifying, but anti-aircraft defense is scarce and the British attacks will most certainly increase.

November 13, 1940

The Duce is beginning to seriously lose faith in Badoglio. He has given me orders to keep my eye on him carefully and constantly to find out what he really tells the Germans in his coming meeting with Keitel at Innsbruck.

Mussolini read me the speech he will deliver to the party chiefs on November 18. It is good, but contains nothing new or different. I shall be absent, because on that day I have a meeting with Hitler; Serrano Suñer will also be present.

November 14, 1940

Antonescu and Sturdza arrive.[475] My impressions of the first man are fair. As to the second, he isn't even worth talking about. Mussolini has called him "one of those types who performs Russian dances."

The interview at the Palazzo Venezia was rather dull. Antonescu strongly attacks the decision at Vienna, and says that the verdict was given on the basis of a colored sheet of paper printed by the Hungarians. If the colors had been reversed the verdict would have been favorable to the Romanians. I did not want to go on arguing, but I must confess that he was not very courteous in speaking with one of the two arbiters.

Farinacci tells me that Mussolini, in speaking of the Greek affair, told him that "even Count Ciano gave him wrong information," and then, speaking of the Fascist party, that "Count Ciano had made a present of Muti to the party." Farinacci said that he protested vigorously. I shall only answer that I had the same information as Mussolini about Albania, and regarding Muti it should be said that from January 1 on I constantly denounced his incompetence and recommended that he be replaced at once.

November 15, 1940

It seems that the Greeks have resumed their attack all along the front, and with considerable forces. Up to now we have resisted very well. This is also confirmed in a letter from Starace, which, with all its realism, is not pessimistic. Above all, he blames Visconti Prasca, who had stately too lightly that everything was ready to the last detail, while, as a matter of fact, the organization of our forces was altogether defective.

The King does not like colored shirts very much, whatever their shade. Yesterday, at the court, he told me, "These Romanians in their green shirts are really ridiculous. They remind me of the hotel porters in old Russia."

In the evening the news from Albania is more serious. Pressure continues, and resistance is more difficult. And then we lack guns, while Greek artillery is modern and well handled.

Under the circumstances, Comrade De Vecchi is thinking seriously of offering his resignation as Governor of the Aegean, and yet he was one of the most active, in fact the most active, in encouraging Mussolini about the war against Greece. But now that he realizes the time has arrived for the rats to scuttle he wants to be the first to land.

November 16, 1940

We are putting up a strong resistance in Albania.

Departure of the Romanians, who, on the whole, have not made a lasting impression.

November 17, 1940

I leave for Salzburg. News from Albania is uncertain; an eventual withdrawal is not to be excluded.

November 18-19, 1940

A rather enigmatic Ribbentrop meets me in Salzburg. Before lunch, in his house at Fuschl, he decides to talk; that is, to announce that Hitler will speak on the situation created by the Greek crisis. The Germans are gloomy, and it is not difficult to understand why. I had lunch with Serrano and Ribbentrop. Serrano is outspoken. He chats away with a freedom the Germans don't like, criticizing especially the German effort to get together with the French. He thinks this understanding is difficult and he doesn't believe that Laval is the right man to bring it about.

In the afternoon I saw Hitler at the Berghof. A long tea with Serrano and the others, and then a personal conversation with Hitler, Ribbentrop, and an interpreter. I outlined the conversation in a letter to the Duce. There was a heavy atmosphere. Hitler is pessimistic and considers the situation much compromised by what has happened in the Balkans. His criticism is open, focused, and final. I try to talk to him, but he does not allow me to proceed. Only in the second part of the conversation, that is, after Hitler approved of eventual negotiations with Yugoslavia, does he become warm and cordial, at times almost friendly. The idea of an alliance with Yugoslavia excites him to the point that while his pessimism at first appeared too black now his optimism seems too rosy.

He tells me some secrets: that Horthy even urged him at the time of his trip to Italy to raise the question of Trieste, because he wanted to launch Hungarian nationalist claims on Fiume. (Can I believe all this?) "For the moment," Hitler added, "it is necessary to dissemble with the Hungarians, because we need their railroads. But the moment will come when we shall speak clearly." (However much he dissembles, the Hungarians know his ideas very well.) From the hotel I write a long letter to the Duce. I emphasized the Yugoslav affair, because I am convinced that it will be very much to the liking of the Germans at this moment. I believe that Mussolini will raise strong objections, at least he will refuse all military help in the matter before he has exacted his revenge on the Greeks.

Alternative news of defeats and victories on the Albanian front. I fear that we shall have to withdraw to a pre-established line. The loss of Corcia is certainly not the loss of Paris, but it will give a name to the battle and help the enemy beat propaganda drums against Italy. This is why I hope that we may hold on to Corcia.

On my way to Vienna by train.

November 20, 1940

Signature of the document by which Hungary joins us. Romanian and Slovakian signatures will follow. I do not attach much importance to these states joining; they are vassals of Germany, or practically so. In fact, they weaken the tripartite agreement itself, and seem to be the useless bits of ersatz diplomacy of our victory. In Germany they talked too much about everything being finished by October, and in fact the Viennese people, who always have their witticisms ready, said, "They were right: oil, butter, and meat are finished." Austrian morale is low.

A few not very interesting words with the Hungarians.

Again a conference with Hitler. He speaks exclusively of Yugoslavia and is satisfied that the Duce has given his consent, in principle. He plans to call the Regent, Paul, to Berlin, and to propose the big deal to him. He is ready to favor the rise of Paul himself to the throne. His wife is ambitious. This seems difficult to me. Paul is not enough of a Serb in spirit and ways to be loved by his people. At the end, Hitler has one of his characteristic fits of emotion. "From this city of Vienna, on the day of the Anschluss, I sent Mussolini a cable to assure him that I would never forget his help. I confirm it today, and I am at his side with all my strength." He had two big tears in his eyes. What a strange man! He hands me a sealed letter.

November 21, 1940

Hitler's letter to the Duce is in the same vein as the first part of the conference—critical and full of concern. I expected a violent reaction from

Mussolini. Instead, there is nothing. He does not seem to attribute any importance to a document which, indeed, has a great deal. I find the Duce calm, determined, unconcerned. What is happening in Albania saddens but does not disturb him. He is critical of our military men, of Badoglio, and announces an imminent change of guard in the military sector.

During the evening Soddu announces that he intends to abandon Corcia and withdraw on the entire front. And yet Greek pressure seems to be less. Mussolini intervenes to get him to reconsider, but the machine is in motion and it cannot be stopped now.

November 22, 1940

Mussolini is preparing his answer to Hitler's letter—on rereading it he realized its full import. "He really smacked my fingers," is how he concludes. The answer is brief and calm. He accepts Hitler's political and military proposals.

Pavolini recounts confidentially what Badoglio said to him: "There is no doubt that Jacomoni and Visconti Prasca bear a large share of responsibility in the Albanian affair, but the real blame must be sought elsewhere. It lies entirely in the Duce's command. This is a command that he, the Duce, cannot hold. Let him leave everything to us, and when things go wrong let him punish those responsible." Pavolini dutifully informed the Duce about it. The Duce's reaction was like a flash. He called Badoglio names like "enemy of the regime" and "traitor," which are strong epithets for him to use about his own Chief of Staff in wartime.

November 23, 1940

Sebastiani revealed to me this morning that the Duce is studying the military *Annuario*,[476] in order to find substitutes for Badoglio and Soddu. His eye seems to have rested on the names of Pintor and Orlando, the latter being an unknown. Mussolini himself said nothing to me about it. In any case, even if he asks me, I intend to keep out of it, since I know little about military matters. Personally, I like Messe, and I recall that my father thought well of Gazzera.

In the *Regime Fascista* Farinacci openly attacks Badoglio, thereby precipitating a crisis.

I had a brief telephone conversation with Ribbentrop. Hitler has not yet read the Duce's letter, and therefore can make no reply. I shall talk to him again tomorrow. News from Albania is of an orderly retreat without pressure from the enemy.

November 24, 1940

Nothing new.

November 25, 1940

Soddu confirms improved news from Albania. He feels that the forces under him are sufficient to guarantee a stabilization of the line. The Badoglio crisis is out in the open. Badoglio demands a retraction by Farinacci, couched in such terms that I am certain the latter will blow up the printing press of his newspaper rather than agree. Badoglio insists that if a denial is not published he will leave. Mussolini now wants to sack him. He is moving slowly, because this is his nature in such matters, and because he wants to let time take its course. He speaks about Pintor and Gazzera.

November 26, 1940

Badoglio, after a conference with the Duce, has handed in his resignation. Farinacci persists in his refusal to publish a retraction. We cannot go on this way. When we add to this the fact Badoglio was confronted with Pavolini's written statement, we begin to see the outlines of the situation. Today the ushers at the doors of the Palazzo Venezia were given instructions to accompany the most important Italian big shots into different rooms, in order to prevent a general brawl.

November 27, 1940

The General Staff crisis continues. Mussolini has accepted Badoglio's resignation in principle, but he must still overcome some last-minute uncertainties. He wants to draft a communiqué stating that "Badoglio has handed in his resignation for reasons of health and age." This formula does not suit Badoglio, but Mussolini insists, because this way he intends to nip in the bud the candidacy of "that roguish old madman, General De Bono." Meanwhile, Badoglio has retired, not to his tent, but to the villa of his friend Necchi near Milan. Nevertheless, this is a situation that cannot go on.

From Albania the news from Soddu indicates progressive improvement. News from Starace, on the other hand, is not very optimistic, since he still feels that our situation is hanging by a thread.

I see De Vecchi. He speaks with less logic than usual, and cannot explain his resignation.

He would really like to leave, but knows he will look bad. Notwithstanding his incomparable conceit, he is ashamed, but not to the point of refraining from applying for another job at the same time.

November 28, 1940

Meeting between De Vecchi and Mussolini, which ends without any decision. De Vecchi said that "he is ready to serve elsewhere, but that he expects lots of chevrons on his sleeve." The Duce did not react.

Bad news from Albania. Greek pressure continues, but above all our resistance is weakening. If the Greeks had enough strength to pierce our lines we might yet have a lot of trouble.

November 29, 1940

The Duce has appointed Guzzoni Undersecretary of War and Assistant Chief of the General Staff. In general, this appointment is well received.

Starace, who has just returned from Albania, sees things in pretty dark colors, and passes harsh judgment on the behavior of our troops. Our soldiers have fought but little, and poorly. This is the real, fundamental cause of everything that has happened.

November 30, 1940

Meeting of the Council of Ministers. The Duce talks at length about the situation. He reads the main documents and, while personally assuming responsibility for the political decisions, he hits hard at Badoglio regarding the military results. The Duce's thesis is this: Badoglio was not only in agreement, but was even over-enthusiastic. The political side of the question was handled perfectly; military action was entirely inadequate. He did not conceal the gravity of the situation, meaning the imminent retreat to the south and the enemy's attack now underway in the Pogradec area. "The situation is serious," said the Duce. "It might even become tragic." In the Council of Ministers there was genuine rebellion against De Vecchi when the Chief mentioned his name and read the cables by which he had spurred him on to the attack of Greece.

The Duce called in General Cavallero, and this reveals his intentions. Cavallero is an optimist who does not believe in the possibility of defeat in Albania, having full faith in our ability to take the offensive once more. I record everything but endorse nothing. I am becoming more and more cautious in military matters. The Duce does not mention any appointments or jobs to General Cavallero. He listens to him at length, and invites him to another meeting tomorrow. In the meantime, Badoglio continues to shoot pheasants.

December 1, 1940

News from Albania has improved. We are holding and even counterattacking in the north, while in the south the withdrawal continues without enemy pressure. In his conversation with Cavallero the Duce tells him about his impending appointment as Chief of the General Staff. It is still on hold, delayed until Badoglio returns to Rome.

We have indirect news of German-Yugoslav negotiations. We have not been told anything, although they are discussing matters which concern us.

I can't say that the Germans are very tactful with us.

December 2, 1940

Nothing worth mentioning. A discussion with the Papal Nuncio about the abolition of holidays on New Year's Day, Epiphany, and St. Joseph's. This is a bright idea of the Duce's, who is very proud of it. At my insistence he relented as to the celebration of St. Joseph's Day, but he holds firm on the other two holidays, and especially on New Year's, "since it is none other than the day of the circumcision of Christ, that is, the celebration of a Hebrew rite, which the Church itself has abolished." I wonder whether, in times like these, it is worth irritating the people with whims of this sort.

December 3, 1940

Greek pressure has started again on the Albanian front, and it seems that the 11th Army must now make that withdrawal from Argirocastro and Port Edda, which we had hoped to avoid.

December 4, 1940

Sorice[477] telephones at an early hour that we have lost Pogradec and that the Greeks have broken through our lines. Then he informs us that Soddu now thinks that "any military action has become impossible and the situation must be settled through political intervention." Mussolini calls me to the Palazzo Venezia. I find him discouraged as never before. He says: "There is nothing else to do. This is grotesque and absurd, but it is a fact. We have to ask for a truce through Hitler." This is impossible. The Greeks will, as a first condition, demand the Führer's personal guarantee that nothing will ever be done against them again.

I would rather put a bullet through my head than telephone Ribbentrop. Can it be possible that we are defeated? May it not be that the commander has given up before his men? I am in no position to make military suggestions, but rigorous logic tells me that if a rout has not already started it is still possible to form a bridgehead at Valona and, with fresh forces, create a safety line on the river Skumbini. What is important now is to resist, and to stick to Albania. Time will bring victory, but if we give up it is the end. Mussolini listens to me and decides to make another attempt. He sends Cavallero to the front. Later, he is again discouraged and says, "Every man must make one fatal error in his life. And I made mine when I believed General Visconti Prasca. But how could I have avoided it when this man seemed so sure of himself and when every indication had given us full assurance? The human material I have to work with is useless, worthless."

The idea strikes me that I can perhaps verify the situation through Jacomoni, and I call him on the telephone. I immediately get the impression that in Tirana they are more calm than in Rome. I fear that some misunderstanding lurks in the air. In fact, Jacomoni says that "as a political solution, Soddu had intended a military diversion on the Greek flank, such as a German or Yugoslav intervention." News from the High Command also improved during the day, and Soddu and Cavallero leave for Elbasan, to study the situation on the spot.

During the evening I see the Duce again. He was more relieved. He has had a talk with Badoglio, who meant to withdraw his resignation. Too late. Mussolini asserts that the King himself encouraged him to accept it, saying that, "in his opinion, Badoglio is now too tired."

December 5, 1940

News from Albania indicates that the situation is unchanged. The time gained is entirely in our favor, the more so since the Germans have given us fifty transport planes. In this way traffic is facilitated.

De Vecchi's resignation has also been accepted, and he will be replaced by Bastico. The Duce intends to replace Admiral Cavagnari with Admiral Riccardi. My father's opinion of the latter was not very high.

I succeed in having the Duce restore the New Year and Epiphany holidays. I inform the Papal Nuncio of it. It was not worthwhile to create a crisis with the Vatican in times like these.

December 6, 1940

News from Albania unchanged.

Conference with Marshal Milch, who has come to Rome to settle the question of the Stukas in the Mediterranean. He was calm and optimistic about the situation in general, including the Greek question. Hitler's letter, of which he was the bearer, also differs substantially in content and in form from the one sent from Vienna. The Albanian affair is minimized, considered as heading to a solution, an episode in the big picture where the prospects are good. All this has greatly relieved Mussolini, who is counterattacking, even concerning internal matters. "If, when I was a Socialist," he said, "I had had a knowledge of the work of the Italian middle class, not purely theoretical as learned by the reading of Karl Marx, but practical, based on experience such as I have now, I would have launched a revolution so pitiless that, by comparison, the revolution of Comrade Lenin would have been child's play."

Cavallero has been appointed. Reactions are not good, especially in military circles. The man is heavily criticized. Opinions vary, but no one says that he is stupid.

December 7, 1940

A speech by Zvetkovic marks the beginning of a maneuver for the conversion of Yugoslavia. Stackic also announces that he will soon make a trip to Italy and will be followed shortly by Antic, Minister of the Court. In a conference with Christich I stressed that we are well disposed toward his country, and alluded to the Slavic character of the Vardar Valley. Mussolini is calm, and as firm as a rock. Now that he has removed De Vecchi he is happy to have done it. He put in the despatch the words "at his request," in order to make it clear to all concerned that "at the time when these men should have made a request to reenter the ranks of the Fascists, they have asked to leave them."

Cavallero returns from Albania. He still considers the situation as critical but heading toward a solution. Within a week our lines, which still suffer from slight oscillations, will be definitely stabilized. Within a short time he is thinking of making a local counterattack that would again assure us possession of Corcia, which, from the point of view of prestige, would be a great thing. News from Greece confirms reports that the situation is serious.

December 8, 1940

Nothing new.

December 9, 1940

The Fascist party has launched a counterattack against Badoglio, which is probably exaggerated; they are even talking of treason. Serena[478] has told me what he was doing and explained his tactics. I do not entirely agree.

Every exaggeration is counterproductive because it touches on the honor of the army itself. In fact, Badoglio went to protest to the Duce and obtained a rather friendly reply.

December 10, 1940

News of the attack on Sidi Barrani comes like a thunderbolt. At first it doesn't seem serious, but subsequent cables from Graziani confirm that we have taken a beating. Mussolini, whom I see twice, is very calm. He comments on the event with impersonal objectivity. It almost seems that what has happened doesn't concern him in the least, he being more preoccupied with Graziani's prestige, and ready to overlook the seriousness of what has happened. But it is serious, at home and abroad. It is serious outside of Italy because from the tone of Graziani's cables it does not appear that he has sufficiently recovered from the blow to prepare a counterattack. Inside Italy, the bad news is compounded. Public opinion had already been much too shaken and divided to receive this new and heavy blow.

Hitler's speech did not make a good impression. It is more defensive than offensive, and one feels that Italy plays a very secondary role.

December 11, 1940

Things are really going badly in Libya. Four divisions can be considered destroyed, and Graziani, who reports on the spirit and decision of the enemy, says nothing about what he can do to parry the blow. Mussolini becomes more and more calm. He maintains that the many painful days through which we are living must be considered inevitable in the changing fortunes of every war. He still hopes that Graziani can and will stop the English advance. If it can be stopped at the old boundary, he thinks the situation will not be serious; if the English should reach Tobruk, then he thinks "the situation would become tragic."

During the evening news arrives that the *Catanzaro* division did not hold against the English push but was itself torn to pieces. Something is the matter with our army if five divisions let themselves be pulverized in two days.

December 12, 1940

We are easing up in Albania. Doing poorly in Libya. Graziani cables little news and gives no details. He has not yet recovered from the blow he has suffered, and besides, it seems that his nerves are quite shaken ever since the attempt on his life in Addis Ababa. They tell me that even in Italy he was so much afraid of assassination attempts that he had his villa at Arcinazzo guarded by at least eighteen carabinieri. In Libya he had a shelter built in a Roman tomb at Cyrene, sixty or seventy feet deep. Now he is upset and cannot make decisions. He pins his hopes on the possible exhaustion of the adversary, and not on his own strength, which is a bad sign. The Duce now feels the seriousness of events. "In Libya we have suffered a real defeat. This time it will not be said that politics is to blame. I have left the military authorities the greatest freedom of action. The King was very gloomy this morning."

I have seen von Mackensen. He came on a pretext. Naturally we spoke about the situation, and I did not conceal how matters stand. He has shown solidarity and understanding. Ansaldo reports that von Ribbentrop has done the same in a conference he had with him in Berlin. During the evening Sebastiani suggests that I should go to the Palazzo Venezia.

December 13, 1940

A catastrophic cable from Graziani has arrived, a mixture of excitement, rhetoric, and concern. He is thinking of withdrawing to Tripoli, "in order to keep the flag flying on that fortress at least," but he is inclined to accuse Rome, meaning Mussolini, of having forced him to wage a war "of the flea against the elephant."

I visit Mussolini and find him very much shaken. I have nothing to tell him, but desire only by my presence to make him understand that I am with him more than ever. He realizes how the country will take the blow. He listens to my suggestion about doing something to raise the morale of the people. We must speak to the hearts of the Italians. We must make them understand that what is at stake in the game is not Fascism—it is our country, our eternal country, the country of all of us, which is above men and times and factions.

The morning news seems better, and the Duce is relieved. For my part I am skeptical, since the strength of the attack and the feeble resistance of the troops do not give us grounds to hope for anything good. I do not at all believe, as the Duce does, that the English will be satisfied to eject us from Egypt and stop at the border. They have more far-reaching objectives.

December 14, 1940

News from Libya seems to improve. Graziani sends fewer cables and is not as gloomy as before. Soddu continues to send disturbing reports from Albania, while Cavallero's telephone calls are quite calm. Mussolini says, "Five generals are prisoners and one is dead. This is the percentage of Italians who have military characteristics and those who have none. In the future we shall create an army of professionals, selecting them out of 12 or 13 million Italians—those in the Po Valley and in part of central Italy. All the others will be put to work making arms for the warrior aristocracy."

During the evening bad news again. While I am dining at the German embassy the Duce telephones to inquire about a crisis in the French government.[479] The Germans don't seem too concerned about it. Their attitude toward us is grim. In German eyes one does not yet read the verdict of guilty but surely finds in them many questions.

December 15, 1940

I find the Duce calm but indignant toward Graziani because of a long recriminatory cable in which he talks "man to man" and scolds the Duce for having allowed himself to be betrayed by his Roman military staff, for never having listened to him, and for having pushed him into an adventure leading us beyond human capabilities and into the realms of destiny. Mussolini reads it to me and says, "Here is another man with whom I cannot get angry, because I despise him." The Duce still believes that the British advance can be stopped at the approaches to Derna.

In Albania there was also a retreat, which Cavallero considers not to be serious and of purely tactical value. He believes that his reserves are sufficient to stop the gap.

I receive the Marchesa Graziani. She is beside herself. She has received a letter from her husband containing his will, and in it he says that "one cannot break steel armor with fingernails alone." He asks for a massive intervention of the German air force in Libya, which might still change the present rout into a victory. Even if this idea were taken into account, would the Germans risk sending their planes on such short notice without time to prepare for replacements and transports? I don't think so. The only thing that is certain is that Marshal Graziani has lost his self-control.

December 16, 1940

A lull in Albania and in Libya, where, however, the enemy is preparing for an attack on Bardia. A meeting with the Duce concerning the request to Germany for raw materials. The sad story begins. We are not asking for too much, but it is always hard to ask for anything, especially now.

December 17, 1940

Again a bad withdrawal in Albania toward Clisura and Tepeleni. The Duce has prepared a letter, a harsh letter, to Cavallero, with an order to the troops to die at their positions. "More than an order from me," he wrote, "it is an order from our country." Let us hope that this lash will have its effect.

In the city the rumor has spread of a great Italian victory with tens of thousands of prisoners and hundreds of tanks destroyed. In a flash the rumor has swept the country. There is no truth to it. It is a maneuver, cunning and base, to break down our morale. They tell me that after Caporetto, too, the same thing happened, and that the country was inflamed by the hopes aroused by false news and was then plunged into an even gloomier desolation. A prelude to the war of nerves.

December 18, 1940

I confer at length with Cavallero, who has returned from Albania. He is clearly optimistic. He not only thinks that some kind of surprise is possible, but he also believes that the critical phase is almost over, and he is planning to strike the first offensive blow at Clisura the day after tomorrow. This is to be followed by another in the Tomorizza Valley. He thinks that by February 1 he will have completed preparations for an offensive that should bring us back to Corcia; from there on he will press the offensive as rapidly as possible. In this spirit, he attaches little importance to the vicissitudes that our lines have suffered in the last few days.

Little news from Libya, where English forces continue to press us around Bardia. Nevertheless, its means of defense are such that if Bergonzoli holds firm the English will not have an easy task.

I received and addressed the National Council of the Veterans' Association. It does not take many words to kindle the faith that is in the hearts of all Italians, and which only awaits an opportunity to express itself.

December 19, 1940

I cannot say that what has happened has proved Cavallero right. The Siena division, which was operating on the shore line, was torn to pieces by a Greek attack. The position is dangerous. Once they enter the valley of Sciuscizza the march on Valona is easy and natural, and it is not difficult to see how heavy a loss the fall of Valona would be. Mussolini is irritated because he feels that our forces are not fighting back and their officers' morale is low. To this must be added the fact that when Soddu speaks to the Duce he says one thing, and when he talks to Sorice he says another. For him, the important strategy is not the one directed at the Greeks, but the one directed at the Palazzo Venezia.

December 20, 1940

Jealousies among generals are worse than among women. One should hear Soddu's telephone calls to Sorice. He demolishes all the generals. Geloso has softening of the brain, Perugi is a disaster, Trionfi is bankrupt. Today, for some unknown reason, he speaks well of Vercellino, saying, "Poor Vercellino. He is such a dear. He came to see me and he wept."[480]

The Duce has prepared a message for Hitler. He presents things as they are and asks for German intervention in Thrace through Bulgaria. I don't think that Hitler can do this before March. In any case, the message will not be sent immediately. The Duce awaits Cavallero's report and probably also the results of our counterattack at Tepeleni, where two fresh divisions have arrived, the Cuneo and the Acqui.

Churchill gave a tough speech. It is, naturally, hard on us, for he says cruel things about the value of our forces in Libya, where the situation continues to be serious. It is a clever speech, in which many hints can be read between the lines.

December 21, 1940

Nothing new or noteworthy on both fronts.

Mussolini, who feels a little better, has a long conversation with the military attaché, Marras, in my presence. It deals with possible German military help. Marras reaches these conclusions: (1) before March Hitler can engage in no actions in Thrace; (2) it is useless to ask for German troops in Valona because they could not arrive within a month; (3) they might consider sending two armored divisions to Libya. The Duce agrees with these points.

December 22, 1940

Cavallero, who is the fellow who always sounds the optimistic note, says that the counterattack on the coast line will be ready tomorrow or the day after. We do not expect great results, but hope to reduce pressure on Valona. This would be a success, because Valona represents a strategic objective of the first order for the Greeks and the English, and also because we shall retake the initiative.

December 23, 1940

Nothing new, but I find the Duce rather irritated over Saturday's withdrawal, contrary to Cavallero's expectations. Instead of lessening, the pressure on Valona is now increasing. The Duce no longer believes what Cavallero says. "These generals have become," affirms Mussolini, "like those country innkeepers who paint a rooster on the wall and under it write 'When this rooster begins to crow, to you credit I'll bestow.' I, too, will grant the military men credit when they prove by some action that the situation has changed." Then, speaking of the rather indifferent behavior of our troops, he added, "I must nevertheless recognize that the Italians of 1914 were better than these. It is not flattering for the regime, but that's the way it is."

December 24, 1940

It is snowing. The Duce looks out of the window and is glad that it is snowing. "This snow and cold are very good," he says. "This is how our good-for-nothing men and this mediocre race will be improved. One of the main reasons I have requested the reforestation of the Apennines has been to make Italy colder and more snowy."

A long conference with Melchiori, who has returned from Cyrenaica. He is Graziani's liaison officer, hence, pretty much in the middle of things. In his opinion the situation has clearly improved, and we shall no longer have any sudden surprises. Graziani openly accuses Badoglio of treachery, and says that even in his gloomiest hours the only thing that prevented him from committing suicide was his strong desire to drag Badoglio to the dock one day.

December 25, 1940

Christmas. The Duce is somber, and speaks again about the situation in Albania. He appears more tired than usual, and this saddens me very much. The energy of the Duce at this time is our greatest resource. He no longer believes in Cavallero. He says that his optimism is like that of someone whistling in the dark. In fact, Cavallero reports from Tirana that "the height of the crisis has passed, and now there is a complete change of spirit in the troops."

December 26, 1940

Nothing new.

December 27, 1940

The usual story in Albania, and this displeases the Duce. He is right. Notwithstanding Cavallero's bright words one cannot read the situation clearly. He promises this offensive of the valley of Sciuscizza, but it does not happen, and we would not be surprised if once again the Greeks should launch theirs first.

December 28, 1940
   Nothing new.

December 29, 1940
   I went to Cortellazzo for the inauguration of the village dedicated to my father. A simple and brief ceremony.
   In Venice I saw little and can say little about how the people feel. Some degrees below freezing, and the lagoons are covered with ice; therefore, the Venetians are unwilling to show any interest in politics.

December 30, 1940
   During my absence the Duce conferred the command of the armed forces on Cavallero, and has recalled Soddu. For some time he had been dissatisfied with Soddu's temperamental mood swings. One day everything rosy, and another everything black. The final blow came when the Duce learned that Soddu, even in Albania, was devoting his evening hours to composing film music.

December 31, 1940
   Cavallero transmits a copy of a letter addressed to the Duce, in which he asks his permission for a large offensive action along the coast. It is like asking the hare to run. No one more than the Duce gnaws his lips on account of this interminable defensive that day after day forces him to swallow bitter pills.
   Parini at the Palazzo Venezia. He speaks of what the party is doing for the troops. His opinion of the future is rather bright, but he is very tough about the past.

1941

January 1, 1941

The year started with a bad scare about Mother's health. A heart attack put her dear life in danger. Then she improved, but all this has left me in great anxiety.

The Duce has received a long letter from Hitler; it contains a complete survey of the situation. The Führer is confident about the future prospects of the war, but he thinks that many decisions are still necessary and he enumerates them with his usual precision.

I write to Alfieri to acquaint him with our negotiations with Russia, and also to inform Ribbentrop. These are no longer at the stage of broad and superficial conversations; the Russians wish to go to the bottom of many fundamental and important issues, about which I would consider it imprudent for us to commit ourselves without first having agreed with the Germans.

Cavallero announces as imminent his attack along the coast.

January 2, 1941

News from Hungary leads us to believe that internal conditions in Greece are serious. The Greek military attaché in Budapest supposedly said that there is very little his country can do now. On the other hand, Bulgaria seems to have decided to align itself with the Axis. Filof will soon go to confer with the Germans.

January 3, 1941

Prince Hesse, on Hitler's behalf, asks about the Duce's true feelings toward the Führer, since certain attitudes on the part of the military have created the impression in Germany that the Duce is showing some coolness. I replied that never before has the Duce been more grateful to Hitler for his solidarity and for his friendship—a reply that corresponds to the truth 100 percent.

During the conversation with Hesse, Guzzoni telephones, saying that a British attack on Bardia makes the situation there extremely precarious. This is painful, but it should not surprise us. To think that, after its initial success, the British attack could be exhausted was, in my opinion, comforting but very wrong.

I inform Mackensen, who is traveling to Berlin about our negotiations with Moscow.

January 4, 1941

A meeting of the Council of Ministers. The Duce makes a long presentation about the military situation in Libya as well as in Albania; the first rather somber, the second somewhat optimistic. In reality, the attack on Bardia seems to have fully succeeded, for only two hours after the fighting began Bergonzoli considered the situation of the stronghold very critical. The Duce read all the documents, including Graziani's cables written "during the time that this man had lost his senses, or at least his mind." He is very hard on all the marshals, except Pecori Giraldi, for whom he has great respect. He confines himself to naming De Bono, adding quickly afterward, "I want you to note that I have said nothing about him." On the whole he seems to be unmoved and hopeful of a solution, after which "a third wave will come, the most formidable of all, one which will upset institutions and men who have revealed their real nature at this hour, and of whom I am now quietly preparing the lists."

Grandi is displeased and terrified because of a letter sent to him by Farinacci, who invites him to come out in the open and drop his self-imposed and ambiguous reserve of the past two months.

January 5, 1941

Ever since 4 p.m. yesterday Bardia radio has been silent. We know what is happening only from the British communiqués. The resistance of our troops was brief—a matter of hours. And yet there was no lack of weapons. The guns alone numbered 430. Why didn't the fight last longer? Is this still a case of the flea against the elephant? "A peculiar flea," says Mussolini, "One that between Sidi el Barrani, Bardia, and Tobruk, had at its disposal more than a thousand guns. One day I shall decide to open the dikes and tell the whole truth to the Italians who have been befuddled by too many lies. After my speech of January 3, I shall speak again on February 3—one of those speeches that draw blood. I am waiting only until Cavallero succeeds in striking a first blow at the Greeks, then I shall speak."

During the evening news arrives that Bardia, though cut in two, is still resisting. For how long? It would be important if we could wear out the British and prevent their carrying out more ambitious programs, such as the recent successes might very well have inspired.

I cabled Alfieri for a Hitler-Mussolini meeting somewhere between the 12th and the 19th. Up to this point Mussolini has procrastinated. He does not like to meet Hitler, burdened by these numerous failures, until they have been at least partially redressed.

January 6, 1941

After a long time I saw the King again. He is worried and shaken by the situation in Libya. He does not believe that the forces arrayed at Tobruk and on the approaches of Derna are sufficient to stop the British advance. He is incredulous with regard to Germany. And even when I talk to him about Hitler's perfectly loyal attitude toward us he is skeptical. "He has treated you courteously only because he had to and could not do otherwise," he said. "But he is a German like the others, and will deal with Italy only on the basis of a brutal utilitarianism. Nor do I believe that Hitler has the power to do anything he wishes. The military element is strong in Germany, and even Bismarck, who was truly exceptionally intelligent, had to submit to it." Then he went on to criticize our military organization. "For too long a time a chair has been called a palace in Italy," he said; "but this does not change the fact that a chair remains a chair. So it happens that our divisions, small and unarmed, are divisions in name only." Then he mentioned an eventual British landing in Italy, which explains why he is against any excessive weakening of the home front. In spite of all this he maintains that the war will end in a German victory, because Hitler has unified the European continent against England.

January 7, 1941

The fall of Bardia has again shaken public morale. The internal situation becomes grim once again. "This is a washing," says Mussolini, "and it will require at least a week to dry." During the meeting of the Council of Ministers the Duce surveyed the situation without comment, soberly, fearlessly, with a calm that these days seems really superhuman. He read the list of the generals and colonels who have been replaced in the course of recent weeks because of their lack of human or professional value, reaching extremely bitter judgments regarding the army and its personnel. Finally, he proposed an order of the day, which was approved by unanimous vote. The final sentence is significant: an appeal to the deeper Italian masses, "proletarian and Fascist." The hostile and complaining middle class is playing a dangerous game. It does not know Mussolini and is not aware that he can take an awful amount of punishment, and is capable, at the same time, of harboring the deepest resentment. If he wins, in fact *when* he wins, the obstructionist bourgeoisie will have to deal with the old Socialist from Romagna it has succeeded in awakening.

Cavallero confirms his decision to attack soon, maybe tomorrow. It will be a limited attack, but one which under the circumstances would have great moral value.

January 8, 1941

The Duce has told Pavolini, Bottai, Ricci, and me as well, that the time has come for some Fascist leaders to go and fight. He is right; immediately following the trip to Germany I shall resume my command of my group in Tirana. The Duce on the other hand feels that the Greek campaign will end within two to three months and says "the politicians who have been accused of wanting the war must prove that they are capable of fighting it."

January 9, 1941

Nothing new of any importance except for a new Greek attack towards Clisura, but that was of no consequence. According to the military these are the last flashes of a flame that is about to burn out. Let's hope this is the case, because up to now their conclusions have always been mistaken.

January 10, 1941

In my presence the Duce received the German ambassador, who has just come from seeing Hitler about the date of a meeting between the two leaders. It is decided for Sunday, the 19th, at Berchtesgaden. Mussolini is in an excellent mood because the air and naval battle, now in progress in the Sicilian channel, is going very well. A British aircraft carrier and two destroyers are in flames. And this is not the end of it. The Duce says: "At last the moon has changed; a good one has appeared." He speaks of the need of always telling the people the truth, in the first place in order to raise morale, and, second, to win its confidence. "The people must know that life is a serious thing and that war is the most serious thing in life."

January 11, 1941

Yesterday evening's news about the air and sea battle was perhaps exaggerated. We cannot as yet establish whether the English carrier has been sunk or not. On the other hand, from Cavallero we are not getting very good news on the course of events in Albania. Clisura is lost. In itself this means nothing. It is a mass of huts in more or less dilapidated condition, but it is a name, and British-Greek propaganda is already sounding all the trumpets of the press and radio. It also proves that the wall of resistance, that famous wall which we have been expecting for seventy days, has not yet been formed. Our troops, even the fresh ones, hold out until Greek pressure starts, but they yield ground rapidly under attack. Why? Mussolini finds that the entire situation is an inexplicable drama, even more serious because it is inexplicable. Cavallero, with whom I have spoken by telephone, does not hide the gravity of what has happened, but he does not feel that the situation at Berat, and hence at Valona, has been compromised. He continues to speak of the famous attack along the coast; however, we see no concrete evidence of this.

January 12, 1941

Nothing new.

January 13, 1941

Tomorrow morning Mussolini is going to Foggia to meet the generals from Albania. He feels the moment has come to make some decisions, especially because Guzzoni is very insistent that the offensive should take place along the coast. He thinks that this will have the effect of exploding the Greek offensive plans and even of bringing us back to the old border.

The movement begins in Bulgaria. The closeness of the German troops already gives the impression that the tempo of events is about to quicken.

Magistrati feels that Bulgaria will not openly align itself with the Axis but will allow itself to be invaded without too much opposition, even of a perfunctory character.

January 14, 1941

Nothing new. I conferred with von Mackensen to organize the Duce's trip to Berchtesgaden.

Alfieri, in a very secret letter, informs me that the campaign against me of the last few weeks has made the rounds, though now it is all over, he says, even in Germany. This does not surprise me. The Germans harbor an old resentment about my non-belligerency and cannot entirely conceal this resentment even when they try to save appearances. This is the case especially with Ribbentrop. Ever since Salzburg, 1939, our relations have changed, and my bet with Joachim on British-French intervention is completely forgotten. I made the mistake of being right. Useless for them to split hairs about whether or not I was for the war with Greece; one thing is certain—I wanted no war at all.

January 15, 1941

No important news.

January 16, 1941

During the morning I had a meeting with the King; in the afternoon, another with the Duce. The King, who maintains an attitude which is more than cordial toward me, said that with the German descent into Thrace, he considers the end of the Greek affair imminent. On the other hand, he feels that the situation in Libya is serious and thinks that the defense of Tobruk is a very serious mistake. It will have no practical results, and will only further weaken our already limited forces, while a courageous retreat on the coast line of Derna might have allowed us to resist, perhaps even victoriously. The Duce has returned from Puglia, where he conferred with Cavallero. He is somber and pessimistic. The front is not yet stabilized, notwithstanding the fact that we have sent many men and much materiel. The military sector is completely bankrupt. "Greece," he says, "was a political masterpiece; we succeeded in isolating that country and having it fight against us all alone. Only the Italian army failed us completely." He is concerned about his trip to Germany. He feels that he will meet Hitler under conditions of obvious inferiority.

On the Clisura front another Greek attack takes place. Let's hope that our troops will hold.

January 17, 1941

The topic of the day is the Duce's decision to mobilize by February 1 all the high Fascist officials—the government, the Grand Council, the Chamber, and the party. When Serena made some objections about the practical feasibility of the project, he answered that what he, the Duce, intends to undertake by working directly with the bureaucracy is an interesting experiment in government. We shall see. Nevertheless, in all higher government circles there is a good deal of dissatisfaction over the decision and the way it was taken.

In the anteroom of the Duce this morning I heard statements and comments that surprised me. There is something in all of this government machinery that does not function well and it would be wise not to ignore it. Some people, such as Bottai, go so far as to speak of a real "*coup d'etat* on the part of the Duce in order to get rid of Fascism and rely on other political forces." I do not believe all this. The more time passes the more I am inclined to disregard anything too complicated. But the decision is certainly ominous, and perhaps this is not the time to undertake experiments "on the domestic front."

Cavallero is not going to Germany because a Greek attack is taking place. Guzzoni replaces him on the trip. I don't like this very much. I don't like him. He is a man who stirs up trouble, untrustworthy, and, besides, it is humiliating to present such a small man with such a big paunch and with dyed hair to the Germans.

January 18-21, 1941
Departure for Salzburg. Mussolini arrives at the train frowning and nervous. He is shaken by the news from Albania. Nothing too dramatic, but once again we have had a kick in the pants, losing many prisoners to the enemy. The serious thing is that it involves the "Lupi di Toscana," a division which has an excellent reputation and a grand tradition, that landed only a short while ago in Albania, and on which we had placed much hope. The Duce talks at length about all this. He repeats his pessimism concerning the army and the Italian people. He can't explain any of it. He keeps repeating, "If anybody had predicted on October 15 what actually happened later, I would have had him shot." Then he changes the subject. He is very much amused by reading a comedy, which has had great success in Germany, entitled *Cherry Trees in Rome.* The subject matter has to do with Lucullus and tries to prove that even a great strategist can have refined tastes and love comfortable living. Mussolini attributes the success of this comedy to a hidden vein of political satire, which escaped Nazi censorship.

He repeats one of his slogans to the effect that the German people more than any other love their food, their drink, and their entertainment, and says that, when he has time for it, he, too, will give himself over to self-indulgence.

We arrive at a small station. I think it is Puch. Hitler and his chiefs of staff are waiting for us on the platform in the snow. The weather is fair and the cold not too intense. The meeting is cordial, and, what surprises me most, spontaneously cordial. There are no lingering condolences in the air— condolences that Mussolini feared. There is, without delay, a meeting between Hitler and the Duce, and also one between me and Ribbentrop. A written report of the latter was presented. I am briefly informed about the other by Mussolini himself, who says that he found a very anti-Russian Hitler, loyal to us, and not too definite on what he intends to do in the future against Great Britain. In any case, it is no longer a question of landing in England. Hitler said that the undertaking would be extremely difficult and that if it failed the first time it could not be attempted again. Added to this there is the fact that while England now fears the loaded pistol of invasion, after a failure she would know that Germany holds only an empty pistol.

Mussolini said that he brought Hitler up to date on Italian matters, including the undecided attitude of the King, which, however, has no influence, and finally, also, about the Badoglio case, which Hitler compared to the Fritsch case. On the whole, the Duce is satisfied with the conversation. I am less so, especially because Ribbentrop, who in the past had always had an attitude of bravado, now, in answer to a definite question of mine on the length of the war, said that he sees no possibility of ending it before 1942. And how about us?

Subsequently, many conversations take place, the most important on Monday in the presence of military experts. Hitler talked for about two hours on his coming intervention in Greece; he dealt with the question primarily from a technical point of view, placing it in the general political context. I must admit that he does this with unusual mastery. Our military men are impressed.

Guzzoni, with his tightly stretched paunch and his little dyed wig, according to Alfieri, made a poor impression on the Germans. He expressed surprise about Hitler's deep understanding of military matters.

Result of the visit, generally good. There is absolute solidarity between the countries of the Axis, and we shall march together in the Balkans. To us is assigned the hard task of bringing the Spanish prodigal son back home. I wish to add that, in my opinion, if Spain falls away the fault rests mostly with the Germans and their uncouth manners in dealing with Latins, including the Spaniards, who, probably because of their very qualities, are the most difficult to deal with.

On his return, Mussolini is elated as he always is after a meeting with Hitler.

I wrote a letter to Serrano, proposing a meeting in Genoa between the Duce and the Caudillo. We shall soon see the Spanish reaction.

January 22, 1941

The news from Romania worries Berlin. The conflict between Antonescu and the Legionnaires had been anticipated by Hitler because of the ambiguous situation that had been created. Here the Führer has had no hesitation about his choice. His sympathies are for Antonescu, who has shown himself to be "a man of good faith, who is resolved to hold firm the baton of command, and is a very thorough nationalist." In fact, von Ribbentrop telephoned late in the day that instructions have been given to the German minister to support Antonescu in every way. He requests that the same thing be done with respect to Ghigi. Naturally I carry out the request, but I have the vague suspicion that the influence of our minister is not as decisive as that of his German colleague.

Tobruk has fallen. There has been a little more fighting but only a little. The Duce is allowing himself to be lulled by his illusions. I thought it necessary to speak to him with brusque frankness. "At Sidi Barrani," I said, "they spoke of surprise. Then, you counted upon Bardia, where there was Bergonzoli, the heroic Bergonzoli. Bardia yielded after two hours. Then you placed your hopes in Tobruk because Pitassi Mannella, the king of artillerymen, was there. Tobruk has also been easily wrested from us. Now you speak with great faith of the escarpment of Derna. I beg to differ with your dangerous illusions. The trouble is serious, mysterious, and deep." That is what I said, but in reality there is very little mystery in it. The reasons for this frightful collapse of the Italians of today, as opposed to the Italians of 1918, appear very clearly to any modest observer. I was not wrong in not wanting war.

January 23, 1941

In Albania, Cavallero is preparing an offensive action. I am waiting without excessive illusions but with faith. The Greek sector is probably the only one that holds out hopes for some rays of success.

Conversation with Gambara. I had him received by the Duce. Notwithstanding my efforts, I have not succeeded in getting him a command in Albania, although he lived there for four years. The Italian General Staff does not like him; he is not one of them, and he has committed the unpardonable sin of advancing by leaps and bounds in his career, a career to which are linked the names of our victories in Spain.

I have given the Duce a serious and harsh letter from Professor Faccini of Leghorn, whose eighteen-year-old son, mobilized on the seventeenth of January, was sent to Albania on the same day, without knowing what a firearm was. This explains so many things.

January 24, 1941

The Duce conferred with Gambara for a long time and is becoming more and more favorable to the idea of putting him at the head of the army now under Vercellino. It seems to me that Gambara is not in the King's good graces, and probably for this reason the Duce suggests that Gambara ask to be received by the King. I tell this to Gambara, who admits that he has never been to see the King once in his whole career. He will go tomorrow.

Grandi got his orders to report for service. He wasn't expecting it and didn't welcome it at all. In addition to the convenience of staying at home, he attached a political significance to his not being called. So much like his complicated nature. All his hopes now have fallen with one single blow. What remains is the stark fact of having to return at the age of forty-five to pound the snow with his Alpine mountain boots, so worn out that he had considered them done for.

As I expected the day before yesterday, Mussolini is concentrating his hopes on the escarpment of Derna. What has happened up to now has taught very little—at least to him.

January 25, 1941

I say good-bye to the Duce. Tomorrow evening I will join my air group in Bari. He wasn't as friendly as he should have been. But Mussolini in these last few days has begun to feel that the order to send the ministers away from Rome has not met with public approval, and, as always happens in such cases, he becomes more stubborn in his decision and more brusque in his speech. In saying farewell he made certain observations which he might very well have kept to himself.

In the afternoon I saw Donna Rachele. She is very much alarmed at the way things are going. As is her simple nature, she follows gossip and small talk, especially on the subject of money, and has no true sense of proportion. In any case, she thinks that the barometer indicates stormy weather, and she says that everything and everybody take it out on the Duce. She is canny in her own way. She complained that the starlings that she loved to shoot had deserted the pine trees at Villa Torlonia. "With the wind that blows even the starlings have changed direction; they are flying to the trees of Villa Savoia," she said.

Cavallero has attacked in the direction of Clisura, and it seems that everything is proceeding well.

January 26, 1941

Departure. This time, since I have some experience at such departures, I find it hard to leave. I have no apprehensions, only a small amount of conviction, and consequently less enthusiasm. All of my comrades who have been forced into becoming volunteers feel this way, and many do not hide their feelings.

[No entries from January 27 to April 23 inclusive. Ciano had joined his air group in Bari.]

April 24, 1941

I resume my notes. I have made an appointment with Pavelić for tomorrow at Lubliana. The object is to find out what the Croatians think more than to reach any definite conclusions. It will not be easy. In Italy, too, there is strong propaganda in favor of the acquisition of Dalmatia, which is carried out by the usual agitators. To be pro-Dalmatian is a profession for many. Nevertheless, we have prepared two solutions: one that involves a continuous stretch of territory from Fiume to Cattaro, and one limited to historic Dalmatia. This last-named portion should be integrated by a political contract which would practically put the whole of Croatia under our control. The attitude of the Germans in all this is ambiguous. When we met at Vienna they gave us a free hand. But up to what point are they sincere?

With Acquarone we settle on a visit that the King wants to make to Albania. He also talks about the restoration of the Petrovichs in Montenegro. "That perpetually indebted Danilo," as Mussolini calls him, has a son. We must go easy in this, especially so as not to arouse hope in Albania for a dynasty of their own. But the Queen [Elena] is using her influence to push the issue. Meanwhile, I have sent Minister Mazzolini as our representative to Cettigne.

April 25, 1941

In Lubliana. A terrible day. It is raining and there is a freezing wind. The people look distraught but they are not hostile. I see Pavelić, surrounded by his band of cutthroats. He declares that the solutions proposed by us would get him thrown out of government. He makes a counterproposal: the Dalmatia of the London pact, with Trau added, goes to us. Spalato and Ragusa, in addition to some islands, would remain Croatian. His followers are more radical than he. They use statistics to prove that in Dalmatia only the stones are Italian. On the contrary, Pavelić is favorable to the political pact. He doesn't even exclude the possibility of a union under one head, or a monarchy under an Italian prince. He asks for time to think about it for a few days, then we shall meet again.

I see the former Ban[481] of Slovenia. I have known him since the times of Stoyadinovich. He is unhappy over the fate of that part of Slovenia, which has remained under the Germans. Commissioner Grazioli tells me that German treatment of the population is actually worse than cruel. Robberies, armed thievery, and killings occur every day. Churches and convents are looted and closed.

April 26, 1941

Except for Spalato, Mussolini agrees with Pavelić and justly feels that it is better to attract Croatia into our political orbit than to gain a little more territory populated by hostile Croats. With the Duce we prepare the decree for the annexation of Lubliana. It will be an Italian province with broad administrative autonomy, both cultural and fiscal. Our humane treatment, as compared to the inhuman treatment by the Germans, should gain us the sympathy of the Croats. The Duce is also resentful of the German attitude in Greece. The Germans have practically assumed the role of protectors of the Greeks, and there was nearly an incident between the soldiers of the *Casale* division and SS troops of Hitler's regiment at the Perati Bridge.

Even Farinacci telephones me to deplore the attitude of the Germans. If he also complains, it must mean something.

Grandi wrote a letter to Cavallero refusing the nomination as Civilian Commissioner in Greece. It appears that Bottai, on the other hand, would go willingly.

April 27, 1941

Von Mackensen comes to my house at one o'clock in the morning, and together we go to Villa Torlonia, where we find Mussolini half asleep but quite courteous. Hitler says that the Greek general, Tsolacoglu, or some such name, is ready to establish a Greek government in Athens with which we might be able to negotiate the surrender of Greece. He is favorable to this. In fact, he considers all this as a "heaven-sent favor." We must send a delegation to Larissa early tomorrow morning. I suggest Anfuso, and the Duce approves. We are naturally less enthusiastic than the Germans, and I feel I can see in all this the explanation of much of the German attitude in Greece, including what has occurred within the last few days. However, Anfuso, having arrived early in the morning at Larissa, informs us that he finds neither the German nor the Greek delegation present, and that, besides, Marshal List had not in any way been informed of his arrival. This puts the Duce in a good mood, because it proves "that even in Germany things don't run smoothly, and gives us another singularly important event to add to the many that have formed a constellation during these six months of German-Greek relations." Later, List informs us that the two delegations will arrive tomorrow morning.

I request the Duce give the Stefani agency his cable of praise for Cavallero, and he agrees.

April 28, 1941

This Tsolacoglu affair pleases me less and less. Anfuso informs me that it is a matter of recognizing a government which enjoys sound legal backing. Although the territorial occupation of the country by the Axis armies is a fact, it is clear that this general proposes to save the national and ethnic unity of Greece, and German connivance is equally clear. It seems to me that the least we can do is to ask the Germans to let us have the civilian government of the territories that we claim. Otherwise, I fear that what we get out of it will be very small.

Casertano telephones that much progress has been made with the Croats about the borders of Dalmatia and also as to the possibility of instituting a monarchy under a prince of the House of Savoy. I called him to Rome.

The King insists upon a restoration of the monarchy in Montenegro. I fear that this will create tension with Albania, which will demand a national dynasty. But the Duce has already agreed, and I don't want to play the spoilsport. The King of Montenegro will be a nephew of the Queen, a young man whom the Duce calls "a son of many and poor parents." He lives in Lobau, Germany, in obscurity and almost in poverty.

April 29, 1941

With Buffarini I prepare a political map for the creation of the Province of Lubliana. It is inspired by very liberal concepts. It will have the effect of attracting sympathies for us in Germanized Slovenia, where the worst abuses are being reported.

Casertano visits the Duce. The Croatian affair has taken many steps forward. The crown is offered to a prince of the House of Savoy, but there is no compromise with respect to Spalato. Pavelić declares that if he were to relent on Spalato he would have to resign, and with him his entire pro-Italian policy would collapse. The Duce is aware of our real interest, but is stubborn about yielding on the question of Spalato. The same words that he used during the Fiume-Dalmatia conflict [in 1919-20] resurface with the Duce. I am more and more convinced of the need to move the problem toward a political solution, which also seems to me to be the most convenient from the military point of view. Is it really worth the trouble to save a city where the only Italian elements are its monuments, and so lose control over a large and rich kingdom? The rights of the stones are undeniable, but the rights of the living are even stronger.

April 30, 1941
Conference with Roatta. The General Staff warmly advocates a political solution with respect to Croatia, and any extremist step regarding Dalmatia is thought dangerous.

A meeting with the King on the Croatian question. There are no objections on his part to concessions about Spalato. On the contrary, he is pleased. The King is of the opinion that the less of Dalmatia we take the less trouble we will have. "If it were not for a certain understandable sentimentality," he said, "I would be in favor of relinquishing even Zara." He is very happy, on the other hand, about the bestowal of a crown on a prince of his house. If the Duke of Aosta had been in Italy the King would have designated him without hesitation; as things stand, the only choice is between the Duke of Spoleto and the Duke of Pistoia. The King favors the first, because of his physical appearance and also, up to a certain point, because of his intellectual capacities. I found the King in good health, sunburned from his tour of the Alps, and, generally speaking, in a good mood. As usual, he is anti-German.

The Duce replies to Pavelić's letter, accepting the crown, and gives final instructions to Casertano: to insist on Spalato but not to the point of creating a break. Today our paratroopers occupied Cefalu. They are only a few, about 150, and we hope that they will not be thrown into the sea by the local garrison. The Duce is anxious to make the announcement "because since we now have a good number of paratroopers we can, even if it be only one regiment, say that it is a division!" This upsets me. We are at it again, and the lessons of the past have taught us little.

May 1, 1941
All the grumblers who were most critical of the Greek affair are now extremists in the matter of Dalmatia. This is particularly true in the Senate, which distinguished itself during the debates on Albania by its blathering. Senator Felici speaks to me of a sort of petition to the Duce to ask that not even a centimeter of coastline should go to Croatia. I have told Acquarone that it would be timely for him to make clear that it is useless to undertake such an absurd campaign. In the Senate the word of the royal household is very much heeded.

May 2, 1941
Badoglio's second son has died in Libya as a result of an automobile accident. I am sorry. In spite of the fact that Badoglio has given me good cause to dislike him, I am really sorry for the loss of his son.

Casertano telephones that all hope for Spalato is not lost.

May 3, 1941

Mussolini has me read an order of the day which Rommel addressed to our divisional commanders in Libya. He goes so far as to threaten to denounce them before the military tribunals. It seems that, owing to this, some trouble has arisen and I would be surprised if it were otherwise. In Albania, too, where at a certain point our army has had to face considerable obstruction from the Germans, the feeling of resentment toward our allies is marked. The Duce realizes this and gives Farinacci the responsibility of drafting a letter to Hitler to call attention to what has happened. He has chosen Farinacci because he has no official position and because there are no possible doubts as to his pro-German feelings.

May 4, 1941

Casertano reports that Spalato might also be given to us with some reservations on the administration of the city. The Duce is satisfied. It now seems that Pavelić wants to have some preliminary talks with the Duce. I prefer that we reach a quick conclusion, especially because the German attitude toward us with reference to Croatia is anything but clear. Alfieri, for what it's worth, continually sounds the alarm from Berlin, and feels that a meeting between Hitler and Mussolini is necessary to settle the main issues of our claims.

A long speech by Hitler. I am not acquainted with it yet, but Mussolini, who listened to it, judges it with considerable detachment and says that it is a useless speech that it would have been better not to make.

May 5, 1941

Farinacci's letter to Hitler will not be sent. The Duce is satisfied with the Führer's explanation, and, on the other hand, does not like the introduction of Farinacci's letter, bragging about his own exploits in Albania.

We have set a conference between Mussolini and Pavelić for the day after tomorrow. It will take place at the border, as close to Zagreb as possible, because it is not very prudent for Pavelić to be absent from his capital too long. The Duce has put a stop to Dalmatian agitation by the usual overzealous people, many of them acting in bad faith, trying to create expectations that might cause disappointments later on.

As always, Hitler's speech was excellent. I like the oratory of this man more and more. It is strong and persuasive. It was an informative speech, but at the same time one in which no assurances were given. All those who, on the basis of previous declarations, believed that the end of the war would come in 1941, have been bitterly disappointed. For my part I have entertained very few hopes of this kind.

On the advice of the Duce I have written a letter to Serrano Suñer. I congratulate him on his speech and give him advice about Axis intransigence. *Palabras y plumas el viento las lleva.*[482]

May 6, 1941

Departure for Monfalcone. On the train Mussolini is wrapped in thought. We speak at length of the future prospects of the war. I cannot say that now that he has cast aside his optimistic view of a rapid end he has any clear idea of the future. I give him my ideas, including those about a compromise peace that we should welcome, especially now that we have acquired our share of booty. He appears to agree, now that recent vicissitudes, and above all tension with the German troops in Greece, have opened his eyes to many things.

May 7, 1941

We arrive at Monfalcone. It is an overcast and cool day. Pavelić is escorted by some carloads of Ustasche, which give his trip a strange Wild West character. We receive him in a little waiting room at the station. Nothing sensational happened. There is confirmation of the results that have been reached at previous conferences. On some points Pavelić appeals to the generosity of the Duce, and the latter naturally agrees—a matter of customs union and of some bits of territory. On my part, I hold firm on Curzola and Buccari.[483] I want to see a monument erected to my father at Buccari. The ceremony of the offering of the crown will take place on Sunday the 18th.

On the train Mussolini is talkative and in a good mood. He evinces satisfaction with the results obtained and criticizes those who wanted a totalitarian solution of the Dalmatian problem, neglecting that of Croatia. He is particularly amusing when he describes at length the old Italian socialist world. All the men of those days are brought to life in his colorful description. "They were bourgeois," he concludes, "who were terrified of the proletariat and were afraid of only one thing: revolution."

He will take care of the question of the army commands and will sack Guzzoni.

May 8, 1941

Through Acquarone I inform the King of the results achieved, and he decides to leave for Albania the day after tomorrow. Acquarone says the Duke of Spoleto is proud of the task which awaits him, but concerned about losing his freedom. "When we looked for him, to give him the news, we managed to find him, only after twenty-four hours, in a Milan hotel, where he was hiding in the company of a young girl."

Mussolini informs the Council of Ministers of what has been done and what will be done. The Council's approval appears to be complete and enthusiastic. I leave for Tirana, where I will welcome the King.

May 9, 1941

At Tirana. The general feeling is good; the soldiers feel more and more that the Italian effort has worn out the Greeks, and they are proud of it.

May 10, 1941

The King arrives. The weather is bad—cold and rainy—which does not prevent the streets from being crowded with enthusiastic people—sincerely enthusiastic. The King is in a very good mood and is moved. He didn't think that he would find Albania so developed and fertile. In his mind was the memory of that heap of arid, hard rocks which is Montenegro, for which he holds, nonetheless, a great deal of affection, even to the point of wanting to re-establish it with the boundaries of 1914. I do not think this is possible. The Albanians would rebel violently against any such decision. We have enough to do to restrain their ambitions, which now go as far as Antivari and beyond.

The King is very courteous with me. He repeatedly said that it was I who "built up" Albania, and he tried in every way to show his friendliness towards me. He was rather distant with Cavallero, who noticed it and did not conceal his resentment. I had to work hard to get him an invitation to lunch with the King, and I did it because Cavallero's exclusion from such an intimate repast would have given rise to many rumors.

May 11, 1941

All the ceremonies were carried out well. During the evening reception we used the Royal Palace for the first time. Afterward eight cigar lighters, a silver case, and sixty knives and forks were missing. As a start on the part of Tirana high society, that's not bad.

Acquarone has spoken to me of the personal financial situation of the King. I, like everyone else, thought he was very rich. On the contrary, he is not. He probably has something between 25 and 30 million. As for the jewels, they are the property of the Crown, and they are linked to the trust established by Charles Albert in order to safeguard the family from the prodigality of Victor Emmanuel II, who died loaded with debt. The King gives a monthly allowance of 20,000 lire to each of his daughters and keeps 100,000 lire for himself. He is concerned about the expenses by his son, for he foresees "that, like his grandfather, he will always have money problems."

I return to Bari by air and proceed to Rome by train.

May 12, 1941

Mussolini was annoyed because the King, in Tirana, had presided over the Council of Ministers. He was reassured only when I explained that it was more a meeting for the Royal Signature than anything else. The Germans have taken a step in Tokyo, with which we have associated ourselves, inviting the Japanese to adopt a definite anti-American stand. I don't know whether the note will have any great effect. Matsuoka does not conceal his great friendliness and respect for the United States. Phillips, with whom I spoke today, no longer excludes the possibility of intervention by his country, and, as usual, he talks of a very long war. Even the Duce, who had always talked about a blitz war, now believes in a long one, mentioning the year 1948. He bases all this on information given him by Forzano, that buffoon Forzano, who, in Athens, supposedly talked with Marshal List, which I doubt very much.

A strange German communiqué announces the death of Hess in a plane accident. I cannot conceal my skepticism about the truth of this version. I even doubt whether he is dead at all. There is something mysterious about it, even though Alfieri confirms the report that it was an accident.

May 13, 1941

The Hess affair sounds like a detective story. Hitler's substitute, his second-in-command, the man who for fifteen years has had in his grasp the most powerful German organization, has made an airplane landing in Scotland. He fled, leaving a letter for Hitler. In my opinion, it is a very serious matter: the first real victory for the English. At the beginning, the Duce believed that Hess had been forced to make a landing while he was on his way to Ireland in order to start a revolt, but he very soon abandoned this thesis, and he now shares my impression of the exceptional importance of this event.

Von Ribbentrop unexpectedly arrives in Rome. He is discouraged and nervous. He wants to confer with the Duce and me for various reasons, but there is only one real reason: he wants to inform us about the Hess affair, which is now in the hands of the press all over the world. The official version is that Hess, sick in body and mind, was a victim of his pacifist hallucination, and went to England hoping to facilitate the start of peace negotiations. Hence, he is not a traitor; hence, he will not talk; hence, whatever else is said or printed in his name is false. His conversation is a beautiful job of patching things up. The Germans want to cover themselves before Hess speaks and reveals things that might cause a big impression in Italy. Mussolini comforted von Ribbentrop, but told me afterward that he considers the Hess affair a tremendous blow to the Nazi regime. He added that he was happy about it because this will have the effect of reducing German stock, even among the Italians.

Dinner at home with von Ribbentrop and his associates.

The tone of the Germans is one of depression. Von Ribbentrop repeats his slogans against England with that monotony that made Göring dub him "Germany's No. 1 parrot."

It seems that Bismarck, who hates von Ribbentrop, emphasized every phrase of his Minister with heavy kicks under the table at Anfuso, to whom he finally said: "He is such an imbecile that he is a freak of nature."

May 14, 1941

Ribbentrop left after having said good-by to Mussolini during a brief meeting at the Palazzo Venezia. The Hess affair has had no developments so far. British radio says that he spends his time writing, which disturbs Ribbentrop. When Ribbentrop's four-engine plane was taking off, Bismarck said to Anfuso, "Let's hope that they will all crash and break their necks; but not here, or we'll have some unpleasant work to do." That's German national solidarity for you!

In the meantime, in Japan, things are not going the way they should, and still worse in Russia. Ribbentrop himself, when questioned by the Duce, avoided giving a definite answer, and said that if Stalin is not careful "Russia will be despatched in the space of three months." The chief of the SIM, on the basis of information gathered in Budapest, says that the attack is already decided upon, and will begin on June 15; Hungarians and Romanians will collaborate. This may be. But it is a dangerous game and it seems to me without a definite purpose. The story of Napoleon repeats itself.

A long conversation with Spoleto. He is proud of having been chosen as King of Croatia, but has no definite idea of what he is supposed to do and is vaguely uneasy about it. I emphasize that he will be a lieutenant general with a crown at the service of the Fascist Empire. In any case, we will have to keep the reins tightly in our grasp.

May 15, 1941

Contrary to expectations, the speculation by British and American propaganda on the Hess case is quite moderate. The only documents that are really harmful are the German despatches, which are confused and reticent. Alfieri writes that confusion in Berlin is at its height in all circles. He stresses the fact that the Germans, despite their efficiency and determination, are poor sports when fortune turns against them.

A long conversation with the Prince of Piedmont. Although he has been personally courteous to me, yet I have felt that there is considerable bitterness in his heart. For a man so cautious he has frankly criticized the Fascist system in general and the Fascist press in particular. He now lives among the military, and, during the last few months, has absorbed a good dose of poison which has had some effect on him. He does not yet know how to analyze or summarize very well. He has neither the experience nor the acumen of his father, though I consider him a very much better man than his reputation has made him out to be. He recalled what I predicted about two years ago about developments of the Croatian issue.

May 16, 1941

A lull of expectations in the Hess case. Even the British press mentions a mysterious peace mission, going so far as to imply a prearranged agreement between Hitler and Hess. This is in contrast to Ribbentrop's declarations, and also to German agitation, which isn't decreasing.

Augusto Moschi came to see me; he is the nephew of Donna Rachele, who for a long time has held the keys to the heart of his powerful aunt. And now he has been dethroned, his place being taken by Pater, a no-good engineer, who builds houses of sawdust and cardboard. Moschi violently attacks Pater, accusing him of having disturbed the peace of Villa Torlonia with intrigues and evil doings of every kind. He is a sort of puny Rasputin in disguise, who takes advantage of his influence to secure all kinds of personal benefits. Maybe Moschi is exaggerating, but there must be something to it. Edda, who is intelligent and outspoken, pointed out to me some months ago the strange role that Pater was playing with her mother, and concluded by attributing the situation to "the consequences of menopause."

For some months Donna Rachele has been troubled and suspicious, and busies herself like a detective with a thousand things that don't concern her. It even seems that she goes snooping around dressed as a bricklayer, a woman of the people, and God knows what else. All this will end in a huge outcry, and it is good to keep out of it. Pater's influence may be behind Starace's imminent and unjust sacking, since Pater is Starace's bitter enemy. One of the ways in which the Duce explained it to me was to say that he had learned from his wife that Starace sends a militiaman to walk his four dogs. "Italy," said Mussolini, "is still too fed up with D'Annunzio's dogs to tolerate those belonging to Starace."[484]

May 17, 1941

An incident during the departure of the King from Tirana was the only sour note of an otherwise very successful trip. A nineteen-year-old boy, a certain Mihailov, fired a few pistol shots at the royal carriage; the boy, who seems to be half unbalanced, wanted, in this way, to voice his indignation for not having been recognized as a poet by the local authorities. Needless to say that his poems are worth a great deal less than the few lire of subsidy which he had repeatedly received. The King attached no importance to the incident and remained very cool. It appears that he even said to Verlaçi, who was seated at his side, "That boy is a poor shot, isn't he?"

Starace has been ousted, and I must say that nothing was done to make the blow less painful. When he came to see me he was sad and apparently hardened by his sorrow. Unless there are reasons that have escaped me, Starace's sacking and especially the manner in which it was done were unjust.

May 18, 1941

The Croatians arrive led by Pavelić. They are in a good mood and well disposed toward us. I should say that they are better disposed than the Albanians when they were offered the crown. The ceremony is more or less the same as that with the Albanians. In the streets, few undemonstrative people. Not many realize the importance of the event. When His Majesty designated the Duke of Spoleto and the delegates saw him, there was a murmur of approval among them. Let us hope that it will be the same when they hear him speak. Everything took place in due form; also the signing of the Acts, the content of which seemed to those who had knowledge of them to bear a better political message than was expected. It now remains to be seen if what we have built will be lasting. Maybe I am mistaken in my personal impression, but there is a feeling in the air that Italian domination in Croatia is to be temporary. And this is why the public is indifferent. Only one piece of news would really send the country wild with enthusiasm: the news that peace had been declared.

Pavelić is rather sure of himself, and today he is calm and modest, as he was in Rome when living like an expatriate. He asked for some privileges, which are of secondary importance, and advisable for us to grant in order to consolidate his position. During the evening, after one of the usual dinners at Court, formal and boring, the Croatian delegation left.

May 19, 1941

I present two nominations to the Duce: Volpi as president of the Italian Croatian Economic Commission, and Bastianini as Governor of Dalmatia. Both are accepted, and I believe that the public will greet these names favorably. Yesterday's announcements, which were published in the press only today, are meeting with considerable favor, but there is no show of that kind of enthusiasm which one might have expected at other times.

I see Bottai. He is cordial and, I believe, sincere. He would like very much to get away from the job of Minister of National Education, which has overwhelmed him with work for too long without giving him any satisfaction. I believe that deep down his ambition is to be sent as ambassador to Berlin. He would certainly do well, but for the time being at least it is out of the question. I should not want to cause Alfieri grief, even though he didn't know yesterday, after six months of war with Greece, what Florina was.[485]

The Duce, in speaking to me about Bismarck, went on at some length to say that as great and as big as he was he had an intense sentimental life and wrote "schoolboy·letters." From what the Duce said it was not difficult to detect what I should call a personal interest in this side of the Iron Chancellor's private life. . . .

May 20, 1941

Pavelić has found a fairly good situation at Zagreb. One could not ask for more.

Bastianini is going to Dalmatia as Governor. He is cautious, honest, and loyal.

Cavallero informs me of his intentions in his new undertaking. Good. Meanwhile he will sack Guzzoni, the dyed-haired general—and that is perfect!

May 21, 1941

I accompany Mazzolini to see the Duce in order to settle the Montenegrin issue, which is particularly complicated on account of the sentimental interest attached to it by the royal family. It seems that the idea of having Prince Michael for the position is not popular in Montenegro. They do not know him; he has married a French woman and until now has been living in the pay of Belgrade. On the other hand, public opinion is unanimously favorable to the Queen. She is the one who ought to wear the crown of the Petroviches. Such a solution would also be very pleasing to me, because it would tend to place the country solidly in our hands. For the time being the King is recalcitrant. Now we have sent Mazzolini to explain to him how matters stand and we hope that he will give his consent. The King would like to restore Montenegro to its 1914 borders. This is impossible. Albania would start an uprising, and we know from experience how overwhelming is the bitterness provoked by deceit on the part of allies. Versailles teaches us this lesson.

Pavelic made his first speech at Zagreb, which, to judge from the first press reports, seems good. They say that he is an impressive orator.

Grandi has returned to the fold with solemn affirmations of Franciscan devotion and humility. That was to be expected.

May 22, 1941

The King continues to object to the Queen's taking the crown of Montenegro, and suggests instead the son of Prince Roman, who is the son of a Petrovich. Let us hope that the son is better than the father, who is the prototype of a fat head. Moreover, he has an extremely low voice. Mazzolini will try to discuss the matter in Cettigne, but says that it is highly improbable that the idea will be received favorably, for the simple reason that everybody is unaware of the existence of this dear little boy.

May 23, 1941

I went to the country to see my mother. I find her rather well and this makes me very happy.

Then I went to Leghorn. Although the city has always stayed in line, Rodinis[486] tells me that even recent events have caused no enthusiasm. He bases all his opinions on how many copies of our paper are sold, and repeats that circulation has not increased either after our success in Dalmatia nor in Croatia.

May 24, 1941

No news of any importance.

May 25, 1941

The Duce, yielding to Riccardi's insistence, had decided to remove Giannini as Director of Commercial Affairs. Clodius intervened in his favor, courteously but firmly, saying among other things that Giannini's dismissal would further complicate the commitments of both countries on the question of fuel oil. Riccardi is indignant and calls this blackmail. Anyway, the Duce has revoked his order and Giannini remains.

Bismarck let Filippo[487] understand that the Germans are in possession of our secret codes and are reading our cables. This is good to know; in the future, they will also read what I *want* them to read.

May 26, 1941

The King has informed us, through Acquarone, that Prince Roman has no interest in the throne of Montenegro; therefore, we must return to Prince Michael, who is living on Lake Constance. If he, too, refuses, we shall consider a regency. Frankly, I never dreamed we should waste so much brainpower on a country like Montenegro.

No political news. In Crete, military operations are going well and there is a lot of talk around the world on account of the naval victory of the *Bismarck*. In the meantime Otto [von Bismarck] does not at all like the fact that his grandfather's name should be involved in this anti-English struggle, and he feels that the *Bismarck* itself, pursued by the *King George*, is about to pay dearly for its adventure.

I see Bottai. Like everyone returning from Slovenia, he is very anti-German. He is pessimistic about our internal situation, which, in his opinion, is characterized by the formation of two groups, so to speak, that are extra-legal with a strong and dangerous influence on the Duce. On one side are Donna Rachele and Pater (and people in many circles are talking a great deal about this combination), and on the other are the Petaccis and their satellites. Like all *outsiders*,* these people intrigue against those who hold any legal and constitutional power, and this how Bottai explains the cold and almost hostile attitude taken by Mussolini against the Fascist leadership.

The Starace affair made a deep impression on older Fascists, including the enemies of Starace, because everyone sees in this arbitrary and unmotivated punishment a direct personal threat. Perhaps Bottai draws too dark a picture, but it is undeniable that among the Fascists one can observe clear signs of uneasiness.

May 27, 1941

The *Bismarck* has been sunk. This is important especially because of the repercussions it will have in the United States, where it will prove that the ocean is dominated by the Anglo-Saxons. Alfieri has arrived. I can't say that he is a pessimist, but he doesn't show his old optimism. He says, "The war is won. All we have to do is find a way to stop it." This formula is dangerous. Mussolini is still in a bad mood and resents the army. This morning he was tempted to "get out of his car and whip the officers who were entering the Ministry of War—they were so unworthy of the uniform."

In the afternoon the Duce telephoned me asking me to speed up negotiations with Russia, so that we can get a bit of fuel oil. "Otherwise," said the Duce, "in a short time we will be compelled to remain seated."

May 28, 1941

Cavallero has now resolutely taken control of military affairs. From what he tells me I understand that the military undersecretaries will be reduced to the position of managers with respect to men and materiel in their own areas, and this is correct. I have also received Squero, the new Undersecretary of War. He is an upright soldier, timid, modest, and very much surprised at the burden of responsibility that has landed on his shoulders. After the nomination he wept on Cavallero's breast because it seems that he is terrified of speaking in public. And he considers three or more persons as an audience.

---

* In English in the original.

Speech by Roosevelt. It is a very strong document, even though it is unclear as to plans of action. Mussolini thundered against Roosevelt, saying that "never in the course of history has a nation been led by a paralytic. There have been bald kings, fat kings, handsome and even stupid kings, but never kings who, in order to go to the bathroom and the dinner table, had to be carried by other men." I don't know whether this is historically proven, but clearly Roosevelt is the individual against whom the Duce directs his greatest hostility.

May 29, 1941

I accompany Alfieri to see the Duce, who asked him for news about the Hess matter. I must say, to judge from Alfieri's replies, that he knew little about it. Alfieri was the first who, taking the initial communiqué seriously, practically broke his neck to cable Hitler his condolences for the "loss of his favorite collaborator." The Duce later said that, in his opinion, the tone of German-Italian relations had lowered a bit, and from this observation went on to say that Italy is indispensable to Germany, exalting our co-operation and even our military contribution to the war.

The Duke of Spoleto pays a visit. He wishes to take Guariglia with him to Zagreb, and this seems to me an excellent choice. He said nothing of any particular importance, but the tone of his conversation was distinctly anti-German.

I had lunch with Acquarone, who, with great reserve, cautioned me against Cavallero, "who, according to the King, has a tendency to boast and who harbors exaggerated ambitions." But he also said that the King is thinking of nominating the Duce Chancellor of the Empire, and me President of the Council, in order to insure succession in office. But Mussolini, I am sure, will have none of this.

May 30, 1941

Information from Iraq is bad and, what is worse, our planes, a month after the conflict, have not yet gone into action. If there were any need for it, this is additional proof of the lack of preparation of our air force. Things are going better in Crete, on the other hand, where the annihilation of the English seems imminent. Mussolini speaks of a hop on to Cyprus, but I know they are quite skeptical about this at the German embassy. Mussolini has had a violent anti-German outburst about German meddling in Zagreb. "They should leave us alone," he said, "and they should remember that because of them we have lost an empire. I have a thorn in my heart because the vanquished French still have their empire, while we have lost ours." The Duce's bad disposition is the result of this situation. He was very much attached to Ethiopia, which he called "the Pearl of the Regime," and the years 1935 and 1936 the "Romantic Years of Fascism." Now he is trying to console himself by preparing for the reconquest of the empire, but he is the first to grasp the risks and difficulties involved.

Bottai was saying today that Roosevelt is a real dictator, and that our system of government, like those which have always flourished on the shores of the Mediterranean, ought to be interpreted as a tyranny. He is more and more skeptical about the progress of public affairs in Italy.

May 31, 1941

Hitler has sent word that he wishes to meet with the Duce at the earliest possible moment: tomorrow or the day after. Neither the invitation nor the way it was extended pleased the Duce. "I am sick and tired of being summoned by the bell." And he decided on the day after tomorrow for the meeting at the Brenner Pass. We have no idea of the purpose of the meeting, but at first sight I think that it must deal with either one of two subjects: France or Russia.

Sebastiani was sacked by Mussolini, who explained it by saying that his family doesn't like him, and also reproached him for having built a villa at Rocca di Papa. Whoever has seen this villa says that it is a very modest place. The fact is that Sebastiani is also a victim of the campaign against him by Donna Rachele—an exaggerated campaign, even if not altogether unfounded. I myself know the names of persons from whom Sebastiani took money to facilitate the establishment of an industrial plant in Apuania.

Galbiati, who is replacing Starace, comes to pay me his formal visit. He interprets the function of the Militia as a watchdog for the revolution, rather than as an armed force at the service of the country, and says it will operate along that line.

I learn from Bottai that the Duce is exasperated by the publication in the magazine *Minerva*, published in Turin, of a motto by some Greek philosopher or other. The motto reads: "No greater misfortune can befall a country than to be governed by an *old* tyrant."

June 1, 1941

Departure for the Brenner Pass. On the train I had a long conversation with Bismarck on men and things of the Nazi regime. According to him, Göring has lost a good deal of his influence on Hitler because he "admonishes him too much," and dictators don't like that. Von Ribbentrop is very much listened to and Himmler is also very powerful. Lutze's star is rising. Since Hitler proved to be right about the offensive against the Maginot Line, the military men no longer dare open their mouths. The best of them are with the troops, not those who surround the Führer.

The Duce is in quite a good mood, but he cannot understand the reason for this hastily arranged conversation. He fears that the Germans will want to expedite their agreement with France, and that this will take place at our expense. Consequences in Italy from a possible abandonment of our Western aspirations would be very serious and damaging to the prestige of the regime.

June 2, 1941

I have summarized our conversations elsewhere. The general impression is that for the moment Hitler has no definite plan of action. Russia, Turkey, Spain, are all subsidiary elements: secondary or scattering of forces, but it is not there that one can find the solution to the problem. The greatest German hope is now in the action of its submarine fleet, but one does not know what the summer will bring, with its starlit nights and calm sea. A slaughter of ships, some people say. A slaughter of submarines, others think. The Duce, too, is convinced that a peace settlement would be received by the Germans with the greatest enthusiasm. "They are now sick of victories. They now want the Victory—a victory which will bring peace." The atmosphere of the meeting was good. Mussolini says that during the conversation he had privately with Hitler the latter spoke about Hess and wept. The Duce was satisfied with the meeting, especially because he was able to see that for us there was no toning down in Italian-German relations.

An opinion of the Duce on monarchies: "They are like those thick and strong trees, very flourishing on the surface, but hollowed by insects from within. All of a sudden they are struck down by lightning and there is no human power that can prop them up again."

June 3, 1941

On the Duce's instructions I have drafted a letter to Serrano Suñer, emphasizing the advisability of Spain's joining the Tripartite Pact. Mussolini added a personal note to it.

On the whole, the Duce has a favorable opinion of yesterday's conference, while commenting at the same time on Hitler's excessive verbosity. He thinks that personal ties should be strengthened "through pairs." It is my duty, therefore, to establish closer ties with von Ribbentrop. About Keitel the Duce expresses this opinion: "Keitel is a man who is happy that he is Keitel." The opinion expressed by Bismarck is more to the point: "Keitel is an imbecile."

During my absence Anfuso had to put up with a telephone assault from Donna Rachele about certain offenses of the IRCE, which, parenthetically, is not our responsibility but rather the domain of the Ministry of Popular Culture. She didn't express herself in very refined language and said that she will come to the Palazzo Chigi and start "shooting up the place." I don't know who is putting certain things into her head, but I am not going to speak to the Duce because of the high and noble feeling he has of maintaining his prestige in public affairs. But this increasing interference is a serious matter, and perhaps one day I shall be obliged to overcome all my reserve and speak openly to the Duce.

June 4, 1941

Bárdossy arrives—a man whose career has been rapid and ominous, at least for his superiors.[488] I remember him in Vienna a year ago at the meeting on arbitration for Transylvania. He was a modest plenipotentiary in Bucharest. Later, Czaky's death brought him to the government, and Teleki's suicide gave him the presidency. What will become of the Regent? Bárdossy is a person of distinction and restraint, very much the career man. He offers a balanced opinion of the situation and reveals no attitude beyond that inspired by the orthodoxy of the moment. Villani, however, says "that Bárdossy in reality shares the same ideas that he has," which would mean that he hates the Germans. The conversation with the Duce was noteworthy, particularly when Bárdossy went into ecstasy about Hungary's love for Fiume. Then Mussolini, with the air of a sharp old wolf, or some diabolical and over-intelligent animal, said that the Hungarians were to Fiume what the Swiss were to Genoa. Bárdossy was floored by these few words more than by any long conversation.

I saw Donna Rachele. She is in a continuous state of over-excitement for no reason at all. Her arguments are inconsequential. She could live quietly and undisturbed, but instead embitters her days in futile disputes.

June 5, 1941

After spending some time with Bárdossy you see the classical career diplomat come through, a great devourer of buttered canapés at ladies' teas, frequenter of South American legations and the drawing-rooms of unknown countesses. Even his language is that of the traditional chief of mission. He forgets that he is the man responsible for his country's policy, and approaches you with the traditional *"qu'est ce que vous pensez, monsieur le Ministre,"* and so on, which sets those who are career diplomats apart from other mortals. Nevertheless, Bárdossy is a good fellow, and he, too, will pass, like the others, hurriedly and pompously, through the kaleidoscope of Hungarian politics. At any rate, he has left, and his visit to Rome was among the most classically useless ones.

June 6, 1941

Commercial negotiations in Berlin do not offer much satisfaction at this time. Reductions in the coal quota, difficulties in the transportation of oil. Even scrap iron, which we were to receive from France, has been delivered to us only in very small quantities. Mussolini is resentful and this gives an anti-German edge to his words. "This means that in the future we shall wage 'an ersatz war.' I would not be at all sorry if Germany in her conflict with Russia lost many feathers, and this is possible because the Russians are not lacking in armaments, and the only problem is whether twenty years of Soviet propaganda have been enough to create a heroic mysticism in the masses."

I receive Bose, head of the Indian insurgent movement. He would like the Axis to make a statement about the independence of India, but in Berlin his proposals have been received with much reserve. Nor must we be compromised, especially because the value of this young man is not clear. Past experience has yielded rather modest results.

June 7, 1941

Information from Berlin is even less favorable, which increases the anti-German edge in the mind and words of the Duce. In fact, he was even thinking of postponing the speech which he was going to make at the Chamber on the 10th—the anniversary of our entry into the war. "I would be expected to extol our collaboration with Germany, and now this is repugnant to me."

Tassinari informs me about the food situation. It is not good but not very bad, and we may foresee an improvement regarding fats. Prince Michael, who has refused the crown of Montenegro, opened his heart to Consul Serra di Cassano. He does not want to compromise himself because he is convinced that in the end Germany and Italy will be defeated, and for this reason he feels that any present solution is transitory and ephemeral. I do not believe that the Queen is very proud of the opinions of this offspring of the Petrovichs.

June 8, 1941

Starace mopes about his personal misfortunes, but not like a crybaby; he weeps out of anger and, without saying so, out of hatred. I talk to the Duce about him. The Duce's most serious complaint is that Starace wears a distinguished service medal without authorization. The criticism regarding financial doings finds fewer echoes in Mussolini's mind. I was not very successful in defending Starace with the Duce, but it is my impression that the Duce's anger doesn't go very deep. If Starace accepts the Duce's scolding without kicking, in a short time we shall see him rising up to power again.

De Gaulle has entered Syria. What will be the reaction of the French? Mussolini takes it out on the Germans: "They are not intelligent, that is all. They should have occupied all of France at the armistice."

June 9, 1941

No particular news. News from Syria is still quite uncertain, but it seems that a large part of Dentz's army has joined forces with the Gaullists. Which doesn't displease me at all; a Vichy French alliance with the Axis would have been at Italy's expense.

The Hungarian minister of defense, General Bartha, who is visiting Rome, says that a Russian-German clash is more than inevitable—it is actually imminent. He is optimistic as to what is to be expected. He believes that the Russian army cannot resist for more than six or eight weeks, because the human element is "soft." It remains to be seen, however, how twenty years of Communist revolution have influenced the people.

June 10, 1941

What a strange anniversary of our entry into the war! Using as a pretext the increased German meddling in Croatia, Mussolini uttered the harshest charges against Germany that I have ever heard from him. He was the aggressive Mussolini, and hence Mussolini at his best. "It is of no importance," he said, "that the Germans recognize our rights in Croatia on paper, when in practice they grab everything and leave us only a little heap of bones. They are scoundrels in bad faith, and I tell you that this cannot go on for long. I do not even know if German intrigue will allow Aimone to actually ascend the Croatian throne. Besides, I have been thoroughly disgusted with the Germans since the time List signed an armistice with Greece without our knowledge and the soldiers of the *Casale* division, who are from Forlì and hate Germany, found a German soldier barring the road and robbing us of the fruits of victory at the Perati Bridge. Personally, I've had my fill of Hitler and the way he acts. These conferences that begin with the ringing of a bell are not to my liking; when people call their servant they ring the bell. And besides, what kind of meetings are these? For five hours I am forced to listen to a monologue that is quite pointless and boring. He spoke for hours and hours about Hess, about the *Bismarck*, about things more or less related to the war, but he did not propose an agenda, he did not go to the bottom of any problem, or make any decisions. Meanwhile, I continue building fortifications in the Alpine mountains. Someday they will be useful. For the moment there is nothing to be done. We must howl with the wolves. Today at the Chamber I will be nice to the Germans, but my heart is filled with bitterness."

The Duce has shown me his speech. I suggested that he soft pedal on the Turks, who are still allied to the English and who may have some surprises in store for us, especially since French resistance in Syria seems to be petering out.

The reception the Chamber gave to the speech was not noteworthy, and the first comments to reach us are not altogether enthusiastic. But, I ask, could the Duce have acted any differently or better in the present situation?

June 11, 1941

I tried here and there to sound out reactions to the Duce's speech. But even among the die-hard Fascists reactions are not good. Reactions are quite unenthusiastic at the German embassy. Bismarck told Anfuso that some employee or other expressed himself as follows: "I have listened to seventeen speeches by Mussolini. This one is, without doubt, the worst." At lunch Farinacci, Cini, Volpi, and Bottai subjected the speech to intense criticism. The uneasiness lurking in the minds of all party leaders has a lot to do with these acid comments. I cannot agree with them. Perhaps the Duce should have said nothing, but since he did speak, I don't see what other line he could have taken.

The newspapers of the GUF have abused the freedom of discussion which is granted them, and are clamoring against party leaders. They exaggerate—so much so that their criticism is influenced by the absurd and irresponsible grumblings of the mob. Although these youngsters were misguided, it must be said that the regime has also made a mistake; for twenty years it has neglected these young men, and has used them only to deck them out in uniforms, hats, and capes, and herd them against their will into the squares to make a lot of noise at demonstrations.

June 12, 1941

Nothing new.

June 13, 1941

Negotiations in Berlin are dragging. Giannini does not blame the difficulties on the ill will of the Germans, but on a very real scarcity of goods. Mussolini is tempted by black humor. He says that he is glad that the people of Europe experience what German domination means. "We may be willing to let them keep their shirts, but the Germans remove even pieces of hide."

With Jacomoni, the Duce decides on some new directives concerning Albanian policy. A greater autonomy without eliminating the beys, who still count in the country, as recent events have proved, and also to bring some new elements into the government which are closer to the intellectual classes and to the people.

June 14, 1941

In Venice for Croatia's joining the Tripartite Pact. When Ribbentrop arrives he is exceptionally gay and jovial. At dinner in a Venetian inn he is even amused by the vulgar repartee of a waitress. I was astonished, as well as all those who are with me. We didn't discuss politics.

June 15, 1941

As usual, I have had a stenographic report of the conferences made. The ceremony at the Palazzo Ducale was impressive, but the canvas is more important than the frame, since the participation of Croatia has the flavor of homemade tagliatelle. The political value of the event is about zero.

Von Ribbentrop hastens his departure and clearly hinting that this is because of an imminent crisis with Russia. Naturally, he makes no objections to this, approving all of his master's exploits. But he is less ebullient than usual, and had the nerve to recall his enthusiastic praise of the Moscow agreement and of the Communist leaders, whom he compared with those of the old Nazi party.

Pavelić is satisfied with the course of events, and the others also confirm that the situation is consolidated. He already uses the attitudes and gestures of a dictator, at least toward his minions. He is very much of an extremist in social matters. In his discussion with Vittorio Cini he insisted that land must go to the peasants, and that as to industry, we must lead the way to the formation of state ownership of property. All this in ten years. Ansaldo, who gets enraged by such ideas, said, "We must not take the man seriously. Within ten months he will be kicked out!"

June 16, 1941

First I go to Ponte a Moriano, and then to Rome. There isn't much news except the talk by Churchill with the representatives of the invaded powers. He was intransigent and arrogant. He called Mussolini a "tattered lackey." I am unable to find out what the reactions are because the Duce left for Riccione this morning for a short vacation.

June 17, 1941

Nothing important.

June 18, 1941

Long telephone call from Ribbentrop. Two pieces of news: one good and the other not so good. The first is that an agreement has been reached between Turkey and Germany, consisting of neutrality, mutual respect, and peaceful solution of all controversies, and no secret protocols. The second news is the expulsion of all United States consuls from Axis territory, and vice versa. Which means that we are moving headlong toward an open state of war.

The Prefect of Bolzano traveled to Germany to deal with the issue of evacuating non-Italians from Alto Adige. The movement is slowing up under the specious pretext that Hitler has not yet chosen the territory where they are to settle. The Prefect is convinced that the Germans want to mark time, in order to reopen the issue after the end of the war.

Things are better in Libya. The British attack was broken, and we have had a noteworthy success. Bismarck didn't hesitate a minute in making the following comment: "It won't be this sort of thing that will end the war."

June 19, 1941

I conferred with the Turkish ambassador on the possibility of a pact similar to the one concluded with Germany. If anything, we could go even further, since our two countries have close and common interests. The ambassador did not answer, but seemed to be pleased. He is an odd type, with whom I have had little to do so far. In five years I have seen him no more than ten times, and the main topic of our conversations has been the cure of his rheumatism.

June 20, 1941

Nothing new.

June 21, 1941

Many signs create the impression that operations against Russia are about to begin. Bismarck secretly tells Filippo that he is expecting a message from Hitler during the night. The idea of a war against Russia is in itself popular, inasmuch as the date of the fall of Bolshevism should be counted among the most important in civilization. Viewed as a symptom, such a war is not welcomed. An obvious and convincing reason is lacking for such a war. The current explanation is that this new war is a *pis aller,* that is, an attempt to find a way out of a situation that had developed unfavorably and not differently from what had been expected. What course shall this war take? The Germans believe that it will all be over in eight weeks, and this is possible, since military calculations in Berlin have always been better than political calculations. But what if this should not be the case? If the Soviet armies should show the world a power of resistance superior to what the bourgeois countries have displayed, what results would this have on the proletarian masses of the world?

June 22, 1941

At three o'clock this morning Bismarck brings me a long letter from Hitler addressed to the Duce, seeking to explain the reasons for his move [the invasion of Russia], and although the letter begins with the ritualistic assertion that Great Britain has lost the war, its tone is far from the usual euphoria. By telephone I inform the Duce, who is still at Riccione. Then, still early in the morning, I try to contact the Soviet ambassador in order to notify him of the declaration of war. I do not succeed in seeing him until 12:30, since he and all the employees of the embassy have, quite calmly, gone to the beach at Fregene. He receives the communication with rather lackadaisical indifference, but that is his nature. I submit the communication to him without any idle words. The conversation lasted two minutes and was quite undramatic.

Tomorrow Mussolini will send Hitler his answer. The thing that is closest to the Duce's heart is the participation of one of our units, but from what Hitler writes it is clear that he would gladly do without it.

A big outburst by Riccardi about the trends of our economic situation, and he ends with this statement: "At this stage in the affairs of the regime the only thing that might yet surprise me would be finding a pregnant man; aside from this we have seen everything."

June 23, 1941

From Russia initial news of German successes begin to reach us. They talk about seventeen hundred Russian planes destroyed in one night. Cavallero, who conferred with the Duce at Riccione, thinks that the Germans can easily achieve a great victory, and that the Bolshevist armed masses will be scattered, causing a collapse. According to Bismarck, in German military circles they expect to take 5 million prisoners, "5 million slaves," as Otto says. We are sending an expeditionary corps under the command of General Zingales that will operate on the borders between Romania and sub-Carpathian Russia.

Since the Hess affair, all fortunetellers and astrologers in Germany have been arrested.

I see Phillips. He thinks that American intervention is inevitable and coming soon. He desires this intervention against Germany, which he hates, but a war between his country and Italy saddens him a lot.

Churchill has made a speech which, it must be objectively recognized, carries the mark of the great orator. I talked about it with Grandi, who, having lost his self-control for a moment, expressed an extreme admiration for Churchill. "In England," he said, "I had few friends, but Churchill was really a friend."

June 24, 1941

No definite news from the Russian front. Marras cables that the German forward units have met first-line Bolshevik resistance, and are preparing an artillery attack. Our first units will leave in three days. The Duce is very much excited at the idea of this participation of ours in the conflict, and telephones me that tomorrow he will review the troops. I despatch Mussolini's reply to Hitler to Berlin.

June 25, 1941

The Turkish foreign minister has told De Peppo[489] that the proposal of a pact with us has had a favorable reception. Conversations may take place shortly.

Falangist contingents leave Spain for the Russian front. Mussolini does not like this and would like to prevent it, but I do not know what to do since the German-Spanish agreement was reached without our knowledge.

June 26, 1941

At Verona, Mussolini reviewed the first division on its way to Russia. By telephone he called it perfect. Be that as it may, I am concerned about a direct comparison between our forces and the Germans. Not on account of the men, who are, or who may be, excellent, but on account of their equipment. I should not like to see us playing once again the role of a poor relation.

The Japanese want recognition of the government of Wang Ching-Wei, and Berlin now agrees to this. Von Ribbentrop telephones me about it, and adds that he is quite satisfied with the course of operations on the Russian front. In fact, the Germans have made considerable progress, while the Romanians, as could be expected, have allowed themselves to be pushed back.

June 27, 1941

I go to Leghorn to pray at my father's grave. As time passes, his personality becomes greater, not only in my heart, but also in the memory of all those who loved him. Today, as when I was a child, and as always, I strongly feel the need for his protection and his help. I know that he is watching over me.

June 28, 1941

Nothing new.

June 29, 1941

German bulletins describe victories in Russia in simple and exultant terms. Also Ribbentrop telephoned Alfieri that the progress of operations is beyond the most favorable predictions. Notwithstanding this, it seems that Ribbentrop is in a very bad mood; Alfieri explains this is due to German infighting.

Mussolini has returned. He looks well but is in an extremely sour mood. In the Gimma* there was the usual massive surrender, with generals at their head, despite a large amount of arms and equipment at their dis-

---

* A kingdom in Ethiopia.

posal. But even the most modern weapon, as Moltke says, is useless when thrown in the ditch. The Duce is also concerned about the situation in Alto Adige. For some time now the repatriation of non-Italians has almost totally stopped. The letters which arrive from those who have left are filled with threats and insults against us. Mussolini fears "that the Italians will have to learn the hard way that every agreement with the Germans is nothing but a *chiffon de papier*."[490] This, too, he blames on the military, who have ruined our prestige, Graziani in particular.

June 30, 1941

We must settle the matter of the Albanian and Montenegrin borders, otherwise there will be many incidents, especially with Croatia, which, like all new countries, is beginning to toy with imperialism. Pavelić now would like to have the Sanjak of Novi Bazar, an absurd and unfair demand. I am preparing a letter signed by the Duce to reject this request. At the Palazzo Venezia there is a meeting between Mussolini and Pietromarchi; the main points are set down and it is decided that if the Croatians and Bulgarians were to play tricks, the borders will be decided unilaterally by decree.

Mussolini gives vent to another anti-German outburst. He fears that the Germans are getting ready to ask for Alto Adige; he says that he would resist this with armed force, but I do not see that he has the means to carry out such a threat. He was offended, especially by the way the Germans treated him regarding the Russian matter. There was absolute silence on their part and only a "wake-up call" at night to inform him of the accomplished fact. "Even I don't dare disturb my servants at night," said the Duce, "but the Germans make me jump out of bed at any hour without the slightest consideration." The Duce realizes that Hitler doesn't welcome the participation of our troops on the Russian front, but he insists on sending them just the same. I tried my best to change his mind, but he is immovable and convinced that they are "divisions superior to the Germans', both in men and equipment." I know that Rintelen's judgment was very different. The Duce now hopes for two things: either that the war will end in a compromise, which will save the balance of Europe, or that it will last a long time, allowing us to regain our lost prestige by force of arms. His eternal illusion! . . .

July 1, 1941

It seems that at Minsk the Germans are now facing stronger Russian resistance, which is very much to the Duce's liking. He says, "I hope for only one thing, that in this war in the East the Germans will lose a lot feathers. It is false to speak of an anti-Bolshevik struggle. Hitler knows that Bolshevism has disappeared for some time. No code protects private property like the Russian Civil Code. Let him say rather that he wants to vanquish a great continental power with fifty-two-ton tanks which was getting ready to settle his account."

July 2, 1941

A long letter from Hitler to the Duce. It is a summary of the operations, all of which are favorable even though harder than had been foreseen. The Russian deployment of forces was such that one is led to believe that they were preparing to attack. Hitler also proposes a meeting of the two chiefs at his headquarters while operations are still going on. Mussolini liked the idea so much that he accepted immediately.

July 3, 1941

I hope I am wrong, but the star of our Alfieri in Berlin seems to be on the wane. Ribbentrop, who was indignant because of Pavolini's visit to Goebbels, has started a serious and laborious investigation on the origins of this trip, and Dino Alfieri will come out of it with his feathers plucked. The affair has amused the Duce, who "considers the incident quite serious but must laugh at it as at everything, even the dramatic things that happen to Alfieri.[491]"

July 4, 1941

Nothing important.

July 5, 1941

Meeting of the Council of Ministers, financial measures were considered, and then the Duce gave a long dissertation on the political and military situations: the United States will intervene, but its intervention is already taken into account. Russia will be defeated in short order, and this may persuade Great Britain to yield. The Duce was very unhappy over the almost total loss of the empire, "for which loss I [Mussolini] have sworn hatred against the British until the end of time, bequeathing this hatred to all Italians." He shall undertake to reconquer the empire at any cost, even if it should entail the most extreme sacrifices.

Pavelić has replied on the Montenegrin issue: he agrees to establish the 1914 boundaries. I will send the text of the proclamation on the establishment of the borders to Mazzolini, after which the constituent assembly will meet to create the new kingdom of which the same Mazzolini will be the regent. Silimbani[492] makes an interesting presentation of the situation in Tunisia: even the stones are Gaullists, and 80 percent of the middle classes believe in a British victory. They hate the Germans but admire them; they simply despise us.

July 6, 1941

A report from our consul at Innsbruck warns of the resumption of German agitation to take Alto Adige, under the leadership of Gauleiter Hofer himself. The Duce has been flabbergasted and irritated by it. "Note it down in your diary," he says, "that I predict an unavoidable conflict arising between Italy and Germany. It is now obvious that they are preparing to ask us to bring our borders to Salorno and perhaps even to Verona, which will produce a terrible crisis in Italy even for the regime. I shall overcome it, but it will be the hardest of all. I feel this instinctively, and I now seriously ask whether an English victory would not be more desirable for our future than a German victory. Meanwhile, the English are flying over Germany by day. Bruno [Mussolini's son] has told me so, and this pleases me very much. For this reason, since we shall have to fight the Germans, we must not uphold the myth of their invincibility. Nevertheless, I have little faith in our race; at the first bombing that might destroy a famous campanile or a painting by Giotto, the Italians would go into a fit of artistic sentimentality and would raise their hands in surrender. We must thank Graziani; we owe it to him if our prestige is going to pot, as a matter of fact is already destroyed. Once the war is over, he will no longer be Marshal of Italy."

July 7, 1941

Anti-German resentment by the Duce is still keen. "The Germans insist upon the loyalty of others, but they are themselves incapable of being loyal."

I see Della Giovanna,[493] who is back from Germany. His impressions on the situation are mediocre; little enthusiasm, much uneasiness on account of living conditions that are becoming more and more difficult.

The Duce leaves for Puglia.

July 8, 1941

I met Admiral Fioravanzo, who is a young navy ace; he is lively and interesting, though a bit too conceited. He does not conceal his anti-German feelings and is concerned about German hegemony in Europe. He considers our navy still very efficient in dreadnoughts and cruisers, but believes that Italian torpedo boats have received a hard blow from which it will be difficult to recover because of our lack of raw materials. He criticizes our program for naval armaments in which we sacrificed armor for speed.

July 9, 1941

Acquarone comes on the King's behalf with two complaints: first, that in the proclamation to the Montenegrins we mention the Duce but not the King—and this I remedy immediately, since the proclamation has not yet been published. Second, that the Duce reviewed the divisions returning from the front. This, in the past, was always done by the King. I shall talk about it with Cavallero, whom the royal house continues to distrust because, according to Acquarone, "he has ambitions which are more of a political than of a military nature."

The German advance in Russia proceeds at a somewhat slower pace. Resistance is serious; I saw a set of documents sent by Goebbels in which this is clearly evident.

Buffarini paints a very, very dark picture of our internal situation: anti-Fascism is taking root everywhere threateningly, implacably, and silently. He is preparing a documented report, but does not dare show it to the Duce.

July 10, 1941

The Duce has returned to Rome. The Hungarians have annexed the Mura territory which triggered great resentment in Zagreb. I did not hide my disappointment from Villani and told him that Hungary will end badly if she follows this line. A country of 15 million inhabitants and 5 million minorities is inconceivable. The Hungarians will suffer the same fate as all patchwork countries.

Naples is bombed, and Cologne very badly as well. From the Russian front news is quite serious; the Russians are fighting well, and, for the first time in the course of the war, the Germans have to admit withdrawing at two points.

The Bulgarian minister of foreign affairs is ill and his visit to Rome will be postponed. I have the impression that the Bulgarians have little desire to talk to us, preferring that borders be established unilaterally, so that they can always dispute its merits, something they could not do with a regularly signed treaty.

July 11, 1941

I saw the Duce after a few days' absence. He is well and happy about his inspection of the troops in Puglia. "The Tridentina division," he said, "is superb. I say without hesitation that there are no more perfect soldiers in Europe."

Naples was bombed—very bad. Not so much on account of the number of victims as because of the damage, of which the most serious was the fire of the Italian-American refineries. We lost 6,000 tons of oil, and God only knows how much we needed it. The Duce said, "I am happy that Naples is having such severe nights. The breed will harden, the war will make of the Neapolitans a Nordic race." Of this I am very skeptical.

A meeting with Dornberg.[494] He is calm and not enthusiastic. Losses in Russia are heavy, and at length the war may bring us some big surprises. His wife is sprightlier than he, and she does not conceal her judgment of the situation. "This is a war," she said, "that we don't have the strength to win."

News from the Russian front is so-so. The summary bulletin on the battles of Bialystok and Minsk evidently deal with things that should have happened but did not.

July 12, 1941

Nothing new

July 13, 1941

Mussolini is more and more alarmed about the situation in Alto Adige. He had a meeting with Signora de Paoli. She preferred Italian citizenship, although she is of German origin and the mother of a dead soldier with an Italian gold medal. With concrete and unassailable arguments she completely disillusioned the Duce, stating that Germany's real decision is to annex Alto Adige no later than after the war. The Duce repeated his usual anti-German arguments and concluded by saying that he will bring clearly to Hitler's attention the fact that an event of this kind would constitute "the collapse of the regime."

Considerable German progress on the Russian front; the Stalin line has been broken through at various points, and they are moving toward Leningrad, Moscow, and Kiev.

Frau Dornberg is anti-Nazi but she is German, and therefore I must speak with caution. Last night she asked me point-blank, "Is it true that you love Churchill more than Hitler?" To which I replied, "I fear that I do not feel as you do. I love your chief very much." She looked offended!

July 14, 1941

Unrest in Montenegro. Shooting by armed bands, an assault on the royal villa at Budva. It appears that this is not connected to the constituent assembly, but the coincidence of events is at least strange. In the meantime we have postponed the arrival of the Montenegrins in Rome, and on the King's initiative the regency will be assumed by three Montenegrins instead of Mazzolini.

The Duce is furious with the military who "mislead him." They had assured him that the Galileo Factory in Florence would produce eight anti-aircraft searchlights a month, and instead he learned that the first thirteen of them, in two types, would be ready only by the end of December. All this is particularly serious in organizing our anti-aircraft defenses. We have had to stop sending Italian workers to Germany because it was becoming more and more difficult for them to live with the Germans, and fist fights were a daily occurrence.

July 15, 1941

We receive details of the surrender of Debra Tabor.[495] In eight weeks our losses amounted to two killed and four wounded out of four thousand men. The surrender took place with full honors nevertheless. Mussolini affirms that this is one of the "classic Italian *combinazioni.*" They have discovered this form of surrender that saves their hides, and which it is easy to obtain from the mercenary English, who avoid sacrifices and losses themselves.

In Montenegro things are going rather badly. The capital is isolated and all the roads leading to it are blocked by the rebels. We have sent forces there from Albania.

A strange thing from Mussolini: he has scolded Pavolini because in an article by Ansaldo the latter referred to "the war in Russia, under the direction of Hitler, etc. . . ." "In this way," the Duce said, "the Italian people are getting accustomed to thinking that only Hitler is directing the war." I wonder. Are we joking, or are we serious?

July 16, 1941

The Duce is not convinced by the course of events in Russia. The tone of his conversation today was clearly pessimistic, particularly because the British-Russian alliance turns Stalin into the head of Nationalist Russia. He is afraid that Germany is facing a task that is too much for her, and will not reach a complete solution of the whole problem before winter, leading to many unknowns.

July 17, 1941

The Montenegrin insurrection continues; in fact, it takes on larger proportions. If it did not have a deep and bitter significance, it would be grotesque that a war should exist between Italy and Montenegro! We hope that our military men will settle it without having to call for German intervention.

Mussolini, as usual, speaks of the military men bitterly, and says that he likes only one general, I forget his name, who, in Albania, said to his soldiers, "I have heard that you are good family men. That's fine at home, but not here. Here, you will never go too far in being thieves, murderers, and rapists."

July 18, 1941

Anfuso has had an intimate and very interesting conversation with Frau Mollier, the wife of the German press attaché. She revealed that the Russian campaign has caused a deep crisis among the German ruling classes. Hitler went to war believing that the struggle against Bolshevism might lead the Anglo-Saxon countries to end the conflict. Ribbentrop disagreed; in fact, he was convinced that Churchill is ready to make an alliance even with the devil himself if only he can destroy Nazism. And this time he was right. Now the struggle is hard and bloody, and the German people, who are already tired, wonder why. Frau Mollier used harsh terms. She said that Hitler is a *Dummkopf.* In fact, the war is harder than the Germans expected. The advance continues, but it is slow, and harassed by very vigorous Soviet counterattacks. Colonel Amè and General Squero, who reported on the military situation today, believe that the Russians will succeed in maintaining a front even during the winter. If this is true, Germany has begun a hemorrhage on its flank that will have unforeseeable consequences.

July 19, 1941

Some battalions have reached Cettigne, and hence the situation in Montenegro, though it has not been solved, is noticeably improved.

I accompany Villani on his farewell visit to the Duce. The man continues with his anti-German ideas that amuse the Duce at this time and without eliciting any reaction from him. The end of the conversation is less happy. "I am going home because I have reached the age limit," he says. "I'm an old man. I am your age, as a matter of fact one year older." Mussolini did not like this comparison, especially because Villani looks like the very portrait of old age.

We have fixed the Bulgarian-Albanian border by a unilateral decree. Stormy weather in Sofia, where the Cabinet talks of resigning. The approaching and futile visit of the Bulgarian ministers to Rome begins under bad auspices.

July 20, 1941

The Duce continues his anti-German outbursts. Today he said, "Meditating over the words of Villani, I wonder if by now we do not belong to the vassal nations. And even if this is not so today, it will be so on the day of total victory for Germany. They are treacherous, and without any sense of restraint. I have proof that the intrigues in Croatia have all been hatched by the Germans. I predict an unavoidable crisis between the two countries. We must place thousands of guns along the rivers of the Venetian region, because it is from there that the Germans will launch their invasion of Italy, and not across the narrow valleys of Alto Adige, where they would be easily cut to pieces. For the time being there is nothing that can be done. We are on this track, and we must stay on it. But we must hope for two things: that the war will be long and exhausting for Germany, and that it ends in a compromise that will save our independence."

News from the Russian front reports a costly and hard-fought advance. According to some reports from Moscow, intercepted from American-Turkish sources, we learn that disorder is beginning to appear among Soviet troops, and that a collapse might now be near. That may be. However, a heavy price has been paid for it, and even if Russia is beaten, what will become of the rest of the world? Is this a decisive victory? I do not believe it.

July 21, 1941

The Bulgarians arrive: two traditional democratic-parliamentary ministers, whom the raging tempest over Europe forces to deal with dictators, uniforms, and parades. They have come to beg for some border concessions, particularly in the area of the Ochrida and Prespa lakes, indispensable to strengthen their personal situation in their own country. I have held firm, more for reasons of form than out of conviction. Some small concessions may be made at the meeting of the mixed commission. I have seen the King and the Prince of Piedmont, the former more calm and cordial, the latter dissatisfied and critical. Hitler addressed a long letter to the Duce. It is a summary of military operations in Russia, the course of which he thinks is favorable. It is a broad political-military survey, and finally—this is the real reason for the letter—asking to take over our air force and navy commands. I don't know what they can do more or better than we can. Our navy, especially, is giving excellent results in view of its capabilities and equipment. I do not believe that this request will increase fondness toward Germany in many circles.

July 22, 1941

Dummy air raids continue at Rome. It was the Duce who personally ordered an air raid in the capital every time there is one in Naples. He does this because he wants to give the country the impression that a war is taking place. He has also ordered that at the first opportunity antiaircraft should fire in order to make it more exciting. Is all this worthwhile? If we listen to comments on the street, I should say not at all. There is more insistent news about the coming English offensive in Libya. Squero considers that there is something true in the report but doubts that we can resist a mass shock attack.

Matters in Montenegro are going pretty badly. Rebel forces are increased by Croats and Serbs, and our divisions cannot maintain contact with them. All this is grotesque, but it gives one much food for thought.

[*No entries July 23 to September 21 inclusive.*]

September 22, 1941

I return to the Ministry after a long absence, due to a throat infection which compelled me to undergo an operation. Practically two months of inactivity without contacts with the Duce, except for the very sad day of Bruno's death.[496] I found the Chief in good shape, physically and spiritually. He has recovered from the blow. As always, the main point in his conversation is the military progress of the war. He says that the uneasiness of the Italian people is due to the fact that they are not participating in the war on the Russian front on a larger scale. I cannot agree with him. The people are not interested in this Russian war, and the real misery of our people is due to lack of food, fats, eggs, et cetera. But this aspect of the situation is not the one that disturbs the Duce.

However, it does disturb Serena, who, after all, is now responsible—or at least is thought to be the one who is responsible—for the food situation. It was a big mistake on the part of the party to take this problem on its shoulders—one which will be the basis of all complaints, because, if today the situation is disturbing, it is not difficult to envision that it will become more acute later on when the lack of fodder and the scarcity of fertilizers further reduces the harvests and production drops to still lower levels.

September 23, 1941

The event of the day is the issue of private ownership of industrial and state bonds. Revel plays the victim, saying that he knows nothing about it, and that he is against it. The Duce would favor it, but more out of spite than from conviction. According to Revel, the one who inspired this measure is a police informer, a former employee of the Bank of Italy, who has written to Mussolini to the effect that he, Mussolini, doesn't have the courage to do what Giolitti did. Volpi is furious and tries to block the measure with every means at his disposal.

I saw Phillips, who has been called to Washington for consultations. As always he was cordial. We entered into no specific discussion. He merely emphasized that the American press is no longer attacking Italy. He mentioned the Battle of the Atlantic, which he considers already won by the democracies. Von Mackensen also came to pay me a courtesy visit. We did not discuss politics. Generally speaking, he was tranquil and spoke about Italy in cordial terms.

September 24, 1941

The Duce told me that Alfieri warned him about rumors going around about the Duce himself. The rumor is that the Duce returned from Germany with a rather pessimistic impression of the progress of operations, and that he expressed himself in harsh terms about the Germans. (Actually, he has done this even with me sometimes, but more often in my absence.) Alfieri, when pressed about the source of such information, kept his statements on a vague and general level, which made the Duce indignant. "Alfieri lost much ground." Alfieri had spoken to me along these same lines with respect to what was being said about me. I told him off, as I frequently do with this petty braggart. Nevertheless, the Duce was disturbed by it all, and on October 1 he will speak to the Italian-German Association to deny all such rumors.

I saw a report by Cecchi on the treatment of our laborers in Germany. In some camps, in addition to beatings, large watchdogs are used which are trained to bite the legs of those workers who are guilty of only slight transgressions. If a report of this kind became known to the Italian people they would revolt with a violence that few can imagine.

September 25, 1941

I showed Cecchi's report to the Duce. He was shaken by it and requested that I take this up with Mackensen to acquaint him with the seriousness of what has happened. The Duce added "that I should take the step on my own initiative, without informing the Duce, who is supposed to know nothing about it." I did, in fact, talk with Mackensen, who took his cue from my words to attack the presence of our workers in Germany "destined to sharpen the deep irritation which already exists between our two countries."

I saw Cavallero, who, as the good hot-air artist that he is, admits to all the difficulties and concludes with the inevitable "*tout va très bien, Madame la Marquise.*" Actually, the Mediterranean situation is dark, and will become even more so because of the continued loss of merchant ships. Commander Bigliardi, who is in the know and is a reliable person, says that in responsible naval circles they are seriously beginning to wonder whether we shouldn't decide to give up Libya, rather than wait until we are forced to do so by the complete lack of freighters. According to a report by the SIM, of which I have a copy, it appears that armed German units are settling into the main Italian cities. For what purpose? We must keep our eye on them.

September 26, 1941

From other sources, too, news about dogs being sicked on our workers in Germany has reached the Duce, and he was shaken and disturbed by it. "These things are bound to produce a lasting hatred in my heart. I can even wait many years, but in the end I shall square this account. I will not permit the sons of a race that has given humanity Caesar, Dante, and Michelangelo to be devoured by the bloodhounds of the Huns." He suggested that I meet Ribbentrop for discussions and bring this up. I have written a letter making the proposal to comrade Joachim!

A short conversation with Acquarone of no particular interest except the fact that the court atmosphere is becoming more and more somber, down in the mouth, and anti-German.

The new minister of Hungary, Mariassy, is the typical example of the classic career busybody, ceremonious and empty. He wanted to address some political questions to me, and began by asking me if I thought the Axis would win the war! I wonder what kind of an answer he expected in wartime from the Italian foreign minister whom he was meeting for the first time in his life. A fine specimen of an imbecile.

September 27, 1941

Meeting of the Council of Ministers. One should take notice more of the Duce's state of mind than of the measures decided at the meeting. He talked for three hours almost without interruption. His arguments were directed against the bourgeoisie, "against the well-to-do, who are the worst type of Italians." He made a few references to the war and its development, only to say that he now believes that the war will last many years. Bread is rationed at 200 grams, with an increase up to 300 or 400 for heavy laborers. "Let no one think," he said, "that rationing will end after the war. It will stay as long as I want it to. Only in this way will the Agnellis and the Doneganis eat just like the lowest of their employees. If 200 grams are little, then I tell you that around springtime the ration will be even less, and this delights me because we will finally see signs of suffering on the faces of the Italian people, which will be valuable to us at the peace table."

The Duce was delighted by the fact that bonds now bear the names of their owners, but his arguments were hardly convincing and technically meaningless. The Council of Ministers remained silent. Only Revel—who loves to call himself the "Red Count"—was satisfied. Grandi, who accompanied me to the ministry, was horrified by what he called the "white Bolshevism of Mussolini, in which he recognized the editor of *Lotta di Classe*,[497] whom he heard, as a youngster, speak at Imola and whom he felt was utterly foreign to his way of thinking."

September 28, 1941

A long conversation with Gambara. Both the Duce and Cavallero had described him to me as optimistic, confident in the future of Libya. This is not the case at all. He talked to me with a deep sense of responsibility and he sees the future full of clouds and dangers. He thinks that, compared to last year, the situation has greatly improved, but it is only a marginal improvement, and replacements of raw materials are becoming scarce and more difficult to find. Now they are talking about attacking Tobruk. He thinks this is a serious mistake, an action in which we may exhaust our best forces, leaving the door open to the inevitable English offensive. Cavallero supports this plan to please the Germans and the Duce. Therefore, Gambara attacks Cavallero violently, saying that he was unable to secure the army's confidence, and wastes his time in useless political activities instead of proceeding with a real organization of the armed forces. "If we continue like this, we will lose the war. This is also the opinion of Roatta and Squero." Gambara is right. Cavallero is revealing himself a perfect peddler who has found the secret entrance to Mussolini's heart, and who is ready to follow this path of lies, intrigue, and fraud. He must be watched; he is a man who can cause us a lot of trouble.

September 29, 1941
   Nothing new.

September 30, 1941
   Mussolini is elated by the successes of the Expeditionary Corps in Russia. Our naval victory, 90 percent of which is discounted by London, and the prisoners captured on the Eastern Front, have cheered up the Duce. He now sees a rosy future, even from the military point of view. But this represents the endless highs and lows of his personality.
   Phillips is about to leave, and he used some excuse to say good-bye. He talks at length about the depressed state of mind of the Italian people, and ends by repeating America's sympathy for our country—a sympathy which will be indispensable in helping us in our reconstruction. I made no comment, especially since the SIM has secured the American secret code. Everything that Phillips cables is read by our decoding offices, and might therefore be given the wrong interpretation. This, naturally, prevents any possibility of a *rapprochement* with the Americans.
   Today, for the first time, there is a report signed by Alfieri (the real author of the political reports is always Ridomi[498]) in which it is stated that the German people are moving farther and farther away from the idea of a total victory and toward the idea of a compromise peace.

October 1, 1941
   A report from Pittalis[499] in Munich that, while it doesn't paint the situation in dark colors, is certainly not rosy. Of great significance is the clash shaping up between Prussians and Bavarians. The religious factor is certainly of considerable importance, but we must also not neglect the fact that many foodstuffs have disappeared from the Bavarian market because of well-to-do Prussians who have taken refuge in Bavaria. And then there are those who are surprised that Italians are irritated with the Germans when they ransack our warehouses!
   A conference with Admiral Ferreri. He is concerned about the fate of Libya, especially if the sinkings of our merchant ships continue to be as heavy as in September. While in the past the percentage of ships lost had reached a maximum of 5 percent, in September it jumped to 18 percent. Like all our naval officers, he is openly anti-German.
   Inauguration of the academic year of the Italian-German Institute. That simple-minded man, Balbino Giuliano, made a very unconvincing speech on the common traditions of the Italian *Risorgimento* and the corresponding movement in Germany. The presence of the Duce at this unimportant cer-

emony is intended to deny the rumors spread by Alfieri of a cooling of feelings on the part of Mussolini toward his Axis associate.

October 2, 1941
   Nothing new.

October 3, 1941
   Speech by Hitler in Berlin, which was unexpected, or almost. First impressions are that he has tried to explain to the German people his reasons for the attack on Russia and to justify his delay in ending the war, about which he had made very definite commitments. There is no doubt that he has lost some of his vigor. This time there are no fulminating anti-English threats. As for us, we were given no particular attention; he lumped us with the others, and which will not produce a good impression in Italy, where the wave of anti-German feeling is growing stronger and stronger. Plessen has sent to our ministry a verbal note, which is rather strong, pointing out "that in Greece people are starving, and that we are responsible for whatever may take place there." The least I can say is that we are dealing with a puzzling document.
   De Chirico is painting my portrait. This artist is a strange man, opinionated and very timid, at times absent-minded and at times deep and sharp. He has a surprising culture, which runs through his conversation almost without his being aware of it.

October 4, 1941
   Mussolini, who was at Riccione, telephones about Hitler's speech. He does not like it at all, "although he is satisfied as far as he is concerned." He is miffed by the step taken by Plessen about Greece. He says, "The Germans have taken even their shoelaces from the Greeks, and now they attempt to lay the blame for the economic situation on our backs. We can take the responsibility, but only on condition that they clear out of Athens and the entire country."
   The internal situation, which is bad in many sectors, is becoming serious in Sicily. This region, which has suffered all the woes of war and enjoyed none of its benefits, has been particularly annoyed by a personal decision of the Duce to remove Sicilian civil service employees from the island. To the misery of the Sicilians has been added what they consider an outrage. Why this was done I do not know. I met with Gaetani, who wishes to resign his position as vice-secretary of the Fascist party, and weeps when he speaks of conditions in Sicily. I have seen Massi, who is to be transferred to northern Italy, and who refuses to accept. He said, "My father is Genoese and my mother is Sicilian. If she were a Jewess I would be Aryanized. In this case, however, there is no indulgence for me. Is it, then, worse to be a Sicilian than to be a Jew?"

October 5, 1941
   Nothing of importance.

October 6, 1941

Mussolini, judging from what he told me over the telephone from Riccione, is irritated by Hitler's speech. The fact that he has spoken impromptu provides the explanation "of that which otherwise would be unpardonable."

Squero had a long meeting with me about the situation of the army. He is not a man with broad views, but he is honest, and does not bluff. While Cavallero speaks of dozens of divisions that can be ready by winter, Squero thinks that we cannot have more than four or five new ones that are really well equipped. Supplies for Libya are becoming more and more difficult. Only 20 percent of the supplies set aside for September have been shipped and delivered. On the other hand, the number of men is higher: 50 percent.

There is a lot of dissatisfaction because of the food situation. And in some provinces there have been small demonstrations by women, which are difficult to suppress. In Rome they grumble a great deal and are sarcastic. They now call the Campidoglio "Campidaria."[500]

October 7, 1941

Nothing new.

October 8, 1941

Some people can be hard-boiled! When I was in Albania, Verlaçi, in the presence of Jacomoni, talked to me about the Albanian government's intention to offer Cavallero a parcel of Albanian soil. At the moment I thought that it meant the usual urn filled with earth, like the customary earth of the Grappa or water from the Piave, and I had no objection. But when I learned that the offer was not so symbolical, since it dealt with a grant of almost 2,500 acres of land in Fieri, I was definitely against it. This did not please the interested parties, who are now trying to twist things around with a letter from Verlaçi announcing the accomplished fact. I spoke to Cavallero about the matter and I will stop it. But Cavallero is not grateful to me. Just the opposite. He fails to realize that for a man such as himself, whose fame as a strategist is in doubt, but whose reputation as a grafter is known to everyone, accepting such a gift would spell his doom. When bread is being rationed and the people are hungry, is not the time to announce that Cavallero is celebrating a very dubious Greek victory by accepting a present worth a few million.

October 9, 1941

The conditions in Greece, according to Ghigi, are becoming so desperate that there is fear the population will get out of hand. The bread ration is already reduced to ninety grams a day. They have nothing else. If a load of grain does not reach Pireus tomorrow, the ovens will be cold. What is the solution? Ghigi makes no definite proposals, but he states that, in the first place, it is necessary to straighten out the misunderstandings arising from the division of command between ourselves and the Germans which paralyzes many undertakings and burdens the food situation in Athens with too many heavy-eating and arrogant officers. Tomorrow I will see Ghigi again. Today he did not conceal his deep unhappiness but did not explain why, saying only that he would like to be transferred.

News from the German front in Russia is more and more favorable to the progress of operations: as paeans of victory. Will this end up being true, or will we, after so many losses in men and materiel, be reading simply that a new front was formed 100 or 200 kilometers forward? This is what is really important for the entire course of the war.

October 10, 1941

Mussolini has returned and is in a good mood, especially because of his trip to Bologna and Parma, which "received him very enthusiastically, proving once more that they are ultra-political cities." He is cautious regarding the course of operations in Russia. There have been successes, and that is undeniable, but he feels that the communiqués also bear evidence of propaganda for internal consumption, in view of the coming of a winter which will be hard. This opinion is corroborated by some cables from Alfieri, who pours more than a little water in our wine, saying that there is a difference of opinion between the most conservative military men and the politicians, who are sounding the trumpets of victory. The Duce fancies sending troops to Russia. He wants to send another 20 divisions there in the spring, because "in this way our war effort will compare favorably with Germany, and will prevent Germany, at the moment of final victory, from dictating to us as it shall to the subjugated peoples." I also brought the Duce up to date about the Cavallero issue—his property in Albania—and the Duce was deeply and unfavorably impressed.

October 11, 1941

Ghigi discusses the Greek situation honestly with the Duce, which is, in one word, hunger. Anything is possible, from epidemics to ferocious revolts on the part of people who know that they now have nothing to lose. Something will be done. Mussolini has given orders that 7,500 tons of wheat be shipped immediately. A very small amount compared to the needs for November. But we can do no more. The Italians, too, are tightening their belts to the last hole: the one that the Italians call the "*foro* Mussolini"—"the Mussolini hole."[501]

The undersecretary of food administration said that rations must be lowered further because there is no choice but to limit the consumption of food, unless we want to run out of food for a month. Frankly, this would be too much. Meanwhile, what most concerns the Duce is the fact that we are absent or almost absent from the Eastern Front. He wants to send 20 divisions there in October, and Cavallero encourages him to do so. But aside from the fact that in the spring we could never, ever have 20 divisions ready, would it be wise for us to send the little materiel that we still have at home and which is our only protection? The King, who is in San Rossore, is clearly averse to such plans.

October 12, 1941
   Nothing new.

October 13, 1941
   Through Mackensen, Ribbentrop has asked me to join him at Schönhof to go pheasant shooting toward the end of the month.
   The Duce received news that during his trip to the Russian front a German is supposed to have said about him, "There goes our Gauleiter for Italy." An employee of the embassy supposedly overheard that remark. The Duce wrote to Alfieri to find out the truth. Mussolini said, "I believe it. In Germany there exist certain phonograph records. Hitler presses them; the others play them. The first record was the one about Italy being the loyal ally, on an equal footing with Germany, master of the Mediterranean just as Germany was master of the Baltic. Then came the second record, the one about victories, that Europe would be dominated by Germany. The conquered states will be colonies. The associated states will be confederated provinces of Germany. Among these the most important is Italy. We have to accept these conditions because any attempt to rebel would result in our being reduced from the position of a confederated province to the worse one of a colony. Even if they should ask for Trieste tomorrow, as part of German *Lebensraum*, we would have to bow our heads. As a matter of fact, there is the possibility of a third phonograph record, the one which will be published should British-American resistance make our collaboration more useful to the Germans. But that one is yet to come."
   I limited myself to saying that with such a prospect one can easily understand why Italian enthusiasm for this war is so slight.
   Serena is worried about the food situation, and he took it out on the Chief, who, agitated as he is, would—if told—make impulsive decisions on the basis of intercepted telephone conversations and anonymous messages which in a short time cause a dangerous state of disorder. Perhaps the Duce might act differently with me, but I don't share Serena's opinion. Mussolini at times is a little in the clouds, but he is always calm, attentive, and in control of himself. He also has completely recovered from the sorrow of Bruno's death.

October 14, 1941
   Nothing new.

October 15, 1941
   The King sent for me. He had no particular questions to ask, and the pretext that he used with the Duce for his talk with me was the Croatian situation. As usual, he gave a cautious but definite opinion on the situation. He is against sending any more Italian troops to Russia, and he deplores Cavallero's statement about the possibility of forming 96 divisions by spring. He doesn't believe that we have well-supplied army stores "including the three million rifles, which he would like to count for himself, because many of these rifles were given to the Fascist militia, and to the GIL, who stole even the bolts of the rifles." He criticizes the militia; the Mantua Legion was

abandoned by its consul, who returned to his unit only when the engagement was over and was booed by his men, "who, in reality, are nothing but civilians in uniform." The internal situation also disturbs him. Above all, he thinks we must avoid any display of force and all incidents that might exasperate the Italian population, which is already exasperated to the danger point by current restrictions. He fears a German-French agreement at our expense, and he even fears an agreement between London and Berlin. He doesn't trust the Germans, and every time he talks of them he calls them "those ugly Germans."

Today the Duce was influenced by a talk with General Marras, who confirmed the imperialistic plans of certain German social groups, according to whom, after the war, Germany alone will be an armed and industrial power, while the other nations will have to play a more or less agricultural role and become political vassals of Berlin. Mussolini said, "I believe it. The German people are dangerous because they dream collectively. But history teaches that all attempts to unify Europe under a single rule have failed."

Tassinari is very much alarmed and disturbed by the food situation. He fears the worst and would like to pass the buck to a successor, using the excuse of being tired and ill. Naturally, I dissuaded him.

October 16, 1941

I had never met Arpinati and knew of him through my father, who said good things about of him. I met him today and we had a long conversation at the Palazzo Chigi. Before receiving him I informed the Duce, who is very suspicious about this kind of thing. Arpinati is important among the men of the regime. I don't know if this is because of his intelligence, but it is certainly because of his character—a rather rare gift among Italians. He talked about the past and his problems calmly, and, I would say, with pride. He didn't ask to be reinstated or to be forgiven; in fact, without any backbiting he reaffirmed his loyalty to his beliefs, which irritated Mussolini at the time. He is against the corporative system, is anti-Communist, and anti-German, but he realizes that no other policy was possible, because, had we followed a different line of conduct, "we would have been gobbled up like an egg by Germany." He was cautious in his judgments on men: only of Grandi did he say that he is a traitor and that he, Arpinati, "can knock him off his pedestal whenever he wants to."

Marras had a second conversation with the Duce and said that in certain German circles they are making these plans: 1942, liquidation of Russia and attack on Egypt; 1943, occupation of the island [Britain]. I have heard about such programs many times before, and yet . . .

October 17, 1941

The fall of Odessa has saddened Mussolini, who now sees himself taking second place to the Romanians. Every day he vents his anger at the Italian generals, and particularly at Graziani, whom he wants to court-martial. The Riom trial has had an influence on him.

Von Ribbentrop invites me to Germany on the 25th to general headquarters, where Hitler wants to confer with me, and after this to Schönhof
for the usual shooting party

At the Attolicos' a luncheon in honor of Frau Goebbels, who is passing
through, accompanied by a sister-in-law. This is how Bismarck addressed
Anfuso on the subject: "Frau Goebbels is the typical wife of a high Nazi
official. She was first married to a crook, and earned money through prostitution. Later she became the friend of Goebbels, but this did not prevent
her from going to bed with many of the frequenters of the party meetings
at the Sports Palace. Goebbels married her one night when he was drunk.
They have had several children together, and maybe not together, because
Frau Goebbels has continued her former ways. Now she goes around looking for men, and when there are not enough, there is also her sister-in-law,
who is another whore. I am ashamed to think that my wife has anything to
do with such people." This is how a Bismarck talks about the wife of one of
the most outstanding men in the Nazi regime.

October 18, 1941

According to some sources the Germans are beginning to slow down in
front of Moscow. Isn't this a case of their having sung their victory anthem
too soon?

I leave for Ponte Ciano.[502]

October 19, 1941

My day was divided between the countryside and the beach. Nothing
new at Leghorn, but the spirit of the citizens is low. The approach of winter
is viewed with great concern by all. Too many illusions have been built up,
purposely or involuntarily, about the shortness of the conflict and a victory
which was supposed to be easy.

October 20, 1941

Alfieri reports on a long conference with von Ribbentrop, who has sung
his usual song: victory is achieved, the Russian army is crushed, and England has reached the end of her days. And yet at Moscow the armored
divisions are at a standstill facing very strong resistance, and many German
soldiers are bound to die with their mother's name on their lips before the
flag of the Reich flies over the Kremlin. Meanwhile, winter is drawing near,
and military operations will soon become very limited.

October 21, 1941

Funk and Clodius are in Rome. With the first I had a conversation that
was more general than substantial. With Clodius we talked especially about
the Balkan situation. He has returned from Turkey and believes that in Ankara they wish to keep to the middle of the road, hoping for a negotiated
peace. This would be ideal for the Turks: an exhausted Russia, and a Europe
in which the balance of power remains between Britain and Germany.

To Anfuso he said some hard things about our financial status: "Italy is running toward inflation and there is no way to stop its course."

Bottai is increasingly pessimistic. His judgment of the Chief is now violently negative. He said, "My friendship for Balbo was always an argumentative friendship, since our ideas were frequently different. As time passes I must confess that he was right. I remember that he called Mussolini 'a product of syphilis,' and that I used to object to his words. I wonder now if this judgment on Mussolini wasn't correct, or at least very close to the truth. The Duce has decayed intellectually and physically. He doesn't attract me any more. He is not strong-willed; he is weak and ambitious, expecting only to be admired, flattered, and betrayed."

October 22, 1941

This is the anniversary of Maria's death, the dear, unforgettable soul.

Among the many worthless individuals that life produces every day, General Cavallero is easily the most remarkable. Inasmuch as he feels that an ill wind is blowing from my direction, he is now attempting to get around me while seeking favor at the same time. Today, with his artificial, hypocritical, and servile optimism, he was unbearable. He says that he has solved the motorization problem not by giving the troops trucks but by increasing the marching rate of the infantry from 18 to 40 kilometers a day. Crazy stuff. To this I reacted violently, and he was forced to back down. He then went on to assure me that by spring he shall have 92 divisions ready for use. This is a shameless lie. He knows very well that we shall not have even one third of that number. But this way he fires up the Duce's imagination.

The Duce insists more and more on sending forces to Russia, indicating an army of 15 divisions. He has given me instructions to speak to Hitler about this during the meeting that we are to have on Saturday, insisting at the same time that the number of our workingmen in Germany be replaced by soldiers to be sent to the front. Mussolini holds that in this way we shall acquire greater prestige with our ally, who continues to stall in front of Moscow without making headway.

Del Croix openly states his hatred of Germans, and he speaks very freely about the Duce as follows: "For some years now he is missing his mark. He [the Duce] speaks of collaboration with Russia, and the war against Russia breaks out. He says that the march on Rome paved the way for the march on Moscow, but we have not reached Moscow yet. He announces the blitzkrieg, and there is no question but that the war will last many years."

October 23, 1941

Cavallero realizes that he has boasted too much, and came to me to pour some water in his wine, and therefore wiggle out of his previous statements. "It's true," etc., etc., he said, "we can't send more than six new divisions to Russia, and only on condition that the motorized equipment be furnished by Germany." He states that he explained to Mussolini the reasons for his change of mind, but, even if this is the case, the result is quite modest because the Duce confirmed yesterday's instructions that he summed up by saying: "fewer workers and more soldiers." Even regarding food supplies, he said to assure Hitler that Italy can get by on its own. "In 1926, when we had to pay the first installment of our debt to America, one appeal from me was sufficient to bring in the 100 million necessary for the purpose. I am certain that even today, if I made another appeal, many millions of Italians would sacrifice their bread and meat rations."

Aside from the fact that to contribute a few lire is something very different from giving up one's own already meager food ration, is Mussolini sure that things haven't changed deeply in the minds of the Italian people since 1926?

At 8 p.m. I leave for general headquarters, where I shall meet Hitler on Saturday.

October 24, 1941
On my way to headquarters.

October 25-29, 1941
I arrive at headquarters. I am welcomed at the station by von Ribbentrop and by Hitler at the entrance of his fortified cabin. They had told me that he was looking tired and old. This is not true. I found him in top form, physically and mentally. He is very courteous, or perhaps I should say chummy. He quickly has me come into his study, together with von Ribbentrop and Schmidt. I have made a report of the conference to the Duce, and it is filed elsewhere. I have also candidly added my own observations, but now I shall limit myself to jotting down a few episodes and impressions.

Von Ribbentrop speaks in a strangely confidential tone. Usually he is very reserved and dignified, so all this surprises me. He goes so far as to busy himself about my personal comfort, and has sent to my room warm, sweetened milk to help my cough. In Tuscany they say that when people are making more of a fuss than usual is when they are about to cheat you, or you have already been cheated.

He doesn't trust the monarchy. While we were hunting in the woods, von Ribbentrop asked me point-blank, "What is your King doing?" "He is hunting," I answered.

"No, I mean in politics."

"Nothing that is particularly interesting. The King is informed about politics, but does not meddle."

"Yet in court circles they intrigue."

"I can deny that most emphatically. Perhaps, at times, they gossip, and even this to a limited extent. If you knew the people at court you would soon realize that but for one or two exceptions they are not even worth suspecting."

"I am pleased to hear this. But you will not say the same about the Prince of Piedmont. That fellow is hostile."

"Not at all. I can give the most ample assurances regarding the Prince of Piedmont. He is young. He has neither the prestige nor the experience of his father, but he is very respectful of the regime, and is devoted to the

Duce. I beg you, my dear Ribbentrop, don't listen to gossips. They flourish in every country, but are of no account. One must not fish up information from the gutter of public gossip."

The shoot was very beautiful. Everything was perfectly organized. The game was driven by 400 soldiers commanded by their officers, and they all took their task seriously, as if it were a question of ejecting the Russians from the forests of Viasma or Briansk.

If in Italy a party leader dared to assign soldiers for a similar purpose, there would be a tremendous scandal.

At the final dinner Ribbentrop took the floor and spoke very tactfully to the guests and to the organizers of the shoot. He concluded thus: "Next year, my dear Ciano, our game will be better, not only because we shall kill double the number of animals, but also because England will have finally realized that she can no longer win the war. The bag of 1943 will, in the end, be that of peace." For a man like Ribbentrop, who has always, from 1939 on, been announcing victory in fifteen days, this was a big jump to take.

Roosevelt's speech made a big impression. The Germans have firmly decided to do nothing that will accelerate or cause America's entry into the war. Ribbentrop, during a long lunch, attacked Roosevelt.

"I have given orders to the press to always write 'Roosevelt, the Jew'; I wish to make one prophecy: that man will be stoned in the Capitol by his own people." I personally believe that Roosevelt will die of old age, because experience teaches me not to give much credit to Ribbentrop's prophecies.

On our way to the station Ribbentrop repeated something that I have heard many times: "Hitler's New Order in Europe will insure peace for a thousand years." I remarked that a thousand years is a long time. It is not easy to hang a couple of dozen generations on the achievements of one man, even if he is a genius. Ribbentrop ended by making a concession: "Let's make it a century," he said. For my peace of mind I was satisfied with the reduction, which was certainly considerable.

Dornberg, a bit drunk, said to my staff: "Our next colony in Europe will be Hungary. I have hopes of becoming its governor." In spite of the wine, I think that, unfortunately, he was talking seriously.

My general impression of Germany is good; the country is in fine shape. The people are calm, well-fed, well-dressed, well-shod. When Americans speak of an internal collapse they are mistaken, or, to say the least, they are premature in their judgment. Germany can hold out for a long time yet, especially since there is the spirit of victory; under such conditions a revolt will not break out.

I have come across a train filled with our workingmen—long beards, open shirt collars, bottles of wine, some guitars. They are similar to the immigrants I used to see sixteen years ago in South America. Nothing has changed. Sympathy and esteem for us in Germany are in inverse ratio to the number of our men working in any particular district.

The sight of prisoners of war is a sad spectacle. They can be found everywhere in the open country, and serve in farming families where men are lacking. Dornberg says, "Every German has his Frenchman," which is equivalent to saying that he has his cow or his horse. They are bound to the soil—slaves. If they touch a woman they are shot. And yet they have the blood of Voltaire and of Pasteur.

October 30, 1941

I reported to the Duce. He wished me to send the King a copy of the report I sent from Germany.

Mussolini stated this morning that now he believes less than ever in the intervention of the United States. "It is quite clear that Roosevelt is barking because he cannot bite." Could he be right?

October 31, 1941

Nothing new.

Just now, late in the evening, I read that the American destroyer, *Reuben James*, was sunk last night west of Iceland. It appears that there were many victims. I fear that the incident this time is of the kind that will provoke, or at least accelerate, the crisis.

I have been told that the Marchesa Fanny Patrizi is about to be arrested under suspicion of espionage. She is an American, well known in Rome for her escapades and her blondish beard. She is the lover of the United States' military attaché, which caused much alarm to the Sherlock Holmes of the information service. It's possible they could be right: anything can happen. But rather than politics her affair with the American officer can be explained by a craving for the fast life now that she is past her prime and it's not as easy for her to keep up the tempo of her past love life.

November 1, 1941

A letter has arrived from Hitler, but I have not discussed it at length with the Duce because this morning the translation had not yet been available and I did not know its contents. What struck Mussolini more than anything else was that the Führer, throughout the long text, referred only very little to our army divisions. Little politics and a lengthy examination of the military situation. But it was a fragmentary and casual examination that does not forecast future undertakings by the Axis, but rather tends to point out the blows which England may strike at us. He is obviously concerned about us. We had too much trouble during the past winter to be able to face another lightly. He fears English landings in Corsica, Sicily, and Sardinia, and offers, beginning today, all his support like someone who does not know what a successful blow by the English may do to us. Fundamentally, the Germans don't trust us, and in my opinion this letter is the proof. Nevertheless, it is the document of a man who is aware of what might happen and who is very much worried. He knows that he is playing a difficult game with a strong and dangerous opponent. The letters that arrived after the French campaign had quite a different flavor.

A long conversation with the chief of police, Senise. This is the first time I have spoken with him at length. Until now our meetings have been fleeting and we both had rather a wary attitude. After all, he is a policeman. But today I was amused. He is a Neapolitan, both intelligent and ignorant, a strange mixture; he follows his natural instincts and is an investigator; a good man deep down, but also a superficial and gesticulating chatterbox. It is enough to think that a man like him is the chief of police in the twentieth year of Fascism, to be convinced that in this country, *plus ça change et plus c'est la même chose*. He might better have been a minister of the Bourbon kings. In brief, he tells me that the internal situation is restless, but not dangerous; that Mussolini likes to be deceived by crooks who are always successful with him; that Buffarini is a hypocrite and a thief because he demands money for the Aryanization of the Jews, and used to take money from Bocchini, a bigger thief than he, if that can be possible, and that the Duce's new secretary, De Cesare, is a big jinx as well as being an idiot. The information is not really very important, but I shall see him more often because it is amusing.

November 2, 1941
Nothing new.

November 3, 1941
The Duce is furious with Pavelić, because he claims that the Croats are descendants of the Goths. This will have the effect of bringing them into the orbit of the German world. Even at the present time we have clear signs of this maneuver.

A ceremony of the Garibaldi legion on the Janiculum to honor the soldiers who died in 1849. Mussolini delivered a short talk, filled with dark threats against the French. This will not please the French, and will perhaps please the Germans even less.

November 4, 1941
Nothing new.

November 5, 1941
Cavallero speaks to me about the arrival of Marshal Kesselring in Italy. He will take command of the joint forces operating in southern Italy and on the Ionian Islands, which means all combat forces. Even Cavallero realizes that this will have ugly consequences in the country. But personally he would like, at least, to draw one advantage from it, and hints that if he is granted the rank of marshal the trouble might in part be avoided. Mussolini has swallowed the bitter pill. He realizes the meaning of this within the big picture of the war and for the country, but, like a good player, he takes the blow, and pretends that he doesn't feel it.

I accompany Ghigi to see the Duce, and he draws a very dark, realistic picture of the Greek situation. He confirms that within a short time there might be free-for-all shooting in the streets. We must clarify our position with the Germans: it is either them or us. This double harness situation complicates everything, and prevents the solution of all problems. Mussolini has offered Ghigi some good words, and nothing more. Perhaps he couldn't offer anything else.

November 6, 1941

Anne Marie Bismarck told Anfuso that when General Rintelen went to see the Führer on the Eastern Front he was approached by the German marshals and generals, and that a sort of meeting took place. During the meeting they begged him to find some way of making Hitler understand that the way the war is conducted in Russia is pure madness, that the German army is gradually wearing out, that it cannot hold on, and that, finally, he is leading Germany to the brink of ruin. It seems that this is the unanimous opinion of all the military leaders, but that no one dares say so to Hitler. Naturally, Rintelen, too, was careful not to do so. But if this is the case—and it is probable that it is—it is serious, because in Germany the generals still count a great deal.

Today Mussolini said, during one of his usual anti-German outbursts: "We can do nothing against Germany for the time being. We must bide our time. It is a country that no one can vanquish militarily, but it will collapse through lack of internal equilibrium. For us, it is a problem of 'holding out' and waiting until this takes place."

November 7, 1941

I had not seen the Prince of Piedmont for a long time and today he was very cordial. He wanted to know about Germany, and listened with a great deal of interest, making an effort to appear impartial, while his prejudice against our allies was clear: he considers them insufferably crude. Then the Prince spoke about the armed forces. He is, or thinks he is, competent; therefore, his judgment of the past is severe. He blames Badoglio, but repeats that it was a mistake to sack him using the argument of "any old Farinacci." Badoglio has by now disappeared from the memory and the hearts of the army, but the moral crisis created by his departure still exists, and it will take time and care to heal it. The Prince's judgment on Cavallero was almost favorable.

I again called Mackensen's attention to what is happening in Mitrovica, in the Kosovo region, where, with the complicity of German propaganda, there has arisen a small local government composed of refugee elements from Albania. This creates confusion and disorder, attracting all those who wish to disturb relations between ourselves and the Germans. Mackensen agrees. But what can he do about it?

Stalin has made a weak speech full of absurdities, such as the one "that the Russian forces proved themselves to be strong and the German forces weak." But, quite aside from this, it is clear that he intends to fight and resist.

November 8, 1941

The figures sent by our embassy in Washington on American war production have impressed Mussolini, who asked that a chart be prepared comparing present production with preceding months. Actually, the increase is impressive.

It seems that von Plessen, during a dinner in the home of Clemm, asked a lady point-blank, "When will the revolution begin in Italy?" To which the lady replied calmly, "As you know, we follow you in everything. Therefore, it will take place after it happens in your country." What a charming atmosphere! After all, Baroness von Clemm herself told Anfuso that the Germans have a right to a warm-water outlet, and so one day they will claim Trieste. Anfuso gave her the twofold advice, not to discuss politics, and to dedicate her energies to another occupation at which the Baroness is notoriously something of an expert.

November 9, 1941

Since September 19 we had given up trying to get convoys through to Libya; every attempt had cost a high price, and the losses suffered by our merchant marine reached such proportions as to discourage any further experiments. Tonight we tried it again; Libya needs supplies, arms, fuel, more and more every day. And a convoy of seven ships left, accompanied by two 10,000-ton cruisers and 10 destroyers, because we knew that at Malta the British had two battleships ready to act as wolves among the sheep. An engagement occurred, the results of which are inexplicable. All, I mean *all*, our ships were sunk, and one or maybe two or three destroyers. The British returned to their ports after having slaughtered us. Naturally, today our various headquarters are pulling out their usual inevitable and imaginary sinking of a British cruiser by a torpedo plane; nobody believes it. This morning Mussolini was depressed and indignant. This will undoubtedly have deep consequences in Italy, Germany, and, above all, in Libya. Under the circumstances we have no right to complain if Hitler sends Kesselring as commander in the south.

November 10, 1941

The photographs taken by our reconnaissance planes show four English ships moored in the port of Malta. Notwithstanding, it is reported in the bulletin that one of the cruisers has been struck. Pricolo insists upon it, and uses the argument that this ship had gone to moor near the dry dock. This is equivalent to declaring that a man is probably slightly dead because he has gone to live near the cemetery. Clowns, tragic clowns, who have brought our country to the current condition of accepting, in fact, of requesting, outside intervention to be protected and defended!

From now on, until the Germans come, the English air force will dominate our skies almost like their own. I have asked Cavallero what will be done to the admiral responsible. Until last night Cavallero did not even know his name. I reminded him that the democratic Italy of Ricasoli had the courage to court-martial Persano when, after the battle of Lissa, he cabled that he dominated the seas. I also told this to Mussolini, who was still discouraged, and is right in considering yesterday the most humiliating day since the beginning of the war. "I have been waiting for a piece of good news for 18 months now, and it never comes. I, too, should be proud to send a cable like the one Churchill has sent his admiral, but it has been too long that I have been vainly trying to find the opportunity."

November 11, 1941

Irritation and misery for what has happened persist in the country and with the Duce. Mussolini is exasperated and takes it out on the Croatians from Spalato who throw bombs at our soldiers: "I, too, will adopt the method of taking hostages," he said. "I have given orders that for every one of our men who is wounded, two of theirs must be shot, and every one of our dead, twenty of theirs." But he won't do it.

Galbiati, returning from Greece, said that Greece is not yet at the point of starvation, but will be shortly. The rebellion will begin when the first children starve to death.

Jacomoni proposes that we change the Albanian government. Kruia in the place of Verlaçi. Which means a further concession to the extremists of Albanian Nationalism. Up to now the results of this policy have not been good; things went better when Benini concentrated authority in Rome. In any case, Mussolini has agreed, and we shall see what will happen.

I read *Parlo con Bruno,* written by the Duce. It is a collection of articles and various writings held together by Mussolini's style. But this style is very different from that of the book about Arnaldo.

November 12, 1941

At navy headquarters they were outraged by what has taken place in the Mediterranean, but with the present leadership it is impossible to expect anything better. Bigliardi has described to me the different phases of the encounter. All of this would be inexplicable if we didn't know that Admiral Brivonesi is said by Cavagnari to be unfit for any command. After the battle Bigliardi was reached by telephone by Riccardi, who told him that in order to neutralize the bad impression in our country it was imperative to send out a bulletin about successes in the Atlantic. But where were these successes? Relying upon some very uncertain information, a bulletin was drawn up which attributed the sinking of two steamers totaling 10,000 tons to the submarine *Malaspina.* The only real sinking was that of the Italian submarine which has been missing from its base for ten days. The deputy head of the general staff, Admiral Sansonetti, picked up his pencil and increased the 10,000 to 30,000, because "this would create a greater effect." Comments are superfluous. The navy has the reputation of being serious and honorable and cannot tolerate certain actions without going through a deep crisis. Besides, the whole navy knows and repeats that Admiral Riccardi owes his position to the protection of Signora Petacci,[503] and this is certainly not a rumor that will increase the navy's prestige.

November 13, 1941

Tassinari is more pessimistic than ever in his forecasts. If Germany cannot, or does not want to give us 500,000 tons of cereal, it will be necessary to reduce by one half the bread and pasta rations beginning from March 1 to the end of June. Now, Mussolini is absolutely against asking the Germans for wheat; he feels humiliated by military developments, including the arrival of Kesselring, and does not wish to add any more reasons for being grateful, and therefore being even more humiliated.

We have had to change the way we pay our foreign diplomatic agents, because we have no more foreign exchange. The end of the conflict is still so far away.

Anfuso is leaving. He will go as minister to Budapest. He wanted this very much, and now he has been satisfied. I am sorry he is leaving, not so much for his work as because of his companionship.

November 14, 1941

Alfieri transmits a communication from von Ribbentrop regarding the behavior of our men working in Germany. We must recognize that among them is a noticeable percentage of hoodlums, idlers, and intemperate types. Even the Germans make a clear distinction between the northern and southern workingmen, and say that the first do between 80 and 90 percent of what a German workingman can do and the second not more than 40 percent. Hatred against Germany must be exacerbated, in view of the fact that they have gone so far as to repeat aloud, "We shall all march together against the Germans." Von Ribbentrop's communication is harsh but frank, and therefore praiseworthy, but not to the point of my thanking von Ribbentrop as Alfieri would like me to do.

November 15, 1941

Change of guard in the air force command. It is about time. Pricolo had greatly disillusioned us, and had shown himself to be increasingly short-sighted, envious, and mean. Fougier is replacing him. At least he is likable and a real pilot, not a dirigible officer. He will have Casero, my old faithful Casero, his chief of staff, who is certainly an officer who takes his duties seriously. With him things should be better.

November 16, 1941

In Genoa for the dedication of the monument to my father. It was a simple ceremony, an intimate one, which is how I wanted it because I don't feel that this is a time to assemble people in large gatherings. The statue is huge but not very well done; it is by Prini, a Genoese sculptor who yesterday moved us to pity because he had recently lost a son who was a submarine commander. I recalled when my father lived in Via Corsica in 1919 he made Genoa the center of his activities. To see his likeness perpetuated in marble is for me today a sad but pleasing sensation.

November 17, 1941

No news during my absence. Mussolini tells me that he has persuaded Rommel to hasten the attack on Tobruk and that it is to begin some time this month. I recall that Gambara has expressed himself as distinctly opposed to this because he fears that when we attack Tobruk this will be followed by an English attack on our flank at Sollum, which he feels we cannot resist.

Cavallero informs me that the Duce has ordered an inquiry into the conduct of Graziani. The head of the commission is old Thaon de Revel, and General Ago, General Marmi, and National Counselor Manaresi are also part of it. This idea had been fixed in his head for some time. But is this really the time to stir up a hornets' nest?

The King wants the Duke of Spoleto to leave Rome, and Mussolini will inform him through Russo.[504] In fact, the behavior of this young man is quite absurd. He is living with the Pignataro girl and brings her to his private railroad car. He frequents restaurants and taverns and gets drunk. A few nights ago, in a restaurant near Piazza Colonna, he put a twisted towel around his head in imitation of a crown, amid the applause of the waiters and of the owner, a certain Ascensio, who divides his time between the kitchen and jail. Ascensio happens to be the Duke's best friend. He is a fine man to be a king!

November 18, 1941

A serious matter: Bismarck has told Anfuso that there is some alarm at the German embassy because it found out that Pricolo has been removed by the government because he opposes Kesselring's arrival in Italy. This is completely false. Bismarck, when pressed, declared under the seal of absolute secrecy that the information had been passed on to Rintelen by Cavallero, who boasted of the service that he had thus rendered Germany. There is no need for comment. This fact is enough to prove what Cavallero is. The real truth is that he had quarreled with Pricolo for entirely different reasons, and that he has tried to besmirch him like this.

Mussolini tells me that he has learned from His Majesty that the King of the Belgians has married the daughter of the Governor of Liége, whom the King had himself openly criticized because he had gone to meet the Germans. The King now lives at Vienne in his castle, and he has no interest public matters. "Another sovereign who has been terminated," says Mussolini, who is more and more anti-monarchist. "This proves that dynasties are a useless inheritance of the past which nations can no longer tolerate."

Meeting at the Palazzo Venezia about negotiations with France. Although it is not the best situation, I have expressed the opinion that we must do something, especially since the Germans are conducting a conciliatory policy and are grabbing everything.

November 19, 1941

Casertano gives the Duce and me a rather discouraging account of the situation in Croatia. The instability of Pavelić's power, domestic intrigues, and growing German meddling are the elements that make the life of the new state uncertain and our influence precarious. There is no longer an Italian-Croatian problem but an Italian-German problem regarding Croatia. It is a controversial problem, but we do not wish nor can we afford to make it such.

Bartoli is painting my picture. He is a truly great artist. He is human. His feet are on the ground, and he refuses to follow styles and trends in which he does not believe, even if they could bring him fame and easy money. Besides, he has a rare wit and vivacity. He does not dare discuss certain subjects, but rumor has it that his witticisms are very keen. I know that he recently drew a cartoon in which one sees the Lion of Judah leaving the station of Rome, while Mussolini says politely to him, "Let us hope the next time you will remain longer." He is pitiless, but those who know him assure me that Bartoli is a good patriot and a sincere Fascist, even if he indulges in biting satire.

November 20, 1941

English attack in Libya. At some points resistance is effective, at others, the offensive penetration has been rapid and deep. Cavallero is optimistic and considers the situation as "normal." This is reflected in Mussolini's attitude. I am especially fearful of the lack of supplies and the weakness of our air force, which, during this initial attack, has suffered serious losses.

Riccardi takes the opportunity of the selection of a commercial attaché to Spain to violently attack Dr. Petacci[505]—the brother of that notorious woman[506]—who, in his opinion, is a crooked speculator. To support his assertions he repeats this phrase of Inspector General of Police Leto:[507] "Dr. Petacci is doing the Duce more harm than fifteen battles."

The Germans at Frascati have set their sights on the College of Mondragone, and want to requisition it as a barracks. This is an extremely unpopular measure, that will harm five hundred families. The Papal Nuncio has protested, adding that the presence of the Germans at Frascati will prevent the Vatican from carrying out its plan to keep Rome safe from bombing.

November 21, 1941

The battle of Libya is in full swing and our military leaders are optimistic. Churchill in one of his speeches has been outspoken about the objectives of the action but very cautious as to the course of the operations. Nevertheless, we must admit that it is a disturbing speech. The Duce doesn't share this opinion.

Serrano has sent me a long letter ending with the proposal of a meeting in Genoa in December. I shall speak about it with the Germans in Berlin. I shall leave tomorrow night, and if they do not raise objections the meeting with Serrano might take place.

November 22, 1941

No decisive news regarding the Libyan battle. Cavallero is still tranquil; Mussolini is definitely satisfied as to how things are going. On the other hand, von Rintelen appears to be worried. The convoy which was to cross last night directly to Tripoli by following the route east of Malta has not succeeded in passing. The boats under attack by torpedo planes turned back toward Taranto, and at the same time two cruisers, the *Trieste* and the *Duke of Abruzzi*, were struck by torpedoes. Fortunately they were not sunk. There is no doubt that the task of moving supplies is most difficult, and that keeps us in anguish.

I leave for Berlin this evening. There are few instructions from the Duce: I must insist on the question of the troops to be sent to Russia. I am to clarify Germany's intentions as to Croatia and Greece. I must not discuss the food problem, and I must reach an agreement about an eventual meeting between Darlan and myself.

November 23, 1941

On my way to Berlin.

November 24-26, 1941

I have made notes on my conferences and on my impressions of Berlin. Here I add something more indiscreet.

The atmosphere of the anti-Comintern meeting was truly singular. The state of mind of the delegates differed very much. Serrano Suñer was aggressive and sharp but quite pro-Axis. The accusation the Germans level against him of having prevented Spanish intervention is unfair. He really hates the English, the Americans, and the Russians. But he cannot behave properly with the Germans and is ironical with them. Bárdossy looked resigned and as often as he could he launched a modest and cautious dart against Germany. Mihail Antonescu is a novice in foreign politics. Until a short time ago he was an unknown lawyer in Bucharest; now he represents his country, and he does a pretty good job. But he remains a Romanian and looks shady. The Danish representative was like a fish out of water—a little old man in a morning coat who wondered why he was there but who, on the whole, was glad to be present because things might have gone worse.

The Germans were playing the host, and they made everyone feel it even though they were especially polite to us. There is no way out of it. Their European hegemony has now been established. Whether this is good or bad is neither here nor there, but it does exist. Consequently, it is best to sit at the right hand of the master of the house. And we are at the right hand.

Göring was very much offended because of some secondhand gossip concerning our embassy. After venting his feelings to me the air was cleared. He was impressive when he spoke about the Russians, who are eating each other and have also eaten a German sentry in a prison camp. He recounted the incidents with the most complete indifference. And yet he is kindhearted, and when he spoke of Udet and Mölders, who have died recently, tears came to his eyes.

A dramatic episode: Göring told me that hunger among the Russian prisoners had reached such an extreme level that in order to march them toward the interior it is no longer necessary to have armed guards; it is enough to put at the head of the column of prisoners a camp kitchen, which emits the fragrant odor of food; thousands and thousands of prisoners trail along like a herd of famished animals. And we are in the year of grace 1941.

An amusing episode: the Spanish Blue Legion is sturdy but undisciplined and restless. The soldiers suffer from the cold and they want women. Anti-erotic pills, which work so well on the Germans, do not have the least effect on them. After many protests the German command authorized them to visit a brothel and had contraceptives distributed among them. Then came a countermanding order: no contact with Polish women. The Spaniards in protest inflated the contraceptives and tied them on the ends of their guns. Thus one day in the suburbs of Warsaw one saw a parade of 15,000 contraceptives displayed by Spanish legionaries.

The battle of Marmarica has raised us in the esteem of the Germans. For the first time they speak of Italian bravery and of our military contribution. The optimistic outlook on the development of operations was more pronounced in Berlin than in Rome, where we remain cautiously reserved. Two days ago the Führer considered the battle as being won.

November 28, 1941
Return by train.

November 29, 1941
I hand the Duce my report. He is satisfied but in a hurry, and we shall discuss it tomorrow. I accompany him in his car to Villa Torlonia.

The battle of Marmarica has aroused more interest in the Italians than any other episode of this war. This is as it should be. If we win this battle, the English situation may become very insecure, perhaps untenable. Within a short time we may also have favorable and unforeseen developments. England would have to face four crises and all of them of great magnitude: public opinion at home, American disappointments, a more clear-cut separation from the French, and, finally, a loss of face in the East, with repercussions in Turkey and even in India.

November 30, 1941
Cavallero sums up the Libyan situation. He is aware of its gravity but is neither pessimistic nor optimistic. The hardest problem is that of supplies. This evening we are going to try to get a convoy of five steamships through by breaking the blockade. How many will make it?

December 1, 1941
Out of the entire convoy two ships arrived, one was forced to beach at Suda Bay, and two were sunk. The result is not brilliant. But it might have been worse. The Libyan situation has crystallized somewhat, but the English are receiving reinforcements. Cavallero defines it as difficult but logical. God only knows what he means. Experience teaches me that when generals hide behind unintelligible jargon it means that they have a guilty conscience.

I have protested to the Papal Nuncio about the publication in the *Osservatore Romano* of some photographs showing that our prisoners in Egypt are having a great time—soccer games, concerts, gaiety. Mussolini is concerned about it. "It is a well-known fact," he says, "that they are inclined to let themselves be taken prisoners. If they see that their comrades are having such a good time over there, who can hold them back?"

On the advice of the police, who do not guarantee that they can maintain order, I postpone my trip to Zagreb until a better time. This time it will be Pavelić who will return to Italy—to Venice I believe.

December 2, 1941

Another of our ships has been sunk, almost at the entrance of the port of Tripoli. It was the *Mantovani*, loaded with 7,000 tons of gasoline. It cannot be denied that the blow is a hard one. The battle—for the moment—has no new developments, but it is clear that time is working against us. My meeting with Darlan has been arranged with Vacca Maggiolini. It will take place in Turin on Thursday. This will be the first political contact with the French since the beginning of the war. I do not believe, however, that very much will come of it, and Cavallero's hope to have free transit to Bizerte seems to me doomed to failure.

The Duce is concerned about the food problem. He is now convinced that we lack five hundred thousand tons of grain to cover our needs. We must borrow it from Germany. We might be able to pay it back in July, since our harvest, on account of climatic conditions, comes two months before theirs. But Mussolini cannot make up his mind to write to the Führer to make the request, and I can understand this. If we could do without this help it would be most fortunate, but it seems to me that it is absolutely necessary. The fact is that even those responsible for domestic order, Serena, Buffarini, et al., believe that any additional food restrictions would surely cause disorders.

December 3, 1941

A stunning move by the Japanese. The ambassador asks to be received by the Duce, to whom he reads a long declaration on the progress of their negotiations with America, concluding that they have reached a dead end. Then, invoking the pertinent clause of the Tripartite Pact, he asks that Italy declare war on the United States as soon as the conflict begins, and proposes also that we sign a pact with Japan agreeing to not make a separate peace. The interpreter who was taking down these requests was shaking like a leaf. The Duce gave general assurances, reserving the right to get together with Berlin for our response. The Duce was pleased by the communication, and said, "So now we come to the war between continents, which I have predicted since September 1939." What does this new event mean? For the moment Roosevelt has succeeded in his maneuver, unable to enter the war directly and immediately, he is doing so through an indirect route—forcing the Japanese to attack him. Now that every possibility of peace is receding farther and farther into the distance, to speak of a long war is an easy, very easy, forecast to make. Who will have the most stamina? This is the way the question should be put.

The reply from Berlin will be delayed because Hitler has gone to the southern front to see General Kleist, whose armies continue to fall back under the pressure of an unexpected Soviet offensive.

December 4, 1941

Berlin's reaction to the Japanese step is extremely cautious. Perhaps they will go ahead, because they can't do otherwise, but the idea of provoking American intervention is less and less to the Germans' liking. Mussolini, on the other hand, is happy about it.

I receive a massage from Gambara. Naturally, he is offended because Rommel was given command, but aside from this he sees the situation as delicate and filled with unknown factors. Nistri,[508] who is a true Fascist and an intelligent officer, is very pessimistic, and adds by word of mouth the things Gambara did not wish to write, that is that the exhaustion of our forces is noticeable, that enemy infiltrations reach every point of Cyrenaica, and that, finally, we are in no condition to resist another offensive by the British. "Our men go to their deaths gloriously," he concludes, "which does not change the fact that they die."

December 5, 1941

A night interrupted by Ribbentrop's restiveness. After having procrastinated for two days he now can't wait to answer the Japanese, and at three o'clock in the morning he sends Mackensen to my house submitting a plan for a Tripartite Pact regarding Japanese intervention and the agreement not to make a separate peace. They wanted me to wake up the Duce, but I didn't do it, and the Duce was very pleased.

I gave Mussolini a copy of Gambara's letter, in which, however, I omitted the anti-Rommel statements. The Duce is now so proud of having given the command to the Germans that he would have been very angry at Gambara—and Cavallero is urging him on. He dislikes Gambara. They have completely different personalities. One is a soldier, the other is a politician.

December 6, 1941

A few words to answer Gambara, words of friendship and good wishes. But things in Libya are not going well, and I fear that sad days are close at hand.

December 7, 1941

Dark news from Libya. Our forces are no longer able to attempt a long resistance; they must break contact with the enemy, and break it decisively, in order to try to defend the Djebel. Mussolini is calm; in fact, he talks about the possibility of a counterattack. Cavallero, on the other hand, is unclear, and thinks that everything depends on obtaining the port of Bizerte from the French. I am supposed to speak to Darlan about it on Thursday, but during the evening Mackensen comes to tell me on Ribbentrop's behalf that I must start no such negotiations with the French. This is what Hitler wants, communicated to Mussolini through Rintelen.

Hitler is right: Tunisia is 101 percent Gaullist; any unwelcome pressure would in itself increase the separation that is developing between the French Empire and the government of Vichy. But without Bizerte Libya is lost, according to Cavallero.

This morning the Duce was very much irritated by the small losses in eastern Africa. Those who fell at Gondar in November number 67; the prisoners are 10,000. One doesn't have to think very long to see what these numbers mean.

December 8, 1941

A telephone call at night from Ribbentrop; he is jumping with joy about the Japanese attack on the United States. He is so happy, in fact, that I can only congratulate him, even though I am not so sure about the advantage. One thing is now certain: America will enter the conflict, and the conflict itself will last long enough to allow all her potential strength to come into play. This is what I told the King this morning, when he, too, expressed his satisfaction. He ended by admitting that in "the long run" I could be right. Mussolini was also happy. For a long time now he has been in favor of clarifying the position between America and the Axis.

It seems that in Libya things are going a little better. In the Duce's judgment the gloom of the last forty-eight hours has passed. Cavallero, as well as Admiral Riccardi, announce to me a great naval operation against the blockade for the 12th, 13th, and 14th of this month. All the ships and all the admirals at sea. May God help us!

Mackensen sends me the summary of the meeting between Göring, Pétain, and Darlan. It accomplished nothing, only words, suggestions, advice. I don't think my meeting will produce any better results.

December 9, 1941

I go to Turin to await the arrival of Admiral Darlan.

December 10, 1941

I took notes on my meeting with Darlan. My impression of the man was good. He is a small man, energetic, willful, and rather boastful, who talks without holding back, and calls a spade a spade. He is a military man, who is beginning to develop a taste for politics, and because he is French, he does it with a certain finesse. Is he sincere? I can't say, except for one thing: he hates the British. Some ways of speaking and some expressions cannot be simulated. On the other hand, he has no choice, and he says so: if the British should win the war, his fate would not be a happy one.

Results of yesterday's meeting: none, except a clearing of the air which, with the French, it is not difficult to achieve. The mere fact of having a meeting is enough. In order to have bad relations with them, all we have to do is not meet. And this has always been the recipe used by Mussolini as a recipe for a break. He himself, in speaking to them, was unable to prevent a *rapprochement*. Even the population of Turin was cordial with the guests; applause was not wanting, though it was scattered.

News of the amazing Japanese naval victories continues to arrive. Against this the land fighting in Libya and in Russia is not going well. Such are the incredible surprises of this war.

December 11, 1941

Mussolini shows very little interest in my discussions with Darlan. It is the American war that interests him. At 2:30 p.m. I receive the chargé d'affaires, a good man, somewhat timid, with whom I have had little to do. He thinks that I have called him to discuss the arrival of certain newspapermen, but I disillusion him immediately. He listens to the declaration of war, and turns pale. He says, "It is very tragic." Then he hands me a personal message from Phillips. Feeling that zero hour was approaching, he had cabled to express his gratitude and his good wishes. Phillips is an honest man, and he loves Italy. I know that for him this is a day of mourning.

Mussolini gave a speech from the balcony—a brief and cutting speech, which fell on a great crowd. A very pro-Japanese setting. News of the naval victories has excited the Italian imagination. The demonstration, however, was not very enthusiastic. We must not forget that it was three o'clock in the afternoon, the people were hungry, and the day was quite cold. These are all elements which do not create enthusiasm.

In the evening Ribbentrop asks that we join a German proposal that the countries of the Tripartite Alliance declare war on the United States. How about Spain?

December 12, 1941

The Vichy press spoke warmly about the welcome given the French in Turin, and this grated on the Duce's nerves. I gave Mackensen the report of my conversations with Darlan, underlining the need to send a political representative to Vichy for the purpose of depriving the Armistice Commission of the political functions which do not belong to it, and which generals do not always know how to handle successfully.

December 13, 1941

The usual naval woes. Tonight we have lost two 5,000-ton cruisers: the *da Barbiano* and the *Giussano*, and also two large passenger ships, the *Del Greco* and the *Filzi*, loaded with tanks for Libya. This happened even before the great convoy (accompanied by battleships) had put out to sea. What is happening in the navy is baffling, unless what Somigli says is true, and that is, that our general staffs are possessed by an inferiority complex that paralyzes all their activities. The fact is that our naval losses become more serious every day, and I wonder whether the war won't outlast our navy.

The minister of Cuba came to declare war. He was very emotional, and was disappointed that I did not share his emotion. But, after having had the good fortune, or is it the misfortune, to declare war on France, on Great Britain, on Russia, and on the United States, could the good man really expect me to turn pale on learning that Sergeant Batista was mobilizing against us the forces of the Republic of Cuba on land and sea and in the air? Ecuador, also, has declared war, but I had my secretary receive the minister.

December 14, 1941

Cavallero justifies our naval defeats with an impudence that can't be equaled. He has become the defender come what may of Admiral Riccardi, and this morning I got an earful which I shall never forget. It is strange that this Piedmontese general should have the mentality of a Neapolitan parliamentarian.

Mussolini is tranquil. This morning he chatted for a long time with me in an impersonal and argumentative way. He vented his wrath on Christmas, Christmas gifts, and on all holiday gifts in general. He says that the offering of gifts is the alibi of the rich to justify their good fortune in the eyes of the poor. The fact is that these days the people feel the lack of food more than ever, and complain, but Mussolini, as is his custom, takes it out even on the Almighty when things go wrong.

I leave for Venice, where I will meet Pavelić. He will ask for many things, but I already know that I shall have to refuse them all. I shall use good manners, and sugarcoat what I have to say, but the substance will have to be negative.

December 15-16, 1941

I have had the usual stenographic transcriptions made of the meetings.

Impressions. Pavelić is growing more and more confident as he continues to rule. He is more resolute, casual, and calm. He dominates his ministers completely and even treats them harshly. In my presence he scolded his Minister of the Treasury, who blushed to the roots of his hair and lowered his head.

It all depends on the Germans. If they keep their obligations according to which Croatia has become a zone of Italian influence, a great deal can be accomplished by us yet. If, on the contrary, they should again try to force our hand and press their penetration, there is nothing for us to do but to haul down our flag and return home. The Croatians are very friendly toward us. Pavelić also likes us, but all of them are terrorized by the Germans, and it does not even occur to them to offer resistance to any pressure from Berlin.

The question of the monarchy has been set aside for the moment. That does not displease me, especially because I still think that it is possible to have a real union under our King. Naturally, all this is premature, and we should always have to give the broadest guarantees with reference to local independence.

The army, diplomatic corps, police, courts would be separate but part of this geared to an imperial system which in the beginning would be more easily realized in practice than by setting constitutional terms.

In summary, it seems to me that the boat continues to float with some difficulty, and that it begins to unfurl some timid sails. We are far from the end, but something has been achieved, and as for the future, everything will depend upon us and the men who work for us in Croatia.

Venice was sad, empty, tired. Never have I seen it so squalid. Empty hotels, deserted streets. Fog. Misery. Darkness. I have only vague memories of the Venice of the other war, but it was not at all like this. If nothing else, there was the sentimental attraction of a city on the front lines.

December 17, 1941

I confer with Mussolini, who was very skeptical about the progress of things in Croatia. He is happy about it, especially since the Germans have asked us to assume territorial and military control over the entire country. This is certainly because of the fact that the Germans have to withdraw their divisions, because in Russia the winter threatens to be hard, and Serbia gives them too much trouble, although it also proves that Croatia is really considered in Berlin as part of our *Lebensraum*. Mussolini wants to accept the proposal immediately. Roatta, who two days ago replaced Cavallero, who is in Libya, is favorable, but asks if he may not study the proposal because he fears that the available military forces may not be sufficient, and he does not want to start something he cannot finish.

Things are not going well in Libya. Even Mussolini is beginning to admit it, and he blames Rommel, who, he believes, spoiled the situation with his recklessness. Today the entire fleet is at sea, and Riccardi believes that a clash with the British is inevitable. He says that we are definitely superior in quantity and quality, and he promises success—the success we have been waiting for so long in vain. Can it be that our luck will change?

December 18, 1941

The convoy has gone through without battle and without trouble. On the other hand, the situation is reaching a crisis point in Cyrenaica. Headquarters and motorized forces are withdrawing to Agedabia, while the infantry is turning toward Benghazi, where the general staff is thinking of forming an armed camp to resist as the English did at Tobruk. Can this be possible in view of the fact that we do not have control of the sea as they had? I am somewhat skeptical about it.

A meeting at the Palazzo Venezia to extend our occupation to all of Croatia. On the military level it is a question of manpower. We must send in many forces because a revolution may break out in the spring once the foliage makes it impossible to get across the forests offering cover and concealment. If we undertake to garrison the country we must do it 100 percent. However, this does not concern me and I am not getting involved in it. Politically I have expressed my opinion that we must do things very simply: communicate to the Croatians that on account of a special decision of the Axis command the Germans are leaving and we are arriving. We should avoid at all costs presenting the decision as a success gained by us. That would mean pitting all Croatians against us.

December 19, 1941

News is still bad in Libya, in spite of the official optimism of our general headquarters. May God confound the slavish optimists! They are the ones who have cooked our goose. They have ruined us. In the meantime,

Rommel announces that with his armored units, he will fall back into Tunisia, because he does not wish to be made prisoner by the British. All this while Cavallero continues to swear that nobody can make him fall back from the line of the Sirte, and Mussolini believes him.

I saw Verlaçi, who spat venom when talking about Jacomoni, and this is natural, because he was shown the door. It is the way in which it was done that most offends him. He would have wanted longer notice, but this, too, would have been a double-edged sword. He says that now matters are troubled in Albania, and that the people are dissatisfied. He might be exaggerating, but there must be something to it. However, when I asked him what remedy he could offer, he had none to suggest. Jacomoni, with whom I conferred at length, is not pessimistic, and believes that, with some good moves, we can set our ship on course again. So far he has never been mistaken.

December 20, 1941

Mussolini is satisfied with the way the war is going in Russia. He talks about it openly. The failure of the German troops cheers him. "As long as this doesn't go too far," I suggested. He even called Alfieri to Rome to learn more about it. Nothing new in Libya beyond what had been forecast yesterday. The *official slogan** is that if the Littorio division is brought to the African shore we shall be in Sollum in a few days. Let's hope so.

Mackensen informs us that the Germans not only approve our sending a representative to Vichy, but are also favorable to our sending an ambassador to Paris, in a position identical to that of Abetz. I asked Buti if he was willing to go, but up to now he has raised many objections. Truly, I can't understand it.

December 21, 1941

The Duce approves the sending of an ambassador to Paris and the choice of Buti. The latter has now overcome his instinctive timidity and has accepted. I have informed von Mackensen of all this and intend to draw up an official communiqué with him.

I am informed by Cavallero of the development of operations in Cyrenaica. As usual, he finds everything "logical." He says that it is thanks to him that all our infantry has not fallen into the hands of the English. He repeats that we shall hold firm at Agedabia and he denies any danger to Tripolitania. Let's hope he's right. On the other hand, he considers the situation of the Germans on the Russian front quite difficult. Bismarck has communicated to D'Aieta that Brauchitsch has been sacked. It's the sign of a serious crisis. It must be added that in Germany the General Staff has real importance and an enormous following in the country.

Goebbels' and Hitler's messages have not made a good impression. The humble but pressing request for warm clothing for the soldiers on the East-

---

* In English in the original.

ern Front is in direct contrast to the arrogant tone that up to now had characterized their speeches. It also proves the Germans are unprepared for a winter struggle.

December 22, 1941

The sacking of Brauchitsch is on the agenda. English and American radios talk of nothing else. The German embassy is staggered by the news. Mackensen expressed no opinions, but did not conceal his concern. Bismarck didn't conceal his joy, and turning to Anfuso he said: "We have come to the fifth act of the great tragedy. This goes to show that Hitler is a blundering ass." The young man is exaggerating, but he isn't the only one in Germany playing at opposition. The crisis is in the regime itself; it isn't only between men, and I must add that the General Staff supports its chiefs. Cavallero also told me that General Rintelen is very reserved on the subject.

Mussolini does not attach very much importance to the matter. He believes, in fact, that in the last analysis it will be positive because "this war has proven that only political armies have something to say, and now Hitler is making his army more political." I wonder if this is the right moment to do it—between frostbite and Russian defeats. Mussolini has again attacked Christmas. He is surprised that the Germans have not yet abolished this holiday, which "reminds one only of the birth of a Jew who gave to the world debilitating and devitalizing theories, and who especially contrived to trick Italy through the disintegrating power of the Popes." He has forbidden newspapers from mentioning Christmas, yet all you have to do is to look out of the window to see that the people remember it and love it just the same.

December 23, 1941

I accompanied Verlaçi to see the Duce. He did not behave well. He strongly attacked Jacomoni, requesting that he be replaced by Guzzoni, who, in a few months, would be capable not only of eating up Albania, but all the Balkans as well. He naturally detests Kruia, but he does not have any solid arguments against him. He confines himself to saying that a country cannot be governed by a man who is the son of a servant by whom Verlaçi himself had been served a cup of coffee in the home of Essad Pasha. Verlaçi is a feudal lord, and things that may appear to be prejudices to us are sacred principles to him.

Serena and Tassinari have insulted each other in the presence of the Duce, and almost came to blows in the anteroom. It seems that the Duce is almost ready to put thumbs down on Serena, encouraged by Buffarini, who, as always, is working in the dark. He is a snake. I have seen a letter he has sent with the *curriculum vitae* of Serena's eventual successor. The Duce opened it in my presence. Buffarini denied to me having sent such a letter, but I believe more in my eyes than in his word.

Von Mackensen comes, on von Ribbentrop's advice, to ask my personal opinion on the approaching three-man meeting with Darlan. He says that we must discuss politics. I answer that such a conference, if it has an exploratory character, should not turn out to be harmful but could be useless.

December 24, 1941

Nothing new on foreign politics or on the war fronts.

At home, attention is beginning to concentrate on the case of Serena, who for two days has not been received by the Duce. Candidates are cropping up. Riccardi has his name proposed by Osio, but the Chief has not spoken to me about the dismissal and I am not taking any initiative on the matter. I would indeed consider a Riccardi secretariat a real disaster.

Serena, whom I saw in the afternoon, continues to say that it was a plot by Buffarini, who now has the Duce in his hands and maneuvers through indirect and disloyal channels. He [Serena] suggests that on the pretense of charity he is giving more than 100,000 lire a month to the Petacci woman, upon whom, meanwhile, he exerts influence by means of a certain Donadio, whose role is not clear. Indeed, Serena says that a racket of the Petaccis has been formed around the Duce, manipulated in the background by Buffarini and served by De Cesare, who is gaining more influence every day and acts in a sinister manner. He is not worried about himself. He wants a decision as soon as possible because he does not consider it good for the dignity of the party that the secretary be allowed to stew for such a long time.

December 25, 1941

Alfieri writes that the disasters on the Russian front have gone farther than is desirable for us. I glean this from the Germans at the embassy. They are very much discouraged. The Duce, who in the beginning underestimated the problem, now says that it is serious and that perhaps it will have further consequences.

The Pope has delivered a Christmas address and naturally it did not please Mussolini because he found that out of the five points it contains at least four that are directed against the dictatorships. This is unavoidable, in view of the anti-Catholic policy of the Germans. Isabella Colonna told me last evening that she had recently spoken with Cardinal Maglione, who told her that at the Vatican the Russians are preferred over the Nazis.

Anyway, the Duce increasingly reveals his anti-religious attitude. The Christmas holidays provides him with a pretext. "For me," he said, "Christmas is nothing more than the 25th of December. I am the man who in the entire world feels these religious anniversaries the least." To prove it he has made a list of appointments that is longer than usual. This year, however, the crowds in the churches are overflowing.

December 26, 1941

Serena and Tassinari have been replaced. The first is going to the front, and the second is returning to his university teaching. Pareschi, who is a technician, and who seems good to me, even though he talks too much and is ambitious, is going to the Ministry of Agriculture; a certain Vidussoni, who has a gold medal, is 26 years old, and a candidate for a law degree, will become General Secretary of the Fascist party. I know nothing else about him. This is obviously a bold experiment, and we hope that fortune will be a faithful companion to audacity this time. I know nothing about him, and haven't even seen him.

Vacca Maggiolini has come to tell me that he has received instructions from the Duce to begin conversations with the French with a view to obtaining Tunisian ports, such conversations to be carried out on a political level. This surprised me for two reasons: in the first place, because our understanding with the Germans is different, or at any rate nothing has been settled with them; and, in the second place, because just a few days ago Mussolini told me that Vacca Maggiolini is an imbecile who should not be involved in politics. To Vacca Maggiolini, who asked me what to do, I naturally gave the advice that he should follow the instructions of the Duce to the letter.

December 27, 1941

Council of Ministers. The Duce summarizes the military and political situation. He says nothing that is new to me. He predicts a very long war, lasting at least four or five years, and that humanity is moving toward complete "proletarization." He clearly underestimates America and her real weight in the conflict.

I received Vidussoni, whose appointment has aroused a unanimous feeling of astonishment. From the golf caddies to Count Volpi, everybody is commenting on it sarcastically. Until now very few knew him. Bottai, Russo, Host Venturi—all have taken the trouble to say that he is a fool. I cannot yet judge. I have talked with him for about a half-hour, and the conversation remained more or less vague. He seems enthusiastic and loyal, but he is a novice. He will sweat blood in that environment of old whores which is the Fascist party. I have denied that he is a creature of mine, as was beginning to be rumored. Not at all. Let it be clear that he emerged from mind of Mussolini as Minerva sprang from the brow of Jupiter.

Gambara, in a letter addressed to me, assures me that if "supplies" arrive Tripolitania can be saved, and he takes it out on Rommel, who, "as leader, is a beast."

December 28, 1941

Indelli reports from Tokyo that the Prime Minister of Japan has made some discreet allusions to the possibility of a separate peace between the Axis and U.S.S.R. Mussolini has dashed headlong into an examination of the problem and is very favorable. The vicissitudes of the war, particularly the recent ones, have convinced him that Russia, that ocean of land, may have innumerable surprises in store. He is right. I do not believe a separate peace is possible. The manner of the German attack, the German declaration as to the objectives of the anti-Bolshevik war, the development of events, all seem to preclude this possibility.

We learn from Berlin of an English landing in Norway and of a Russian landing in Crimea. There is no alarm, the German embassy reports, but the two incidents are not at all underestimated.

The Germans have changed their minds on the Croatian question. They will no longer withdraw their troops, but offer only military collaboration with us. Perhaps this is not bad, because in the spring Bosnia, Serbia, and Montenegro will give us plenty of headaches.

December 29, 1941

Mussolini says that he will write to Hitler regarding the issue of the Tunisian ports; either France comes to an agreement with us and grants them, or it will be necessary to take them by force. I hope that he doesn't write the letter, because it wouldn't produce good results.

Bismarck talked to D'Aieta about the nomination of Vidussoni. It has made a very bad impression in German circles, and particularly at the embassy, where they have had an opportunity to know the youth and to see that he is poor material

December 30, 1941

The letter to Hitler on the question of Tunisian ports was written and sent through Rintelen. I am certain that Hitler's reaction will not be good, especially since news from the Russian front has been anything but favorable. Even Mussolini is concerned about it. He believes, and with good reason, that the physical factor is predominant, and that the Germans will succeed in creating a wall of resistance against Russian pressure only if they are in good physical condition. This is his chief conclusion, but it is certain that the German situation is not very rosy at this moment.

Mussolini asks me to go to Bologna to speak there on January 3. He realizes that Vidussoni's nomination has shaken the old Fascism and now he wants to do something that will reduce the reaction.

December 31, 1941

At the Russian front things still not so good.

I see Kesselring, with whom I have a more or less formal conversation.

1942

January 1, 1942

Cavallero comes to see me on a number of pretexts, but actually because he wants the Germans to know through me that he is not responsible for the idea proposed by the Duce of attacking Tunisia. As a matter of fact, it was he who put it in the Duce's head.

A long letter from Hitler arrives. It crossed the Duce's letter. It is a long summary of how things have gone in Russia; mostly excuses, not explanations. The tone is courteous and vaguely subdued with regard to Italy. Very different from the tone used last year about this time when we had our Albanian problem.

Alfieri came to the Palazzo Venezia. He paints a vague and disjointed picture of the situation in Germany. He knows nothing and says nothing, and does it with many words.

January 2, 1942

Nothing new here. From our embassy in Berlin news from the Russian front gets steadily worse, but Mussolini doubts that it is accurate.

Speaking with Alfieri he said, "Tell the Germans that three years from now Italy will still be in the war under exactly the same conditions as today."

It's a pleasure to find a dissenter now and then. Today Barella said that the appointment of Vidussoni has been well received by the country!

January 3, 1942

I was in Bologna for the celebration of January 3[509] and made a rather long speech at the Medica theater. I curbed publicity for my speech for the following reasons: I had nothing new to say, I think the less one says at the moment the better; all my government comrades were talking in other cities and it wasn't advisable to arouse or increase any jealousies due to a disparity in treatment. The audience listened with attention and applauded warmly, but wanted to be convinced. Even a Fascist audience reasons, doesn't get excited, wants to understand things. The warmest acclamations were for Hitler and for the King. The Duce, in Bologna, is part of the family.

During my return I met von Mackensen on the train returning from Germany. He didn't say much but was somewhat low; the retreat in Russia weighs heavily on every German, almost as if it were a personal misfortune.

January 4, 1942

The Duce has unusual praise for my Bologna speech. There is no news except the sailing of a convoy which is carrying our weapons and hopes for the resistance in Libya.

January 5, 1942

Mussolini today repeats his praise of my speech, but he shows me a clipping from the *Resto del Carlino*, and criticizes my Fascist salute, which was not according to regulations. Is there really nothing better to think about? Vidussoni comes to see me. After having discussed a few odd things, he makes some political allusions and announces savage plans against the Slovenes. He wants to kill them all. I take the liberty of observing that there are a million of them. "That does not matter," he answers firmly "we must imitate the Ascari[510] and exterminate them!" I hope he will calm down. Now they say that the motto of the party is no longer "*Libro e Moschetto*" but "*Libro e maschietto.*"[511]

The convoy reached Libya without being attacked by air or sea. This will stimulate resistance.

The police recommend that I not travel to Zagreb: the local situation is bad and there is some shooting nearby. On the other hand, I don't want to disappoint Pavelić, who was expecting me to come. I cabled Casertano for his opinion.[512]

January 6, 1942

Mussolini is indignant with the Germans for two reasons—because General Schmidt, who was made prisoner at Bardia, declared to the correspondent of the *Daily Herald* that he could not hold out because he was commanding Italian soldiers. But it appears that it was Schmidt himself who took the initiative of giving up. And because the Germans in Romania, according to Antonescu's communication, took for themselves the oil which was meant for us. This is why Mussolini called them "highway robbers."

Our liaison officer with the Second Army in Croatia transmits bad news on the situation and troop morale. Some units let themselves be captured without firing a shot.

Ravasio comes to pay me a visit. He was appointed deputy-secretary of the party by the Duce, with instructions to function as "supervisor of moral orthodoxy and policy of the party" an assignment which is obscure, difficult, and not well defined. Ravasio, whom I know very slightly, has the reputation of being a Savonarola, who, in the Cova Café and the columns of the *Popolo d'Italia*, has uttered thunderous threats against the impure [members of the Fascist Party]. But who are the so-called impure? It is so easy to engage in paper demagogy, but, in reality, whom are we supposed to be accusing? Let them first name names and prove guilt; then, and only then, let them bring out the rope and the soap. I put the question up to Ravasio, and he himself was able to give me no more disturbing example than a butcher who dug up and sold a dead hog, which had been declared infected by a veterinarian. A bad thing, to be sure, but not a matter to justify an accusation against the entire class of Fascist leaders.

January 7, 1942
Nothing new.

January 8, 1942
Nothing new.

January 9, 1942
Anti-Italian demonstrations at Zagreb. Everything tends to discourage the trip. It shall take place at another time.

Mussolini is concerned about the fate of the four ocean liners, which are supposed to go to Ethiopia to bring home a first group of Italians. He fears that the British will stop the ships in Lisbon on their return and seize them. I do not think so. I rule out that the British government will want to be guilty of breaking promises. In any case, since the Duce feels as he does, I cannot take the responsibility upon myself, and I leave the decision up to him.

Acquarone talks to me about the Duke of Spoleto. The Duke doesn't give a damn about Croatia, and wants only money, money, and more money. On the whole, it is in our interest to give him at least a little. I shall propose to the Duce that we give him a hundred thousand lire a month.

January 10, 1942
Mussolini holds firmly to his point of view regarding the ships we should be sending to Ethiopia. However, he does not want to shoulder the burden of a rejection and he gives these instructions: we should postpone a decision in this case without breaking off negotiations.

My article on Albania has received favorable comments and, strangely enough, even the German press has mentioned it as an expression of Axis policy. Nevertheless, it does not appear that that is really their line of conduct in the occupied countries.[513]

January 11, 1942
There is nervousness in Germany. The denial issued to the foreign press about disorders at home proves it. The Duce deplores it. He says, "I, for example, never denied that I fought a duel with the heir to the throne. The people would have really begun to believe it." Alfieri sends bad military news and cables that the divisions withdrawn from the Russian front are stationed in occupied territories, but not brought back to the Reich fearing that they will spread propaganda. Romano from Vienna also informs me that the general state of mind is very bad and that many soldiers have committed suicide rather than return to the Russian front.

January 12, 1942

The Duce protests against the conduct of the German soldiers in Italy, especially the non-commissioned officers, who are arrogant, quarrelsome, and often drunk. Last night in Foggia two of them forced their way into the house of a man who was about to go to bed and said to him, "We have taken possession of France, Belgium, Holland, and Poland. Tonight we are going to take possession of your wife." To which the man replied, "You can take possession of the whole world, but not of my wife. I haven't any. I'm a bachelor." In their disappointment they broke all the furniture before they withdrew. If they go on in this way even Mussolini, who protested to Rintelen, predicts some "vespers."

Generally speaking, nothing new. The Japanese are doing well, the Germans not at all well in Russia, and we, in Libya, so-so.

January 13, 1942

Politically these are rather empty days. From the military point of view attention has turned toward the Russian front, where problems continue for the Germans. Alfieri, who as a rule paints everything in rosy colors, is also beginning to admit openly that in Russia they are swallowing a bitter pill. The retreat continues under the growing pressure of the enemy. The Duce does not seem to be very worried, but considers the situation very serious. He criticizes Hitler for the entire Russian campaign and says that he has distributed his communiqués. "He has used big figures to shock people like that big animal Roosevelt," he said, "and the results have been sinister. In fact, they are both big animals and belong to the same race of mules."

Buti is received by Mussolini before going to Paris and listens to these instructions: he is to take no political initiative. He should try to stimulate economic and commercial exchanges; not do very much in the cultural field except to send some of our products to France, such as books, plays, films; and not take anything from the French.

I have seen von Mackensen. I had not seen him for ten days, since he has been ill. As always happens to the Germans when times are bad, he appeared dejected. I tried to inject some energy into him.

January 14, 1942

On my way to Budapest. Brief stop at Vienna. The city is sad and tired-looking. Romano confirms that the people are not in a good mood.[514]

January 15, 1942

Elsewhere I have noted my impressions of and my conversations with the Hungarians, but since my notes were reaching many different people I was very cautious. The truth is that the Hungarians are exasperated with the Germans. You can't remain long with any Magyar before he speaks ill of Germany. All of them are like that, from the Regent to the last beggar on the street.

Admiral Horthy said, "The Germans are a brave people, and I admire them for this, but they are also an unbearable, tactless, and boorish people."

Kanya was even more cutting. Bethlen weighed his words, but in talking about German interference he was so violent, even though restrained, that I can't describe it.

January 16, 1942
In Budapest. Military ceremonies, and a free afternoon.

January 17, 1942
I was hunting at Mesohegeys. It was a good hunt, but not as rich as the one of 1938. Ribbentrop had already killed most of the wild game, and the Regent was too tired to engage in a long hunt.

January 18, 1942
With the Italians in Budapest, a patriotic ceremony at Fascist headquarters. I left in the evening.

January 19, 1942
On the train to Rome. I stopped in Venice for supper.

January 20, 1942
I report to Mussolini on my trip. He seems to be interested in what I said in my report and what I say personally to him. In turn, he gives me the latest news.

France. The Führer does not want to accept the terms, which Vichy lays down for placing Tunisian ports at our disposal. He is right. They are exaggerated. Besides, I have never doubted Hitler's intentions on this issue.

Rio de Janeiro. America is insisting that all South American countries break relations with us. If this happens, the Duce believes that it would be in our interest to declare war immediately. This way we shall impose upon the United States the burden of a military defense on a huge front. "They want a white war," says Mussolini, "but they will get a red one."

Libya. The situation is precarious. Our supplies are scarce, while British forces are extremely well supplied. The Duce fears that it will not be possible to hold the present line. He discussed this with Cavallero, proposing a withdrawal to the Sirte-Homs line. Cavallero has written a memorandum opposing this. Nevertheless, Mussolini has not yet abandoned his project and will come back to it again.

Today the Duce was in a good mood but looking tired.

The King has added to the noble title of Buccari that of Cortellazzo. I am proud of this because of the memory of Father.[515]

January 21, 1942
Cavallero, on his way to Libya, explores the situation with me. Naturally he persists in his official optimism. He uses propaganda slogans, such as "We will resist," "They shall not pass," and "The difficulties will strengthen our will," which displease me when mouthed by a general. Anyway, he says,

1. that the Russian push on the Eastern Front is almost over; 2. that in Libya we shall be able to resist an eventual British attack; 3. that the preparation of the Italian army continues at a favorable pace. We shall see to what extent Cavallero is right.

January 22, 1942

I went to see the King. He was not very talkative. As always he is anti-German. He criticized the organization of the Italian army.

I received General Roatta on his farewell visit. He was bitter but dignified. He said he realized that his association with Cavallero could not continue because "Cavallero is a man who loves to create and believe in illusions, while Roatta always wants to keep his feet on the ground." He says that the war is now in its critical phase; even for Libya he isn't at all confident, and fears that we shall soon have more British pressure, which we shall not be able to resist. He is happy about his new command in Croatia. In the spring he will get plenty of fighting. Roatta may not be a very pleasant person, but he is the most intelligent general I know.[516]

Osio, founder of the Lavoro Bank, was kicked out of his job. He came to tell me, and, although he is a strong man, he had tears in his eyes. The reason for his dismissal is unclear, but it appears that Osio made some unorthodox comment, and some say he had a quarrel with Petacci's brother over business matters. In fact, Osio talked about it a bit too freely, calling him [Petacci] "Lorenzino de Medici."[517]

Today Grandi could no longer contain himself and said, "I don't know how I was able to disguise myself as a Fascist for twenty years." Arpinati tells me that Grandi plays the unruly liberal and monarchist in Bologna. He told me that the King frequently invites him to lunch. I asked Acquarone if this were true, and he denied it most categorically.

January 23, 1942

News from Rio de Janeiro is contradictory regarding the decisions of Argentina and Chile. I fear that notwithstanding controversies these countries will also line up against us in the end. Mussolini is almost happy about it. I confess that I am very distressed. Not only because every hope of peace is vanishing, but also because I think with sadness of the collapse of so much good will created by our industrious immigrants during a hundred and twenty years of work. In some places undoubtedly the memory of the mother country is pretty much forgotten, but in many others they still love Italy with a deep nostalgic attachment. If war comes, many Italian tears will be shed.

News from Russia is bad. The Russian advance continues at an accelerated pace, with growing strength. Alfieri, in one of his reports, which betrays the style of Ridomi, describes the internal German situation in dark colors, though he does not reach pessimistic conclusions. It is still too early to say, but, as Grandi mentioned yesterday, a Beresina wind is blowing. In contrast to this we are doing better in Libya, according to our military people.

January 24, 1942

The Duce was quite disturbed by Alfieri's report, which "really doesn't confirm anything." On the other hand, he is happy about the progress of operations in Libya, and about our naval traffic, even though the *Victoria*, which was the jewel of our merchant fleet, was sunk today.

Mezzasoma wants to leave the party, hoping to become editor of the *Nazione* in Florence. He isn't wrong. He cannot get along with Vidussoni. Somebody wrote an anonymous letter in which all the secretaries of the party are given titles: Turati is called an epileptic and a dope fiend; Farinacci, one who inflicts wounds upon himself to escape military duty, and also a thief, and so on down the line to Vidussoni, who is called the perfect champion of Fascist youth, depraved, ignorant, and moronic. Naturally they exaggerate, and a great many unfair rumors about Vidussoni are being spread. However, I cannot say that he has yet displayed any evidence of qualities which would justify his appointment. I believe the Duce himself will soon see that he is dealing with a pupil unworthy of his teacher.

Pareschi would like to get grain from Hungary. They will not give it to us, particularly since they fear that the Germans, whom they hate, intend to impoverish them further. Yet in Hungary there is an abundance of everything. The only thing lacking is the desire to make war.

January 25, 1942

Again Mussolini complains of the behavior of the Germans in Italy. He has before him the transcript of a telephone call by one of Kesselring's aides, who, speaking with Berlin, called us "macaroni" and hoped that Italy, too, would become an occupied country. The Duce is keeping a dossier of all this, which "is to be used when the moment comes." In the meantime, he reacts strongly against the request by Clodius to have still more Italian workers in Germany. They would like to raise the number from 200,000 to 325,000. It is too much. Moreover, it is impossible because, aside from other considerations, our own labor supply is running short and we shall soon have to call new classes to the colors.

The breaking of diplomatic relations with South American countries begins. Today it is Peru, tomorrow it seems it will be Uruguay and Brazil. I have seen the Argentine ambassador, who has just returned from Buenos Aires. His country has held firm and will still hold firm, but will not be able to resist isolation for an indefinite period. We must, therefore, expect the breaking off of relations with all of South America. He indicated the possibility of discriminating between Germany and us. I unhesitatingly dispelled all his illusions on this point. The Duce would never accept it, nor would it be in our interest.[518]

January 26, 1942

Hunger grows in Greece. We can give very little, but our means of transportation to get it there are even less. The Italian merchant fleet doesn't have a single ship it can place at our disposal. We shall have to turn to the

Italian Red Cross and have them try to get some ships. The Duce has agreed to this solution.

We are getting on well in Libya. The Germans are intensifying their propaganda about it to raise morale at home, which is quite low because of the way things are going on the Russian front, where the Germans continue to be beaten.

January 27, 1942
Nothing new.

January 28, 1942
Göring has arrived in Rome but I have not seen him. In the first place this is because the visit is of a military character and our military men have insisted on monopolizing his time. In the second place, it is because this paunchy individual has for some time—that is, from the time of the granting of the Collar to von Ribbentrop—taken on a haughty attitude toward me that I don't like very much. When I was in Berlin the last time he received me with an almost regal ceremony, to which he did not try to add any personal cordiality. He knows that my address is the Palazzo Chigi. If he wants me, he knows where to find me.

The Duce has told me that Göring said when arriving by train, "We are having hard times." Cavallero later telephoned to inform me that Göring is optimistic about the possibilities of reaching an understanding with France. How much truth is there in that?

I have read Churchill's long speech very attentively. It is clear that times are hard for them as well, and that many disappointments are in store for the future. But it does not seem that he is faltering in his decision to carry on the struggle to the end.

January 29, 1942
The Duce talked with Göring for almost three hours yesterday. Schmidt took the conversation down as usual. I shall try to get it, but it is not that easy to get it from them. Göring is bitter about things in Russia and takes it out on the German generals, who have little or no sympathy for the Nazis. He thinks that problems will last throughout the winter, but is just as convinced that Russia will be defeated in 1942 and that Great Britain will lay down her arms in 1943. I took all this with a grain of salt. Göring is skeptical about the possibilities of an understanding with France, which is taking every opportunity to boycott the armistice, remaining irretrievably hostile at heart. Göring reached an agreement for the attack on Malta. In a few days the intensive air bombardments will begin, then it will be decided whether we can or cannot land. The Duce summarizes his impressions as follows: state of mind toward us, very good; general morale, pretty good.

Brazil has broken diplomatic relations. Mussolini wanted me to tell the chargé d'affaires who made the declaration that he, Mussolini, has the memory of an elephant, and someday he would make them pay dearly for it. But how? And when?

January 30, 1942
   Nothing new.

January 31, 1942
   Nothing new.

February 1, 1942
   Nothing new.

February 2, 1942
   Mussolini is very happy about operations in Libya. He wants us to push them because, from some intercepted American messages, it appears that the English forces are somewhat disorganized.

   For the first time since his presentation visit two years ago I have seen the ambassador of Chile. He does not believe that his government will ever go so far as to break diplomatic relations with the Axis. The new President-elect, Rios, notwithstanding the fact that he belongs to the popular front, will follow the same line. Nevertheless, the ambassador is doing his best to influence him in this respect, especially since he is profoundly convinced of British-American defeat.

   Luncheon with Göring at Cavallero's. As usual he is bloated and over-bearing. He said nothing that is especially noteworthy. The only thing, and indeed it is very sad, is the slavish behavior our leading military men display toward him. Following the example of that perfect clown, Cavallero, who would even go so far as to bow to the public lavatories if this would be helpful to him, the three heads of our military staff acted today in the presence of that German as if he were their master. And he pontificated blissfully. I know that it is futile, but I swallowed a lot of bile—more bile than food.

February 3, 1942
   The Duce has me read two letters, which Melchiori sent from Libya. They are typical of this unpleasant character, two reports accusing our command and in praise of Rommel. I do not know whether he is right or wrong, but I distrust the individual and everything he does. Nevertheless, there is nothing more humiliating than Melchiori's behavior, he who has placed himself at the service of the Germans and is cheating the Italians. Mussolini, who has taken the letters seriously, railed strongly against Gambara and Bastico, especially because Gambara is reported to have said at a dinner—but I do not believe it—"Mussolini has sold Italy out to Germany. I hope to live twenty years longer in order to command an army when we shall fight the Germans."

   In addition, I have received a long report from Gambara on the situation in Libya. It is an interesting document that is worth keeping. Gambara was against Rommel's withdrawal as he is now against his rapid advance. We shall see if and to what degree he is right.

February 4, 1942

Göring is leaving Rome. We had dinner at the Excelsior Hotel, and during the dinner Göring talked only about the jewels he possesses. In fact, he had some beautiful rings on his fingers. He explained that he bought them for a relatively small sum in Holland after all jewels were confiscated in Germany. I am told that he plays with his gems like a little boy with his marbles. During the trip he was nervous, so his aides brought him a small cup filled with diamonds. He placed them on the table and counted them, lined them up, mixed them together, and was happy again. One of his top officers said yesterday evening: "He has two loves—beautiful objects and making war." Both are expensive hobbies. He wore a great sable coat to the station, something between what automobile drivers wore in 1906 and what a high-flying prostitute wears to the opera. If any of us tried something like that we would be stoned in the streets. He, on the contrary, is not only accepted in Germany but perhaps even loved for it. That is because he has a dash of humanity.

February 5, 1942

No news of any particular importance. Now that the pendulum is swinging in our favor and against the British in Libya, the Vichy government is anxious to smile at us. We must take it for what it is worth.

On his arrival from Germany I accompanied De Cicco to see the Duce. He described the situation with considerable optimism. Hitler is nervous, and the people are strong and determined to fight to the end. I think he is fundamentally right, even though Lanza, the secretary of Legation, who has been in Berlin a few years, paints a darker picture. According to him, hopes for a total victory went up in smoke on the Russian steppes, and the Germans now aim for a negotiated peace.

I found out that the Prince of Piedmont will be chosen to command an Italian army in Russia. Is this a good thing? Is it wise to send him? I would think long about it before answering.

I see Ravasio. He found some pretext to come to see me, but in reality he wanted to explain his own situation and that of the party. His friction with Vidussoni, or rather with the people around him, was inevitable, and it can clearly be seen in outline. Ravasio will explode before long because he feels that he is being attacked from above and wants to react, but Vidussoni has put him in a modest corner of the Department of Propaganda. Ravasio knows that Vidussoni is a dumbbell, and is convinced that it will go from bad to worse. He wants no responsibility, not having been at fault. This all makes the situation of the party more precarious, and it is already very shaky and weak.

February 6, 1942

Nothing new.

February 7, 1942

Meeting of the Council of Ministers. Mussolini makes a rather brief statement on the progress of the war in Libya and concludes with his usual attack on our generals. On the other hand, he praises Rommel, who is always in his tank leading the attacking columns. The Bersaglieri are enthusiastic about him and give him their feathers, carrying him in triumph on their shoulders, shouting that with him they are sure they can reach Alexandria. The measures taken today are of no particular importance, but Revel announced a new loan in order to reduce circulation of money, declaring that after the end of the war interest on state bonds will be lowered considerably.

Grandi, while accompanying me to the Ministry, leveled his usual criticism on the social policy of the regime and also took it out on the King, who, he said, has become senile. I had to raise my voice to stop him because, aside from everything else, this is not true.

Complaints from von Mackensen about an article by Admiral Ducci in which it is shown that it would be to the advantage of the British to make a landing in northern Norway. According to Mackensen it seems that his arguments are excellent. But for this very reason couldn't he say anything more idiotic?

February 8, 1942

The German objection has resulted in the ban of the newspaper *Oggi*. When the Duce mentioned it to me I encouraged him to ban it. It was the organ of very questionable individuals, who accepted the regime but with many ill-concealed reservations. As usual these second-rate and discontented intellectuals are headed by Bottai, who boasts that he has accredited an ambassador, whose name he conceals, to the house of the Petaccis.

Admiral de Courten, who commanded a convoy for Tripoli, told me of his struggle against torpedo planes. It is due to a stroke of good fortune that all of his division was not lost. De Courten has a very optimistic view of the development of the naval war. There is only one dark spot—the lack of oil. Just now we have barely a hundred thousand tons, and only a negligible quantity comes to us from abroad. This immobilizes the navy, particularly the large ships, which, as matters stand, could enjoy a total supremacy in the Mediterranean.

February 9, 1942

Attolico died suddenly, and this saddens me very much. Not only for personal reasons (since was bound by strong friendship to poor Maria), but also because I greatly valued working with him. Of all the ambassadors who have worked with me through the years he was among the most intelligent and certainly the most courageously honest. In Berlin he predicted the power of the new Reich and favored the understanding and friendship between the two regimes. He didn't believe in the supposed miracles of blitz warfare, and fought tenaciously, first of all against the outbreak of the conflict; second, against our entry into it. We owe it to him in large measure if in September we did not immediately join the Germans, and thereby incur the consequences which would have followed. With Attolico, we lose a man who in other times would have been called *"un grand commis de l'état."* Bottai wanted to take his place at the Holy See. The Duce was against it. He said, "I refuse to believe that at forty-six years of age Bottai would want to end as a sacristan. Besides, he still has to carry through the educational reform which he invented and which he would now like to sidestep. We shall appoint Guariglia, whom I regard highly both for his intellect and for his character."

Baldur von Schirach is in Rome. He is convinced we will have a long war. He is an optimist who doesn't exaggerate. He sees in our food situation the main cause for alarm.

February 10, 1942

I have received El Gailani, the Prime Minister of Iraq, who started the anti-English movement and now travels between Rome and Berlin to lay the foundation of future Arab nations. The Germans are cautious and do not wish to sign any pact with him for the present. He is a lively and determined man, who enjoys a great influence among his people, both through his rank and personality. He believes in the victory of the Axis and says that when our forces arrive at Tiflis the English will not be able to prevent an insurrection of the peoples subject to them. He is skeptical about the Turkish attitude. Except for some military leaders the Turkish people heartily favor the English and hope they will win. I must add that Bismarck, while speaking with Vitetti this morning, led him to understand that Germany is preparing to attack Turkey, which is necessary if the Germans want to reach the oil wells. But is this calculation right? It appears that Bismarck sees things on the dark side. He has always been that way, and the development of events in Russia cannot but have encouraged him. At this point, little by little, he will reveal something more.

News from the Eastern Front is again alarming. The Russians are attacking everywhere, and a new and clear withdrawal of the line is to be expected.

Vidussoni has appeared for the first time at dinner at the German embassy. He had rigged himself out in a blue striped shirt and a red tie and handkerchief. He was not very much at ease.

February 11, 1942

Attolico's funeral was proof of the esteem and affection in which he was held.

In the afternoon there was a ceremony for the inauguration of the headquarters of the Association of the Friends of Japan. Much to everybody's surprise, the Duke of Pistoia wanted to say something, since he had prepared a clever little speech. I must say the speech was violent. Anyway, it was delivered in a tone unexpected and unusual for a Royal Highness.

February 12, 1942

The British have torpedoed one of our tankers, the *Lucania*, en route from Taranto to Genoa to join the convoy of ships earmarked for the evacuation of our compatriots from East Africa. The ship was traveling according to plan and under the agreement with Great Britain. They really broke their word, and there is no justification for it. The Duce and the navy, which were always against the idea, now take advantage of what has happened to drop the entire undertaking. Frankly, I can no longer oppose them. I should have made myself personally a guarantor of British good faith, but after what happened yesterday this becomes very difficult.

1 handed Mackensen the text of a cable from the American military attaché in Moscow, addressed to Washington. It complains about failure to deliver arms promised by the United States, and says that if the U.S.S.R. is not aided immediately and properly she will have to consider capitulating. Still, up to the present, Soviet attacks have continued at a stepped-up pace, and it is now a question of the Germans either holding or abandoning the whole sector of Vitebsk-Smolensk. Alfieri cables that the German position is not serious because it responds to modern criteria of elastic defense, but I must confess that his arguments do not convince me.

February 13, 1942

The submarine which torpedoed the *Lucania* has been rammed and many of those picked up from the latter have been saved. We must, therefore, eliminate the hypothesis that a drifting mine sank it.

The Duce, as usual, is irritated at the military. In order to send two divisions to Russia in March, we must ask the Germans for anti-tank guns, anti-aircraft batteries, and motorcars. Notwithstanding this, Cavallero has presented Mussolini a list showing that we are producing 280 anti-tank guns a month. When this figure was questioned he confessed that it was not correct but represented our theoretical possibilities, and, in pencil, in front of the Duce himself, he corrected the 280 to 160. This was a tremendous reduction. Like the Jews in Campo dei Fiori.* Mussolini was indignant and explained that the only reason he did not throw him out was because after so many changes he realizes that they are all equally deceitful. He said, "Only Squero is sincere. He is a fool, but an honest man."

I received Marshal Kwaternik, who handed me a letter from Pavelić. He wants to meet the Duce. I believe this can be done in Rome, but not very soon.

February 14, 1942

Nothing new.

During the evening, at Clemm's home, Mrs. Ninon di Belmonte tells me a story that I still can't believe. Two things are clear: that Revel has lost his head over Ninon, and that Revel hates the banker Armenise. His hatred is unreasonable, unmotivated, but nonetheless unyielding similar to that of Cataline. Armenise, who was beginning to feel the weight of this persecution, turned to Ninon, to whom he was introduced by Rudolfo Borghese.

---

* Peddlers' market in Rome.

Ninon took up Armenise's cause. Well, Revel not only swore that he will do nothing against him, but also that within a week he will see him to re-establish cordial relations. "He was blushing and sorry," said Ninon, of this fifty-year-old minister, "like a child caught in a naughty prank. But now that he promised me, I am certain that he will behave." Here is an episode which illustrates certain negative aspects of present-day Italy more than innumerable volumes could.

February 15, 1942

Mussolini has not yet made up his mind to break off negotiations with England regarding the evacuation of Italians from East Africa. He prefers to take his time. He is opposed in principle to dispatching our ships, but realizes it would be too serious a responsibility to refuse.

I write to Bárdossy to buy some wheat. Pareschi and Pascolato[519] have come to speak to me about the cereal-production situation. They consider it bad. By March it will be necessary to reduce rations by fifty grams, but this will not be enough to carry us through.

The Duce is much more optimistic. He believes that enough wheat will be produced, and that in any case his appeal to the people will make them patient and understanding.

February 16, 1942

Kruia has come to Rome for the first time since the installation of his cabinet at Tirana. When he was appointed there was considerable criticism: among the Italians because he is considered too nationalistic, among the Albanians because he is of humble origin and the Albanian tradition is still feudal. Verlaçi said of him, "I shall never be able to respect a man whose father waited on me in the house of Essad Pasha." It is too early to pass judgment on the Kruia experiment. So far things have gone well, and even the indignation that had been aroused in many Albanian circles has died down. It was feared that he would be an extremist, but instead he has been moderate. Now that he is in power he, too, realizes that *"la critique est aisée, mais l'art est difficile."* He has not asked me for anything unexpected, except some small changes on the Montenegro border and some modifications to the flag. They do not want the eagle "imprisoned" between the lictors' fasces and the knots of the House of Savoy. The question is a delicate one and not to be too easily dismissed.

Churchill gave a speech today, which I should call firm but serious. The fall of Singapore has been a great blow to the British Empire. "I should like to know," Mussolini said today, "what effect the sight of four English officers, presenting themselves with a white flag to surrender, has had upon those whimsical Orientals. Had it been us, no one would have given it any importance, but they are English!"

February 17, 1942

A conversation between Mussolini and Kruia. The Albanian president talked about the situation, sounding an optimistic note. Mussolini emphasized his desire to grant the Albanians a more and more liberal and autonomous local regime. This is the only policy possible—one that bears good fruit. Otherwise, Albania, too, would be a breeding place for revolt and intrigues like the other occupied countries. Revel, as might be expected, told me that he received Armenise and put an end to the cruel rivalry with a long embrace. And to think of what they say about women . . .

February 18, 1942

With Gailani to see Mussolini. Gailani strongly insisted on having a treaty and a declaration of independence for the Arab states. The Duce kept him guessing, because for some time the Germans have been opposed to gestures of this sort. Mussolini said that he will make this declaration when it can have an immediate effect, that is, when our military forces are close enough to the Arab countries for the words to be immediately followed by deeds. What once appeared fantastic now seems possible. The Japanese victories are shattering British resistance by the hour and may perhaps prepare a more rapid and successful conclusion which so far we could not foresee. In fact, the Anglo-Saxon situation has never appeared to me as desperate as it does now. But I believe they will hold on. Yesterday I announced at a luncheon for Kruia and in the presence of all the ministers, a formula which was well received. We are not born young; we become young.

February 19, 1942

An address by Senator Kruia at the Rome city hall. He spoke of the Italian-Albanian union, but it was more a theoretical and academic rather than a political speech. The party should have organized things better. The hall was half empty.

Muti told me that Farnesi, Vidussoni's chief of staff, candidly told him that his boss is "an imbecile," and he is very worried when Vidussoni has to do anything without the help of his staff.

February 20, 1942

Alfieri sends a strange cable, saying that Ribbentrop is predicting that England will ask for an armistice to save what can still be saved. Can it be that the Germans are actually beginning to realize the fearful tragedy that this war represents to the white race? It would be a good thing, but I can't believe it.

This morning Mussolini showed some concern about coal and steel. We lack these things, and the Germans carry out their commitments to us only partially. "Among the graveyards," says Mussolini, "I shall someday build the most important of all, one in which to bury German promises. They have delivered nothing, or almost nothing, of what they promised. For this reason it is better not to insist. I persuaded Cavallero not to ask for the anti-tank guns and the anti-aircraft guns for our divisions going to Russia. I prefer to take the risk of taking twelve batteries from the Rome defenses." Naturally, he took it out on the Italian bourgeoisie, "which never troubled itself to develop the resources of the country," and which "he is sorry not to have physically exterminated in 1911."

Horthy's son was appointed Vice-Regent of Hungary. Anfuso cables that the enthusiasm of the assemblies was moderate. The man is not at all up to the job. He is a gentleman, modest and courteous, but nothing more. Through this move Hungary tries to take out an insurance policy of an anti-German sort. I don't know if they have guessed right. In Berlin there is much coolness, and I am told they will not send congratulations to the Vice-Regent.

February 21, 1942
    No news.

February 22, 1942
    From Prague our consul general reports that the deputy of the Reich Protector is treating our nationals if not worse than the Czechs certainly not much better. I showed the report to Mussolini, who is indignant and wants Alfieri to protest with some moderation, to von Ribbentrop. "And after this the Germans have the gall to protest against Japanese exclusivism. I much prefer the yellow people, even if the Japanese were to arrive as far as the Persian Gulf."
    The coal situation is very bad. This month will be exceptionally good if we reach 540,000 tons, which is one third of our needs. If we go on in this way, by April we shall have consumed all the available supplies for the railroads.
    Rome is full of rumors about the Duce's violent anti-Vatican statements. In fact, he has said some things, but more theoretical than political, more historical than contemporary—such as the Duce has uttered many times. Vidussoni, who is a perfect imbecile, has interpreted them literally and repeated them in various quarters. He even told d'Aieta that he was getting ready for an attack on the Vatican. Hence the scandal. This happens when children play with matters of importance.

February 23, 1942
    I hadn't seen the King for some time. I found him in poor health, hardly able to stand up.
    He said nothing of any real importance, but reaffirmed his old thesis that the fall of Russia will knock England and America out of the war. I again stated my doubts.
    The Duce is worried about the rumors being circulated regarding his statements on religious matters, and has asked me to have Guariglia deny them. Evidently Vidussoni, who has few ideas, and very confused ones at that, has a bee in his bonnet about the Vatican. When Guariglia introduced himself to Vidussoni a few days ago at city hall, as soon as he heard him say "Ambassador to the Holy See," he ostentatiously turned his back to him. He had mistaken him for the Papal Nuncio.
    I accompanied Clodius to the Palazzo Venezia. He offered some explanations on the failure to deliver coal. He said the winter was exceptionally cold, there was a shortage of labor and railroad transportation; the Russian front alone absorbed five thousand more locomotives than had been fore-

cast. But in the future things will go better. This, at any rate, he was good enough to promise us in the name of the Führer.

February 24, 1942

Mussolini voices one of his new theories on war. Wars are necessary in order to see and appraise the true internal composition of a people, because during a war the various classes are revealed: the heroes, the profiteers, the indolent. I objected that in any case war is a selection in reverse, because the best die.

A speech by Roosevelt. A calm, measured, but nonetheless determined speech. It doesn't sound like the speech of a man who is thinking of suing for peace soon. Still, this strange belief is spreading. Even in Italy a good many honest people believe it.

The Papal Nuncio wants to know if it is true that Padua University is preparing to offer Goebbels and Rosenberg honorary degrees. Honoring the two most bitter opponents of Catholicism in the city of Saint Anthony would be extremely obnoxious to the Church. However, the rumor was baseless.

Bismarck talked to d'Aieta in a very pessimistic tone. In Germany they all believe that another winter of war would be unbearable. Everybody is convinced of this, from the supreme heads of the army to the men close to Hitler. But no one dares tell Hitler. Therefore, they ought to find some way of reaching an understanding with the Anglo-Saxons, especially since the Japanese advance is a disaster for the white race. The Germans can do nothing along this line. They are much too hated. They are "black sheep." Thus the Italians should assume the role of world peacemakers. According to Bismarck there isn't one intelligent German who doesn't believe this.

February 25, 1942

There are some signs of friction between the Germans and Japanese. For example, the latter frowned on some proposals made by von Ribbentrop, who, as usual, is taking on the role of Grand Master of the Tripartite Alliance.

Mussolini, who is pro-Japanese, mostly because of his anti-German stance, expresses his satisfaction. "The Japanese are not a people," he said, "with whom the Germans can take liberties such as getting the Emperor or the Prime Minister out of bed at two o'clock in the morning in order to announce decisions that have already been made and carried out."

A strange attempted murder at Ankara: von Papen, who was passing by, was knocked down but is unhurt. We shall see what De Peppo thinks of it. But from here, offhand, I would not be surprised to learn that the Germans have a hand in it and that they are beginning to pave the way for a crisis with Turkey. I have many doubts as to the timeliness of this crisis.

February 26, 1942

It is perhaps a stroke of fate, but every time the Germans issue a communiqué that everything is going well on the Eastern Front, they get a thrashing. Today has been the turn of Viasma, which has fallen, and, judging from the Russian-English radio, the Russian thrust is continuing rapidly.

The Duce has issued a decree for the mobilization of civilians. For the time being it will include men between eighteen and fifty-five; later it will be the women's turn. However, there is some uneasiness because people do not understand what it is all about. In fact, they are afraid that it will be an imitation of the forced-labor decree imposed upon the Germans. Lombrassa will be in charge of the service as undersecretary. His name is a guarantee of moderation and competence.

The son of Oriani has become the mouthpiece of the dissatisfaction existing in many Fascist circles over the line taken by the regime, especially in its social policy. "Let us turn back to the beginnings," is the motto of the old members of the party. The beginnings were anti-Bolshevik, traditionalistic, in defense of the family, of private property and marked by respect for the Church. Now, on the other hand; we are slipping more and more to the left, and I fear that this Vidussoni, who does not understand anything, will attempt to drive the party recklessly. Vito Mussolini, who had a conversation with him yesterday, and who is a cautious young man, told me that he was surprised by the idiocy, the ignorance, and the meanness of the secretary of the party.

February 27, 1942
Nothing new.

February 28, 1942
Nothing new.

March 1, 1942
The English agree to our demands after the torpedoing of the *Lucania*. They again give the broadest guarantees, and to replace the *Lucania* they will release one of our confiscated oil tankers. Our navy, which would like to boycott the undertaking at all costs, raises objections. It wants the tanker to be an English tanker. Unless this is done they say we shall have one tanker less once peace comes. Mussolini, although he is not enthusiastic about the repatriation of the Italians, has reacted against this foolish objection. "Either we shall win the war," he commented, "and we shall have tankers to throw away, or we shall lose it and they will not even leave us eyes to weep with."

Notwithstanding the report by Alfieri, which assures us that the situation on the Eastern Front has stabilized, we receive news of continuous offensive thrusts by the Russians, which at some points are quite deep. Even Mussolini is now worried. "It's all right that the Germans have told me that they have 300 divisions ready. But even admitting that this is so, of what human material are these divisions composed? What is their true morale? Everything depends on the answers to these questions." Very bad news on the Duke of Aosta's state of health. He has miliary tuberculosis, and hence his fate is sealed. Mussolini is not interested, and even the royal house does not seem to be very much moved by it.

March 2, 1942

Jacomoni reports on the situation in Albania. In general it is good, considering the times. But there is one matter that has attracted my attention: the weakness of our military forces. We barely have four divisions, each one composed of two regiments and the regiments composed of two battalions; a small number of carabinieri, not a single tank. These are the forces that are garrisoning Albania. Now it is clear that if a blow were struck from the outside and if enemy propaganda succeeded in arousing large parts of the interior, we would be unable to hold worth a damn. We must not forget that all the Balkans are up in flames, that Albania has been under Italian rule for only three years, that we are at war with America and England, who have great resources, and with Russia, a master of subversion. I shall speak very seriously about all this with the Duce. It is obvious that before sending new forces to Russia we must assure ourselves of holding what we have.

Pareschi considers the present food situation improved and he makes these forecasts for the future: the coming crop will be good because the earth is still well supplied with the fertilizers that were used generously for the Battle of Wheat; bad crops in the future because of lack of fertilizer.

New and strong Russian attacks along all sectors of the front. The German communiqué is toned down and our divisions are also having serious problems.

March 3, 1942

The Duke of Aosta is dead. With him disappears a noble figure of a Prince and an Italian, simple in his ways, broad in his outlook, human in his spirit. He did not want this war. He was convinced that the empire could hold out for only a few months, and, besides, he hated the Germans. In this conflict, which drenches the world in blood, he feared a German more than an English victory. When he left for Ethiopia in May 1940, he had a premonition of his fate. He was determined to face it, but was filled with sadness. I communicated the information to the Duce, who expressed his regret laconically.

In the afternoon Bismarck telephoned to say that his government was preparing to launch a campaign against the English Secret Service because of the Duke's death. He added that he personally thought that the plan was in "bad taste." He is right. There is nothing to support this accusation; on the contrary, it's quite absurd. I brought this to the Duce's attention, and he expressed himself against it. The only value of the plan is to measure the intelligence and morality of the person who proposed it. Mussolini is more and more pro-Japanese as the Germans now appear to be less so. He would like to write an article praising the Japanese people who, after centuries of misery and with their faces turned to the future, have, in a few months, reversed their situation, passing "*dall'ago al miliardo*."[520] The Duce considers what is happening in the Orient and in the Pacific as cast in stone.

March 4, 1942

I took Jacomoni to see the Duce, so that he might speak openly to him. The internal situation is fundamentally good, but outside our borders there are a thousand dangers which can quickly change the state of mind of the population. The indispensable condition for calm is power—to have power. Now we lack it. Probably more because of the duty of his office than out of conviction, the Duce said that he does not share our fears. In any case, he will send a third regiment and some companies of light tanks which serve quite well in the city. Jacomoni, who hadn't seen the Duce for many months, found him heavier and with signs of exhaustion in his face. As a matter of fact it seemed to me that the Duce more tired than usual today.

Buffarini is very much concerned about the food situation. From every district in Italy we hear alarm bells and cries of grief, and he believes that the situation is rapidly getting worse. To the scarcity of food must be added the steady rise in prices, which makes life really unbearable for all classes of people who live on fixed incomes.

The death of the Duke of Aosta made a great impression on the country. There was sincere sorrow shared by all. A young working-class boy, whose brother is a prisoner, said to me, "Today my mother cried. All the mothers of prisoners are weeping today."

March 5, 1942

Nothing new.

March 6, 1942

Mrs. Margherita Campello, who is a friend of one of Gambara's secretaries said that when he, Gambara, was replaced in his Libyan command, his aides in Rome were arrested and his office was searched by General Maravigna and by the carabinieri. This was a blow delivered by Cavallero, who hates Gambara. I telephoned Cavallero to learn about this, but, as usual, he sidestepped everything, saying that he knew nothing about it and that it was the Ministry of War which had acted without his knowledge. He concludes by admitting that they are on the trail of illicit business activity by Gambara's aides, but Gambara has nothing to do with it and he will go to Bolzano to command the army corps. He must not stay in Rome. He must not confer with anyone. We shall see where this will end, but there is no doubt that Cavallero has sought help from the Germans to strike at our valorous general who was careless enough to talk too much. It appears that at an officers' mess in Libya he said, "I hope to live long enough to command an Italian army marching on Berlin."

Vidussoni pays me a long visit to bring me up to date on his plans for the party. I was cautiously reserved; he can't last long.

Heavy bombing of the industrial area of Paris by the British and, consequently, an attempt by German propaganda to arouse French resentment. But Buti informs us that the French are not aroused, or aroused in a different way.

March 7, 1942

The Duce, who is dissatisfied with the way things are going, said, "This war is not for the Italian people. The Italian people do not have the maturity or the consistency for such a tremendous and decisive test. This war is for the Germans and the Japanese, not for us."

Luigi Cortese, Consul General in Geneva, informs us that fear of invasion is over in Switzerland because no one any longer believes in a complete German victory. In fact, the forecasts are of an entirely different nature. It is believed that, having once more banged her head against Russia in the coming offensive without achieving a decisive success, Germany will have to give up before winter. Feeling toward Italy has improved a lot. In fact, it is quite favorable for certain future possibilities which are hopefully being fostered in Switzerland.

Mussolini received Revel's report following the investigation of Graziani. It appears to be very hard on Graziani. The Duce will give me a copy of it. Mussolini does not know whether to have him court-martialed or get rid of him administratively through retirement. I would be in favor of the latter solution in time of war. The Duce accuses Graziani of having been responsible for three serious losses to the country: a blow to its military prestige, the arrival of the Germans into Italy, and the loss of the empire. The Duce now feels that we must attack Tobruk, or else the British will deal us another blow.

Japanese admirals have informed us that they intend to proceed toward India. The Axis must move toward them in the Persian Gulf.

March 8, 1942

Nothing new.

March 10, 1942

Casero has me read a report from our air force information office. It is filled with dire pessimism. According to it Germany must conclude its war with Russia within a few months, because it is clear that the population will not stand for another winter of war. How much truth is there in this?

Meanwhile, there has been a strange development. Prince Urach, of von Ribbentrop's press bureau, has come to Rome requesting to see d'Aieta. He made strange statements about Japan, with an ambiguous coloring and a bittersweet flavor. It is all very well for the Japanese to win because they are our allies, but after all they belong to the yellow race and their successes are achieved at the expense of the white race. It is a leitmotif which appears frequently in conversation with the Germans. D'Aieta even had the impression that in a roundabout way Urach was trying to sound out our feelings about a separate peace between the Axis and England. Urach also said that the defeat of Russia still appears to be a very hard task. D'Aieta restricted himself to generalities and did well.

I telephoned Bova-Scoppa to further postpone my trip to Romania. I see from intercepted cables from the Romanians that they are making difficulties, and that they would like to give my trip an anti-Magyar character. Hence there is nothing to be done.

March 11, 1942

The Duce reacted sharply to Urach's statements. He confirmed, on the contrary, his extreme pro-Japanese attitude. "After all, is it that important if the enrichment of the Japanese comes at the cost of the European standard of life? Such materialistic reflections betray traces of Marxism in the German soul, even though it is National Socialist."

This morning, at the Sudario, there was a requiem mass for the Duke of Aosta. Only members of the Court were invited, and, of course, also the bearers of the Collar of the Annunziata. The royal family was seated in a pew which was hidden from our view. The ceremony had just begun when the door opened and a woman in mourning entered, bent and aged. It was Donna Rachele. She took the first seat she could find, and wept throughout the entire ceremony. At the close of the service I called for her car, but it wasn't there. I offered her mine, but she refused. She came on foot, and she left on foot. I told the Duce, who was very much surprised. He didn't know that his wife would go to an intimate ceremony of the royal house. "This is the first time such a thing has happened," he said. But that old woman who was weeping in the Church of the Sudario today was not the wife of a great leader. She was simply the mother of a 20-year-old lieutenant killed in his airplane.

March 12-13, 1942

Nothing new.

March 14, 1942

Council of Ministers. There are no important measures except the regulation of registered bonds. This issue prompts the Duce to make some extremist economic and financial declarations which end with a dark threat "to dig up another regulation, which has been ready for eight years, which, in just two clauses, modifies the entire situation of property in Italy, in case there is any attempt to oppose this law."

Further restrictive measures are adopted, because of the state of war, and in particular it is planned to limit the travel of private persons as much as possible. To go from one place to another will require a permit from the Prefect with a written justification for the trip.

March 15, 1942

At a meeting with Indelli the Japanese have defined their plans. No attack on India, which would scatter their forces in a field that is too vast and unknown; no attack upon Russia; an extension of the conflict toward Australia, where it is obvious that the Americans and the English are preparing a counterattack.

I saw Ando, the Japanese counselor, before he left. He is returning to Tokyo. I gave him a very friendly message for his government, especially since the Japanese are sensitive and suspicious about the German attitude. Here, as well, the pro-Japanese slant is stressed by some just to spite Germany. I do not approve of this. No one can accuse me of being strongly pro-German, but I still prefer the white to the yellow race . . . and then Japan is far away and Germany is close, very close.

Bastianini paints an ultra pessimistic picture of the Croatian-Dalmatian situation. Except for the militia our armed forces are deplorable. They show no energy and no spirit. Anti-Fascism is general and widespread among them. Bastianini predicts many dark hours in the spring and summer. He is always rather pessimistic.

March 16, 1942

New and violent Russian attacks make the situation on the Eastern Front from Kharkov down rather uncertain. Mussolini does not hide his concern.

The Swedish minister issues a report on Greece on behalf of his government. The English are ready to open their blockade and to allow the Greeks 15,000 tons of wheat per month. They naturally ask for some guarantees. I do not know whether the Duce and the Germans are willing to accept the terms proposed. I shall work in their favor because it is the only way some millions of innocent and unfortunate human beings can escape certain death.

A long conversation with Pareschi about the food situation. It is not good. The recent 25 percent cut in the bread ration was greeted with despair, even though there have not been many signs of protest. Pareschi, who has all the enthusiasm of a convert, looks hopefully to the future and believes that some of his measures will at least accomplish much to improve the situation, if not change it completely. Nevertheless, all the most favorable forecasts are based on the help of fate and depend on a number of ifs and buts. The facts are that fertilizers are reduced to one third, manual labor is lacking, agricultural implements are wearing out, and fuel is lacking.

March 17, 1942

Nothing new.

March 18, 1942

Nothing new.

March 19, 1942

Pavolini, on his return from a conversation with Goebbels, paints a pretty dark picture of the situation in Germany. Even his German colleague, who in the past has maintained a haughty tone, has had to pipe down this time. He spoke of a crisis in the regime, and about "walking on the razor's edge," and even when he discussed the future beyond this dark period he could be only cautiously optimistic. They are no longer talking about destroying Bolshevism; they will be satisfied if they reach the Caucasus.

The words "resistance" and "tenacity" have replaced declarations about "overwhelming victories," "dictated peace," and "New Order." Pavolini also told a funny and telling story, quite telling actually for the Nazis as well as for their lackeys. When Goebbels sent Farinacci a bust of Hitler the statuette was brought over by Gauleiter Esser, who brags about his Italian. In handing over the gift, this is what he said: "Your Excellency Farinacci, Minister Goebbels has entrusted me to bring you this envelope."[521] The story is making the rounds in Germany, and the first to tell it and laugh is Goebbels himself. Farinacci would laugh less.

This morning Mussolini discussed the Italian internal situation, and had to admit that the Italian people are not in the least in favor of the war. He explains it by saying that immediate incentives are lacking, such as can be easily understood by the common folk. He believes, therefore, that our propaganda line should simply be to flaunt the banner of defeat as a threat. Our enemies would show no generosity, and we would be reduced to slavery for a century. But the people aren't even convinced of this. In Milan they are saying, "As long as we can end the war, let's at least win it."

March 20, 1942
    Nothing new.

March 21, 1942
    Nothing new.

March 22, 1942
    A young man called me on the telephone a few days ago, using the name of the secretary of the party, asking to see me, because he had some "important disclosures to make about a plot." I received him. He is a boy from Trieste, Armando Stefani, twenty years old, a member of the GUF, lean, intelligent, nervous. He said that he had been approached by a journalist, Felice Chilanti, who suggested that he join a super-Fascist insurrectional movement, for the purpose of eliminating all rightist or conservative elements in the party, and to impose upon the Duce a strong socialist policy. Everything was thought out—attacks, the arrest of the ministers, the death of Ciano. The young man was very much worried about it, and so he hurried to tell me. I wouldn't attach too much importance to this except for the fact that the police believed there might be something to it. We must get to the bottom of this matter, and with a bit of concentration camp, or even jail, the hotheadedness of these young men will be cooled off. But this gives rise to a question: Why is all this happening? Might these not be clearly anti-Fascist beginnings, which dare not display the flag of revolution openly, but try to hide under the emblems of the party itself? Are these not elements which the party itself is lovingly nursing within its ranks, and which, in the opinion of some, are being kept under control by flattery and adulation, but in reality are being encouraged to follow a path which instead ought to be deplored and condemned?

March 23, 1942
    Nothing new.

March 24, 1942

I brought the Duce a report on Germany by Luciolli.[522] Even Mussolini said that he "had not read anything so significant and far-reaching in a long time." He is right. After mentioning the miserable internal situation of the country, Luciolli explains how there could be no political support for the military side of the war. They talked a lot about a New Order, but did nothing to bring it about. All of Europe today is languishing under German occupation. The enemies of Germany have multiplied infinitely, even though they can do no more at the moment than hate and hold their peace.

Luciolli says that in Germany they are now considering a possible defeat. For this reason they want all the countries of the continent to become exhausted, so that even in case of defeat the Germans will remain relatively strong. The Duce was struck by this idea, and said that by the end of 1943 he intends to have fifteen perfect divisions ready in the Po Valley. Very good. I replied that this is now a war of attrition, the progress of which is not easy to predict. Anything is possible. Therefore, it is necessary to prepare our forces, and to keep them *at home*. Some day, maybe not too far away, a small but solid army at one's disposal might decide the fate of Europe.

Cavallero came to see me, and I had a slight argument with him about the Gambara issue. An embrace solved the argument; but is he sincere?

March 25, 1942

Some interesting cables from Turkey. De Peppo has spoken to various personalities, and although there is some difference of opinion on the military situation, they agree in believing that the German-Russian conflict will end by forcing Turkey to face the alternative it would like to avoid. But De Peppo is not in a position to answer the question whether Turkey is with us or against us. However, it appears from numerous sources that the ties between Turkey and the Anglo-Saxon world are growing stronger and stronger.

March 26, 1942

Colonel Amè is very worried about the German situation. He bases his opinion not only upon the information that reached him from our SIM agents stationed in Germany, but also upon what he was told personally by his German colleague, Admiral Canaris; the internal situation is serious both from the material and moral viewpoint. The army is bitter and in disagreement with the political elements. There is little confidence in the spring offensive and in any case the feeling that no conclusive success can be attained. The German people are tired of "victories" and no longer believe in "victory."

The Duce also, in commenting on the steps taken by Hitler to detach the SS from the regular army to create a single large unit, sees the symptoms of a deep and perhaps incurable uneasiness.

A speech by Churchill to the Conservatives. As usual he was quick to recognize the disasters that have occurred, but he reiterated his determination to carry on to the end and his certainty in ultimate victory. We must honestly recognize in Churchill an orator of unusual power, capable of deeply moving the people.

March 27, 1942

A long conversation with Squero about the Gambara matter. In spite of Cavallero's thousand insinuations Gambara is a perfect gentleman with a clear record. He came out of the investigation as clean as a whistle. Cavallero had set everything up for the purpose of wreaking vengeance on a brave critic, and to eliminate a bold young general who might have overshadowed him. In any case, Squero will act in defense of Gambara.

Squero is certainly a fine person. He may not be a genius, but he is sincere and honest. Mussolini also trusts him 100 percent, and he is right.

March 28, 1942

Awarding of posthumous gold medals to the dead flyers. Balbo's son, who without looking like him yet reminds one of his father, received his father's decoration without batting an eye, pale and proud. Then it was the turn of Bruno's widow. She carried little Marina, who extended her arms toward her grandfather. There was sincere emotion in the air. Mussolini's expression was stonelike and did not change. He decorated Bruno's wife, the wife of his Bruno, as though she were just another of those who have been bereaved. Somebody asked whether the Duce was superhuman or in-human. He is neither one nor the other. He was simply conscious of the fact that at that moment any weakness would have an echo in a thousand hearts. Later, for only a moment, when Marina was going away, I saw a light in his eyes—a light that fully betrayed everything that his iron will had sought to hide. I felt myself very close to his heart and to his sorrow.

In Venice we have had the first popular demonstrations occasioned by the bread shortage. Many people who had used all their ration stamps before they became due are protesting because the bakers refuse to sell. The Duce was resentful and sad; he gave orders that the crowds be scattered by using leather scabbards. But this is an ugly occurrence which proves that many calculations regarding food were wrong and the coming weeks may hold some other bad surprises in store.

March 29, 1942

Today there have been bread riots at Matera, where groups of women broke into the Littorio Club and were dispersed by the carabinieri, who were forced to fire in the air. These are serious symptoms, especially since the harvest is far away and the available food supply scarcer and scarcer. Buffarini is expecting similar riots throughout the country and has sent a cable of instructions to his prefects, which begins with the words "Keep calm." He wants to avoid bloodshed, and he is right.

Gastaldi, the former Federal secretary of Turin, whom I hardly know, comes to me with the story of his dissensions with a partner, and up to this point there is nothing bad. But, as usual, the Petacci family is mixed up in the matter, which he discusses freely. It meddles and grants political protec-tion, threatens from above, intrigues from below, and steals at all points of the compass. The commanding general of the carabinieri, Cerica, had spoken to me about this confidentially a few minutes before. Without a doubt this scandal will spread and involve the person of the Duce. But what can one do to warn him, especially as two of his most intimate collaborators, De Cesare and Buffarini, are rolling in money in this decaying atmosphere of the Late Roman Empire? Nevertheless, as far as I am concerned, I want to keep out of this, and out of respect for the Duce I abruptly cut short anyone who speaks to me about it.

At a meeting of the party Directorate yesterday Mussolini was violently critical of the youth and favorable to the older squad members of the party. Is he beginning to realize the deep and widening crisis within the party?

March 30, 1942

Agostini violently attacked Cavallero. According to him, Cavallero has already chosen the new commander of the carabinieri, which he would like to control for ulterior motives. There is a great deal of exaggeration, but a substratum of truth, in Agostini's words.

Vidussoni goes to Venice to discuss with Axmann[523] the foundation of a European Youth Association, which would be under the honorary presidency of Schirach. Vidussoni would like to ask for an Italian presidency side by side with the German. I am certain that Schirach will not be favorably inclined, since this is his baby. I do not hide my doubts on the matter from Vidussoni, but the young man, who is as ignorant as he is conceited, insisted on his point of view. Let him break his neck if he wants to.

March 31, 1942

Nothing new.

April 1, 1942

The Duce has learned from an industrialist of Alto Adige that the following joke is circulating in Germany: "In two months we shall win the war against Russia, in four months against England, and in four days against Italy." He has asked me to obtain confirmation from Alfieri while "on his part he is beginning to prepare new divisions, because it is not known what surprises are in store for 1943." Mussolini is also very much concerned by a report from Anfuso regarding the behavior of two groups of Italians in Budapest who have gone to Hungary for the agricultural fair. Drunken brawls in nightclubs and raids on all the ham on sale in the shops. This incident gave rise to a violent Mussolinian tirade against the middle class.

Pareschi is rather optimistic about our present harvest. On the other hand, he makes increasingly dark forecasts for the coming years.

April 2, 1942

The Prefect of Naples, Albini, reports that the Neapolitan situation is bad, but the Neapolitans are people who are accustomed to tightening their belts and suffering; hence, there is nothing to be feared, at least until some new and serious incident develops.

General Hazon, of the carabinieri, reports that the general situation has improved, but the country has lost faith in the party, which is no longer an important element in national life. The army remains hostile toward Cavallero, although it recognizes that there is no general who enjoys a real and unquestionable prestige and who, therefore, deserves to replace him. The appointment of Gariboldi as commander of the troops in Russia has made a good impression. It was known that he was a personal enemy of Cavallero and his appointment was not expected.

Farnesi expressed concern about the food situation and was critical of the attitude of young men. The centers of infection are the classes on political leadership at the universities where one finds some ambitious, crooked, and untrustworthy individuals. From now on they will be scattered at various jobs in distant cities, and the university newspapers will be placed under the supervision of serious and responsible persons.

Borri, Prefect of Genoa, reports that the city is in good shape, but the lack of food supplies is beginning to be worrisome.

Geloso, commander of the troops in Greece, reports that public order is good, public health in danger, the food outlook a little better for the future.

April 3, 1942
Nothing new.

April 4, 1942
A move by the Japanese ambassador to get us to take a step with the Holy See. At the time it established diplomatic relations with Japan it did the same with Chiang Kai-shek. The Japanese prefer that the Chinese minister should not come at all or that his arrival be postponed for some time at least. I do not know what we can really do, but I have promised the ambassador to act on his request.

April 5, 1942
Mussolini does not want to accept the 13,000 tons of wheat which Pareschi got Hungary to promise him. He considers this a pittance and believes that we can produce enough food without a further reduction in rations.

Del Drago[524] returns from Paris. In Berlin there is nothing new on the surface, while, on the other hand, Paris is really in a sad state. In some German circles he was told that after the offensive on the Eastern Front, which will practically liquidate Russia, they are hoping to obtain a compromise peace with the Anglo-Saxon countries.

Today I went to mass at Santa Maria degli Angeli. A devout crowd filled the church. I do not at all believe, as some would like to have it, that Italy is not a fundamentally Catholic country.

April 6, 1942
When Göring was in Rome we spoke of the possibility of having returned to Italy certain Italian paintings now in France, particularly those that belonged to Jews and were seized by the Germans. Among the names that

were mentioned in the conversation was that of Rothschild, who owned many Boldinis. Today Göring sent me a Boldini as a gift, and his letter began as follows: "Unfortunately, there was nothing left in the Rothschild house . . . " If, someday, this letter is found, it will appear that it was I who instigated him to sack the homes of Jews and that he was sorry that he had arrived too late. This is an example of the political sharpness of the Germans.

The Vichy government is attempting a typically French form of blackmail regarding the repatriation of the Italians in East Africa. Whereas it had previously approved of the embarkation of our nationals at Djibouti, it now raises many objections unless we repatriate at the same time 150 French civilians and 650 military men. While it is possible to agree about the civilians, it is not possible for the military. Meanwhile, I believe that we should give them a haughty answer. We shall see about it later.

We have received news of a Japanese air attack on Colombo. Does this represent a first move toward India? I believe, rather, that its object is to impress the Indians during the Cripps negotiations, which just now seem to be moving in the general direction of a partially favorable conclusion.

April 7, 1942

Nothing new.

April 8, 1942

Somebody was talking about illiteracy in certain Italian regions, when Mussolini said: "Even if this were true, what is the difference? In the fourteenth century Italy was populated by nothing but illiterates, and this did not prevent the flowering of Dante Alighieri. Today, when everybody knows how to read and write, we have instead the poet Govoni, who, while not exactly insignificant, is certainly something less than Dante."

The Prefect of Rome informs me that the Duce is indignant because he sees too many young men walking around the streets of the capital. He has given orders that they be inducted into the army. But what will be done with them? How will they distinguish between the unemployed and those who must walk the streets on account of their occupations? I recall that in Peking, when old Chiang Tso-Lin was in need of soldiers, he would block off a few streets and his soldiers would then seize all male citizens who were passing by, shave their heads and immediately put them into uniform. Protests were to no avail. The problem of conscription was reduced to a problem of street traffic. Are they thinking of adopting in Rome the ways of that old Pekinese despot?

I see Gambara, who is indignant but not embittered by Cavallero's hostility. It seems that they are going to send him to Russia. If this happens, I am sure that his name will once again become a synonym for success.

April 9, 1942

Alfieri has come to Rome on leave. He does not report anything particularly important, but is less optimistic than usual and thinks that the summer offensive can have only a limited success.

On the other hand, the statements made by Bismarck to Blasco d'Aieta in strictest confidence are more interesting. I summarize them briefly. By October, no matter how things go, Germany must make peace. The army cannot and will not take the initiative at that time, in the first place because it is not according to its tradition, and also because it has had its back broken by the removal of its best military leaders. There are many disturbances within the party. Himmler himself, who was an extremist in the past, but who now holds the real pulse of the country, wants a compromise peace. By October England will be ripe for negotiations, especially if the Germans would consider the possibility of an anti-Japanese collaboration for the reconquest of Asia by the white race. Italy should take the initiative within the Axis to take the war to a diplomatic level. Are these the imaginings of our Bismarck, or are they signs of real trends within German public opinion? I lack the information to form an opinion, but it is noteworthy that Otto spoke after Admiral Canaris' visit to Rome and the many conversations he has had with him. Personally, I believe that the strength of German resistance is far greater.

April 10, 1942

Conversation between the Duce and Alfieri. Mussolini talked less to seek information than to reaffirm his complete optimism on the progress of the war as well as its conclusion. He gave as much evidence of anti-German sentiment as of pro-Japanese feelings. He was in a happy mood, and talkative. Speaking of Charlemagne, he said that he admired his virility above all, since he agrees with the French philosopher who said, "Genius is a question of genitals."[525]

Host Venturi told me about the origin and explanation of the abolition of railroad sleeping cars, restaurant cars, and first-class cars. It is Mussolini who took this step to place everybody on the same level, and against the opinion of the technicians. Mussolini said that he now feels the old revolutionary spirit more than ever. Meanwhile, the trains are filled with disorder of every sort, since the crowd is enormous and the accommodations limited. In Trieste last evening the Undersecretary of the Postal Service had to be placed in his train through the window, since all the corridors were filled to the point where no one could get through. Naturally the government hasn't gained any prestige through this incident.

April 11, 1942

Mussolini visits the Society of the Friends of Japan. He likes more and more to declare himself "the first pro-Japanese in the world," but he gives to his affirmation a distinct anti-German character. He uttered a few words of warm sympathy, and concluded: "The Italian soldiers and the Japanese soldiers and the *other armies* of the Tripartite Alliance will wage war until victory."

De Peppo from Ankara summarizes the situation thus: The Turks will not fight against us and they may, perhaps, be on our side if the fate of the war brings success to the Axis armies. Enemy Number 1 is Russia, fear Number 2 is Germany. The Turkish ideal is that the last German soldier should fall upon the last Russian corpse. We are still very much under suspicion. In order to remove this suspicion it will be necessary to withdraw from the island of Castellorizzo, which is considered our offensive point in Turkish territory. But we cannot do that now. This gesture, at such an inopportune moment, would be interpreted as a sign of weakness and would lead to results that would produce the opposite effect to what we are seeking.

April 12, 1942
 Nothing new.

April 13, 1942
 The Hungarian Chief of Staff comes to visit me, followed step by step by Cavallero. He says nothing of any interest.

 I had a long conversation with Donna Edvige.[526] She asked to see me about a small favor, but this was obviously just a pretext. She really wanted to give me her impressions on the situation, listen to my own, and especially unburden her heart about a matter which has now become a national problem: the Petacci family. She tells me, with much intelligence and great affection for her brother, what everybody is saying. She adds that she has proof in her hands concerning the shady business transactions of the Petacci clan, and the scandal resulting from them. She has made up her mind to confront the Duce about it and discuss the situation. I was very reserved, and told her what she already understands very well—my delicate position in the matter. Edvige told me that she had already talked about it last year, when it was said that Mussolini was going to the Cammilluccia to play tennis. He had admitted going there, but definitely denied the tennis part.

 Revel unburdened himself about the situation and expressed concern over the Duce's state of health, saying that he saw him at times in such obvious pain as to be alarming. He wanted me to do something about it. But what? In the first place I am convinced that he is very well, and then, who has the courage to speak to him about a personal matter?

April 14, 1942
 The Japanese have proposed a tripartite declaration on the independence of India and Arabia. Initial reactions in Berlin are unfavorable. The Japanese initiative is not welcome in regions closer to Europe. Mussolini, on the other hand, wanted to approve the proposal immediately.

April 15, 1942
 Laval is at the head of the government in France. This is the result of long German efforts, of which we have always been kept in the dark. Only after it was over did the German representative in Paris inform our ambassador of what had happened, yet the matter concerns us directly. What promises have been made to the French in order to reach this conclusion? At whose expense? We shall see. For the moment it is hard to predict anything. But one thing is certain: Laval does not represent France, and if the Germans think they can conquer French hearts through him, they are mistaken, grossly mistaken once again.

April 16, 1942
   Nothing new.

April 17, 1942
   Nothing new.

April 18, 1942
   The Laval government is formed. It is a government of undersecretaries and of unknowns. It remains practically a Pétain-Darlan government. Thus France prepares for all three outcomes: a British victory, de Gaulle; a German victory, Laval; a compromise, Pétain. Hopefully all this will not end to our disadvantage.
   The Americans have bombed Tokyo and other Japanese cities. This is their first offensive action since the beginning of the war. I do not think that, for the moment, they can do great things, their preparation being far behind; but as time passes they will make their weight felt more and more—especially in the air.

April 19, 1942
   Mussolini was very much surprised by an order of the Führer which postpones to May 2 the national German holiday because it would have been on a Friday. He is right. These Germans, he says, who bark against Catholicism, demonstrate themselves to be slaves of a prejudice which is clearly Christian in origin. But, above all, they show that they lack nerve, and are not sure of what they are doing.

April 20, 1942
   A strange speech by Goebbels on the occasion of Hitler's birthday. He talked in rather gloomy terms to reaffirm his faith in ultimate victory. But why did he have to make this speech, if, as is repeated in many quarters, the coming of spring allows the Germans to look to the Eastern Front with greater confidence? Even Mussolini, who is ordinarily inclined toward optimistic interpretations, commented bitterly on Goebbels' speech.
   Anfuso, on his return from Budapest, also talks in a lower tone. The Hungarians say that German preparation for the offensive is not what is claimed, and that on the Southern Front supplies are low.

April 21, 1942
   The Germans intend to procrastinate for a few days in replying to the Japanese about the declaration of independence for India and Arabia.
   Bismarck tells d'Aieta that the German Consul General in Milan receives many insulting letters. The last one ran like this: "We hear that you are looking for a new residence. We offer you one which is very beautiful, and worthy of you, of your people and of your leader. The address is so and so." The Consul General went solemnly to the address indicated, and found himself at the entrance of the city jail.

Jacomoni makes a rather good report on the Albanian situation. The only difficulty is the shortage of building supplies, which makes it impossible for us to continue our public works.

April 22, 1942

The Duce informs me that Marshal Kesselring, on his return from Germany, brought Hitler's approval for the landing operation on Malta. It appears that bombing from the air has really damaged the island. This does not, however, change the fact that the coastal defenses are still intact. Therefore, in the opinion of some naval experts, the undertaking is still dangerous and would in any case require many losses.

April 23, 1942

I accompany Jacomoni to see the Duce to discuss the question of the Albanian flag. The flag as it is now, the eagle framed in the fasces and topped by the crown of Savoy, is offensive to the Albanian Nationalists, who demand respect for their own national symbols. We now revive the old flag, which will have on the standard the Fascio Littorio and the blue band of Savoy. Naturally, before making the Duce's decision public I shall confer with the King.

Ambassador Boscarelli has died in Buenos Aires. As a diplomat he was my first friend in Rio de Janeiro, and had always kept alive his affection and devotion for me. He wasn't gifted with exceptional talent, but he was honest, a good worker, and courteous—all things which made him a very useful diplomatic agent. His death makes me very sad.

April 24, 1942

The Japanese military attaché, in talking to Prunas, vented his violent criticism of the German attitude and the German way of conducting political warfare—which is all wrong, according to the Japanese. If the Germans continue at this pace, they will have some painful surprises. I showed the Duce my notes on the subject and his comments were favorable to the Japanese.

During the evening Mackensen brings a proposal to the Duce that he meet the Führer at Salzburg by the end of the month. Mussolini would like to delay until May 1. Hitler sends word by telephone that the delay is not possible "for reasons independent of his will." The meeting is thus set for the 29th and 30th.

Riccardi vented his feelings about Petacci's brother and his gang. He says that he talked openly to the Duce about it. I limited myself to listening. This is a buzz saw I don't want to put my finger into.

April 25, 1942

Nothing new.

April 26, 1942

Nothing new.

April 27, 1942

A long speech by Hitler. It is difficult to comment upon it because by now all his speeches are more or less the same. The tone is not very optimistic. More than anything else he looks to the past, how and why the Russian winter was so severe and they were yet able to overcome it. But there is not a hint of what we all are waiting for—the end of the war. On the contrary, he declared that he is making every preparation to face the possibility of another winter on the Russian front with more adequate forces. Then he asked for full power over the German people. He already exercises complete power, but by appealing for it in this way he has aroused the feeling that the internal situation in Germany requires still more rigid control. In general, the speech has had a depressing effect in Italy, while Mussolini has judged it to be "an excellent and strong speech."

Marcello Vaccari, the Prefect of Venice, speaks to me of the extravagances of the young Petacci, how he has caused a big scandal in Venice, and how Buffarini had suppressed the reports of the carabinieri which Vaccari himself had given him. According to what Petrognano has said, Buffarini is financing Miss. Clara Petacci with 200,000 lire a month, and in this way Buffarini secures his complete impunity. However, now there is really too much talk about the affair.

April 28, 1942

We leave for Salzburg. This is a meeting that was requested by the Germans, and for which, as usual, they have given us no indication of an agenda. During the trip Cavallero talks to me about the Malta operation. He realizes that it is a tough nut. The preparations under way are being made with a maximum of attention and care, and with the conviction that the attack must take place. This is to give the maximum incentive to those concerned with planning. But whether the operation will take place, and when, is another matter, and in this regard Cavallero makes no commitment. As is his nature, he hides behind a great quantity of ifs and buts. He talks about the future progress of the war. We must win during this year or, at least, place ourselves in a position to win. Otherwise, the dangers will continue to increase.

April 29, 30-May 1, 2, 1942

Arrival at Salzburg (the Puch station). The usual scene: Hitler, Ribbentrop, the usual people, the usual ceremony. We are housed at the Klessheim Castle. This is a grandiose building, once owned by the prince-bishops of Salzburg, which has now become a guesthouse for the Führer. It is very luxurious and well arranged: furniture, hangings, carpets, all coming from France. They probably did not pay very much for the furnishings.

The atmosphere is extremely cordial, which makes me suspicious. The courtesy of the Germans is always in inverse ratio to their good fortune. Hitler looks tired; he is strong, determined, and talkative. But he is tired. The winter months in Russia have weighed heavily upon him. I see for the first time that he has many gray hairs.

Hitler talks with the Duce, I talk with Ribbentrop, but in two separate rooms, and the same record is played in both. Ribbentrop, above all, repeats his usual propaganda piece. I have recorded the conversation elsewhere. Napoleon, the Beresina, the drama of 1812, all this is brought to life in what he says. But the ice of Russia has been conquered by the genius of Hitler. This is the strong dish that is served up to me. But what about tomorrow? What does the future hold? On this issue Ribbentrop is less explicit. An offensive against the Russians in the south with the oil wells as a political and military objective.

When Russia will have exhausted her oil supplies she will be brought to her knees. Then the British Conservatives, and even Churchill himself, who, after all, is a sensible man, will bow in order to save what remains of their battered empire. Thus spoke Ribbentrop. But what if all this doesn't happen? What if the English, who are stubborn, decide to go on? What course must we follow to change their minds? Airplanes and submarines, says Ribbentrop. We go back to the 1940 formula. But that formula failed then and was shelved in the attic. Now they pull it out once more, and, after having dusted it thoroughly, they want to offer it to us again. I am not convinced by it, and I say so to Ribbentrop, much to Alfieri's dismay. Alfieri understands very little of what he hears but always says yes.

America is a big bluff. This slogan is repeated by everyone, big and small, in the conference rooms and in the antechambers. In my opinion, the thought of what the Americans can and will do disturbs them all, and the Germans shut their eyes in order not to see. But this does not keep the more intelligent and the more honest from thinking about what America can do, and they feel shivers running down their spines.

In regard to France they feel more doubt than friendship. Laval, too, is hardly convincing. The true spirit of the French is more clearly expressed by the gesture of the typesetter who risked his life to print the newspaper with the name of Pétain changed to Putain, * than by all the words of the collaborationists in the pay of Vichy. In Germany they have no illusions, and are always ready to slug anybody who moves.

Hitler talks, talks, talks. Mussolini suffers, since he is in the habit of talking and, instead, practically has to keep quiet. On the second day, after lunch, when everything had been said, Hitler talked uninterruptedly for an hour and forty minutes. He omitted absolutely no argument: war and peace, religion and philosophy, art, and history. Mussolini automatically looked at his wristwatch, I had my mind on my own business, and only Cavallero, who is a phenomenon of servility, pretended he was listening in ecstasy, continually nodding his head in approval. Those, however, who dreaded the ordeal less than we did were the Germans. Poor people. They have to take it every day, and I am certain there isn't a gesture, a word, or a pause which they don't know by heart. General Jodl, after an epic struggle, finally went to

---

* *putain*: French for "whore."

sleep on the sofa. Keitel was reeling, but he succeeded in keeping his head up. He was too close to Hitler to let himself go as he would have liked to do.

One does not see any physically fit men on the streets in the cities and towns of Germany. Women, children, and old men only. Or else foreign laborers, slaves of the earth. Edda, who visited a camp of our Italian workers, found one who had been wounded on his arms by a brutal guard with a scythe. She told Hitler, who had a fit of anger and ordered all sorts of arrests and investigations. Which, however, will not change the course of things.

Losses in Russia are heavy. Ribbentrop says 270,000 dead. Our General Marras raised it to 700,000. And between amputations, frostbite, and the seriously ill who will not recover by the end of the war, the figure rises to three million.

The British air force is striking hard. Rostock and Lübeck have been literally razed to the ground. Cologne has been heavily hit. The Germans react and strike back at the English cities but with less violence. Which only partly consoles the German population, accustomed as it has always been to dish it out but never to take it.

This leads many of them, who have devastated half of Europe, to weep about the "brutality of the English, who make many innocent Prussian families homeless." The worst of it is that they really feel this way.

Mussolini is satisfied with the trip and by his conversations with Hitler. This always happens. But, although he doesn't say so openly, this time he is led to reflect deeply about many things which are not yet apparent, but that one can sense in the air. This is the way he summarized the situation: "The German machine is still formidably powerful, but has suffered great wear. Now it will make a new and imposing effort. It must reach its goal."

The trip didn't arouse very much interest in Italy, and the war goes on. Real interest would come if people could begin to see peace in the offing. But peace has already been brushed aside by Hitler's speech, which could not have produced a worse impression. Everybody expected the announcement of the offensive against the Russians. Instead, he announced an offensive against the German people.

May 3, 1942

Yesterday a meeting of the Council of Ministers. The Duce summarized the results of his trip in a brief address. Grandi found it "discomforting."

In agreement with Berlin, we reply to Tokyo that the moment has not yet come to make a declaration about Arab and Indian independence. It would be a platonic gesture with no practical results, and could have negative consequences. Only if and when the armies of the Axis have reached a point where they can impose the declaration of independence with armed force can they indulge in such a gesture.

I have given the Duce the stenographic report of my conferences with von Ribbentrop. I had given it a somewhat controversial flavor and thought that this would displease him. Instead, he found it satisfactory and has kept it because tomorrow he wants to show it personally to the King.

D'Aroma[527] has come to tell me, with a tragic and mysterious air, all those platitudes that everybody knows about the situation of the regime and the Duce. Nonsense. Naturally, the moment we are going through doesn't call for elation, nor for many reasons could it be so, but the people's approval for the person of the Duce is unanimous. In order to sense this one had only to be at his train window during his trip from Tarvisio to Rome. There was not a person who, on recognizing the Duce, did not show signs of happy exaltation. Exactly like before. And so, then, must we really take a few professional gossips seriously?

May 4, 1942

I report to the King on the trip and tell him that the Duce will personally hand him the memorandum I dictated. As usual, I speak quite frankly, and the King shows that he appreciates it. But today he looked more tired than usual. He made some anti-German remarks. "If they did not need us they would cast us aside like old rags. I always tell the Duce that we must not trust those ugly Germans, and I know that he does not like my comments." However, in general he expresses himself calmly about the development of the conflict and is convinced that in England the situation is graver than it is thought to be.

I also speak to the King about the issue of the Albanian flag. We talk about modifying it by removing the fasces and the crown of Savoy, and putting these symbols on the standard. He accepts reluctantly.

I receive Bose, head of the Hindu Nationalists. He is unhappy upon learning that the declaration in favor of independence for India has been postponed *sine die*. He believes that in this way we are acting in favor of Japan, which will move on its own account without considering the interests of the Axis. He now thinks that British domination in India is coming to an end. British forces are small and Indian troops have no desire to fight. Naturally, we must take these declarations by Bose for what they are, because he is trying to bring grist to his mill.

May 5, 1942

The English have occupied Madagascar. It was to be expected, especially since Laval had announced to the four winds that he desired Japanese occupation in order to forestall that of the Anglo-Saxons. Mussolini even thinks that Laval took this step in order to press the English to act and that he established an alibi in advance. He wanted Berlin informed of his suspicion.

I go with Bose to see the Duce. A long conference without any new developments, except the fact that Mussolini allowed himself to be persuaded by the arguments put forth by Bose to obtain a tripartite declaration in favor of Indian independence. He has cabled the Germans proposing— contrary to the Salzburg decisions—proceeding at once with the declaration. I feel that Hitler will not agree to it very willingly.

Conference with Monsignor Bernardini, Papal Nuncio in Berne. He is very hopeful for a compromise peace in the fall, after the offensive in Russia. I disillusioned him. Germany is, and will be, extremely intransigent for a long time. Not even from a distance do I see what could be a good basis for discussion by the two parties in conflict. I advised the Holy See not to embark on a course that is surely bound to fail.

May 6, 1942
   Nothing new.

May 7, 1942
   Nothing new.

May 8, 1942
   A great naval battle is taking place in the Coral Sea. Both sides claim great successes, but as yet we have no details as to how things have really gone.
   An important item in the orientation of Italian political and social life: Vidussoni wanted to close the golf courses. I questioned him, and he, who is very simpleminded and is never able to find a way out, answered candidly that he intended to do this because "golf is an upper-class sport." That's a fine reason! He sounds almost like those people we beat up in 1920 and 1921. The matter itself has relatively little importance, but it has a great deal of importance as an indication of what is to be expected in the future. However, they must not exaggerate, because there are many people who are beginning to get annoyed. Let us not ask for greater rights than others merely because we wear a collar and wash our feet. But let us not be also ready to accept this deprivation just because of the reasons given. The Italian middle class is the one that endures the greatest sacrifices, that wages war, and that makes up the backbone of the country. Must we really strike at it every day and harass it to the point of turning it into an implacable enemy of the regime? I consider it a great mistake because nothing is gained and one does not even earn the gratitude of the simple people, which as lower classes are inconsistent and changeable as the sands.

May 9, 1942
   It is not yet clear how things have gone in the Coral Sea. The British-American communiqués, although they admit some unspecified losses, make loud claims of victory. On the other hand, the Japanese do the same. It is to be noted that the declaration of the Japanese General Staff placed the honor of the Emperor himself at stake. Therefore, they should not lie, although war lies are more or less like those that do not compromise a woman's honor—permissible lies.
   I accompanied Dindina[528] to the altar for her first communion. She was as pretty as a dream and was very moved. I, too, was somewhat touched.

May 10, 1942
   Mussolini has left for Sardinia on a military inspection trip. He will be absent one week.
   Senise makes his usual violent attack on Buffarini, who, according to him, is at the bottom of all the filthy doings in Italy. Now he hopes he has

finally caught him by the throat, through the scandal regarding the Aryanization of the Jews. The gang, which apparently was headed by Pre fect Le Pera,[529] was actually directed by Buffarini, who gorged himself with the profits. Buffarini has a bad conscience, and is trembling.

Senise has also sent me the reports of the questioning of those four bad boys who wanted to stage a *coup d'état*, starting it in a manner of which I greatly disapprove, that is, with my assassination. More than their perversity, it is their idiocy which is impressive. They talked about these projects in the presence of people they had met for the first time and who were obviously police spies. I think that, except for one, all the rest should be set free with a kick in the rear. They deserve no more. The Duce, talking about the matter, said to Senise: "I do not know whether the appointment of Vidussoni was a good or a bad thing." Well, it was a bad thing. But it is interesting that the question is being raised so soon.

May 11, 1942

A violent speech by Churchill. He threatens to use gas against German cities in case Hitler uses gas on the Russian front. I hope that neither one nor the other will carry out such a sinister plan.

Hungarian uneasiness is expressed by this little story making the rounds in Budapest. The Minister of Hungary declares war on the United States, but the official who receives the communication is not very well informed on European matters and hence asks several questions.

He asks, "*Is Hungary a republic?*" "No, it is a kingdom." "*Then you have a king?*" "No, we have an admiral." "*Then you have a fleet?*" "No, we do not have any sea." "*Do you have any claims, then?*" "Yes." "*Against America?*" "No." "*Against England?*" "No." "*Against Russia?*" "No." "*But against whom do you have these claims?*" "Against Romania." "*Then will you declare war on Romania?*" "No, sir. We are allies."

There is a great deal of truth in this series of paradoxes.

May 12, 1942

Cavallero outlines our program for carrying on the war in the Mediterranean. At the end of the month Rommel will attack in Libya with the aim of defeating the English forces. If he can, he will take Tobruk and will go as far as the old boundaries; if not, he will limit himself to forestalling an attack by the enemy by striking first. Then all the forces will be concentrated for an attack on Malta. The Germans are sending a parachute division commanded by General Student and are providing us with technical supplies for the assault. It will take place in July or August at the latest. Afterward it will no longer be possible because of the sea. Cavallero declares, "I know that it is a difficult undertaking and that it will cost us many casualties, and I know, too, that I am staking my head on this operation. But I am the one who wants it because I consider it absolutely essential for the future development of the war. If we take Malta, Libya will be safe. If not, the situation of the colony will always be precarious. I shall personally assume command of the operation. The Prince of Piedmont was considered, but for many reasons it was decided to leave him out." Cavallero does not conceal the fact that he hopes to derive a great deal of personal glory from this operation. But I believe he will never go through with it.

I saw the King at the exhibit of the German Academy. The works are few and rather second-rate.

May 13, 1942

Colonel Casero does not share Cavallero's easy enthusiasms about the attack on Malta. Malta's anti-aircraft defense is still very efficient, and their naval defense is completely intact. The interior of the island is one solid nest of machine guns. The landing of paratroopers would be very difficult; a great part of the planes are bound to be shot down before they can deposit their human cargo. The same must be said for landings by sea. On the other hand, it must be remembered that only two days of minor aerial bombardment by us were enough to make their defense more stubborn. In these last attacks we, as well as the Germans, have lost many feathers. Even Fougier considers an eventual landing operation with much anxiety, and the German General Lörzer did not conceal his open disagreement. The supporters of the undertaking are Kesselring and Cavallero, the latter going through his usual tricks to place the responsibility on the shoulders of others.

Arpinati asks for a small favor. He is, as always, calm and dignified, and not at all anxious about his personal position. He does not consider the internal situation of the country very good, and blames two things: the close union with the Germans, whom he does not like, and any display of what may appear as leftist tendencies.

May 14, 1942

Nothing new.

May 15, 1942

In Rome there is a good deal of gossip about the fact that there was a dance last Saturday in the Senni home, which was attended by a young secretary of the American embassy. No one of those present had the courage to react against it, which is extremely deplorable. It seems that several of the attachés of our Ministry for Foreign Affairs were present, and for this reason I have asked the chief of police to make a careful investigation. Naturally, this gesture by a few inconsiderate, irresponsible persons is causing a lot of commotion and is discrediting an entire class of people, which, as a matter of fact, are giving their share of blood and faith to the conflict.

May 16, 1942

Mussolini returns. He is very happy about his trip and what he has seen. He doesn't seem at all tired; in fact, he is sunburned and thinner. He talks with enthusiasm about the people of Sardinia, from whom he didn't hear a single protest about the scarcity of bread, or one plea for peace, "which would not have been lacking in the Po Valley, where there have been too many political experiments." Even regarding the defense of the island, his visit has given him reasons for assurance: good troops, efficient armaments, and, in the areas of a possible invasion, "enough malaria so as to decimate British troops in a few days, just as those of Frederick Barbarossa were decimated, when they stopped between Portonaccio and Ponte Galera."

Fougier vents his rancor against Cavallero, whom he accuses of being a dangerous clown, ready to follow every German whim without dignity, and a liar. He wanted to discuss his feelings with the Duce, but I dissuaded him, at least for the time being. Things are not yet ripe for Cavallero's dismissal, which, however, will be necessary at the proper time. Fougier also mentions Rommel's plans to attack on the 28th, and to drive forward as far as the valley of the Nile. Cavallero, who in Rome says that he does not want such a risky offensive, sings a different song in Derna, encouraging Rommel to "make the maximum effort."

May 17, 1942

Starace. A brief visit to recommend two persons to me. He is calmer than before, which makes me think that he has found some satisfaction—if nothing else of a material kind.

Gariboldi. He will leave shortly for Russia to take command of the expeditionary army. I have known him for many years, from the time of the capture of Addis Ababa. I have never had a very favorable opinion of him. Just now he seems even more tired and aged, notwithstanding the bleached-blondness of his thick mustache, trimmed *fin de siècle*. Cavallero has insisted on appointing him in order to get rid of Messe, who was beginning to acquire too much importance in the eyes of the Duce and of the country. Cavallero is a faithful follower of the theory which calls for the decapitation of poppies that grow too high. Gariboldi has been to Germany and has returned generally satisfied, but without clear ideas as to what is brewing in the kettle. However, he does not consider that the total liquidation of Russia will be possible before the coming of winter, which raises some very serious problems for us since we shall soon have 300,000 men on the Eastern Front.

May 18, 1942

The Duce telephones me to tell Edda "to talk to no one, absolutely no one, about what she saw and observed in Germany." The explanation is that the King told him, "Everyone in Rome knows that in a German hospital there is an Italian laborer with his fingers cut off, and that your daughter energetically protested to Hitler." The Duce is concerned about this remark by the King, and realizes that it is a maneuver to feed the anti-German resentment of the Italian people, using in a specific case an important name. "The King, who always plays the part of the anti-German," said Mussolini, "has given a daughter to a German, his son to a Belgian woman of the German race, and in his House marriages with Germans can be counted by the dozens."

In Slovenia things are not going so well. The High Commissioner asks us to send 24,000 men. It appears that the streets of Lubliana are now unsafe for our troops; every doorway and every window hides potential dangers.

All the youngsters who attended the dance in the Senni home, together with the American secretary, are now the object of Mussolini's just anger. Some of them, including the lady of the house, have been handcuffed. "The first to thank me," said the Duce, "should be her husband, because while he was fighting this whore was receiving the enemy in her home and was dancing with him."

May 19, 1942

The English would like to send some hospital ships to Malta. Our navy is favorable in principle, but the Germans are against it. The Duce decides against it, "especially because his experience has taught him the many things it is possible to hide in hospital ships when the blockade would otherwise prevent their passage. Last winter we were able to deliver some timely supplies of gasoline to Benghazi by using white ships."

Captain Dollmann, the SS man in Rome, has told d'Aieta that Himmler would like to come to Rome in October to talk things over with me, after the offensive in Russia that will certainly be brilliant but not decisive, making it necessary to prepare ourselves for a winter which will be hard, both materially and psychologically. Interesting statements, especially because Himmler is the only man who really knows the mood of the German people.

May 20, 1942

The Duce attached no importance to Dollmann's move. "Very well," he said. "We shall talk about it later. We know already that absolutely nothing will happen in Italy."

General Amè has secretly sent me two reports from General Marras on the morale of the German army. According to the reports, it is bad from every point of view, discouragement has taken hold of everyone, and the idea of an unavoidable winter on the Russian front brings real despair to the military. Suicides are numerous among those who prefer death to returning to the front. Marras doesn't reach any conclusion, but these are his premises.

British radio suggests that Rommel's preparations for his coming offensive in Libya have not gone unnoticed.

May 21, 1942

Mussolini has influenza. For the first time in many years I am told that he will not come to his office. I speak to him briefly over the telephone. His voice is hoarse and he has a bad cough. He must be in a very bad mood.

I speak with Colonna[530] and some attachés who have returned from the United States. They say nothing sensational. They all agree in stating, first, that the United States is not now in a position to do a great deal along military lines; second, that her industrial preparation is formidable and that within a few months we shall see a production of incalculable proportions; third, that the war is not popular, but that everyone is determined to fight even for twenty years, in order to get things settled; fourth, that feelings toward Italy are not at all hostile.

May 22, 1942
Nothing new.

May 23, 1942
The Duce telephoned indignantly, charging that the Japanese ambassador, Shiratori, made certain unacceptable statements: the dominion of the world belongs to Japan, the Mikado is the only god on earth, and that both Hitler and Mussolini must come to accept this reality. I remember Shiratori during his short stay in Rome. He was a fanatical extremist, but, most of all, he was very uncouth.

Bismarck has confirmed to d'Aieta that Himmler is playing a personal game by inciting people to grumble. Is this true? For the time being I think that the rumor must be accepted with a lot of caution.

May 24, 1942
Nothing new

May 25, 1942
Nothing new.

May 26, 1942
Mussolini is now interested only in the coming offensive in Libya, and he is definitely optimistic. He maintains that Rommel "will reach the Delta" unless he is stopped, "not by the British, but by our own generals." Even for the taking of Malta he makes good "forecasts." "A surprise has been prepared which will give tremendous results." But he didn't say what the surprise is.

Serrano wants to come to Italy and Mussolini is in favor of the trip. I suggest that the meeting take place at Leghorn toward the middle of June. I don't think we shall have important things to say, but it is good not to lose this Spanish card, which has cost blood and gold.

The situation between Hungary and Romania is more and more tense. Mariassy sent a note today, which is something of an alarm signal. I confess one suspicion, and that is that the Hungarians may be showing such concern in order to avoid any deep commitments to the offensive against Russia.

May 27, 1942
Sorrentino,[531] on his return from Russia, gives his impressions and makes forecasts for the future. The first are not pleasant and the second not comforting. The brutality of the Germans, which has now reached the proportions of a endless crime, stands out so vividly and so movingly from his words as to make one skeptical of its truthfulness. Massacres of entire populations, raping, killing of children—all this is a matter of daily occurrence. Against this there is the cold Bolshevik decision to resist and fight to the end, certain of victory. On the other hand, German morale is lower than might be imagined. "The coming four months may mark the beginning of a catastrophe, the like of which has never been seen."

Fougier sends the first news of Rommel's attack in Libya. There is action by the air force and the advance of armored columns, but it is too early to give even a partial account of what is happening. It appears that Rommel has somewhat reduced his original program, which was very comprehensive. Now he wants to reach the Nile Valley.

Bismarck told d'Aieta that food rations in Germany will soon be cut 25 percent. Anne Maria Bismarck told me very candidly yesterday evening, "I am pro-German because I married Otto, but I am anti-Nazi."

May 28, 1942

I understood that the Duce asked to see the statements that I was going to make to the Senate on Saturday, so I sent him a copy of my speech. I hate to make speeches these days. One runs the risk of being called a liar or of being banal.

Pittalis, returning from Munich because of his appointment as ambassador to Buenos Aires, paints the German situation in dark colors. In 1942 it is necessary that careful decisions be made because the people have made every extreme sacrifice, and no more sacrifices can be expected of them. I must say that Pittalis, up to now, had, if anything, been guilty of optimism.

Venturi, Minister of Communications, says that sleeping cars and first-class cars will shortly be put back into operation on the Italian railroads. The experiment of abolishing them—one demagogically flavored—did not have good results, but just the opposite.

Pavolini tells me that the Duce will have a deserter, who is a condemned murderer, shot in broad daylight at the Coliseum. I ask myself whether this lugubrious publicity will be of any help to the morale of the Italian people, whose psychology is a great deal more complex than is generally believed.

May 29, 1942

My speech to the Senate is approved by the Duce, without changing a word, which is something unusual for him, especially since he is in a very bad mood because of the drought, which threatens to reduce the harvest by a million or so quintals of wheat.

May 30, 1942

I spoke to the Senate. It appears that they liked the speech very much, because the senators, who are usually critical and reserved, were rather enthusiastic. They applauded a lot and stood throughout the last part of my speech. Mussolini wanted a detailed report of the session and didn't hide his satisfaction.

In the afternoon I leave for Leghorn.

May 31, 1942

In Leghorn. A day of rest and fishing. But this does not spare me from complaints about food, which is in very short supply. Wine is lacking, and so is everything else. Renato, my fisherman, lost thirty pounds in a few months, and he tells me that the members of his family are losing weight at the same rate. In spite of this the mood is good and there is faith in the future.

I had a long and interesting conversation with Carboni. At the moment he is commanding one of the assault divisions, which is to participate in the Malta operation. He is decidedly against it. He is convinced that we shall have heavy losses and nothing will come of it. He takes it out on Cavallero, whom he considers to be an intriguer and a man in bad faith. He is very pessimistic also about the Russian front. He doesn't think that during the summer the Germans can undertake any operations of far-reaching proportions. It is a war of position rather than anything else. From this he draws the most sinister conclusions for the German future. Carboni is a very capable general. One must not forget, however, that he was dismissed by the SIM because of his anti-German attitude, and that his mother was American.

June 1, 1942

The King praised my speech, after I sent him the complete text through Acquarone. As usual he takes it out on the Germans, whom he considers capable of all sorts of deceit and treachery. He shows interest in France and in the restoration of the Spanish monarchy, which he naturally approves, though at the same time he judges the future King with considerable reserve. He praises the future Queen, "who has a big nose, but a lot of common sense and clear judgment." He has modified his ideas about the future outlook. At first he believed in a British collapse, but he does not talk about it any more and believes "that we must reach a compromise peace because no one will win, and the nations will add to their war sufferings the dissatisfaction of much inevitable disillusionment."

Mussolini repeats his praise of my speech and speaks with restraint about our offensive in Libya. According to him the main clash has not yet taken place because of the scarcity of supplies for the mechanized units. At the German embassy, on the other hand, they are not satisfied with the course of events. It now seems that Tobruk has become an impossible objective and yet Cavallero was speaking of Cairo! True enough, on the day the attack began he went to bed with a very convenient bout of influenza.

June 2, 1942

The offensive in Libya has not yet taken a definite turn. On the whole, the Duce is optimistic, but at the High Command they are a little less so. Mussolini also thought of going to the front, but "he wouldn't like a repetition of what happened in Albania, when they made him a witness to an unfortunate battle."

Riccardi talks to me very critically about the Petacci family and about the business deals of Dr. Marcello Petacci. It appears that he had an open quarrel with them, and a violent exchange of words over the telephone. He showed me an interesting document. A noncommissioned officer of the carabinieri wrote in a report to his superiors that "a certain individual (whose name I do not remember) is a crook, but also the lover of a certain Petacci, sister of the Duce's mistress; therefore I can't touch him." This is incredible but true; I saw it with my own eyes.

Gambara writes that he has been retired. This is Cavallero's victory. Gambara asks for neither favor nor pity, but speaks sincerely. Was it necessary to hurt the man who covered our flag with glory in Spain?

June 3, 1942

Optimism prevails at the Palazzo Venezia on the progress of operations in Libya. The Duce talks today about the imminent siege of Tobruk and about the possibility of carrying the action as far as Marsa Matruk. If these are roses...they will bloom. The Duce was very hostile to the Vatican because of an article appearing in the *Osservatore Romano* signed by Falchetto. The article discussed Greek philosophy, but the real purpose was obvious. Guariglia will take the matter up with the Secretariat of State of the Vatican. "I hate priests in their cassocks," said Mussolini, "but I hate even more and loathe those without cassocks, who are vile Guelfs, a breed to be wiped out."

I had lunch with Bottai. He said more or less the usual things, adding that as a matter of personal experience he found the Duce "spiritually and intellectually very low" in the last few months. I don't know on what he bases his impressions.

The Germans have prevented Alfieri from going to Cologne, and stopped him at the station in Düsseldorf. The city is so damaged they prefer that our ambassador not see it. Essen was also bombed last night, and, it would seem, quite as heavily as Cologne.

According to Colonel Casero, the battle of Libya has become stationary, turning into a battle of attrition.

June 4, 1942

Cavallero describes the results of the Libyan battle as being "considerable," which, for anybody who knows the mysterious language of this mountebank general, means that things have gone very badly. He summarizes the situation as follows: it was a good thing we attacked, because the enemy was preparing to attack. But who says so? He goes on to say that we used up their materiel and thus won a tactical success. In reply to a question he says he doesn't believe that we can reach Tobruk or any more distant objectives, but this does not prevent us from entertaining hopes (sic!). It is a bit early to judge. We shall know later if this offensive of ours was good or bad.

I saw Messe on his return from Russia. He sees red because Cavallero made the old and stupid Gariboldi commander of the army over his head, in spite of Messe's excellent record. Like everybody else who has had anything to do with the Germans, he hates them, and says that the only way of dealing with them would be to punch them in the stomach. He thinks the Russian army is still strong and well armed, and that any idea of a complete collapse of the Soviets is absolute utopia. The Germans will still have some successes, perhaps some big successes, but they will solve nothing, and the winter will catch them still in the field with an even greater shortage of supplies. Messe draws no conclusions, but does not conceal his doubts, which are very serious.

June 5, 1942

Grandi tells me that the Council of Ministers tomorrow, in connection with the increase in the income tax, will introduce the oath as a way of ascertaining income, with all the consequences that this implies. This means that for the first time in the history of our tax system they are thinking of jailing tax evaders. This might work in countries educated in fiscal matters, but not with us, where everyone would be forced to take false oaths. If we closed our eyes to this, we would become ridiculous, or, wishing to apply the law, we would have to enlarge our jails to the point where half of the budget would go for the maintenance of prisoners. Thus Revel, after having taken everything from the Italians, also wants to take their honor . . .

June 6, 1942

Meeting of the Council of Ministers. Mussolini rails violently against the merchants, 132,000 of whom have already been denounced. He accuses them of constituting another army which stabs the state in the back while it is engaged in a very hard war. Thus there will be new and tougher penalties added to those already in existence. On the other hand, the tax oath, invented by Revel, was stillborn. The provision has been withdrawn. Naturally, it will be pulled out again, because the "Red Count," as they call this new Philippe Egalité Minister of Finance of ours, loses no opportunity to impose his demagogic policies.

Cavallero judges the situation in Libya as "logical." This is an adjective which he has now pulled out and dusted off and which he hasn't used since the time he was being beaten in Albania. In the meantime, he stays in bed with his strange and rather suspicious illness.

June 7, 1942

Nothing new.

June 8, 1942

Nothing new

June 9, 1942

The SIM has uncovered an espionage network inside the German embassy. Dr. Sauer, a cultural attaché, has already been arrested and has confessed. He made it clear that he did not act for money but out of hatred for Nazism and Fascism. He turned over to the Swiss military attaché information of a military nature. It also seems that a German colonel, an aide of von Rintelen, is also mixed up in the affair. The Duce commented bitterly on the matter and fears that it may damage the position of von Mackensen, the ambassador. Bismarck, who has spoken on the subject with d'Aieta, did not attach much importance to what has happened. He says that Sauer is a pederast and that he has been induced by his vice to commit this serious offense.

On Mussolini's orders the newspapers have attempted to show for some days that during World War I the food situation in the country was worse than it is today. It is a sort of propaganda that produces the opposite effect to what was intended. We were all living then, and our memories are too fresh to accept these statements. Pavolini has, in fact, told me that the Duce complains that the newspapermen do not know how to carry on this campaign efficiently. The facts are that all those approached by Pavolini have refused to write what was asked of them.

June 10, 1942

A ceremony at the monument to the Unknown Soldier to honor the naval heroes. As usual, the sailors and the cadets of Leghorn made a superb showing. However, the public showed little enthusiasm. No applause all along the parade.

In Dalmatia the situation is very tense. The rebels, after having overwhelmed one of our brigades at Knin, are advancing toward Zara. Bastianini, who hurried to Rome, says that there isn't a minimum of forces to engage the rebels, thus their occupation of Dalmatia is to be feared. In the region of Fiume, also, there is a great deal of unrest. I talked with Testa, who is an energetic man who knows how to take on responsibility. Now Mussolini is furious with him, because without even a semblance of a trial he hanged five rebels whom he found wearing the shoes of our dead soldiers. Aside from the hangings, which are not really in our tradition and bring to mind the Austrian methods of bygone days, Testa succeeds in keeping order, and the rebels tremble at the very mention of his name.

Argentina protests strongly against the sinking of the *Victoria* by Axis submarines. Ambassador Malbran, who is pro-Italian and who has always been an optimist, now begins to see difficulties in the future relations between our two countries.

June 11, 1942

Bir Hacheim has been taken. The garrison resisted strongly, because there were many French, Italians, Germans, and Jews convinced that there would be no pity for them. Now we shall see if the action can be followed up or will stop with this local success. This morning the Duce expressed the opinion that it will be difficult to occupy Tobruk. The action to date has cost us great losses.

I spoke with Mussolini about Gambara. It appears that Cavallero wishes to make an investigation even into the Spanish war period. This is a shame, because in Spain Gambara was the only general who brought glory to our colors. The Duce agreed and will put a stop to this shameful behavior. Every day Cavallero is becoming more and more harmful to the army and to the country.

Pareschi is optimistic about the food situation, even though the heat of the last few days has greatly damaged the grain harvest. At any rate, he is convinced that the coming winter will be less hard than the last.

Bismarck telephoned Blasco [d'Aieta] about a twenty-year alliance between America, England, and Russia, and about an American commitment to open a second front against the Germans. This is like an injection to keep the Russians on their feet. Further news is necessary before forming an opinion on the matter.

June 12, 1942

Mussolini is more and more irritated against the *Osservatore Romano* because of certain articles signed by Falchetto in which he reads—and there really is—a subtle vein of poison against the regime. He has decided to have its director, Count della Torre, arrested. I insisted that this act, which is bound to create a great crisis with the Vatican, must be avoided, especially now that we have no need of crises. He wasn't convinced, but I hope that he will reconsider his decision.

Lequio's[532] reports connect Serrano's visit even more to the question of the monarchy. Serrano has his visa for Switzerland, where the King of Spain is at this time. Mussolini is very much against the restoration of the monarchy and spoke along this line for a long time today. But nothing can be done about it. The monarchy will not solve anything, but all the Spaniards want it. Therefore, if such a thing should happen, it is better that it take place with us rather than without us or against us. From Leghorn I shall take Serrano to luncheon with the King of Italy at San Rossore.

I saw Serena. He is just back from Croatia. He speaks despondently about the morale of the army. He says, however, that a formula to improve it exists: kick out Cavallero. Every passing day he is less respected and even more hated. General Guzzoni told me the same thing, but he is too much involved in the matter to be objective.

I learned from Bigliardi that the destroyer *Usodimare* has been mistakenly sunk by one of our own submarines.

June 13, 1942

Nothing new. Off to Leghorn. Bad weather.

June 14, 1942

Nothing new.

June 15, 1942

Serrano arrives. The city greets him with an open heart and a tremendous southwest wind.

June 16, 1942

At lunch with His Majesty. The conversation is conventional, but the King makes a very shrewd statement, which I must set down. Serrano states that England, through Samuel Hoare, spends ten million pesetas a month for British propaganda in Spain. The King commented, "This is a lot of money, but fortunately experience teaches that a great part of these funds sticks to the fingers of the propagandists, and those who are to be propagandized get only the crumbs. This is a good thing, otherwise God only knows how many revolutions there would be."

June 17, 1942
Nothing new.

June 18, 1942
Nothing new.

June 19, 1942
I return to Rome. I made some notes of my conversations with Serrano. The Duce is still at Riccione.

June 20, 1942
I thought that after the successes in Libya and at sea I would find the Duce in a positive mood. Instead, he is reserved in his judgment and outlook. Nor does he give way to easy optimism. He is preparing to go to Africa if Tobruk is taken.

General Carboni has come to Rome to discuss the Malta operation, which has been set for the next new moon. He is convinced, technically convinced, that we are heading for an unheard-of disaster. Preparations have been childish; equipment is lacking and inadequate. The landing troops will never succeed in landing, or, if they land, they are doomed to total destruction. All the commanders are convinced of this, but no one dares to speak for fear of reprisals by Cavallero. But I am more than ever of the opinion that the undertaking will not take place.

The Duce receives Serrano, who repeats more or less what he said at Leghorn. Mussolini expresses hostility to monarchies, which are potentially the natural enemies of totalitarian revolutions. He believes that in Spain the King will soon want to stifle Falangism. He cites some Italian precedents that tend to prove his point of view. As for the war, he predicts the success of the Axis with absolute certainty, but foresees a very long war. He speaks of four or five years. He will see Serrano again before his departure. In today's conversation the Duce was particularly incisive and vivacious.

June 21, 1942
Tobruk has fallen and the British have left us with 25,000 prisoners. This is a great success for us and opens new developments. On the other hand, I learned from a conversation with Bigliardi that the results of our aerial-naval battle were a great deal more modest than had been announced. The merchant ships were, in fact, hit, and many were sunk, but the British losses were limited to a cruiser, probably sunk, and a destroyer, sunk.

Riccardi renews his broadsides against Clara Petacci. He also denounces an illegal traffic in gold, involving Buffarini, who lends his name to it. Riccardi, who is very violent and stubborn, is capable of starting a scandal. We shall see what develops.

Amè is pessimistic in judging the internal British-American situation, but more so in judging the German situation. He, too, repeats the formula about the coming decisive four months. I think three months will be enough to see into the future.

June 22, 1942

The Duce is in an excellent mood and is preparing to go to Africa. In reality he was the man behind the decisive attack, even against the opinion of the High Command. Now he fears that they may not realize the magnitude of the success and therefore fail to take full advantage of it. He trusts only Rommel. From Rome a restraining cable has already been sent, advising that they should not venture beyond the line of Fort Capuzzo-Sollum.

There is, on the other hand, some hesitation about the Malta undertaking. Mussolini wrote to Hitler, saying that if we did not have at our disposal forty thousand tons of oil, we should have to postpone it indefinitely.

This morning Petacci's sister was married in Rome, and the event was talked about throughout the city. There was talk of expensive and fantastic gifts, forests of flowers, and Lucullan banquets. Much of it is probably fantasy, but there is a great deal of talk and this is what counts. The Duce said to Pavolini: "While we are talking, a marriage is going on at Santa Maria degli Angeli. It is good from an economic point of view, but bad for the girl, who had prospects of a successful career in the movies. I hope, at any rate, that the newspapers will have the sense not to talk about it. Only the *Messaggero*, where her father writes a column, can make the announcement." It is interesting that Mussolini discussed the matter openly with a minister.

June 23, 1942

A second conference between Serrano and the Duce. Nothing very important except the affirmation by Serrano that, should Portugal be attacked by the Anglo-Saxons, Spain would not hesitate to come into the war. In this connection there already exists an agreement between Franco and Salazar. From the Duce comes the striking statement that he, "like all Italians, is an Apostolic Roman Catholic, and that he does not believe that Rosenberg's theories will be successful after the war."

According to some intercepted cables from the American observer at Cairo, Fellers, we learn that the English have been beaten and that if Rommel continues his action he has a good chance of reaching as far as the Canal Zone. Naturally, Mussolini is pressing for the attack to continue.

The promotion of Rommel to marshal raises some problems of organization—in other words, the promotion of Bastico and Cavallero to the same rank. I have told the Duce what I think. "Bastico's promotion will make people laugh; Cavallero's will make them indignant." A real shake-up has taken place over the clandestine traffic in gold with Spain through the diplomatic pouch. I have confiscated eighteen kilos and given them to the police. The information came from Riccardi. The persons mixed up in it all belong to the Petacci gang. Buffarini is also involved in it. I make no further comment.

June 24, 1942

The question of the gold and the Petaccis is becoming more severe. Riccardi talked about it with the Duce, with whom Buffarini had already tried to speak in self-defense. According to Riccardi, Mussolini is very indignant at what has happened and has given orders that the guilty be punished according to the law, irrespective of the persons and without pity. According to Buffarini, on the other hand, the Duce was angry with Riccardi for having made a scene about the issue, which should have been treated differently and with discretion. To complicate matters, the name of the notorious Dr. Petacci has now appeared. Dr. Petacci has come out into the open to address a violent letter to Buffarini, Riccardi and the Duce, in which he lays claim to special merit—"Fascist and national merit"—for having gone into such an operation, and insults all those who are trying to place obstacles in his path. The whole affair cannot end too easily. It will be interesting to see who will foot the bill.

In Libya, Rommel's action is progressing at full speed. The rosiest forecasts can now be made.

June 25, 1942

After having toured the airfields to distribute decorations, the Duce has returned to Rome.

Victory has encouraged our forces in Libya and they are now preparing to besiege Marsa Matruk.

Serrano has left, after an eleven-day visit. A too lengthy trip is never useful; it creates boredom. Perhaps reciprocal, certainly unilateral.

June 26, 1942

Mussolini is happy about the progress of operations in Libya but unhappy over the fact that the battle is identified with Rommel, thus appearing more and more as a German rather than an Italian victory. Also Rommel's promotion to field marshal, "which Hitler obviously decided to underscore the German character of the battle," causes the Duce much pain. Naturally, he takes it out on Graziani, "who was always seventy feet underground in a Roman tomb at Cyrene while Rommel knows how to lead his troops with the personal example of a general living in his tank." For the moment Mussolini makes no forecasts but hopes that "before fifteen days are over we can establish our commissariat in Alexandria." He paints the Russian situation in darker colors: Russia, "where the Bolshevists have put into execution the tactics of Lenin, who instructed the proletariat to fight house to house against the bourgeois armies, thus obliging them to abandon their artillery and aviation, to use only guns and bombs." Our services have prepared a declaration of independence for Egypt, changes in government, et cetera. We shall talk about it after Marsa Matruk has been taken.

I go to Leghorn on the anniversary of my father's death.

June 27, 1942

At Leghorn for the ceremonies in memory of my father; my memory of him is increasingly keen and sacred.

June 28, 1942

At Leghorn. Seashore and fishing. Operations in Libya are moving very fast. Marsa Matruk has fallen. The way to the Delta is now open.

June 29, 1942

Mussolini has left for Libya. I see Riccardi, who gives me a long account of his conversation with the Duce on the Petacci gold matter. It seems that the Chief is very indignant and has ordered Dr. Petacci to abstain from any such dealings in the future. We shall see. I do not know whether Riccardi has, perhaps, exposed himself too much. He said something that impressed me, "While I was speaking with the Duce I had a humiliated man facing me. We were no longer on the same level. I was two steps higher up." With Mussolini, it is very dangerous to believe that one is two steps above him.

June 30, 1942

I have had considerable difficulty in preventing Riccardi, for economic reasons, from creating a real political crisis with Switzerland, which I definitely want to avoid at this time. I succeeded, but it was a heavy and annoying discussion.

In Libya we are doing well, and our information creates the impression that the English are going through a serious crisis.

July 1, 1942

I leave for Leghorn, where I intend to spend a few days of rest at the beach. News from Africa is still excellent.

July 2, 1942

Mussolini cables, giving instructions to contact the Germans on the question of the future political government of Egypt. Rommel is to be the military commander, and an Italian is to be civilian commissioner. I am asked to suggest a name. I suggest Mazzolini, who was our last Minister at Cairo. Blasco d'Aieta speaks with von Mackensen. If I had met with the Duce I would have dissuaded him from making a move, which sounds too much like putting the cart before the horse.

July 3, 1942

Hitler answers that he agrees so far as Rommel is concerned, but he is postponing his answer about the Italian delegate, also in relation to the question of German representation. At any rate, he does not consider the question "urgent." He is not wrong, because a sudden and not unforeseen English reaction compels us to mark time before El Alamein. At the High Command in Rome they are very optimistic, and convinced that the lull is altogether temporary.

July 4, 1942

Cavallero has been made a marshal, evidently to offset the impression produced by Rommel's promotion. The effect is negligible. The move is received with unanimous disfavor, especially in military circles.

July 5, 1942

Nothing new. We are still marking time in Libya. In Russia, on the other hand, the German offensive is moving slowly and with great difficulty. Either resistance has increased considerably or the force of penetration of the German army is no longer what it was.

July 6, 1942

I have returned to Rome. There is some concern going around due to the lull before El Alamein. It is feared that after the impact of the initial attack is spent Rommel cannot advance farther, and whoever stops in the desert is truly lost. It is enough to think that every drop of water must come from Marsa Matruk, almost 200 kilometers of road bombed by enemy air force. It is reported to me that in military circles there is violent indignation against the Germans because of their behavior in Libya. They have grabbed all the booty. They thrust their claws everywhere, place German guards over the booty, and woe to anyone who comes near. The only one who has succeeded in getting plenty for himself, naturally, is Cavallero, and he has sent the goods to Italy by plane. This information is correct. Colonel Casero, the head of the air force staff, gave it to me. There is no question about it, Cavallero may not be a great strategist, but when it is a question of grabbing, he can even cheat the Germans.

July 7, 1942

Francesco Coppola,[533] who, despite his advanced age, faced the long journey to East Africa in order to find his daughter, has returned disconsolate and alone. His daughter has been detained in Somaliland and may come home with the next Red Cross ship if there is to be one. Coppola has given a very unbiased account of his trip. The Italians, after the English occupation, for the most part maintained a very praiseworthy attitude. They do not complain about the treatment they receive. In general, the English have been fair, and the Abyssinians also, especially in the large towns. It seems that the Negus has taken strong measures to protect the life and property of Italians, perhaps in the hope of establishing a future *modus vivendi* with us. The English, with whom Coppola had to deal during his trip, likewise behaved well. In general, they are not very enthusiastic about the war, and their morale is moderate.

Cavallero, who has left Libya for a brief visit, is 100 percent optimistic on the coming resumption of operations. He is certain that the superiority of the Axis forces will take us to Alexandria immediately and in a short time to Cairo and the Canal. Meanwhile, the Germans have agreed that the civilian commissioner of Egypt should be an Italian, a matter they had previously raised some objections about.

July 8, 1942

I met with Sebastiani, Mussolini's former secretary, whom I have not seen for some time. He is upset because a request for an audience was not granted by the Duce. He attributes his misfortune to the sinister influence of the Petaccis. Sebastiani is a reserved man, and for the first time he spoke to me about this matter. He believes that the Duce will find it difficult to deal with the situation that has arisen. ("The girl is not bad, but the other members of the family are a bunch of exploiters!") For some time he has been convinced of the necessity of breaking away. Once he said to Sebastiani, "This affair, too, will soon end." Pavolini thinks otherwise. He states that Mussolini took more interest in the marriage of the Petacci woman's sister than in the marriages of his own children. He even telephoned at midnight to learn the contents of the article in the society column of the *Messaggero.*

July 9, 1942

Again to Leghorn for ten days. I have not had any political contacts except a visit from Admiral Riccardi, who outlined a project to block the Sicilian passage, and one from Buffarini, who makes rather gloomy forecasts about the wheat harvest.

July 20, 1942

In Rome. Mussolini, too, will return during the evening. His return, together with news from Libya, convinces the public that many rosy dreams about Egypt have faded, at least for the time being. We shall now see if our deployment at El Alamein is wise or not. Some people on the General Staff are considering the advisability of a retreat.

Tamaro sends news from Switzerland about British-German conversations that are supposed to be taking place at Lugano. He supplies a wealth of details. On behalf of the Germans, those present are said to be Seyss-Inquart, Rintelen, et al.; representing the English personages of more or less equal rank. Tamaro even enclosed some snapshots, but I honestly did not recognize anyone. How much truth is there in this? It's difficult to say. Nevertheless, it all has a strong flavor of a dime novel. But it is best to keep our eyes open. One never knows.

July 21, 1942

The Duce is in a good mood, especially because he believes that within two or three weeks we can resume our forward march into Egypt and reach the great goals of the Delta and the Canal. He is so certain of it that he has left his personal baggage in Libya as a guarantee of a quick return. (Bismarck, on the other hand, in view of information from General Rintelen, considers that our offensive is postponed for a long time, because the exhaustion of our troops has been very considerable, and because the reinforcements that have reached the English are greater than forecasted.)

Naturally, Mussolini has been absorbing the anti-Rommel spirit of the Italian commander in Libya, and he lashes out on the German marshal who, by the way, did not pay him a visit during the three weeks and more Mussolini spent there. The attitude of the soldiers is also obnoxious. German motor vehicles do not yield the right of way to anyone, even to our generals, and at the smallest opportunity of acquiring a little booty they grab everything. The Arabs behave very badly. "The policy of Balbo failed completely, and the only good thing done by him is the Balbia."[534] He told me that he had found strong nuclei of New Zealand prisoners with "hangman faces and so far from reassuring that he always kept his gun close at hand." He said little about Russia, but he is convinced that for the time being operations are far from being decisive.

July 22, 1942

Mussolini has written a letter to Hitler: an account of his stay in Libya and his visit to Athens. The main purpose of the letter was actually to straighten things out on the matter of our *Sabratha* division, because Rommel had sent a cable to Germany where he was very critical of it—a cable for which "Mussolini will never forgive him." The tone of Mussolini's letter did not please my office colleagues. There were too many bureaucratic expressions, such as "I have the honor of transmitting to you," "I allow myself to call your attention to," which gave to the writing, according to them, the character of a report by a subordinate to his superior. Mussolini is now irritated at the Germans. He deprecates their systematic plundering of Greece, and when I called them "Lanzi" he, who usually dislikes my phraseology, agreed with enthusiasm, adding, "Perhaps many Germans deplore the fact that they couldn't invade Italy, in order to grab everything we have. But had they done this, they would have lost the war." Mackensen pays me a visit on some pretext or other. He eulogizes Cavallero, "who, in addition to technical competence, has also great political instinct and is a real friend of Germany." Friend? No, a servant. Mackensen doesn't believe that the offensive can be resumed before October, and makes many reservations. De Cesare also said the same thing. This concerns me more because De Cesare is a jinx. During a trip to Libya his spell worked well: among the Duce's party, four people died in a plane crash.

July 23, 1942

I recounted to the Duce the forecasts made by the German ambassador. After two days of pretended assurance Mussolini has lowered his mask and has spoken clearly. He is furious with the military, who "for the second time have made a fool of him by making him visit the front at unfavorable moments." (Of course he is alluding to his trip to Albania.) This time he had given orders to Cavallero to send, by cable, in plain language the word "*Tevere*" when Cavallero was certain about the advance of our troops toward the Canal. The password "*Tevere*" arrived on Friday, June 27. The Duce had to delay his departure for two days because of a cyclone. Only when he was on the spot did he realize that things were not going well, and that even "Rommel's strategy had its ups and downs." The promotion of Cavallero to field marshal could not be avoided because he found himself "between Rommel and Kesselring like Christ between the thieves." In any case, Bastico will also be nominated field marshal, and other generals after him, and "he doesn't exclude even Navarra, his doorkeeper." Forecasts are now very cautious; Mussolini thinks we must avoid any retreat because otherwise we would not know where we would end up.

July 24, 1942

The tone of the Duce's conversation is increasingly anti-German. Today he gave vent to his feelings on two points: a statement by General Marras on the low esteem in which our military contribution is held by the German General Staff, and the lack of understanding of our needs and of our industrial aspirations. "The people," Mussolini said, "are now wondering which of the two masters is to be preferred, the English or the Germans." I reminded him what François-Poncet said upon leaving my room on the day of the declaration of war: "*Ne creusez pas des fossés trop profonds; n'oubliez pas que les allemands sont des maîtres durs.*"[535] I agree with him.

The Germans have occupied Rostov. From many sources the opening of a second front in France by the British-Americans is reported to be certain. In Berlin, according to what Alfieri cables, the matter is not causing concern, but annoyance.

July 25, 1942

Nothing new. The Duce is leaving for Riccione.

July 26, 1942

The Mufti issues harsh criticism against Gailani. As was to be expected, the two have quarreled, and the one who added fuel to the fire was Minister Grobba, the German head of the Arab Service of the *Auswaertiges Amt.* The incident is especially important if operations in Egypt are to resume favorably.

July 27-30, 1942

In Leghorn.

July 31, 1942

I return to Rome.

August 1, 1942

Buffarini was summoned to Riccione by Mussolini because the situation in Sicily is very worrisome; the peasants are refusing to hand over their grain, and in many cases they fired on those who were supposed to collect it. On the basis of reports from the Health Service Buffarini called Mussolini's attention to the fact that among the working class edema caused by malnutrition is appearing. Even at Piombino, according to Aiello,[536] similar cases are occurring.

Bottai pays me a visit. He has nothing to tell me, but he is more anti-Mussolini than ever. If he talks this way to me, I can imagine what he must say to his own friends!

August 2, 1942

We are warned from Lisbon that the Royal Air Force will soon bomb Milan heavily. I don't know whether this will happen, but it is likely, and, in a certain sense, quite logical. I inform Buffarini.

Edda attacked me violently, accusing me of hating the Germans, saying that my hatred for the Germans is known everywhere, especially among the Germans themselves, who are saying that "I am physically repulsed by them." I cannot understand why Edda should be so excited about it, nor who discussed it with her. Generally when she does this somebody has influenced her. I said little or nothing in reply. After all, she knows very well how I feel about the matter. And I am not the only one....

August 3, 1942

Nothing new.

August 4, 1942

Ambrosio, chief of the General Staff, tells me: (1) in Libya we shall not be able to resume our movements until the end of October; however, the prospects are good because English reinforcements are slower than had been expected while our reinforcements, especially the Germans (and this concerns the General Staff for obvious reasons), are arriving regularly; (2) operations in Russia are developing well, and German operations against the Caucasus are expected to continue even during the winter; (3) personally, he does not believe in a victory that will liquidate our enemies. However, he thinks that Russia will probably be detached from the Allied camp, after which Great Britain and America will be obliged to come to terms. This, in summary, is the military-political thought of our General Staff today.

Lombrassa foresees a strong increase in the labor shortage, and this is why, within a short time, the mobilization of civilians will begin on a large scale. I have advised him to remove from forced civilian service that odious flavor of punishment, which has so far been attached to it. The citizen should know that civilian service is on the same moral level as military service. Hence, we must do away with contemptible gossip, referring to such citizens as being pederasts, cardsharpers, dandies, and such people we normally despatch to Carbonia. It is not becoming and proves nothing.

August 5, 1942

A letter arrives from Hitler for the Duce. I send it to Riccione unopened.

August 6, 1942

There is great optimism on the possibilities in Libya according to General Marchesi, commander of the air squadron. Rommel is preparing to attack, and without a doubt he should settle matters within the space of ten days. Objectives: Cairo, Alexandria, Suez. The action is to begin between the 20th and 26th of this month.

A less rosy picture is painted for me by Renato Ricci. He talks about the industrial and food situations as they will be during the coming winter. He predicts that we shall have to tighten our belts; nothing compared to last winter.

Arpinati asks a favor for some of his friends. He describes the situation in Romagna as dull and dubious, attributing this in large measure to the fact that too many women of the Mussolini family are poking their noses into the local situation. To these is now added the Petacci woman, who, in Rimini, where she is staying at the beach, passes judgment, orders people about, and is given to intrigues. Her spokesman and agent is a certain Spisani, a third-rate dancing teacher. Funny anecdotes are reported. It appears that Miss. Petacci recently traveled to Budapest, which is likely, because she is trying to get a divorce. To someone who asked her for news of her trip, she replied, "I had neither receptions nor parties. I went there absolutely incognito."

August 7, 1942

At Forlì to attend the placing of Bruno's remains in a vault. On the train I spoke with Vidussoni. Besides being rather unintelligent, he displays brazen ignorance. He spoke "of the history of Fascism by Oriani," but meant Orano. But to him it's all the same. He said that he did not know who "De Chirico was, because for two years he had been too busy reading modern writers." What makes things worse is that he no longer holds his tongue; he talks too much and insists on having his say.

Mussolini wanted the ceremony in the cemetery of San Cassiano to be a family affair. There were eight of us in the crypt—his closest relatives and the widow. There was a lot of sadness, a sort of catacomb atmosphere, and three tombs of gray stone—for the two parents of Mussolini and his son. On Bruno's tomb a painting of him, gay and smiling, increases sadness. The mass was short, and performed by a priest who drew out the Latin *s*'s like those of his Romagnolo dialect. The Duce was apparently impassive but inwardly tormented. After the ceremony he kissed Bruno's tomb and, indicating the empty space between Bruno and the altar, said a number of times that that was to be his place. We then went to Rocca and to Carpena. Mussolini wanted to visit the places of Bruno's childhood. He was angry because the members of his family had accepted a basket of foodstuffs from the peasants. "I do not intend to return from the tomb of my son with chickens and pears," he commented. He was right.

August 8, 1942

Mussolini is back in Rome. I had a long conversation with him about certain matters, which had been delayed during his absence. Generally speaking, Hitler's letter was of no great importance, and with regard to Greece he avoids any and all commitments. It is the food situation which concerns the

Duce. Not at this time, since vegetables and fruit allow a temporary well-being, but later, during the winter, everything will be scarce and perhaps it will be impossible to increase the bread ration. There are cases of malnutrition in some provinces. It isn't too pervasive a phenomenon, but it is ugly. Mussolini thinks about it more than he talks about it, and more than he would have others believe. His stomach cramps have returned; the old ulcer has come to life again. This means that he is worrying.

Pareschi, who is usually optimistic, is far from being encouraging at present. He would like to find foodstuffs abroad. But it is useless. I believe that this year we shall receive very little, perhaps nothing. There will be suffering also on account of the cold. There is no coal, and wood will be rationed.

Alfieri took a useless trip to the Russian front, where he saw Hitler. He learned nothing specific, and for this reason he chatters a lot. Mussolini, too, thinks that Alfieri has come to the end of his usefulness; maybe not today, but in any case I must be ready with his successor.

August 9, 1942
Nothing new.

August 10, 1942
News of the day: the taking of Maikop by the Germans and agitation in India. Mussolini attributes to both facts a great deal of importance. The first will relieve the Axis, but not immediately, and not completely, of the pressing oil problem. The second could, in the Duce's opinion, provoke an Asian crisis. If Japan should decide to march on India, great and surprising developments might be expected. But will Japan do it? From here it is not possible to forecast, considering the fact that China, according to what Ambassador Taliani[537] cables today, is more than ever of one mind in being anti-Japanese; and even Wang Ching-Wei, the Laval of Nanking, has given up trying to bring about a *rapprochement* between the two peoples. In my opinion, the struggle between China and Japan will be eternal. There will be lulls, it will have vicissitudes favoring first one side and then the other, but it will never quiet down. More than a political fact, it is a biological fact, and biologically China is very strong.

August 11, 1942
Meeting of the Council of Ministers. The measures considered dealt with ordinary administration, but they nonetheless gave Mussolini a cue to make certain interesting statements regarding his trip to Libya, on the fall of the empire, and on the progress of the war. He was more optimistic than ever in his forecast for the future: the war has already been won because the Anglo-Saxons, having divided their forces on so many fronts, cannot seriously engage in any offensive action.

Grandi was pessimistic in commenting on the Duce's statements. Grandi is very much disturbed by the internal situation and said that for the first time in twenty years he has asked for carabinieri to protect his villa. He exaggerates. He hates Cavallero. "That rascal," he said, "is preparing himself to become the Italian Pétain and would like to kill us all. But we shall bump him off first."

A great English convoy, well escorted, is sailing from Gibraltar to the East. Our air and naval forces have already taken position. Tomorrow will be a hard-fought day.

August 12, 1942

The air and naval battle is in progress. For the time being details are not available. Fougier and Casero are not too pleased. The Germans have announced the sinking of the English aircraft carrier *Eagle*, but there are many reasons to doubt this. By tomorrow at dawn a naval engagement is expected. However, we are in a position of inferiority. The big ships cannot leave port because of a gasoline shortage and lack of light escort craft.

August 13, 1942

All attention is concentrated on the battle in the Mediterranean. It appears that things are developing rather well for us, but we have paid with the loss of the *Bolzano*, and damage suffered by the *Attendolo* was a high price. At the moment only four ships of the convoy have reached Malta. Mussolini is moderately satisfied with the results, "because the guns of the navy were not engaged in the battle."

August 14, 1942

No news.

August 15, 1942

The Roman midsummer holiday; the city is empty as usual. It seems that this morning at the railroad stations, as the trains were leaving, there was behavior worthy of barbarians. The people do not wish to change their habits, if they can get away with it, and everybody wants to have a good time. The war? They want to forget it.

A long conversation with Buti, who, according to his personality, delivers what he has to say in mouthfuls and morsels, saying nothing that commits him too much, and is very reticent. This is more or less what he thinks: French hatred is growing by leaps and bounds against the Germans, not against us. But nothing will happen; in any event, they will not go beyond their present demonstrations: shootings, sabotage, nothing more. The government believes in a victory of the Axis; the people believe in a victory of the Allies. Everybody despises De Gaulle, as a person, but the country is Gaullist at heart. The blow has been heavy for the French, and this is more evident in things generally than it is in individuals. The French have remained what they were before: same habits, same ideas, same prejudices. They cannot explain why, but they are convinced that in the future they will still have a great deal to say. Naturally they look more toward Moscow and Washington than toward London. "The feeling of the French with regard to the British is identical to the way the Italians regard the Germans." For once he couldn't have been more explicit.

August 16, 1942

Resistance on the Russian front seems to stiffen. In any event, there are no indications of a collapse either possible or imminent. From a Turkish cable, intercepted by our services, it would seem that the standard of life in Russia is quite good and the spirit of the people hopeful. "Emaciated faces," cables Ambassador Zobune, "I have seen only in Vienna and Munich. In Kuibyshev everybody lives well and eats very abundantly." He relates that the real enemy of the diplomatic set is boredom, and that in order to defeat it everybody has resorted to drink with great determination. I must say that I have seen many of my colleagues get drunk even without this excuse.

A discussion between Giannini and Clodius for the maintenance of food supplies to our Expeditionary Corps in Russia. The Germans want to place it entirely on our shoulders, contrary to existing agreements. Giannini insisted strongly, but the German embassy in Rome has brought the matter up and we shall see what Mussolini will decide.

Bulgarian frontier break-throughs into Albania. It appears that the Germans are behind this; they have their eyes on the mines of Jezerina.

I am dissatisfied, and now believe that I shall recall Tamaro, Minister to Switzerland. He is mixed up in a policy of resentment and I believe that it is in our interest, present and future, to be friendly with Switzerland.

August 17, 1942

In Leghorn.

August 25, 1942

I leave Leghorn for Budapest, for the funeral of Stephen Horthy, who was killed in an airplane accident.

August 26, 1942

I arrive in Budapest. The city is in mourning and very sad. From the windows and from the archways long black streamers are hanging, which contrast with the enamel blue of the sky. The Regent is the first person I see. Our meeting at the gateway is casual. He is very much touched, and leaves at once. Later he receives me in his study. He speaks with relative calm, and would like to discuss general politics. But he is still upset by his sorrow for the loss of his son, and is thinking of the succession. The death of Stephen today seems to indicate the collapse of what he has accomplished so far. He has no clear ideas, but from various hints I take it that he is thinking of having the designation go to his son's son, who is a baby one year old. Nonsense. Everybody in Hungary, even those who were favorable to the vice-regency of Stephen Horthy, is very much opposed to a solution that would tie the hands of the Magyar people for a period of twenty or thirty years. Kallay tells me this himself, and in Hungarian politics he is a strong follower of the Regent.

I have drawn up a statement on the conference with Kanya. It has been suggested that a solution would be to have Victor Emmanuel III become the nominal sovereign of both countries. I have noted my remarks and objections elsewhere. I believe the idea is impossible, or at least very premature.

August 27, 1942

Hungarian ceremonial funerals have a certain oriental and imposing quality. Much commotion and many tears, but more for the grief of the mother than for the loss of Stephen Horthy.

Long conversations with Ribbentrop. His courtesy is really unusual. He comes to see me first, invites me to lunch, steps back at every doorway, even though with the Hungarians he wants to make it clear that he occupies first place, contrary to every right and tradition. (The Hungarians, who hate the Germans but who tremble in their presence, try to please him by suggesting that precedence be determined according to the French alphabetical order of nations: Allemagne, Italie, et cetera. Much ado about nothing!)

Ribbentrop's tone is moderate, even though he continues to be optimistic. The German *"Krieg ist schon gewonnen"*[538] of the old days has now become [in English] "We cannot lose this war." He is obviously coming off his high horse. He gave no particulars, but he judges Russia to be a hard nut, very hard, and thinks that not even if Japan should attack her would she be entirely knocked out. He makes no forecasts about the length of the war; it might have a rapid conclusion, "but one must not count too much on that."

He repeated his invitation for the usual hunting party at Schönhof toward the end of October.

August 28, 1942

In Venice. A visit to the biennial. Paintings and sculpture are very interesting. In general, the Spanish pavilion is the best. We had two painters who are important: De Chirico and Sciltian.

August 29, 1942

I report to Mussolini on my trip to Budapest and give him notes on the meeting with Kanya. The Duce's reaction is 100 percent negative. The main reason for this is concern over the Germans. He is convinced—and he is right—that Hitler, even if he were to accept such a thing, would bill us for it, and would make us pay dearly as soon as possible. The second element has to do with the growing hostility of Mussolini toward the monarchies and toward our own monarchy. "I entertained a similar proposition regarding the Duke of Aosta, but with him dead nothing else will be done."

With the approval of the Duce, Grandi had arranged for a trip to Spain. Now I have received instructions to tell him to forget about it. Grandi understood the idea and has postponed the trip without objection.

August 30, 1942

Ghigi sends an SOS from Greece. The Germans are still insisting on astronomical indemnities, the government threatens to resign, trouble may begin any minute. In any case, I advise Mussolini not to take any initiative. He had promised the Greeks to plead for them with Hitler, and wrote him a letter, but Hitler refused. One cannot fail twice without losing too much prestige. This argument of mine led Mussolini to expatiate on an article that appeared in a German magazine. The New Order is described in detail, including the role of all peoples, as well as the allies of Germany. No liberty, no rights, except that of serving the nation "who will be at the head." I cabled Alfieri to learn whether the ideas in the article reflected those of the leading classes in Germany. I think that even if the answer is no it means yes.

August 31, 1942
Yesterday evening at eight o'clock Rommel attacked in Libya. He has chosen the day and the hour well, at a time when no one was expecting the attack and whisky had begun to appear on the English tables. Mussolini expresses no opinion, but is basically optimistic. Cavallero, who had shown no signs of life for a long time, telephones to give me news of the operation. As usual he wavers between "yes" and "no." He does not wish to compromise himself, but intends to remain sufficiently near to gather the fruits of victory, if there are any. Churchill, according to what the Turkish ambassador has cabled to his government, has said that if Rommel had not attacked in two weeks he would have taken the initiative in the operations. He believes that English forces are sufficient for any situation, but wishes to adopt a phrase used by Stalin: "Anything is possible, since war is war."

September 1, 1942
There is no big news. In Egypt the English are withdrawing toward the sea, offering a minimum of resistance. Mussolini believes that they want to resist on the coast, where they can have the support of the naval forces.
Jacomoni makes a rather reassuring report on the Albanian situation. All we need is the certainty of a minimum of food to maintain order in the country, notwithstanding the fact that enemy propaganda is now aiming at Albania, which represents the only oasis of peace in all the Balkans. From documents that have come into possession of the government it seems that the English are attempting to start uprisings and disorders in order to be able, at the moment of peace, to compromise those who were in favor of union with Italy, and to destroy any legal basis to the relations between the Albanians and us.

September 2, 1942
Rommel is stopped in Egypt because of a lack of fuel. Three of our oil tankers have been sunk in two days. Cavallero maintains that this will not change the course of operations, and that other means will be found to deliver the gasoline. Instead of the oil tankers, which are too easily identified, ordinary boats and hospital ships can be used. (This is an old system that goes well as long as it works.) Nevertheless, Cavallero repeats that Rommel's push is meant to reach the Canal this time.

September 3, 1942
Rommel's pause continues, and, what is worse, the sinking of our ships continues. Tonight there have been two. Cavallero repeats his optimistic

declarations, and says that within a week the march will be resumed. Rintelen, who has just arrived from Libya today, is less sure. Everything, not just fuel, is lacking. Hence, action this time is, according to him, a little risky, and may turn out well or badly. Mussolini is in a dark mood. He does not express himself; in fact, he has been silent on the subject of Egypt for three days. Once more he suffers from stomach pains. Yesterday he had himself examined by a radiologist. There was nothing serious the matter with him, except gastritis, but it is painful and debilitating. Today, while he was conferring with Jacomoni and me on the Albanian situation, he was unable to hide his pain. Yesterday the Duce sent a cable to the industrial workers. He praised them and violently threatened other greedy, odious, and egotistical groups. Everybody thought that he was aiming at the middle class, as usual, but, on the contrary, he was striking at the farmers, who, "after the regime has followed a policy in their favor for twenty years, take everything and are greedy for money to the point of deserving the worst punishment, the infliction of which would, after all, result in benefiting only the state. Nevertheless, this year no one will die of hunger, and if many Italians have to grow lean, it will be good for them."

September 4, 1942

What is happening in Libya is not clear. Rommel is drawing back his left flank under the attack of the British air force even before enemy tanks go into action. Tonight two other ships were sunk. Our supply problem is difficult. Rintelen maintains that the offensive should be postponed indefinitely. Casero is of the same opinion.

A governmental crisis in Spain. It had become inevitable. I was convinced of this in Leghorn when I heard how Serrano was talking about Franco. He spoke of him like someone speaks of a moronic servant. And he said this openly, in the presence of everybody. It is too early to say what the consequences of this development will be. The only indication might be the choice of Jordana, and this is not favorable. Jordana has always been a man not wholeheartedly with the Axis and a sympathizer with France and Great Britain. On the other hand, lately, many events prove that the Iberian peninsula is beginning to entertain doubts about the future, and wishes to remain on friendly terms with everybody. Maybe Serrano will come to Rome. I am not enthusiastic about the idea, because Serrano is an intriguer and a gossip, and may be the cause of great embarrassment. We must be extremely careful about him.

September 5-7, 1942

Three days with the flu.

September 8, 1942

Bigliardi informs me about the reasons that led Rommel to cancel the offensive: the vast increase in numbers and quality of British-American supplies; the superiority of the Allied air force; lack of supplies in general and of fuel in particular.

The first sign of the direction in which Jordana is going in Spain: the submarine *Giuliani*, which is being repaired at San Sebastian, with many dead and wounded on board, has for all practical purposes been interned. When this happened under Serrano Suñer our submarines could come and go into Spanish ports as if they were public parks.

September 9, 1942

I call Mussolini's attention to the Albanian situation. More than of the inevitable undercurrent of discontent, I am concerned about our lack of troops. There are 4 divisions, but in name only; actually, 11,000 men. Under these circumstances, any kind of surprise is possible. Cavallero, to whom I communicated the alarm, could do nothing more than give me 50 tanks; not enough. The Duce sounds off one of his periodic attacks on the army, with which everything is going badly and nothing is improving. He talks also about operations in Libya. The idea of an offensive is now shelved, at least for some time. Let us hope that the enemy will not take too much advantage of it. Then, he is also angry with Rommel, who, according to English sources, has cabled, accusing several of our officers of having revealed some of his future plans to the enemy. As always, victory finds a hundred fathers, but defeat is an orphan. Now they are quarreling in Libya, and Kesselring ran to Berlin to complain about Rommel. They are talking about a possible recall of Rommel.

Gambara emerged unscathed from the investigation directed against him. He will get another command. I am happy about it, because he is a patriotic Italian and a soldier, and for these very reasons they were trying to stab him in the back.

Churchill has spoken after a long silence. It is an unruffled speech, and for the most part, optimistic.

September 10, 1942

I accompany the secretary of the Albanian National party to see the Duce.

Casero summarizes the issue of airplane production concerning ourselves, the Germans, and the Allies. The proportions are changing every day to our disadvantage and on a large scale.

September 11, 1942

I leave for Leghorn, where I will stay until September 23.

September 22, 1942

This is what happened during my stay in Leghorn.

Fougier describes our airplane production in dark colors. Between Germany and ourselves we produce less than one-fifth or one-sixth of what the Allies produce. The enlistment of pilots is also short and falling off. During the summer of 1943 the Allies will definitely have control of the skies.

D'Aieta reports to me a very confidential conversation with Bismarck, who now is sure that Germany will be defeated but will go on to the "bitter end." Italy will find a way out; and to this end may contribute the measured policy that I have always maintained toward England and America. It is because of this policy that Ribbentrop especially, and the Germans in general, hate me. If "they should win the war, my head would be the first one they would want." There are also many Italians who denounce me to the German embassy as being pro-English. Mackensen reports on everything, but he comments about me in a friendly way.

Bottai stayed with me for two days. He also sees a dark future. According to his nature, he indulges in useless details. He says that the war is illegal, because the Grand Council was not consulted. He is, as always, hostile to Mussolini. He calls him "a self-taught man who had a bad teacher, and who was a worse student."

September 23, 1942

I find nothing new in Rome. On this first day I have no conversations of any importance. I talk with Mackensen about organizing certain celebrations for the Tripartite Pact. Ribbentrop misses no occasion to exalt this beloved child of his.

Guariglia says nothing new on Myron Taylor's trip.[539] It is clear, at any rate, that at the Vatican they keep us informed only about what they want us to know. The only interesting thing is that the Germans have asked the Pope to intervene to stop the bombing of German open cities. The word "Coventrize" was coined in Germany, as I recall!

September 24, 1942

The lull on the two fronts has undoubtedly made a bad impression on public opinion. For the first time people are no longer asking themselves about the length of the war, but about its progress. That is how people with whom I have had occasion to talk express themselves.

A brief conversation with Arpinati, who recommends to me an employee of the Office of Corporations. Arpinati makes few comments regarding the general situation, and what he says is not interesting. The few conversations I have had with him give me the impression that this man has a very average mind. They say that he is an honest man. This may be true, but that is all there is to him.

Albini is skeptical about the situation in Naples. There is a lot of misery, a great deal of hunger, and concern that bombings on a large scale will resume.

Ricci wants me to get a little more involved with the internal situation, which, according to him, is at its lowest point. But why should I get mixed up in it? Under what pretense?

September 25, 1942

I had a few more conversations, and all those whom I spoke to were depressed. Morgagni, who is anything but a friend of mine, was more explicit than the others. Things are not going well at the front, and very badly inside the country. What, then, will the future bring? I limited myself to replying that while I was always cautious when others are optimistic, I am calm and quiet when others are in despair. I don't know how, nor can I say why, but I am certain that things cannot go completely wrong for us. Bastianini also sees everything painted black. But this is his usual way, and I don't remember ever having had a conversation with him in which he didn't make some forecasts. He isn't a great intellect and doesn't see very far ahead; what he sees is always so damn dark.

The most pessimistic report that has come to us from Germany lately is from the young Consul Farinacci. What would his father think?

From Berlin through Alfieri, who approves of it, comes the proposal that we give Myron Taylor a "solemn booing." How foolish! I can't say whether it is more ridiculous or disgusting. It would appear that the inventor of this idea was that cripple Goebbels. It doesn't even deserve an answer.

September 26, 1942

I receive a letter from Edda, which disturbs me a great deal. I attach it to this page.

Dear Gallo: I arrived last evening at eleven, after a terrible trip. I was told, with that idiotic inconsistency which makes mine the most impossible of families, that they were all leaving today, but that if I wanted to remain I could . . . My mother has no sense of humor. However, she says and does the funniest things . . . Anyway, this is not why I am writing you. My father is not well. Stomach pains, irritability, depression, et cetera. My mother draws a rather dark picture. In my opinion it's the old ulcer again. (His private life of the last few years gives us much to think about, its effects, et cetera.... Well, let's not talk about it.) They took X-ray pictures of every kind—all negative—but a doctor was never called. When, having called for Frugoni, they learned that he would not be in Rome until the 4th, they gave it up and . . . let it all slide! I have known few such scatterbrained people. Please get on the job yourself. If it isn't Frugoni, then let it be Pontano; if not him, then somebody else, anything so that my father is seen and examined and examined properly. Communicate with my mother and help her. So far the only measures taken have been blasphemy and curses. In an illness, a clinic is to be preferred, though, naturally, with a certain secrecy. Even though it was a beautiful day, I had a sense of suffocation and fear. Maybe because I am so tired that I feel as if I were poisoned. Tonight I haven't slept a wink, because, as the song says, "All through the night in vain, with candle in hand, I hunted the ugly beast." On my unprotected bed hundreds of mosquitoes charged forth. That's Capri for you. Some time today I shall leave for Castrocaro, where I hope to sleep. The children, as you will see, are well. The governess has been given her instructions. Hurray for Colonel Oliva![540] Dear Gallo, let's take it as it comes, chin up! I urge you to get to work about the doctors, et cetera. I embrace you affectionately,

EDDA

Tomorrow I shall see Donna Rachele and will decide what can possibly be done. Under the circumstances, an ill Duce would be really disastrous.

Alfieri cables that the German Chief of Staff, Halder, has been sacked. Halder is an important figure in the German military world. An ugly sign.

September 27, 1942

I see the Duce again, after a long absence. I find him thinner but solid, and his appearance doesn't seem to confirm Edda's troubled impression. As always he is calm, but he realizes that military events have cut deeply into the morale of the population, especially the Stalingrad resistance, which makes clear in the minds of the masses the great attachment of the Russian people to the regime—a thing proved by the exceptional resistance and spirit of sacrifice. I have had a visit from Rommel, who said that he is leaving on a six weeks' furlough. Mussolini is convinced that Rommel will not come back. He finds Rommel physically and morally shaken. I didn't conceal from the Duce my view of the situation, summing it up as follows: "We are starting the winter in a state of mind in which, at the worst, we should be at the end of the winter."

A dinner for the Tripartite group. A rather heavy atmosphere. The only noteworthy event was Cavallero's *faux pas* when, to endear himself to the Japanese ambassador, he gave him news of successes at Stalingrad. When Cavallero's English and that of Horichiri mixed together, the result was that Stalingrad had fallen. The rumor spread through the hall, until the Germans, to Cavallero's great shame, immediately denied it. Bottai heard the Japanese general offer the German assistant military attaché his congratulations for the victory. The German, in his rough Italian, answered dryly and in a military style, "Nonsense."

September 28, 1942

Nothing new.

September 29, 1942

Host Venturi is concerned about the many sinkings of our merchant fleet. Replacements are slow and totally inadequate. As of now, we have little more than a million tons left in all. At this rate the African problem will automatically end in six months, since we shall have no more ships to supply Libya. Venturi will give me a detailed report in a few days.

September 30, 1942

From Berlin and Vienna we get very pessimistic reports. Even Alfieri, as is his nature, with many buts and maybes, says that things are not going well, and that the summer offensive has failed to accomplish its purpose. The bombings are terrorizing the German population, often paralyzing daily life.

D'Agostino, Director of the Lavoro Bank, will go to Switzerland soon. I give him many good-will messages for his banker friends. I believe in the future function and possibilities of Switzerland, and am convinced that we must cultivate Swiss friendship.

October 1, 1942

Hitler has spoken. *Quantum mutatus ab illo.*[541] Last year, at about this time, he also gave a speech that was a paean of victory. Now, at best, it may be said that he has made a defensive address. As usual on such an occasion, Alfieri is silent.

Pareschi gave me a very realistic note on the food question today. Winter will be harder than expected, and if the Germans do not really give us a hand we do not know where to get an adequate food supply.

October 2, 1942

No new event of any importance, but both from within and without pessimistic reports continue to reach us. From without, it is especially our consuls in Germany and our Balkan legations that give us discouraging news. From within, almost everybody is. Today, for example, I met Federzoni and Del Croix. Both have just returned after their vacation. Well, they spoke as if they had had some previous understanding, the same observations, the same forecast, and identical regrets.

October 3, 1942

Nothing new.

October 4, 1942

Castellani sends me the results of the diagnosis that he made of the Duce. Naturally in this case, too, Castellani has discovered his usual amoeba. As for myself, I believe he invented it. Nevertheless, Mussolini, although he feels some slight pain, looks well, and his capacity for work has not at all diminished.

Otherwise there is nothing new.

October 5, 1942

Nothing new.

October 6, 1942

Clodius is in Rome to discuss the Greek financial question, which is becoming more and more thorny. If it continues at this rate sensational and unavoidable inflation will result, with all its consequences. Ghigi foresees that the situation will be very bad. The amount of Greek money in circulation is 160 billion. Before the war it was 9 billion. The Greeks are required to supply 53 billion a month. All this is absurd, but the German army does not intend to reduce its interest rate. Clodius agrees with us, but can do nothing about it. He will return to Berlin to confer with his superiors. He makes no comment on the general situation, but says only that by the end of October the cycle of summer operations may be considered at an end, and that this year the Russian front will cause "much less anxiety than last winter."

October 7, 1942

Dr. Kesterer, the man whom Himmler calls "The Magic Buddha," and who cures everything through massage, told me today that Himmler and von Ribbentrop are at loggerheads, but that the first is powerful and the second will be sacked because he is "insane and ill." Hitler hardly ever receives him. This must be true in part, because von Ribbentrop energetically opposed Himmler's trip to Italy, and even now demands that the program of the visit be reduced to its bare essentials.

Mussolini is disturbed over the gossip about the arrival of Myron Taylor in Rome. All this gossip is unimportant and unfounded, because we know nothing as to what he has said and done. But all this talk is a provocation and I am certain that in the future it will make any visits to the Vatican by Anglo-Saxon visitors more difficult.

October 8, 1942

Mussolini is very much disturbed by the attitude of the Germans in occupied countries, especially in Greece. The claims that have been set forth are quite absurd. This means that the Germans are trying to create disorders and complications at all costs. The Duce said, "I have no qualms about the military course of the war. There will be neither surprises nor second fronts, but if we lose the war it will be because of the political stupidity of the Germans, who have not even tried to use common sense and restraint, and who have made Europe as hot and treacherous as a volcano." He is thinking of speaking to Himmler about this next Sunday, but he will not get anywhere.

I receive Count Capodistria, mayor of Corfu. He is a serious, restrained, and distinguished old man, and expresses himself in excellent Italian. He declares that the Ionian populations would like to have some administrative freedom, but that they do not at all want to return to the odious Hellenic government, and prefer to link their destinies to those of Italy. A plebiscite on this issue today would give almost unanimous results. The work of Parini has been highly praised and he really deserves it.

October 9, 1942

A long conference with General Amè, head of the SIM, who was clearly pessimistic. All the information and the conversation lead one to conclude that the Anglo-Saxons are preparing to land in force in North Africa, whence, later on, they intend to strike against the Axis. Italy is geographically and logically the first objective. How long shall we have the strength to resist a determined, strong, and methodical air and naval offensive? On the Russian front there will be no important news, and if there were it would probably not be in our favor.

The situation inside Germany is heavy and oppressive. Prospects cannot be good and, according to him, that is what the majority of the officers think who are not drawing any conclusions. They observe but do not talk, and do not offer any forecasts. Amè reported these and other things to Cavallero who, however, pretends to be too deaf to understand.

Clodius informs me that Germany is ready to reduce its claims to 18 or perhaps 15 billion a month, but that Gotzamanis rejects even these proposals.[542] I shall have a meeting in my office tomorrow. Mussolini is convinced of the harmful uselessness of the Ministry of Currency and Exchange and has promised me that he will abolish it soon. That will be an excellent move.

October 10, 1942

Council of Ministers. Routine matters. But this did not prevent the Duce from repeating his optimistic statements about the future. His opinion, as well about the morale of the Italian people, is very assured. "We cannot expect enthusiasm from a people who know that they must still face heavy sacrifices before victory, and must show discipline, obedience, tenacity— virtues which they have beyond all measure."

In the afternoon a meeting to discuss Greece. Clodius withdraws the proposals which he had made through official channels. On the other hand, Gotzamanis explains that Greece can no longer yield anything for the simple and clear reason that it has nothing to offer. If we continue on the present course the most complete bankruptcy will take place within two months. Today the middle class must already give up its jewels, its beds, at times its daughters, in order to survive. Hence, we face uprisings and disorders, the size of which it is impossible to estimate accurately at this time. But nothing can make the Germans change their absurd and idiotic attitude, and the worst of it is that we Italians must suffer 80 percent of the consequences.

Mussolini's health is unchanged. We do not notice anything special and he says nothing, but he suffers severe stomach pains. Castellani now thinks he has had a recurrence of his ulcer condition.

October 11, 1942

I receive Himmler at the station. He has just returned from the front. He does not hide his joy at being in a beautiful city again and under a blue sky. The memory of the front is a nightmare to him, and he doesn't hide it. At Castel Fusano I see the Prince of Piedmont. He scolds me because I have not been to see him for a long time. He says little about the situation and speaks as he must in public, somewhat optimistically, but when I speak frankly about today and tomorrow he becomes expansive and recalls that I had the courage to say the same thing two or three years ago. He tells me that he has seen Mussolini, who said that 1943 will be a hard year for the Axis but that 1944 will be more favorable and that 1945 will bring us victory, but in repeating this the Prince did not hide his skepticism.

A long conversation with Himmler. He says nothing very important, but what counts is the extremely reserved tone of his conversation. He is no longer the Himmler who in Munich in 1938 was unhappy because an agreement had been reached and war appeared to be averted. Now he speaks of the difficulties, of the sacrifices, of what has been done, and, above all, what remains to be done. He wanted to find out a lot about Italy. In particular he wanted to know about the monarchy and about the Vatican. He praised the loyalty of the first and the discretion of the second.

October 12, 1942

Nothing new in politics. The Duce was about to leave for Rocca, but had to postpone his trip because of a bad attack of gastritis, which compelled him to stay in bed.

October 13, 1942

I met Castellani, who talked to me about the Duce's health. His diagnosis, and that of Frugoni, would seem to indicate that the old ulcer has reappeared, and is now complicated by an acute attack of dysentery. Castellani maintains that the Duce must have a long rest, but denies that there is anything to worry about. I am happy about it, because now, more than ever, the Duce's health is indispensable.

October 14, 1942

Himmler leaves. He is very much satisfied by his visit to Rome: he needed to be in a civilized atmosphere for a while after long, horrible days at the front. He didn't say much, but I must also add that he was very moderate.

Göring will come to Rome in a few days to pick up his wife, who is in Naples. He told me he would only be in Rome for two hours, that he wants no one at the railroad to welcome him, and wants to be received by Mussolini on Monday at 11 a.m. (sic!).

October 15, 1942

Nothing new.

October 16, 1942

The Spaniards ask that we accept Fernandez-Cuesta as ambassador. I met him immediately after the fall of Madrid and he made a good impression. It appears that he did very well in Brazil. In any event, he is to be preferred to Serrano Suñer, who evidently didn't know his place and had turned the Spanish embassy into a dangerous center of gossip.

The Germans inform us that Sapuppo in Copenhagen is making defeatist statements, and that therefore it is desirable that he be recalled. I have taken measures for his recall, without attempting to defend him. And this because Sapuppo is essentially a fool, and it is always hopeless to defend fools.

According to the Duce's entourage we are told that he may not be in condition to receive Göring on Monday. In any event, he will have to receive him at home, and the Duce is somewhat embarrassed on account of the modesty of his living quarters. Yesterday, however, I was told that he was almost well, and his voice over the telephone seemed strong and assured.

October 17, 1942

After a conference with Ghigi, Giannini, and Baldoni,[543] I telephoned the Duce about the real situation in the Greek negotiations. Tough going! The Germans, with utter obtuseness, insist on demanding a crazy sum which in the space of a few months would cause the total collapse of the drachma. Even before this we shall have a political crisis, because the Greek government will resign, and then we can hold the country only by force of arms. The Duce agrees with me, and expresses himself in harsh terms against the Germans. He goes so far as to say that "the only way to explain such a savage attitude on the part of the Germans is that they are convinced that they have lost, and since they have to die, they want to create general confusion."

But a little later Ribbentrop telephoned to tell me that he has sent new proposals to Rome through Neubacher.[544] He added that things were going very well on the Stalingrad front, where yesterday they had made great progress. He was ostentatiously cordial and repeated many times that we ought to get together.

October 18, 1942
Nothing new.

October 19, 1942
Mussolini was getting ready to go to the Palazzo Venezia to receive Göring when Mackensen informed us that the Reichsmarshal had been stricken tonight by violent dysentery which did not "allow him to leave his throne, even for ten minutes." The expression isn't very respectful, but it was used textually in the message. Bismarck also repeated it, in a more ludicrous tone. It must be recognized that such an ailment is not particularly becoming to the glamorous vanity of the Reichsmarshal.

Neubacher, appointed by Ribbentrop as special commissioner for Greek economic and financial affairs, has arrived Rome. We shall appoint one of our own with the same powers. I suggested D'Agostino,[545] who has the necessary qualifications, and he was accepted. The Duce was favorable to a solution that "probably will help us find the thread to unravel the skein."

Jacomoni makes a rather favorable report on the Albanian situation. He believes that the critical period is now over, and that, with some forceful gesture against the rebels, it may be possible to bring order and tranquility back to the country.

October 20, 1942
Nothing new.

October 21, 1942
A meeting about Greek economic affairs, attended by Mackensen, Neubacher, D'Agostino, Ghigi, and Gotzamanis. Neubacher is the only one who is convinced that big things can be accomplished. The others are quite skeptical, especially Gotzamanis, who undoubtedly is the one who knows the conditions and the possibilities of his country best. I more or less share his skepticism, but naturally avoid saying so.

October 22, 1942

To Leghorn for the anniversary of the death of my poor dear Maria.

October 23, 1942

Genoa has been heavily bombed by the English air force, though the number of planes was no more than twenty. Anyway, we should realize that, as time passes, bombing will become our daily fare.

I see Farinacci and Bottai. They are both exasperated by the internal situation, which is aggravated by the total inadequacy of the party, in connection with which there is much talk about a report by the Federal secretaries of a meeting presided over by Farnesi at Lucca, during which the "Petacci affair" was officially discussed—whether it was a good thing or whether it was an evil, what was being said about it, etc. I wouldn't believe it, except that Aiello himself, who is serious, and who confirmed it to me, with some others, spoke up to end this obscenity.

October 24, 1942

The British have attacked in Libya. For the moment news is favorable to us. No progress was made on land. But von Stumm, the over-all commander who had taken the place of Rommel, is dead. Genoa and Milan were again the targets of heavy bombing.

October 25, 1942

Bismarck tells me that in German military quarters they view the situation in Libya with a certain optimism, provided the British offensive doesn't last too long. Our supply problem is very difficult, and reserves are entirely inadequate. This is confirmed by Colonel Casero, who says that we have no fuel stocks in Libya, even to the point where we are shipping fuel by air from Italy.

Politically, nothing new, except a short letter from Alfieri, who speaks of "the lead weight which now physically and psychologically hovers over the capital of the Reich." The Duce, who wanted to speak before a large gathering of party leaders on the 29th, has given orders to cancel everything. What's the reason? There are three current interpretations: (1) that his doctors have forbidden the strain of a long speech; (2) that he does not wish to say anything until the Libyan offensive is resolved; (3) that he intends to make big changes in the party, and, logically, he wishes to speak to the new leaders. Personally, I incline toward the second interpretation.

October 26, 1942

Today I saw the Duce for the first time in two weeks. He has lost a lot of weight, but his eyes are clear, his voice firm, and he looks bold. I would say that the ailment, in drying up his face and body, has made him more youthful. There wasn't anything of great importance to say, and that is clear, because there is silence in the field of foreign policy. The Duce was irritated with Myron Taylor and with the Vatican. He attributes the heavy bombing of our northern Italian cities to the reports of the American envoy. "This buffoon," he said, "returned to America to report that the Italians are on their last legs, and that with one or two hard blows they can easily be beaten." Anyway, "he learned these things from the Holy See, where information comes by way of the parish priests. But," says the Duce, "there they don't see that the people who follow the priests are the least courageous, and the worst, always ready to weep and beg." In any case, he wanted me to let the Vatican know that "Concordat or no Concordat, if Myron Taylor tries to return to Italy he will end up in handcuffs."

I do not share the Duce's conclusions as to the reasons which have led the Anglo-Saxons to aim these hard blows at Italy. Maybe Myron Taylor is involved, but very little. It is rather the entire offensive plan of the Americans and the British which is being applied.

In Libya it seems that they are holding up well, but with heavy losses, and with the hope that pressure will not be kept up too long.

October 27, 1942

Ley has come here to head the National Socialist Mission to the Twentieth Anniversary of the March on Rome. Vidussoni brings him in to see me. Ley is vulgar, both in appearance and in the way he thinks. In fact, he is such a bum that I wonder how he was ever able to reach a position of leadership. He says nothing new, but adds a new lie to the propaganda line: the whole Stalingrad action has cost the Germans only three thousand dead. I wouldn't believe it, even if he multiplied it by ten.

Pavolini informs me that the Duce talked to him about the incident which occurred during the report of the Federal secretaries at Lucca, when they discussed the "Petacci affair." He faced the argument squarely and said that no one has the right to "investigate and judge the emotional life of anybody else," and then he went into the history of the Renaissance to show that all men had their love affairs. He was annoyed at the party. He has every reason to be.

October 28, 1942

The Twentieth Anniversary celebration. It was just one ceremony, the inauguration of the new quarters for the Exhibit of the Revolution. Mussolini appeared in public for the first time since his illness. In the open, in uniform, surrounded by many people, he seemed thin and more tired than two days ago at the Palazzo Venezia. He was welcomed in a way that I would call affectionate. But the organization of the ceremony was far from being up to par, lacking even the least sense of camaraderie among its members. The fact is that the current party secretariat is composed of unknown men, to whom we are, in turn, unknown. This explains the coolness of the ceremony. It explains also a good many of the serious difficulties of the internal situation. On this very day of the recurrence of the Fascist celebration, the inefficiency of the party is felt more strongly than ever, because incapable, discredited, and questionable men head the party.

The battle in Libya continues to be tough. We are holding on tenaciously. To listen to the High Command, the only danger is in our lack of stocks and transportation. The tactical situation is good, the logistic situation dangerous. I am no technician, but I believe that in a battle of this kind logistics will play the decisive role.

October 29, 1942

Another oil tanker was sunk this evening. This is a black mark on the situation in Libya. Bismarck has learned from Rintelen that Rommel is optimistic about the military quality of the troops, but that he is literally terrified by the supply situation. Just now not only is fuel lacking but also ammunition and food.

The mood of the Chief is good. We have spoken of a certain Roseo, who has gone to intrigue at Court for a separate peace. He will be handcuffed. The Duce gave me a letter from Hitler on the twentieth anniversary of the founding of the Fascist party, which is extremely laudatory and sugarcoated. Mussolini expressed himself in harsh terms against the Genovese people, who are "certainly the most hostile to the war and who have shown moral weakness." On the other hand, he praised the Neapolitans, who have become fatalistic by centuries of difficulties and misery to the point of composing ironical songs about the English during the bombing raids.

A long visit from Donna Edvige Mussolini. She judges the internal situation with much common sense and is concerned about the future. She serves as a mouthpiece for what is said in various circles and would like me to take the Ministry of the Interior. She believes—and she is right—that we must give our policy a more humane character, but for nothing in the world would I want to go to the Ministry of the Interior.

October 30, 1942

Nothing of any particular importance.

October 31, 1942

General Ambrosio, who in the past was very optimistic, is now notably less so. With regard to Libya, he maintains that if the British continue to develop a battle of attrition it will be difficult for us to avoid a retreat; and with regard to Russia, he fears that during the winter there will be a Soviet counteroffensive and that it will start against our armies. Although everything has been done to assure our troops decent living conditions, we must expect greater difficulties than last year, because now they have no native houses to live in, nor have they the coal that was available in the Donetz basin. All this leads General Ambrosio to modify his rosy predictions of the past.

I received the Swiss banker, Vieli, to whom I offered many olive branches. I strongly believe in the present and future European function of Switzerland. Furthermore, we have great need of her now.

Alessi informs me that Petacci's brother wrote a letter to Prefect Tamburini, saying that Castellani had made the wrong diagnosis and cure for the Duce. He wanted Tamburini to put pressure on Donna Rachele, with whom he has cordial relations, to persuade her to call in a new doctor.

November 1, 1942

Sorrentino, who is an intelligent journalist, even if odd and a little bit sectarian, returns from a long stay in Russia definitely pessimistic. To listen to him, even the sanctum sanctorum of the German spirit—the army—is weakened by its worst enemy: a doubting mind. "This year we were fighting to avoid defeat. It hasn't gone very well." Now the Germans themselves believe in defeat, and perhaps many among them even hope for it.

I spoke to our Minister in Lisbon, Fransoni, who is not exactly an ace, but who is an honest man. The attitude toward the Axis has changed a lot in Portugal, and all the Anglo-Saxon preparations lead one to believe that in a short while a powerful blow will be delivered in the Mediterranean to strike at Italy, which is thought to be the Achilles' heel of the Axis. Mussolini has written a letter to answer Hitler's. He concludes by setting the date of a meeting in Salzburg at the end of November.

At golf I meet Senator Castellani, who speaks positively about the Duce's health. The crisis is over, convalescence may still require some time, but it will only be convalescence.

November 2, 1942

The Duce is in a very good mood. Maybe because the progress of operations in Libya is quite satisfactory. He vents his displeasure at the *Osservatore Romano*, which is hurling anti-dictatorial darts, and this leads him to observe that Catholicism and Christianity are on the decline "because they wish to make people believe a number of things which do not agree with our modern concept of life. For example, at a certain point I decided that even regarding miracles it was necessary to adopt autarchy, and I referred this to the Vatican. As a result, they launched the Madonna of Loreto in competition with that of Lourdes, and one must agree that they did a swell business."

Farnesi has come to see me. He feels the earth giving way beneath him, and would like to build some bridges. I did not conceal from him that on many issues I disagree with the present leadership of the party, for reasons of substance and form, but I haven't slammed the door on them. I think they will have a short tenure, and for my part I am not going to help them keep their jobs. But I don't think it is sensible to start internal dissension within the party at a moment like this.

November 3, 1942

A new and more violent English attack makes our Libyan position very dangerous. Our forces are wearing out and supplies are arriving as if delivered through an eyedropper. We really seem to be condemned to fight wars overseas. That crook Cavallero continues to give the watchword of optimism at headquarters, but on the sidelines they see the future very black, and are already thinking of withdrawing to defend Tripolitania. Rommel thinks the situation is "very serious." This, at any rate, is what Bismarck reports. Bismarck is in deadly fear of betraying himself, and urges that his confidential information be given to no one.

November 4, 1942

After a long interval I see Cavallero in the Duce's antechamber. He tells me how things are going in Libya. Two days ago Rommel supposedly wanted to begin his withdrawal, but Hitler nailed him to the spot with the order to "show the troops the way of victory or death." Mussolini did the same with our forces. Now the battle is in full swing, and Cavallero, who is usually unduly optimistic, is reserved, though he adds quickly that "his faith is intact." I believe little in any of the virtues of this faker, and his type of faith especially convinces me least of all. From Gibraltar we learn that a great convoy is being prepared, which even includes monitors with 381-caliber guns. This suggests the possibility of a landing in Morocco.

The Duce is angry at the Vatican because of the attitude of the *Osservatore Romano,* and he wishes to "break a few wooden heads." He has had this in mind for a long time, especially since the party encourages him along this line. I disagree with this, and, up to now, I have succeeded in avoiding any crisis with the Vatican. But now he wants to give personal instructions to Guariglia, who will come with me to the Palazzo Venezia tomorrow. I do not think this is really the time to create a new problem, and such a serious one, especially now that without a doubt the prestige of the Church is very high.

November 5, 1942

The Libyan front collapses. Mussolini telephones early in the morning to have me postpone Kallay's trip to Rome. In fact, this is not the moment to welcome any guests. Later I see the Duce at the Palazzo Venezia. He is pale. His face is drawn; he is tired. But he still keeps calm. He judges the situation to be serious, but he still has some hope that the English can be held on the line of Fukra-El Qattara. (Even Cavallero, who is really the one responsible for all our troubles, affirms, on the other hand, that no attempt at resistance can be concentrated except on the Sollum-Halfaia line.) The Duce also speaks with Guariglia about relations with the Vatican, and has calmed down a great deal since yesterday, giving instructions for a completely moderate step. I see Grandi and some others. The news from Libya makes them unhappy, but does not surprise them. For some time a sense of irrepressible pessimism has overtaken the Italian people.

November 6, 1942

The Libyan retreat is looking more and more like a rout. We know nothing of our 10th Army Corps, cut off by the English forces, and even the detachments that are withdrawing are massacred by bombing from the air. Even the Duce thinks that as matters stand Libya will probably be lost, and he quickly adds "that from some points of view this represents an advantage because this region has cost us our merchant fleet and we can better concentrate on the defense of Italy itself." Nevertheless, we cannot say to-day on what line we will attempt to resist, even if we do not consider pos-sible attacks from the west, where a convoy of exceptionally large propor-tions is advancing.

Mussolini asked me if I was keeping my diary up to date. When I an-swered affirmatively, he said that it will serve to prove how the Germans, both in the military and political fields, have always acted without his knowl-edge. But what does his strange question really hide?

I have seen Gambara, Fougier, Pirelli, and Admiral Maugeri. They are all staggered by the news from Libya, and today even the most optimistic tem-peraments see the future in dark colors. The rank and file, on the other hand, believe that this time it is a question of one of the usual seesaw races across the desert.

November 7, 1942

Today the Duce views the situation more favorably. A certain amount of resistance which Rommel has offered the English at Marsa Matruk, as well as the arrival of reinforcements in Libya, lead him to believe that some change may take place in the course of events.

But what will he do, or, rather, what will the various convoys do that have left Gibraltar and are eastward bound? There are various scenarios. According to the Germans, the provisioning of Malta or an attempt at land-ing in Tripolitania in order to fall upon Rommel's rear. According to our General Staff, the occupation of French bases in North Africa. The Duce, too, shares this opinion; in fact, he believes that the Americans, who will meet almost no resistance from the French, will undertake the landing. I share the Duce's opinion; in fact, I believe that North Africa is ready to hoist the Gaullist flag. All this is extremely serious for us.

November 8, 1942

At 5:30 in the morning von Ribbentrop telephoned to inform me of American landings in Algerian and Moroccan ports. He was rather nervous, and wanted to know what we intended to do. I must confess that, having been caught unawares, I was too sleepy to give a very satisfactory answer.

The reaction of the Duce was lively as usual. He speaks at once of a landing in Corsica and of the occupation of France. But what forces are there for such undertakings? In the opinion of the most responsible people of our General Staff this is not at all feasible, but the Germans are certainly ready. Officially, I have not learned anything from the Germans. I know from Anne Maria Bismarck that at the embassy they are literally terrified by the blow, which is very severe and above all totally unexpected.

During the evening I see General Amè, who brings me up to date. There is still resistance in the cities, but pressure from the Gaullists and the Ameri-cans will soon overcome the small amount of French resistance. Amè be-lieves that within the coming week the Allies will have extended their domin-ion over all the colonies, including Tunisia, and that within two weeks they will be able to attack Libya from the west. The situation resulting from this is extremely serious. Italy will become the center of attack by the Allies in the offensive against the Axis. Amè says that army morale is dramatically low.

November 9, 1942

During the night von Ribbentrop telephoned. Either the Duce or I must go to Munich as soon as possible. Laval will also be there. It is time to assess our line of conduct toward France. I wake up the Duce. He is not very anxious to leave, especially since he is not yet feeling at all well. I shall go, and these are the instructions: if France is ready to collaborate loyally it will receive all possible aid from us; if, on the other hand, it plays hot and cold, we are going to adopt preventive measures: occupation of the free zone and a landing in Corsica.

In Munich I find von Ribbentrop at the station. He is exhausted, thin, and courteous. Laval, who is making a long trip by car, will arrive during the night.

I have my first conversation with Hitler this evening. He harbors no illusions on the French desire to fight, and now among the rebels there is General Giraud, who has brains and courage. Hence, we must reach our supreme decisions before it is too late. He, Hitler, will listen to Laval. But whatever he says will not modify his own precise point of view: the total occupation of France, landing in Corsica, a bridgehead in Tunisia. Hitler is neither nervous nor restless, but he does not underrate the American initiative and he wants to meet it with all the resources at his disposal. Göring does not hesitate to declare that the occupation of North Africa represents the first point scored by the Allies since the beginning of the war.

November 10-11, 1942

Hitler, Göring, von Ribbentrop, and myself at the Führerbahn. Decisions have been made to move, especially because the position of Admiral Darlan at Algiers is quite ambiguous and leads one to suspect some understanding with the rebels. A conference with Laval is almost superfluous, because he will be told nothing, or almost nothing, of what has been decided.

Laval, with his white tie and middle-class French peasant attire, is very much out of place in the great salon among so many uniforms. He tries to speak in a familiar tone about his trip and his long sleep in the car, but his words go unheeded. Hitler treats him with frigid courtesy. The conversation is brief. The Führer is the first to speak and asks pointedly if France is in a position to assure us landing points in Tunisia. Laval, like a good Frenchman, would like to discuss it and take advantage of the opportunity to obtain concessions from Italy. I do not have time to interrupt because Hitler, with the firmest decision, declares that he does not intend to take up at this time a discussion of Italian claims, which are more than modest. Laval cannot take upon himself the responsibility of yielding Tunis and Bizerte to the Axis, and he requests that he be faced with a *fait accompli*; meaning that we draw up a note to Vichy in which it is stated what the Axis has decided to do.

The poor man could not even imagine the kind of *fait accompli* that the Germans were about to hand him. Not a word was said to Laval about the impending action—that the orders to occupy France were being given while he was smoking his cigarette and conversing with various people in the next room. Von Ribbentrop told me that Laval would be informed only the next morning at eight o'clock that on account of information received during the night Hitler had been obliged to proceed with the total occupation of the country. Laval owes it to me if a communiqué was not published in which, even though it was not stated in so many words, it was implied that Laval had given his assent to all the measures decided by the Axis. And yet the words loyalty and honor are always on the lips of our dear Germans!

I return to Rome. I find Mussolini nervous because our military operations are not proceeding as they should. Those in Corsica are carried out with a flotilla of cutters, which is crazy, and Vercellino[546] has requested a five-hour delay before moving. In Libya, also, Rommel's withdrawal continues at an accelerated pace. Now Mussolini thinks that we shall have God to thank if he can succeed in stopping at the old Agedabia line. I see a few people, and gather the impression that the events of the last few days have been a sad blow to the country, which, for the first time, is asking many questions without getting answers.

November 12, 1942

The march of the Italian and German troops is proceeding in France, and also in Corsica, without encountering any opposition. The French people have certainly changed completely. I thought there would be some gesture of opposition, at least for the honor of the flag. But nothing of the kind. Only the French navy informed us that the fleet would remain loyal to Vichy, and that it does not want the occupation of Toulon by the Axis. The Germans agreed and also, the Duce, willy-nilly, who, however, does not trust their word of honor and thinks that someday we shall wake up to find the port of Toulon empty.

We shall see what will happen in Tunisia, where the first German contingents are supposed to arrive tonight.

Rommel continues to withdraw from Libya at breakneck speed. There is a great deal of friction between Italian and German troops. At Halfaia they even fired on one another, because the Germans took all our trucks in order to withdraw more rapidly, leaving our divisions in the middle of the desert, where masses of men are literally dying of hunger and thirst.

Churchill has made a great speech in the House of Commons. It is clear from what he said that all the British and American forces will hurl themselves on Italy for the purpose of knocking us out of the fight.

November 13, 1942

Nothing new.

November 14, 1942

This evening conversations are taking place with the Germans. Von Mackensen is the bearer of a message to be sent to the French troops and to the population of Tunisia, as well as a plan for an answer to the Spanish government on the entire problem of the American landings. With this kind of stuff he might have allowed me to sleep in peace. In fact, I advised von Mackensen "to find some good sleeping pills for von Ribbentrop, who has insomnia and pesters too many people."

I see Messe, who has returned from Russia. His opinion regarding the Eastern Front is that the Bolsheviks do not have the strength to attempt action on a large scale, but have enough to hold almost the entire German army on the steppes. His diagnosis regarding Africa is worse. He does not believe that it is possible to maintain a new line, and hence considers the loss of Tripolitania inevitable. Neither does he believe that the attempt to establish a bridgehead in Tunisia can have any lasting success.

Buti reports that the Germans have arrested Weygand. The Duce enthusiastically approves of this.

November 15, 1942

The Japanese chargé d'affaires asks for news on the situation, and in such a way as to make it clear that his government is very anxious to know the whole truth on the European-African situation. I reassure him, of course, within the limits that are possible.

Today the Duce views the situation with greater optimism, and is irritated at Cavallero, who, having been sent by him to Libya, came back quickly without having seen anything. His return, as the Duce himself asserts, is due to worry about his personal safety.

Otherwise, nothing new.

November 16, 1942

Nothing new.

November 17, 1942

The Duce is convinced that during the next few days, for better or worse, the crisis in Africa will come. An American column is at Sfax, or in the vicinity; other columns are advancing on Bizerte and Tunis. The French attitude is very ambiguous, and we must expect hostility rather than indifference. Will the Axis forces be able to resist the blow? It will all depend on what can be transferred to Tunisia in the next few days. At present not much has been done, and German support is very much smaller to what was hoped and promised. If Tunisia should fall, we would lose our last defensive bastion, and the Italian situation would become extremely difficult in a short time. The Duce seems thoughtful, and today his face showed fatigue.

Galbiati tells me what he is doing so that the militia can face any internal crisis decisively and successfully. I am not entirely convinced of what he says. I believe that the police and carabinieri represent all that is left to guarantee our institutions.

Spain is beginning to mobilize. What for? I think that above all she wishes to warn both sides that she is ready to defend her territories against anyone who wants to violate them.

November 18, 1942

The Consul General at Tunis, Silimbani, has left Tunis with the attachés of the consulate. Admiral Salza, the commander of the armistice commission in North Africa, has also returned to Italy. Silimbani says over the telephone that the situation in Tunis is untenable, that the Americans are advancing unopposed, and that the city is already practically in the hands of the Gaullists, who will stage an uprising on the first appearance of the Stars and Stripes. The Duce was not informed of this; then he telephones me later, asking whether Silimbani has had orders to leave from the Ministry for Foreign Affairs. He added that Salza had returned temporarily and for other reasons. He says that the military situation is "becoming clearer." Has Silimbani gone crazy or is Cavallero lying, as usual?

The Papal Nuncio protests about some stupid article by Farinacci, according to which the Holy See and Myron Taylor are to blame for the bombings. The Vatican is not going to stand for such an accusation and is ready to stir up a lot of trouble. Mussolini instructs me to ask Farinacci for a retraction. Farinacci reacts, saying that he got the information from the Duce himself. We shall see about it tomorrow.

November 19, 1942

I see the King, after not having seen him for a long time. I find him physically well and spiritually tranquil. He keeps me for a long conversation—an hour and twenty minutes. He wants to be informed about everything that was done at Munich, and explores the situation fully. He asks particularly for news about Spain, Switzerland, and Turkey. He says very little about what has happened and is happening in the Mediterranean, but is particularly concerned about the scarcity of troops in Italy, and especially in Rome, where even the Grenadiers have been removed. He asks me to insist with the Duce that some troops be returned to Italy, begging me at the same time not to tell him that the King asked this, "because otherwise he might suspect secret dealings." He defends the armed forces passionately, pronounces no judgment on Cavallero, but "if they are thinking of a new head of the armed forces, they should consider the oldest who are the best," and he cites "Ago, Amantea, and Geloso." He speaks favorably about Guzzoni. As always, a certain amount of Germanophobia is not lacking in his words. On the progress of the war he repeats a rather generic statement of faith, but he asks me many questions about Washington and London, advising me to cling to any thread which may yet be reknotted, "even if it is as thin as a spider's web."

I saw Del Croix. He is unhappy, but not surprised by the situation. He, too, condemns the absence from Italy of our best divisions. He rails against dictatorship of the type of the Roman, Marius, "because, with us, all plebeian dictatorships have degenerated into tyrannies," and he adds that the single great merit of Marius was that of having beaten the Teutons.

November 20, 1942
Nothing new.

November 21, 1942
Council of Ministers dealing with routine matters. At the end the Duce spoke to summarize and to throw light on the present situation. In brief, he said: (a) that the food situation is a great deal better than forecasts, which had been very gloomy; (b) that the military situation in Cyrenaica is such as to lead to stopping the enemy at Agheila Marada, and perhaps to get the upper hand, while the trend of operations in Tunisia is favorable to the Axis; (c) that the internal situation is excellent, except for the alarmists; (d) that Hitler, acting on a suggestion made by him, has agreed to send 100 anti-aircraft batteries for the protection of our cities, which are suffering severe punishment every night from the RAF.

Tonight, in fact, it has been Turin's turn, and the city was the target of bombing that was heavier than any other attacks, including those on Genoa. This now raises serious problems: the evacuation of the cities, the question of supplies, and the reduction of the industrial potential in Italy. It is useless to harbor illusions. All this has a considerable bearing on morale, and the spirit of resistance is weaker than one might expect. We must not confuse endurance with resistance; they are two very different things.

November 22, 1942
The Duce remarks that His Majesty talked to him about replacing Cavallero, mentioning the same names as he did with me, but Mussolini, who is again optimistic these days, says that we should not make changes in our command while we are engaged on two fronts.

A Russian offensive on the Don has achieved noteworthy success, and deserves the most cautious attention.

November 23, 1942
Bismarck says that General von Pohl, returning from Libya, was pessimistic, notwithstanding the fact that "Rommel is in a good mood." From the confidential talks that Colonel Montezemolo of our General Staff has had with our foreign office liaison officer, it appears that the Germans intend to make another try at saving Tripolitania, while we believe that it would be more useful to concentrate everything on the defense of Tunisia. This causes a certain uneasiness in our High Command, except, naturally, Cavallero, who, having become the servant of the Germans, puts his personal interests before the interests of his country.

In the country, pessimism and concern are growing beyond all measure. One cannot speak with any person of any class or station in life without hearing the same thing.

November 24, 1942

All of West Africa has joined the Darlan movement. The fact is extremely important. A large reserve of men passes over to the Allies as well as the base of Dakar, and a considerable part of the navy. Reactions are just beginning to come in, but the event is important.

Alfieri from Berlin. He still harps upon the official optimism in German circles. Personally, he seems to be concerned because he believes that the Italian people may consider him one of those mainly responsible for our entry into the war. He does not even suspect that the Italian people merely consider him a fool.

New and more accurate X-rays of the Duce, which tend to prove that his trouble is caused by a rheumatic localization in the spinal column. If this is true, as I hope it is, within a short time he can completely recover his health.

November 25, 1942

Nothing new.

November 26, 1942

Information from Africa is, generally, worse. Both in Tunisia and in Tripolitania the position of our forces is becoming more critical; at the same time pressure from the enemy increases. Last night 40 American tanks reached the gates of Tunis. Fougier, who is a realist and an honest man, thinks that within a few days we shall be driven from Tunis, and within a month from all of Africa. Mussolini, too, must more or less have the same idea, since he said over the telephone to me about the commercial agreement with Romania, "We should not insist too much on increasing our quota of gasoline. I believe that next year our needs will be markedly less."

Von Mackensen communicates to me the details of a letter from Laval to Hitler. He offers full French collaboration with the Axis, but what does a Laval from the Auvergne represent in reality? How can he speak for France? The German answer was cautious indeed. Not Hitler, but von Ribbentrop thanked Laval in vague terms, and another conference has been postponed without setting a date.

The Russian attack on the Volga-Don basin continues, and it appears that the results are really very important. But on this matter we know nothing very specific. We must accept what the Germans tell us.

November 27, 1942

The important event of the day is the occupation of the port of Toulon by German troops. During the night a communication reached the Duce from Hitler regarding the decision taken. Communication took place through the military, and I was kept in the dark about everything until noon, when Cavallero telephoned me. No one knows yet how things have gone. Two things are certain: that there was some resistance, and that the French navy is completely scuttled. I do not yet know the French reaction to what has happened, but in any event it would not appear to increase sympathy for Laval and for the Germans. For us Italians there is one advantage—that in any case a naval power in the Mediterranean has been eliminated for many years. The need to carefully preserve our own navy becomes more and more evident.

November 28, 1942
Nothing new.

November 29, 1942
I go to Leghorn.

November 30, 1942
Göring comes to Rome without advance notice. From what is said by General Staff officers, the trip was prompted by the fact that Rommel has left Libya secretly to see the Führer. We reacted and the assistant German military attaché has been told that if an Italian general had behaved in this way he would have been brought before a court-martial. Now Göring comes to settle the trouble, but this dispute is not merely a matter of form. Rommel does not consider it possible to hold Tripolitania and would like to withdraw into Tunisia at once. Bastico is of the opposite opinion, and among the members of the Italian General Staff many share Bastico's ideas. We shall see what decisions come out of the conference that is to be held today at the Palazzo Venezia.

Amè is very pessimistic about our resistance in Tunisia. Taking everything into consideration, he thinks that we shall be dislodged in about ten days. By Christmas we shall be out of Libya. This raises very serious problems for us.

Churchill makes a speech relating particularly to Italy. Unfortunately, I do not see what means are at our disposal today to frustrate his program of a scientific and destructive offensive against our country. In these last few days Turin has suffered more extremely painful ordeals.

December 1, 1942
I have seen the Duce again after a ten-day interruption, during which he stayed at Villa Torlonia for health reasons. Physically he is thinner, but energetic and lively. Tomorrow he will address the Chamber. The occasion for this is Churchill's attack, and he intends "to debate with him without, however, resorting to insults as he has done.[547] Besides," he added, "Churchill's address honors me because it proves that I am the real antagonist of Great Britain." Then he told me about his conversation with Göring. They will send three armored divisions to Africa, the *Adolf Hitler*, the *Hermann Göring*, and the *Deutschland*—"three names that mean much to German honor." In Libya the situation is confused. Everything is in the hands of the English, who, by quickly taking the initiative, can easily dislodge us from our present line of defense. We are planning to make Buerat the line to which we shall retreat, and it has the advantage of placing the Sirte desert in front of us

rather than in our backs. In general, I found the Duce optimistic both regarding the war and the internal situation. The officers in Göring's party speak with assurance. They declare themselves convinced that within three months German armored forces will reach Morocco. With respect to the conflict in Russia they also make rosy forecasts.

Cables arrive from Bova-Scoppa in Bucharest that demonstrate the nervousness caused by the information from the Don River front. The Conducator Antonescu is accused of having involved Romania too much in a struggle in which it has no direct interest.

December 2, 1942

After a long silence Mussolini has spoken to the Chamber. The reception of the speech by the National Councilors was very warm, even though it was easy to recognize people in the hall who privately disagree. Physically the Duce appeared quite thin, but nonetheless vigorous and at times as fiery as ever. The speech? It is too early to say what effect it will have. But it is clear that it does not introduce new facts or opinions, nor indeed could it have done so. It will not be difficult for English propaganda to refute it effectively, even if it does not avail itself of Mussolini's glaring slip about the "dinner jackets worn by the English while drinking their five o'clock tea." (Edda was aghast at this *faux pas*. She knows the English and knows how they will laugh at it, and she immediately wrote me a letter to have the newspaper version corrected.)

Bismarck spoke confidentially to d'Aieta about Göring's visit. He says that the Germans are the first to be convinced that there is nothing more to be done in Africa, and that all the promises made by Göring are bound to be left up in the clouds. But it is a matter of saving Rommel's reputation, who has a big name in Germany and is one of the military men most loyal to the Nazis. Hence Göring's main goal is to create confusion and give documentary proof that the blame for everything rests upon our poor organization of transports, ships, railroads, et cetera. For this reason he has begun to snub everyone, including Admiral Riccardi. Bismarck added that the military technicians of the embassy are surprised at the amount of nonsense which the Reichsmarshal has been capable of putting together.

December 3, 1942

Scammacca[548] confirms our opinion that Göring has made an extremely bad impression, even on our officers in the High Command. Colonel Montezemolo, secretary of the meeting of the four marshals (Göring, Kesselring, Rommel, and Cavallero), said that he was surprised by the "proud ignorance" displayed by the Reichsmarshal. Now, Göring has gone to Naples, declaring that he intends to appoint "as Superintendent of Transportation the secretary of the party in Naples, who is a young and active man, and who thinks as he does." For the sake of history, Federal secretary Milone, an excellent chap, is a doctor. Can it be that Göring is really thinking of appointing himself the Reichsprotektor of Italy?

December 4, 1942
Nothing new.

December 5, 1942
Guariglia has spoken with Maglione about the bombing of Rome. The Holy See is doing its best to avoid it, and the British and Americans have been informed that the Pope, the Bishop of Rome, could not stand by helplessly during the destruction of the Eternal City. The English Minister, Osborne, answered that Rome is not only the city of the Catholics, but also the headquarters of the Italian High Command, a large German command, many airports, as well as a very important railway convergence point. The Allies, therefore, assume full freedom of action, at least against military objectives. Cardinal Maglione therefore pointed out that the removal of the commands from Rome would strengthen the Holy Father in his task. I informed the Duce of this, but as yet I don't know his reaction. On the other hand, I have learned that the King is favorable to this and he himself had thought of such an action.

Göring continues to preside over meetings to which he invites even civilian politicians, Buffarini, technical ministers, et al. Buffarini reports that the meetings are banal and useless, and he is rather disgusted at the servile attitude of Cavallero toward the Reichsmarshal. Yesterday, when Göring arrived at the High Command, our military chiefs received him in the courtyard. This made the young officers present indignant, and they have reported it to me.

December 6, 1942
The Duce has dictated a brief summary of his conferences with Göring to me, which I have preserved elsewhere. No conclusion has been reached in the political field, but in the military area the Reichsmarshal has observed that our efforts will have to be increased if we wish to avoid further grief in Africa. We, too, had reached this conclusion without the need of his precious insight.

In principle Mussolini is not against the transfer of the High Command elsewhere, "so that it may not be said that he has remained under the big umbrella of Catholicism to protect himself from English bombs."

Von Mackensen officially invites the Duce to go to Germany between the fifteenth and twentieth of the month. Laval will attend the second part of the conference. Tomorrow the Duce will give his answer.

D'Aieta has had a long conversation with the Prince of Piedmont. In general, it was satisfactory even though he is inclined to see the situation in dark colors everywhere.

December 7, 1942
Conference with the King. We went into detail about the situation. We spoke of the advisability of transferring the High Command elsewhere in order to avoid the bombing of Rome and, accepting my suggestion, he told me that he will propose Fiuggi to the Duce as the most suitable site.

Then he mentioned a bit of advice once given by his grandfather, King Victor Emmanuel II. In speaking with people, one must say two things in order to be assured of a good reception, "How beautiful your city is!" and "How young you look!" The King maintains that in his long experience they never fail. But some minutes later, when he began saying nice things to me about Leghorn, I took the liberty of interrupting, and this amused him.

The Duce agrees to the trip to Germany at the time proposed, but without enthusiasm.

December 8, 1942

The Duce has said that he will go to Germany only on one condition: namely, that he be allowed to take his meals alone in his apartment, "because he does not want a lot of ravenous Germans to notice that he is compelled to live only on rice and milk." But, I may add, his health has considerably improved during the last few days, so that it appears almost normal.

He is optimistic about the African military situation, especially because he has decided not to defend the Agheila-Marada line in Tripolitania, but to fall back to Buerat so as to leave in front of the English the 400 kilometers of the Sirte desert.

December 9, 1942

New and effective bombing of Turin by the RAF.

I see Amè on his return from Nice, where he met Admiral Canaris. He repeats his usual pessimism, which he bases above all on news coming from Russia regarding Soviet attacks and German exhaustion. For Africa, also, he makes dark forecasts, though for the distant future.

Amè, for his part, sees the situation with a little more optimism than he did ten days or so ago. This, naturally, only in the immediate future; his ideas have not changed looking further ahead.

But the demonstrations of bad strategy shown by the British and Americans in Tunisia lead him to believe that the fight will still be a long one. The Duce, to whom Amè reported Canaris' concern, showed no interest in it. In fact, he asserted his confidence in quick victory.

Franco spoke in very friendly terms about the Axis. Mussolini sent him congratulations through our ambassador, but "he does not intend to move a finger to accelerate the intervention of Spain in the war, because it would be more of a hindrance than a help."

December 10, 1942

No news.

December 11, 1942

Nothing new.

December 12, 1942

The removal of our commands has been decided and I shall pass on the news to Guariglia so that he may inform the Holy See. The bombing of

Rome must be absolutely avoided; the population is very much disturbed, and the two air raids of yesterday were enough to create deep apprehension.

December 13, 1942

The British have attacked in Libya. For the moment we are resisting well, but this disturbs the withdrawal from the Buerat line.

Mussolini is calm. This morning he was going through the reports from the censorship office and reached some very pessimistic conclusions on humanity. Two things, he believes, have really eternal value, "bread and testicles." The rest are pipe dreams, ideals, sacrifices—nothing.

Notwithstanding the fact that we let the Germans know that we did not consider Cavallero's presence advisable at the coming meeting at Klessheim, they have still insisted that he come. It becomes more and more obvious that they consider him their man.

Guariglia talked to the Vatican about the removal of the command. It appears that Osborne insists especially on the removal of the Germans. When Guariglia told Monsignor Montini that even the Duce would leave the capital, the Monsignor replied, "I think he will have to make another march on Rome to come back."

Jacomoni is quite optimistic on the Albanian situation, in spite of the many incidents that are taking place. He believes, and with good reason, that it depends solely on international events. He would change Kruia, but he doesn't regret the experiment. "He is a man," he said, "who, in our own interest, we had to use as much as possible."

December 14, 1942

Ribbentrop informs us that "due to operations in the East" it is advisable to postpone the meeting at Klessheim for a few days. He is not definite about when the meeting will take place, but hopes that it will still be possible before Christmas.

The British attack is rather heavy in Libya, but our greatest difficulty is due to the scarcity of fuel. Our navy has also suffered severe losses these days.

December 15, 1942

Nothing new.

Late in the evening Mackensen asks to see me. New proposals are made for the meeting. Hitler cannot leave the High Command, nor can he postpone the meeting. And since he does not want the Duce to face such a long trip, almost to the old borders of Lithuania, he invites me to go as soon as possible with Cavallero. He tells us beforehand that the conversations will be important and will last a day or so. I will answer him tomorrow.

December 16, 1942

As I had anticipated, the Duce does not feel inclined to face such a long trip, nor does he care to interrupt his electrotherapeutic treatment, which seems to be working very well for him. I shall have to go, and this time will have precise instructions. Mussolini is especially anxious to have Hitler know (and he has already spoken about it with Göring) that he considers it extremely advisable to reach an agreement with Russia, or at least to settle upon a defensive line that can be held by small forces. 1943 will be the year of the Anglo-Saxon effort. Mussolini feels that the Axis must have on hand all the troops it needs in Africa, in the Balkans, and perhaps even in the West. I shall note elsewhere the instructions received and shall have stenographic notes made of the conference. Just now it is interesting to note that Bismarck has told d'Aieta that the Führer has tried to avoid the meeting with the Duce, because he does not want to engage in general political discussions. It seems that we shall speak about France only if Laval is present.

Things are going badly in Cyrenaica, where the English have succeeded in making our retreat somewhat disorderly, while obliging us to fight under the worst tactical and logistic conditions.

The Duce confirms the removal of the German commands from Rome, and I give instructions that Cardinal Maglione be informed immediately. Perhaps it will be worthwhile to put the negotiations that have taken place in writing. We shall never have the assurance from the English that they will not bomb, but I continue to be optimistic.

December 17, 1942
On my way to Hitler's headquarters.

December 18, 1942
I recorded my conversations in the forest of Görlitz and made notes of my general impressions. Now, a few details, as usual.

The atmosphere is heavy. To the bad news there should perhaps be added the sadness of that humid forest and the boredom of collective living in the barracks of the command. There isn't a spot of color, not one vivid note. Waiting rooms filled with people smoking, eating, chatting. Kitchen odor, smell of uniforms, of boots. All this is in great measure needless, at least for a mass of people who have no need to be here. First among them is Ribbentrop, who compels the majority of his employees to live a troglodyte life for no reason and which, in fact, prevents the normal workings of the Foreign Ministry.

When I arrived no one tried to conceal from me or from my associates the unhappiness about the news of the break-through on the Russian front. There were open attempts to place the blame on us. Hewel,[549] who is very close to Hitler, had the following conversation (in English) with Pansa. Pansa: "Had our army many losses?" Hewel: "No losses at all; they are running." Pansa: "As you did in Moscow last year?" Hewel: "Exactly."

December 19-20, 1942
Laval made a trip that he could have spared himself. After two days on the train they first sat him at a tea table, then at a dinner table, and did not let

him open his mouth. The moment he tried to speak the Führer would inter-rupt him and deliver a long dissertation. (I believe that at heart Hitler is happy at being Hitler, since this allows him to talk all the time.) Altogether, Laval is a disgusting Frenchman—the most disgusting of all Frenchmen. To get into the good graces of the German bosses he doesn't hesitate in betray-ing his own compatriots and to defame his own unhappy country. He said one clever thing, that for him it is difficult to govern France, since every-where he turns he hears people cry out, "*Laval au poteau!*"[550]

And yet the Germans do feel the charm of the French! Even of this Frenchman. Except for Hitler, all the others were milling around trying to talk to him, or get close to him; it looked like the entrance of the great fallen lord in a circle of newly enriched peasants.

Ribbentrop also did his best, but he ended with a *faux pas*. He reminded Laval that his "eminent compatriot" Napoleon had once been in that same forest.

If I am not mistaken, Napoleon was there under entirely different cir-cumstances.

A fact that should be remembered: in June 1939 Cavallero went to Ger-many bearing a letter from Mussolini. Now Keitel, recalling that meeting, said that they had already then decided on the war against Poland, even down to the setting of the date. And all this, naturally, while they were com-mitted to a period of at least three years of peace with us.

December 21, 1942
    Return trip

December 22, 1942
    I return to Rome. I find considerable panic over the news from the Russian front, especially since the Duce, in speaking to people of a possible peace with Russia, had kindled many hopes.

Mussolini is also in a rather bad mood. I turned the report on my trip over to him, in which I clearly state what I think. In my verbal comments, also, I do not conceal my unfavorable impressions. I speak to him about Cavallero and of the servility he shows in his relations with the Germans. The Duce says: "The usefulness of Cavallero is over. A few years ago he had a keen brain, but that is no longer true." However, he does not allude to the person who is to replace him. He invites me to send His Majesty a copy of my report.

Colonel Stevens has commented on the radio on my trip to Germany, which is quite amusing. He recalls my speech at the Chamber on December 16, 1939, and says that I am the person best qualified to speak plainly to the English because I did so since that time.

December 23, 1942
    Nothing new.

December 24, 1942

The King has words of approval for my report on my return from Germany. He is indignant about the fact that Ribbentrop has asked for part of our light fleet. The tone of the King's conversation is, as always, anti-German, but he says nothing in particular and concludes with the usual formal and unconvincing affirmation of victory.

We are at loggerheads again on the issue of the bombing of Rome. From an intercepted British cable we learn that in addition to the departure of the Duce and the commands from Rome, Eden also wants that of the King and the entire government, with Swiss officials controlling the evacuation. Naturally Mussolini reacted vigorously and is preparing to refuse. Yesterday I was in his room while he was listening to the Pope's speech on the radio. He commented on it with sarcasm, "The Vicar of God, who is the representative on Earth of the Ruler of the Universe, should never speak; he should remain in the clouds. This is a speech of platitudes which might better be made by the parish priest of Predappio."

News from Russia still bad, but at the High Command they believe that this time the Russians will not succeed in taking strategic advantage of their initial successes.

December 25, 1942

Darlan has been assassinated in Algiers, with three pistol shots. Are the Gaullists, the English, or the Germans to be blamed? He was shot by a young man, twenty years of age, and hence either a fanatic or an agent. Perhaps we shall find out the truth. However, it is interesting to note the cold indifference with which the English press has commented on the news.

Fougier is very deeply pessimistic. As far as he is concerned the war is already lost; in fact, it was lost some time ago, and now the only thing that remains is to find the way to end it as soon as possible and with the least possible harm to us. In his opinion the scarcity of equipment has become so acute as to render any kind of serious military operation inconceivable— at least for the air force.

December 26, 1942

Horia Sima, head of the Romanian legion, has arrived in Italy. Since he got out of Germany with a false passport, Himmler is demanding his extradition. For my part, I advised the Duce to grant his extradition forthwith, especially since his presence here would create friction with Antonescu. And then, all things considered, there will be one less crook.

Today Princess di Gangi, who had a cordial friendship with the Duce, opened her heart to me on the Petacci affair, without any suggestion from me, talking, as she said in her Sicilian accent, "like in the confessional." According to her, Mussolini has had enough of Claretta, her brother, her sister, and all of them, but he can't get rid of them because they are bad people, ready to blackmail and create a scandal. In speaking with the Princess di Gangi, the Duce is supposed to have said that he once loved the girl, but that now she is "revolting" to him. How much truth is there in this and how much of it is dormant feminine jealousy? Anyway, the Princess blames the Petaccis for everything that is going badly in Italy, including the Duce's ailments, which to me, frankly, seems a bit exaggerated.

December 27, 1942

I go to Leghorn to say good-by to Emilia, my dear old faithful Nanny, who is slowly dying. To the weight of her eighty-two years is added that of many ailments. I have loved her very tenderly. Yesterday afternoon was one of the unhappiest days of my life.

December 28, 1942

No news of any importance in Rome. I don't see the Duce because he is in bed with a kind of flu. His health is not what I should like it to be.

Mackensen sends me in the name of the German government the cable answering Laval, regarding what he asked for in the forest of Görlitz. It has to do with very modest concessions, entirely matters of form. Not hard to agree with as far as we are concerned.

December 29, 1942

Buffarini shows me written reports of the Rimini police which the Duce asked for today. It is nothing more than a mediocre and banal piece of gossip spread in Tirana by people I don't know and who gossiped about me, saying that I was seeking to become the Duce's successor and other such absurdities. I told Buffarini to show the reports immediately to Mussolini, who will easily judge them for what they are worth. I am only sorry that there are people who bring such silly reports to the Duce, and that he, after knowing me for so many years, can listen to them even without taking them seriously.

Buti is here in transit. He says nothing really new. All of France is now convinced that Germany will lose the war, and everybody awaits the day. Laval is despised, but he is tolerated because they fear the worst; meaning, they fear Doriot, who is considered a gangster. Buti found a picturesque simile in talking about French-German relations: a wagon driver who whips his mule yelling "collaboration, collaboration!"

December 30, 1942

Donegani[551] rushed to the Palazzo Chigi to advise against the proposed customs union with Germany. In reality somebody had mentioned it, though I can't remember who, but the idea had been bluntly rejected because of the enormous loss which would result for our country is too obvious. It would be like opening the doors of our house while the doors of others remained locked. The Germans have taken enough from us. Are they still not satisfied?

A good point on the question of the bombing of Rome: from an intercepted cable we learn that the Americans have said no to Eden's draconian request, declaring that they do not intend to bomb the city of St. Peter because there would be more disadvantages than advantages for the Allies. Thus it seems to me that the matter can be shelved. At least for the time being.

December 31, 1942

Emilia died tonight. With her dies another part of my youth. Perhaps no one in the world has lavished upon me such a sweet and constant tenderness. In her opinion I have never grown up; man, youth, adolescent, it was all the same. She surrounded me with the same concern that she had for me as a child. She was generous, honest, and extremely faithful. Today I have suffered the deepest sorrow of my life, after the death of Father and that of Maria.

I received Colonel Montezemolo, sent to me by Cavallero with the Duce's approval, to explain what is to be done in Tripolitania; namely, to evacuate it. It is impossible to send sufficient supplies and reinforcements. Everything that goes to Libya is used up in Tunisia and supplies are already very scarce. Now Cavallero's order of the day is: optimism regarding Tunisia, pessimism regarding Tripolitania. Only a few days ago he was an optimist about all sectors. We shall see. Montezemolo, whom I asked about his personal opinion on our prospects in Tunisia, answered: "I believe that we shall be able to resist for a long time." He did not wish to compromise himself.

An interesting conference with Colonel Luca, who has just returned from Constantinople.[552] As is well known, he is a very good friend of Saragioglu. The latter told him two or, rather, three things: that what is happening to the Axis is no longer seen with optimism in Turkey; that Russia would not be adverse to making a separate peace; that Turkey would behave just like the Bulgarians with respect to Germany if England violated her neutrality. I have asked Luca for a written report.

1943

Nothing particularly new except a great flowering of cables from the German Nazi chiefs which are very courteously worded. It is a sign of the times.

I did not like very much Hitler's message to the German people and the one he sent to the armed forces. They reveal a great deal of concern, which is logical, but it is not wise to announce it to a public which is already puzzled.

January 2, 1943

Pietromarchi has had a long conference with the Pope. Without assuming any obligation, the Holy Father said that he now believes that the danger of the bombing of Rome has been averted. He also informed whom it may concern that his reaction would be energetic and immediate. He has found more understanding in Washington than in London, and this is logical. He did not give any opinion about the situation but shows that he is informed as to what the Ministry for Foreign Affairs is doing to prevent massacres and ruin in the occupied territories. He ended by sending me his greetings and his blessing.

I took Colonel Luca to see the Duce. The former is now convinced that we cannot make a separate peace with Russia. Two months ago he considered it feasible, but now that the Cossacks are advancing on the Donetz basin and Yeliki Lukki has fallen, Stalin would seek to impose impossible terms. However, he feels that before long the situation may offer better prospects. That the situation on the Russian front is very depressing is confirmed by Antonescu, who considers German mistakes as "strategic and hence susceptible of having serious consequences."

I have prepared a memorandum for the Duce on the real situation in Croatia, Dalmatia, and Montenegro as it is developing after our understanding with the Chetniks. It is very precarious and dangerous.

January 3, 1943
Nothing new.

January 4, 1943
The Duce asked me to give von Mackensen a copy of a cable Turkish Ambassador Zorlu sent to his government from Kuibyshev. It is a description of the Soviet situation. It seems impartial and quite informative. According to him, the war weighs heavily on the Russians, but Russia is still strong and, in the judgment of the diplomatic corps in Kuibyshev, Axis stock is falling.

I am thinking about gifts for Göring on his fiftieth birthday. The Duce is giving him a gold sword carved by Messina (which was originally meant to go to Franco, but times have changed). I will give him a Star of San Maurizio studded with diamonds (originally meant for Zog and kept in the safe all this time). The personal indifference of the Duce to personal possessions is moving. At home he owns only one good piece: a self-portrait by Mancini, which was a gift from the painter. Well, when he heard that a gift had to be made to Göring and that the Ministry of Fine Arts had difficulty in locating something worthwhile, he immediately thought of giving his Mancini. I had to argue a lot to change his mind.

January 5, 1943
I see the Duce after two days. I find him tired. Edda says that the pains in his stomach have increased even though he takes only liquid food. He is depressed about the situation in Libya. He realizes that the loss of Tripoli will cut deeply into the morale of the people. He would like a desperate house-to-house defense like that of Stalingrad. He knows that this will not happen. Furthermore, it is impossible. The city can be broken into from all sides, and can be shelled from the sea. He has harsh words for Cavallero and for "that madman Rommel, who thinks of nothing but retreating into Tunisia."

January 6, 1943
I talked with Roatta and Geloso. With the first we discussed the Chetnik problem. He also realizes the danger that the Chetniks represent now and will represent in the future. He declares that in order to carry out the German plan of extermination we need a great many more troops than both we and Germany can afford. I believe that, as things stand, he is not wrong. But what about tomorrow? The fact is that military forces are scarce. In Africa, Russia, and the Balkans, the occupied countries, everywhere new and greater forces are needed. At times I have the impression that the Axis is like a man who is trying to cover himself with a bedspread that is too small. His head is cold if he warms his feet, and his feet freeze if he wants to keep his head warm.

Geloso, too, draws a rather modest picture of the situation in Greece. He thinks, however, that the forces at his disposal are sufficient to repel a British attack, at least in the initial phase. Both of these generals see a gloomy future, and, without confessing it openly, make unhappy forecasts.

Alfieri sends a long report on the German situation. For the first time he comes to pessimistic conclusions without even bothering to suggest palliatives. This must be hard for him, since he has been the zealous representative of unconditional optimism.

January 7, 1943

Japan wants to sign economic agreements with Germany and us, in which the living spaces of the three countries would be defined and specific preferential tariffs agreed upon. Since our position of inferiority is obvious I stalled.

Pirelli talks to me with all his cards on the table. He describes his conversation with a Swiss banker who just arrived from London, and frankly admits that he now believes that the war has been won by the Allies. He gives no news; he confirms the fact that it is easier for us to find understanding in Washington than in London.

General Dalmazzo views the Albanian situation with remarkable tranquility so long as there is no attack from the outside. This would bring many painful surprises.

January 8, 1943

I have seen the Duce again after three days and find him looking worse. It seems that Frugoni, too, in these last few days has expressed his concern. But in my humble opinion, what is harming his health more than anything else is his uneasiness about the situation. He feels rage in his heart over the abandonment of Tripoli and suffers from it. As usual, he hurled bitter words at the military men who do not make war with the "fury of the fanatic, but rather with the indifference of the professional."

I have lunch with Bottai and Farinacci. Both are furious. In speaking of the loss of Libya, Bottai says: "After all, it is another goal that has been reached. In 1911 Mussolini uttered his 'get out of Libya.' After thirty-two years he has kept his word."

The impudent Dr. Petacci has sent me through Di Giacomo[553] a letter which in peremptory terms advances the candidacy of his partner, Vezzari, to the embassy in Spain. Vezzari is an old jailbird, an ignorant man, a swindler, and obscene. I have rejected the letter. If it were not that Mussolini is unwell and I do not want to worry him I would speak it to him about it. But there will be time to do so.

January 9, 1943

Vittorio[554] speaks to me about the Duce's health. In the last few days he has had very severe gastric pains, which is serious, because they drastically reduce his consumption of food. All the doctors agree in saying that there is no organic problem. Vittorio, and I as well, are convinced that the source of the disturbance is nervousness.

Wang Ching-Wei declares war on the Allies.[555] The event is of no practical importance, even though we play it up with large headlines for home consumption. I speak candidly to the Duce about it. As far as Italy is concerned, we are giving up our concession at Tientsin which is not very important, but was, nevertheless, a heritage of the past and is personally very dear to me.

January 10, 1943

I think the Germans would do well to watch the Romanians. I see an about-face in the attitude and words of Mihail Antonescu. The sudden desire for conciliation with Hungary is suspicious to me. If the Russian offensive had not been so successful I doubt that all this would have taken place. There is something peculiar going on in Finland as well; to be watched.

Göring, to whom Martin Franklin[556] today handed the first Gold Star of the Roman Eagle, expressed his thanks so vociferously that his childish joy was obvious.

January 11, 1943

Von Mackensen telephoned during the night on Ribbentrop's orders to inform us that Pétain was preparing to leave Vichy, to go to his villa near Marseilles. The move is suspicious: preparations for an escape to Algeria? In any case, orders have been issued to the troops to watch the movements of the old marshal closely, and the French government was told that it would be best for Pétain not to move. Mussolini telephoned me early, requesting further details, which I didn't have. Then, suddenly, he left for Forlì. His departure can be explained by his bad health; and as the meeting of the Council of Ministers, planned for the 16th, has been postponed indefinitely, this will cause unavoidable gossip.

Marshal Antonescu, talking with Bova-Scoppa, mentioned something about the German secret weapon, which is supposed to do wonders: a multiple-barreled electric gun; no armor could withstand its blow. Any truth to it? Is this the weapon that Hitler alluded to in his speech? Or is it the usual hot air?

January 12, 1943

The Prince of Piedmont has sent for d'Aieta to tell him that in military circles the action I undertook to avert the bombing of Rome has been favorably received, but he adds that everyone now wants the removal of the German commands, who are shilly-shallying about it. Blasco d'Aieta showed the Prince the transcript of my report on my recent trip to the German High Command.

A long conference at the Colonna residence with Monsignor Montini, who, from what is said, is a really close collaborator of the Holy Father. He acted cautiously, reservedly, and like an Italian. He did not express any opinion on the military situation but said only that in the Vatican they think that the struggle will still be hard and long. He added that in so far as he is able to do anything in favor of our country he is completely at our disposal. I spoke to him of the importance that we must attach to the internal order of our country at all times, and he agreed. The Church will always work in this direction. Though he is anti-Bolshevik, he nevertheless expresses admiration and surprise at what Stalin has been able to do. He said: "One thing is important: whatever the future may bring, our people have given singular proof of strength, faith, and discipline. These are qualities that will bring about a complete revival."

January 13, 1943

Senator Kruia has resigned. The governor[557] is planning to replace him with Ekrem Libohova, who was Minister for Foreign Affairs under Zog, or with Kensal Vrioni. In fact, it is planned to return to the government of the beys, who still have a considerable influence in the country and are in a position to strongly influence public opinion.

Suardo tells me that he once asked Senator Borea d'Olmo, who had been Cavour's secretary, his own personal reminiscences of the great statesman. "He used to eat a great deal," was the only answer that he got. Some ideas come to mind spontaneously.

January 14, 1943

Nothing new.

January 15, 1943

Mussolini telephones, wishing to know if it is true that I went to a luncheon at Farinacci's home with Bottai, Scorza, and Tarabini. It is very true. But also nothing could have been more insignificant. Farinacci had invited me to see his new country home; a bad luncheon, a banal conversation. Evidently somebody is trying to sow distrust and suspicion in the mind of the Chief, and I am sorry that he could fall for it even for a moment.

January 16, 1943

Among our interceptions there is a cable in which a conversation between the German General von Thoma and Montgomery is summarized. If it is true it is serious. Von Thoma said that the Germans are convinced they have lost the war, and that the army is anti-Nazi because it holds Hitler completely responsible. By order of the Duce I gave a copy of it to von Mackensen. There must be some truth to it because Thoma, passing through Rome, said more or less the same thing to Bismarck.

Edda spoke with Frugoni about the Duce's health. A consultation with Cesabianchi will take place tomorrow at the Castle of Rocca. Although the ailment is of such long standing, Frugoni said there is every reason to believe that the Duce will be all right. This is good news.

January 17, 1943

Nothing new.

January 18, 1943

During the night a cable from Tirana, in which the police inspector sounds the alarm: they can't form a government, the rebellion is growing, and we must hand over power to the military. No news from Jacomoni. Now one thing is clear: either somebody is too cool or too nervous. I call him on the telephone, and in his customary veiled way he says things are quite bad, especially because Marka Gioni, the Catholic leader of Scutari, wants everything or nothing—either the whole government or no collaboration on his part. Jacomoni will not be blackmailed and solves the crisis with Ekrem Libohova. This is a return to the government of the beys, that is, the local aristocratic families. I inform the Duce, who was rather disturbed, and advised Jacomoni in any case to take precautionary measures with the military authorities. We shall see what will come of this situation, but it is clear that even in Albania we are getting the reflection of events on the larger chessboard. And these events are not good. They are bad in Russia, with the German retreat taking on ever greater proportions, and they are bad in Libya, where the threat against Tripoli appears more and more imminent.

I receive a rather reassuring letter from Frugoni about the Duce's health.

January 19, 1943

It has been a very oppressive day. News from all sectors is bad. The retreat in Russia continues and seems to have become a rout in some sectors. In Libya, infantry divisions are abandoning Tripoli and marching to the west, while the rear guards are trying to delay the cautious but unstoppable advance of Montgomery. I speak with Mussolini over the telephone. He seems discouraged. Since the Germans have informed us that they can no longer send the armored forces they promised to Tunisia, he is thinking of finding a corrective in an eventual declaration of war on the Anglo-Saxon powers by the Bey. I tried to explain that this is impossible, useless, and ineffective. But he insists, and wants me to summon Silimbani to Rome for a conference.

Bova-Scoppa has sent a report on his long conference with young Antonescu, who has returned from German headquarters. The latter was very explicit about the tragic condition of Germany and foresees the need for Romania and Italy to contact the Allies in order to establish a defense against the Bolshevization of Europe. I shall take the report to the Duce and will make it the topic of a conversation which I have been planning for some time. Let us not bandage our heads before they are broken, but let us look at the situation realistically and remember that charity begins at home.

January 20, 1943

A long and interesting conversation with Ambrosio and Vercellino. These two generals, both worthy and honest men, and of patriotic integrity, are very anxious about what is about to happen. Convinced as they are that Germany will lose the war, and that there is nothing left for us but destruction, death, and disorder, they ask how far we intend to go. Naturally they violently attack Cavallero—Cavallero who lies, consorts with the Germans, and steals all he can. I promise that I will speak frankly with the Duce, concealing nothing from him; this is what I can and must do in order to be at peace with my own conscience.

In fact, taking my cue from Bova's report, I told the Duce what I thought. The Duce began by replying that "he was sure that the Germans would hold tenaciously." Then he listened to me attentively. He naturally rejected Antonescu's offer, saying that "the channel on the Danube is not the way we must follow." But he did not react when at a certain point I said openly that we, too, should try to make some direct contact.

Physically he is the same as three weeks ago. He seemed a little thinner but looks well. Obviously he is depressed.

We have chosen De Peppo for Madrid and Rosso for Ankara. They are both good.

January 21, 1943

As I anticipated, Mussolini asked to read the Bova report. He described Antonescu's language as biased and he reaffirmed in terms much stronger than those of yesterday his decision to march with Germany to the end. In addition he hopes "that five hundred Tiger tanks, five hundred thousand men in reserve, and the new German gun can still reverse the situation." Even concerning Africa he uses the most optimistic language: "Our Libyan forces are entering Tunisia and we still have many trump cards to play." I do not know what these can be. I speak candidly about Albania: what we are doing is merely to apply hot bandages. We must send more and more troops. It is now clear that we have lost the Albanians' consensus as well as their trust. Only force will win—not to be used in the beginning, but at least we should show that it is there.

General Amè is darkly pessimistic. He is convinced that 1943 will witness the collapse of Germany. He believes that we must begin to think about ourselves, perhaps not immediately, but certainly within a short time. As for Cavallero's successor, whom Mussolini intends to appoint very soon, he believes that Ago is the best candidate.

January 22, 1943

The Duce thinks that today's German military bulletin is the worst since the beginning of the war. And it certainly is. A rout at Stalingrad, retreat everywhere along the front, and Tripoli about to fall. It appears that Rommel has again maneuvered in such a way as to save his forces leaving Italian troops in the lurch. Mussolini is very much irritated, and plans to have it out with the Germans. He is very unhappy about the fall of Tripoli, but he remains convinced that we can counterattack from Tunisia and retake it. Thus he continues to lull himself with many dangerous illusions, which distort his clear vision of reality—a reality which is now obvious to everybody. Naturally, Cavallero and his entourage are the ones really responsible for the creation of this fool's paradise.

January 23, 1943

Meeting of the Council of Ministers. After the administrative agenda Mussolini talks about the military situation. The negative point is the allied initiative on all land fronts, the positive side is the success of the submarine campaign. He puts a great deal of emphasis on this. (But really I can't understand why the Axis, where power is represented by the German army, should find its reasons for hope on the seas!) The Duce makes no forecasts. He says, instead, very firmly that this war will last "another three or four years."

Today the communiqué announced the fall of Tripoli. On many faces, the most humble and the most sincere, I saw deep lines of pain. Many hopes are now focused by our propaganda on Tunisia. I fear that these are all false hopes.

January 24, 1943

General Messe informs me of a conference he had yesterday with the Duce in the presence of Cavallero. He has been made commander of the Italian forces that are flowing into Tunisia. "Commander of the scattered forces," so Messe defines his job. He considers it a left-handed blow struck at him by Cavallero to get rid of him, since he, too, must be convinced that there are no prospects for us in Tunisia and wants Messe to lose his reputation in a desperate gamble or even to end up in a prison camp. What surprised Messe was the language used by Mussolini, who spoke of certain successes, offensive possibilities, African recoveries, et cetera, et cetera. All this is because that Cavallero paints a situation which is far removed from the truth and is deliberately deceiving the Duce.

January 25, 1943

The Royal Signature. His Majesty had a heavy cold, his voice was raucous, and he coughed. He spoke in rather general terms, avoiding any reference to the situation. As a matter of fact, he indulged in some perfunctory optimism, without missing the opportunity for a dig at the Germans. He talked at length about Giolitti, praising his callousness and ignorance. Giolitti managed Parliament like no one else in the world. He had a notebook, each page of which was dedicated to some deputy, where he wrote the all there was to know about each man. Not a single deputy ever escaped Giolitti's blackmail. The King himself read the page having to do with Eugenio Chiesa, who was particularly sensitive to threats because of an old bankruptcy. To demonstrate Giolitti's ignorance, His Majesty said that when he proposed that Michetti[558] be made a senator, Giolitti asked who he was, and then cabled the Prefect of Naples to secure information about "a certain Michetti."

Today's German communiqué is depressing, and announces the evacuation of Voronezh.

January 26, 1943

Nothing new.

January 27, 1943

Favagrossa confers with me on our supply situation. There are no changes, either good or bad, but now that a major effort must be made in the field of production, he thinks that there will be a considerable depletion of the stocks available. However, our contribution to the production of weapons is very modest: more than half and less than three quarters of one percent of world production.

Bismarck was received by the Duce, to whom he brought a horse offered to him by the city of Bremen. Mussolini talked about a theory which he had once told me about, according to which German bulletins are purposefully pessimistic in order to prepare more pleasant surprises for the German people. Bismarck does not share this theory, and was very much surprised by it.

We receive news of the Casablanca meeting for the first time[559] It is too early to judge, but it seems to be a serious thing, very serious indeed. I neither share nor approve the easy ironies of our press.

January 28, 1943

The Duce continues to interpret the Russian situation rather optimistically. He believes that the Germans have the men, the resources, and the energy to dominate the situation, and perhaps to turn it to their advantage.

Even for Africa he doesn't see things in gloomy colors. But he speaks more and more unfavorably about Cavallero.

One cannot say that the Duce's ideas are different from those of Colonel Battaglini, Chief of Staff of the Third *Celere* Division, just back from Russia. He painted the darkest picture possible, and though it was the first time he talked to me he said that the only way left to save Italy, the army, and the regime itself is a separate peace. This is an idea that is taking root. It was mentioned to me with some approval, even by Mussolini's sister.

January 29, 1943

I go to see the Duce with our Consul General in Tunis, Silimbani. He reports with some objectivity on the situation, which he considers serious. He does not see how, without the help of very considerable armored forces, it is possible to hold the thin strip of land to which we are now clinging when the double British-American pressure begins. The meeting will continue tomorrow.

Anfuso has written from Budapest a keen and interesting letter which Mussolini praised very much. There are no actual facts as yet, but many indications lead one to believe that Hungary has already had some contacts with the Anglo-Saxons. Besides, Mariassy asked d'Aieta with a good deal of anxiety today if it were true that the Romanians had been negotiating with the English and that conversations were under way in Lisbon. D'Aieta denied this but, what do we really know about it?

Grandi is insisting that I send foreign service officer Casardi as First Secretary to Madrid. It may be a coincidence, but Casardi is half English, has an American wife, and was with Grandi when Samuel Hoare, who is now ambassador to Spain, was Secretary for Foreign Affairs.

January 30, 1943
Ambrosio replaces Cavallero as Chief of Staff. This is a good change, imposed by honesty, by events, and by the resentment of all Italians against a man who has always lied for his own self-interest and for the sake of his career. Ambrosio is respected by the army. He isn't considered a thunderbolt, but anyway, under present conditions, I don't think that even a Napoleon Bonaparte could work miracles. What is important is that at the head of our armed forces there be an Italian, a patriot who looks at reality with honesty, and who intends to put the interest of the country above everything else. Ambrosio, to judge from the conversations I have had with him, is that kind of man.

January 31, 1943
The sacking of Cavallero has produced joy among Italians and disappointment among the Germans. Bismarck has become the mouthpiece of the latter, and praises the excellent collaboration which the marshal had given to the German armed forces. Naturally, I said that the event did not have any political significance: reasons of an internal and military nature had determined it. Besides, the Germans had changed their chief of staff three times and the removal of Admiral Raeder took place only yesterday.
In a conference with me Ambrosio confirms what we had discussed the last time we met. He is an honest man who will act in the interests of the country rather than in his own interest.
The event of the day: a meeting between Churchill and Turkish government officials. De Peppo and Alfieri do not attach too much importance to the meeting. Mussolini, when informed by telephone, said that this proves the weakness of the English "if Churchill must go to the trouble of begging for Turkish help." I cannot share this much too optimistic interpretation. It is the Casablanca plan that is finding its application, and Turkey is too important a base not to be exploited. I am not yet sure that the Turks have been neutralized as Berlin believes or says.

February 1, 1943
Mussolini delivered a very proud speech for the Twentieth Anniversary of the Fascist militia. It wasn't an optimistic speech; he talked not of victory, but of fighting.
News from Albania is disturbing; the government of Libohova is also up to its own tricks. The men who were most faithful to us are trying to jump ship. Even Vrioni. Even Verlaçi. These are signs of the times.
I think that before long it will be necessary to place all power in the hands of the military.

February 2, 1943
Nothing new.

February 3, 1943

I talked to the Duce about three problems:

Albania. The situation is such that I think it is necessary to replace Jacomoni. For a certain period he did very well, but now his policies are irrelevant. We need a man who can talk about force, and who can also use it. I propose Guzzoni or Pariani, two generals who know the country and are well regarded. Mussolini said he would think about it and decide.

Cavallero. His replacement has alarmed the Germans. He was their servant. Now they fear that with his departure the whole system will be changed. I reassure Bismarck, but I think it would be good for the Duce to write to Hitler on the matter.

Tunis. Silimbani is pretending that he is sick, and does not want to go back. No use pushing him; he has made enough of a fool of himself. I will send Bombieri instead, who was consul general for many years.

A meeting with Missiroli. He informs me in detail of the opinions expressed by eminent men of the past about today's situation.

February 4, 1943

A long visit with Thaon de Revel. He had been one of the most ardent interventionists, who believed 100 percent in a German victory. Now he is facing a crisis, a real crisis. He opened his heart to me with a sincerity that is unusual in politics. He expects the country to be saved by the monarchy. He is even ready to seek the help of his uncle, the Grand Admiral, who seems to have a great deal of influence with the King.

In the afternoon I go to the Royal Palace for the registration of the birth of Princess Beatrice. His Majesty had a bad cold and looked tired. The Prince of Piedmont was very cordial, and we had a brief conversation. He sees things very clearly, and no wonder he is disturbed.

February 5, 1943

At 4:30 in the afternoon the Duce calls me. The moment I enter the room I understand that he is very much embarrassed. I can guess what he is about to tell me. "What are you going to do now?" he begins, and then adds in a low voice that he is changing his entire cabinet. I understand the reasons. I share them, and I do not intend to raise the least objection. Among the various solutions of a personal nature that he offers me I decisively reject the governorship of Albania, where I would be going as the executioner and hangman of those people to whom I promised brotherhood and equality. I choose to be Ambassador to the Holy See. It is a quiet job that may, moreover, open up many possibilities for the future. And never as much as today has the future been in the hands of God. To leave the Ministry for Foreign Affairs, where for seven years—and what years—I have given my best, is certainly a hard and sad blow. I have lived too much, in the full sense of the word, between those walls not to feel the anguish of my removal. But that does not matter. I know how to be strong and to look at tomorrow, which may require even greater freedom of action. The ways of Providence are at times mysterious.

February 6, 1943

The Duce telephones quite early in the morning, holding up my nomination to the Holy See. "They will say that you have been kicked upstairs, and you are too young to be kicked upstairs." But since I had expected Mussolini's vacillations, I had already sent Ambassador Guariglia very early to ask the Secretariat of State to accept my nomination. What's done is done. The Duce accepted the *fait accompli* without enthusiasm.

Acquarone informs me that the King knew nothing about my leaving the government when he saw me on Thursday. The King is happy about my appointment to the Vatican. Acquarone is personally enthusiastic about it.

February 7, 1943

Nothing new except the official announcement of my appointment to the Holy See.

February 8, 1943

I hand over my office at the Ministry for Foreign Affairs. Then I go to the Palazzo Venezia to see the Duce and take leave of him. He tells me "Now you must consider that you are going to have a period of rest. Then your turn will come again. Your future is in my hands, and therefore you need not worry!" He thanks me for what I have done and quickly enumerates my most important services. "If they had given us three years' time we might have been able to wage war under different conditions or perhaps it would not have been at all necessary to wage it." He then asked me if I had all my documents in order. "Yes," I answered. "I have them all in order, and remember, when hard times come—because it is now certain that hard times will come—I can document all the treacheries perpetrated against us by the Germans, one after another, from the preparation of the conflict to the war on Russia, communicated to us when their troops had already crossed the border. If you need them I shall provide the details, or, better still, I shall, within the space of 24 hours, prepare that speech which I have had in my mind for three years, because I shall burst if I do not deliver it." He listened to me in silence and almost agreed with me. Today he was concerned about the situation because the retreat on the Eastern Front continues to be almost a rout. He has invited me to see him frequently, "even every day." Our leave-taking was cordial, for which I am very glad, because I like Mussolini, like him very much, and what I shall miss the most will be my contact with him.

[*No entries from February 9 to December 22, 1943.*]

[Final entry—*December 23, 1943*]

If these notes of mine see the light one day, it will be because I took precautions to safeguard them before the Germans, through base trickery, turned me into a prisoner. It was not my intention, while I was writing these hasty notes, to release them to the press just as they are; rather it was my desire to note events, details, facts which would have been useful to me in the future. If Providence had granted me a quiet old age, what excellent material for my autobiography! They do not, therefore, constitute a book, but rather the raw material with which the book could have been prepared later.

But perhaps it is in this skeleton form and in the absolute lack of embellishment that the real merit of these diaries can be found. Events are photographed without being touched up, and the impressions reported are the first ones, the most genuine, unencumbered by the criticism or the wisdom of later years. I was accustomed to jot down the main happenings day by day, hour by hour, and perhaps at times repetitions or contradictions can be found, in the same way in which life very often repeats and contradicts itself.

Certainly if I had not suddenly been deprived of the opportunity to expand these notes, I should have wished, on the basis of other documents, or my personal recollections, to amplify the chronicle of certain days which had particular and dramatic influence on the history of the world.

I should have liked to fix the responsibility both of men and governments with a greater wealth of detail, but unfortunately this was impossible, even though there might come to my mind, in these last hours, so many details that I should like to make known to those who tomorrow will analyze and interpret events.

The Italian tragedy, in my opinion, had its beginnings in August 1939, when, having gone to Salzburg on my own initiative, I suddenly found myself face to face with the cynical German determination to provoke the conflict. The alliance had been signed in May. I had always been opposed to it, and for a long time I made sure that the persistent German offers were allowed to drift. There was no reason whatever, in my opinion, for us to be bound in life and death to the destiny of Nazi Germany. Instead, I favored a policy of collaboration, because given our geographic position we can and must detest the 80 million Germans, brutally set in the heart of Europe, but we cannot ignore them. The decision to enter the alliance was taken by Mussolini, suddenly, while I was in Milan with von Ribbentrop. Some American newspapers had reported that the Lombard metropolis had received the German Minister with hostility, and that this was proof of Mussolini's diminished personal prestige.

Hence his wrath. I received by telephone the most peremptory orders to accede to German demands for an alliance, which for more than a year I had left unanswered and had thought of keeping that way for a much longer time. That was how "The Pact of Steel" was born. A decision that wrought such a sinister influence upon the entire life and future of the Italian people was due entirely to the spiteful reaction of a dictator to the irresponsible and worthless utterances of foreign journalists.

However, the alliance had a clause; namely, that for a period of three or four years neither Italy nor Germany would create controversies capable of upsetting the peace in Europe.

Instead, in the summer of 1939 Germany advanced its anti-Polish claims, naturally without our knowledge. Moreover, von Ribbentrop repeatedly denied to our ambassador Germany's intention to push the dispute to its final conclusion. Despite these denials I was somewhat incredulous and wanted to be sure, and, on August 11, I went to Salzburg. It was at his residence at Fuschl that von Ribbentrop, as we were waiting to be seated at the dinner table, told me about the German decision to set a match to the European powder keg. This he told me in much the same manner that he would have used about an inconsequential administrative detail.

"Well, Ribbentrop," I asked as we were walking together in the garden, "what do you want? The Corridor or Danzig?"

"Not that any more," he said, gazing at me with his cold metallic eyes. "We want war!"

I felt that the decision was irrevocable, and in a flash I saw the tragedy that threatened humanity. The conversations, not always cordial, which I had with my German colleague lasted for ten hours that day. Those that I had with Hitler lasted for as many hours during the two days that followed. My arguments made absolutely no impression on either of them. They were like water on a duck's back. Nothing could have prevented the execution of this criminal project long meditated and fondly discussed in those somber meetings the Führer had every evening with his inner circle. The madness of the Chief had become the religion of his followers. Every objection was ruled out when it was not turned to ridicule. Hitler went so far as to tell me that I, a man from the south, could not comprehend how much he, as a Germanic man, needed to grab the timber in the Polish forests...

Their calculation was fundamentally wrong. They were convinced that both France and England would remain passive while they slit Poland's throat. Convinced of this, Ribbentrop insisted on making a bet with me during one of those gloomy meals at the Österreich Hof in Salzburg. If England and France remained neutral I would give him an Italian painting. If those Powers intervened he would give me a collection of ancient armor. There were many witnesses to this bet. Not long ago Ambassador Mackensen and I were discussing the incident. But von Ribbentrop has preferred to forget the bet and has never paid up—unless he believes that he is fulfilling his debt by having me shot in his name by a platoon of wretches in the pay of the enemy.

After Salzburg, during the period of Italian neutrality and during the war, the policy of Berlin toward Italy was nothing but a web of lies, intrigue, and deceit. We were never treated like partners, but always as slaves. Every move took place without our knowledge; even the most fundamental decisions were communicated to us after they had been carried out. Only Mussolini in his supreme cowardice could, without reaction, tolerate this and pretend not to see it.

We were informed of the attack on Russia half an hour after German troops had crossed the eastern border. Yet this was an event of no secondary importance in the course of the conflict, even if our understanding of the matter differed from that of the Germans.

The preceding Sunday, June 16, I was with von Ribbentrop in Venice to discuss the inclusion of Croatia in the Tripartite Pact. The world was filled with rumors about an impending act of aggression against the Soviets, despite the fact that the ink was not yet dry on the friendship pact signed between the Germans and the Soviets. I asked my Axis colleague about it in a gondola while we were going from the Hotel Danieli to a dinner given by Count Volpi in his palace.

"Dear Ciano," said von Ribbentrop with studied deliberation. "Dear Ciano, I cannot tell you anything as yet because every decision is locked in the impenetrable bosom of the Führer. However, one thing is certain: if we attack them, the Russia of Stalin will be erased from the map within eight weeks."

Thus, in addition to a notable case of bad faith against Italy, there is also a blatant misconception of reality, sufficient at least to help lose a war . . . .

I am aware of the fact that in this explanatory note, which was meant to be no more than that, I have allowed myself to drift into narrating some facts which are not altogether negligible nor should be forgotten.

Within a few days a sham tribunal will make public a sentence which has already been decided by Mussolini under the influence of that circle of whores and pimps which for some years have plagued Italian political life and brought our country to the brink of the abyss. I accept calmly what is to be my infamous destiny. I take some comfort in the thought that I may be considered a soldier who has fallen in battle for a cause in which he truly believed. The treatment inflicted upon me during these months of imprisonment has been shameful and inhuman. I am not allowed to communicate with anyone. All contacts with persons dear to me have been forbidden. And yet I feel that in this cell, this gloomy Verona cell where I am confined during my last days of earthly life, I am surrounded by all those whom I have loved and who love me. Neither walls nor men can prevent it. It is hard to think that I shall not be able to gaze into the eyes of my three children or to press my mother to my heart, or my wife, who in my hours of sorrow has revealed herself a strong, reliable, and faithful companion. But I must bow to the will of God, and a great calm is descending upon my soul. I am preparing myself for the Supreme Judgment.

In this state of mind which excludes any falsehood I declare that not a single word of what I have written in my diaries is false or exaggerated or dictated by selfish resentment. Everything is just as I have seen and heard it. And if, as I prepare to take leave of life, I consider allowing the publication of my hurried notes, it is not because I expect posthumous rehabilitation or vindication, but because I believe that an honest testimonial of the truth in this sad world may still be useful in bringing relief to the innocent and punish those who are responsible.

December 23, 1943, Cell 27 of the Verona Jail.

Notes

1. The sections of the *Diary*, that were added back based upon the Swiss edition, were retranslated into Italian from the French.
2. Published in English under the title *Ciano's Diplomatic Papers*, Oldhams, London, 1948.
3. The two existing biographies [in 1980], the one by Duilio Susmel, *Vita sbagliata di Galeazzo Ciano*, Palazzi, Milan, 1962, and the one by Giordano Bruno Guerri, *Galeazzo Ciano una vita 1903/1944*, Bompiani, Milan, 1979, are basically journalistic in their conception and fail to offer a true historical perspective.
4. Maurice Ingram, chargé d'affaires of Great Britain in Rome.
5. Fulvio Suvich, Italian ambassador to Washington.
6. Arturo Bocchini, Chief of the Italian police.
7. Giacomo Medici del Vascello, Undersecretary of State; Italo Balbo, quadrumvir of the March on Rome and Governor of Libya and Don Aspreno Colonna are mentioned because of an incident caused by statements made by Medici about Balbo.
8. Achille Starace, General Secretary of the Fascist party (PNF).
9. General Pietro Badoglio, Chief of the General Staff.
10. General Luigi Russo, Chief of Staff of the Fascist Militia.
11. General Ettore Bastico, Chief Commander of the Voluntary Troops Corps in Spain.
12. Luigi Federzoni, President of the Senate.
13. Sir Eric Drummond (Lord Perth), ambassador of Great Britain to Rome.
14. Masa Aki Hotta, Japanese ambassador to Rome.
15. Dino Alfieri, Minister of Popular Culture.
16. Osvaldo Sebastiani, special secretary to Mussolini.
17. Filippo Anfuso, Chief of Staff at the Ministry of Foreign Affairs.
18. Milan Stoyadinovich, Yugoslav Prime Minister.
19. Samuele Cupini, aviator, winner of the Paris-Istres-Damascus race.
20. Pedro Garcia Conde, ambassador of Nationalist Spain in Rome.
21. Admiral Domenico Cavagnari, Minister of the Navy.
22. Augusto Rosso, Italian ambassador to Moscow.
23. General Alberto Pariani, Army Chief of Staff.
24. Count Paolo Thaon di Revel, Minister for Finance.
25. Boris Stein, Soviet ambassador to Rome.
26. Giuseppe Bastianini, Undersecretary at the Ministry of Foreign Affairs.
27. Renato Ricci, Undersecretary at the Ministry of National Education, Chief of the ONB (Opera Nazionale Balilla).
28. Giuseppe Bottai, Minister of National Education.
29. Count Massimo Magistrati, Councilor at the Italian embassy in Berlin, Ciano's brother-in-law.
30. Edda Mussolini Ciano, Mussolini's daughter, wife of Galeazzo Ciano.
31. Jacques Doriot, head of the "Parti Populaire Français" (PPF).
32. Lt. Colonel François de La Rocque, head of the French movement "Croix de Feu."

33. Ulrich von Hassel, German ambassador in Rome.
34. Gino Buti, Director General for Europe and the Mediterranean area at the Ministry of Foreign Affairs.
35. Luca Pietromarchi, head of the "S" (Spain) Department at the Ministry of Foreign Affairs, Minister Plenipotentiary.
36. Stanley Baldwin, former British Prime Minister.
37. Sir Samuel Hoare, former British Secretary of State at the Foreign Office, then Home Secretary.
38. Pierre Laval, former Prime Minister of France.
39. Vladimir Poliakov, British journalist.
40. Neville Chamberlain, British Prime Minister.
41. General Francisco Franco, head of the Spanish Provisional Nationalist Government.
42. Jules Blondel, French chargé d'affaires in Rome.
43. Refers to Massimo Magistrati.
44. Margherita Sarfatti, writer, friend of Mussolini.
45. Roberto Farinacci, State Minister.
46. Niccolò Castellino, Deputy, President of the Authors and Publishers Association.
47. Curzio Malaparte (Curzio Suckert), Italian writer.
48. Felice Guarneri, Minister of Currency and Exchange.
49. Alessandro Lessona, Minister of the Colonies.
50. Rexists, supporters of the Belgian Nationalist movement "Rex" lead by Léon Degrelle.
51. Vittorio Cerruti, Italian ambassador to Paris.
52. Carlo Galli, Italian ambassador to Ankara.
53. Mario Appelius, Italian journalist, deputy editor of the newspaper *Il Popolo d'italia*.
54. Dino Grandi, Italian ambassador to London.
55. Gen. Francesco Berti, Italian Commander in Spain, then Chief Commander of the CTV (Corpo di Truppe Volontario).
56. Colonel Gastone Gambara, Italian commander in Spain.
57. F. Marinotti, Italian industrialist.
58. Renato Bova-Scoppa, General Secretary of the Italian Delegation in Geneva, and Minister Plenipotentiary.
59. Ciccino (Fabrizio), son of Galeazzo Ciano.
60. General Attilio Teruzzi, Italian Commander in Spain.
61. Zenone Benini, Fascist Deputy, Vice President of the Metal Works and Mechanic Corporation.
62. Anthony Eden, British Foreign Secretary.
63. Yvon Delbos, French Minister of Foreign Affairs.
64. Ruggero Farace, official at the Ministry of Foreign Affairs.
65. Catherine Romanov, Imperial Princess of Russia, daughter of Queen Elena of Italy.
66. Count Giuseppe Volpi, President of the Industrial Confederation, Minister of State.
67. Vittorio Cini, Italian industrialist, and Senator.
68. Alberto Pirelli, Italian industrialist, Minister of State.
69. Colonel Sante Em. (Emanuele), head of a section of the SIM.
70. Erkem Libohova, Albanian Minister of Foreign Affairs.

71. Prince Prospero Colonna, former Mayor of Rome.
72. Tommaso Tittoni, former President of the Senate, before the Fascist take-over.
73. Bruno Mussolini, son of Benito Mussolini.
74. Attilio Biseo, Commander of an air force squadron in Spain.
75. Yovan Doucich, Minister of Yugoslavia to Rome.
76. Guido Buffarini-Guidi, Undersecretary at the Ministry of Internal Affairs.
77. Piero Parini, Director General of Italians Abroad.
78. Attilio De Cicco, official at the Ministry of Foreign Affairs.
79. Nicolas Franco, brother of the *Caudillo*, in charge of military negotiations.
80. Pellegrino Ghigi, Minister of Italy in Vienna.
81. Francesco Salata, former Minister of Italy in Vienna.
82. Rocca delle Caminate, country estate belonging to Mussolini, near Forlì, in his native province of Romagna.
83. Amedeo di Savoia, Duke of Aosta.
84. Cesare Maria De Vecchi di Val Cismon quadrumvir of the March on Rome, Governor of Dodencanesus.
85. Pablo de Azcaráte, former assistant secretary general of the League of Nations, head of the delegation of the Spanish Republican Government in Geneva.
86. Augusto Turati, former secretary of the Fascist party.
87. Marshal Rodolfo Graziani Viceroy of Ethiopia.
88. Charles de Chambrun, former ambassador of France in Rome.
89. Renato Prunas, Councilor at the Italian embassy in Paris, then chargé d'affaires.
90. Lowentau(?), probably Marvin Loventhal.
91. Pierre Dupuy, editor of the French newspaper *Le Petit Parisien*.
92. Vincenzo Fagiuoli, Italian businessman, spokesman of the Mercury Alliance Italy-Spain, he also was involved in the matter of the Djibouti-Addis Ababa railway.
93. E. Visconti, former mayor of Leghorn, director of the Siele company, controlled by Fagiuoli.
94. Pietro Arone di Valentino, Italian ambassador to Warsaw.
95. Joseph Beck, Polish Minister of Foreign Affairs.
96. Ion Logusiano, Romanian Minister to Rome.
97. Heinrich Himmler, German chief of police and head of the SS.
98. Antonio Benni, Minister of Communications.
99. Joachim von Ribbentrop, German ambassador, special representative of the Führer.
100. Konstantin von Neurath, German Minister of Foreign Affairs.
101. Bernardo Attolico, Italian ambassador to Berlin.
102. Prince Philip of Hesse, husband of Princess Malfada of Savoy, Hitler's go-between for communications with Mussolini.
103. Pietro Gerbore, official at the Ministry of Foreign Affairs.
104. Mario Renzetti, Italian Consul General in Berlin.
105. Mrs. Patrone, mother of an Italian arrested in Russia.
106. Grigoriev, Soviet agent arrested in Italy.
107. Dindina, nickname of Ciano's daughter Carolina.
108. Rudolf Hess, Hitler's deputy for the National-Socialist Party.
109. Markov, Soviet agent arrested in Italy.
110. Frau von Hassel-Tirpitz, wife of the German ambassador Rome.

111. Julius Streicher, editor of the anti-Semitic newspaper *Der Stürmer*.
112. George II of Schlesvig Holstein Souderbourg Glucksbourg, King of Greece.
113. Luigi Aldrovandi Marescotti, ambassador, head of the Italian delegation to the Nine-Power Conference at Brussels.
114. Admiral Romeo Bernotti.
115. Radu Irimescu, Romanian Minister of the navy and air force.
116. Kalman de Kanya, Hungarian Foreign Minister.
117. Vincenzo Lojacono, Italian ambassador to Brazil.
118. Alfred Wisochy, Polish ambassador to Rome.
119. Pertinax, French journalist (pseudonym of André Géraud).
120. Giovanni Ansaldo, editor of the Leghorn daily newspaper *Il Telegrafo*, owned by the Ciano family.
121. Arrigo Solmi, former Minister of Justice.
122. Guido Schmidt, Austrian Foreign Minister.
123. Kurt von Schuschnigg, Austrian Chancellor.
124. Getulio Vargas, President of Brazil.
125. William Phillips, American ambassador to Italy.
126. Giulio Barella, administrator of the newspaper *Il Popolo d'Italia*.
127. Don Juan of Borbon, heir and claimant to the throne of Spain.
128. Chiang Kung-Pao, envoy of Marshal Chiang Kai-shek to Rome.
129. Chiang Kai-shek, President of the Yuan Chinese Executive.
130. Giuliano Cora, Italian ambassador to China in Chunking.
131. T. V. Soong, Foreign Minister of the Chinese government.
132. Francesco Scardaoni, Paris correspondent of the newspaper *La Tribuna*.
133. Baron Okura, Japanese industrialist, head of a mission to Italy.
134. Lord Halifax, British Foreign Secretary.
135. General Hermann Göring, Prussian Prime Minister, Reich Air Minister.
136. Sebastiano Visconti-Prasca, military attaché to Paris.
137. Alessandro Pavolini, President of the Fascist Confederation of Professionals and Artists.
138. Carlo Del Croix, President of the Association of Disabled Veterans.
139. Amilcare Rossi, President of the National Veterans Association.
140. César Campinchi, French Minister of the Navy.
141. Theodor Hornbostel, Austrian Minister Plenipotentiary, director of political affairs.
142. José Antonio de Sangroniz, head of the Secretariat for Foreign Relations of the provisional Spanish Junta.
143. Hjalmar Schacht, former Finance Minister of the Reich.
144. Giovanni Battista Marziali, Prefect of Bologna.
145. Felice Felicioni, President of the *Dante Alighieri Society*.
146. Guido Baroni, Italian journalist.
147. Alberto Perego, Italian Consul to Singapore.
148. Sir Percy Loraine, ambassador of Great Britain to Ankara.
149. Giuseppe Cardinal Pizzardo, substitute state secretary of the Holy See.
150. Rino Parenti, federal secretary of the Fascist party in Milan.
151. Paul, Prince Regent of Yugoslavia.
152. Alexander I, King of Yugoslavia (1888-1934).
153. Crespi, cotton manufacturers from Lombardy. The name or word that follows is not identifiable.
154. Giovanni Engely, Italian journalist, correspondent of the "Telepress" agency in Rome.

155. Wilhelm Röder, Hungarian War Minister.
156. Blasco Lanza D'Aieta, an official on Ciano's staff.
157. Marchioness Delia di Bagno, wife of a foreign ministry official.
158. Sandro Sandri, Italian journalist, killed in a Japanese attack on a Chinese ship.
159. Massimo Pilotti, assistant general secretary at the League of Nations.
160. Guido Viola, Italian ambassador to Nationalist Spain.
161. Paul van Zeeland, former Prime Minister of Belgium.
162. Marzio Ciano, Galeazzo's son.
163. Egon Berger Waldenegg, Austrian Minister to Rome.
164. Frederick Villani, Hungarian Minister to Rome.
165. Joseph Goebbels, Nazi Minister for Propaganda.
166. Koloman Daranyi, Hungarian Prime Minister.
167. Koço Kotta, Albanian Prime Minister.
168. Degna Marconi, daughter from Guglielmo Marconi's first marriage.
169. Prince Fumimaro Konoe, Japanese Prime Minister.
170. Enrico Mizzi, head of the Italian Nationalist Party in Malta.
171. Guido Crolla, Councilor at the Italian embassy in London.
172. Bonifacio Pignatti di Custoza, Italian ambassador to the Holy See.
173. Eugenio Cardinal Pacelli, Secretary of State of the Holy See.
174. Jean Verdier, Cardinal and Archbishop of Paris.
175. Sir Robert Vansittart, main diplomatic councilor at the British Foreign Office.
176. Giacomo Auriti, Italian ambassador in Tokyo.
177. Koki Hirota, Japanese Minister of Foreign Affairs.
178. Leonardo Vitetti, Director of General Affairs at the Ministry of Foreign Affairs.
179. Mario Frusci, Italian Commander in Spain.
180. Ugo Sola, Italian Minister to Bucharest.
181. Giovanni Preziosi, editor of the anti-Semitic magazine *La Vita Italiana*.
182. Stefan Bethlen, former Minister of Foreign Affairs, and Hungarian magnate.
183. Admiral Candido Bigliardi.
184. Eric Trautmann, German ambassador to China.
185. Giuseppe Valle, Undersecretary of the Air Force.
186. Giovanni Host Venturi, Italian Minister of Communications.
187. G. Ingianni, Director General of the Merchant Marine.
188. Achille Lauro, Italian shipbuilder.
189. Lord Perth (formerly Sir Eric Drummond), ambassador of Great Britain to Rome.
190. Count Serafino Mazzolini, Italian Minister to Cairo.
191. Francesco Jacomoni, Italian Minister to Tirana, Albania.
192. Durini, Italian noble family.
193. Francesco Borgongini-Duca, Papal Nuncio of the Holy See to Italy.
194. Catholic Action: lay organization authorized by the Lateran Pact.
195. Baron Francesco Paolucci de Calboli, Italian ambassador.
196. Karl von Clausewitz, German General, strategy theorist.
197. DIE - Directorate of Italians Abroad.
198. Eugenio Maury, Undersecretary of Post and Telegraph in the Sonnino government.
199. Nunzio Nasi, Minister in the Giolitti government.
200. Octavian Goga, Prime Minister of Romania.
201 Corneliu Codreanu, founder of the Romanian Iron Guard.

202. Franz von Papen, German ambassador.
203. General Alessandro Pirzio Biroli, Governor of Amhara, Ethiopia.
204. Frank Gervasi, American journalist, correspondent of *The Washington Times* in Rome.
205. Prince Don Piero Colonna, Governor of Rome, deceased at the time.
206. Gian Giacomo Borghese, Roman Prince, nominated Governor of Rome.
207. Costantino Patrizi, Roman nobleman.
208. Gyula Gömböes, former Prime Minister of Hungary.
209. Bose Subhas Chandra, head of the most anti-British faction within the Hindu Congress Party.
210. Paul Ruegger, Minister of Switzerland to Rome.
211. Giuseppe Motta, President of the Swiss Confederation.
212. Tewfik Rustu Aras, Foreign Minister of Turkey.
213. Monsignor Celso Costantini, Secretary of the Congregation rites at the Holy See.
214. Emilio De Bono, Marshal of Italy, quadrumvir of the March on Rome.
215. General Aldo Ajmonino, aide-de-camp of the Prince of Piedmont.
216. In English in the original.
217. Giovanni Bonmartini, Italian industrialist.
218. Nicola Pascazio, Italian journalist.
219. General Federico Baistrocchi, former Undersecretary of War.
220. General Alfredo Dell'Olio.
221. General Pietro Gazzera, Governor of Gimma in Ethiopia.
222. Bochko Christich, Yugoslav Minister to Rome.
223. Mehemed Spaho, Yugoslav Communications Minister, head of the Muslim community.
224. Werner von Blomberg, former German War Minister.
225. Guido Manacorda, Italian professor of German.
226. In English in the original.
227 Hubert Lagardelle, French diplomat.
228. General Zeff Sereggi, King Zog's aide-de-camp.
229. Dario Lupi, Undersecretary of the Little Entente in Mussolini's first cabinet.
230. George Ward Price, English journalist, *Daily Mail* correspondent in Rome.
231. Eduard Beneš, Czechoslovakian Prime Minister.
232. Ferdinand of Savoy, Duke of Genoa.
233. Giovanni Rizzo, Prefect at the service of Gabriele D'Annunzio.
234. Giacomo Matteotti, Socialist Member of Parliament, assassinated by the fascists in 1924.
235. Carlo Formichi, Professor of Sanskrit, member of the Academy of Italy.
236. Seif al-Islam Hussein, Prince of Yemen; son of Iman Yahia, the heir apparent.
237. Sir Neville Henderson, British ambassador to Berlin.
238. Artur Seyss-Inquart, leader of the Austrian Nazis.
239. Marquess Antonino di San Giuliano, Foreign Minister in 1905 and 1914.
240. Giovanni Giolitti, Prime Minister many times until 1921.
241. Pier Adolfo Cittadini, official at the Italian Foreign Ministry.
242. Isabelle of France, Duchess of Guise, wife of the claimant to the throne of France.
243. Johann von Plessen, Councilor at the German Embassy in Rome.
244. Engelbert Dollfuss, Austrian Chancellor, until his murder in 1934.

245. "Nel mezzo del cammin…" Ciano is quoting from the first line of Dante's *Divine Comedy*.
246. Leopold von Saxon Coburg, President of the German Veteran's Association.
247. Leandro Arpinati, former Undersecretary to the Interior; placed under arrest by Mussolini.
248. Giannantoni Ettore, Commander of the "Teramana" Legion during the March on Rome.
249. Ettore Muti, head of the Fascist Militia (MVSN).
250. Hans Georg von Mackensen, German ambassador to Rome.
251. Count André De Kerchove of Deuterghem.
252. Count F. du Chastel de la Howarderie.
253. Attilio Teruzzi, Minister of Italian Africa (new name of the Ministry of the Colonies).
254. Hussein Ragip Bajdur.
255. Peter Metaxas.
256. Raffaele Bastianelli, Italian surgeon.
257. Dankward Bülow-Schnante, attaché at the German embassy in Rome.
258. Paul Gentizon, French-Swiss journalist, *Le Temps* correspondent in Rome.
259. Ermete Zacconi, Italian actor.
260. Léon Blum, Prime Minister of France.
261. Giuseppe Cobolli-Gigli, Minister of Public Works.
262. Leo Amery, Member of the House of Commons.
263. Leslie Hore Belisha, British War Minister.
264. Virginio Gayda, editor of the newspaper *Giornale d'Italia*.
265 Mustafa el Sadek Bey.
266. Camille Aymard, French journalist.
267. Adalberto Guerra-Duval.
268. General Pietro Piccio, air force attaché at the embassy in Paris.
269. Pierre-Etienne Flandin, former Prime Minister of France.
270. Paolo Monelli, Italian journalist.
271. Hsu Shao Ching.
272. Georghe Tatarescu, former Prime Minister of Romania.
273. Adalberto of Savoy-Genoa, Duke of Bergamo.
274. Countess Geraldine Apponyi of Hungary.
275. Georges Bonnet, French Foreign Minister.
276. Frantisek Chvalkovsky, Czech Foreign Minister after the Munich Conference (September 29, 1938).
277. Irgens Joannes.
278. Eberhard von Pannwitz.
279. In English in the original.
280. Sem Benelli, Italian playwright.
281. Joseph Paul-Boncour, former French Prime Minister and Foreign Minister.
282. Iacopo Gasparini, former Governor of the colony of Eritrea.
283. Emilio Settimelli, journalist, former editor of the *Impero*.
284. Silvio Crespi, industrialist, Italian Delegate at international conferences.
285. Konrad Henlein, head of the SDP (Sudeten German Party).
286. Milàn-Astray, Commander of the Tercio (Spanish Foreign Legion).
287. José Maria Pemán, Spanish journalist.
288. Hiraide Hideo.
289. Boleslav Wieniawa.

290. Umberto Ajello, Fascist party Secretary of Leghorn.
291. Colonel Giuseppe Piéche, commander of the Italian Carabinieri in Spain.
292. Giuseppe Talamo, Italian Minister to Bulgaria.
293. Edouard Herriot, former French Prime Minister, Mayor of Lyon.
294. Antonio Tamburini, Consul General of Italy in Lyon.
295. Hans Frank, German Minister of Justice.
296. Pietro De Francisci, former Minister of Justice.
297. Bela Imredy, Prime Minister of Hungary.
298. Viktor Lütze, commander of the Nazi SA (Sturm Abteilungen).
299. Admiral Arturo Riccardi, Undersecretary of the Navy and Navy Chief of Staff in 1940.
300. Maurice Caron de Beaumarchais, former French ambassador to Rome, 1927-1933.
301. General Augusto Agostini, Commander of the Fascist Forest Militia Corps.
302. Baldur von Schirach, Chief of the Hitlerjugend.
303. "berreter," meaning "Verräter" (traitors).
304. Fritz Weidemann, executive secretary of the Führer.
305. "You eat well in France." (sic)
306. Rino Alessi, editor of the paper Il Piccolo of Trieste.
307. Paul Cremona, correspondent of The Christian Science Monitor in Rome.
308. Father Pietro Tacchi-Venturi, Jesuit priest, intermediary between Pope Pius XI and Mussolini.
309. Mondini, lieutenant colonel.
310. Pater, Italian constructor.
311. Francesco Franzoni, Italian Minister to Prague.
312. Sir Noel Charles, councilor and later chargé d'affaires at the British embassy in Rome.
313. Luigi Barzini, Sr., was at the time special correspondent in Spain for the paper Il Popolo d'Italia.
314. Lord Walter Runciman, representative of the British government on a mission to Czechoslovakia to resolve the Sudeten problem.
315. Jague, Spanish Nationalist General.
316. Juan Vigon, Spanish Nationalist General.
317. E. Manuel Malbran, Argentine ambassador to Italy.
318. Aldo Borelli, editor of Il Corriere della Sera.
319. Ugo Sola, Italian Minister to Romania.
320. Quartarella: the location in the woods near Rome where the body of murdered Socialist Member of Parliament Giacomo Matteotti was discovered in 1924. The word was synonymous with a deep crisis for the Regime.
321. General Ugo Cavallero, Commander in Chief in Italian East Africa.
322. Count Carlo Sforza, Foreign Minister in Giolitti's Cabinet (1920).
323. Raffaelle Casertano, official at the Foreign Ministry.
324. See note 170 above.
325. General Efisio Marras, military attaché at the Italian embassy in Berlin.
326. Edouard Daladier, Prime Minister of France.
327. Dr. Milan Hodza, Prime Minister of Czechoslovakia.
328. Admiral Miklos Horthy, Regent of Hungary.
329. Boleslav Wieniawa, Polish ambassador to Rome.
330. Colonel G. B. Nulli, officer in the "S" (Spain) office of the Foreign Ministry.
331. Ruggiero Palmieri.
332. Jan Masaryk, son of the former President of the Republic of Czechoslovakia.

333. Jankovic Rodivoye, Yugoslav Minister to Albania.
334. Magaz Pers, Marquis of Magaz.
335. General Wilhelm Keitel, Commander in Chief of the German army.
336. André François-Poncet, French ambassador to Berlin.
337. Alexis Léger, General Secretary of the French Foreign Ministry.
338. Hugh Wilson, official at the Foreign Office.
339. Mamoru Shigemitsu, Japanese ambassador to London.
340. The sentence is reproduced verbatim. Ciano probably intended to say, "it is not worth crystallizing situations, etc…"
341. Count Charles de Chambrun, former French ambassador to Rome.
342. Magda de Fontanges shot and wounded Count de Chambrun, whom she held responsible for separating her from Mussolini, "the one love of her life."
343. Kworchak (probably Dworchak), Slovak pro-Hungarian agitator.
344. Pierre Lyautey, French Nationalist leader, son of the Marshal.
345. Lieutenant-Colonel Corrado Valfre di Bonzo.
346. Colonel L. Szabo, Hungarian military attaché to Rome.
347. Count Istvàn Czaky, Hungarian Foreign Minister.
348. Luigi Barzini, Jr., journalist on the editorial staff of *Il Corriere della Sera*.
349. Otto von Erdmannsdorf.
350. Ferenc Szalazy, leader of the Hungarian National-Socialist Party.
351. José Calvo Sotelo, deputy at the Spanish Cortès, murdered in 1936.
352. Mustapha Kemal Pasha Ataturk, President of the Republic of Turkey.
353. Regarding the statements made in this book, on this and the following pages, about the idea of killing King Zog of Albania, Ambassador Jacomoni, who read some passages of the *Diary* published in daily newspapers, transmitted a message where he wishes to point out: "that from the trial held in front of the High Court of Justice on the foreign policy of the Regime it clearly emerged how the idea of violently eliminating King Zog, opposed by Jacomoni himself, was to immediately discarded, because not only did Ciano no longer consider it but, regarding that Monarch, the policy until the end was to seek new and improved agreements with absolute respect for his person, who was protected until the moment he crossed the Albanian border." (Note reproduced in the Capelli 1953 edition.)
354. Lieutenant Colonel Hiraide Hideo and Commander Arisue Seizo.
355. Giuseppe Mastromattei, Prefect of Bolzano.
356. Emanuele Filiberto of Savoy-Genoa and Lydia of Ahrenberg.
357. Boris III of Saxony-Coburg-Gotha, Tsar of Bulgaria.
358. Giovanna of Bulgaria, Tsarina, and daughter of Vittorio Emanuele III.
359. Count Pal Teleki, former Hungarian Prime Minister.
360. Hermann Neubacher.
361. Pignatti di Custoza, Italian ambassador to the Holy See.
362. Raffaele Guariglia, Italian ambassador to Paris.
363. In English in the original.
364. Albert Heymans.
365. Carneekis Valdemarcas.
366. "And let this be a seal to undeceive all men." (*Divine Comedy*, Inferno, XIX, 21.)
367. Vittorio Mussolini, eldest son of Benito Mussolini.
368. Luigi Vinci Gigliucci, Italian Minister to Budapest.
369. Brauner Vladimir.
370. Antonio Mosconi, Senator, the Chairman of the National Bank of Albania.
371. A. Gambino, Managing Director of the National Bank of Albania.

372. Emanuele Pugliese, retired Army Corp. General.
373. O. Aranha, Foreign Minister of Brazil.
374. K. Ritter, German ambassador to Brazil.
375. General Mario Bernasconi, Italian Commander in Spain.
376. Paolo Orano, writer and Fascist deputy.
377. F. Grunwaldt-Cuestas, Minister of Uruguay to Rome.
378. V. A. Johnstone-Hope, Marquis of Linlithgow.
379. Sir Percy Loraine, British ambassador to Rome.
380. The handwriting of this name is uncertain, but from the context it is thought to be that of the secretary of the German embassy, von Strautz.
381. Louis Alexandre Berthier (1753-1815), Commander of the Italian army, later Marshal of France under Napoleon.
382. Alberto Giannini, Italian journalist, editor of *Il Becco Giallo*.
383. Eigi Amau, Japanese ambassador to Rome.
384. Tullio Cianetti, President of the Industrial Worker's Confederation
385. Lord George Ambrose Lloyd, British High Commissioner for Egypt and the Sudan.
386. See note 92 above.
387. Paul Baudouin, French banker and politician.
388. Gherardo Casini, director of the Italian press.
389. The tenth anniversary of the Lateran Pact (February 11, 1929).
390. Fernand de Brinon, journalist and president of the committee "France Allemagne."
391. Mario Indelli, ambassador to Yugoslavia.
392. This could be Henri De Man, Belgian professor and former cabinet minister.
393. Filippelli, important Fascist official and journalist, who exposed the facts of the murder in 1924 of Matteotti, a Socialist leader in the Chamber of Deputies.
394. Francisco de Jordana, Spanish nationalist Foreign Minister.
395. The coat of arms of the Fascist party.
396. Count Pal Teleki, Prime Minister of Hungary.
397. Ubaldo Rochira, Italian Consul General in Vienna.
398. Marshal Josef Pilsudski, leader of Poland after the First World War.
399. Obviously the Chamber of Fasces and Corporations, the new name of the Chamber of Deputies.
400. Shiratori was the Japanese ambassador to Rome.
401. Chinese politician.
402. Emil Hacha was the President of the Czechoslovak Republic; Frantisek Chvalkovsky was Minister of Foreign Affairs of Czechoslovakia.
403. "a Dio spiacenti ed ai nimici sui." (*Divine Comedy*)
404. The Masonic lodge in Ferrara, where Balbo was prominent.
405. Pietro Acquarone was Minister of the Royal House, managing the King's household.
406. Baron Carlo De Ferraris, Chief of Staff to Count Ciano.
407. Giacomo Suardo, President of the Senate.
408. Refers to Sir Noel Charles.
409. Vladimir Macek, Croat nationalist.
410. General Luigi Gabrielli, Italian military attaché to Albania.
411. Blasco Lanza d'Aieta, head of the secretariat and later Ciano's Chief of Staff at the Ministry of Foreign Affairs.
412. Tommaso Perassi was legal advisor to the Ministry of Foreign Affairs.

413. Luigi Cardinal Maglione, Secretary of State of the Holy See.
414. Shevket Verlaçi, Albanian Premier.
415. Cinkar Markovic, Yugoslav Minister of Foreign Affairs.
416. Zenone Benini, Undersecretary for Albanian Affairs.
417. See note 82.
418. Grigore Gafencu, the Romanian Minister of Foreign Affairs.
419. General Giacomo Carboni was Italian military attaché in Paris.
420. An allusion to one of the characters in the comedies of the Italian playwright Goldoni.
421. In English in the original.
422. General Werner von Brauchitsch, Chief of Staff of the German army.
423. On May 24, 1915 Italy entered World War I on the side of the Western allies and declared war on Austria-Hungary and Germany.
424. The Spanish ambassador.
425. Ramon Serrano Suñer, Spanish Interior Minister and Franco's brother-in-law.
426. Aide-de-camp of King Victor Emmanuel III.
427. Costanzo Ciano, Galeazzo's father, died on June 27, 1939. He was also President of the Chamber of Fasces and Corporations.
428. *Il Telegrafo* was the main daily newspaper of Leghorn and property of Costanzo Ciano.
429. Arnaldo Mussolini, the Duce's brother, had died in 1931.
430. Giacomo Acerbo had been a minister in the government at various occasions.
431. Massimo Magistrati.
432. Ernest Koligi, Albanian Minister of Instruction and later President of the Albanian parliament.
433. Queipo de Llano, Spanish Nationalist general.
434. Ernest von Weizsäcker, German Undersecretary for Foreign Affairs.
435. General Carlo Favagrossa, Commissioner and later Minister of War Production.
436. Amedeo Giannini, ambassador, senator, and General Director of the Ministry of Foreign Affairs.
437. Ciano is mistaken and must be referring to Romania, not Ukraine.
438. Charles Lindbergh, U.S. aviator, famous for his 1927 solo crossing of the Atlantic.
439. Emanuele Grazzi, Italian minister to Greece.
440 General Ioannis Metaxas, Prime Minister of Greece, as well as Foreign Minister and Minister of War.
441. A communiqué dated September 20 issued in Rome and Athens announced that both countries continued to have friendly relations. As proof the Italian government announced that its troops were moving away from the Greek border with Albania. The Hellenic government also took similar steps.
442. Romanian Prime Minister Calinescu was murdered in Bucharest on September 21 by elements of the banned "Iron Guard." King Carol named a military government under General Argeseanu that took draconian measures as reprisals and lasted only from September 21 to September 28.
443. Francesco Saverio Nitti, former Italian President of the Council of Ministers from May 1919 to May 1920.
444. Hitler gave the speech at the Reichstag on October 6, 1939. A peace initiative had been announced in the western capitals. Hitler stated that the pact between Germany and the Soviet Union would last a long time and that no

attempt made by the democracies could weaken it. He was proposing in very vague terms a European conference to give a new structure to the nations of the continent.

445. Count Ciano's sister, who was married to Count Massimo Magistrati, was near death.

446. On October 19, 1939 the representatives of England and France signed a mutual assistance treaty with Turkey at Ankara. This treaty was the conclusion of a long series of negotiations between the three governments and was signed just as negotiations between Russia and Turkey were being suspended, having failed to reach any tangible results.

447. King Leopold III of Belgium visited The Hague on November 6 to meet with Queen Wilhelmina. The next day the two sovereigns sent a message to the belligerent countries in which they offered their mediation for possible peace negotiations. On November 10, King Carol II of Romania also joined in the message from the Belgian King and the Queen of Holland.

448. Ciano refers to the fact that the Germans did not permit foreigners to live in the restricted industrial area of Posen.

449 Dr. Robert Ley, German minister, head of the "Labor Front."

450. Dino Grandi, former Minister of Foreign Affairs and ambassador to Great Britain, was appointed President of the Chamber of Fasces and Corporations.

451. Marshal Ion Antonescu was to become Prime Minister and "Conducator," or leader of Romania.

452. King Leopold III of Belgium.

453. "Hateful to God and to His enemies." A quotation from Dante.

454. The famous Buccari raid by the Italian navy against the Austrian navy during World War I, led by Ciano's father.

455. Colonel Giuseppe Teucci, Italian air force attaché in Berlin.

456. Henri de Kerillis, French journalist; editor of the Paris daily newspaper *L'Epoque.*

457. Umberto Albini, Prefect of Genoa and later of Naples; in February 1943 he was appointed Undersecretary of the Interior.

458. Giuseppe Bodini, Chief of Staff of the GIL.

459. Bertoldo is the Wise Fool in Giulio Cesare Croce's famous comic literary work, *Bertoldo, Bertoldino, and Cacaseno.*

460. General Ubaldo Soddu, Undersecretary for War.

461. Casto Caruso, Italian Consul General in Prague.

462. Alessandro Melchiori, Fascist party leader and Lieutenant General of the Militia.

463. "The Lord giveth and the Lord taketh away."

464. Italian newspapers had just published a map of Europe according to French plans, which, it was said, Paul Reynaud had given to Sumner Welles, where Italy was shown to have its 1914 borders.

465. Paul Reynaud, Finance Minister in the Daladier government and later Prime Minister.

466. Francesco Giunta, a Fascist deputy in parliament since 1921, was later Undersecretary to the Prime Minister.

467. Grandi refers to the speech he gave in London the year before in the presence of the German ambassador on specific orders from Rome.

468. Guelfo Zamboni was the Councilor at the Italian embassy in Berlin.

469. As soon as news about German aggression towards the three countries was made public, Pius XII sent cables to each of the rulers of Holland, Belgium, and Luxembourg expressing his wish for the reestablishment of their freedom and independence.

470. Freidrich Werner von der Schulenburg, German ambassador to Moscow.

471. After the Ethiopian war Graziani had been promoted to Marshal.

472. Mihail Manoilescu, Romanian Foreign Minister.

473. Pellegrino Ghigi, Italian Minister to Bucharest.

474. On October 12 Berlin announced that following a request by Romania a German military mission would travel to Bucharest and that German Luftwaffe aircraft would defend the oil fields.

475. Marshal Ion Antonescu, Prime Minister and Prince Luca Sturdza, Foreign Minister of Romania.

476. Official publication listing the officers of the armed forces by age and seniority.

477. General Antonio Sorice, Chief of the Cabinet of the Minister of War.

478. Adelchi Serena replaced Ettore Muti as Secretary of the Fascist party.

479. Pétain had fired Pierre Laval from the Vichy Cabinet.

480. Generals Carlo Geloso and Mario Vercellino were the commanders of the Armies in Albania; Trionfi and Perugi were division commanders.

481. Governor.

482. "The wind carries away both words and feathers."

483. The "Beffa di Buccari" is famous in the annals of World War I on account of a brilliant maneuver by the Italian navy against the Austrian navy, directed by Admiral Costanzo Ciano, the father of the author of the *Diary*. It was because of this feat that the Admiral was awarded the title of Count of Cortellazzo.

484 D'Annunzio became the laughingstock of the Italians when he had his many dogs paraded on leash by liveried flunkies.

485. Florina, a Greek village, was the scene of critical fighting.

486. Rodinis, administrator of Ciano's daily newspaper, *Il Telegrafo*.

487. Filippo Anfuso.

488. Laszlo Bárdossy had replaced Count Czaky (who died on January 27, 1941) as Hungarian Minister of Foreign Affairs and, following the suicide of Count Teleki on April 3, 1941, became Prime Minister of Hungary.

489. Ottavio De Peppo, Italian ambassador to Turkey.

490. "scrap of paper"

491. Allusion to the fact that a German officer thrashed Alfieri.

492. Giacomo Silimbani, Italian Consul General in Tunis.

493. Ettore Della Giovanna, newsman at the weekly *Tempo*.

494. Alexander von Dornberg, Chief of Protocol of the German Foreign Ministry.

495. Ethiopia.

496. Bruno, Mussolini's son, died in an airplane accident in Pisa while experimenting with a new type of plane.

497. *La Lotta di Classe*, a Socialist newspaper, of which Mussolini was once editor.

498. Cristano Ridomi, press attaché at the Italian embassy.

499. Francesco Pittalis, Italian Consul General in Munich.

500. A pun: *Campidaria*, "live on air," and *campi d'olio*, "live on oil."

501. The Italian word *foro* means both "forum" and "notch," or "hole." Hence the pun about the Foro Mussolini.

502. Ponte a Moriano had changed its name in honor of Ciano's father.

503. A reference to the mother of Mussolini's mistress, Claretta Petacci.
504. Luigi Russo, Undersecretary to the Prime Minister's office.
505. Dr. Marcello Petacci, Claretta Petacci's brother.
506. Claretta (Clara) Petacci, Mussolini's mistress.
507. Guido Leto, Inspector General of the Police and head of the OVRA.
508. Pier Francesco Nistri was General Gambara's deputy.
509. See the text of the speech in *Relazioni Internazionali*, January 10, 1942.
510. Ascari: fierce Italian colonial troops from Eritrea.
511. Libro e Moschetto (Book and Rifle): the pun is on the word *Maschietto*, meaning "little boy."
512. Raffaele Casertano, Italian Minister to Zagreb.
513. Ciano had published an article, "La Nuova Albania," in the first issue of the Albanian edition of the weekly *Tempo*. (See *Relazioni Internazionali* of January 17, 1942.)
514. Guido Romano, Italian Consul General in Vienna.
515. Ciano would now be called Cavaliere Galeazzo Ciano, Count of Cortellazzo and of Buccari. Both Cortellazzo and Buccari were the places where Admiral Ciano had distinguished himself in the First World War.
516. General Mario Roatta was head of General Staff of the army and had just been appointed troop commander in Croatia.
517. Lorenzino, nephew of Lorenzo the Magnificent, who murdered his brother.
518. On January 15 the Panamanian Conference met in Rio de Janeiro to decide the attitude its member states would take the following the United States' entry in the World War. The conference was to end with the approval of a resolution recommending to all the American republics to break relations with Italy, Germany, and Japan.
519. Carlo Pareschi and Michele Pascolato were, respectively, Minister of Agriculture and Deputy Secretary of the Party.
520. "From a Needle to a Billion"—the title of an Italian light opera.
521. *Busta* (envelope) instead of *busto* (bust). A comical misunderstanding for Italian speakers.
522. Mario Luciolli, Secretary at the Italian embassy in Berlin.
523. Arthur Axmann, head of the Nazi youth organizations.
524. Marcello Del Drago, Councilor at the Italian legation in Paris.
525. "Le génie c'est les génitaux."
526. Mussolini's eldest sister.
527. Nino D'Aroma, newsman and former Fascist federal secretary for Rome.
528. Dindina Ciano was Galeazzo's only daughter.
529. Prefect Antonio Le Pera, General Director of the office of Demography and Race section of the Ministry of the Interior and the main enforcer of Italian racial and anti-Semitic policy.
530. Ascanio Colonna, Prince of Paliano, former Italian ambassador to Washington.
531. Lamberti Sorrentino, newsman at the weekly magazine, *Tempo*.
532. Francesco Lequio, Italian ambassador to Spain.
533. Francesco Coppola, professor at the University of Rome and a member of the Academy of Italy.
534. The via Balbia was the coastal highway built by Italo Balbo as governor of Libya.
535. "Do not dig trenches that are too deep; don't forget that the Germans are hard masters."

536. Umberto Aiello, Fascist party secretary in Leghorn.
537. Francesco Maria Taliani de Marchio, Italian ambassador to China.
538. "The war is already won."
539. Myron C. Taylor was President Franklin D. Roosevelt's personal representative to the Holy See.
540. The following passage is from a letter sent by Lieutenant-Colonel Francesco Oliva, addressed to the publisher Rizzoli, dated May 24, 1963:
    "This writer, a Lieutenant-Colonel of the carabinieri reserves, detached for service at the Ministry of Foreign Affairs since June 1935, was ordered to serve as aide-de-camp from August 1942 to August 1943 of Minister and Ambassador Count Ciano. The episode referred to by Countess Edda in her letter to her husband is related to the request made to this writer to convince the reluctant governess of the Ciano children to ask to be replaced for health reasons. The request was granted. Naturally, Countess Edda was very much satisfied and wished to inform her husband of the outcome."
541. How much he's changed.
542. Gotzamanis, a minister in the Greek government, traveled to Rome to discuss issues relating to the occupation of his country.
543. Corrado Baldoni.
544. Hermann Neubacher, Bürgermeister of Vienna.
545. Alberto D'Agostino, head of the Lavoro Bank.
546. General Mario Vercellino, commander of the Italian army on the western border.
547. On November 30, 1942 Churchill had spoken at length about Italy in his radio address. He had also said the famous words: "One man and one man alone has brought Italy to this point."
548. Baron Michele Scammacca, an official at the Ministry of Foreign Affairs.
549. Walter Hewel, an old follower of Hitler from the early days of National Socialism and a diplomat who was part of the Führer's inner circle.
550. "Death to Laval!"
551. Guido Donegani, President of the Montecatini Company.
552. Colonel Ugo Luca, military attaché in Turkey.
553. Probably Giacomo Di Giacomo, national councilor and former President of the Confederation of Artists and Professionals.
554. Mussolini's eldest son.
555. Wang Ching-Wei, President of Nationalist China.
556. Martin Franklin, former Italian ambassador and senator, had been expressly sent to Berlin to deliver the decoration to Göring.
557. Francesco Jacomoni, Governor of Albania.
558. Michetti was one of the most famous artists in Italy at the time.
559. The Casablanca Conference between Roosevelt and Churchill when the "unconditional surrender" formula was announced.

Index

SUMNER WELLES (1892-1961), author of the original Introduction to the first American edition, published by Doubleday in 1946, was a career diplomat and Undersecretary of State in the administration of President Franklin D. Roosevelt, from 1937 to 1943. Welles, a close associate of the President, undertook a fact-finding mission to Europe in February and March 1940, when he had various meetings with Ciano and Mussolini. He left the State Department in 1943 and published several books and many articles about U.S. foreign policy.

RENZO DE FELICE, author of the Preface to this edition, was one of the most eminent 20th century Italian historians. He is best known not only for *The Jews in Fascist Italy: A History*, published in English by Enigma Books, but also for his monumental 8-volume biography of Mussolini, published by Einaudi. De Felice was born in 1929 in Rieti, near Rome. He studied with the two distinguished modern Italian historians, Federico Chabod and Delio Cantimori, and then taught history at the universities of Salerno and Rome. De Felice died in 1996.

ROBERT L. MILLER, the translator and editor of *Diary 1937-1943* by Galeazzo Ciano, is the founder and publisher of Enigma Books. Mr. Miller also translated *The Jews in Fascist Italy: A History* by Renzo De Felice (Enigma Books). Mr. Miller is a former professor of French and Italian at Saint Peter's College and Herbert Lehman College of CUNY. He was also vice president of Berlitz Publishing and of Macmillan Publishing Company, as is currently the president of Language Publications, Inc. He holds a Licence-ès-Lettres in History from the University of Paris, an MA from Middlebury College, and did graduate work at New York University.

STANISLAO G. PUGLIESE, co-editor of this translation, is Associate Professor of History at Hofstra University and a Visiting Fellow at the Italian Academy for Advanced Studies at Columbia University. He is the author of *Carlo Rosselli: Socialist Heretic and Antifascist Exile*, Harvard University Press 1999, and *Italian Fascism & Antifascism: A Critical Anthology*, Manchester University Press 2001.

Acknowledgements

The publisher wishes to thank the following people: Dr. Stanislao Pugliese; Carol Lazar of Doubleday-Broadway; Giovanna Canton of Rizzoli Corriere della Sera; Asya Kunik; Charles Miller; Jay Wynshaw.